Ke

The
Legislative Process
in the
United States

The Legislative Process in the United States

Third Edition

Malcolm E. Jewell
University of Kentucky

Samuel C. Patterson
University of Iowa

Random House, New York

Third Edition
987654321
Copyright © 1966, 1973, 1977 by Random House, Inc.

Library of Congress Cataloging in Publication Data

Jewell, Malcolm Edwin, 1928–
  The legislative process in the United States.

  Bibliography: p.
  1. Legislative bodies—United States.   I. Patterson,
Samuel Charles, 1931–   joint author.   II. Title.
KF4933.J4 1977   328.73   76-46383
ISBN 0-394-31265-1

Manufactured in the United States of America. Composed by Datagraphics, Inc., Phoenix, Arizona. Printed and bound by R. R. Donnelley & Sons Co., Crawfordsville, Ind.

Text design: R. Lynn Goldberg

Preface

We are living in an executive-centered world, a world of presidents and governors, prime ministers and premiers, kings and potentates. They dominate our political communication, our discourse, and our imagination. They are the prime focuses of our electoral struggles; they are credited with the creation of the great public policies by which we live; they negotiate the questions of peace and war; to a very considerable extent, they set the policy agendas for legislatures and, for that matter, for all public institutions.

This has not always been so. The seventeenth century produced the doctrine of legislative supremacy, and in parts of the Western world this doctrine was to be found in practice during the eighteenth and nineteenth centuries. The classical notion that legislatures have the task of making broad public policy, which the executive and the courts enforce, was a matter of common practice during the early decades of the American republic. But in the twentieth century, the broad outlines of public policy tend to be formulated by executives. The policy-making process of the American national government now depends indispensably upon the President. He and the bureaucracy that is at least nominally under his command create the principal elements of public policy, and his program becomes the agenda for Congress. At the state level, the governor's program is usually, if not always, the central feature of the legislative process. The modern democratic legislature has become a response-oriented institution. It responds not only to the electorate organized into constituencies but also to the executive, upon whom it necessarily depends.

The modern legislature may be more than ever subordinate to and dependent upon the executive, but it is nonetheless an important institution in a democratic political system. Although the legislature is far less independent of the executive than it was in simpler times, legislative and executive activities are interdependent, and the legislature can check, frustrate, delay, reject, and modify the policy extensions and inventions of the executive. What is perhaps more important, the legislature provides a critical connecting link between the people and the bureaucracy. Explanation of this linkage, of the functions of legislative systems and their instrumental activities, is a fundamental part of political science.

Ultimately, legislative analysis ought to accomplish at least three tasks of explanation: it ought to be descriptive of the structure and function of a particular legislative system at a point in time; it ought to be developmental, explaining behavioral patterns over historical time; it ought to be comparative, testing explanations that are apparently adequate for one legislative system against those of others. Success in any one of these tasks of explanation depends upon success in the others. In this book, we have sought to describe, develop, and compare a set of legislative systems for one society, the United States. We have taken as our universe of legislative systems those for which the national and state legislatures are the central nuclei. Every legislative body is, in a variety of ways, unique. A science of legislative systems utilizes structural-functional analysis, developmental analysis, and comparative analysis to identify uniformities in patterns of legislative behavior. Explanation of the unique can often be immensely important in the analysis of uniformities of behavior. The United States Congress is unique in many ways; it is, after all, the only national legislature in the country. There are fifty state legislative systems, with many variations among them that are important and deserve careful attention. Yet these legislative systems, embedded in a culture that is remarkably even across the land, exhibit far more similarities than differences; and comparative analysis makes it possible to investigate both. It would be foolhardy to assert that Congress is not significantly different from the state legislatures or that the legislatures of California and New York are not different from those in Nevada and South Dakota, but this is no reason to neglect the marked advantages of comparative treatment.

If these comments are taken as prefacing a definitive analysis of American legislative systems, the reader will be disappointed. Like its predecessors, this edition remains an exercise in taking stock of meager knowledge in the face of the overwhelming task of learning that lies ahead. We regard each edition as an interim report, not as an authority to provide absolutes for teaching. No one is more clearly aware of its flaws than we are. The research available about American legislatures is slim indeed, although it is rapidly growing. In some chapters we have had, of necessity, to rely principally upon data about Congress; in others research about state legislatures is more fully developed. There is almost no theory about legislative behavior to provide limits to the number and variety of relevant variables for analysis. We have tried to be systematic where that has been possible, but we have often had to proceed by example when systematic analysis did not exist. Our book raises as many questions as it provides tentative answers; it urges new research as much as it uses old.

Yet we feel that there is much to be said for taking stock of legislative research now, however imperfect it is. A field of study can be improved by trying to organize it and beginning to theorize about it. We have adopted the general approach of structural-functional systems analysis as the principal mode of our analysis and have outlined it in Chapter 1. We have utilized this scheme as a peg on which to hang our analysis, but we have not attempted to select only those kinds of research that fit the scheme. Our paradigm calls for research that has not yet been done, and where our chart did not indicate our course, we have used dead reckoning. Next, we analyze the development of American legislatures as institutions. We proceed to describe and explain significant aspects of the process and product of legislative recruitment, dealing with the mechanics of election and the attributes of those who are selected. We then move to the legislative institution itself, its organization, structures of leadership, bureaucracy, and procedures. We look at three sets of participants in legislative systems who are not themselves legislators: executives, lobbyists, and constituents. We next examine the legislature as a normative system, describing legislative norms and roles. Finally, we view the legislature as a system of action, examining the activities of roll-call voting, committee work, and legislative oversight, as well as the relationship of the legislature to the judiciary.

We have synthesized a wide range of legislative research, adding some new analysis, reorganizing the old, and frequently relying upon fragmentary data or isolated studies with complete awareness of their limitations. This sort of synthesis thus constitutes a guideline and incentive for future research rather than an encyclopedia of established truths.

By the time a book reaches its third edition, its authors have accumulated many debts. Our indebtedness to those whose research we have used and to publishers who have given us permission to make use of quotations is evident in the footnotes. Beyond this, over the years we have received tremendous help from our departmental colleagues at Iowa and Kentucky, from students in our courses on the legislative process, from colleagues around the country who have given us generous comments about the book, and from critical readers for Random House who have helped, we hope, to make each edition of this book better than its predecessor. By now, our debts have grown too large to thank everyone by name, but we are, nevertheless, especially mindful now of the corporate nature of this enterprise.

Our major indebtedness is intramural; the help from our wives ranged from the tangibles of typing and proofreading to the intangibles of encouragement and patience. Special appreciation is due to Polly Ann Patterson for her careful work on the index. Finally, we note that this book is a joint venture in its entirety; the authors are solely and equally responsible.

Lexington, Kentucky   M. E. J.

Iowa City, Iowa   S. C. P.

Contents

Tables

Figures

The Legislative System

There are a number of ways in which we might describe, analyze, or conceptualize legislative institutions and their activities. The traditional literature about legislatures has been largely descriptive: they were viewed largely as lawmaking machines and were described principally in terms of their constitutional powers and responsibilities, their organizations, and their procedures. More recent analytical literature about legislative bodies has focused on the policy process, adding to the emphasis of the older treatments an analysis of some of the "outside" forces impinging upon legislative decision making. The rediscovery of political-interest groups by political scientists in the period immediately prior to World War II marks the beginning of the development of case studies in legislative analysis with this kind of focus.

In the last few years, political scientists have adopted a more sociological perspective on legislative behavior and have sought to understand legislative institutions in the context of a more inclusive legislative *system,* which in turn is embedded in, reacts to, and affects the wider political system. It is this general perspective that we adopt here. We cannot ignore legislative traditions, history, organization, and formal procedural rules because these are important factors in the behavior of legislators. Nor can we ignore the importance of legislative policy-making processes. Legislative enactments have important social, political, and economic consequences; therefore, we must seek to understand and explain the underlying processes by which such enactments are made.

We realize that the conceptualization set forth in the following two chapters does not cover all the important elements of legislative processes in the United States, but it is a step toward a more comprehensive conceptualization of American legislative behavior, and it does help both to synthesize the accumulated research on the legislative process and to lay a foundation for further research and theory development. We present these chapters in a modest and tentative spirit. They display our point of view; they provide reference points for the substantive chapters that follow; and taken as independent entities, they constitute a kind of pre-theory of legislative systems.

CHAPTER ONE

The Legislature in a System

The legislator is a central political leader in the American political system, and his work is fundamental to any understanding of the processes of policy formation. Legislative systems and processes are basic phenomena of the American polity. Legislative behavior takes place at all levels of government—national, state, county, municipal, school district. Since local legislative bodies differ in many ways from those at the national and state levels, and since there is not enough research on them to make possible a comparative analysis of all levels of legislative activity, in this volume we focus solely on the legislative process in Congress and in the fifty state legislatures.

Because we believe that the behavior of legislators cannot be understood apart from the institutional or structural setting in which that behavior takes place, we have taken as a central concern here the legislature as an institution. The legislature is a highly institutionalized human group, with time-honored traditions and practices that affect the attitudes and behavior of its members. But the legislative system is more than a collection of formal rules, procedures, and units of organization. It is a social system in which individuals interact in terms of normative expectations derived both from within and from outside the legislature itself. The legislature is a group of individuals whose behavior as elected representatives is given both flexibility and restraint by the obligations and expectations imposed upon members by the system.

THE LEGISLATIVE SYSTEM

The terms *legislature, legislative system,* and *legislative process* are basic to our discussion and require definition.[1] A *legislature* may be defined as the collection of individuals who are elected as members of the formal parliamentary bodies prescribed by national and state constitutions. Other political actors who have some part in the legislative process and who often interact with legislators include lobbyists, constituents, the executive and his spokesmen, administrative agents, political party leaders, staffs and other expert groups, and so forth. When we refer to the *legislative system,* we mean to include those individuals and groups outside the legislature as well as the legislators themselves. The total legislative system configuration is represented in Figure 1.1.

FIGURE 1.1   Legislative System Configuration

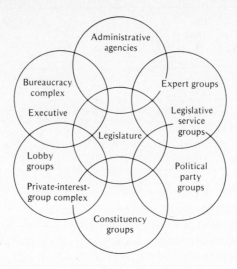

Although each of these actors might be described as being part of the legislative system, each also engages in some activities that have no legislative significance. Political party leaders are not a part of the legislative system when they are running campaigns for county offices, nor is the Agriculture Department when it advises farmers on better methods for growing crops, nor is the lobbyist for an association of bicycle manufacturers when he is engaged in a promotional campaign aimed at the consumer. Most constituents are far too busy earning a living, killing their crabgrass, and watching television to be more than minimally engaged in the legislative system. Therefore, in order to encompass the entire legislative system in our study, we must decide which activities of these outside actors are to be included. To do this, we must define *system* more precisely.

A *system* consists of a number of individuals who interact with each other in a situation that may lead to the achievement of some goal or set of goals defined in terms of culturally structured and shared symbols.[2] Along these lines, David Easton conceptualizes the political system in general as composed of the multiplicity of social interactions involved in the policy-making process oriented toward the goal of the authoritative allocation of values for a society.[3] The keys to defining a system are the terms *interaction* and *goals.* Thus, those who are outside the legislature enter the legislative system when they are interacting with legislators, sometimes when they are interacting with other outsiders, *and* when the purpose of this interaction is related to the legislative process. The lobbyist is a part of the legislative system when he calls on a congressman or when he writes to constituents in his organization urging them to write their congressman. The President is acting within the legislative system when he stresses at a cabinet meeting the necessity of clearing all patronage appointments with appropriate members of Congress. The county party chairman is an actor in the legislative system when he seeks a campaign contribution from a trucking official who wants legislation raising weight limits on the highways.

Most of these actors are also identifiable within other systems, such as the executive or bureaucratic, the electoral, and the judicial. In the strictest sense, these are all subsystems of the wider political system. It is obvious that they overlap and that for purposes of political analysis there may be various ways of defining and delineating these systems.[4] Moreover, the political system is not complete within itself but is a component in the social system that we define as society. Although the problems of defining and distinguishing various systems may become quite technical and complex, extending the study of the legislative system beyond the confines of the legislative chambers to encompass all those with some interest in influencing what the legislature does is necessary if we are to understand the broadest dimensions of the legislative system.

A distinction must be made between legislative system and the more common term *legislative process*. *Legislative process* refers to movement in the legislative system from one point in time and space to another. Although the notion of process is dynamic and has to do with the general process of social change, the legislative system itself may be viewed at one point in time in terms of its structure and functions. The term *legislative behavior* refers to the actions and the reciprocal expectations of the individuals in the legislative system. When we discuss legislative processes or legislative behavior, we do not aim to confine our analysis to lawmaking in the narrow sense of that term.[5] Legislative groups perform a variety of activities that are not strictly lawmaking nor policy-making in character; at times, lawmaking may be only a subsidiary activity. But each of these activities can be expected to serve some purpose for the polity.

FUNCTIONS OF THE LEGISLATIVE SYSTEM FOR THE POLITY

If you were to ask a number of legislators what the purpose of the legislature is, you might get a variety of answers: "Our job is to pass laws." "We have to represent the people." "It's all a matter of compromising the different interests." Each answer would be correct, but in itself would give an incomplete picture. A very substantial part of legislative activity is directly related to the mechanical operation of enacting legislation. This is what the spectator sees from the galleries, what the lobbyist may seek to influence, and what is reported day by day in the press. The making of laws is of interest to the political scientist who wants to analyze the strategy of participants, the reasons for passage or failure of a bill, or the substantive content of legislation. A considerable portion of this book deals directly with the process of lawmaking. In the traditional division of power among the legislative, executive, and judicial branches of government, the task of lawmaking belongs to the legislature. Only in the most formal sense, however, is this a realistic way of distinguishing the work of the legislature from that of other parts of government. Administrative decisions, often formalized and published as orders and rules, constitute another part of the law. The contribution of the judiciary to lawmaking includes common law, the interpretation of statutory law, and constitutional law. Moreover, if we define lawmaking as exclusively the legislature's task, how can we explain the fact that most bills are drafted by executive departments or by pressure groups?

We must try to get behind the manifest activity of legislative systems—namely, lawmaking—in order to understand their functional consequences for the polity. What functions does the legislative system perform that contribute to the maintenance of the political system?[6] We shall define the functions of the legislative system broadly as the *management of conflict* and the *integration of the polity.*[7] Defined as such, these are obviously functions performed by all components of government. As we define these functions more exactly, we can show how, as performed in practice by legislative systems, they are distinct from the same functions in other parts of the political system.

Conflict Management

A legislative system is deeply involved in the problems of maintaining order, of attempting to assure a relatively high degree of stability in political relationships, and of creating and sustaining substantial equilibrium in the polity. In pluralistic societies, group conflicts are a characteristic phenomenon. Whenever human associations proliferate and people raise conflicting claims to scarce status, power, and resources, some techniques for resolving conflict are essential. In such cases, a primary task of government is to provide various arenas in which such conflicts can be resolved.

One of the major functional consequences of the legislative system is the management of political conflict. Other political subsystems—both the administrative and the judicial—share this function. In the legislative systems of this country, these conflicts are most characteristically resolved by some form of compromise. The technique of compromise is used by executives and even by judges; it is not unique to the legislature. But the legislative system may be distinguished by the extent to which compromise, as a mode of conflict resolution, is institutionalized in the system.

We speak of the legislative function as being the management rather than the resolution of conflicts because, in a sense, few political decisions are final. Kenneth E. Boulding, for instance, has observed:

> In one sense, in a successful political process all decisions are interim. We live in a perpetual state of unresolved conflict. A decision is a partial resolution of conflict. It should never be a complete resolution. The majority does not rule; a majority decision is simply a setting of the terms under which the minority continues the discussion—a discussion which presumably goes on forever or at least for the lifetime of the organization.[8]

There are at least four ways in which the legislative system contributes to the management of conflict: the *deliberative,* the *decisional,* the *adjudicative,* and the *cathartic.* Often the legislature deliberates without making a decision in the positive sense of taking action. But the process of deliberation itself and the rules under which deliberation takes place contribute to the reconciliation of divergent interests. When the legislature makes a decision, deliberation facilitates acceptance and thus holds conflict to a minimum. "The chief function of debates," according to David B. Truman, "is as a part of the process of adjustment. . . .

Formal debates facilitate acceptance of the final decisions, not necessarily by the immediate participants but by those on the periphery."[9]

Deliberation in the legislative system is not confined to formal debate on the floor nor is participation limited to members of the legislature. Deliberation may be carried on in the hearing rooms, the offices of legislators, or in the lobbies and cloakrooms surrounding the chambers. These informal modes of deliberation are sometimes the most important ones, but the formal procedures for deliberation serve the purpose of ensuring that there will be time and opportunity for a variety of interests and viewpoints to be heard. The rules and procedures that permit hearings and extensive debate are among those that facilitate deliberation. It is noteworthy that one of the most frequent criticisms of state legislatures is that they do not permit adequate deliberation. Sometimes sessions are brief; hearings are infrequent; debate is sketchy; and the majority is very strong in the legislature. If the only purpose of the legislative system were lawmaking, this kind of criticism would be pointless. One indication of the essential part the legislative system plays in managing conflict is that if the legislature becomes a rubber stamp or a law factory, there may be no other arena in which adequate deliberation is possible.

Legislative decisions are both tentative and likely to represent compromises that have been reached after deliberations among legislators and other relevant participants in the legislative system. Earl Latham has described the process:

> Every statute tends to represent compromise because the process of accommodating conflicts of group interests is one of deliberation and consent. The legislative vote on any issue tends to represent the composition of strength, *i.e.,* the balance of power, among the contending groups at the moment of voting. What may be called public policy is the equilibrium reached in this struggle at any given moment, and it represents a balance which contending factions or groups constantly strive to weigh in their favor.[10]

Latham proceeds to point out, however, that in this process of the resolution of conflict, "the legislature does not play the inert part of cash register, ringing up the additions and withdrawals of strength, a mindless balance pointing and marking the weight and distribution of power among the contending groups." Instead, the legislature is itself a group with an identity of its own, composed of members who themselves have a multiplicity of group identifications.

Furthermore, both legislative deliberation and decision-making are likely, because of their functional places in the process of compromise, to be diffuse and ambiguous. As Truman points out:

> The imperative of compromise among groups, between group demands and the "rules of the game," explains ... the ambiguity of many legislative formulas. ... But ambiguity and verbal compromise may be the very heart of a successful political formula, especially where the necessity for compromise is recognized but is difficult to achieve in explicit terms. Ambiguity may postpone or obviate the necessity for a showdown and as such has an important political function.[11]

In effect, the equivocal nature of much of what goes on in legislative systems tends to prevent the polarization of many issues; this equivocation therefore often serves as a mechanism for resolving conflicts. At the same time, where highly divisive issues are operating in the environment, legislative equivocation may lead to or intensify conflicts and promote a deepening of crises.

Frequently, the decisional routines of American legislatures involve little more than the ratification, often by unanimous vote, of decisions effectively made by other structures in the legislative system. Interest-group leaders or local officials, for example, may make agreements that they bring to the legislature for approval. In such cases, the legislative body merely ratifies or registers a reconciliation of conflicting interests made at an earlier stage in the decisional process and, perhaps, arrived at entirely outside the legislature itself.

A variety of legislative structures facilitate the resolution of conflict in legislative systems. Dual partisanship in many legislative bodies provides the structure for contending forces; where two-party competition does not prevail, as in the case in many American states, bifactional or multifactional rivalry may be at least a partial substitute for partisanship in terms of providing structure for conflict and its resolution. We shall assess the partisan and factional structure of American legislatures in Chapters 7 and 16. Both within and without the legislature proper, political-interest groups constitute divisive elements; we consider their representatives in detail in Chapter 12. As the conflicts confronting the legislature have become more complex, the executive has increasingly taken the initiative in proposing ways to resolve them, a process described in Chapter 11. In some legislative systems, the vigor and effectiveness with which the executive has played this part have led to criticisms that the legislature has lost its share in decision making. But legislative authority to make decisions remains unquestioned. Specialization and division of labor in the legislative system facilitate the crystallization and the resolution of conflict. The committee structure of a legislature involves a specialization of tasks, and the tendency to accept the specialists' judgments contributes to conflict reduction. Legislative committees are dealt with in both Chapters 8 and 17. Finally, the rules of the legislature, both written and unwritten, are not neutral in the reconciliation of conflicting interests. Controversies over principles and issues are often converted into conflicts over means and are thus more readily resolved. Truman has suggested how much of the conflict in legislatures focuses on struggles over procedures, technical rules of debate, the power to limit debate, committee assignments, calendars, timetables, and the like.[12] For instance, with reference to the use of the legislative calendar as a focal point for the resolution of intermediate conflicts, Arthur F. Bentley has observed that "most bills that become laws do so after a fight with other bills for space on the calendar, rather than after a fight with an opposition of a more direct kind."[13] Again, other rules of an unwritten kind, such as the seniority rule for the selection of committee chairmen, tend to remove areas of potential contention from the realm of conflict altogether.

Essentially adjudicative routines are frequently performed by American legislatures. Much of the private-bill process in the Congress is largely adjudicative in nature, in the sense that individual grievances (conflicts between individuals and the authorities) are settled thereby. Similarly, the work of some legislative committees has been essentially adjudicative, as when hearings before investigating committees have in effect been trials, during the course of which sanctions have been applied.

A final mechanism for the facilitation of conflict resolution in the legislative system is the cathartic, or safety-valve, mechanism, which can be found in a variety of legislative structures. The public hearing, for example, can be a cathartic mechanism, and has been viewed as "a quasi-ritualistic means of adjusting group conflicts and relieving disturbances through a safety-valve."[14] In a public hearing, the spokesmen for conflicting interests have an opportunity to let off steam and to get their complaints, arguments, and pleas out of their system. And legislators, at a public hearing or during floor debate, may do the same. The legislature cannot accede to the demands of all interests, sometimes not even partially, but it can grant these interests a hearing—perhaps not obtainable elsewhere—which can be an important factor in the management of conflict. To discover the consequences of shutting off this safety valve, we have only to recall the demonstrations in the 1960s in the streets of several southern cities by black Americans who had been unable to obtain not only the policies they sought but even a hearing in state or local legislative systems.

Integration

The legislative system serves to facilitate the unification of the polity and contributes to its effective operation by providing support for it. Any political system is subject to stress. Groups that are dissatisfied with the way in which conflicts have been resolved may become alienated from the system and unwilling to accept the political decisions emanating from it. Ultimately, this is the path to revolution. Unless ways can be found to provide support for the political system, the demands that are placed upon it cannot "be satisfied or conflicts in goals composed."[15] The legislative system functions in order to engender a spirit of loyalty or patriotism, but it also provides support in a more immediate sense, for example, when interest-group leaders endorse legislative programs and voters select legislators at the polls. An equally important contribution of the legislative system is to provide support for the executive and judicial systems, thereby contributing directly to the integration of the polity. Three closely related ways in which the legislative system contributes to the integration of, and support for, the entire political system are: *authorization, legitimation,* and *representation.*

One of the characteristics of a written constitution is the specific delegation of formal authority to different components of government. In American constitutions, the legislative branch is given various kinds of authority over the executive branch. One of the most important of these is the budgetary process, through which the legislature authorizes the executive to collect taxes and expend funds. The earliest English parliaments were summoned by monarchs to authorize the collection of taxes because these monarchs were seeking support for their regimes. The battle cry of the American Revolution—"No taxation without representation"—was simply a negative statement of the principle that legislative authorization of taxation functions to provide support for a political system. The legislature authorizes the executive to act in a variety of other ways: to reorganize itself, to select its major officials, to regulate the economy. Authorization also involves legislative oversight of bureaucratic activity, which is discussed in Chapter 18. Theodore J. Lowi has contended that in this oversight the modern legislature engages in its most important activity "as a place where the needs of the bureaucracy are continually being balanced against the prevailing special interests in the community."[16] If this is the most important task, it is also the one that is not being fully performed by many state legislatures; and this failure could contribute to the relatively low level of support accorded to some state governments by the public. Similarly, legislative systems in the United States authorize the courts to assert jurisdiction, to create their organizational machinery, and to qualify their members.

The legislative system functions for the integration of the political system not only by authorization but by legitimation. The constitutional and traditional base of the legislature and the orderly procedures that it follows make legislative action appear legitimate; it has the quality of rectitude. It is regarded by the public as right and proper. When the legislature gives other agents of government permission to act (i.e., when others are authorized to exercise power), their exercise of authority is legitimized in the process (i.e., they have the right as well as the power to act). The importance of this function can be illustrated by the consequences that follow when Congress questions the legitimacy of governmental actions. When congressmen question the right of the Supreme Court to adjudicate certain topics (such as legislative apportionment), or when a committee or one house of Congress approves legislation to withdraw a subject from the Court's jurisdiction, the result is to weaken popular support for the Court, even though its legal authority remains unchanged. In a similar sense, the courts not only invalidate some legislative acts but also strengthen the appearance of legitimacy and, consequently, public support for most pieces of legislation.

The legislative system contributes to the support of the polity by virtue of its representative character. Legislators are the spokesmen for, and are empowered to act for, constituencies as a result of the legitimacy of their selection as representatives. But the pervasiveness of the representative role goes beyond the legislative body itself. Other participants in the legislative system (the lobbyist, the administrative agency, the chief executive, the party leader) play representative roles. The legislative system is a system of interaction in which individuals are expected to act for their clienteles. The legislator represents a geographically designated group of individuals, although he may act for wider interests as well. The lobbyist represents interests and associations, often economic, that may be nationwide. The executive represents the political forces that are at least temporarily dominant in the polity as a whole. The administrative agent represents a segment of the bureaucracy and often its wider clientele as well. The party leader represents the controlling elements of the political organization at the electoral level. Representation provides the channels for, and mediates the interaction among, the many participants in the legislative system.[17] Legislative acts have authority and are regarded as legitimate in part because of the representative quality of the system. The nature of representation in the legislative system is explored in more detail later in this chapter.

Historically and traditionally, it is the legislature that has provided support for the political system through representation. But as modern government has grown more complex, elaborate techniques for representing interests have been developed within the administrative agencies and even in the courts. Compared with the administrative system, the legislative system has more traditional methods of formal representation and a more elaborate network of informal representation; but the techniques are common to both because an urban, industrial society requires representation at many levels.

During the 1960s, the adequacy of representation of population by Congress and the state legislatures was subjected to severe criticism. The struggle through the courts and the legislatures to secure equal population apportionment and districting for legislatures is discussed in Chapter 19. Although the techniques of apportionment affect only the formal aspects of representation, these have a critical effect on the access to the legislators of other participants in the legislative system. Some have argued that at both the state and national levels, the executive and the judicial systems have provided more adequate representation than the legislative system has.[18] It is true that groups that have been denied effective representation in the legislative system, such as urban dwellers and blacks, have turned to the executive and judicial systems, both of which have often been more accessible to them.

FUNCTIONAL MAINTENANCE OF THE LEGISLATIVE SYSTEM

We have so far described the functions of the legislative system for the polity and the contributions that it makes toward preserving the political systems in the nation and in the states. Now we must ask: What are the requirements for maintaining it as a viable system capable of supporting the entire political system? The legislative system in a democracy, like the democratic political system of which it is a part, does not live a charmed life; it is capable of collapse. There are many examples of legislative systems abroad that have collapsed and, in doing so, have usually brought about the collapse of the entire political system. The legislative systems in the United States, although varying in effectiveness, have remained viable. Why? What characteristics have made this possible? Although more research and more theoretical analysis are necessary before it becomes clear what aspects of the legislative system may properly be described as essential to its preservation, this technique of cataloging and analyzing the functional requisites of a legislative system offers a useful, if incomplete and tentative, approach to the understanding of legislative life. For example, an internally well-integrated, closed legislative system may, under conditions like those of Fourth Republic France, contribute to the disintegration of the polity.

Recruitment

To develop and persist, a legislative system must establish mechanisms for the recruitment and selection of personnel. The extensive knowledge available about the selection of legislators is summarized in Chapters 3 and 4. The recruitment mechanisms for American legislators involve apportionment (allocation of seats), districting (territorial demarcation), and election. These mechanisms have non-random political effects, which are summarized in Chapter 3. Our analysis deals only with the recruitment of legislators themselves and not with that of others involved in the legislative system (lobbyists, party leaders, executives, and the like), since for some almost nothing systematic is known about their selection, and since such added description would make our analysis unmanageable in size.

Communication

Channels of communication have to be available if a legislative system is to be maintained. In the legislative system, communications networks are highly complex and highly differentiated in form. Knowledge of the internal and external communications channels that characterize legislative systems is very limited, fragmentary, and unsystematic. Our analysis deals with communication obliquely in terms of structure in Part III, where the exposition is concerned with legislative organization and procedure; more directly in terms of strategy in Chapters 11 and 12, where we discuss executive leadership and pressure groups; and specifically, though impressionistically, in Chapters 12 and 13, where we deal with legislator-lobbyist and legislator-constituent communication.

Normative Regulation

A legislative system must have enforceable, sanctioned standards of proper conduct by which participants are expected to abide. Legislative norms must exist that regulate the means of taking action and of effective expression and that control disruptive forms of behavior. The formal, written rules of procedure provide one set of norms, a set that must be known before legislative behavior can be understood. Legislators abide by the rules; they can be, and are, punished for violating them. The rules also have significant political effects and are thus part of the strategy of political conflict. We deal specifically with the written rules in Chapter 10. The unwritten rules of the game, however, are frequently of equal importance to an interpretation of legislative life. They govern the circumstances under which the written rules can be violated in the pursuit of system goals, and they prescribe, proscribe, and prohibit action in the legislative system beyond the formal rules. These unwritten but highly institutionalized rules are treated in Chapter 14.

Integration of Subsystems

A legislative system must adequately integrate its subsystems and the systems tangentially related to it. Although the standards of adequacy are not fully known, it is clear that the parts must work together. The legislature is usually the central arena wherein the internal integration of the system is accomplished. It is very doubtful, for instance, whether the American legislature could operate adequately without minimal cooperation from lobbyists, the executive, party leaders, significant constituents, judges, and bureaucrats. Such individuals belong to the legislative system when they play roles related to legislative action. Similarly, the internal subsystems of the legislature itself (i.e., committee structure and party organization) must be minimally integrated. The practical and theoretical problems involved in an analysis of this function are great. We shall develop the present knowledge in this connection at various times throughout this book, and shall particularly endeavor to demonstrate the meshing of forces from the point of view of the legislative product in Part VI.

Shared Goal Orientation

It does not seem likely that a legislative system could exist unless its participants shared a goal or a set of goals. The goal orientation of the legislative system may be crucial to the distinction between it and other political subsystems. It may be said that the principal goal orientation of a legislative system is the resolution of group conflicts. As Bentley observed many years ago, "If we take these legislative bodies as they stand today, we shall find in all of them group oppositions which form the body and soul of their activity."[19] Other observers of the legislative system in action have made similar comments. For instance, the whole orientation of Bertram M. Gross's study of the legislative system was the concept of the legislative "struggle," and he referred to the legislative process as "combat on the legislative terrain."[20] The conflicts in legislative systems over differing instrumental goals provide the substantive content of legislative processes, but the resolution of conflict itself is characteristic of the legislative system. The sharing of goals among participants (e.g., the resolution of conflict) may be said to be functional for the maintenance of the system. The resolving of conflict itself has wider significance, and we shall deal with it in our discussion of role conflict.

Role Allocation

Allocation of roles is requisite for the maintenance of a legislative system. We shall examine the available knowledge on legislative role differentiation and assignment in Chapter 15. However, the role concept is so fundamental to our whole analysis of American legislative systems that it must be expanded at some length in this introductory chapter.

The term *role* first came into general usage in the social sciences as a result of the theoretical work of the anthropologist Ralph Linton.[21] In its simplest form, the role concept is a theoretical analogy to the parts that actors play in a drama, although of course in a Shakespearean play the dramatic actors read fixed lines, whereas social roles are more flexible and less clearly defined. For the purpose of this analysis, a *role* is defined by the total pattern of expectations, including the person's own expectations, having to do with the "tasks, demeanors, attitudes, values and reciprocal relationships" that the actors have with respect to a position in the social structure.[22] A role "is defined by what others expect of the person filling it," as well as by what the individual expects he ought to do as the occupant of a position.[23]

A distinction must be made between role, which is defined by the expectations of individuals, and *role behavior*, which refers to the actual behavior or performance of specific individuals as they play their roles.[24] It is clear, for instance, that actors in a system may have certain expectations about the nature of proper behavior in particular positions in the structure of the system; and yet specific individuals may add to, subtract from, or otherwise transform the expected pattern of behavior in their actual role performance.

Roles are inexorably related to the social norms that prevail in particular social structures.[25] The norms of a social group, the "ought" behaviors that group members come to expect, are to a considerable extent organized around roles. Thus, roles will consist of the expected rights, duties, and obligations of occupants of positions in the structure of a system.

Although it is difficult to discuss the role concept except in relation to positions in the social structure, it should not be assumed that each position has associated with it one and only one specific role. In complex social structures, a particular position will involve a whole set of behaviors that are more or less expected of individuals occupying that position. Thus, for instance, the father in a family has a given position in the family structure but may behave differently in his role with respect to a teenage daughter, an adult son, or the baby in the family.

Position is a static abstraction that refers to "a place in a structure, recognized by members of the society and accorded by them to one or more individuals."[26] Obviously, an individual occupies positions in a variety of social structures; that is, he holds multiple positions.[27] A role, on the other hand, is dynamic. Linton first defined role as "the dynamic aspect of status."[28] It refers to the expected behavior of occupants of a position, although "not to all their behavior, as persons, but to what they do as occupants of the position."[29] In this way, the concept of role links the individual personality with the social system of which he is a part.[30]

Roles have mutual and reciprocal implications. The majority floor leader and the rank-and-file member have similar but not identical perceptions of the leader's role. Moreover, the viewpoints of each concerning the leader's role affect their respective attitudes concerning the legislator's role as a member of the legislative party. The pattern of expected role behavior in a social structure may be defined as a system, but this means neither that there is perfect harmony among all the participants in a system concerning their roles nor that the entire pattern of roles can be fully comprehended or described completely.[31]

The participants in a system may differ in their role expectations concerning a legislator, a lobbyist, or some other occupant of a given position. There may be widespread agreement that certain kinds of behavior are prohibited by the norms in the system or that other behavior is required. In still other cases, the expected behavior may simply be preferred. For example, in a legislative system, acceptance of a bribe from a lobbyist may be flatly prohibited by legislative norms (as well as by law), yet accepting certain favors from lobbyists may be frowned on by some legislators and tolerated by others. If there is too much difference in the viewpoints of participants concerning norms and roles, the resulting confusion and misunderstanding can be dysfunctional for the system.[32]

Role can be used as a basic unit in an analysis of legislative behavior. The role concept is also central to the problem of defining the boundaries of the legislative system, which may be said to be the limits of the legislative role system. Although it must be pointed out that political subsystem boundaries are likely to be vague and will usually "shade off" rather than show a clear-cut line of demarcation, the boundaries will tend to be drawn between actors who play system roles and actors who do not.[33]

Actors in the legislative system are susceptible to *role conflict*, which is "the situation in which incompatible demands are placed upon an actor because of his role relationships with two or more groups."[34] A legislator may be a member of an organized interest group in his constituency, a political organization in his constituency or state, or a series of groups in the legislature, including the House, a party group in the House, legislative committees, voting blocs, or even a national party.[35] In each of the organized groups to which the legislator belongs, he may play a variety of roles. Groups with which the legislator identifies but in which he does not actually have membership may be *reference groups* for him. A reference group is a comparison group, a group to whose norms the actor refers for his behavior.[36] Either membership or nonmembership groups may be reference groups for the legislator, but "functioning in terms of a reference group that is different from the group in which one is participating physically is especially well-illustrated by the behavior of political representatives."[37]

The role expectations (the rights, duties, and obligations associated with the role) of a legislator in the variety of groups of which he is an interacting member or the norms of groups of which he is not a member but to whose standards he refers for his own behavior may be conflicting. It has been suggested that the resolution of political conflict in the legislative system is related to the extent of role conflict.[38]

A variety of institutional mechanisms may be employed by the legislator in an attempt to integrate or reduce role conflicts. He may utilize a hierarchy of role obligations and avoid sanctions by employing an equally high or higher claim. He may assert that the conflict was an accident, that circumstances beyond his control prevented his playing the approved role. He may take refuge in the legislative rituals of etiquette, tact, or procedure, which will tend to reduce social frictions. He may employ a segregation of roles by repudiating his role in one group, playing off one group against another, stalling until pressures subside, redefining his role or roles, leading a double life, absenting himself from the field when conflict approaches, or, in some extreme cases, becoming physically or mentally ill.[39]

Also, the legislator may reduce role conflicts by compromise or bargaining.[40] Compromise appears to be a characteristic mechanism for role-conflict reduction by those who play the legislative role. According to Robert A. Dahl and Charles E. Lindblom, the legislator, as a leader "whose control depends upon successful bargaining," tends

to have attitudes toward the control process substantially different from those of other American leaders, like those in business and administration, whose control depends upon a successful use of hierarchy. Probably the role both attracts and shapes the men who play it. ... In any case the role calls for actions such as compromise, renunciation, face-saving of oneself.[41]

Furthermore, it seems likely that there are some norms shared by actors in the legislative system which "serve to rank the relative importance of various roles or spheres of behavior, thus serving to mitigate potential conflicts between inconsistent role definitions."[42] Such norms link the reference-group behavior of legislators to their roles and role conflicts.

We have far from complete knowledge of legislative role systems and can by no means fulfill the specifications for analysis suggested in these paragraphs. We have begun to accumulate specific data, however, and we shall see in Chapter 15 some of the concrete role allocations in several American legislative systems.

Socialization

A legislative system must have formal or informal mechanisms, or both, for the socialization of members. Participants have to learn how they ought to behave, what are the written and unwritten rules of the game, and what are the potentialities and limitations of their roles. We shall deal only briefly with the socialization processes (Chapters 3 and 13), which political scientists and political sociologists are only beginning to investigate. The problem of socialization for the legislative system becomes most visible and acute with respect to the incorporation of new members into the legislative body, although socialization strains may be just as difficult for the initiate lobbyist, the new President or governor, or the bureaucrat.[43]

When the new legislator enters the legislative system, he enters a group with time-honored norms, and he must undergo a socialization process in order to learn the role system of which he is to be a part. In several state legislatures, a formal training period is held prior to the legislative session in order to begin the socialization of new members.[44] Indeed, "the tyro who reaches the capitol breathing fire after a vigorous campaign soon finds that he can accomplish nothing until he learns how to get along with his colleagues."[45]

Woodrow Wilson, in his classic treatise on Congress, suggested some of the difficulties of the socialization process for new legislators. He contended:

> The newly-elected member, entering its [the House] doors for the first time, and with no more knowledge of its rules and customs than the more intelligent of his constituents possess, always experiences great difficulty in adjusting his preconceived ideas of congressional life to the strange and unlooked-for conditions by which he finds himself surrounded after he has been sworn in and has become a part of the great legislative machine. No man, when chosen to the membership of a body possessing great powers and exalted prerogatives, likes to find his activity repressed, and himself suppressed, by imperative rules and precedents which seem to have been framed for the deliberate purpose of making usefulness unattainable by individual members. Yet such the new member finds the rules and precedents of the House to be. It matters not to him, because it is not apparent on the face of things, that those rules and precedents have grown, not out of set purpose to curtail the privileges of new members as such, but out of the plain necessities of business; it remains the fact that he suffers under their curb, and it is not until "custom hath made it in him a property of easiness" that he submits to them with anything like good grace.[46]

Shared Meanings

In order for a legislative system to operate and to maintain itself, the individuals who are involved must tend to see things in about the same way. More than a minimum level of knowledge is required; the participants must share meanings and have the capacity to understand one another in the legislative situation. For a variety of reasons, legislatures seem to be characterized by a high degree of shared cognition among a very high proportion of their participants, a characteristic that becomes clear when the high degree of morale is observed in legislative groups. "It is pleasurable," writes Harold F. Gosnell, "to be with one's own kind," and so "legislators draw together in their misery of exposure to the populace."[47]

Because legislators and others in the legislative system tend to define situations in about the same ways, legislative bodies tend to develop styles of life, characteristic climates or atmospheres.[48] Some legislative bodies, notably the United States Senate, are usually solemn, deliberate bodies. They function on the basis of traditionally established norms of decorum and etiquette. At the other extreme, perhaps, is the kind of atmosphere Dayton D. McKean found in the New Jersey legislature in the late 1930s. He describes the turmoil in the following way:

> A visitor going to the State House in Trenton some Monday night to observe the legislature in session would be struck by the crowds of men in the corridors, most of them in small groups of five or six, talking earnestly and smoking furiously. On an average evening there are about two hundred of these men, and perhaps twenty-five women. Some of them are political hangers-on, some are public employees, some are politicians from different parts of the state, but the greater part of them is composed of representatives of various state associations. The visitor would notice that they congregate thickest near the doors of the Assembly and Senate chambers, where many of them seem to be trying to get inside. . . .
>
> By the time the legislature convenes at eight-thirty o'clock the floor of the house is packed with people, all talking vigorously. The clamor is deafening. In the confusion each legislator who is present is surrounded by men and women, all trying to convince the man of the soundness of their views. Some thrust printed or mimeographed material into his hands or pile it on his desk.
>
> When the Clerk begins to call the roll most of them have to leave the floor. A few manage to stay by having press passes, by being former members, or simply by avoiding the sergeant-at-arms until he has made his rounds.[49]

No doubt most legislative groups operate in an atmosphere of considerably more solemnity than that described by McKean. The architecture of the buildings, the floor plan and furnishings, and the other accouterments of the situation tend to make the legislature a solemn body most of the time. Even so, legislative groups have days when humor and horseplay break the monotony of a long session.

Another aspect of legislative atmosphere is that of morale. Generally speaking, legislators are more like each other than they are like their constituents in education, dress, age, social class, and so forth. The claims that are made on the new legislator by his other group memberships must be adjusted to those of the legislative group. This adjustment is at least partially strengthened and facilitated by the morale of the legislative body. Truman writes:

> The morale of legislative groups is often marked, even when mutual confidence of the members is not productive of the most widely approved results. . . . Politicians of quite different opinions and of at least nominally opposed political party are likely nevertheless to understand and respect a colleague's fears and triumphs. . . . They speak a language which the uninitiated can never quite understand; they have had roughly parallel experiences that set them a little apart from those whose struggles have been of a different order. These commonalities help to support the conforming influences of the legislative group.[50]

Indeed, Garland C. Routt observed that "the *esprit de corps* displayed by legislative bodies, especially the smaller ones, is probably not rivaled by any other formally organized self-governing body."[51]

Empirical evidence does not clearly explain the cohesiveness of legislative groups, which may extend to the protection of group prerogatives by stubborn opposition to all the recommendations of the executive or to rivalry and suspicion between houses of a bicameral legislature. But the phenomenon has been observed often and discussed frequently by legislators themselves. It may have been stated in classic form by Speaker Champ Clark when, in 1915, he responded to a resolution commending him for his long record of impartial service by saying:

> A man who has never been in the Army has no adequate concentration of and never can understand the feeling that soldiers who have fought shoulder to shoulder have for each other; but, next to that, men who fight together in this legislative body have a feeling approximating that of the soldiers' feeling for each other.[52]

And the morale of legislative bodies goes beyond mere affect to shared definitions of the situation.

DEMAND AND SUPPORT INPUTS

The American legislature receives and processes *demands* for policies, services, or reassurance that are made upon the government. These demands may come from legislators' constituents, from organized interest groups, from state and local governmental bodies, from party organizations, or from the chief executive or agencies of the national bureaucracy; or they may arise from the exigencies of the times and environment. Thus, labor unions demand that Congress pass increases in the federal minimum wage; cities demand increased federal funding for pollution control; local governments demand increases in their share of tax funds for roads from the state legislature; citizens demand tighter legislation to provide law and order; the governor or President submits a detailed program of legislative action; and so on. Since the American legislature is a relatively autonomous institution exercising substantial, independent political power, its role in converting demands made on it into public policy or into authorization for the performance of governmental services is more prominent than that of legislatures in other political systems.

The American political process has regularly been analyzed and interpreted from a *demand-input* point of view. However, demands constitute only one type of input to the legislative system. In addition to demands, legislatures receive inputs of *support*. Of course, demands made upon legislatures may be accompanied by a degree of support for those individuals in or components of the legislature who can be expected to receive particular kinds of demands favorably. The responsiveness of the legislature to demands is likely to be in some measure proportional to the support offered or expected. Political parties, interest groups, and individual political leaders, among others, seek to build support for certain political alternatives in order to influence the decision-making processes of the legislature. However, support directed toward the legislature as an institution is not limited to a focus upon specific policy alternatives. Easton points out that

> if demands are to be processed into binding decisions, regardless of whose demands they are, it is not enough that support be collected behind them so as to impress the authorities with the need to adopt them as a basis for decisions. Basically, a large proportion of political research has been devoted to just this matter. Studies of voting behavior, interest groups, parties, and legislative analysis have all sought to reveal the way in which support is distributed, shifted, and mobilized behind varying demands (issues) or behind personalities and leadership groups seeking positions of authority. But if the authorities are to be able to make decisions, to get them accepted as binding, and to put them into effect without the extensive use of coercion, solidarity must be developed not only around some set of authorities themselves, but around the major aspects of the system within which the authorities operate.[53]

The legislative system constitutes one discrete subsystem of the polity around which support may become focused, producing conditions under which legislative decisions can be implemented without resort to extensive coercion. It is this type of support, directed toward the legislature as such, that has not been the subject of very extensive systematic research.[54]

Support for political institutions may take a number of different forms. It may be *specific* or *diffuse*. Specific support from members of a political system "flows from the favorable attitudes and predispositions stimulated by outputs that are perceived by members to meet their demands as they arise or in anticipation."[55] Diffuse support is that reservoir of good will which a system may engender, not dependent upon any particular output, and which in the extreme mode is typified by unquestioning loyalty or patriotism. Easton also suggests that support for political structures like legislatures may be *overt* or *covert*. The first involves some kind of action in the form of observable behavior; the latter involves attitudes, sentiments, predispositions, or frames of mind. Finally, support may be *direct*, linking the public with the political elite in some immediate way, or *indirect*, mediated by some communication links between public and elite.[56] It seems highly probable that the functional effectiveness of the legislative system (its capacity to contribute to the integration of the polity and to manage conflicts) is in some important measure dependent upon relatively high levels of diffuse support, perhaps largely covert and indirect, in the community.

THE FUNCTION OF LEGISLATIVE OUTPUT

The functions of the legislative system for its maintenance and for the larger polity are highly related. The adequate performance of one set of functions facilitates the performance of the others. Thus, adequate conflict management facilitates integration for the political system, and the relationship is reciprocal. Similarly, the more effectively the legislative system maintains itself as a viable system of interaction among roles, the more effectively it functions for the polity as a whole. This interrelatedness is demonstrable in terms of the legislative output. The concrete output of a legislature includes decisions, public policy, services, supervision, and information. Such output has functional consequences for the integration of the political system in that "one of the major ways of strengthening the ties of the members [of the polity] to their system is through providing decisions that tend to satisfy the day-to-day demands of these members."[57] Legitimate, representative, authoritative legislative decisions facilitate the resolution of conflict among contending interests in the polity. John C. Wahlke maintains:

> The general legitimacy of the legislature as a decision-making system ultimately depends upon the character of its output. So does the assuasion or exacerbation of individual and group tensions or conflicts in society which potentially threaten to rupture the bonds of political community and destroy the basis of government itself. The degree of stability, or lack of it, and the potentiality of degeneration, solidification, or transformation of the total political system are also affected by the character and quality of legislative output.[58]

The consequences of legislative output for the general political system ultimately affect the legislature itself through feedback in such forms as electoral effects and communications to legislators (see Figure 1.2).

Legislative output has direct consequences for the legislature as well. As Wahlke has said:

> A given decision or decisions may so alienate one group of legislators as to affect drastically the course of all future deliberations and debate. That is, the state of conflict, tension, and group cohesion within the legislature itself is directly affected by its own output and its process of arriving at that output. In the same way, legislators' sense of concern, apathy, or efficacy may be affected by prolonged stalemate or continuing dissatisfaction with the legislative product on the part of individual legislators.[59]

That is, there is a direct feedback from output to the legislature itself, which may be dysfunctional for the operation and maintenance of the legislative system. Output feedback can also have effects upon nonlegislator components of the legislative system. For instance, legislative output of certain kinds may intensify the lobbying demands of some groups, reduce those of others, or force interest groups to concentrate their attention on some other political subsystem. Finally, the output of the legislature may have direct and indirect effects on the support accorded to the legislative institution.

FIGURE 1.2 Functional Consequences of Legislative Output

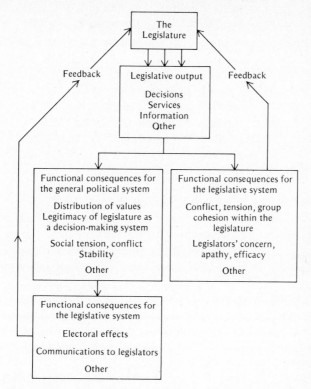

SOURCE: John C. Wahlke et al., *The Legislative System* (New York, 1962), p. 27.

LEGISLATIVE REPRESENTATION

Representation is a very general characteristic of human behavior. In fact, it might be said that all forms of human interaction are representative in the sense that "every individual is the natural representative of his own person."[60] Social, political, and economic institutions, where interpersonal relationships have become organized, stable, and accepted, typically manifest representative characteristics. The managers and directors of corporations represent the stockholders or some portion of them. Trade-union leaders represent union members.[61] In intergroup relations of all kinds, social groups are "linked together by persons who act as representatives for these groups."[62] The father may represent the family, or the elder male may represent the family clan in relationships with other kinship associations.[63] The college administration may represent the faculty and students to the public or to the legislature, and the school teacher may be represented by the principal.[64] Representative roles are played by a wide variety of individuals in our society, and functional social interaction and accommodation would seem inconceivable without them.

Political representation (i.e., representation of the body politic by political leaders) is also a very general concept. Political leaders are always representative in some sense, whether the political system in which they operate is closer to the authoritarian or to the democratic end of the continuum of political control. It is difficult to imagine how any kind of political regime could long survive unless it represented the people in some way or another. Thus, it is not improbable to suppose that all political systems have representative qualities and that representation stretches back historically to the earliest modes of political control.

Earlier, we dealt with representation as a mechanism for political integration, but we have as yet left its precise definition unspecified. There is a great deal of ambiguity in the literature about its definition.[65] Without enveloping ourselves in the contradictions and obfuscations about this term, we should like to suggest that representation is a functional mechanism that is multidimensional. There are three distinct dimensions of representation: the *authority* dimension, the *symbolic* dimension, and the *instrumental* dimension.[66]

The *authority* dimension of representation relates to the authorization of a person or persons to represent others. In the lawyer-client relationship, for instance, it is easy to see that the lawyer is a representative in the sense that he has been authorized by his client to represent him. The authorization of representation may be very formalistic and legalistic. The United States Congress and the American state legislatures are authorized representatives, and their authority is specifically granted in their respective constitutions and statutes. In the case of Congress, for example, legislative authority is granted in Article I of the United States Constitution, and Section 8 of that article sets forth detailed authority for particular kinds of enactments.

Thomas Hobbes, the renowned seventeenth-century English political philosopher, thought of representation primarily in terms of formal authorization. In *Leviathan,* he expressed his view that in the relationship between represented and representative, representatives "have authority from them so far-forth as is in their Commission, but no farther."[67] Also in *Leviathan,* Hobbes spelled out in detail his notion of the strictly contractual relation between citizen and representative:

> But if the Representative be an Assembly; whatsoever that Assembly shall Decree, not warranted by their Letters, or the Lawes, is the act of the Assembly, or Body Politique, and the act of every one by whose Vote the Decree was made; but not the act of any man that being present Voted to the contrary; nor of man absent, unlesse he Voted it by procuration. It is the act of the Assembly, because Voted by the major part; and if it be a crime, the Assembly may be punished, as farre-forth as it is capable, as by dissolution, or forfeiture of their Letters, (which is to such artificiall, and fictitious Bodies, capitall,) or (if the Assembly have propriety,) by pecuniary Mulct. For from corporall penalties Nature hath exempted all Bodies Politique. But they that gave not their Vote, are therefore Innocent, because the Assembly cannot Represent any man in things unwarranted by their Letters, and consequently are not involved in their Votes.[68]

Some modern writers have held closely to the Hobbesian view of representation.[69] Such writers would answer the question, "Who are the representatives?" with the reply, "Whoever are authorized in advance to act in behalf of their constituents and bind them by their decisions."

Analysis of the authority dimension of representation draws attention to the technique of election and its operation in a system of accountability.[70] Elections provide a way in which authorization can be given to representatives, who are, in some regimes, held accountable to the electorate for their stewardship by means of regular elections. We can give substantial attention to legislative elections in the United States as techniques for conferring authority because we are dealing with relatively democratic legislative systems. But elections provide only one means of conferring authority on representatives; in less democratic regimes, status or the mere threat of physical force may perform the same function. In addition, when we are dealing with the Congress and the state legislatures in the United States, we have under consideration conditions wherein authority to represent is formally conferred; but there is no theoretical reason why such conferral might not be tacit or even unconscious.

The *symbolic* dimension of representation has to do with the image of the representative or the legislative body as "standing for" the polity. In political mythology, the representative body is sometimes seen as a microcosm of the nation, a kind of body politic writ small, a miniature of the society as a whole; the importance to political integration of such symbolism should not be minimized.[71] Again, the legislator is a symbol for his constituents; he is expected to be the kind of person his constituents want him to be. As Alfred de Grazia has said:

> The representative embodies the traits, the outlook, even the sins, of the larger group. Furthermore, if the larger group has anything to say about it, the representative *ought* to possess some large measure of identity of characteristics with the group qualities, or at least some large measure of agreement with the group norms. How familiar in many societies are terms like "foreigner," "hick," and "snob" directed at representatives who lack such qualities. In American society there are unacknowledged qualifications of name, nationality, occupation, and education for many offices; such prerequisites for acting as a representative are none the less effective for not being incorporated into the written laws. Electors often demand these qualifications and, therefore, they often exist.[72]

Representation may be defined in its symbolic dimension as a condition in which an individual is represented "when the characteristics and acts of a person in a position of power in the society are in accord with the desires, expressed and unexpressed, of the individual."[73]

Symbolic representation places emphasis upon the character of the representative, the recruitment process, and the manner in which legislative membership is apportioned. To what extent are representatives similar to the larger group in their characteristics? In some democratic systems, constituents "have been known to select representatives *by reason* of their superior class position rather than to reject them because of it [because] the society's norms for representation may have demanded special differences rather than identity."[74] Such norms are often combined with expectations that maintain the political fictions of the folksy strategy because representatives are well aware of them. Democratic Senator

Robert S. Kerr, an oil millionaire from Oklahoma, used to board an airplane in Washington dressed like a New York banker and emerge in Tulsa in a baggy white suit and floppy hat. It is said that Huey Long, Louisiana's "Kingfish," wore silk pajamas to bed but quickly put on an old-fashioned nightgown one night when newspaper photographers came to the executive mansion to photograph him signing a bill. Such symbolic identification is also an important factor in the political appeal of dictators.

The symbolic dimension in representation also draws attention to the apportionment of legislatures. Apportionment and the drawing of legislative district boundary lines are important techniques of representation, and they have become especially controversial in the United States. No device of representation extends equally to all individuals, and none is politically neutral. "The process of apportionment," de Grazia says, "is a point of entry for preferred social values. The existing system of apportionment, whether legal, illegal, or extra-legal, institutionalizes the values of some group in a society."[75]

The *instrumental* dimension in representation refers to the action of representatives. Representatives are expected by their constituents to act for them, to be their instruments for getting things done.[76] In these terms, representation may be defined as a way of acting or an expectation about how a representative ought to act in place of, or on behalf of, his constituents. The relationship between the represented and the representative provides the basis for controversy about how the representative ought to act, as well as for recent empirical investigations into the reciprocal role expectations and policy agreements between represented and representative, which we shall explore in detail in Chapter 15.

Political philosophers and legislators have differed dramatically over the question: In what manner should the legislator act in representing his constituents? The classic answer to this is supplied by Edmund Burke's theory of representation. In 1774, Burke, a member of the English Parliament, told the electors of Bristol:

> To deliver an opinion is the right of all men; that of constituents is a weighty and respectable opinion, which a representative ought always to rejoice and hear, and which he ought always most seriously to consider. But *authoritative* instructions, *mandates* issued, which the member is bound blindly and implicitly to obey, to vote, and to argue for, though contrary to the clearest conviction of his judgment and conscience,—these are things utterly unknown to the laws of this land, and which arise from a fundamental mistake of the whole order and tenor of our Constitution.
>
> Parliament is not a *congress* of ambassadors from different and hostile interests, which interests each must maintain, as an agent and advocate, against other agents and advocates; but Parliament is a *deliberative* assembly of *one* nation, with one interest, that of the whole—where not local purposes, not local prejudices, ought to guide, but the general good, resulting from the general reason of the whole. You choose a member, indeed; but when you have chosen him, he is not a member of Bristol, but he is a member of *Parliament*. If the local constituent should have an interest or should form an hasty opinion evidently opposite to the real good of the rest of the community, the member for that place ought to be far as any other from any endeavor to give it effect.[77]

The modern legislator faces similar problems in defining how he should represent his constituents. Consider the remarks made by Senator J. William Fulbright (D-Ark.) in a speech at the University of Chicago in 1946:

> The average legislator early in his career discovers that there are certain interests, or prejudices, of his constituents which are dangerous to trifle with. Some of these prejudices may not be of fundamental importance to the welfare of the nation, in which case he is justified in humoring them, even though he may disapprove. The difficult case is where the prejudice concerns fundamental policy affecting the national welfare. A sound sense of values, the ability to discriminate between that which is of fundamental importance and that which is only superficial, is an indispensable qualification of a good legislator. As an example of what I mean, let us take the poll-tax issue and isolationism. Regardless of how persuasive my colleagues or the national press may be about the evils of the poll tax, I do not see its fundamental importance, and I shall follow the views of the people of my state. Although it may be symbolic of conditions which many deplore, it is exceedingly doubtful that its abolition will cure any of our major problems. On the other hand, regardless of how strongly opposed my constituents may prove to be to the creation of, and participation in, an ever stronger United Nations Organization, I could not follow such a policy in that field unless it becomes clearly hopeless.[78]

The statements of Burke and Fulbright illustrate competing conceptions about how the legislator ought to represent his constituents. They suggest "two possible foci of representation: local, necessarily hostile interests, on the one hand; and a national interest, on the other hand."[79] Burke rejected the local focus of representation and advocated the latter. Senator Fulbright's comments suggest that legislators may often combine the two, depending upon the nature of the issue involved. Burke also linked a particular focus of representation with a certain representational style. He held to the free-agent conception of representation, believing that the representative ought to be guided by his own best judgment, rather than to the delegate notion of representation, in which the legislator is instructed by his constituents and ought to vote their instructions regardless of his own views.

Of course, modern legislative life is not as simple as these comments may suggest. For Senator Fulbright, it is whether or not the issue is fundamental to the national welfare that counts; if it is not, he will accept the mandate of his constituents *as he sees it.* Obviously, many referents may "constitute significant foci of orientation for the representative as he approaches his legislative task."[80] These focuses may be geographical interests, such as the electoral district, the state, or the nation; or they may be political parties, political-interest groups, or administrative agencies.

The development of the modern party systems of Western democracies has had significant ramifications for legislative representation. In some political systems, political parties are, in effect, intermediate representative agencies between the constituent and the legislature. The British parliamentary system is a polity in which, at least in the immediate post–World War II period, the member of the House of Commons was elected by his constituents to be a cog in the party machinery of the Commons. Although party orientations are less pronounced in the United States than in Britain, continental European nations, and some Asian systems, the party representative is to be found in American legislative systems. Illustrations can be cited of the pressure-group-oriented legislator. Senator Henry Jackson (D-Wash.) has, for instance, often been denominated "the senator from Boeing" because of his active representation of the interests of the Boeing Aircraft Company, an important concern in his state. There are other familiar shorthand descriptions of legislators in the United States: oil senators, wheat senators, cotton senators, and so forth. Again, examples abound of legislators whose representative orientation sometimes is in the direction of administrative agencies; Senator Stuart Symington (D-Mo.), a former Secretary of the Air Force, was once said to speak in defense matters from the point of view of the Air Force.

It is possible analytically to keep distinct the focal and stylistic characters of representation and to emphasize that a variety of combinations are theoretically possible. "Burke's linkage of a particular areal focus of representation with a particular representational style constitutes only a special case on a generic series of empirically viable relationships between possible and different foci of representation and appropriate styles of representation."[81] And emphasis upon the focuses and styles of representation permits empirical observation of the instrumental dimension of representation; that is, we are concerned here not with how decisions should be made, whether legislators are authorized to decide, or whether constituents acquiesce, but rather with how decisions are actually made.

This chapter does not constitute a functional theory of legislative systems. A great deal more empirical evidence than is now available is necessary in order to begin the process of specifying relationships among the significant variables suggested here. It is a convenient, if taxonomic, way of looking at legislative life. The chapters that follow are far more eclectic than this chapter may have suggested. We hope that this book will make a contribution toward a better theoretical understanding of legislative systems, but we recognize that the body of knowledge of legislative systems is only beginning to grow significantly and is at present quite inadequate for a fully developed theoretical analysis. The present chapter attempts only to integrate and to make more meaningful what we shall say in those that follow.

NOTES

1.   Much of the material in the next few pages relies heavily upon and quotes directly from Samuel C. Patterson, *Toward a Theory of Legislative Behavior* (Stillwater, Okla., 1962), pp. 16–37.

2.   See Talcott Parsons, *The Social System* (Glencoe, Ill., 1951), pp. 5–6; and *Essays in Sociological Theory* (Glencoe, Ill., 1954), p. 213.

3.   David Easton, *The Political System* (New York, 1953), pp. 129–130. See also Samuel C. Patterson, "The Role of the Deviant in the State Legislative System," *Western Political Quarterly* 14 (1961):460–472; and William C. Mitchell, "The Polity and Society: A Structural-Functional Analysis," *Midwest Journal of Political Science* 2 (1958):403–420.

4.   The problems of drawing lines around behavioral systems are many, and abstracting a subsystem makes its definition somewhat arbitrary. This point is discussed in A. R. Radcliffe-Brown, *A Natural Science of Society* (Glencoe, Ill., 1957), pp. 60–62.

5.   Legislative activities are defined in more traditional terms in Roland Young, "Representative Government and the Legislative Process," in *Research in Political Science,* ed. Ernest S. Griffith (Chapel Hill, N.C., 1948), p. 45; and in the Council of State Governments' study, *Our State Legislatures* (Chicago, 1948), p. 1.

6.   Our analysis of legislative functions relies upon the following: D. F. Aberle et al., "The Functional Prerequisites of a Society," *Ethics* 60 (1950):100–111; Marion B. Levy, Jr., *The Structure of Society* (Princeton, N.J., 1952); Robert K. Merton, *Social Theory and Social Structure* (Glencoe, Ill., 1957), pp. 85–117; Talcott Parsons, *Structure and Process in Modern Societies* (Glencoe, Ill., 1950); David Easton, "An Approach to the Analysis of Political Systems," *World Politics* 9 (1957):383–400; Mitchell, "The Polity and Society," pp. 403–420; Gabriel A. Almond, "A Functional Approach to Comparative Politics," in *The Politics of Developing Areas,* eds. Gabriel A. Almond and J. S. Coleman (Princeton, N.J., 1960), pp. 3–64; John C. Wahlke et al., *The Legislative System* (New York, 1962), pp. 3–28.

7.   See Wahlke et al., *The Legislative System,* chap. 1; and Mitchell, "The Polity and Society," pp. 403–420.

8.   Kenneth E. Boulding, *The Image* (Ann Arbor, Mich., 1956), p. 103.

9.   David B. Truman, *The Governmental Process* (New York, 1951), p. 394.

10.   Earl Latham, *The Group Basis of Politics* (Ithaca, N.Y., 1952), pp. 35–36.

11.   Truman, *The Governmental Process,* p. 393.

12.   Ibid., pp. 322–332.

13.   Arthur F. Bentley, *The Process of Government* (Bloomington, Ind., 1949), p. 493.

14.   Truman, *The Governmental Process,* p. 372.

15.   Easton, "An Approach to the Analysis of Political Systems," p. 390.

16.   Theodore J. Lowi, *Legislative Politics U.S.A.* (Boston, 1962), p. xix.

17.   See, for example, Herman Turk and Myron J. Lefcowitz, "Towards a Theory of Representation Between Groups," *Social Forces* 40 (1962):337–341.

18.   See Loren Beth, "The Supreme Court and State Civil Liberties," *Western Political Quarterly* 14 (1961):825–838.

19.   Bentley, *The Process of Government,* p. 363.

20.   Bertram M. Gross, *The Legislative Struggle* (New York, 1953).

21.   Ralph Linton, *The Study of Man* (New York, 1936), pp. 133–140 and *The Cultural Background of Personality* (New York, 1945), pp. 76–77.

22.   Eugene L. Hartley and Ruth E. Hartley, *Fundamentals of Social Psychology* (New York, 1955), p. 486. Among a score of useful treatments of the role concept is the comprehensive analysis by Neal Gross, Ward S. Mason, and Alexander W. MacEachern, *Explorations in Role Analysis* (New York, 1958). See also Bruce J. Biddle and Edwin J. Thomas, eds., *Role Theory: Concepts and Research* (New York, 1966).

23.   Hartley and Hartley, *Fundamentals of Social Psychology.*

24.   Ibid., p. 486.

25.   We are here employing the familiar definition of *norm* of George C. Homans. "A norm . . . is an idea in the minds of the members of a group, an idea that can be put in the form of a statement specifying what the members or other men should do, ought to do, are expected to do, under given circumstances," where "any departure of real behavior from the norm is followed by some punishment." See George C. Homans, *The Human Group* (London, 1951), p. 123.

26.   Theodore M. Newcomb, *Social Psychology* (New York, 1950), p. 280.

27.   Merton refers to the individual's occupancy of a number of positions as his "status-set." See *Social Theory and Social Structure,* pp. 369–370.

28.   Linton, *The Study of Man,* p. 114.

29.   Newcomb, *Social Psychology,* p. 280.

30. See Parsons, *Essays in Sociological Theory,* p. 230.

31. Newcomb, *Social Psychology,* p. 286; and S. F. Nadel, *The Theory of Social Structure* (Glencoe, Ill., 1957), pp. 59–60.

32. Hartley and Hartley, *Fundamentals of Social Psychology,* p. 547; Parsons, *The Social System,* pp. 234–235.

33. See Talcott Parsons and Edward A. Shils, eds., *Toward a General Theory of Action* (Cambridge, Mass., 1954), p. 192.

34. John T. Gullahorn, "Measuring Role Conflict," *American Journal of Sociology* 61 (1956):299.

35. See "Research in Political Behavior," *American Political Science Review* 46 (1952): 1028.

36. Merton, *Social Theory and Social Structure,* pp. 225–386.

37. Hartley and Hartley, *Fundamentals of Social Psychology,* p. 465.

38. Samuel A. Stouffer suggested that "it may be the very existence of some flexibility or social slippage—but not too much—which makes behavior in groups possible." See Samuel A. Stouffer, "Analysis of Conflicting Social Norms," *American Sociological Review* 14 (1949):717.

39. These alternatives have been adapted from Jackson Toby, "Some Variables in Role Conflict Analysis," *Social Forces* 30 (1952):323–327.

40. This is the emphasis of the analysis of Robert A. Dahl and Charles E. Lindblom, *Politics, Economics and Welfare* (New York, 1953), p. 329.

41. Ibid., p. 334.

42. Merton, *Social Theory and Social Structure,* pp. 31–33.

43. See, for example, Bernard Schwartz, *The Professor and the Commissions* (New York, 1959).

44. See, for example, York Y. Willbern and Donald H. Clark, "Pre-Legislative Conferences in Indiana," *State Government* 32 (1959):43–46.

45. Truman, *The Governmental Process,* p. 343.

46. Woodrow Wilson, *Congressional Government* (New York, 1956), pp. 59–60; first published in 1885.

47. Harold F. Gosnell, *Democracy: The Threshold of Freedom* (New York, 1948), p. 233.

48. See Hartley and Hartley, *Fundamentals of Social Psychology,* pp. 396–400.

49. Dayton D. McKean, *Pressures on the Legislature of New Jersey* (New York, 1938), pp. 50–51.

50. Truman, *The Governmental Process,* p. 344.

51. Garland C. Routt, "Interpersonal Relationships and the Legislative Process," *Annals of the American Academy of Political and Social Science* 195 (1938):130.

52. U.S. Congress, *Congressional Record,* 63rd Cong., 3d sess., p. 5520.

53. David Easton, *A Systems Analysis of Political Life* (New York, 1965), pp. 157–158.

54. See G. R. Boynton, Samuel C. Patterson, and Ronald D. Hedlund, "The Structure of Public Support for Legislative Institutions," *Midwest Journal of Political Science* 12(1968):163–180; and Samuel C. Patterson, G. R. Boynton, and Ronald D. Hedlund, "Perceptions and Expectations of the Legislature and Support for It," *American Journal of Sociology* 75 (1969):62–76.

55. Easton, *A Systems Analysis of Political Life,* p. 273.

56. Ibid., pp. 159–161, 225–229.

57. Easton, "An Approach to the Analysis of Political Systems," p. 395.

58. Wahlke et al., *The Legislative System,* p. 26.

59. Ibid., p. 27.

60. Ferdinand Tonnies, *Community and Association* (London, 1955), p. 203.

61.   See Avery Leiserson, "Problems of Representation in the Government of Private Groups," *Journal of Politics* 11 (1949):566–577.

62.   Turk and Lefcowitz, "Towards a Theory of Representation Between Groups," pp. 337–341.

63.   See Francis X. Sutton, "Representation and the Nature of Political Systems," *Comparative Studies in Society and History* 2 (1959):1–10.

64.   See R. Jean Hills, "The Representative Function: Neglected Dimensions of Leadership Behavior," *Administrative Science Quarterly* 8 (1963):83–101.

65.   For an exhaustive discussion of many definitions extant, see John A. Fairlie, "The Nature of Political Representation," *American Political Science Review* 34 (1940):236–248, 456–466; and Charles E. Gilbert, "Operative Doctrines of Representation," *American Political Science Review* 57 (1963):604–618.

66.   The best contemporary treatment of political representation can be found in Hanna F. Pitkin, *The Concept of Representation* (Berkeley and Los Angeles, 1967). See also J. Roland Pennock and John W. Chapman, eds., *Representation* (New York, 1968). These dimensions are expressed in somewhat different terms in A. H. Birch, *Representative and Responsible Government* (London, 1964), pp. 13–22.

67.   Thomas Hobbes, *Leviathan* (London, 1953), p. 84; first published in 1651.

68.   Ibid., p. 119. See Hanna F. Pitkin, "Hobbes's Concept of Representation," *American Political Science Review* 58 (1964):328–340.

69.   See, for example, Karl Loewenstein, *Political Power and the Governmental Process* (Chicago, 1957), pp. 38–39; Edward M. Sait, *Political Institutions: A Preface* (New York, 1938), pp. 476–478; and a discussion of a variety of philosophical positions in Gosnell, *Democracy,* pp. 124–142.

70.   See, for example, Henry J. Ford, *Representative Government* (New York, 1924), p. 157.

71.   On symbolic images, see Boulding, *The Image,* pp. 109–110. Boulding points out that "political images include not only detailed images of role expectations. They also include what might be called symbolic or personalized images of institutions themselves. A symbolic image is a kind of rough summation or index of a vast complexity of images of roles and structures. These symbolic images are of great importance in political life."

72.   Alfred de Grazia, *Public and Republic: Political Representation in America* (New York, 1951), p. 5.

73.   Gosnell, *Democracy,* p. 130.

74.   de Grazia, *Public and Republic,* p. 6.

75.   Alfred de Grazia, "General Theory of Apportionment," *Law and Contemporary Problems* 17 (1952):256–267; quotation at 257.

76.   See, for example, Carl J. Friedrich, *Constitutional Government and Democracy* (Boston, 1941), p. 260.

77.   Louis I. Bredvold and Ralph G. Ross, *The Philosophy of Edmund Burke* (Ann Arbor, Mich., 1960), pp. 147–148.

78.   Center for the Study of Democratic Institutions, *The Elite and the Electorate* (New York, 1963), p. 6.

79.   Heinz Eulau et al., "The Role of the Representative: Some Empirical Observations on the Theory of Edmund Burke," *American Political Science Review* 53 (1959):742–756; quotation at 744.

80.   Ibid., p. 744.

81.   Ibid., p. 745.

CHAPTER TWO

The Development
of American Legislatures

As representative assemblies go, American legislatures have quite long histories; and it is difficult to understand contemporary legislative politics fully without some knowledge of how legislatures came to be what they are. At the same time, the systematic study of the history of American legislatures, even the Congress, is very incomplete. Despite this, we attempt in this chapter to trace some of the important and measurable lines of development of these institutions. To do so reasonably briefly, we have adopted the working assumption that an institution's development can be traced by examining the degree to which that institution has adapted itself to changes in the environment, the relative independence or autonomy of the organization, and the extent of the internal complexity and unity of the organization.[1] A legislature that is at once highly adaptable, autonomous, complex, and coherent can be said to be highly developed. In general, American legislatures are much more highly developed, or institutionalized, than they were in the eighteenth century; but, of course, there has been considerable irregularity in their development. Institutionalization is not inevitable, nor has it been, in the case of American legislatures, a steady, upward, linear progression, for institutions can decline, decay, and disappear. As we probe the main dimensions of institutionalization for American legislatures, we will suggest elements of decay as well as features of development.

INSTITUTIONALIZATION OF REPRESENTATION

In the more than 200 years of their existence, American legislatures have undergone significant developmental change as representative bodies. The fact that they have been in existence for a fairly long period of time suggests that these institutions have been relatively adaptable to changing forces in the environment. Internally, these institutions have become more complex in their organization and procedures. With relative and changing degrees of success, American legislatures have tended to become autonomous organizations, existing without domination by other agencies, such as party organizations or political executives. And these legislatures have become increasingly coherent in the sense that today there is a greater degree of consensus or unity on basic organizational norms than existed in the early years of the Republic. Finally, decision making by American legislatures in the conduct of their internal business affairs has become relatively more universalistic, dependent more upon objective criteria, the "merits" of the case, and less upon particularistic considerations, such as those of purely personal or partisan advantage. In these respects, it may be said that American legislatures have, more or less, become more highly institutionalized.

In taking relative adaptability, complexity, autonomy, coherence, and universalism as desiderata for legislative institutionalism, we really are suggesting five underlying developmental dimensions along which we may roughly locate American legislatures:

1. Autonomy _____ Subordination
2. Complexity _____ Simplicity
3. Universalism _____ Particularism
4. Coherence _____ Disunity
5. Adaptability _____ Rigidity

To the extent that these dimensions can be taken to imply fairly explicit modes of measurement, it should be possible, in principle, to make estimates of the degree of autonomy-subordination, complexity-simplicity, universalism-particularism, coherence-disunity, and adaptability-rigidity of a given legislative institution at a given point in time. Such a pattern of locations on these five dimensions, if taken as a whole, would constitute an empirical statement of the level of institutionalization of the legislature. Again in principle, such a pattern could be identified at different points in time in order to isolate developmental patterns in legislative institutionalization. A system for explaining developmental variations in patterns of institutionalization would constitute an important nucleus for a theory of institutional development. In this process of pattern identification, it should be possible to find waxing and waning in the location of the legislature along any one dimension of institutionalization. Thus, to speak of a legislature as having achieved a high level of institutionalization is to take institutionalization as a summary variable that combines the location of the legislature on the five discrete dimensions.

This is heady stuff, indeed, and neither the data nor the mechanics for handling it in a way that could adequately fulfill this prescription is presently available for American legislative bodies. However, some rough measurements can be used to illustrate the development of American legislatures along these dimensions. To the extent that it is possible, an examination of the development of American legislatures helps to explain how they evolved, irregularly to be sure, from fairly provincial and simplistic representative mechanisms in the eighteenth century to relatively professionalized and sophisticated legislative institutions in the twentieth century.

LEGISLATIVE DIFFERENTIATION AND INDEPENDENCE: AUTONOMY-SUBORDINATION

Nelson W. Polsby has pointed out that "one aspect of institutionalization is the differentiation of an organization from its environment."[2] In concrete terms, this means that a legislature may be said to be autonomous when it is different enough from the larger structure of political authority to exhibit a separate and distinctive career structure for its own members and to have a relatively independent internal system of leadership. Such a legislature may be said to have established its boundaries.

> The establishment of boundaries in a political organization refers mostly to a channeling of career opportunities. In an undifferentiated organization, entry to and exit from membership is easy and frequent. Leaders emerge rapidly, lateral entry from outside to positions of leadership is quite common, and persistence of leadership over time is rare. As an organization institutionalizes, it stabilizes its membership, entry is more difficult, and turnover is less frequent. Its leadership professionalizes and persists. Recruitment to leadership is more likely to occur from within, and the apprenticeship period lengthens. Thus the organization establishes and "hardens" its outer boundaries.[3]

The little illustrative evidence that is available quite clearly indicates the development of American legislatures along this dimension.

The Congress of the early nineteenth century was a fluid institution, indeed, when considered as a bounded career system for its members. It exhibited a relatively low level of autonomy in the sense that members moved fairly freely in and out of the institution. The fluidity of the early Congress is described by James S. Young:

> Instead of a stable community membership, one finds a society of transients. Almost none of the members acquired homes in the capital or established year-round residence there. They merely wintered in Washington, spending more time each year with constituents than with each other. Each new Congress, moreover, brought a host of new faces to the community, drastically reconstituting its membership every two years. For the first four decades of national government between one third and two thirds of the congressional community left every two years not to return. . . . New faces appeared and familiar ones departed with considerably greater frequency than in today's Congress. . . . While there were a few for whom the Hill was more than a way station in the pursuit of a career, a man's affiliation with the congressional community tended to be brief. . . .
>
> Thus, for all the forced social intimacy of their community life, the rulers on Capitol Hill were largely strangers to each other. "We never remain long enough together to become personally acquainted." "There are many individuals in this House whom I do not know, for I have never met them in the House or out of it." "Friendships . . . we had few and limited opportunities to cultivate," recalled another legislator, and those "were soon broken by our subsequent separation in different and often far-distant states."[4]

The congressional membership became increasingly stabilized during the nine-teenth century, as can be seen by the increase in the years of service of members of the United States House of Representatives and Senate shown in Figure 2.1. Although more often than not in the nineteenth century, over half of the member-ship of the House was made up of new entrants, by the post–World War I era, only about a fifth or less of the membership was neophyte. Figure 2.1 indicates that before the Civil War, representatives served only slightly more than two years on the average, and senators about four years; but in the late 1860s, an unmistakably steady increase in the tenure of congressional membership began. By the 1960s, representatives were serving an average of more than nine years, and senators more than ten years.

The early Congress simply did not provide a very stable or attractive career channel for its members. Few members found service in Congress appropriate as a career in which they might engage for a long period of time. A career in other political offices, notably at the state level, must have been regarded by many temporary congressmen as more attractive. In fact, it may have been more desirable from the standpoint of a political career in the early nineteenth century to serve in the Massachusetts General Court or the Virginia House of Burgesses than to remain a member of the United States Congress. In the first half of the nineteenth century, service in the United States Senate was cut short by many members who left office before the expiration of their terms; many of these senators then took office at the state level. About ninety senators resigned from

FIGURE 2.1   Increases in the Tenure of Congressmen, 1789–1971

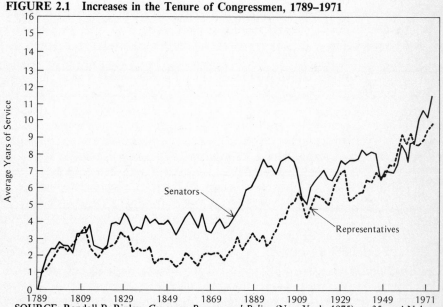

SOURCE: Randall B. Ripley, *Congress: Process and Policy* (New York, 1975), p. 35; and Nelson W. Polsby, "The Institutionalization of the U.S. House of Representatives," *American Political Science Review* 62 (1968):146. Reprinted from *Congress: Process and Policy* by Randall B. Ripley. By permission of W. W. Norton & Company, Inc. Copyright © 1975 by W. W. Norton & Company, Inc.

the Senate from 1790 to 1819, and another ninety resigned from 1820 to 1849. Thereafter, resignations declined rapidly, so that only about thirty members resigned from 1850 to 1879; about twenty, from 1880 to 1909; and fewer than twenty, from 1910 to 1939. Before 1850, more than a fourth (48 out of 180) of the senators who resigned did so to take state office; afterward, less than 10 percent of the few who resigned did so for this purpose.[5] Thus, like the House of Representatives, the Senate, by the end of the nineteenth century, became an institution that exhibited a highly bounded career structure, clearly differentiated from other kinds of political careers.

Although it is not clear when a bounded career system in an institution becomes hidebound, it does seem clear that a Congress that had no turnover of membership might be stagnant and unresponsive and thus reflect institutional decay. A very large majority of present congressional districts are electorally safe for the incumbent party. There are many reasons for this condition (see Chapter 4) which do not necessarily entail deliberate manipulations, but theoretically it would be possible through the device of pervasive gerrymandering of districts to rig congressional elections in a way that produced no turnover of seats beyond replacing deceased members. Far from representing evidence of institutionalization, the results of such deliberate rigging could produce institutional deterioration. When legislative autonomy becomes isolation, when the representative body becomes a "house without windows," then it fails to adapt to changes in the environment.[6] Therefore, autonomy and adaptability interact, and the degree of autonomy a representative institution can viably develop has to be tempered by the maintenance of adaptability. Unfortunately, the study of legislative institutionalization is not sufficiently sophisticated to make it possible to determine precisely when the critical nexus between these two modes of development occurs.[7]

In general, state legislatures have much less stable memberships than Congress; and in many states, high turnover of members appears to have taken place for the past quarter of a century (see Chapter 3). At least in this respect, therefore, it is possible to venture the assertion that Congress is at a much higher level of institutionalization than the state legislatures are. During the period from 1957 to 1963, the average percentage of members of the United States House of Representatives serving a first term was 14 percent; and the comparable percentage for the Senate was 12 percent. In contrast, in 1963, two-thirds of the lower houses of state legislatures were composed of more than 30 percent first-term members.[8] At the same time, it is possible to observe institutionalized tendencies on the part of state legislatures in terms of differentiation of channels for political careers. For example, between the 1880s and the end of World War II, the average number of terms a member of the Michigan legislature served nearly doubled. It should be possible to trace this kind of development in many states, especially New York, California, Illinois, or Ohio, which have quite highly institutionalized legislatures.

Another measure of legislative autonomy is the specificity and stability of leadership roles within the legislature. A legislature highly dominated by leadership from outside agencies (such as the chief executive, lobbyists, and extralegislative party leaders) is not as institutionalized as one that has developed internal leadership roles. The early American Congress was relatively subordinate to the President and the executive branch of the national government. Until the Third Congress, such concerted congressional leadership as there was came from Alexander Hamilton, who was not a member of Congress at all, but rather served as Secretary of the Treasury.[9] During most of the Jefferson administration, the President was able to serve as the effective legislative leader, managing the factions in the Democratic-Republican party in Congress.[10] Contemporary reports document the inchoate character of leadership in the incipient Congress. James Asheton Bayard, the Federalist senator from Delaware, said of leadership in the House of Representatives in 1806: "The fact is that the House of Representatives is so completely disorganized, having no man to lead them, and being split into twenty different opinions, that there is little prospect of their adopting or pursuing any regular plan." Federalist Congressman Josiah Quincy of Massachusetts said of the House in 1808: "No one pretends to see the course, or to be able to preside over the destinies of the House or the nation. . . ." Joseph Story, Democratic congressman from Massachusetts, reported of the House in 1818: "There is no rallying point for any party. Indeed, every thing is scattered. Republicans and Federalists are as much divided among themselves, as the parties formerly were from each other."[11]

By the second decade of the nineteenth century, Congress had developed internal committee and party leadership to a point at which it had come to be a relatively autonomous institution. But it took quite a long time beyond that for stable leadership careers to develop. The speakership of the House does not appear to have developed as a formidable position of party leadership until after the Civil War.[12] And throughout the nineteenth century, congressmen were chosen Speaker even though they had very brief previous careers in the House. Although Henry Clay is something of an exception, having been elected Speaker in 1811 during his first term as a member of the House, twenty-five of the thirty-three Speakers in the nineteenth century were elected to the leadership position after only eight years of service or less. Since 1899, long service in the House has generally been prerequisite to elevation to the speakership; eleven of the thirteen twentieth-century Speakers served more than twenty years in the House prior to their election as Speaker.[13]

The development of the roles of party floor leaders in Congress had to be associated with the crystallization of partisanship in the House and Senate, which reached its zenith in the later years of the nineteenth century. Because the House Committee on Ways and Means handled the burden of legislative work before the Civil War, the chairman of that committee was usually designated as the majority leader by the Speaker; and when the legislative work load shifted to the Committee on Appropriations after 1865, its chairman was ordinarily designated as floor leader. From 1896 until 1910, the chairman of the Ways and Means Committee once again served as majority leader. It was not until 1919, after the congressional reforms of 1910–1911 that took the selection of majority floor leader from the Speaker and shifted it to the party caucus, that a separate majority-leader role, distinct from a committee chairmanship, developed. Oscar Underwood (D-Ala.) was the first floor leader to be elected by the party caucus.[14] The role of the minority party leader in the House did not clearly emerge until the early 1880s, when the defeated candidate for Speaker clearly was the opposition leader; since 1911, minority floor leaders have been elected by the minority party caucus.[15] It was not until the end of the nineteenth century that party whips came to occupy a formal role in the party leadership of the House.[16]

Party leadership developed in a much more erratic manner in the Senate, where emergent floor leaders could not be discerned until the mid-1880s. Before that time, individual senators had been prominent as leaders on important questions of the day; and even after 1885, when party caucus chairmen fulfilled the roles of floor leaders, they were not always major leadership figures. But the modern practice of "electing a single Majority Leader or Minority Leader who would serve during an entire Congress and presumably would be reelected did not become established until the period between 1911 and 1913."[17] Soon thereafter, the positions of majority and minority whips became established, although the whip organization of the Senate has never been as important to the structure of leadership as it is in the House of Representatives.

Since the firm establishment of congressional floor-leadership roles in 1911, those who have held the position of leader have previously served a number of terms. Table 2.1 shows the average years of service as floor leader and the mean number of years in the House or Senate before election as floor leader for the period since 1900. Although House leaders have, on the average, served longer prior to elevation to floor leadership, the leadership in both houses has normally gone only to experienced members. And even though the average length of service as floor leader ranges from only five to eight years, Joseph Martin (R-Mass.) served as minority leader for sixteen years, and John McCormack (D-Mass.) served as majority leader for eighteen years. Of the twenty House members who served as floor leaders between 1911 and 1971, nine became Speaker of the House. Thus, congressional leadership has become stable in the sense that regular leadership career patterns have developed. The autonomy of Congress as an institution is indicated in this differentiation of leadership roles.[18]

The development of bounded career patterns for legislative leaders in the state legislatures has been subjected to very little systematic analysis, but it is clear that in general, these bodies exhibit lower levels of institutional development in this

TABLE 2.1   House and Senate Leaders in the Twentieth Century

HOUSE AND PARTY	MEAN YEARS OF SERVICE AS FLOOR LEADER	MEAN YEARS IN HOUSE OR SENATE BEFORE ELECTION AS FLOOR LEADER
Senate		
Democrats	5.6	8.3
Republicans	5.2	13.8
House of Representatives		
Democrats	5.3	18.6
Republicans	8.3	15.6

SOURCE: Randall B. Ripley, *Congress: Process and Policy* (New York, 1975), pp. 127–128. By permission of W.W. Norton & Company, Inc. Copyright © 1975 by W.W. Norton & Company, Inc.

regard. In the post–World War II era, there has been a turnover in the position of presiding officer either every two years or every two to four years in almost half of the state legislative bodies; in most of the remainder, an occasional leader has been able to serve a longer term; but in only fourteen bodies has any leader served for twelve years or more (see Chapter 6). As recently as the mid-1950s, as many as three-fifths of the state legislatures did not have a regular floor leader.[19] And in a few states, mainly in the South, the legislative leadership, largely chosen by the governor, could not be said to be independent of executive control.[20] In general, as John C. Wahlke has argued, it appears that "compared with the more familiar picture of leadership in the United States Congress, the picture of leadership in American state legislatures is often blurred and indistinct."[21]

DEVELOPMENT OF INTERNAL STRUCTURE: COMPLEXITY-SIMPLICITY

Although the development of the internal complexity of American legislatures may be measured roughly in several ways, the centrality of the committee system justifies our concentration on its development. One of the first students of congressional committees, Lauros McConachie, saw them in a rather prophetic way as prime indicators of the institutionalization of the American legislature. According to McConachie, the legislature

> from simple and unnoticed beginnings . . . expands with an individuality of its own into a complex organism . . . from the chaos of the beginning, from the nebular dust of scattered business, select committees group themselves into huge growing nuclei, the first standing committees, which, spinning more and more rapidly, begin to throw off new spheres, other standing committees.[22]

Although fairly sophisticated committee structures developed in some American states in the late eighteenth century, the early United States Senate functioned as a whole body, and the House adopted the procedure of conducting its business through the committee of the whole. Ralph V. Harlow has described early House practice:

> The outstanding feature of procedure in the House was the important part played by the committee of the whole. Much of the business in the House of Delegates of Virginia was transacted in that way, and the Virginians were influential enough to impose their methods upon the federal House, in spite of the grumbling opposition on the part of members from other sections. The rules were so framed as to permit almost unrestricted freedom of debate, and every member was given unlimited opportunity to satisfy his own craving to talk, and incidentally to convince his watchful constituents at home that he was not neglecting their interests. As a matter of fact, this extensive use of the informal session was not wholly bad from the democratic point of view. The House was so small that it was a genuine deliberative assembly, in which national questions could be discussed and considered from every possible angle. It was in committee of the whole that Congress worked out the first

tariff bill, and also the main outlines of such important measures as the laws organizing the executive departments. After the general principles were once determined, select committees would be appointed to work out the details, and to frame bills in accordance with the decision already agreed upon in committee of the whole.[23]

Internal institutional complexity goes hand in hand with the variety and technical intricacy of legislative problems, the size of the legislative body, and the professionalization of the legislative membership. The amateur legislators of the early Congresses were able to manage the moderate number and manageable form of policy demands by way of general consideration in committee of the whole, followed by closer scrutiny in small, temporary, select committees if these became necessary. The increasing organizational complexity of Congress over the nineteenth century is evidenced by the growth of specialized, permanent, autonomous standing committees.[24]

In the House, most of the earliest committees had housekeeping duties; but eight major committees now in existence date back to the first three decades of the House: Interstate and Foreign Commerce (1795), Ways and Means (1795), Interior and Insular Affairs (1805), Post Office and Civil Service (1808), District of Columbia (1808), Judiciary (1813), Veterans' Affairs (1813), and Government Operations (1816). The present committees on Agriculture, Armed Services, and International Relations (for a long time called the Committee on Foreign Affairs) were established in the early 1820s; and the present Public Works Committee was created in 1837. Immediately following the Civil War, the House established the committees on Appropriations, Banking and Currency (now called Banking, Currency, and Housing), and Education and Labor. The House Rules Committee was created in 1880; and the Committee on Merchant Marine and Fisheries, in 1887. Since World War II, five new House standing committees have been established: Un-American Activities, subsequently called Committee on Internal Security (1945); Science and Astronautics, now called Science and Technology (1958); Standards of Official Conduct (1968); and Budget (1975). In January 1975, the House abolished the Internal Security Committee, and elevated the Select Committee on Small Business to a standing committee. Although standing committees developed somewhat later in the United States Senate, the pattern there was much the same as in the House.[25]

The proliferation of congressional committees over the nineteenth and early twentieth centuries is an indicator of the increasing complexity of the internal organization of the House and Senate. For the House, the average number of committees increased regularly from about fifteen in the first decade of the nineteenth century to nearly sixty in the first decade of the twentieth century. The peak number in the House was reached in 1925, when there were sixty-one standing committees. The Senate, ultimately more prone to create specialized standing committees, had seventy-four such committees by 1913.[26] But after the 1920s, the sheer number of standing committees in Congress cannot be considered a meaningful indicator of the development of internal complexity. Both in the 1920s and in the mid-1940s, the committee structures of the houses of Congress were streamlined by reducing the number of standing committees, consolidating and rationalizing their jurisdictions, and increasing the size of their memberships. These major reorganizations did not diminish the organizational complexity of the congressional houses; rather, they both reflected the increased professionalization of the Congress and provided the structural setting for a somewhat different form of specialized committee proliferation in the propensity of committees to subdivide their legislative work through the creation of subcommittees. Standing and select committees of Congress were sometimes created or retained largely to provide office space and clerical assistance for members. Such was the case for the Senate committees on Revolutionary Claims, Indian Depredations, Transportation Routes to the Seaboard, and Disposition of Useless Papers in the Executive Departments and for similarly minor House committees.[27] The professionalization of the Congress, permitted by the construction of office buildings and the provision of staff assistance, made these sinecure committees unnecessary. More professionalized congressional handling of the federal budget, exemplified by the adoption of the Budget and Accounting Act of 1921, was reflected in the consolidation of committees with appropriations functions. The Legislative Reorganization Act of 1946, hailed by its leading architect as a "modernization of the standing committee system," reduced the number of standing committees from thirty-five to fifteen in the Senate and from forty-eight to nineteen in the House.[28] Since then, committees dealing with space sciences and the budget have been added in both houses. The House has added committees on congressional ethics and small business, and the Senate has added a committee on veterans' affairs.[29]

The internal complexity of Congress reflected in the proliferation of specialized subcommittees is not, of course, a phenomenon noticeable only since the passage of the Legislative Reorganization Act of 1946. Several major House committees (Appropriations, Ways and Means, District of Columbia) were divided into standing subcommittees as early as the 1890s.[30] Although unfortunately there is no definitive historical study of congressional subcommittees, it is clear that there was a substantial increase in their numbers after the 1946 Reorganization Act reduced the number of full committees. As Table 2.2 shows, before the act, there were a total of 180 subcommittees in intracameral or joint committees of Congress; but by 1975, the number had grown to 299. In the Ninety-fourth Congress (1975–1976), only three Senate committees had no subcommittees (Aeronautical

TABLE 2.2   Congressional Subcommittees, 1945–1975

| YEAR | NUMBER OF SUBCOMMITTEES | | | |
	House Committees	Senate Committees	Joint Committees	TOTAL
1945	106	68	6	180
1959	121	100	8	229
1961	131	109	13	253
1968	139	104	15	258
1970	138	104	15	257
1975	146	139	14	299

SOURCES: George Goodwin, Jr., *The Little Legislatures: Committees of Congress* (Amherst, Mass., 1970), p. 46; and *Congressional Staff Directory* for 1959, 1961, 1970, and 1975.

and Space Sciences, Budget, and District of Columbia); four (Appropriations, Commerce, Judiciary, and Labor and Public Welfare) had more than ten subcommittees. In the House, three committees (Budget, Rules, and Standards of Official Conduct) had no subcommittees; four had ten or more (Agriculture, Appropriations, House Administration, and International Relations).

It is very difficult to make developmental generalizations about state legislatures because almost no historical research has been done on them. State legislative committees developed in the late eighteenth century; Harlow showed that the "period between 1776 and 1790 . . . is the time when standing committees really came into extensive use" in state legislatures.[31] Committee systems developed especially rapidly during this period in Massachusetts and South Carolina, and the early development of revenue committees throughout the states is particularly interesting.[32] By the end of the nineteenth century, the complexity of committees in state legislatures more or less paralleled that of the Congress, so that Paul Reinsch could say in 1907: "It is a notable fact that during the last few decades both the number of committees, and the average of membership, have increased rapidly."[33] We should note here that analysis of contemporary state legislatures indicates generally lower levels of institutionalization in comparison with Congress; in Chapter 9, we will discuss the relatively weaker role of state legislative committees in comparison with congressional committees. It is possible that the development of significant specialized committees in the state legislatures was attenuated in the nineteenth century by the dominance of political party machines in many states and perhaps, also, to some extent by the distorting effects on state legislatures that increasingly in the nineteenth century resulted from their inordinately time-consuming task of electing United States senators.[34] For twentieth-century developments, it can be said that there has been a general decline in the number of state legislative standing committees. The average number of committees in the lower houses of state legislatures declined from thirty-nine in 1931 to twenty-seven in 1960–1961 and to seventeen in 1973. The number of state senate committees declined over the same time period from thirty-two to twenty-two to fourteen. (For more detailed figures, see Chapter 8.) This reduction in the number of state legislative committees represents not institutional decay but rather institutional streamlining. Until recently, the typical state legislature had a small number of committees that handled most of the work and a large number of committees that did very little. One consequence was a large number of committee assignments for the average member and a serious imbalance in the actual work load of legislators. One of the high-priority items in most recent campaigns for state legislative reform has been to improve the committee system by reducing the number of committees, redistributing the work load, and improving the staffing of committees. The increase in the quantity and quality of committee staffs, which was dependent on a reduction in the number of committees, provides another measure of increasing institutionalization of state legislatures. Although there has not been much proliferation of subcommittees at the state level, the changes in the number and structure of state committees constitute a development in institutionalization comparable with the reforms in congressional committee structure inaugurated in the 1946 Legislative Reorganization Act.

AUTOMATED DECISION RULES:
UNIVERSALISM-PARTICULARISM

An institution is a highly predictable setting. When legislative organizations come to deal with organizationally disintegrative problems in a relatively predictable, automatic way, they can be said to have become institutionalized. The handling of contested elections and the use of seniority in the selection of committee chairmanships provide important examples of the development in the American legislature of universalistic criteria for dealing with issues that are potentially full of conflict. Here we will confine our illustrations to the Congress because, in general, state legislatures do not use seniority as the basis for the selection of committee chairmen (this matter is at the discretion of the Speaker) and because little is known in a systematic way about contested elections to state legislatures. It will have to suffice to suggest that in both respects, state legislatures are poorly institutionalized in comparison with Congress.

The decline in the turnover of membership of Congress and the development of stable, autonomous committees made possible at the end of the nineteenth century an automated rule for the selection of committee chairmen that would remove the selection from partisanship within the legislative houses and from the outside influences of executive or interest-group pressure. The change is described succinctly by Neil MacNeil:

> In the latter part of the nineteenth century, a shift took place in the House's attitude toward committee assignments. The House came to feel, institutionally, that the longer a man familiarized himself with a given subject, the more he could know about that subject and the better he could deal with it. It was the beginning of individual specialization in the House, a concept that has grown stronger ever since. It was the beginning also of the seniority concept, of granting the individual Representative a formal "right" to the committee assignment he held, a right that carried over year after year, so long as he continued to be elected to the House. Out of this grew the right of the most senior majority party member of a committee automatically to become its chairman.[35]

The so-called seniority rule is an informal, unwritten legislative norm (see Chapter 14). It has been invoked as a matter of practice in the houses of Congress for a long time, although the practice crystallized in the House following the rule changes in the 1910–1911 session when the Speaker lost the power to appoint committee chairmen. Since that time, committee lists and chairmanships have been adopted by the political party caucuses, although these lists are first prepared by the respective party committees on committees.[36]

Quite a thorough analysis of the practice of seniority in the United States House of Representatives has been made by Polsby. He calculated the proportion of the time seniority was followed in the selection of committee chairmanships between 1881 and 1963. The results of this investigation are shown in Figure 2.2. Polsby summarized the analysis by saying that:

FIGURE 2.2   Development of Seniority in the United States House of Representatives, 1881–1963

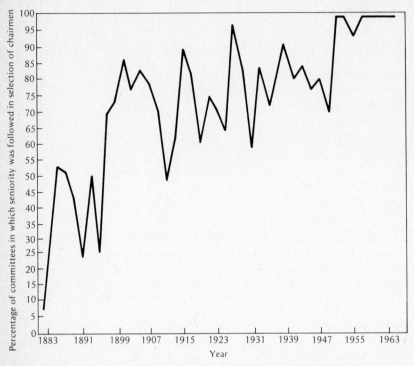

SOURCE: Nelson W. Polsby, Miriam Gallaher, and Barry S. Rundquist, "The Growth of the Seniority System in the U.S. House of Representatives," *American Political Science Review* 63 (1969):793.

In the period between 1881 and 1911, a large number of committees and a discretionary system of appointment in which seniority and political considerations played a part produced a pattern of relatively frequent violations of seniority. Many of these were responsive to the necessity for new Speakers, after a party turnover in the House, to organize a majority coalition in the committees. After 1911 the system responded at first to the centralized decisions enforced by the Democratic caucus, and later to piecemeal bargaining and tinkering, as Representatives with many committee assignments adjusted their workloads with respect to a large number of narrowly focused committees. This produced some violations of seniority, but within a context providing much less power and discretion for party leaders in the House. After 1946, both the discretionary rights of leaders and the rich array of minor committees disappeared with the "streamlining" of the committee system, and thus from 1946 onward, the rule of seniority is virtually never breached.[37]

Although the political consequences of the seniority rule for the selection of committee chairmen are substantial, the rule itself is automatic. Insofar as it goes, it does not matter whom the representative's friends are, which interest groups support him, or whether he has the favor of the President or the Speaker; the committee member of the majority party with the longest continuous service on the committee becomes the chairman. That the rule is not inviolable was indicated in 1975, when several seniority chairmen were replaced by actions of the House Democratic caucus. In the future, the House may be less willing than it was to allow senior members to become chairmen automatically, requiring seniority chairmen to be formally selected by the majority party caucus (see Chapter 8).

In the matter of handling of contested elections by Congress, the Constitution makes each house of Congress "the judge of the elections, returns and qualifications of its own members" (Article I, Section 5). When two or more persons claim to have been legally elected to the same House or Senate seat, the contest may be handled in one of two ways. First, it may be dealt with on the particularistic grounds of pure partisanship, regardless of the merits of the case; the majority party in the house may seat the contestant of its own party. Second, the contest may be dealt with in a universalistic way, on the merits of the case, based upon careful investigation of the facts irrespective of the party affiliations of the contestants.

In the House of Representatives, there were 557 election contests between 1789 and 1964. The proportion of seats contested reached a peak during the Civil War era, remained at quite a high level through the 1890s, and then dramatically declined in the twentieth century. Since the late 1930s, less than 1 percent of House seats have been contested.[38] In the Congresses of the nineteenth century, it seems clear that election contests for House seats were almost invariably decided on the basis of purely partisan advantage, regardless of the merits of the cases. Speaker Thomas B. Reed said in 1890 that "probably there is not an instance on record where the minority benefited" in House decisions on election contests. Senator George F. Hoar, who as a House member served on the Committee on Elections, reported of the House in the 1870s that "whenever there is a plausible reason for making a contest, the dominant party in the House almost always awards the seat to the man of its own side." And DeAlva Stanwood Alexander concluded that "of these three hundred and eighty-two contests submitted up to and including the 59th Congress [1907], only three persons not of the dominant party obtained seats."[39] In contrast, at least since the 1920s, it can be said that "contested elections are settled with much more regard to due process and the merits of the case than was true throughout the nineteenth century."[40]

Contests in the seating of senators have also occurred; there have been more than 130 since 1789, although only 26 have occurred since 1916. In the nineteenth century, celebrated cases of contested Senate seats appear to have arisen because of purely partisan considerations. In describing ten cases that arose between 1857 and 1899 on the basis of allegations of bribery or corruption, George H. Haynes asserts that "a reading of the reports of the investigating committees leaves no question that in most instances not a desire for truth and justice, but party policy determined the bringing of the charges and the zeal with which they were pressed."[41] But it appears that the Senate never dealt with such cases in as partisan a way as the House did in the nineteenth century. Speaking of the Senate as a whole and of its Committee on Privileges and Elections (created in 1871), Haynes concluded that "since the same party has control of the Senate and of this frankly political committee, it is but natural that the decisions have generally favored the dominant party; but certainly partisan advantage has not governed election contests in the Senate so almost universally as it did for a century in the House."[42] The record appears to indicate that at least since Reconstruction, Senate election contests have generally been decided, insofar as the evidence made it possible, on the merits of the case.[43]

DEVELOPMENT AND SPECIFICATION OF NORMS: COHERENCE-DISUNITY

Although we discuss legislative norms more extensively in Chapter 14, it can be said here that a highly institutionalized legislative body is one in which there is relatively wide consensus on the unwritten rules of the game, or standards of proper conduct, among members. Where substantial disunity exists, where there is a great deal of disagreement over expectations of members' conduct, where there is not "general acceptance of the functional utility of the rules for enabling the group to do what a legislature is expected to do," the legislature's institutionalization level can be said to be low.[44]

The institutionalized legislature is, thus, one in which there is a substantial degree of reciprocity, courtesy, and predictability among representatives. This condition has been shown to characterize the contemporary United States Senate and the state legislatures in Ohio, Tennessee, New Jersey, and California.[45] With respect to standards of interpersonal courtesy, Donald R. Matthews said of the post–World War II Senate that " a cardinal rule of Senate behavior is that political disagreements should not influence personal feelings."[46] Congressman Clem Miller's "overwhelming first impression as a member of Congress" was "the aura of friendliness that surrounds the life of a congressman. . . . Almost everyone is unfailingly polite and courteous."[47] Congressman Jerry Voorhis found that "Congressmen are friendly souls."[48] These remarks illustrate the relatively high levels of consensus in contemporary American legislatures about interpersonal relations in the Congress.

There is fairly abundant evidence that the coherence of the United States House of Representatives in the nineteenth century with respect to levels of reciprocity, courtesy, and predictability in interpersonal interactions was weak, indeed, in comparison with the contemporary House. In the early nineteenth-century House, John Randolph of Virginia threatened Samuel W. Dana of Connecticut. The incident is recounted by William Plumer:

> Mr. Dana has every day attended the House & has expected Mr. Randolph would insult him by spitting in his face, kicking pulling his nose striking him with a horse whip, or some such method. Mr. Dana had been prepared to receive such an insult, not indeed tamely—but in such a manner as to cause the haughty Virginian to repent of his folly & insolence. Mr. Dana has carried weapons of defence in his pocket—a pistol with a spring bayonet—his friends have been near him—to see that the adherents of Randolph should not join in the assault.[49]

Alexander described an incident that took place in the early 1800s:

When Matthew Lyon, of Kentucky, spat in his face, [Roger] Griswold [of Connecticut, a member from 1795 to 1805] stiffened his arm to strike, but remembering where he was, he cooly wiped his cheek. But after the House by its vote failed to expel Lyon, he "beat him with great violence," says a contemporary chronicle, "using a strong walking-stick."[50]

Alexander also referred to a number of such episodes in the mid-nineteenth century:

Upon resuming his seat, after having replied to a severe personal arraignment of Henry Clay, former Speaker White, without the slightest warning, received a blow in the face. In the fight that followed a pistol was discharged wounding an officer of the police. John Bell, the distinguished Speaker and statesman, had a similar experience in Committee of the Whole (1838). The fisticuffs became so violent that even the Chair could not quell it. Later in the day both parties apologized and "made their submissions." On February 6, 1845, Edward J. Black, of Georgia, "crossed over from his seat, and, coming within the bar behind Joshua R. Giddings as he was speaking, made a pass at the back of his head with a cane. William H. Hammett, of Mississippi, threw his arms round Black and bore him off as he would a woman from a fire. . . .

. . . When Reuben M. Whitney was before a committee of investigation in 1837, Balie Peyton, of Tennessee, taking offense at one of his answers, threatened him fiercely, and when he rose to claim the committee's protection, Mr. Peyton, with due and appropriate profanity, shouted: "You shan't say one word while you are in this room; if you do I will put you to death." The chairman, Henry A. Wise, added; "Yes; this insolence is insufferable." As both these gentlemen were armed with deadly weapons, the witness could hardley be blamed for not wanting to testify before the committee again. . . .

. . . "These were not pleasant days," writes Thomas B. Reed. "Men were not nice in their treatment of each other."[51]

Congressman Lawrence M. Keitt of South Carolina was involved in a House fracas in the late 1850s:

[Galusha M. Grow, of Pennsylvania] had passed to the Democratic side of the chamber, and while there John A. Quitman, of Mississippi, asked leave to speak. Grow objected. Keitt, who stood near, said roughly: "If you are going to object, return to your own side of the House." Grow answered: "This is a free hall. Every man has a right to be where he pleases." Keitt, coming near, said: "I want to know what you mean by such an answer as that." Grow replied: "I mean just what I said. This is a free hall and every man has a right to be just where he pleases." Thereupon Keitt seized Grow by the throat, exclaiming: "I will let you know that you are a — — black Republican puppy." Grow knocked up his hand, saying, "No negro driver shall crack his whip over me." Keitt again grasped him by the throat, and Grow knocked him down.[52]

J. C. Clements describes the situation in 1890:

For unseemly thrusts and controversies between the Chair and the members in their places, and between members on the floor, and the general exhibition of ill-nature, the session has been unprecedented. A conspicuous illustration of this was given ... during the debate ... when coarse vulgarity, vile epithets and even physical blows were resorted to.[53]

Normative coherence appears to have developed in the Senate well before it did in the House, although commentators have reported a few serious confrontations in the Senate. In 1850, Senators Benton of Missouri and Foote of Mississippi "had clashed sharply in debate. While Foote was replying in kind to Benton's provocative speech, Benton rose angrily from his seat and strode toward Foote's chair. Seeing his threatening approach, Foote stepped toward the secretary's table, at the same time drawing and cocking a pistol. Members interfered. Benton returned to his seat and Foote surrendered his pistol."[54] Then there is the now-classic story of Congressman Preston Brooks of South Carolina who, in 1856, incensed by a speech by Senator Charles Sumner, entered the Senate chamber, "denounced him and broke a thick walking-stick over the Senator's head."[55] But in these and other similar cases, members expressed apologies to the Senate, the Senate censured participants, or both.[56]

DEVELOPMENT OF LEGISLATIVE PARTIES: COHERENCE-DISUNITY

The national capital was moved to Washington in 1800, but the Congress that went into business there was a frail and fragmented body, indeed. As an organization designed to resolve conflicts through the formulation of legislative policy, it was very much undeveloped. As Young has shown, the basis for fragmentation in the Jeffersonian Congress was largely to be found in the boardinghouse patterns of living among congressmen.[57] Members lived in boardinghouses near the capitol during the brief congressional sessions, and tended to vote cohesively within these boardinghouse groups. By about 1816, the development of committees further contributed to the fragmentation of the legislature. Coherence in the formulation of public policy in legislative bodies tends to be provided by political party formations, especially when two large parties confront one another. Yet, in the early Congress, party coherence was very minimal, since "party solidarity in the Jeffersonian Congress meant the achievement of agreement ... among men who had chosen to have as little to do with each other as possible."[58] Young found that "one searches the community record in vain for evidence that common party affiliation was the basis of any associational activity whatever in the everyday life of Capitol Hill."[59] He quotes James Fenimore Cooper's observation:

> The practice is for those who arrive first to choose their seats, and the choice is invariably respected.
> There is no such thing known as political division of seats. Members of the same politics certainly often choose to be placed near to each other, and sometimes the entire representation of a particular State is seen as near together as possible. But there is no rule in the matter.[60]

Young draws the following conclusions from his analysis of the congressional establishment of the early 1800s:

Quite irrespective of whatever party cohesion occurred on policy issues, the gross imbalance between conflict-producing and conflict-resolving behaviors and attitudes compels the conclusion that the congressional community was a fundamentally unstable social system. No impression emerges from the community record of Capitol Hill in the Jeffersonian era more clearly than the impression of a community lacking adequate means to resolve or stabilize the conflicts generated by its own structures and values, let alone those conflicts imported into it from the outside, to which, as a governing community, it was peculiarly susceptible. . . .

. . . To perform the inherently governmental function of resolving conflict in the polity at large, there must be some means for resolving conflict among the governors themselves, and some disposition to do so. There must be some means for displacing disintegrative conflict with harmless or constructive conflict. . . .

Such means, commensurate with the sources of conflict, are not discernible in the congressional community of Jeffersonian times.[61]

The development of political party coherence in Congress occurred slowly over the nineteenth century.[62] By the end of the century, historical accounts suggest that the Senate had become quite a highly politicized legislature in party terms. Although David J. Rothman's conclusions probably are overstated, his general point is well taken:

The Senate experienced the most vital changes in its history during the three decades that followed the end of Reconstruction. Both parties became firmly established, and a new concern for order and discipline accompanied their stability. The increased importance of party government sharply differentiated the institution at the opening of the twentieth century from its predecessors. The battlelines for control of the Senate parties were clearly delineated; the strategic posts were known, their strength predictable. . . . By 1900 the United States Senate had become modern, enjoying a life of its own.[63]

The House clearly developed as a highly partisan body by the end of the nineteenth century.[64] It is possible to trace the development of party coherence in policy formation by the House fairly precisely. An analysis of the proportion of party votes taken in the House in the first sessions of Congresses from 1867 to 1953 is given in Figure 2.3. In this context, a *party vote* is defined as a roll call on which at least 90 percent of the members of one party voted together against at least 90 percent of the members of the other party. As Figure 2.3 shows, the level of party voting in the House reached a peak about the turn of the century, a time when the House became highly institutionalized in other respects. In the twentieth century, party voting in the House has irregularly declined; by the 1930s, although political party affiliation accounted for the voting behavior of congressmen more often than any other single factor, the pattern of policy coherence had begun to trifurcate. Largely because of the sectional split in the Democratic membership of the House and the resultant rise of the southern conservative third force, which sometimes votes with the northern Democrats, sometimes with the Republicans, levels of strong interparty voting diminished to about 5 percent of the recorded collective decisions of the House membership.[65]

Another way to get a snapshot view of the development of party coherence in the Congress is to examine patterns of seating in the legislative chambers. As

FIGURE 2.3   Party Voting in the United States House of Representatives, 1867–1952

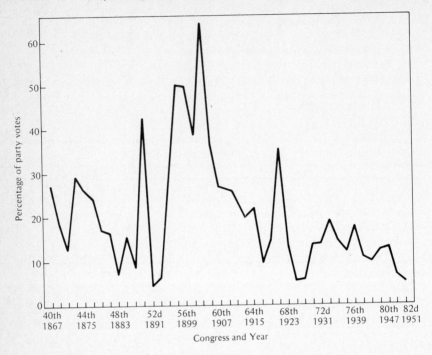

SOURCE: For 1881–1913, party voting scores are from David W. Brady and Phillip Althoff, "Party Voting in the U.S. House of Representatives, 1890–1910: Elements of a Responsible Party System," *Journal of Politics* 36 (1974):756. For other years, scores were provided by Professor David Brady, University of Houston.

James Fenimore Cooper noted in describing the Jeffersonian Congress, members did not tend to sit in clear party groups in the early 1800s. As Figure 2.4 suggests, the incidence of *seating aggregation* (the tendency of party members to sit together in the legislative chamber) was not very great even by 1863. By 1911, even though members of the House drew lots for choice of seats, Democrats and Republicans tended to sit in distinctive groupings, and they continued to do so afterward, even though specific seats were no longer assigned. In some state legislatures, it is possible to distinguish very similar patterns that demonstrate the development of party coherence through the analysis of legislative seating patterns over time.

RESPONSIVENESS OF THE LEGISLATURE: ADAPTABILITY-RIGIDITY

In general, a legislative institution that adapts to crises and responds effectively to challenges from its environment can be said to be relatively institutionalized. A legislature that closes itself off from its environment becomes a "house without windows"; it thus fails to adapt to new conditions and demands and can be said to be poorly institutionalized. Whether a particular legislative body is, in fact,

FIGURE 2.4 Seating Aggregation in the United States Congress, 1863–1911

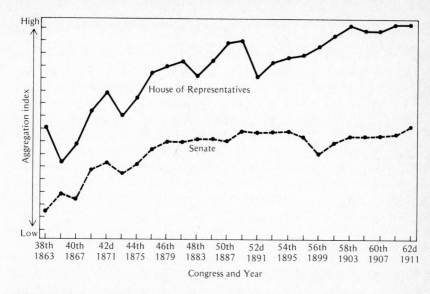

SOURCE: Samuel C. Patterson, "Party Opposition in the Legislature: The Ecology of Legislative Institutionalization," *Polity* 4 (1972):352

responsive to its environment will always be a matter of some controversy in the short run because those whose political interests are not satisfied at a given moment in history are likely to assert the claim that their failure to achieve what they want is not a result of their own lack of political support, effectiveness, or competence but rather that it reflects a fundamental failure of adaptation by the legislative institution itself. But assessments of the adaptability of legislatures cannot rest purely on the issue of whose ox is gored.

At the same time, it cannot be denied that the adaptability of American legislatures is extraordinarily difficult to assess with the kinds of evidence available on a systematic basis, and the available evidence is open to conflicting interpretations. Of the United States House of Representatives, Polsby has argued that "it seems reasonable to conclude that one of the main long-run changes . . . has been toward greater institutionalization."[66] Although he warns that legislative institutions are "continuously subject to environmental influence and their power to modify and channel that influence is bound to be less than all-encompassing," the thrust of Polsby's interpretation of the development of Congress is that it has been highly responsive, in the main, to changes in, and new demands from, the political environment.[67] However, using essentially the same kind of evidence, Samuel P. Huntington has attempted to argue that "Congress's legislative dilemma and loss of power stem from the nature of its over-all institutional response to the changes in American society" and that "during the twentieth century Congress has insulated itself from the new political forces which social change has generated and which are, in turn, generating more change."[68] Although we ignore at our peril holistic assertions about the adequacy of the adaptation of American legislatures to social, economic, and political change, and although we are very much aware that the adaptation of these institutions has been uneven, sometimes tenuous, and often painfully slow, it can be demonstrated that American legislatures have, in many respects, adapted to their environments. In the absence of any substantial theory about the causes or consequences of legislative adaptability, we can only present selected illustrations of this dimension of legislative institutionalization.

Changes in the composition of American legislatures, especially in the nineteenth century, seem clearly to represent responsiveness to demands for wide participation in political life and to indicate the democratization of the legislatures. It appears that in the very early years of the Republic, such democratizing pressures were at work on American legislatures and that responses to crises of participation were substantial. For example, the composition of the memberships of state legislative bodies shifted after the American Revolution, reflecting the representation of a wider spectrum of the population. Jackson Turner Main has shown that, in both northern and southern states, the legislatures' postrevolutionary memberships were much more drawn from among farmers and the middle class than from the upper class. He says for example:

> The economic upper class of well-to-do men, which in New Jersey had held three fourths of the seats before the war, saw its control vanish; indeed two thirds of the states' representatives in 1785 had only moderate properties. The typical legislator before the war held at least 1,000 acres; in 1785 the median was about 300 acres. Merchants and lawyers were all but eliminated from the legislature, retaining only a half-dozen seats. The colonial elite, once controlling one third of the votes of the house, now had one eighth; the overwhelming majority of the new legislators were men who had been unknown before the war and whose ancestry, where ascertainable, was uniformly undistinguished. Fully two thirds of the representatives were ordinary farmers, presumably men of more than average ability and sometimes military experience, but clearly part of the common people.[69]

Although changes in the economic status of legislators in the 1770s can be interpreted easily as reflecting responses to demands from the political environment for the democratization of the state legislatures, occupational changes in the composition of American legislatures over the long run are not so easy to explain. The dominant feature of the occupational composition of the houses of Congress and of many American state legislatures has been the preponderance of lawyers (discussed in greater detail in Chapter 3). The incidence of members of the United States House of Representatives who were lawyers is shown in Figure 2.5. About a third of the members of the First Congress were lawyers, but then the proportion rapidly escalated to about three-fourths in the 1840s, only to decline in the twentieth century. Although varying explanations have been offered for the importance of lawyers in the American political elite, no adequate historical interpretation has been attempted.[70] However, it is possible that the increase in the number of lawyers in the House in the early decades of the nineteenth century reflected congressional adaptation to the needs for skills appropriate to policy making for a rapidly expanding nation and for recruits to the legislative elite with sufficient social status to assure the viability of the developing legislature. Furthermore, lawyers may have been more dispensable for legislative office relative to other business and professional occupations in the early part of the nineteenth century than they have been in the twentieth century. The House came to demand more and more time from its members, and in a land of farmers and small merchants who presumably found it difficult to leave their jobs to spend a period of months in Washington, the dispensability of the lawyer, his ability to leave his place of work for fairly long periods of time without undue damage to his profession, may have been relatively more important.

Not much data are available on the occupational composition of the Senate over a long period of time, but it does not seem likely that the main patterns of the composition of the membership have changed much in the past three-quarters of a century. As Table 2.3 shows, a comparison of post–World War II senators with those serving at about the turn of the century suggests that the proportion of lawyers has declined in the Senate as well as in the House, but otherwise differences between these two cohorts in occupational background or political experience have been small.

What is most notably lacking over the history of the United States Congress is any significant membership drawn from among farmers and workers in the population, sectors of the population more conspicuously represented in Western European parliaments.[71] Presumably, the most direct explanation of the contrast

FIGURE 2.5   Changing Occupational Composition of the United States House of Representatives

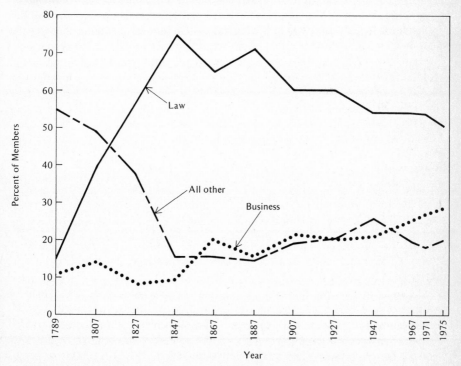

SOURCE: Roger H. Davidson, *The Role of the Congressman* (New York, 1969), p. 38; *Congressional Quarterly Weekly Report*, January 15, 1971:128–133; *Congressional Quarterly Weekly Report*, January 18, 1975:122–127.

TABLE 2.3   Occupational Backgrounds and Political Experiences of United States Senators, 1895–1905 and 1947–1957 (In percentages)

CHARACTERISTIC	1895–1905	1947–1957
Occupational background		
Lawyers	64	54
Other professionals	13	9
Proprietors, officials	19	29
Farmers	5	7
Political experience		
Governor	18	25
Congressman	39	30
State legislator	50	47
Major law-enforcement office	11	15
No previous political experience	10	9
Number	159	180

SOURCE: George H. Haynes, *The Election of Senators* (New York, 1906), pp. 71–99; and Donald R. Matthews, *U.S. Senators and Their World* (Chapel Hill, N.C., 1960), pp. 55, 282-283.

in the representation of farmers and workers between the United States and Western European countries lies in the fact that a substantial working-class political party never developed in the United States.[72]

If changes in the occupational composition of American legislatures provide a clue about their adaptation to demands from the political environment for democratization, there is some evidence that begins to suggest congressional adjustments to shifting forces in the federal system and the changing shape of the electoral environment. Especially since the turn of the twentieth century, national forces in the electorate have come increasingly to influence both turnout at the polls and the partisan division of the vote in congressional elections, exemplified especially when congressional and presidential elections coincide.[73] It seems very likely that the decline of constituency forces and the increase of national forces over the congressional vote have contributed greatly to the modern relationship between the President and Congress, facilitating the adaptation of Congress to the increasing legislative role of the chief executive in an accelerating technological society. At the same time (roughly between 1870 and 1920), the political competitiveness of elections in congressional districts declined sharply; and this change in the electoral environment, most notably marked by the critical election of 1896, must have had a major role in the development of congressional seniority norms and the professionalization of congressional leadership. As Walter Dean Burnham observes:

> Before the mid-1890s, there was very large fluctuation in the proportion of committee chairmanships selected on seniority grounds; the norm had simply not been fully institutionalized. Afterward, a high and relatively stable reliance on seniority came quite abruptly into being. It would be surprising indeed if the sudden upward shift in this reliance on seniority were not somehow related to the essentially negative public-policy purposes of the new majority coalition.[74]

The congressional response to centralizing forces in the United States in the late nineteenth and early twentieth centuries is exhibited quite conoretely in the changes in the process of selecting United States senators. Prior to the passage of the Seventeenth Amendment in 1913, senators were elected by the state legislatures, not by direct popular vote. However, as William H. Riker has shown, the peripheralizing processes of legislative instructions to senators and state legislative election of Senate members disintegrated after 1860; first the public canvass for the Senate, widely practiced in the 1880s, and then direct election recognized and ratified the degree of centralization of the political process by the turn of the century.[75] Parenthetically, the struggle to elect United States senators seems to have had a very retarding effect on the development of state legislatures in many states, particularly after the Civil War, when election deadlocks in the legislatures became increasingly common.[76] The importance of the change to direct election of senators in the adaptation of the Senate is suggested by Rothman's description of the unpopularity of the Senate in the 1890s:

> During these years, for the first time, a sentiment that the government stood distinctly apart from the people gained widespread popularity. The notion spread that an unbridgeable gap divided the interests of the officeholder from his constituents. In point of fact, the nation was growing larger. More and more Americans lived in areas remote from Washington; others, congregating in cities, were not likely to meet or become friendly with their representatives, let alone their senators. Communications could not keep pace with the expansion and proceedings in the capital seemed more remote than ever. Then too, the nation was undergoing a complex development. Heterogeneous immigrants, giant industries, aggregates of capital, and amalgamations of workers were some of the new and strange components of modern America. A general malaise gripped the country, and every innovation excited hostility. Efforts to exclude newcomers, to break up corporations, to discourage the unions increased. And in politics identical fears provoked the movement to abolish the authority of party organization.[77]

The direct election of senators was a part of the process of dismantling the political party machines that, in many states, came to control the election of senators by the legislatures; and thus, it reflects an effort to make the Senate more responsive to its constituency.

It is easier to anchor in some empirical evidence the adaptation of American legislatures to diffuse demands for representation than it is to identify the waxing and waning of legislative responsiveness to specific policy demands. It is fairly clear that the early Congress had not developed much capacity to manage tensions or to contribute to political integration. Young has described the Congress of the early 1800s:

> Instability of membership; the constant circulation of short-time servers through the community; cultural, political, temperamental, occupational, ethnic, and age disparities between the members, inflamed into personal animosities by close-quarters confinement on Capitol Hill; permissive rules of debate and dogged adherence to the practice of internal democracy; the absence of formal leadership roles; a compulsion to garrulity and contention; policy-making conducted in a hubbub of irrelevant activities—all these would seem more than enough to offset whatever advantages smallness of size and negligibility of citizen pressures upon the legislative establishment gave to those who would mobilize Congress for policy action.[78]

By the 1840s, party government in Congress appears to have developed to a point at which conflicting political demands and interests could be reasonably well articulated and compromises achieved among contentious sections of the country. Major issues, mainly arising in connection with black slavery and economic programs, were managed remarkably well by the incipient congressional parties, although sectional hostilities always were latent; and, of course, the Civil War represents a major failure of the political apparatus to manage conflict.[79] The post–Civil War mechanisms of consensus and compromise themselves served to produce political conflict because the congressional party system, highly developed by the 1890s, frequently operated in ways designed to avoid controversial public issues that were not malleable to the system of congressional compromise.[80] Quite rapidly, the proliferation of policy demands brought about by industrialization and two world wars facilitated the gravitation of policy initiative to the executive bureaucracy.

In the twentieth century, the party system of the Congress of the 1890s degenerated; but it is possible that the decline of the system of policy formulation by party government which evolved to the 1890s and the subsequent decentralization of the congressional institution came about less by presidential aggrandizement or some inherent deficiency of Congress than by a rather fundamental change in the American society itself. The rise of the technological society, it may be argued, required new modes of policy-making institutions. According to Ernest S. Griffith:

> It was [the] nontechnical character of public questions [in the nineteenth century] that lent itself to their resolution in an atmosphere of "principle" and party loyalty rather than through study and discussion. The average member knew, or thought he knew, the answers. Where principles were not immediately forthcoming, party supplied them. Party cohesiveness was practicable in an age of few, but persistent, major issues. . . . The contrast with the present day is tremendous. Congress functions in a different world.[81]

The post–World War II institutionalization of Congress has been most notable in its response to the technological complexity of modern legislation, evidenced by the rapid development of professional staffs for Congress and its committees (see Chapter 9). There is some evidence that the increasing professionalization of Congress has contributed to the passage of legislation that is more responsive to modern social needs and demands. In very recent years, substantial progress has been made in strengthening the capacity of state legislatures to deal with the complexities of modern society, notably through extending the time limits on sessions, streamlining legislative structure, and improving professional staffing.[82]

Any realistic assessment of the adaptability of state legislatures, however, must lead to the conclusion that they adapted to the needs of the twentieth century very slowly. Partly as a result of legislative scandals in the late nineteenth century, rigid constitutional limits on the length and frequency of sessions were imposed on most legislatures. As late as 1964, only nineteen state legislatures held regular annual sessions; and in many states, either annual or biennial sessions were limited to sixty or ninety days. State legislatures had the authority to initiate constitutional amendments easing these restrictions, but they were slow to do so.

As the number and variety of legislative bills escalated and the budgets increased, most state legislatures lacked one resource that was essential to cope with these changes: enough time to do the job. State legislators have also been very slow to provide themselves with the necessary tools for their job; professional staff, secretarial help, minimal office space, and computing equipment are very recent developments.

The state legislatures were also slow to adapt in one other important respect. As most states grew increasingly urban and metropolitan, the legislatures continued to be dominated by rural members, men who were frequently unfamiliar with the problems of the cities and suburbs and were unresponsive to the needs of citizens of those areas. As we describe in Chapter 19, state legislatures in the first sixty years of the twentieth century either ignored state constitutional mandates to reapportion or adopted constitutional amendments designed to preserve rural control of legislatures. The reapportionments of the 1960s were not even belated evidence of adaptation by the legislatures, since they were imposed by outside institutions: the federal and state courts.

The state legislatures have, indeed, modernized themselves in many respects in the 1970s. Reapportionments brought about some alterations in the character of these legislatures; such things as federal revenue sharing brought increased legislative responsibilities, and policy demands brought to bear on the legislatures increased. The state legislatures began to streamline rules and procedures, increase salaries for legislators, improve fiscal and legislative committee staffs, and oversee the administration of state programs by the executive branch of the state government. In 1975, forty-two states had adopted formal or informal arrangements providing for annual legislative sessions. In many states legislative committee systems have been streamlined by reducing the number of committees, adopting uniform committee rules and so-called "open meeting" laws, and providing for the continuation of committee operations in the interim between legislative sessions. The professionalization of the state legislatures in the 1970s has represented a major adaptation of these institutions to their increasingly important role in a society undergoing urbanization and industrialization.[83]

NOTES

1. We adopt the approach of Huntington in our analysis of legislative institutionalization. See Samuel P. Huntington, "Political Development and Political Decay," *World Politics* 17 (1965):386–430; and *Political Order in Changing Societies* (New Haven, Conn., 1968), pp. 1–92.

2. Nelson W. Polsby, "The Institutionalization of the U.S. House of Representatives," *American Political Science Review* 62 (1968):145.

3. Ibid., 145–156.

4. James S. Young, *The Washington Community, 1800–1828* (New York: Columbia University Press, 1966), p. 89.

5. William H. Riker, "The Senate and American Federalism," *American Political Science Review* 49 (1955):462–463.

6. For an important illustration, see the example of the case of the parliamentary institution in France described in Constantin Melnik and Nathan Leites, *The House Without Windows* (Evanston, Ill., 1958).

7.   See Samuel P. Huntington, "Congressional Responses to the Twentieth Century," in *The Congress and America's Future,* ed. David B. Truman (Englewood Cliffs, N.J., 1965), pp. 5–31.

8.   Duane Lockard, "The State Legislator," in *State Legislatures in American Politics,* ed. Alexander Heard (Englewood Cliffs, N.J., 1966), pp. 103–106.

9.   See Ralph V. Harlow, *The History of Legislative Methods in the Period before 1825* (New Haven, Conn., 1917), pp. 120–164.

10.   See Young, *The Washington Community,* pp. 179–210.

11.   Quoted in ibid., p. 136.

12.   See Randall B. Ripley, *Party Leaders in the House of Representatives* (Washington, D.C., 1967), p. 12.

13.   Polsby, "The Institutionalization of the U.S. House of Representatives," pp. 148–149; and Young, *The Washington Community,* pp. 131–132.

14.   Floyd M. Riddick, *The United States Congress: Organization and Procedure* (Manassas, Va., 1949), p. 86; George B. Galloway, *History of the House of Representatives* (New York, 1961), pp. 107–110; and Ripley, *Party Leaders in the House of Representatives,* pp. 24–27.

15.   Ripley, *Party Leaders in the House of Representatives,* pp. 28–29.

16.   Ibid., pp. 33–41.

17.   Randall B. Ripley, *Power in the Senate* (New York, 1969), pp. 24–35; see also George H. Haynes, *The Senate of the United States* (Boston, 1938), pp. 480–483.

18.   For studies of party leadership in the contemporary Congress, see Charles O. Jones, *The Minority Party in Congress* (Boston, 1970); and Randall B. Ripley, *Majority Party Leadership in Congress* (Boston, 1969).

19.   Belle Zeller, ed., *American State Legislatures* (New York, 1954), p. 195.

20.   See Malcolm E. Jewell, *The State Legislature: Politics and Practice,* 2d ed. (New York, 1969), pp. 72–73.

21.   John C. Wahlke, "Organization and Procedure," in *State Legislatures in American Politics,* ed. Alexander Heard, p. 141.

22.   Lauros G. McConachie, *Congressional Committees* (New York, 1898), pp. 123–124.

23.   Harlow, *The History of Legislative Methods in the Period before 1825,* pp. 127–128.

24.   McConachie, *Congressional Committees,* p. 124. For an analysis of the state of congressional committees in the mid-1880s, see Woodrow Wilson, *Congressional Government* (New York, 1956); first published in 1885. For analyses of the modern congressional committee system, see John D. Lees, *The Committee System of the United States Congress* (London, 1967); William L. Morrow, *Congressional Committees* (New York, 1969); and George Goodwin, Jr., *The Little Legislatures: Committees of Congress* (Amherst, Mass., 1970). For a general historical treatment, see Joseph Cooper, "The Origins of the Standing Committees and the Development of the Modern House," *Rice University Studies* 56 (1970):1–167.

25.   Goodwin, *The Little Legislatures,* pp. 3–13; Galloway, *History of the House of Representatives,* pp. 64–67; and Haynes, *The Senate of the United States,* pp. 271–284. The history of the Senate Finance Committee is traced in some detail in U.S., Congress, Senate, Committee on Finance, *History of the Committee on Finance,* 91st Cong., 2d sess., 1970.

26.   Goodwin, *The Little Legislatures,* p. 13.

27.   Haynes, *The Senate of the United States,* pp. 280–284. Haynes quotes one senator as saying that "there are six of the standing committees of the Senate that have never had a bill, or a resolution or a particle of business before them within the memory of a living man that I know of" and that "they were created simply to give secretaries to members

of the Senate and a committee room." Haynes points out that "in 1917 the Committee on Transportation Routes to the Seaboard—which was said not to have had a meeting in thirty-eight years—numbered in its membership Senators of the grade of McCumber, Lodge, Sheppard, and Martin" (p. 283).

28. George B. Galloway, *The Legislative Process in Congress* (New York, 1953), pp. 276–278.

29. On congressional ethics, see Robert S. Getz, *Congressional Ethics* (Princeton, N.J., 1966), especially pp. 117–142. On the space sciences committees, see Vernon Van Dyke, *Pride and Power* (Urbana, Ill., 1964).

30. McConachie, *Congressional Committees,* pp. 135–136.

31. Harlow, *The History of Legislative Methods in the Period before 1825,* p. 78.

32. Ibid., pp. 61–78.

33. Paul S. Reinsch, *American Legislatures and Legislative Methods* (New York, 1907 p. 163.

34. See ibid., pp. 164–165; and George H. Haynes, *The Election of Senators* (New York, 1906), especially pp. 191–195.

35. Neil MacNeil, *Forge of Democracy: The House of Representatives* (New York, 1963), p. 125.

36. See Galloway, *History of the House of Representatives,* pp. 67–69. The role of seniority in the United States Senate is described in Haynes, *The Senate of the United States,* pp. 294–305; and David J. Rothman, *Politics and Power: The United States Senate, 1869–1901* (Cambridge, Mass., 1966), pp. 50–61. For a good general treatment of the subject, see Barbara Hinckley, *The Seniority System in Congress* (Bloomington, Ind., 1971).

37. Nelson W. Polsby, Miriam Gallaher, and Barry S. Rundquist, "The Growth of the Seniority System in the U.S. House of Representatives," *American Political Science Review* 63 (1969):806–807. See also Michael Abram and Joseph Cooper, "The Rise of Seniority in the House of Representatives," *Polity* 1 (1968):53–85; and Walter Dean Burnham, *Critical Elections and the Mainsprings of American Politics* (New York, 1970), pp. 100–104.

38. Polsby, "The Institutionalization of the U.S. House of Representatives," pp. 163–165; and Galloway, *The Legislative Process in Congress,* pp. 357–358.

39. Haynes, *The Senate of the United States,* p. 126; and Polsby, "The Institutionalization of the U.S. House of Representatives," pp. 161–162. See also DeAlva Stanwood Alexander, *History and Procedure of the House of Representatives* (Boston, 1916), p. 323; and MacNeil, *Forge of Democracy,* pp. 135–137.

40. Polsby, "The Institutionalization of the U.S. House of Representatives," p. 163.

41. Haynes, *The Election of Senators,* p. 56.

42. Haynes, *The Senate of the United States,* p. 126. See also Galloway, *The Legislative Process in Congress,* pp. 358–366.

43. Haynes describes Senate action in several major contest cases in *The Senate of the United States,* pp. 127–168.

44. John C. Wahlke et al., *The Legislative System* (New York, 1962), p. 168.

45. Ibid., pp. 141–169; and Donald R. Matthews, *U.S. Senators and Their World* (Chapel Hill, N.C., 1960), pp. 92–117.

46. Matthews, *U.S. Senators and Their World,* p. 97.

47. Clem Miller, *Member of the House,* ed. John W. Baker (New York, 1962), p. 93.

48. Jerry Voorhis, *Confessions of a Congressman* (Garden City, N.Y., 1947), p. 26.

49. William Plumer, *Memorandum of Proceedings in the United States Senate,* ed. E. S. Brown (New York, 1923), p. 276. We are indebted to Nelson Polsby for calling attention to these references, drawn from the extensive citations in the unpublished version of "The

Institutionalization of the U.S. House of Representatives" (Paper presented at the Annual Meeting of the American Political Science Association, New York City, 1966).

50.   Alexander, *History and Procedure of the House of Representatives,* pp. 111–112.

51.   Ibid., pp. 115–116.

52.   Ibid., p. 125.

53.   J. C. Clements, "What Congress Has Done," *North American Review* 151 (1890): 533; quoted in the unpublished version of Polsby's "The Institutionalization of the U.S. House of Representatives."

54.   Haynes, *The Senate of the United States,* p. 186.

55.   Ibid., p. 187.

56.   See Dean L. Yarwood, "Norm Observance and Legislative Integration: The U.S. Senate in 1850 and 1860," *Social Science Quarterly* 51 (1970):57–69; and "Legislative Persistence: A Comparison of the United States Senate in 1850 and 1860," *Midwest Journal of Political Science* 11 (1967):193–211.

57.   Young, *The Washington Community,* pp. 87–109.

58.   Ibid., p. 124.

59.   Ibid., p. 125.

60.   Ibid. The quotation is from James Fenimore Copper, *Notions of the Americans: Picked up by a Travelling Bachelor,* vol. 2 (Philadelphia, 1828), p. 30.

61.   Young, *The Washington Community,* pp. 151–152. For an analysis of party polarization before the turn of the nineteenth century, see Rudolph M. Bell, *Party and Faction in American Politics* (Westport, Conn., 1973).

62.   For a cursory history of party government in the House, see Galloway, *History of the House of Representatives,* pp. 128–159.

63.   Rothman, *Politics and Power,* pp. 71–72. See also William G. Shade, Stanley D. Hopper, David Jacobson, and Stephen E. Moiles, "Partisanship in the United States Senate: 1869–1901," *Journal of Interdisciplinary History* 4 (1973):185–205; and Jerome M. Clubb and Howard W. Allen, "Party Loyalty in the Progressive Years: The Senate, 1909–1915," *Journal of Politics* 29 (1967):567–584.

64.   See Paul DeWitt Hasbrouck, *Party Government in the House of Representatives* (New York, 1927); David W. Brady, *Congressional Voting in a Partisan Era* (Lawrence, Kans., 1973); and David W. Brady, "Congressional Leadership and Party Voting in the McKinley Era: A Comparison to the Modern House," *American Journal of Political Science* 16 (1972):439–459.

65.   For very interesting analyses of the role of legislative parties in the contemporary era, see W. Wayne Shannon, *Party, Constituency and Congressional Voting* (Baton Rouge, La., 1968); see also Julius Turner, *Party and Constituency: Pressures on Congress,* ed. Edward V. Schneier, Jr. (Baltimore, 1970), and Chapter 17 of this book.

66.   Polsby, "The Institutionalization of the U.S. House of Representatives," p. 164.

67.   Ibid., p. 168; and Polsby, *Congress and the Presidency* (New York, 1964).

68.   Huntington, "Congressional Responses to the Twentieth Century," p. 8.

69.   Jackson Turner Main, "Government by the People: The American Revolution and the Democratization of the Legislatures," *William and Mary Quarterly* 23 (1966):401.

70.   For a discussion of the role of lawyers in American politics, see Heinz Eulau and John D. Sprague, *Lawyers in Politics* (Indianapolis, Ind., 1964); and Donald R. Matthews, *The Social Background of Political Decision-Makers* (Garden City, New York, 1954), pp. 28–32.

71.   For European contrasts, see Hans Daalder and S. Hubée-Boonzaaijer, "Sociale Herkomst en Politieke Recrutering van Nederlandse Kamerleden in 1968," *Acta Politica* 5 (1969–1970):292–333, 371–416; Mattei Dogan, "Les Filières de la Carrière Politique en France," *Revue Française de Sociologie* 8 (1967):468–492; and Henry Valen, "The Recruit-

ment of Parliamentary Nominees in Norway," *Scandinavian Political Studies* 1 (1966): 121–166.

72. For the best single discussion of the absence of a working-class party in the United States, see Leon D. Epstein, *Political Parties in Western Democracies* (New York, 1967), pp. 138–145.

73. See Donald E. Stokes, "Parties and the Nationalization of Electoral Forces," in *The American Party Systems: Stages of Political Development,* eds. William N. Chambers and Walter Dean Burnham (New York, 1967), pp. 182–202.

74. Walter Dean Burnham, *Critical Elections and the Mainsprings of American Politics* (New York, 1970), pp. 100–106; quotation at p. 103.

75. Riker, "The Senate and American Federalism," pp. 452–477.

76. See Haynes, *The Election of Senators,* pp. 36–70; and *The Senate of the United States,* pp. 81–117.

77. Rothman, *Politics and Power,* pp. 257–258.

78. Young, *The Washington Community,* p. 97.

79. For interesting analyses of the congressional response to major policy demands in the middle of the nineteenth century, see Joel H. Silbey, *The Shrine of Party: Congressional Voting Behavior, 1841–1852* (Pittsburgh, 1967); Thomas B. Alexander, *Sectional Stress and Party Strength* (Nashville, Tenn., 1967); and W. R. Brock, *An American Crisis: Congress and Reconstruction, 1865–1867* (New York, 1963).

80. See Rothman, *Politics and Power,* pp. 262–263.

81. Ernest S. Griffith, *Congress: Its Contemporary Role* (New York, 1961), pp. 68–69.

82. For a very systematic analysis of the effects on legislative policy output of levels of professionalization of state legislatures, see John G. Grumm, "Structural Determinants of Legislative Output," in *Legislatures in Developmental Perspective,* eds. Allan Kornberg and Lloyd D. Musolf (Durham, N.C., 1970), pp. 429–459.

83. Recent changes in the state legislatures are summarized in Karl T. Kurtz, "Legislative Organization and Services," in *The Book of the States 1974–1975,* vol. 20 (Lexington, Ky., 1974), pp. 53–65.

Selection of Legislators

part II

The selection of legislators involves both the process of recruitment and the electoral process. Recruitment includes the socioeconomic characteristics of legislators, their motivations, and the activities of political leaders. Primary and general elections provide a link between the electoral and legislative systems.

A substantial amount of information has been accumulated about the characteristics of national and state legislators. It is known that they are not typical of their constituents, that they are better educated and have larger incomes, and that they are drawn disproportionately from certain businesses and professions. Considerably less is known about how potential candidates—those who possess the necessary background qualifications—become actual candidates, to what extent they are recruited or are encouraged by others to run.

Legislative elections at the state level have become more competitive as a result of the increasingly competitive nature of state party systems. Research on legislative elections at both national and state levels is beginning to shed some light on the causes and consequences of primary and electoral competition, the influence of national and state election trends on outcomes, and the costs and tactics of legislative campaigns.

Students of political behavior and of parties and elections are interested in recruitment and elections generally. The interest of legislative specialists in these topics grows out of the assumption that the selection process has some effect on legislative behavior and output. We attempt in this section to focus attention on those aspects of the selection process that have an impact on legislative behavior and output—topics covered in subsequent sections of this volume.

CHAPTER THREE

The Recruitment of Legislators

One of the most persistent popular beliefs in our political culture is in the openness of the political system. The log-cabin image, the notion that anybody can become President, and the unpopularity of class interpretations of politics are indicative of the egalitarian orientation of many Americans. Although the American political system is relatively open to participation and activism by a wide range of citizenry, it is also a rather highly selective system in which recruitment to public office emphasizes certain well-defined strata of the population.

The American legislature is not a representative body in the sense that all elements of the population are included as legislators in direct proportion to their relative size. Partly as a result of the processes of their selection, and partly as a result of more diffuse factors in the political system, American legislators tend to be distinctly different in their social origins and political experiences from the population at large.

CHARACTERISTICS OF LEGISLATORS

Social Origins

One basis upon which to differentiate American legislators from the general population of the country is social origin. Typically, the American legislator has grown up in rural or small-town areas. The malapportionment of many state legislatures and the advantages given to rural areas of the country in the drawing of congressional district boundaries were factors that contributed to the recruitment of legislators who were essentially small-town boys. With the exception of the New Jersey legislators, less than half the members of the legislatures shown in Table 3.1 grew up in cities; and about one-quarter of them (one-third in Tennessee) were raised on farms. At the national level, an even higher proportion of legislators had rural and small-town origins. In 1959, 64 percent of the members of the United States Senate had grown up in rural or small-town environments; only 17 percent had been raised in a medium-sized city; and 19 percent had grown up in a metropolitan center. Reapportionment of state legislatures and congressional redistricting since 1962 probably have attenuated the small-town

TABLE 3.1 Where State Legislators Grew Up, 1957 (In percentages)

PLACE	CALIF.	N.J.	OHIO	TENN.	WIS.
City	45	62	45	22	40
Small town	23	32	28	34	29
Farm	21	5	24	33	25
Combination of above	11	1	3	11	6
Total	100	100	100	100	100
Number	110	78	162	119	89

SOURCES: John C. Wahlke et al., *The Legislative System* (New York, 1962), p. 489, for California, New Jersey, Ohio, and Tennessee legislatures; data for the 1957 Wisconsin assembly in this and subsequent tables come from unpublished material collected by Patterson.

and rural character of American legislatures, so that by the Ninetieth Congress, for instance, members of the United States House of Representatives born in rural areas and small towns were apparently not overrepresentative of the general population.[1]

Donald R. Matthews has shown that in the period from 1947 to 1957, more than two-thirds of the United States senators were born in rural areas or small towns and that "the most consistently overrepresented birthplaces ranged in size from 2,500 to 5,000 inhabitants." The small towns of this size "produced twice as many Democrats and four times as many Republicans as one might expect on the basis of chance."[2] Except for a few states (like California) with substantial immigrant populations, the vast majority of state legislators have been born in the states that they serve as legislators. In many states (including California), a higher proportion of legislators have been born in the state than is the case for the states' populations generally. The same pattern holds for Congress: 71 percent of the members of the United States House of Representatives for the Seventy-seventh Congress had been born in their states; 24 percent had been born in another state; and 5 percent were foreign born.[3] Thus, the American legislator tends not only to have had a rural or small-town upbringing but also to have been born in the state he serves.

The legislator tends to have deep roots in his district. Although aspirants to the legislature in the United States are not universally required by law to be residents of the districts they represent, this is invariably the case. New York is the only state without a legal residency requirement for state legislators, and there is no requirement that United States congressmen be legal residents of their states and districts.[4] The process of recruitment of legislators tends to place great weight upon extended residence in the district. This tendency is reflected clearly at the state level. For example, in the five states shown in Table 3.2, well over half of the members of each state's 1957 legislature had lived in their districts at least 80 percent of their lives, or more than thirty years. More than 73 percent of the members of the 1958 session of the Pennsylvania legislature had been born in the county from which they were elected, and nearly 69 percent had lived all their lives in the county of their birth; 55 percent of both houses of the 1957 Georgia legislature were born and had lived all their lives in the districts they represented; and 56 percent of Colorado legislators who served from 1957 to 1966 had resided more than twenty years in their districts. More than 60 percent of Oregon

TABLE 3.2   Length of Residence in District, State Legislators, 1957 (In percentages)

LENGTH OF RESIDENCE	CALIF.	N.J.	OHIO	TENN.	WIS.
All their lives	14	60	65	53	39
80 percent of lives, or over 30 years	42	23	23	23	30
20–29 years	15	7	7	11	10
10–19 years	19	10	3	9	12
Less than 10 years	10	—	2	4	9
Total	100	100	100	100	100
Number	118	79	162	119	89

SOURCE: Wahlke et al., *The Legislative System,* p. 488.

legislators elected in 1966 had lived in their districts at least twenty years.[5] The American legislator is usually a "local boy," and legislative careers in the United States are generally closed to newcomers in the community. A small-town or rural heritage and long residence in the community tend to confer representative legitimacy upon aspirants to legislative office in this country.

Family Background

The political recruitment process in the United States gives disproportionate weight to those who have middle-class and upper-middle-class family backgrounds. The extent to which political leaders are drawn from such families increases from the lower political levels to the higher ones and is most marked among legislators who serve in the United States Congress. There, commonly more than half the members come from families in which the father had a professional or business occupation, in contrast with the occupational distribution of the fathers of people in the general population. Table 3.3 shows the occupations of the fathers of legislators in several states and in the United States Senate and the occupational distribution of the labor force in 1900. About 60 percent of the members of the Senate came from families in which the father was a professional or a businessman. The sons of farmers most accurately represented the labor force in 1900, but the higher proportion of farmers' sons in the Senate reinforces the image of legislators as largely rural in background.

At the state level, a smaller (in comparison with Congress) but still substantial proportion of legislators were drawn from families where the father's principal occupation was a profession or a business; and a higher proportion came from families in which the father was a skilled or an unskilled worker. Table 3.3 shows the percentages in each occupational category of legislators' fathers for six states. Less than half of the fathers of legislators in the first four states engaged in professional and business occupations, and only 31 percent were farmers or farm managers. An even smaller proportion of Wisconsin legislators' fathers were businessmen and professionals, and a higher percentage were skilled workers. In Pennsylvania, a higher percentage were professional men and workers, and a smaller percentage were farmers. But even for state legislators, middle-class and

TABLE 3.3   Occupations of Fathers of American Legislators (In percentages)

OCCUPATION	CALIF., N.J., OHIO, TENN. (1957)	WIS. (1957)	PA. (1957)	U.S. SENATORS (1947–1957)	LABOR FORCE (1900)
Professional	18	17	12	24	6
Proprietor, official	29	14	30	35	7
Farmer, farm manager	31	25	16	32	22
Other	28	38	42	9	66
Total	100	100	100	100	100
Number	504	100	106	180	—

SOURCE: Wahlke et al., *The Legislative System*, p. 489; Frank J. Sorauf, *Party and Representation* (New York, 1963), p. 78; Donald R. Matthews, "United States Senators: A Collective Portrait," *International Social Science Journal* 13 (1961):623.

upper-middle-class occupational heritages were considerably overrepresented when legislators were compared with the labor force generally.

Occupational Status

The occupational composition of the American legislative bodies is such that candidates in some occupations have a better chance of legislative service than others do. American legislators tend to have highly prestigious occupations prior to their election to the legislature. By and large, those in the professional and business occupations dominate the legislative halls in the United States, at both state and national levels (see Figure 3.1). Some occupations often represented among legislators are dispensable for politics in the sense that those engaged in such occupations can take time out from their professional or occupational activity to participate in politics with a minimum of sacrifice.[6] The nature of law, real estate, insurance, farming, and many business occupations is such that those involved can, without seriously endangering their livelihoods, be away from their businesses for short periods of time to serve in the state legislature or run for Congress.

Well over half of the members of all the legislatures shown in Figure 3.1— except those of Iowa in 1967, Nebraska in 1963, and Minnesota in 1951—were businessmen or professionals. There is some variation among states, with a higher proportion of business and professional people in the legislatures of the more highly urbanized states of California, New Jersey, Ohio, and Pennsylvania, and a smaller proportion in the less-urbanized states of Iowa and Nebraska; but the occupational recruitment of legislators does not follow rural-urban differences very well. At the national level, the preponderance of professional and business occupations greatly increases, with more than two-thirds of the members of Congress in the professional category.

The proportion of farmers in state legislatures varies in terms of the urbanization of the states, from none in the 1968 Rhode Island house to as many as 47 percent in the 1966 Nebraska senate. Furthermore, the number of farmer-legislators seems to have declined in some states and remained relatively stable in others. In Iowa, where the proportion of farmers has been higher than in most other state

FIGURE 3.1   Occupations of American Legislators

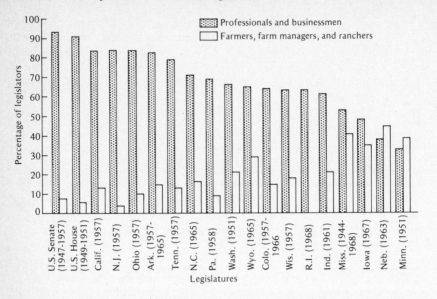

SOURCES: P. Beckett and C. Sunderland, "Washington State's Lawmakers: Some Personnel Factors in the Washington Legislature," *Western Political Quarterly* 10 (1957):195; Elmer E. Cornwell, Jr. et al., *The Rhode Island General Assembly* (Washington, D.C., 1970), p. 18; Victor S. Hjelm and Joseph P. Pisciotte, "Profiles and Careers of Colorado State Legislators," *Western Political Quarterly* 21 (1968):701; K. Janda et al., *Legislative Politics in Indiana* (Bloomington, Ind., 1961), p. 3; Alex B. Lacy, Jr., ed., "Power in American State Legislatures," *Tulane Studies in Political Science* 11 (1967): 11, 92; Donald R. Matthews, *The Social Background of Political Decision-Makers* (New York, 1954), p. 30; Samuel C. Patterson, ed., *Midwest Legislative Politics* (Iowa City, Iowa, 1967), p. 22; Frank J. Sorauf, *Party and Representation,* p. 71; D. P. Sprengel, "Legislative Perceptions of Gubernatorial Power in North Carolina" (Ph.D. diss., University of North Carolina, 1966), p. 38; S. A. Stoiber, *Legislative Politics in the Rocky Mountain West* (Boulder, Colo., 1967), p. 113; W. P. Tucker, "Characteristics of State Legislators," *Social Science* 30 (1955):94; and Wahlke et al., *The Legislative System,* p. 490.

legislatures, 50 percent of the members in 1961 were farmers, a ratio that was virtually the same as it had been before World War II, but that declined to 35 percent by 1967. In 1951, 39 percent of the members of the Minnesota house were farmers, compared with 37 percent in the period from 1925 to 1935. In the same ten-year prewar period, 24 percent of the members of the Indiana house and 28 percent of the Washington house were farmers, compared with 21 percent in both bodies in recent sessions.[7] The proportion of farmers in the houses of Congress is comparatively small.

Lawyers constitute an occupational category among legislators that deserves special attention. Attorneys have played a prominent role in the American political system since the early days of the Republic. Twenty-five of the fifty-two signers of the Declaration of Independence and thirty-one of the fifty-five members of the Continental Congress were lawyers. The legal profession provided 70 percent of the presidents, vice-presidents, and cabinet officers between 1877 and 1934, 50 percent of the United States senators from 1947 to 1957, 56 percent of the members of the United States House of Representatives from 1949 to 1951, nearly half of the state governors between 1870 and 1950, and about a quarter of the members of the state legislatures since 1900.[8] The overrepresentation of lawyers as an occupational group in the legislature is particularly marked because lawyers have never constituted more than .2 percent of the labor force and now account for about .1 percent of the work force in the country.

The proportion of lawyers in the houses of Congress has remained stable at well over half the membership in recent years. And in state legislatures, the overall proportion of attorneys has not varied much. Charles S. Hyneman found that between 1925 and 1935, 28 percent of the members of thirteen lower and twelve upper houses of state legislatures were attorneys; Belle Zeller found that in 1949, 22 percent of the members of forty-eight state legislatures were lawyers.[9]

The Senate in the United States has tended to contain a higher proportion of lawyer-legislators than the House of Representatives. In the Eighty-fifth Congress, for example, 65 percent of the members of the Senate and 55 percent of the members of the House of Representatives were attorneys.[10]

There is a considerable amount of variation in the numbers of lawyer-legislators among states. In some states, legal training appears to be more congenial to a legislative career than it is in others. Furthermore, the lawyer composition of a state's legislature may vary over time. For example, if the pre-1935 and post-1935 periods are compared, the number of lawyers in the Illinois senate has increased substantially. In the pre-1935 period, a third of the senators in Illinois were lawyers; but in the twenty-year period thereafter, the average proportion of lawyers was over 40 percent. Accurate information about the occupational characteristics of state legislators over time has never been gathered for all states, and thus, systematic state-by-state comparisons are not possible.

Lawyer-legislators differ from legislators who are not lawyers in a variety of ways. They are somewhat less occupationally mobile than nonlawyers in the sense of the number of different types of occupations held prior to legislative service, but there is evidence of the greater political mobility of lawyers subsequent to legislative service.[11] They tend to come from higher-status family backgrounds in terms of their fathers' occupations. Lawyers tend to have had more prelegislative political experience and to be more highly involved in politics, more self-motivated for a political career, and more professional politically in viewing legislative service as only a step to other political offices. In their legal-professional ability, legislator-lawyers do not appear to differ significantly from lawyers in the general population. Furthermore, where evidence is available, it appears that lawyers are distributed about equally between the Republican and Democratic parties and between rural and urban parts of the states.[12]

It is often argued that the lawyer brings a special kind of skill to politics. The nature of legal training itself may tend to prepare its recipients for representative roles. The lawyer's occupation is the representation of clients. He makes no great change when he moves from representing clients in his private practice to representing constituents as a legislator. In general, lawyers may find legislative service more congenial to their previous training and occupational experience than those who come to the legislature from other occupations. The occupational strains associated with a legislative status may be reduced among lawyers; they may be more receptive to the bargainer or negotiator role so commonly played in the American legislature.

But the professional skills developed by lawyers cannot by themselves explain the dominance of lawyers in the legislature. "In a highly competitive society," asks Matthews, "who can, with the least danger, leave their jobs for the tremendous risks of a political career?"

> Among the high-prestige occupations it seems to be the lawyers. Certainly, other professional men find the neglect of their careers for political activity extremely hazardous. To those in professions where the subject matter is rapidly changing, a few years of neglect of their vocations and their skills would be either lost or outmoded. The active businessman, be he an individual entrepreneur or a member of a corporate bureaucracy, would find the neglect of his vocation for politics no asset to his primary occupational interest. These barriers to political participation either do not exist or are decreased in significance for the lawyer. The law changes relatively slowly. The lawyer, as Max Weber argued, is "dispensable," he can most easily combine his occupation, on a part-time basis, with political activity. Moreover, this activity can be a positive advantage to his occupational advancement— free and professionally legitimate advertising, contacts, opportunities to meet important lawyers of his region result from his political activities. Finally, lawyers possess a monopoly of public offices relating to the administration of law and the court system. Since in America "every political question tends to become a legal question," the offices of judge and prosecuting attorney provide lawyers (and lawyers alone) relatively easy entry into the political world and important springboards to higher offices.[13]

American legislatures are thus dominated by professional men, especially lawyers, businessmen, and farmers. Other occupational groups, and in particular those in the skilled labor or manual worker categories, are very markedly underrepresented among legislators. The recruitment of legislators is very selective in terms of occupational status. Although the legislative system is by no means closed, legislators clearly tend to be drawn predominantly from high-status occupations.

The American legislator tends not only to enter politics from a high-status occupation but also to be characterized by a high degree of occupational mobility. Although a great deal more evidence about the intergenerational and intragenerational occupational movement of legislators is needed, the data available indicate that legislators are more upwardly mobile than the population in general. It might be said that the legislator is on the make occupationally. He tends to have a higher-status occupation than his father, and he tends to exhibit more changes in his own occupational career than the ordinary jobholder.

Data for state legislators in California, New Jersey, Ohio, Tennessee, and Wisconsin indicate the substantial intergenerational mobility of legislators. Heinz Eulau and David Koff found that of 325 legislators from the 1957 sessions of the legislatures in the first four states named above, 32 percent could be classified as occupational "mobiles" vis-à-vis their fathers' occupations.[14] These legislators had moved substantially ahead of their fathers in terms of occupational status. Using a somewhat different basis of classification, it was found that 46 percent of the members of the 1957 session of the Wisconsin assembly could be seen as occupationally mobile in comparison with their fathers' occupational status.

If the occupational mobility of the legislator is viewed in intragenerational terms, there is evidence to suggest that American legislators are highly mobile in their own career experiences. There is, for instance, evidence that the variety of occupational experiences of American congressmen increased uniformly from the early nineteenth century until after World War I.[15] More recent findings about United States senators in the period from 1947 to 1957 show enough of the presenatorial occupational career pattern to indicate their increasing movement into high-status occupations.[16] Table 3.4 indicates the occupational categories of senators in this period at the levels of their first occupations, their principal occupations before senatorial service, and their occupations at the time of their entry into the Senate. The table reiterates the extent to which United States senators are recruited from high-status occupations no matter where in their careers one looks. Even so, the prelegislative occupations of senators are clearly characterized by increasing movement from lower-status work into professional and business occupations.

Religion, Race, and Ethnic Origin

Protestant Anglo-Saxons are substantially overrepresented among American legislators; blacks, Jews, and foreign-born Americans are significantly underrepresented. The religious composition of most state legislatures and both houses of the Congress is predominantly Protestant. The Senate is more Protestant than the House, and there is considerable interstate variation in the proportion of Protestants in state legislatures. For example, 94 percent of the members of the Mississippi legislature who served from 1944 to 1968 were Protestants, but nearly half (about 45 percent) of the Louisiana legislators from 1964 to 1968 were Catholics.[17]

The relationship between the proportions of Catholics in the population and in the legislature may vary a good deal. Certainly, it seems unlikely that the Catholic population is overrepresented in an American legislature, but in some

TABLE 3.4 Occupations of United States Senators, 1947–1957 (In percentages)

OCCUPATION	FIRST OCCUPATION AFTER SCHOOL	PRINCIPAL OCCUPATION	OCCUPATION AT TIME OF ENTRY INTO SENATE
Professional	68	64	82
Proprietor, official	13	29	15
Farmer	4	7	2
Low-salaried worker	8	—	—
Industrial wage earner	6	—	1
Servant, farm laborer	1	—	—
Total	100	100	100
Number	180	180	180

SOURCE: Matthews, "United States Senators: A Collective Portrait," p. 628.

states the proportions are similar. In the 1957 Wisconsin assembly, for example, 32 percent of the members were Catholic, and 32 percent of the state's population had Catholic religious affiliation. In the United States Senate, the country's Catholic population is underrepresented. Only 11 percent of the senators serving from 1947 to 1957 were Catholic; in 1952, 21 percent of a sample of the population identified themselves as Catholic; and the claimed church membership reached 34 percent of the population. The number of Jewish members in every American legislative body is small and underrepresents the Jewish population in every known case.

The number of black legislators has increased considerably since the early 1960s. There were 17 blacks in the Ninety-fourth Congress (16 representatives and 1 senator), more than at any time in the nation's history but still well below the proportion of blacks in the national population (about 11 percent). Similarly, the proportion of blacks in state legislatures has increased; the number of states with black legislators went from 27 in 1966 to 41 in 1973. There were 238 black state legislators in 1973, compared with 154 in 1966 and only 36 in 1960.

In addition, American legislators are overwhelmingly born in the United States and are heavily Anglo-Saxon in ethnic origin. Very few members of Congress have been foreign born. Of 9,618 people who served in Congress from 1789 to 1949, only 374 (4 percent) were born outside the United States. Such individuals tend to have come from northwestern European countries; up to 1949, 82 percent of all the foreign-born congressmen had been born in Canada, England, Germany, Ireland, and Scotland. Furthermore, 75 percent of the second-generation United States senators who served from 1949 to 1957 were of northwestern European ancestry. However, in some states, ethnic representation has undergone significant change. For instance, in 1900, about half of Rhode Island's population was Yankee; but 89 percent of the members of the state house of representatives were of Yankee stock. By 1968, Yankees constituted less than a third of the population and only 27 percent of the legislators; Irishmen (32 percent of the legislators) and Italians (20 percent) were somewhat overrepresented.[18]

Educational Level

No characteristic of American legislators is better documented than the fact that they are among the most educated occupational groups in the United States. Table 3.5 shows the levels of educational attainment of members of several state legislatures and of the United States Congress. More than half the members of these state legislatures had attended college, and a third or more were college graduates. Oregon legislators elected in 1966 were an especially well-educated group, more than a third of whom held post-graduate degrees. About 80 percent of the members of Congress are college graduates. As the table indicates, the legislators in each case were proportionately much better educated than the populations they represented.

The relatively high educational level of American legislators can be accounted for, in part, by their relatively high class origins. But at least more United States senators than other members of the white adult population of the country attended college, regardless of their class origins. Although the middle-class and

TABLE 3.5 Educational Level of American Legislators (In percentages)

EDUCATION	CALIF. (1957)	N.J. (1957)	OHIO (1957)	TENN. (1957)	WIS. (1957)	IND. (1961)	GA. (1961)	COLO. (1957–1966)	ORE. (1966)	U.S. HOUSE (1966)	U.S. SENATE (1966)
Elementary school only	– (33)	– (47)	4 (43)	4 (60)	8 (52)	7 (46)	12 (50)	3 (29)	2 (21)	–	– (33)
Some high school	15 (45)	13 (38)	19 (42)	22 (29)	24 (34)	20 (41)	16 (37)	17 (47)	6 (53)	7	4 (49)
Some college	31 (11)	24 (6)	19 (7)	28 (6)	23 (7)	26 (6)	32 (7)	24 (12)	22 (13)	14	13 (9)
College graduate	54 (8)	63 (7)	58 (6)	46 (4)	45 (5)	47 (5)	40 (6)	56 (15)	70 (12)	79	83 (9)
Total	100	100	100	100	100	100	100	100	100	100	100
Number	120	79	162	120	100	99	259	182	51	435	100

NOTE: Numbers in parentheses indicate proportions of the total relevant populations in each category.

SOURCES: Hjelm and Pisciotte, "Profiles and Careers of Colorato State Legislators," p. 701; Janda et al., *Legislative Politics in Indiana*, p. 3; Charles O. Jones, *Every Second Year* (Washington, D.C., 1967), p. 49; Hugh M. Thomason, "The Legislative Process in Georgia" (Ph.D. diss., Emory University, 1961), pp. 82–83; Whalke et al., *The Legislative System*, p. 489; Lester G. Seligman et al., "Patterns of Recruitment" (Chicago, 1974), p. 121.

upper-middle-class parent in the United States is better able to assure a college education for his children, the educational system is sufficiently open to all, so that at the level of the Senate, legislators achieve a high educational level almost regardless of status differences.

Age and Sex

The legislative recruitment process in the United States tends to select the middle-aged (men in their forties and fifties) for legislative careers. In general, the median ages of members of the senates are higher than those of members of the lower houses, although in some states the age differences between the two houses are not great. Also, members of the national houses tend to be older in terms of median ages than members of the comparable state bodies.

The age of the candidate for legislative office may be independently significant in the selection process. The legislative candidate in his fifties may have an advantage over one in his forties in terms of his capacity to project a politically desirable image of wisdom and experience. It has been demonstrated with age data for one congressional election (1958) that winning candidates for the United States House of Representatives had higher average ages than losers. Age fluctuations occurred between "safe" and "marginal" congressional districts in that younger men tended to be elected from the more politically competitive areas. The available evidence is consistent with the hypothesis that "middle-agedness is part of the electorate's image of a Congressman."[19] A similar phenomenon may occur at the state level.

Although the vast majority of American legislators is male, the recently increased political consciousness of women has meant some acceleration of the recruitment of women to the state legislatures. In 1973–1974, 457 women were serving in the legislatures of the states (about 6 percent), about 100 more than ten years previously. Similarly, the proportion of women serving in Congress has been increasing, after some decline in the 1960s. Nineteen women served in the Ninety-fourth Congress (1975–1976), all in the House of Representatives. No woman has served in the Senate since Senator Margaret Chase Smith (R-Maine) lost her reelection attempt in 1972. While in the 1950s and 1960s about 40 percent of the women in Congress were widows replacing their husbands, the women elected in the 1970s have overwhelmingly been candidates in their own right; only three of the women in the Ninety-fourth Congress succeeded their husbands.

POLITICAL SOCIALIZATION

The family environment provides an arena for the politicization of the individual. Although some legislators develop their interest in politics as adults and some perhaps only after they have been elected to office, most begin to develop political interests at a time when they are greatly influenced by their families. Certainly, legislators tend to have been raised in highly politicized family milieux. In their interviews with legislators in California, New Jersey, Ohio, and Tennessee, Wahlke et al. found that a high proportion of members of each legislative body (from 41 percent in New Jersey to 59 percent in Ohio and Tennessee) had relatives in politics; and they concluded that "state legislators tend to come from families which are much more involved in politics than the average American family."[20] From one-third to nearly one-half of the legislators in these states indicated as agents in their political socialization their primary group associations, principally family members.

Probably largely because of the highly politicized family environments in which they are raised, very large percentages of American legislators report significant political interests dating back to childhood and adolescence. The accumulated data for legislators in ten states and a group of congressional leaders in regard to their reported time of initial interest in public affairs are displayed in Table 3.6. Substantial majorities of legislators in every case reported that their initial political interest took place as preadults. More than half of the members of the 1957 legislatures in California, New Jersey, Ohio, and Tennessee who recalled early political interest also reported substantial family political activity; whereas only about 7 percent of their colleagues who perceived their initial interest in the political world as an adult experience reported family political activity.[21] Furthermore, the analysis of data from these four states indicates that "pre-adult political socialization is associated with a different pattern of events than deferred socialization."[22] Legislators who recalled childhood and adolescent political interest were much more likely than those whose political interests developed after college or at the time of their entry into public life to have perceived the study of politics in school and participation in school politics as important contributions in ushering them into the world of legislative politics. Those legislators who were initiated to political interest as adults were, on the contrary, more inclined to view their involvement in the largely nonpolitical activities of civic, vocational, and religious groups as leading to political activity. The evidence from the above-mentioned states also supports the generalizations that preadult socialization of legislators is more likely to be brought about by involvement in or reaction to presidential, senatorial, or gubernatorial campaigns or administrations and that both admiration for politicians and ambition for political power are more closely associated with preadult socialization. Those legislators who develop political interests only in adulthood tend to respond more to the local conditions or issues than to major national political campaigns and to seek legislative office more out of a sense of duty or indignation than out of admiration for politicians or out of political ambition.[23]

There is some evidence that legislators who develop or acquire political interests prior to adulthood are both more likely to be self-motivated in their political careers and more likely to participate in legislative bargaining processes than are their colleagues whose interest in politics is an adult phenomenon. For example, in studying legislators from Massachusetts, North Carolina, Oregon, and Utah in 1966, Harmon Zeigler has shown that early political interest is quite powerfully correlated with self-starting legislative careers. In these states, legislators who reported that their earliest recollections of interest in politics had occurred before the age of twenty were much more likely than those whose political interests were adult ones to have embarked on a political career on their own, without the necessity for encouragement to run for office from friends, interest groups, or party organizations.[24] Zeigler's data also indicate that "legislators who have been

TABLE 3.6 Earliest Recollections of Political Interest of Legislators (In percentages)

TIME OF INITIAL POLITICAL INTEREST	CALIF. (1957)	N.J. (1957)	OHIO (1957)	TENN. (1957)	IOWA (1965)	MASS. (1966)	N.C. (1966)	OREG. (1966)	UTAH (1966)	MICH. (1967)	CONGRESSIONAL LEADERS (1963)
Preadult	64	60	64	61	62	54	70	57	75	61	59
Adult	36	40	36	39	38	46	30	43	25	39	41
Total	100	100	100	100	100	100	100	100	100	100	100
Number	110	57	150	98	119	244	164	84	90	44	78

SOURCES:: Ronald D. Hedlund, "Legislative Socialization and Role Orientation: A Study of the Iowa Legislature" (Ph.D. diss., University of Iowa, 1967), p. 292; Allan Kornberg and Norman Thomas, "The Political Socialization of National Legislative Elites in the United States and Canada," *Journal of Politics* 27 (1965):768; Kenneth Prewitt, Heinz Eulau, and Betty H. Zisk, "Political Socialization and Political Roles," *Public Opinion Quarterly* 30 (1966–1967):571; John W. Soule, "Future Political Ambitions and the Behavior of Incumbent State Legislators," *Midwest Journal of Political Science* 13 (1969):445; and Harmon Zeigler and Michael A. Baer, "The Recruitment of Lobbyists and Legislators," *Midwest Journal of Political Science* 12 (1968):506.

politicized in their youth are more likely to have high interaction rates with lobbyists than those who were not."[25] Thus, dealing with lobbyists and perhaps with other actors in the legislative system is more congenial to legislators whose own lives have been highly politicized relatively early in their experience.

But having emphasized the importance of findings about the effects of early political socialization experiences on the recruitment and predispositions of American legislators, we need to add a comment or two about the apparent influence of preadult socialization versus adult socialization experiences on the orientations legislators take toward their job and the policy decision making in which they engage. Kenneth Prewitt, Heinz Eulau, and Betty H. Zisk posed the following questions: "Is there a relationship between the nature of an incumbent's initial political socialization and how he views his incumbent duties? Do events and images associated with an early career stage restrict the choices made at a later stage?"[26] Their analysis of data gathered from interviewing legislators in California, New Jersey, Ohio, and Tennessee indicated a consistent absence of any important relationship between initial political socialization and the orientations of incumbent legislators to their jobs. Legislators ushered into politics in their preadult years and those who developed political interests only as adults did not differ in the ways in which they conceived of their jobs as elected representatives with respect to the styles of representation they adopted, their attitudes toward political-interest groups, or their orientations toward the purposes of legislative representation. In addition, Donald D. Searing's research on the effects of the social-background attributes of state legislators on their political attitudes raises very serious doubt about the effects of early socialization experiences on the policy attitudes of legislators. If anything, the socialization contexts of adult experience are more predictive of legislators' political attitudes than their preadult experiences are.[27]

The evidence now available about the political socialization of legislators supports the following conclusions: (1) Legislators tend to be recruited from among those raised in highly politicized families, and a substantial majority indicate preadult interest in politics; "explicit political awareness in youth sets one apart from colleagues with respect to personal contacts, images formed, global and particular events, and predispositions associated with the socialization experience."[28] (2) The early political socialization of American legislators is not related very strongly, if at all, to major aspects of the legislator's orientation toward his role as a representative or to political attitudes. This conclusion suggests that:

> intervening between initial political socialization and incumbent behavior are political experiences that condition subsequent behavior irrespective of factors associated with initial socialization. These experiences interrupt the career sequence and retard or even reverse patterns formed during earlier stages. Recruitment and induction experiences may be of this kind; such experiences are closer in time and in kind to those of the incumbent officeholder. They serve as guidelines for the incumbent's present behavior. In addition, institutional considerations and pressures undoubtedly provide direction as the officeholder relates to his constituency, his party, or his interest groups; and his interactions within the legislative . . . setting may be the primary factor accounting for how he evaluates his own performance.[29]

We shall have more to say about these intervening conditions in the sections that follow.

RECRUITMENT OF STATE LEGISLATORS

Although investigations of the social-background characteristics and the political socialization of legislators have explained a great deal about the kinds of people who ultimately become members of legislative bodies, these studies have revealed rather little about the process of recruiting legislative members. It sometimes is suggested that people come to be recruited as legislators because of their high socioeconomic status, that high-status people tend to gravitate to legislative office. Again, it has been suggested that because legislators tend to be people who are politicized very early in life and have substantial political experience as adults, their unique political socialization leads them to legislative office. Finally, some have thought that people who become legislators share special political motivations, that they are seekers after power, prestige, status, or deference. Certainly, it is very clear that legislators differ greatly from the general electorate in their social status, political socialization, adult political experiences, and sometimes in their political motivations. But there is a real question about whether legislators differ from others in the politically active stratum of the population in these respects. A detailed study carried out in Iowa demonstrated that with regard to these characteristics legislators do not differ significantly from other political leaders. Party leaders, lobbyists, and the most attentive constituents in legislative districts were found to be very similar to legislators in terms of their socioeconomic status, political socialization, or motivation.[30]

Legislative recruitment is the active process of selecting certain persons to serve as legislators from among those who are politically active. Sometimes this may be a matter of self-selection. These self-recruited candidates, sometimes called *self-starters,* "enter the primary like entrepreneurs, eager to get ahead by their own efforts."[31] Other legislative candidacies come about through recruitment contacts, and in some degree such candidates are *drafted.* Some of these candidates for the legislature are conscripted from among the ranks of loyal party activists; sometimes prestigious persons not actively associated with party organizational efforts are co-opted as legislative candidates; and occasionally political-interest groups may get one of their own spokesmen to seek a legislative seat.

Some studies of legislative recruitment have indicated that a fairly large proportion of state legislative candidates are self-starters. For instance, polls of legislative candidates in Pennsylvania and Wisconsin have suggested that one-fourth or fewer of the candidates were asked to run by someone else.[32] However, the sharp distinction that is frequently made between self-starting and recruited candidacies may be a rather artificial one. Frank J. Sorauf has argued that many candidacies are likely to involve both elements:

> Under the flattering stimulus of party hints and overtures, the candidate-to-be may develop ambitions or may at least make the party's will his own. By the same token, he may become the object of party encouragement only after he has carefully hinted his availability or his contemplation of a candidacy.[33]

In their study of legislative recruitment in Iowa, G. R. Boynton and Samuel C. Patterson concluded that there were few pure self-starters and that "matching the available people to the available legislative offices is, at least to a substantial extent, a matter of recruiters making contacts."[34] As the Iowa study demonstrated, these recruiters include party leaders; but they may also include interest-group leaders and influentials in local communities who are not part of the formal party apparatus.

The extensiveness of recruitment contacting for the state legislature may vary in different kinds of political milieux. For example, in his study of legislative politics in Pennsylvania, Sorauf emphasized that party organizations in metropolitan areas play a much more active part in the recruitment of legislative candidates than small-town and rural parties do. This appears to be true in other states as well. Sorauf says that the strong, active metropolitan organizations

> present an impressive picture as they sort out the petitions of their many willing candidates. . . . Screening activities in these majority parties begin well in advance of the primary filing date. Although the party leadership may initiate its own recruitment and screening chores, party committeemen and other worthies carry to the leadership the cases for their favored candidates. . . . Eventually the party insiders, usually an executive committee, meet to fashion a slate which reflects a balanced appeal to all the interests and localities in the constituency.[35]

The party is concerned with finding a winning candidate, but where it is well-enough entrenched to assure victory, the legislative nomination becomes a pawn in the adjustment of claims by party groupings and a reward for faithful party workers. Potential candidates who fail to get the party's support may be expected to bow out of the race and wait for another opportunity.

Outside the metropolitan areas, the recruitment process may often be a haphazard one. Where the party is dominant in a constituency, active recruitment may be unnecessary; as one Kentucky county chairman said, "We never have a scarcity of candidates." In such areas of rural or small-town one-party dominance, the leadership may see no need to interfere in candidate selection unless the self-starting candidates are inept or the candidacies have threatened to provoke serious divisions in the party. Polls taken in both Kentucky and the plains states have indicated that most county chairmen occasionally find it necessary to encourage a candidate to run in the primary against someone who has already filed, presumably for reasons such as these.[36] In constituencies where the party is weak, the situation for legislative recruitment is very different. In many states (like Pennsylvania), "in the hard-core minority parties, recruitment often involves little more than the harried efforts by the chairman and a few henchmen to fill the party ticket."[37] Rural-urban differences such as these were sharply pinpointed in the Iowa study, which showed that recruitment contacts by party leaders were more extensive in urban legislative districts than in rural constituencies.

As has been suggested, the extensiveness of active recruitment of legislative candidates may differ not only between rural and urban constituencies but also between politically competitive constituencies and safe constituencies. These two sources of variation in recruitment contacting, although related, are not the same thing because not all urban districts are competitive and not all rural districts are safe. Generally speaking, the available evidence supports what might easily have been surmised: active legislative recruitment is more likely to be found in competitive districts than in safe ones. The most detailed illustration of the tendency for the degree of legislative recruitment to vary with the political competitiveness of constituencies is found in Lester G. Seligman's analysis of legislative recruitment in Oregon. He showed that in competitive districts "the candidacy market place was wide open" and that legislative recruitment was undertaken by a relatively wide variety of party leaders, factions, and nonparty groups. The majority party in safe districts was less involved in candidate recruitment, although in these districts, the hopeless minority party often was found to be involved in conscripting ticket fillers. The analysis of legislative recruitment in Iowa also supplied systematic evidence that legislators from competitive districts report recruitment contacts substantially more often than those from safe constituencies and that local community influentials report having made more recruitment contacts in competitive districts.

In sum, legislative recruitment at the state level cannot be accounted for very well by virtue of social distinctions, differences in politicization, or political motivation. These variables distinguish elites from mass publics, but they do not distinguish very well among elites. They contribute to the conditions under which the politically active subculture in the political system can exist. Political recruitment is a process in which people enter the politically active stratum, but *legislative* recruitment takes place largely within the politicized stratum, where it is a matter of opportunity, availability, and recruitment contact. There are finite numbers of seats available in the state legislatures in any one election year, and a limited number of people who want the job, are able to seek the office, and are wanted by others. It is in such a configuration that legislative recruitment occurs.

RECRUITMENT OF CONGRESSMEN

A very high proportion of state legislators enter the legislature without having served in any previous political office, and turnover of membership in state legislatures is very high.[38] Candidate recruitment, therefore, is a matter of substantial importance; a lot of recruiting needs to be done. Recruitment of congressmen, however, is a much more constrained activity because incumbency is far more prevalent and career paths through previous political offices are far more likely to be expected on the part of candidate recruiters. In the years following World War II (from 1949 to 1967), only 36 percent of the members of the United States House of Representatives had not previously served in a major office; and only 9 percent of postwar (from 1947 to 1957) United States senators had had no previous experience in public office. For members of Congress, the predominant previous public-office experience was that of state legislator; 36 percent of postwar representatives and 21 percent of senators had been state legislators.[39]

Since most congressional incumbents seek reelection, and since a high proportion of them normally win, the congressional recruitment problem may be considered, to a very large extent, a matter of recruiting losers.[40] What evidence there is about the recruitment of nonincumbent congressmen indicates a substantial role for political party recruitment contact. For instance, in their analysis of 238 defeated candidates in the 1962 congressional election, Robert J. Huckshorn and Robert C. Spencer found that two-thirds of the losers considered party leaders a major influence in their decisions to run for Congress; and 64 percent reported specific contacts with party leaders prior to their announcements of candidacy. This investigation further showed that the decision to run for Congress often stemmed from a desire to further the organizational development of the candidate's party in the congressional district or to serve as a "ticket-filler" and that organizational-development activities seemed to account for much of the recruitment activities of party leaders.[41] The most detailed analysis of a congressional-recruitment milieu is Leo M. Snowiss's description of the selection of congressional candidates in the Chicago area. He shows, especially for the Democratic party, the pervasive role of the party organizational apparatus in the recruitment of congressional candidates. Writing of the congressional districts in the inner city of Chicago, Snowiss says:

> Long-standing membership in the organization has been the single most important criterion of selection. The congressmen have been chosen by party regulars from among party regulars. They have risen through the party apparatus following career lines shaped by the distribution of power and the existence of established traditions. The party tends to funnel certain racial, ethnic, and religious groups to specific organizational and public positions. A given office may be reserved for Irishmen, or particular ward organizations may by tradition be awarded specific offices or patronage jobs. And offices are traded as patronage in bargains among different factions within the party. In this manner, prospective careers are determined and paths to Congress established.[42]

Whether the recruitment systems in which congressmen are selected are of the political machine or the nonmachine type appears to have a clear effect on the subsequent congressional careers of the persons chosen. Thus, "irrespective of district marginality, non-machine Democrats tend to enter Congress with a career-potential advantage of two to three terms" because they tend to be younger on entry to Congress. At the same time, "the non-machine congressmen . . . have tended to represent districts whose electoral marginality gives the least promise of long careers in the House."[43]

OPPORTUNITY AND AMBITION

Recruitment to political office is, among other things, a combination of the availability of an office and an individual's desire to seek the office. Opportunities for legislative office are by no means invariant across the country or from one level of government to another. The availability of legislative office varies from state to state and from state legislature to Congress. The opportunity structure for legislative recruitment presents such a variable pattern because of substantial variations in patterns of office incumbency, the absolute number of offices available, the frequency of elections, and probably also the differences in patterns of behavior on the part of recruiters. The structure of legislative opportunity is largely outside the control of prospective legislative candidates and also bears little relationship to patterns of interparty competition.

At the state level, opportunity for office is relatively high, in large measure because of the high incidence of turnover of legislative seats. Table 3.7 illustrates the turnover of membership in state senates and houses of representatives from 1963 to 1973. Over this period about one-third of the members of the legislative houses were new members. In any one year shown in Table 3.7, there were considerable variations in the proportions of new legislators among the states; for example, in 1973 more than half the members of the lower houses in Iowa, Maine, Nevada, New Jersey, Texas, and Utah were first-termers, while the turnover was a fifth or less in California, Hawaii, and New Mexico. The high average turnover in 1967 reflected the consequences of widespread changes in legislative district boundaries brought about by reapportionment. In any event, the high turnover of legislative seats in the states indicates substantial opportunity for legislative office at that level.

Turnover of congressional seats is much lower than is generally the case at the state level. Since the Eighty-fifth Congress, about 12 percent of the senators and 14 percent of members of the House of Representatives have been new members. The 1974 congressional election produced an unusually high turnover in the House, so that ninety-one new House members entered the Ninety-fourth Congress (21 percent).

A more precise analysis of opportunities for legislative office at both state and national levels is available in the estimates developed by Joseph A. Schlesinger.[44] Schlesinger calculated opportunity rates for United States senators and representatives in each state by combining frequencies of personnel change and differential terms of office for twelve-year periods from 1914 to 1958. He chose to calculate opportunity rates for twelve-year periods in order to provide a common denominator for various offices with terms of different lengths; twelve years is a time period that could conveniently be considered to be a "political generation."

These calculations of the legislative opportunity structure demonstrate that in general, United States House seats are more available than United States Senate seats and that state legislative offices are considerably more available than congressional offices. That is to be expected. What would not have otherwise been so apparent is that for each legislative office, there is considerable variation in opportunity rates among states. Thus, opportunities to be a United States senator during the period analyzed varied from an average of four-tenths of a time in a

TABLE 3.7　State Legislators Serving First Terms (In percentages)

LEGISLATIVE CHAMBERS	YEARS						AVERAGE 1963–1973
	1963	1965	1967	1969	1971	1973	
Senates	30	31	42	24	25	37	32
Houses	35	38	45	31	32	30	35

SOURCES: Alan Rosenthal, "Turnover in State Legislatures," *American Journal of Political Science,* 18 (1974):611; and *The Book of the States 1974–1975,* vol. 20 (Lexington, Ky., 1974), p. 69.

given twelve-year period in Virginia to as much as one and a half times in an average twelve-year period in Delaware. Although in general, opportunities are greater for United States House seats than for United States Senate seats, in a number of states, the differences are not great in spite of the greater frequency of election of House members. For example, opportunities for House membership are not much better than prospects for Senate membership in states like Texas, Arkansas, California, or North Carolina. Finally, although in general opportunities for state legislative office are considerably better than opportunities for congressional office, differences among states are considerable; and in some states they are not much better. This is the case, for instance, in Louisiana and New York, and nearly so in Wyoming. Schlesinger's analysis makes it possible to see that recruitment to legislative office operates within rather finite boundaries set by the opportunity structures of the states.

Once elected to legislative office, members tend to aspire to reelection. In 1957, for example, over three-fourths of the New Jersey state legislators and about 90 percent of the Wisconsin assemblymen who were interviewed indicated plans or expectations to run for their legislative seats again.[45] Of the ninety-six freshman Connecticut state legislators whom James D. Barber interviewed in 1959, 65 percent indicated a willingness to return for three or more sessions of the legislature.[46] In 1967, John W. Soule interviewed ninety-seven of the 110 members of the Michigan House of Representatives and found that 82 percent of the members under sixty years old were willing to return for three more legislative sessions.[47]

Defeat at the polls accounts for only a minority of American legislators who do not return to subsequent legislative service. For instance, Barber found that in Connecticut in the post–World War II era:

> election defeat accounted for less than 26 percent of retirements from the House in the seven elections between 1946 and 1958. Thus by far the largest proportion of retirements may be classified as pre-election turnover. Paradoxically, when incumbents *do* run for reelection, they are far more likely to win than to lose. Incumbents won 982 times and lost in only 219 cases in Connecticut reelection contests during this period.[48]

In New York, where postwar state legislators left mainly to seek political advancement, a considerable proportion moved into the government of New York City (35 percent of the Democratic legislators in the 1951 session).[49] The level of aspiration for higher public office among state legislators seems, in general, fairly high. Wahlke and his associates found that approximately one-third of the legislators in California, Ohio, New Jersey, and Tennessee aspired to hold other political offices.[50] And 59 percent of the members of the 1969 Michigan house apparently aspired to higher political office.[51]

In seeking other public offices, state legislators compete with those who enter politics from different channels. Still, it is important to take note, at least by way of illustration, of the extent to which state legislators migrate to other key offices. Schlesinger studied the career patterns of state governors from 1870 to 1950; he found the state legislature an important, if declining, recruiting ground for governorships. Between 1940 and 1950, 41 percent of the governors had had legislative experience, although only 13 percent had served in the state legislature immediately prior to election as governor.[52] Leon D. Epstein found that in Wisconsin "between 1925 and 1955, almost one-third of the U.S. Senators, governors, other state constitutional officers, and U.S. Representatives . . . were former state legislators."[53] Furthermore, in the last quarter century, it appears that about one-fourth of the members of the United States House and roughly one-fifth of the members of the United States Senate have served as state legislators in their first public office.[54]

Why are politically active people ambitious to achieve legislative office, to remain members of the legislative body, or to move from one legislative body to another? No full and systematic analysis of ambition of this kind has been done, but some clues are available. Not to be overlooked is the fact that the pay is now reasonably good. The annual salaries of members of Congress were increased in 1975 to $44,625, representing a 5 percent increase over their previous pay of $42,500. The median biennial compensation of state legislators has grown from about $4,000 in the early 1960s to $14,520 in 1972–1973. In California, New York, and Illinois legislators now receive a biennial salary of $40,000 or more, and in Michigan, Ohio, Pennsylvania, and Wisconsin, the biennial salary is more than $30,000. At the other extreme, the New Hampshire constitution limits legislators to a $200 salary for the biennium.[55] But less-tangible incentives for legislative ambitions clearly are available and used. Legislative services can be shown to fill private needs of personality, to supply the "joys of belongingness," the pleasure of prestige and approval, the satisfaction of participating in the decision-making process. For example, for the highly ambitious and active Connecticut legislators whom Barber calls "Lawmakers":

> the satisfactions that Lawmakers derive from being in the House show an emphasis on the prescribed tasks of the body as a source of reward. . . . Lawmakers achieve satisfaction from *producing desired legislation.* Lawmakers show a pressure for completion, for following through and finishing legislative tasks. . . .
>
> Secondly, Lawmakers are concerned that the *decision process be rational,* especially in the sense that deliberations are well-organized, long enough, and germane to the issue at hand. They derive pleasure from participating in persuasion "on the merits," not bullying or emotional propaganda or calls to duty. . . .
>
> Thirdly, the Lawmaker's attitude toward others is one of *acceptance based on insight.* Part of this insight consists of a consciousness of shared goals . . . being sought in a shared situation. . . . In addition, Lawmakers seem to have unusual empathic abilities. . . .
>
> All things considered, the most probable sequel to the Lawmaker's initial legislative experience is a lifetime of political involvement, in or out of the General Assembly. Perhaps this, rather than any particular piece of legislation, is the one most promising outcome of the Lawmaker's first session.[56]

NOTES

1. Andrew Hacker, "The Elected and the Anointed: Two American Elites," *American Political Science Review* 55 (1961):541; and Leroy N. Rieselbach, "Congressmen as 'Small Town Boys': A Research Note," *Midwest Journal of Political Science* 14 (1970):321–330.

2. Donald R. Matthews, "United States Senators: A Collective Portrait," *International Social Science Journal* 13 (1961):622.

3. Madge M. McKinney, "The Personnel of the Seventy-seventh Congress," *American Political Science Review* 36 (1942):68.

4. The federal Constitution, in Article I, Section 2, requires only that a representative shall, "when elected, be an inhabitant of that state in which he shall be chosen."

5. Frank J. Sorauf, *Party and Representation: Legislative Politics in Pennsylvania* (New York, 1963), p. 74; Hugh M. Thomason, "The Legislative Process in Georgia" (Ph.D. diss., Emory University, 1961), p. 74; Victor S. Hjelm and Joseph P. Pisciotte, "Profiles and Careers of Colorado State Legislators," *Western Political Quarterly* 21 (1968):704; and Lester G. Seligman, Michael R. King, Chong Lim Kim, and Roland E. Smith, *Patterns of Recruitment: A State Chooses Its Lawmakers* (Chicago, 1974), p. 128.

6. See H. H. Gerth and C. Wright Mills, eds., *From Max Weber: Essays in Sociology* (London, 1948), p. 85.

7. Charles S. Hyneman, "Who Makes Our Laws?" *Political Science Quarterly* 55 (1940):560–561.

8. Donald R. Matthews, *The Social Background of Political Decision-Makers* (New York, 1954), p. 30; "United States Senators: A Collective Portrait," p. 628; and Joseph A. Schlesinger, "Lawyers and American Politics: A Clarified View," *Midwest Journal of Political Science* 1 (1957):28.

9. Hyneman, "Who Makes Our Laws?" p. 557; and Belle Zeller, ed., *American State Legislatures* (New York, 1954), p. 71.

10. *Congressional Quarterly Student Guide* (Washington, D.C., 1957), p. 8.

11. See Mapheus Smith and Marian L. Brockway, "Mobility of American Congressmen," *Sociology and Social Research* 24 (1940):519–520; and Paul L. Hain and James E. Piereson, "Lawyers and Politics Revisited: Structural Advantages of Lawyer-Politicians," *American Journal of Political Science* 19(1975), 41–51.

12. See David R. Derge, "The Lawyer as Decision-Maker in the American State Legislature," *Journal of Politics* 21 (1959):408–433; "The Lawyer in the Indiana General Assembly," *Midwest Journal of Political Science* 6 (1962):19–53; and Heinz Eulau and John D. Sprague, *Lawyers in Politics: A Study in Professional Convergence* (Indianapolis, Ind., 1964).

13. Matthews, "United States Senators: A Collective Portrait," p. 629.

14. Heinz Eulau and David Koff, "Occupational Mobility and Political Career," *Western Political Quarterly* 15 (1962):511

15. See Smith and Brockway, "Mobility of American Congressmen," p. 514.

16. See Matthews, "United States Senators: A Collective Portrait," p. 625.

17. Alex B. Lacy, Jr., ed., "Power in American State Legislatures," *Tulane Studies in Political Science* 11 (1967):58, 93.

18. Murray G. Lawson, "The Foreign-born in Congress, 1789–1949: A Statistical Summary," *American Political Science Review* 51 (1957):1183–1189; Matthews, "United States Senators: A Collective Portrait," p. 624; and Elmer E. Cornwell, Jr. et al., *The Rhode Island General Assembly* (Washington, D.C., 1970), pp. 16–17.

19. David B. Walker, "The Age Factor in the 1958 Congressional Elections," *Midwest Journal of Political Science* 4 (1960):1–26; quotation at p. 7. See also Sorauf, *Party and Representation,* p. 66.

20. John C. Wahlke et al., *The Legislative System* (New York, 1962), p. 82.

21. Kenneth Prewitt, Heinz Eulau, and Betty H. Zisk, "Political Socialization and Political Roles," *Public Opinion Quarterly* 30 (1966–1967):573.

22. Ibid., p. 574.

23. Ibid., pp. 575–578.

24. Harmon Zeigler and Michael A. Baer, "The Recruitment of Lobbyists and Legislators," *Midwest Journal of Political Science* 12 (1968):507; and *Lobbying: Interaction and*

Influence in American State Legislatures (Belmont, Calif., 1969), especially pp. 38–59. See also Allan Kornberg and Norman Thomas, "The Political Socialization of National Legislative Elites in the United States and Canada," *Journal of Politics* 27 (1965):761–775.

25.   Zeigler and Baer, "The Recruitment of Lobbyists and Legislators," p. 510.

26.   Prewitt, Eulau, and Zisk, "Political Socialization and Political Roles," p. 578. See also Charles G. Bell and Charles M. Price, " Pre-Legislative Sources of Representational Roles," *Midwest Journal of Political Science* 13 (1969):254–270; and Malcolm E. Jewell, "Attitudinal Determinants of Legislative Behavior: The Utility of Role Analysis," in *Legislatures in Developmental Perspective,* ed. Allan Kornberg and Lloyd D. Musolf (Durham, N.C., 1970), pp. 460–500.

27.   See Donald D. Searing, "The Comparative Study of Elite Socialization," *Comparative Political Studies* 1 (1969):471–500. See also Lewis J. Edinger and Donald D. Searing, "Social Background and Elite Analysis: A Methodological Inquiry," *American Political Science Review* 61 (1967):428–445.

28.   Prewitt, Eulau, and Zisk, "Political Socialization and Political Roles," p. 581.

29.   Ibid., p. 582.

30.   See Samuel C. Patterson and G. R. Boynton, "Legislative Recruitment in a Civic Culture," *Social Science Quarterly* 50 (1969):243–263.

31.   Lester G. Seligman, "Political Recruitment and Party Structure: A Case Study," *American Political Science Review* 55 (1961):77–86; quotation at p. 85.

32.   See Sorauf, *Party and Representation,* p. 99; Leon D. Epstein, *Politics in Wisconsin* (Madison, Wis., 1958), p. 205.

33.   Sorauf, *Party and Representation,* p. 103.

34.   Patterson and Boynton, "Legislative Recruitment in a Civic Culture," p. 254.

35.   Sorauf, *Party and Representation,* pp. 57–58.

36.   See Malcolm E. Jewell and Everett W. Cunningham, *Kentucky Politics* (Lexington, Ky., 1968), pp. 60–61, 122–125.

37.   Sorauf, *Party and Representation,* p. 57.

38.   For example, 71 percent of the Colorado legislators serving from 1957 to 1966 had no previous public-office experience. See Hjelm and Pisciotte, "Profiles and Careers of Colorado State Legislators," p. 707. See also Wahlke et al., *The Legislative System* (New York, 1962), pp. 95–97; Epstein, *Politics in Wisconsin,* p. 191; W. P. Tucker, "Characteristics of State Legislators," *Social Science* 30 (1955):94–98; and Sorauf, *Party and Representation,* p. 83.

39.   Matthews, "United States Senators: A Collective Portrait," p. 630; and Michael L. Mezey, "Ambition Theory and the Office of Congressmen," *Journal of Politics* 32 (1970):567–569.

40.   Congressional winners and losers do not differ much in their social-background characteristics or ideological postures, although winners do appear to incline to be differently affected by the election outcome than losers in their perceptions of their constituents. See Jeff Fishel, "Party, Ideology, and the Congressional Challenger," *American Political Science Review* 63 (1969):1213–1232; John W. Kingdon, *Candidates for Office: Beliefs and Strategies* (New York, 1968); and Chong Lim Kim, "Political Attitudes of Defeated Candidates in an American State Election," *American Political Science Review* 64 (1970): 879–887.

41.   Robert J. Huckshorn and Robert C. Spencer, *The Politics of Defeat: Campaigning for Congress* (Amherst, Mass., 1971), pp. 49, 66, 74.

42.   Leo M. Snowiss, "Congressional Recruitment and Representation," *American Political Science Review* 60 (1966):630.

43.   Ibid., p. 639.

44.   Joseph A. Schlesinger, *Ambition and Politics: Political Careers in the United States* (Chicago, 1966), pp. 37–56.

45.   Wahlke et al., *The Legislative System,* p. 122.

46.   James D. Barber, *The Lawmakers* (New Haven, Conn., 1965), p. 20.

47.   John W. Soule, "Future Political Ambitions and the Behavior of Incumbent State Legislators," *Midwest Journal of Political Science* 13 (1969):442. For an analysis of the political ambitions of local legislators, see the reports of the research on city councilmen in the San Francisco Bay area in Kenneth Prewitt, "Political Ambitions, Volunteerism, and Electoral Accountability," *American Political Science Review* 64 (1970):5–17. See also Kenneth Prewitt, *The Recruitment of Political Leaders: A Study of Citizen-Politicians* (Indianapolis, Ind., 1970), especially pp. 175–203.

48.   Barber, *The Lawmakers,* p. 8.

49.   Leonard Ruchelman, *Political Careers: Recruitment Through the Legislature* (Rutherford, N.J., 1970), pp. 100, 115–127.

50.   Wahlke et al., *The Legislative System,* pp. 129–130.

51.   Soule, "Future Political Ambitions and the Behavior of Incumbent State Legislators," p. 444.

52.   Joseph A. Schlesinger, *How They Became Governor* (East Lansing, Mich., 1957), p. 51.

53.   Epstein, *Politics in Wisconsin,* p. 117.

54.   For some documentation, see McKinney, "The Personnel of the Seventy-seventh Congress," p. 71; and Matthews, "United States Senators: A Collective Portrait," p. 630.

55.   Council of State Governments, *The Book of the States, 1974–1975,* vol. 20 (Lexington, Ky., 1974), pp. 59, 71.

56.   Barber, *The Lawmakers,* pp. 35–37, 181–182, 211. See also Soule, "Future Political Ambitions and the Behavior of Incumbent State Legislators," pp. 447–450.

CHAPTER FOUR

Legislative Elections

Congressman A comes from a district in the Deep South that consists of small towns and farm areas. When Congressman A was first elected fourteen years ago, he won a narrow victory in the Democratic primary following the retirement of the incumbent. In the next three primaries, he won by increasing margins. Since that time, he has been unopposed in the primaries, and he has never had a Republican opponent. His personal popularity and the strength of his personal organization in the district seem to preclude effective opposition.

Senator B, a Democrat, was elected to his first term six years ago in a large northern industrial state. He narrowly defeated a veteran Republican senator in a year when the Democrats were making electoral gains across the country. Since that time, a popular Republican governor (who may run against him) has been elected, and there are other signs of Republican revival in his state. Senator B's prospects in the forthcoming election are precarious.

Legislator C is a Republican senator who represents a medium-sized city in the legislature of a midwestern state. Long active in party organizational work, he agreed to run for senator four years ago in a normally Democratic district because the party was having difficulty filling that position on the slate. He was swept into office when his party's candidate for governor scored a surprisingly strong victory. Legislator C has no elaborate campaign plans because he believes that the outcome of his reelection contest depends largely on the coattails of the governor, who has promised to make several campaign appearances in his city.

No congressman or state legislator can be described as typical. These three examples illustrate the variety of situations that confront a legislator when he faces reelection. Districts vary greatly in size. United States senators represent fifty states that range in population from 300,000 to 20 million; most congressional districts have between 450,000 and 500,000 people. Although reapportionment has minimized the variations in population of districts within states, the average district is much greater in some states than in others. The average state senate district in California has a population of about 500,000, larger than many congressional districts; at the other extreme, the average member of the lower house in New Hampshire represents less than 2,000 people. United States senators face reelection every six years, and United States representatives, every two years. State senators serve four-year terms in thirty-eight states and two-year terms in twelve states; representatives serve four-year terms in only three states and two-year terms in the rest. Legislative campaigns are affected by the nature of the districting system, the intensity of primary and two-party competition, and the candidate's dependence upon the party and its major candidates for assistance. We shall explore each of these factors in order to determine how it influences legislative elections.

An understanding of the factors affecting elections is important for several reasons. First, it helps to explain the recruitment of legislators and the variation among legislatures in turnover and personnel. The power structure in Congress and in some state legislatures is a product of variations in electoral districts; congressmen from safe districts with a minimum of competition have acquired the seniority essential for holding the positions of power. Above all, the electoral situation that confronts a legislator affects his role. Congressman A, with his secure electoral base, has greater freedom to choose his role; and he is likely to respond to the demands of his congressional colleagues and the norms established in Congress and in his committees. Senator B has less freedom; if he can determine what his constituents want, he must give them priority in his resolution of the inevitable role conflicts that confront him. Legislator C, if he believes that the governor's coattails are essential to his political survival, may define his role in accordance with the expectations of the governor and may thus contribute to a high level of party unity in the legislature.

To understand the problems faced by legislative candidates and how the votes for a party get translated into seats in the legislature, it is necessary to understand what method of representation is being used. Proportional representation methods come closest to giving a party a number of seats proportionate to the vote it receives. Although this method is common in Europe, the only such plan at the state or national level in this country is in the lower house of the Illinois legislature, where it is called cumulative voting. Each house district there has three seats, and each voter has three votes, which may be cast in a variety of ways, including more than one vote for a single candidate. Under this method in most districts the stronger party elects two members and the minority is virtually guaranteed one member. But this method encourages the parties to run only as many candidates as they expect to get elected, and consequently it has reduced the level of competition.

Any districting technique other than proportional representation substantially benefits the majority party because it wastes the votes of minority parties. Minor, or third, parties are severely handicapped because they rarely have a plurality, even in a small district, and thus cannot elect legislators. The minority, or second, party is handicapped by a single-member district plan; it is hurt even more by multimember districts, even without any attempt at gerrymandering by the majority party. In a large county, if several multimember districts are used, minority pockets of strength are likely to be swallowed up by the majority; and if all legislators are elected at large, all the minority party's votes may be wasted. In a single-member district system, if a minority party's strength were evenly distributed throughout a state, that party would be a minority party in every legislative district and would be unrepresented in the legislature. In practice, the minority party has concentrations of strength that enable it to elect some legislators; but in single-member districts, more of its votes are wasted than the majority party loses. The exact relationship between the percentage of votes and the percentage of seats for each party in a single-member district system depends on the distribution of party strength and the number of districts with uncontested elections. Data from congressional elections suggest that as long as both parties get between 40 and 60 percent of the national vote, a gain of 1 percent in the total popular vote will result in a gain of about 2.5 percent in House seats.[1]

Figure 4.1 illustrates the effects of districting in a hypothetical metropolitan county containing 120,000 voters (70,000 Democrats and 50,000 Republicans). Under a proportional representation system, the county would elect seven Democratic and five Republican legislators. If the voters in each party were unevenly distributed throughout the county and twelve districts were established, with no attempt at gerrymandering and with exactly 10,000 voters in each, the result might be the one shown in Figure 4.1. The Democrats would carry nine districts, and the Republicans would carry only three (D, H, and L). The Republicans would have wasted 32,000 votes in the nine districts they lost, but the Democrats would have wasted only 12,000 votes in their three losing districts. If the county were divided into three or four multimember districts, the Democrats could win all the seats by incorporating each of the Republican areas (D, H, and L) into a larger Democratic district.

COMPETITION IN PRIMARIES

A congressman or state legislator faces two potential obstacles when he decides to run again: the primary and the general election. His role as a legislator and, in the long run, his power in the legislative body are affected by the frequency and strength of the opposition he encounters in hurdling these two obstacles.

Congressional Seats

With rare exceptions (mostly in southern Republican parties) members of Congress are nominated in direct primaries. It is unusual for an incumbent to be defeated in a congressional primary. In twelve election years from 1952 to 1974 (involving over 300 elections), only 5 percent of the incumbent senators who

FIGURE 4.1   Division of a Hypothetical County into Twelve Legislative Districts with 10,000 Voters Each, Indicating the Number of Democratic and Republican Voters

A 7,000 D 3,000 R	B 7,000 D 3,000 R	C 6,000 D 4,000 R	D 4,000 D 6,000 R
E 7,000 D 3,000 R	F 6,000 D 4,000 R	G 6,000 D 4,000 R	H 4,000 D 6,000 R
I 7,000 D 3,000 R	J 6,000 D 4,000 R	K 6,000 D 4,000 R	L 4,000 D 6,000 R

sought renomination were beaten in a primary. From 1956 to 1974 less than 2 percent of the incumbent representatives were denied renomination in the primary.[2] After one or more six-year terms, a United States senator becomes so well known to constituents and develops so much political strength in his state that he is nearly invulnerable in the primary. Although the representative must face the voters every two years, he has the advantage of representing a smaller district. He usually is able to develop a reputation and cultivate support by careful attention to local needs. After several terms in office, the representative may not even be challenged in the primary. It should be pointed out that state and local party leaders usually discourage primary challenges to a senator or representative who has proven to be a successful vote getter and has developed enough congressional seniority to help his state or district.

If there is no incumbent running, the intensity of competition in congressional primaries depends to a large extent on the parties' prospects in the general election. V. O. Key, Jr., surveyed senatorial primaries from 1920 to 1960 and found that about half of them were closely contested (with the winner getting less than 60 percent of the vote) in states that were safe for a party. There were slightly fewer close primaries in competitive states, and only about one-fifth were close in states dominated by the opposite party. Data for House districts during the 1950s showed even greater contrasts; almost two-thirds of the primaries were close in safe districts, and only one-fifth were close in districts controlled by the other party.[3] There is seldom any surplus of candidates to run in either party's primary when a district is controlled by a veteran congressman. However, when a veteran congressman retires, there is likely to be a scramble for the nomination in his party among candidates who have been waiting impatiently for him to retire.

State Legislature Seats

The proportion of one-party districts is greater in many state legislatures than it is in Congress, and consequently, it becomes particularly important to determine whether the primary serves as an adequate substitute for the general election in safe legislative districts. In state districts where the voters usually have little, if any, choice in general elections, are they likely to have a choice in the majority party primary? On the surface, it would seem that the answer is yes. Studies of a number of states, by Key and others, have shown that state legislative primary competition increases with the prospects of victory in the general election (as we have noted that it does in congressional primaries).[4] When a party is virtually certain of victory, candidates have a greater incentive to run. The prospect of a close election reduces the incentive and often leads to efforts by the party organization to preserve unity. When election prospects are dim, candidates may have to be drafted by party leaders, who are lucky if they can find *one* candidate. As Frank J. Sorauf points out, when electoral victory is unlikely, "the overriding criterion for the legislative candidate is simply the willingness to run as a sacrificial candidate."[5] Data collected from several northern states in the 1940s and 1950s showed that there were primary contests in one-half to three-fourths of the safe districts, one-third to two-thirds of the marginal districts, and, in most cases, less than one-third of the hopeless districts. This does not necessarily mean that the voters always have some choice in either the primary or the general election, however. In Wisconsin, from 1946 to 1956, there was no majority party primary contest in nearly half of the 15 percent of cases where there was no general election contest.[6]

The likelihood of victory in the general election is not the only factor that affects the level of primary competition. Key has suggested that competition is likely to be lower in rural areas because less effort and fewer resources are necessary to monopolize party control than would be required in large urban areas characterized by a multiplicity of power centers. Control by a small clique in a rural county may be easily preserved if there are too few persons interested enough in politics to present an effective challenge. Studies have shown that legislative primary competition is greater in the urban than in the rural areas of some two-party states (such as Wisconsin, Michigan, and Ohio), with the pattern consistent in both marginal and safe districts.[7]

Urban-rural differences are more easily discerned in those parts of the South that have been under solid one-party control. A study of eight southern and border states during the 1950s and early 1960s showed that in most of these states, there was a higher proportion of contested primaries and of closely contested primaries in metropolitan than in nonmetropolitan counties, although the differences were not consistently large. (The relatively small number of districts that had two-party competition during that period were excluded from the comparison.) In at least two states, Alabama and Louisiana, there was substantially lower competition in those rural counties that had a large proportion of nonvoting blacks (prior to the large-scale registration of blacks in those states). It appeared that white politicians might be trying to minimize the competition and open political controversy that might lead to increased black registration and voting. It should also be noted that during the 1950s and early 1960s, there were substantial differences among the southern states in the levels of primary competition that could not be explained by urban-rural differences, incumbency, or similar factors and that apparently resulted from differences in political styles and traditions in the states.[8]

Do incumbent state legislators, like congressmen, develop the political strength to discourage primary competition? In most states for which studies have been made, the evidence shows that there are fewer contested and less closely contested primaries when incumbents are running, but the drop is less pronounced than in congressional races. There are sharp variations in the proportion of incumbents who seek renomination. In southern states, it has varied from four-fifths to one-third, with the lower proportions usually being found in states that make some use of *rotation agreements* (agreements among county party leaders to rotate the seat among counties in a district). Moreover, the presence of an incumbent is most likely to discourage competition in those southern states where incumbents are most likely to run. In other words, in districts where incumbents usually seek renomination, there is likely to be a backlog of eager candidates when an incumbent finally decides not to run again.[9]

What are the chances of an incumbent losing in a state legislative primary? In northern two-party states, the survival rate appears to be relatively high, although lower than it is for congressmen. Data from Michigan show 5 percent losing; in Wisconsin, 14 percent lost in a series of elections. In southern states that have been dominated by a single party, the primary is a more serious obstacle and one that varies from state to state. During the 1950s and early 1960s, 35 to 40 percent of the incumbents who ran were beaten in Louisiana and Alabama; 20 to 25 percent lost in South Carolina, Florida, Kentucky, and Tennessee; and less than 15 percent lost in Texas and North Carolina. In these southern states, the variation in losses by incumbents parallels the variation in other measurements of primary competition.[10]

TWO-PARTY COMPETITION

Congressional Seats

There are three major factors that affect the outcome of elections for both congressional and state legislative seats: incumbency, the partisan balance in the district, and national or state political trends. In any election year there are some districts that appear to be safe for one party because of the political strength and experience of the incumbent and/or the partisan allegiance of a large majority of voters in the district. There are some national or state elections in which the political trend is so favorable to one party, perhaps because of the popularity of its top candidate, that it is able to capture some seats that were regarded as safe for the other party.

In the twelve election years from 1952 to 1974 only about 16 percent of the incumbent senators who sought reelection were defeated in the general election (in addition to 5 percent who lost in the primaries). In ten election years from 1956 to 1974 only 6 percent of the incumbent representatives who ran lost general elections (in addition to 2 percent who lost primaries), but the figure was as high as 11 percent in 1964 and as low as 1 percent in 1968. The rate of loss for freshman representatives during this period was almost 15 percent; for other incumbents it was only 5 percent. One-third of the defeated incumbents were freshmen.[11] Another group of incumbents who were vulnerable to defeat were those whose districts were changed drastically by redistricting and particularly those unfortunate enough to be placed in a district with another incumbent.

Senators face a possible challenge at the polls only one-third as often as representatives, but the data show that they are twice as likely to be defeated in a primary or a general election. Most states are larger and more heterogeneous than most congressional districts, and it is more difficult for a senator to build a secure political base by assiduous attention to the needs of his constituents. Moreover, the proportion of closely competitive two-party states is much larger than the proportion of closely competitive House districts (Table 4.1). The defeat of an incumbent may result from his failure to work hard and take full advantage of an incumbent's inherent advantages, from a change in the partisan loyalties (or boundaries) of his district, or from a change in national political trends. The greater vulnerability of freshmen results from the relatively short period of time they have to make themselves well known and to establish a record in the district and also from the fact that some of them may have been swept into office as a result of a strong national trend in a district that normally votes for the other party. The highest rates of defeat for freshmen in recent years were in 1966 and 1960, immediately following elections that had unusually strong trends in favor of one party.

One way in which nonincumbent candidates attempt to overcome the advantage enjoyed by incumbents is to run a second or third time in a district. This gives them the opportunity to become better known to the voters, to build up an organization, and to learn from the mistakes of the first campaign. There are no systematic, long-term studies of repeating candidates, but an analysis of the 1972 and 1974 House elections provides some indication of the extent and success of this strategy. There were forty-two nonincumbent candidates in 1972 who had run before in the district, and forty-seven such candidates in 1974 (counting the same person only once even if he were a repeater both times). Of these eighty-nine candidates, fifty-four had run once before, eight had run twice before, thirteen had run unsuccessfully in the district primary before, and fourteen were former congressmen from the district. Most, but not all, of the repeated efforts were in consecutive elections. In some cases it was clear that the candidate had never stopped running from one election to the next, as he kept his organization intact and kept making public appearances. How successful was this strategy? In 1972, 23 percent of the repeaters won (compared to 16 percent of all nonincumbents running), and in 1974, 60 percent won (compared to 21 percent of all nonincumbents).

Table 4.1 shows that the proportion of close elections (under a 55 percent margin) is at least twice as high in the Senate as it is in the House. In both branches there has been a decrease in the proportion of uncontested races, which partly explains the increase in the proportion of contests decided by 60 percent or more. Most of the uncontested seats are in southern states, where the proportion of House seats contested by the Republican party has risen from less than one-third in the early 1950s to about two-thirds in recent years. Many of the safest Democratic seats are in the central city parts of metropolitan areas, and some of the safest Republican seats are in rural sections of Republican states. The propor-

TABLE 4.1   Levels of Two-Party Competition in Senate (1952–1974) and House (1954, 1962, 1970, 1974) (In percentages)

	ELECTIONS WON BY LESS THAN 55 PERCENT	ELECTIONS WON BY 55–55.9 PERCENT	ELECTIONS WON BY 60 PERCENT OR MORE	UNCONTESTED ELECTIONS
Senate				
1952–1960	39	23	26	12
(N = 180)				
1962–1974	44	19	34	3
(N = 245)				
House				
1954	21	21	38	20
1962	17	23	48	12
1970	12	16	61	11
1974	22	16	51	11
(N = 435)				

tion and the location of highly competitive districts vary with national political trends. In a strongly Democratic year, marginal Democratic seats are won by comfortable margins and safe Republican seats become less safe. The data in Table 4.1 may give the impression of less competition than actually exists over a period of several elections. Mayhew notes that 58 percent of all House members in the Ninety-third Congress had carried their district at least once by less than 55 percent, and over three-fourths had had margins of less than 60 percent.[12]

Another way of measuring safe and marginal districts is to look at party turnover in them over time. During the period from 1952 to 1960 there were 38 districts (all southern) in which the Democratic candidate never had an opponent, and 130 more districts (two-thirds of them Democratic) that were always won by the same party with at least 60 percent of the vote; only 95 districts had some partisan turnover during the period.[13] Frequent changes in district boundaries in more recent years have made it difficult to measure long-term turnover, but Mayhew has calculated that over one-third of the House members in the Ninety-third Congress had in their initial election succeeded a member of the other party.[14]

Some districts that consistently elect a congressman of one party are safe because that party has a large majority of supporters in the district. In other cases, however, a congressman succeeds over a period of years in building up a solid majority through the services he performs in the district even though in elections for other offices the district is close or supports the other party. One way of judging how much of the electoral margin is due to the incumbent's own efforts is to compare his vote with that for other candidates. Another way is to see what happens when he retires; often an apparently safe district is lost to the other party when the incumbent retires. A good example is the Wisconsin district held for years by Republican Melvin Laird, by a margin of more than 60 percent (64 percent in 1968). When Laird resigned to enter the cabinet, a Democrat (David Obey) narrowly won the district in a special election in 1969, and then in 1970 Obey carried the district by over 67 percent.[15]

The outcome of congressional elections depends in part on the strength and direction of national political trends. In most election years there is a predominant trend favoring one party or the other. As Table 4.2 shows, the effects of this trend on House elections vary substantially from election to election. The party winning the Presidency usually gains seats in the House, but in 1956 and 1960 the winning party lost House seats; in 1968 it gained only four, and in 1972 it had a modest gain of twelve. In midterm elections from 1950 to 1974 the opposition party always gained seats, but the net gains varied from only two to forty-seven seats. The smallest gains by the opposition in recent years (1962 and 1970) immediately followed elections in which the party winning the Presidency had made few, if any, gains in the House.[16] In some elections (such as 1950 and 1958) only one or two districts had a party turnover that was contrary to the national trend. In more recent years, the election trends have seldom been so one-sided. Even with the Johnson landslide in 1964, the Democratic party lost ten House seats (mostly in the Deep South) and won forty-eight. In 1972 the Republicans won twenty-four seats while losing twelve. Even in the 1974 Democratic landslide there were six Republicans who won Democratic seats, four of them from incumbents. There have been wide fluctuations in the net gains and losses of seats in recent years, but the changes have been smaller and less consistent than in the past. From 1932 to 1948 the winning presidential party always won House seats, usually a substantial number; in midterm elections from 1930 to 1946 (except for 1934), the opposition party consistently gained a large number of seats. The average of all net shifts from 1930 to 1948 was forty-four House seats; the average from 1950 to 1974 was half of that.

Table 4.2 shows that the net changes in the party balance in the Senate have been relatively small since 1950, except for the 1958 election, and have not always been consistent with the direction of changes in the House. There are several reasons for the distinct pattern in the Senate. Senators are better known than representatives and have a better opportunity to attract the attention of voters and persuade them to split their ticket.[17] Moreover, the staggered election of senators to six-year terms may create cross-currents in national elections. For example, the large gains made by the Republicans in the 1946 and 1950 Senate elections (thirteen and five seats, respectively) left very few marginal Democratic seats that would be vulnerable six years later; consequently, Republican Senate gains were negligible in the 1952 and 1956 elections when Eisenhower won presidential races. The last major shift in Senate seats occurred in 1958, when the Democrats made a net gain of seventeen seats. Six years later, in the 1964 Johnson landslide, the Democrats were only able to win two more because most of the remaining Republican seats up for election were very safe ones.

There is evidence that senatorial elections have become more independent of national trends in recent presidential elections. Data collected by V. O. Key for the presidential elections from 1920 to 1948 showed that the party winning the

TABLE 4.2   Results of Congressional Elections, 1950–1974

YEAR	HOUSE					SENATE				
	Members Elected			Gain and Loss		Members Elected			Gain and Loss	
	D	R	Other	D	R	D	R	Other	D	R
1950	234	199	2	−29	+28	48	47	1	−6	+5
1952	213	221	1	−21	+22	47	48	1	−1	+1
1954	232	203		+19	−18	48	47	1	+1	−1
1956	234	201		+2	−2	49	47		+1	0
1958	283	154		+49	−47	66	34		+17	−13
1960	263	174		−20	+20	64	36		−2	+2
1962	259	176		−4	+2	68	32		+4	−4
1964	295	140		+38	−38	67	33		+2	−2
1966	248	187		−47	+47	64	36		−3	+3
1968	243	192		−4	+4	58	42		−5	+5
1970	255	180		+12	−12	55	45		−4	+2
1972	243	192		−12	+12	57	43		+2	−2
1974	291	144		+43	−43	61	39		+3	−3

NOTE: The calculation of gains and losses takes into account special elections and appointments between regular elections.
SOURCE: *Congressional Quarterly Weekly Report* 32 (November 9, 1974): 3105.

Presidency held 95 percent of its senatorial seats and the losing party held only 54 percent of its seats (with or without an incumbent running).[18] A similar comparison of presidential races from 1952 to 1972 shows the winning party holding 83 percent and the losing party holding 74 percent, a much smaller contrast. There has been a similar decrease in the effect of presidential voting on House elections, as more voters appear to be splitting their tickets. According to data compiled by Milton C. Cummings, the proportion of House districts carried by the presidential nominee of one party and the congressional nominee of the other ranged from only 11 to 17 percent during the period from 1932 to 1948, but between 1952 and 1964 it ranged from 19 to 33 percent.[19] In 1972 it reached 44 percent. In 1952 and 1956 Dwight Eisenhower carried large numbers of districts (80 and 127) won by Democratic congressional candidates and lost only 4 districts won by Republicans. In contrast, John Kennedy in 1960 won only 28 Republican congressional districts and lost 83 that were won by Democrats, an unusually weak record. Lyndon Johnson's 1964 record was 113 victories in Republican congressional districts and 32 losses in Democratic districts.[20] In 1972 McGovern lost 190 districts where Democrats won congressional seats, and won only 3 Republican districts, which is why the Democrats kept their majority in the House despite the Nixon landslide. A major reason for these results is the strength of incumbents. Cummings has shown that in elections from 1924 to 1964, 85 percent of the congressional winners in districts carried by the opposite presidential candidate were incumbents.[21]

There have been several recent efforts to measure more precisely the relative effect of incumbency, the party loyalties in a district, and national political tides on the outcome of congressional elections. Erikson has estimated that in the 1954 to 1960 elections the status of being an incumbent in a House race was worth only about two percentage points, but that in the 1966 through the 1970 elections this advantage increased to about 5 percentage points.[22] Kostroski's study of senatorial elections also shows a steady increase in the importance of incumbency. Between 1948 and 1958 its value increased from about three to six percentage points; in the 1960 to 1970 election years it averaged about 11 percentage points. During that same period the importance of party loyalties in the state declined steadily, national political tides became somewhat less important, and idiosyncratic variables (such as the image of candidates and the effectiveness of their campaigns) increased in importance.[23] This means that incumbent senators have a good chance of being reelected, and that their major threat comes less from strong national political tides than from a well-known candidate who is a skillful campaigner.

Survey research studies provide further insight into the fluctuations in congressional voting between presidential and nonpresidential years. Presidential elections attract some voters to the polls who do not have enough interest in politics to vote in nonpresidential elections. If many of them are attracted to a strong presidential candidate and vote a straight ticket, the lower turnout in the succeeding congressional election is likely to result in a drop in congressional seats for the President's party. A study of the 1956 and 1958 elections by the Michigan Survey Research Center showed that the likelihood of voting was more closely related to the strength of party identification in congressional than in presidential years. Consequently, the voters strongly identified with a party constituted a larger proportion of the electorate for congressional races in 1958 than they did in 1956. The proportion of those voting for Congress who were independents (with no party leanings at all) dropped from 9 to 5 percent from 1956 to 1958. In 1970 it was slightly higher, 8 percent. Party identification is likely to have a greater impact on congressional voting in nonpresidential years because there is no presidential candidate with a possible coattail effect and because a higher proportion of the voters are strong party-identifiers.[24]

Studies of the 1958 and 1970 elections shed light on the factors that influence votes for congressional candidates. In 1958, 84 percent of all the votes were cast by party-identifiers voting for candidates of their party; in 1970 this figure dropped to 76 percent, both because there were more independents voting and because more Democrats voted for Republicans than in 1958. The congressional vote in nonpresidential years is usually consistent with party loyalties, but it is seldom a vote of confidence in the record or program of either party. In 1958 only 7 percent of the voters gave an explanation for their vote that included any reference to issues, and these issue-oriented voters were no more likely than others to cross party lines in their voting. In 1970 the relatively small number of voters who perceived a difference between the parties and disagreed with their own party on three major issues showed only a little greater tendency to cross party lines in voting than did other voters. Both years only about half of the voters knew that the Democratic party controlled Congress; those who did not obviously could not make voting decisions based on an accurate assessment of the records of congressional parties.[25]

When voters who are party-identifiers vote for a candidate of the other party, the reason is usually that they know more about that candidate. In 1970 one-fourth of those who knew something about both candidates and one-sixth of those who knew nothing about either voted for the other party's candidate, but 57 percent of those who knew only about the other party's candidate voted for him. The same pattern had prevailed in 1958, although the proportion of those in each category who had shifted their vote was smaller. The level of information about candidates is relatively low, and in many cases is nothing more than name identification. The fact that the level of information about candidates is usually what leads voters to cross party lines obviously helps to explain the success of incumbents, who are often better known than their opponent to the voters of both parties.[26]

State Legislative Districts

Since state legislative districts are almost always smaller than congressional districts, they are likely to have greater homogeneity; and consequently, they are more likely to be dominated by a single party than to be competitive. If competition is measured by party turnover, it is limited to a small proportion of the districts in most states. In states dominated by one party, minority party strength is likely to be concentrated in a few districts of traditional support; and there may be very few districts in which there is any party turnover. Even in closely competitive two-party states, each of the parties may have its strength so concentrated in particular areas that relatively few seats change hands over a period of several elections. Only the landslide victory of a gubernatorial candidate is likely to produce a large turnover of legislative seats.

Because partisan turnover is so limited, it is more useful to compare the proportions of seats in which both parties run candidates. Such competition is more likely to be found in metropolitan areas because both party organizations have greater resources of finance and personnel available, and the large numbers of votes at stake for national and state elections provide both parties with an incentive for presenting a full slate of local candidates in order to stimulate voting. Moreover, urban life is characterized by greater population mobility, which upsets traditional voting habits, and by a variety of economic and social classes, which provides potential voting support for both parties.

A major factor determining whether there will be legislative contests in a district is the strength of local party organizations, which carry much of the burden of recruiting candidates. A party that is well organized at the state level is better able to provide assistance to its local organizations and is more likely to encourage them to run candidates in every district. A party that is relatively weak at the state level is likely to have weaker local party organizations and may have to concentrate its efforts in a smaller number of districts. Key has argued that the direct primary has produced stagnation in local party organizations, which have been deprived of their responsibility for nominations.[27] There is some evidence that the proportion of legislative seats contested by both parties is lower in those two-party states where wide-open primary competition has been common. If there is not a viable party organization that makes an effort to recruit candidates, the likelihood of any candidate's running depends on the party's prospects for victory in the district.

In recent years, the most notable increases in legislative competition have occurred in southern states, such as Florida, Alabama, South Carolina, and Texas. There the Republican party contested few, and in some cases none, of the legislative seats during the early 1950s; but by the mid-1960s, the party was running candidates in as many as half of the districts. Republican candidates appeared first, and had the greatest success, in metropolitan areas, where the party had organizational and financial strength, and where it could solicit the support of presidential Republicans living in the suburbs. Gradually, Republican candidates began to run in larger numbers in the smaller urban and rural districts.[28]

THE CAMPAIGN

Campaigning for the Nomination

The single clearest impression gained from looking at the wide variety of legislative campaigns is that most candidates, whether incumbents or not, are on their own. This impression is even stronger for most, though not all, candidates for the state legislature. In Chapter 3, we described the recruitment of legislative candidates, noting that a large proportion of candidates are self-recruited but that some party organizations, particularly in metropolitan areas, devote a considerable amount of attention to recruitment. The candidate who decides to enter a race without the active support of a party organization cannot expect any assistance from that organization in the primary election. He must raise money and recruit campaign workers on his own. If organizations not connected with the party have encouraged him to run, he may be able to count on them for endorsements or more active support in the primary.

When a party organization actively recruits candidates, it must provide enough support in the primary to ensure that the persons it has recruited will win. Even where the party does little active recruiting, it may endorse primary candidates. One or both parties have provided endorsement to legislative primary candidates in recent years in a number of metropolitan areas, including Denver, Indianapolis, Cleveland, Cincinnati, Louisville, and several cities in New York State. What makes such endorsements effective? The party leadership may pass the word to precinct workers, who then pass the word to voters either by word of mouth or by means of a printed sample ballot. Sometimes an organization may print its slate of candidates in a newspaper advertisement. Very little is known about how the voters react to such endorsement, but those party organizations that make frequent endorsements usually have a high batting average. Until the mid-1960s, legislators in Denver, Cincinnati, and Cleveland were chosen in countywide elections; and voters who were confused by long lists of primary candidates were particularly inclined to rely on party organization slates. In Denver, state law provides that the endorsed candidates will appear on the top line of the ballot, which helps to explain why the voters almost always choose the endorsed candidate.[29]

The method of nomination has some effect on legislative recruitment patterns. One study of four states shows that in states where the party organization is able to control nominations (Connecticut and Pennsylvania) individuals usually serve a longer apprenticeship in other public offices before running for the legislature than they do in states where the nominating process is more open (Minnesota and Washington). Where legislative nomination is dependent on party support, legislative office is part of a professional political career.[30]

The candidate who has the endorsement of a strong party organization may find it unnecessary to do much campaigning during the primary. Does such a candidate lose his independence? If he fails to support the party in the legislature after winning nomination and election with its support, will he be purged in the next primary? This is a possibility, but it is not very likely in most states. In practice, incumbent legislators can usually count on support from a party organization if they seek renomination, and organizational purges of legislators are rare. A number of years ago, party leaders in urban organizations often took an active role in legislative affairs, dictating policy to their legislative delegations and denying renomination to noncooperative legislators. Most local party organizations today seldom intervene in legislative matters, and it is rare to find an incumbent being denied renomination because of his voting record. If this should occur, it would be more likely to result from local conflicts over patronage or a judgment that the incumbent is a particularly weak candidate. Consequently, in those areas where a party organization makes endorsements successfully, the fortunate candidate who wins that endorsement has little to lose by accepting it.

General Election Campaigns

Most candidates for Congress or state legislatures organize their campaigns independently of other candidates who are running for statewide or local office. They maintain separate headquarters, recruit their own workers, and determine their own tactics for the campaign. Legislative candidates may run independently by their own choice, but usually it is because they receive little help from national, state, or local party organizations. Presidential and statewide campaigns absorb the attention and resources of national and state party organizations. The fragmentation of American political party organizations prevents the coordination of congressional campaigns at the national level or of legislative campaigns at the state level. The local party is likely to be more interested in county or city offices, partly because these offer much greater prospects for patronage. As one congressman said, "The sheriff in my county has seventy or eighty jobs to pass out, and everyone is interested in who is sheriff. No one cares about us."[31] Moreover, congressional districts, to an increasing degree, cut across the county and city boundaries that form the basis for local party organizations. In some urban areas with a powerful and active party organization, the congressional or state legislative candidates can ride along on the campaign organized by the party. More often, they discover that they must rely on their own resources. As another congressman remarked, "If we depended on the party organization to get elected, none of us would be here."[32]

This does not mean that legislative campaigns are completely isolated from the electoral mainstream. The legislative candidate recruits his own workers and sometimes develops a corps of supporters that can be relied on year after year, but he usually draws them initially from the reservoir of experienced party workers. If he receives relatively little money from national or state headquarters, he is likely to be offered advisers, literature, campaign kits, ghostwritten speeches, and even training schools. Even the local party headquarters may provide him with some assistance. Legislative candidates often depend on the personal campaigning of the presidential or gubernatorial candidate of their party in the district to provide a boost for their candidacy. The candidate who accepts this kind of assistance from the party and its leaders loses some of his independence and may find it expedient to echo the policy positions being taken by the leadership.

The incumbent has many advantages in a congressional or state legislative campaign. The most obvious one is that he is likely to be better known to the voters; at least most voters will recognize his name and know that he is the incumbent. He also has tactical advantages in campaign planning. He can usually rely on many of the campaign workers and financial contributors who supported his previous campaign.[33] A study of Massachusetts state senate races showed that two-thirds of the campaign workers supporting an incumbent had worked in a previous campaign for him.[34] The incumbent has learned from previous campaigns which groups of voters should be cultivated and which types of campaigning (door-to-door, newspaper advertising, radio and television) seem to work best. Because of his previous experience, he not only has access to larger resources of manpower and money, but he is less likely to waste them during the campaign.

The basic problem faced by most nonincumbents is gaining recognition. One nonincumbent put it this way:

> We had to overcome the fact that nobody in God's name knew who I was. I'd never been in the papers, had never inherited a million dollars, was never a big athlete. That was the first hurdle—try to get some identification.[35]

The nonincumbent not only has to locate campaign workers who are interested in his cause and are not working for other candidates, he must also persuade them that his chances of winning—or at least of running a respectable race—are great enough to justify their commitment of time and effort. Similarly, he must persuade financial contributors that their funds will not be going to waste. Obviously a candidate who knows the district well, who has been active in politics and developed many contacts in his party, and who has worked in other campaigns has an advantage over a complete neophyte.

Campaigns for the United States Senate are frequently large-scale, expensive affairs, comparable to a gubernatorial campaign. Candidates are likely to make extensive use of radio and television, employ professional campaign-management firms, and at the same time follow the traditional approach of campaigning personally in every village and town and speaking to every group, large or small, that they can find. A candidate for the United States House faces a more limited task because his district is much smaller and his resources are more limited. He usually has greater difficulty in attracting public attention and interest. If he is running against an incumbent, his opponent is likely to be well-entrenched. Unless the state party believes the district is a marginal one, it is not likely to provide much assistance to the candidate.

For the average state legislative candidate, elaborate campaign techniques are not only prohibitively expensive but inefficient as well. If he buys radio or television time or newspaper advertisements, he will have to pay for an audience much larger than his constituency, particularly if he is running in a metropolitan area, where costs are high and the audience large. The study of campaigns for the Massachusetts state senate showed that only one candidate (out of thirty-three interviewed) made any use of television advertising, but that most of them employed radio and newspaper advertising, which was much less expensive.[36] The state legislative candidate has one advantage over senatorial and congressional candidates. His district is small enough so that it is feasible for him to reach many of the voters in person, campaigning door-to-door, in the shopping centers, and in small groups. A large proportion of the legislative candidates in Massachusetts used these techniques of personal contact.[37] In addition, a legislative leader who has been active in his community can call on the assistance of a wide circle of friends and acquaintances to play some part in his campaign, from running a mimeograph machine to hosting a coffee in their home. An army of volunteers is important, not only because it provides essential manpower without cost but also because the participants can appeal to their own friends and acquaintances for votes. Massachusetts state senate candidates in most districts had between 150 and 300 persons working for them, many of them with previous campaign experience.[38]

It is difficult to generalize about the costs of legislative campaigns because they vary with the level of the race (national or state), the extent of opposition, and the nature of the district (urban or rural). Moreover, it is difficult to get accurate information about campaign costs. Although some state legislative candidates spend thousands of dollars on their campaigns, there are probably a larger number who spend only a few hundred dollars, relying on their own resources and those of a few friends. If the legislative candidate is relying on personal campaigning rather than on expensive media techniques, his costs may be limited to the printing of one or two leaflets, handbills, or matchbooks for distribution. In the 1968 Massachusetts state senate races, the average candidate who had opposition spent $4,500. He contributed about $1,000 of this himself; raised about $1,600 from individuals (an average of forty contributors); received about $1,300 from his party; and got the rest from private groups of various kinds, notably labor unions.[39]

There are some candidates for seats in the United States House of Representatives, particularly those who are well-entrenched incumbents, whose campaigns are relatively inexpensive; but it is not uncommon for incumbents in safe districts to spend five to ten times as much as their opponents. Some of the highest spending, on the part of both candidates, occurs when there is no incumbent running in a competitive district. A detailed study by Common Cause of spending in the 1974 congressional elections shows the range of spending and the advantage enjoyed by incumbents. Incumbents outspent major party challengers in about 80 percent of the House races in which an incumbent had an opponent and in all but one of the Senate races. A breakdown of the spending by district shows:

Incumbents:
17 percent spent over $100,000,
40 percent spent $50,000 to $99,999,
40 percent spent $10,000 to $49,999,
4 percent spent less than $10,000;

Nonincumbents:
19 percent spent over $100,000 (but half of these were running against other nonincumbents),
24 percent spent $50,000 to $99,999,
31 percent spent $10,000 to $49,999,
26 percent spent less than $10,000.

There were seven candidates for the Senate who spent over a million dollars. The median figure for incumbents was about $470,000, and for nonincumbents was about $350,000.[40]

Those candidates for state legislative and congressional seats who raise their own campaign funds are not dependent on the state or national party for financial aid, and this is one reason why they can be independent of party leadership in their voting records. Of course, any candidate who finds it necessary to accept contributions from private interests loses some of his independence as a legislator. A survey of candidates running against United States House incumbents in 1964 showed that a little more than half thought that they had received "considerable" or "some" help from the national party (financing, staff personnel, literature, etc.), about half reported such help from the local party, and very few got any help from the state party. The same study estimated that in 1964, congressional candidates (incumbents or challengers) for House seats who faced particularly close races might expect to get $4,000 to $5,000 from various national party organizations, with those in less competitive districts getting much less. Other national fund-raising groups, such as labor unions and business or professional groups, might contribute an equal amount to some candidates. In other words, it is very unusual for a candidate to receive more than 10 to 15 percent of his campaign costs from national party or interest organizations.[41]

Both political parties operate national fund-raising committees for Senate and House candidates, and in recent years groups of liberal Democratic senators and representatives have organized separate fund-raising drives for selected candidates. In 1970, the various committees affiliated with the national congressional parties distributed nearly $7 million, but this is a relatively modest amount when spread over so many House and Senate races. There are fewer Senate contests, and the resources of national political committees have often been concentrated on a small number of these, depending on the closeness of the race and the viewpoints of the candidates. In 1970 there were several senatorial candidates who received $25,000 or more from one or more of these national party committees. In addition, there were dozens of national labor, business, agricultural, liberal, conservative, and peace groups that, taken as a whole, contributed more than the national party committee to congressional campaigns in the same election.[42] The financing of congressional campaigns, particularly for the Senate, may be becoming a little more nationalized, but it is not really centralized because there is so much diversity in the sources of financing at the national level.

The most important question to ask about legislative campaign financing is whether differences in the levels of spending determine the outcome of elections. It is also the most difficult to answer. In general we can say that, in state legislative contests, the districts are small enough so that expensive campaign techniques are unnecessary and the level of spending is unlikely to be of critical importance. In races for the United States House, the incumbent has many advantages, one of which is greater access to financial resources. An incumbent who is almost certain of reelection often gets much more funding for a campaign than he needs. A challenger who is believed to have a serious chance of defeating an incumbent in a close district can usually count on substantial support from his party. It is the campaigns for the United States Senate in large states that are expensive enough so that the outcome may be very much affected by differences in spending, particularly in primary races. There have been a number of examples recently of relatively unknown candidates winning senatorial nominations after expensive media campaigns.

Issues and Images

Most legislators recognize that the average voter knows little or nothing about specific political issues or about the legislator's voting record, a fact substantiated by survey research data, and by the legislator's own contacts with constituents. It is difficult for legislative candidates to attract enough public attention during a campaign to persuade a substantial proportion of the voters that a particular candidate's views and his record on specific issues are correct. Many legislators would share one congressman's view of the campaign:

> The people back home don't know what's going on. Issues are not most important so far as the average voter is concerned. The image of the candidate plays a greater role. If voters feel the candidate is conscientious and is trying hard to serve them, then that man has a good chance of coming back.[43]

The image of the candidate is more likely to make an impression on the voter than the issues; however superficial the image may be, voters are more likely to vote for a candidate about whom they know something, as shown by the polls referred to earlier in this chapter. What image does the legislative candidate try to project? He wants to appear conscientious, capable and knowledgeable, zealous on behalf of his district's obvious interests, and able to use his judgment in determining how to vote.[44]

Although they generally recognize the low level of voter interest in and knowledge about issues, most legislative candidates pay some attention—and some devote a great deal of care—to issues. There are probably several reasons for this. Nimmo points out that, "A candidate can do relatively little about the distribution of partisanship in his constituency, but he can maneuver by articulating issues that strengthen his hand. He has at least political control over issues."[45] Kingdon suggests that a candidate must articulate his position on issues to attract the support of interest-group leaders, newspaper editors, and other opinion leaders whose political influence is much greater than that of the average voter. He also notes that from time to time a particular issue will have an important effect on the outcome of an election, but that it is difficult to predict under what conditions which issues will be important—and consequently the candidate cannot afford to ignore the issues and the views of constituents on them.[46]

Several types of issues seem most likely to assume importance in legislative election campaigns and to have some salience for the voters, or at least a significant number of voters. Candidates frequently criticize an incumbent opponent for failing to pay enough attention to his district or not spending enough time in it (in the case of congressmen). Alternatively, they may claim that an incumbent has a high rate of absenteeism when roll-call votes are taken. Incumbents, on the other hand, are likely to stress their experience, their seniority (particularly in Congress), and the specific things they have done for the district. In recent years several issues have stirred up constituent opinion at the state level: busing, abortion, law and order, and the perennial issue of taxes. In congressional campaigns, national economic issues—inflation and recession—and the implications of Watergate have been frequent themes.

The fact that a successful candidate has campaigned on particular issues does not necessarily mean that these issues have been critical to the outcome of the election. Issues may contribute to a political trend that defeats an incumbent in a marginal district without that incumbent's own record being a major factor in his defeat. There are probably relatively few votes cast by an incumbent that are so salient to the voters, or even to opinion leaders, that they contribute to his reelection or defeat. An issue such as abortion is so obviously controversial that any legislator recognizes the risk involved in voting on it if there are serious differences of opinion among his constituents. On other occasions a legislator may fail to realize that his stand on an issue may be risky, until an opponent succeeds in exploiting it. Some Republican congressmen who had emphasized their close ties with and support for President Nixon in earlier years found that this record was costly in the 1974 election.

Because legislative candidates sometimes avoid taking stands on specific issues and because voters are often unaware of those stands that are taken, the outcome of the election seldom provides a legislator with a mandate to pursue specific policies. At most, he is likely to view his reelection as a vote of confidence by the electorate in his judgment and, perhaps, in his general record or image. He may be bound by commitments to organized groups whose votes or financial aid he solicits, but even these commitments may not be very specific with regard to individual bills. The nature of the district he represents, the coalition of interests that elect him, and his own public record are all factors that may limit his freedom of action in legislative voting; but it is unusual for a campaign to be so focused on issues that the campaign in itself has an impact on his subsequent voting record.

NOTES

1.   See Robert A. Dahl, *A Preface to Democratic Theory* (Chicago, 1956), pp. 147–149; and James G. March, "Party Legislative Representation as a Function of Election Results," *Public Opinion Quarterly* 21 (1957–1958):541–542.

2.   Data for the years 1956 to 1966 are from: Charles O. Jones, *Every Second Year* (Washington, D.C., 1967), p. 68.

3.   V. O. Key, Jr., *Politics, Parties and Pressure Groups* (New York, 1964). pp. 438–439, 447.

4.   V. O. Key, Jr., *American State Politics* (New York, 1956), pp. 171–181; Leon D. Epstein, *Politics in Wisconsin* (Madison, Wis., 1958), p. 201; and Frank J. Sorauf, *Party and Representation* (New York, 1963), p. 112.

5.   Sorauf, *Party and Representation,* p. 107.

6.   Key, *American State Politics,* p. 174; Epstein, *Politics in Wisconsin,* pp. 199, 201; and Sorauf, *Party and Representation,* p. 112.

7.   See Key, *American State Politics,* pp. 175–178; and Epstein, *Politics in Wisconsin,* p. 133.

8.   See Malcolm E. Jewell, *Legislative Representation in the Contemporary South* (Durham, N.C., 1967), chap. 2.

9.   Ibid.

10.   See Epstein, *Politics in Wisconsin,* p. 198; and Jewell, *Legislative Representation in the Contemporary South,* pp. 30–31.

11.   Data for 1956 to 1966 are from Jones, *Every Second Year,* p. 68.

12.   David R. Mayhew, *Congress—The Electoral Connection* (New Haven, 1974), p. 33.

13.   *Congressional Quarterly Weekly Report,* 19 (March 10, 1961).

14.   Mayhew, *Congress—The Electoral Connection,* p. 34.

15.   Ibid., p. 36.

16. In midterm elections, the presidential party is most likely to lose districts where the President ran ahead of his congressional ticket. See Barbara Hinckley, "Interpreting House Midterm Elections," *American Political Science Review* 61 (1967):694–700.

17. See Barbara Hinckley, "Incumbency and the Presidential Vote in Senate Elections," *American Political Science Review* 64 (1970):836–842.

18. Key, *Politics, Parties and Pressure Groups,* pp. 549–551. Data for the 1952, 1956, and 1960 elections have been subtracted from Key's figures.

19. Milton C. Cummings, Jr., *Congressmen and the Electorate* (New York, 1966), p. 10.

20. Ibid., p. 48.

21. Ibid., pp. 69–71.

22. Robert S. Erikson, "The Advantage of Incumbency in Congressional Elections," *Polity* 3 (1971):395–405; Erikson, "Malapportionment, Gerrymandering, and Party Fortunes in Congressional Elections," *American Political Science Review* 66 (1972);1234–1245.

23. Warren Lee Kostroski, "Party and Incumbency in Postwar Senate Elections: Trends, Patterns and Models," *American Political Science Review* 67 (1973):1213–1234.

24. See William A. Glaser, "Fluctuation in Turnout," in *Public Opinion and Congressional Elections,* ed. William N. McPhee and William A. Glaser, pp. 19–51; and Angus Campbell, "Surge and Decline: A Study of Electoral Change," *Public Opinion Quarterly* 24 (1960):397–418

25. Donald E. Stokes and Warren E. Miller, "Party Government and the Salience of Congress," *Public Opinion Quarterly* 26 (1962):531–546; and Stanley R. Freedman, "The Salience of Party and Candidate in Congressional Elections: A Comparison of 1958 and 1970," in *Public Opinion and Public Policy,* ed. Norman Luttbeg (Homewood, Ill., rev. ed., 1974), pp. 126–131.

26. Ibid.

27. Key, *American State Politics,* chap. 6.

28. See Jewell, *Legislative Representation in the Contemporary South,* chap. 4.

29. Jewell, *Metropolitan Representation* (New York, 1969), chaps. 2 and 4.

30. Richard J. Tobin, "The Influence of Nominating Systems on the Political Experiences of State Legislators," *Western Political Quarterly* 28 (1975):553–566.

31. Charles L. Clapp, *The Congressman: His Work as He Sees It* (Washington, D.C., 1963), p. 344.

32. Ibid., p. 351.

33. See David A. Leuthold, *Electioneering in a Democracy* (New York, 1968); and John W. Kingdon, *Candidates for Office* (New York, 1968), chaps. 4 and 5. Both are excellent studies of legislative campaigns at the national and/or state level.

34. Jerome M. Mileur and George T. Sulzner, *Campaigning for the Massachusetts Senate* (Amherst, Mass., 1974), p. 85.

35. Kingdon, *Candidates for Office,* p. 110.

36. Mileur and Sulzner, *Campaigning for the Massachusetts Senate,* pp. 135–144.

37. Ibid., pp. 121–128.

38. Ibid., pp. 80–89.

39. Ibid., pp. 89–99.

40. Compiled from data in *Congressional Quarterly Weekly Report* 33 (April 19, 1975):789–794.

41. Jeff Fishel, *Party and Opposition* (New York, 1973), pp. 99–108.

42. *Congressional Quarterly Weekly Report* 28 (December 18, 1970):3022–3031.

43. Clapp, *The Congressman,* p. 373.

44. For a full discussion of issues and images, see Charles O. Jones, "The Role of the Campaign in Congressional Politics," in *The Electoral Process,* ed. Harmon Zeigler and

Kent Jennings (Englewood Cliffs, N.J., 1966); and Kingdon, *Candidates for Office,* chaps. 2, 5, and 6.

    45.   Dan Nimmo, *The Political Persuaders* (Englewood Cliffs, N.J., 1970), p. 24.

    46.   Kingdon, *Candidates for Office,* pp. 114–115.

Legislative Organization and Procedure

part III

At the center of the legislative system is the legislature itself, an institution with certain constitutional powers and traditional procedures, operating with an established structure of subsystems (such as committees) within a particular political environment. The patterns of behavior that are rooted in these characteristics of the legislature seldom permit a quick response to pressures for change that arise outside the legislature. An understanding of the legislative system and the way in which the roles therein are shaped, or an analysis of the legislative process and its output, requires knowledge of the structure of the legislature. The outline of the structure is less useful for this purpose than a description of its operation in practice. Legislative structure varies tremendously in practice, more so than is apparent from a summary of rules or a list of leaders and committees in the different legislatures. It is neither possible nor desirable to describe in detail the structure and operation of 101 legislative bodies, but we can indicate the most common patterns of activity, provide examples from specific legislatures, and, most important, explain why certain structural patterns develop and how these affect the legislative process.

A starting point is the framework of the national or state constitution, which defines legislative structure and powers. There are few constitutional restrictions on Congress, but most state constitutions severely restrict both the substantive jurisdiction and the structural flexibility of the legislature. Few of these constitutional restrictions have been removed in recent years, but other structural changes have been made to improve the ability of both Congress and the state legislatures to cope with the growing demands made on them. The most important of these changes has been the development of bigger and better-trained staffs, particularly in Congress and in some of the larger states.

The legislative system cannot be considered separately from the entire political system of which it is a part, whether at the state or at the national level. The nature of party competition affects not only the selection of legislators, which we have discussed above, but also the structure of the legislature. In a two-party state, the legislature is organized along party lines. If the parties are well organized and cohesive at the state level, there are more likely to be tightly organized party organs in the legislature. The fractures evident in the congressional parties are in part a consequence of the decentralized national party system. If legislative parties are insignificant, the political vacuum in the legislature may be filled by the governor or by some factional leadership group.

Legislative organization is the apparatus of leadership. Leadership is personal, and in smaller legislative bodies, it often appears that the nature of leadership can be defined exclusively in terms of personality, the style and skills of one or a few men. But leadership is also affected by the political environment. The Speaker's role is defined largely by the expectations of the group that selected him, whether that be a party caucus, a small clique of senior legislators, or a large coalition of personally recruited legislators. The floor leader's role is sometimes an ambivalent one because of the demands made on him by both the administration and the legislative party. A floor leader's power is derived both from his own skills and from the degree of cohesion that characterizes the party or faction. Similarly, the use of leadership committees and caucuses depends on both the preferences of the leaders and the existence of sufficient unity in the party to make these devices workable.

Every legislative body has leadership, but it is not necessarily centralized in the presiding officers and the party or factional leaders. If there is a decentralized structure, the other loci of power are the committees. Every legislature uses standing committees; they make possible a division of the work load and specialization in the study of legislation. An analysis of committee structure and of the process by which members are chosen for committees is perhaps the best method available for determining the sources of leadership and the distribution of power in the legislature. In some legislatures, committees are little more than organs of the majority party; in others, they are just as tightly controlled by a clique or faction. In Congress, the seniority principle is so important in the selection process that committees have developed an unusual degree of independent authority. In the House, even the placing of bills on the calendar for floor consideration (of leadership responsibility in most states) is vested in a Rules Committee not firmly controlled by the majority leadership.

A knowledge of legislative rules and procedures is essential to an understanding of the legislative process. Some can be defined and described in terms of their functional utility for the majority party or faction, for the minority, or for the protection of committee authority. Others serve the interests of the legislature as a whole.

CHAPTER FIVE

Organization and Powers of Legislative Bodies

The newly elected member of a legislative body is comparable to the freshman who has met rigid entrance requirements and outlasted strong competitors in order to enter a university. Like the freshman, the legislator discovers that the institution has a history, regulations, and traditions, often long established, that define the limits of his authority and set the pattern for his behavior. The individual legislator, if he remains long enough, and particularly if he attains leadership status, may be able to have some impact on the system or make some change in the rules. But in his day-to-day operations, the legislator must conform to an environment that is the product of history and constitutional law as well as of political tradition. There are common elements in the fifty-one state and national legislatures of this country, but there are also significant variations in legislative environment.

CONGRESS

Constitutional Framework

One constitutional authority, Max Farrand, has written that "every provision of the federal constitution can be accounted for in American experience between 1776 and 1787."[1] The delegates to the Philadelphia convention of 1787 were able to draw upon their experience with the Continental Congress and the Congress under the Articles of Confederation as well as the experience of state legislatures. These in turn were modeled in part on the British Parliament and the colonial legislatures. One of the earliest and least-disputed decisions of the Philadelphia convention was to approve the principle of bicameralism that had been contained in the Virginia plan. Most state legislatures had preserved the colonial practice of bicameralism, which had made possible representation of the colonies in one house and the mother country in the other. As the convention progressed, the agreement on bicameralism facilitated compromises between the proponents of large or small states and between the advocates of greater or lesser popular representation. It also gave more substance to the principle of checks and balances. The bicameral system established at Philadelphia, like those in the states but unlike those in many other countries, is a system in which substantially equal power is given to the Senate and the House. The Senate approves treaties and executive appointments, but the approval of both branches is required for all other legislation and appropriations, with the House initiating revenue bills.[2]

The relationship of Congress to the executive branch was a perplexing problem for the Founding Fathers. Many of them were influenced by the views of Locke and Montesquieu and believed that the separation of powers was an essential defense against tyranny. At the same time, they recognized the dangers of a weak executive, which existed under the Articles of Confederation and in the new state governments. Yet the early proposals at Philadelphia provided for election of the President by the Congress, and in his review of the debates, James M. Burns notes how "one watches suspensefully as the Framers again and again come to the brink of letting Congress choose the President and then teeter off in the reverse direction."[3] The framers finally decided on the awkward mechanism of the electoral college, with Congress given the authority to settle deadlocks; it was only the subsequent growth of the two-party system that avoided deadlocks and guaranteed the President electoral independence of Congress.

In the opening words of Article I, the Constitution provided: "All legislative powers herein granted shall be vested in a Congress." The President, however, was authorized to play both a positive and a negative role in the legislative process. He could recommend for the consideration of Congress "such measures as he shall judge necessary and expedient." He could veto legislation, subject to the authority of Congress to override his veto by a two-thirds vote of both houses. The framers did not foresee the powerful role that the President plays in the legislative process today, but they provided the constitutional framework that makes it possible. In short, the Constitution established a presidential-congressional system in which the two branches are guaranteed independence of each other and in which both play an essential role in the legislative process. This is the most important constitutional fact determining how Congress functions.

Power and Functions

Since the Constitution vests "all legislative powers" in Congress, it is logical that the list of delegated powers of the national government should follow the heading: "The Congress shall have power." There are also a few specific limitations on the scope of legislative power in the original Constitution and in the Bill of Rights. In contrast with legislative authority in most states, congressional authority is broad because the grants of power are broadly described and have been broadly interpreted by the courts, at least in recent years. The substantive scope of congressional authority has grown with the evolutionary changes in the federal system, and today there are relatively few areas in which legislation can be seriously proposed but in which congressional action is inhibited by the Constitution.

Formally, the functions of Congress may be divided into several categories. First, Congress is a lawmaking body, as the Constitution makes explicit by its vesting of legislative power. Closely related are the powers of Congress to levy taxes and to make appropriations, also made explicit in the Constitution. There have been no significant limits on these powers since the Sixteenth Amendment was passed, legalizing the progressive income tax. Allied to this is the power of the Senate to give or to withhold its consent to treaties by a two-thirds vote. The development of bipartisanship as a tactic of presidential leadership has minimized senatorial obstructionism, but it has not eliminated senatorial power in treaty making. Congress, by a two-thirds vote in each house, may recommend constitutional amendments; at the request of two-thirds of the states, Congress "shall call a convention for proposing amendments," although congressional discretion in complying with this latter provision has never been tested.

Congress has authority to supervise the administration of government. This is not explicitly granted in the Constitution, but it can be implied from the impeachment authority, senatorial approval of nominations to executive office, the appropriations power, and the need to investigate the implementation of legislation. Congress has, in fact, regarded this as one of its most important responsibilities and has used its powers, particularly those with regard to appropriations and investigations, with skill and determination to carry out this function. Congress also has responsibility over the judiciary. The Senate must approve judicial appointments, and Congress must establish federal courts (other than the Supreme Court) and prescribe their jurisdiction (except for the original jurisdiction of the Supreme Court). The House has the responsibility for electing a President if no candidate receives a majority of the electoral vote, although it has not exercised this authority since 1824; in such a situation, the House would vote by states, with each state casting one vote. The Senate would choose a vice-president if no candidate had a majority of the electoral vote. Congress also provides for succession to the presidency below the level of vice-president, an issue that has stirred renewed interest in recent years. Congress may regulate the holding of congressional elections (time, place, and manner), and each house is the judge of the election returns and qualifications of its own members. It also passes legislation regarding apportionment of the House.

The House

The casual visitor to Capitol Hill cannot help noticing one of the most important differences between the House and the Senate: the House is a much larger body. One consequence of this is that the House follows more rigid rules regarding debate and the conduct of business. It is too large to be a deliberative body, to give any substantial proportion of the members a chance to speak on issues; as a result, the House does not try to be a deliberative body, seldom devotes itself seriously to debate, and rarely tries to rewrite the committee's version of a bill on the floor of the House. Sometimes there are drastic limits on the amendments that can be considered on the floor. Much of its decision making with regard to amendments is carried on in the committee of the whole, where the quorum requirement is small (100 members, instead of a majority), with the result that important decisions are often made by a small minority of representatives. The greater size of the House also leads to some less-obvious consequences for the member. The work load is more specialized, and with few exceptions, the individual member has little chance to become influential except with regard to a single narrow area related to his committee responsibilities.

The House of Representatives was intended by the delegates in Philadelphia to be the major representative body in the government; its members were the only ones directly chosen by the people. The political party system first developed in the House. After a period of presidential domination under Jefferson, the House emerged as the strongest branch of government under the speakership of Henry Clay. It is impossible to trace with precision the ups and downs of this branch's prestige and influence; the evaluation must be a subjective one. In the decades before the Civil War, however, the prestige of the House appears to have declined as the conflict over slavery and the weakness of Clay's successors in the speakership led to fragmentation of power and deadlock in the House. Webster, Clay, Calhoun, and other congressmen of stature transferred their talents to the Senate. The period from the end of the Civil War through the first decade of the twentieth century was, with few exceptions, one of congressional supremacy and growing House influence. A series of strong Speakers, by enhancing their own power, made it possible for a majority of the House members to conduct business efficiently. The Senate's prestige declined because its members, still elected by state legislatures, came increasingly to be regarded as agents of powerful business interests and unrepresentative of the public.[4]

In the last half-century, however, the House, in comparison with the Senate, has declined in prestige. Effective political leadership in the House was weakened and diversified when the Speaker's powers were curbed in the revolt of 1910–1911. The Senate, on the other hand, became a more important body because following the adoption of the Seventeenth Amendment in 1913, its members were popularly elected and because foreign affairs became increasingly important in American life. One additional factor may have contributed to its decline. In an age of increasing attention to public opinion and the public image, senators have been not only more visible to the public but also more successful in creating favorable images.

The Senate

When students hear the Senate described as a "deliberative body," they sometimes envision it as the scene of repeated filibusters. The use of the filibuster today is unusual, although the possibility of a filibuster is an ever-present factor in legislative maneuvering. When we speak of the Senate as a deliberative body, we mean that, unlike the House, it gives extended and careful attention to the legislation that is reported from committees. The fact that bills are often debated at length on the floor does not mean that mere oratory changes many votes. It means that bills are sometimes substantially changed as a result of the discussion and bargaining that occur, on the floor and off, between the time the bill emerges from committee and the time when it passes.

The Senate was originally intended to be a conservative political institution, vaguely like the House of Lords in Britain today, restraining and moderating the rash impulses of the House of Representatives. The system of election by state legislators was viewed by the framers as a method of assuring that senators would be men of the highest caliber, sensitive to the interests of the individual states.[5] In the half-century following the Civil War, however, this electoral system produced a Senate that was under Republican and conservative control and not responsive to changes in viewpoint or party reference on the part of the voters. The often-used label "millionaires' club," if not perfectly descriptive of the membership as a whole, was an apt name for the Senate majority.

The popular election of senators created, in time, a new Senate and a new breed of senators. The system of equal representation for each state has, at various times in the past, given disproportionate power to such groups as the silver bloc and the farm bloc. A combination of factors, but especially the seniority system, for a time gave the South particular influence in the Senate.[6] Today it is more accurate to describe the Senate as an urban institution rather than as a southern institution. Senators, by the nature of their constituencies, represent a greater variety of interests than members of the House do. The growing number of states in which metropolitan areas play a major or a dominating role has produced the paradox that the Senate, where Montana is represented equally with New York, is more responsive to urban interests than the House is.

The senator as an individual differs significantly from the representative. He is usually more of a generalist or at least a specialist in a larger range of subject matter. He is usually a more important political figure in his state and is far more likely to be an important figure on the Washington political scene. (In recent years, more than a dozen senators have made serious efforts to secure a presidential nomination, but the few efforts by representatives have not attracted significant support.) The senator has a much larger staff, receives more mail, and in general, operates on a much larger scale in his day-to-day work. As we have said, he is less able than the average representative to succeed in carving out a completely safe constituency for himself. It is worth noting that approximately one-third of the senators have previously been representatives.

The Senate differs from the House in its concern with foreign policy. The increasing importance of foreign aid and the reciprocal-trade program has given the House a larger legislative role in foreign affairs than previously, but the Senate alone remains responsible for approving treaties. Throughout its history, the Senate's treaty-making power and tradition as a deliberative body have made it the locus for the great debates over foreign policy. The Foreign Relations Committee remains more prestigious and more influential than its counterpart in the House.

Organizational Change

In 1946, Congress passed the Legislative Reorganization Act, which, among other things, streamlined committees and provided for more adequate staffing. A second Legislative Reorganization Act, passed in 1970, was designed to improve congressional procedures in committee and on the floor and to make public more of the votes taken in both places. In one respect, the 1946 act reflected nostalgia rather than foresight; it provided that except in time of war or national emergency, Congress should adjourn annually not later than the end of July. The 1970 act was more realistic; it provided for a thirty-day recess in August. In recent years, congressional sessions have usually dragged on into the fall; and even in election years, congressional business has sometimes interfered with the campaign.[7] Perhaps the year-long session in 1963 was a portent of the future. On December 24 of that year, representatives trudged through the snow to cast their votes on the foreign-aid bill at a session of the House that convened at seven in the morning, and senators interrupted their brief holiday vacation to return for a final vote on the same bill on December 30.

During the 1973–1975 period a number of changes were made in the committee system, particularly in the House, changes that will be described in some detail in subsequent chapters. In both branches, meetings of committees and conference committees have been opened to the public. The seniority system for appointing committee chairmen has been modified in the House. Although the House rejected a proposed sweeping reorganization of committees, some important changes were made, including more use of and greater independence for subcommittees, as well as some changes in committee jurisdiction. Congress also adopted a new system for handling the budget, a goal established, but never successfully implemented, in the 1946 Reorganization Act.

Congress has become not only a year-round operation but a large and expensive one as well. The appropriation for operating Congress is about $350 million a year, a total that would have financed the entire government in any year prior to the Civil War. In addition to the Capitol, there are two Senate office buildings and three House office buildings, and congressional operations spill over into other nearby buildings that become available.

Political Setting

Congress is one of the best examples of a two-party legislative system in this country. Two political factions can be distinguished as early as the First Congress in 1789. Although there were several Congresses prior to the Civil War in which three parties were strongly represented, the two-party pattern predominated. Since 1873, minor party members have never constituted more than 5 percent of the House or eight members of the Senate; the median number of minor party members has been three in the House and one in the Senate. There has been a remarkable balance of major party strength in Congress. Since 1873, the second party has consistently had at least one-fourth of the membership of the Senate and House, with two exceptions in each branch during the New Deal. There have been only eight other occasions in the House and only six other occasions in the Senate when the second party has had less than one-third of the membership. The normal pattern has been one in which nearly all congressmen belonged to one of the two major parties and in which the second party had at least one-third, and very often almost half, of the congressional seats. Since the Civil War, there have been eight Congresses in which the Senate was under Republican control and the House was under Democratic control; but this has occurred only twice in this century (the Sixty-second Congress, at the start of Wilson's administration, and the Seventy-second Congress, at the end of Hoover's).[8]

The strength of two-party competition may also be measured by the frequency of turnover in majority control; in this respect, congressional party competition ranks lower. Since the Civil War, there have been thirteen changes in majority control in the House and eleven changes in the Senate. From 1865 to 1895, party control was almost equally divided, with frequent alternations in control in the House; but the Republicans controlled the Senate, often by the narrowest of margins, for all but four years. From 1895 to 1931, the Republicans controlled the House, except from 1911 to 1919, and the Senate, except from 1913 to 1919. The Democrats won House control narrowly in 1931 and Senate control in 1933 and have held majorities in each ever since, except for the Eightieth Congress (1947–1948) and the Eighty-third (1953–1954), when the Republicans had majorities in both branches. Thus, since 1895, Congress has operated with one majority party and one usually strong minority party but with little alternation between the two. A major factor in the political environment of Congress today is that the Democratic party has been the majority party, with only two brief interruptions, for over forty years.

The persistence of the two-party system in Congress has implications that may be obvious but should be stressed because they present a contrast to the practices in many state legislatures. The Speaker of the House is the choice of the majority party and serves as a party leader. Responsibility for leadership on the floor of both houses rests with the majority leader. Committee membership is apportioned among Democrats and Republicans according to the proportions of each in the House and Senate. Party loyalties are highly significant in roll-call voting, and party is a significant factor in determining social contacts and friendship groups in Congress. The frequent weakness of party cohesion and the occasional sharp splits within parties should not obscure the central fact that in contrast with some state legislatures, Congress is oriented along party lines.

STATE LEGISLATURES

Constitutional Framework

The bicameral principle found in most early state constitutions was a continuation of the practice in the colonies, where one house was elected and the other represented the interests of the Crown and the colonial aristocracy. There were experiments with unicameralism in several of the early states, Vermont being the last to abandon it (in 1836). The Nebraska experiment with a single house was adopted in 1934 and has proved successful in the eyes of most observers, but in other states there has been little serious interest in following Nebraska's example.[9] In the early state constitutions, the upper house continued to represent the landed interests as a result of higher property qualifications for both electors and members; it was regarded as a necessary check on the popularly elected house by those who feared that the latter would be radical. After property qualifications were abandoned, the principle of bicameralism remained popular because it accorded with the American belief in checks and balances and limitations on majoritarian government. More specifically, bicameralism facilitated the overrepresentation of the minority party or rural interests. It also provided a larger number of points of access for interest groups and particularly suited those groups that usually benefited from obstacles to the passage of legislation. In most states, where there was no constitutional initiative, a constitutional amendment to abolish one house would require legislative approval; in the last analysis, it is the instinct for legislative self-preservation that has maintained bicameralism as the prevailing system.

The powers of a state legislature do not depend on constitutional delegation. As Belle Zeller points out: "The state legislature is a repository of the residual powers of the people. Unless restricted by provisions in the state constitution itself, it can do anything that has not been delegated to the national government or expressly or implicitly denied to the states by the federal Constitution."[10] The early state constitutions were usually relatively brief and contained few restrictions on the legislature other than a bill of rights; colonial experience had led the framers to put their trust in the legislature rather than in the governor, who in the past had represented the king. Duane Lockard says that the early constitutions "establish in many instances virtual legislative supremacy while simultaneously proclaiming the doctrine of separation of powers."[11] As constitutions were rewritten and amended, more and more provisions were added that placed restrictions on the legislature, often as a result of disillusionment with it. Particularly during the late nineteenth and early twentieth centuries, the public developed an impression, too often accurate, of the legislators as inept, corrupt puppets manipulated by powerful interests. Constitutional revisions were designed to minimize the amount of damage that these men could do. Since that time, the quality of legislatures has improved, but with little resulting change in constitutional provisions.

These restrictions on the legislature take many forms. Every constitutional provision that specifies what shall and shall not be done concerning any area of public policy constitutes a limit on legislative power. Many constitutions rigidly dictate the organizational structure of both state and local governments, limit the taxing power or allocate tax revenue to specific purposes, and provide outdated or inflexible solutions for a great variety of problems. The list of constitutional details could be extended for pages; each provision serves as a limit on legislative power.[12] In large part as a result of the detailed nature of constitutional provisions, state courts have interpreted these provisions far more rigidly than the Supreme Court has interpreted the federal Constitution.

Another kind of dilution of legislative power is represented by referendum and initiative, which were adopted, particularly in western states, during the first two decades of the twentieth century as a result of efforts by the Progressive movement. In twenty-two states, laws enacted by the legislature may be subject to a popular referendum if a petition is signed by a substantial number of voters. Twenty-one states permit the statutory initiative, which allows citizens, by signing a petition, to initiate a bill and place it on the ballot. In some states, the bill is placed immediately on the ballot; in others, it is placed on the ballot if the legislature fails to pass it within a given time.[13]

There are many constitutional restrictions placed on the operation of the legislature itself. One of the most serious of these, and the one that indicates the greatest distrust of legislatures, is the restriction on the frequency and length of legislative sessions. In 1964, only nineteen states had regular annual sessions; the rest met only every second year unless a special session was called. But there has been increasing public recognition that the legislature needs more time to do its work, and by 1973 there were annual sessions in forty-two states. Many of the states, however, still impose a constitutional limit on the length of legislative sessions or a limit on the number of days for which legislators can be paid, which is just as effective. In most states, such limits are between sixty and ninety days for either an annual or a biennial session.[14] Rigid limits on the length or frequency of legislative session not only seriously restrict the legislature's opportunities for deliberation but also weaken the effectiveness of its committees and the ability of less-senior members to develop experience and to become acquainted with legislative norms. No single factor has a greater effect on the legislative environment than the constitutional restriction on the length of sessions.[15]

There are many other constitutional provisions that affect legislative structure. Some are important; some, trivial; and some, ignored or evaded in practice. For example, the requirement of more than a simple majority vote for passage of a tax bill, found in at least six states, has a profound effect on legislative-executive relations. Limitations on legislative salaries probably affect the quality of legislators and presumably increase turnover; the legislatures attract men who either have independent incomes or can be expected to devote most of their time and effort to nonlegislative business. Many states have raised legislative salaries in recent years, and some have removed constitutional restrictions on salaries. The range of salaries from state to state is very large, and of course the workload is much heavier in the larger states that have longer sessions. In 1975 the salaries for a two-year period ranged from $20,000 to $47,000 in the top one-fourth of the states, and were less than $4,000 in the bottom one-fourth. Most states also provide an expense allowance, but it is probably not very often large enough to pay for more than the extra expenses required by a legislator's job.[16] It remains true that a large proportion of legislators are underpaid, considering the importance of their responsibilities and the amount of time that they are expected to devote to their job.

Frequently, constitutional provisions concerning legislative procedure were designed to guarantee careful, publicized consideration of bills; but these laudable objectives are often evaded, usually because they are unwieldy in practice. A large number of state constitutions require that a bill be read in full one or more times before passage, and compliance often takes the form of having the clerk read excerpts from the bill at a breath-taking pace, which makes the reading incomprehensible. In more than half the states, a roll call is required on final passage of all bills; but where there are no voting machines, this has often meant that on noncontroversial bills, all those who do not object are simply recorded as voting in the majority.

State constitutions specify either the exact size or the maximum size of the legislature. This rigidity is one of the factors that leads to inequalities when the legislature is apportioned. The size of the legislature is obviously an important aspect of the legislative environment, and it is a varied one. The size of state senates varies from 20 members to 67, but forty of them have between 25 and 50 members. The lower houses vary more widely; there are only three with fewer than 50 members, thirty-nine with 50 to 150 members, and seven with over 150 members. Although most New England states are below average size in terms of both geography and population, five of them have lower houses with 145 or more members, including Massachusetts, which has 240, and New Hampshire, which has 400. This probably results from the fact that the constitutions of these states were written between 1780 and 1820 and have seldom been revised.[17]

State constitutions, although imposing serious limitations on legislative power, often grant powers that are not strictly legislative. One route to constitutional amendment lies through the legislature (with approval at the polls); in the thirty-two states that lack the constitutional initiative, this is the only route. Most states require legislative approval by a two-thirds or three-fifths vote or approval by two successive legislatures. In most states, legislative action is necessary to start the procedure for calling a constitutional convention.

Legislative supervision of the administration varies considerably from state to state. The power of impeachment (the house presents the impeachment charge and the senate tries the case) is a common but rarely used power. Most, but not all, governors must submit some of their appointments to the senate for approval. In some states the legislature has authority that encroaches more seriously on the executive power, either through its ability to appoint certain executives or through the senate's ability to veto the dismissal of certain officials or members of boards. Despite these surface manifestations of strength, most state legislatures are not effective in providing oversight of the administration, largely because of the constitutional restrictions limiting the length and frequency of sessions and because of legislative turnover and poor staffing.[18]

Innovations that Strengthen the Legislature

As a result of constitutional limitations, as well as tradition and practice, the state legislature remains today essentially a part-time body composed primarily of amateurs. This is the source of the sharpest contrast with Congress. Although this description fits every state legislature, there are some states, particularly the large industrial ones, in which the work load faced by the legislature has forced significant changes in its operations. These are the states in which the legislature meets for long sessions every year, pay scales have been raised significantly, and the greatest efforts have been made to provide adequate staffs and office facilities for the members of the legislature, their leaders, and their committees.

Except for the easing of constitutional limits on legislative sessions, most innovations have been made without changing the constitutional framework. The most important and widespread steps have been designed to overcome the limitations of time through institutional devices. In roughly half of the states, legislative leaders are selected, formally or informally, before the session begins, and in most of these committee members are also chosen before the session. About two-thirds of these states permit the prefiling of bills, a step that is particularly important where the session is limited to sixty or ninety days.

Most legislatures have also established some machinery for carrying on legislative business between sessions. At least two-thirds of the states have a legislative council (sometimes under a different name). This is a committee of legislators, usually numbering about fifteen, representing both houses and both parties and usually consisting of legislative leaders and members appointed by the presiding officers of the two houses. The council is assisted by a permanent research staff. The council meets periodically to conduct studies, authorize research projects, and review and approve the findings of the research staff. Some councils simply transmit the research reports of their staffs to the legislatures. Others make specific legislative recommendations on the basis of staff reports. In some states the councils provide the legislature with an alternative to gubernatorial initiative, while in others the council works closely with the governor and serves in effect as an instrument of his leadership.

With the growing importance of committees and improvements in the structure and staffing of committees, there has been increased utilization of interim committees to carry on research, hearings, and discussion of proposed legislation. In some legislatures the interim committees operate as subcommittees of the legislative council and may report their recommendations to it. In other states the interim committees are independent and do most of the work that is done by councils elsewhere. In some states special interim committees are established by the legislature, or its council, to study particular problems. Other states provide that the standing committees in existence during the session will simply continue as interim committees, or the standing committees of the two houses will be merged to form joint committees during the interim. A number of states use both standing and special committees during the interim.[19] Where standing committees continue to meet during the interim, they have much more time to study problems in depth and to conduct hearings, a particularly important consideration in legislatures where the regular sessions are limited to two to four months. The interim committee system also increases the power of committees, particularly if they are adequately staffed. In states where the interim committees operate after the last session of the legislature (and particularly in states with biennial sessions), their influence is reduced because of the turnover that occurs in the legislature and in committees from one legislature to the next. There is no certainty that new members of a committee will be influenced by recommendations made by the committee in the previous interim.

Political Environment

The single factor that is most meaningful in explaining differences among state legislatures is the political environment. In a two-party state, the legislature is organized, and its leaders and committees are selected along party lines. To what extent the party serves as a cohesive force in explaining decision making, whether roles are perceived in partisan terms, whether party caucuses are functional, and whether roll calls follow party lines are questions explored in many of the subsequent chapters. All these considerations are potential characteristics of a two-party legislature. A legislature dominated by a single party is, in reality, a no-party legislature; it cannot be expected that partisan factors will affect any aspects of legislative behavior in such situations. The importance of party varies widely among two-party legislatures, but there are even greater variations between two-party and one-party legislatures. The role of the governor in the legislative process is important enough for gubernatorial control to be included in any catalog of party competition.

The student who is familiar with the literature on state politics must have noted that no two writers use the same criteria in defining categories of party competition in the states.[20] The reason is simply that different criteria are pertinent for different purposes. Since we are describing legislatures, we shall measure, first, both the size of party delegations and the division of partisan control (in terms of party majorities) in the legislature, and second, the partisan affiliation of the governor. Congressional and presidential elections are not relevant. No time period is perfect for our purposes. Party competition is increasing in some states, and this growth could be brought most sharply into focus by using a short time period. But the choice of a longer period can be justified because of the effect of custom on legislative practice. The period from 1953 to 1976 was chosen in order to balance these conflicting factors.

Tables 5.1 and 5.2 illustrate the wide range of partisan composition found in state legislatures. Table 5.1 shows that in three southern states (category A.1), Democratic control is absolute; Republican legislators are seldom, if ever, seen;

TABLE 5.1   States Classified According to Degree of One-Party Control, 1953–1976

CATEGORY	DEMOCRATIC	REPUBLICAN
A.1 One-party states (same party controlling governorship and legislature) with negligible minority representation	Alabama Louisiana Mississippi	
A.2 One-party states (same party controlling governorship and legislature) with more than negligible minority representation	Georgia Texas	
B. States with one party dominant*	Arkansas Florida Kentucky Maryland North Carolina Oklahoma South Carolina Virginia West Virginia	Kansas Vermont

NOTE: Nebraska and Minnesota are omitted because they had nonpartisan legislatures during all or most of period. The time period for Kentucky, Louisiana, Mississippi, and Virginia, which have off-year elections, is 1952–1975.

*Same party controlled both houses of the legislature throughout the period but did not always control the governorship, and (except for Arkansas) the minority party occasionally had over one-fourth of the seats in at least one house.

TABLE 5.2   State Legislatures Classified According to Degree of Two-Party Competition, 1953–1976

STATE	SENATE D	R	Tie	HOUSE D	R	Tie	GOVERNOR-SHIP D	R
C. Limited two-party states*								
Tennessee	24	0	–	22	0	2	20	4
New Hampshire	0	22	2	0	24	–	6	18
North Dakota	0	24	–	2	22	–	16	8
New Mexico	24	0	–	22	2	–	14	10
Missouri	24	0	–	22	2	–	20	4
Wyoming	0	22	2	4	20	–	6	18
Maine	2	22	–	4	20	–	14	8
Idaho	4	20	–	2	22	–	6	18
South Dakota	6	18	–	0	22	2	8	16
New York	1	23	–	6	18	–	6	18
Hawaii	14	4	–	18	0	–	14	4
Rhode Island	18	4	2	24	0	–	16	8
Massachusetts	18	6	–	22	2	–	8	16
D. Two-party states†								
Illinois	2	20	2	6	18	–	12	12
Iowa	6	18	–	4	20	–	10	14
Ohio	4	18	2	6	18	–	12	12
Wisconsin	2	22	–	10	14	–	12	12
Indiana	6	18	–	6	18	–	8	16
Washington	20	4	–	16	8	–	8	16
California	16	4	4	16	8	–	10	14
Alaska	10	6	2	14	2	2	12	6
Colorado	6	18	–	10	14	–	10	14
Arizona	16	8	–	16	8	–	8	16
Montana	20	4	–	12	12	–	8	16
Utah	6	18	–	10	14	–	12	12
New Jersey	4	20	–	12	12	–	18	6
Michigan	4	16	4	10	10	4	10	14
Oregon	18	4	2	12	12	–	4	20
Nevada	10	12	2	20	4	–	14	10
Delaware	14	8	2	14	10	–	12	12
Connecticut	18	6	–	10	14	–	18	6
Pennsylvania	6	16	2	14	10	–	14	10

NOTE: Nebraska and Minnesota are omitted because they had nonpartisan legislatures during all or most of period. The time period for New Jersey, which has off-year elections, is 1952–1975. The time period for Alaska and Hawaii is 1959–1976. Maine had an independent governor for two years.
* Same party controlled both houses during most of the period.
† Neither party had dominant legislative control or domination of the governorship.

and the result is a completely nonpartisan environment. In two other southern states (A.2), Democratic control is just as complete; but in recent years, a large-enough group of Republican legislators has been elected (at least during some sessions) to be identifiable as a minority party.

The next category of states in Table 5.1 (B) are those in which the minority party has captured the governorship at least once but has never gained a majority in the legislature during the period covered. All (except Arkansas) are states in which that minority party has consistently had enough legislative strength (at least in recent years) to be recognizable as a functioning minority party. In most cases, there has been an upsurge in that strength, however spasmodic, associated with the party's success in one or more gubernatorial elections. In all these states, however, one party has dominated the legislature for such a long time that legislative norms and practices are significantly different from those in most two-party states.

Table 5.2 shows that the remaining states (categories C and D) are all competitive in the sense that no party has consistently had a majority in both houses or control of the governorship and that minority legislative parties have consistently been strong enough to have at least a minimal impact on the legislative process. We have divided the states into two categories (C and D) to emphasize the differences in levels of two-party competition. Competition is limited in the first category (C) because the minority party seldom held a legislative majority. In nine of the thirteen states in category C, the minority party never held a majority in one house of the legislature; in none of the states did the minority party control both houses at the same time in more than one session. In some of these states, however, the minority party has captured the governorship a substantially greater proportion of the time than it has won the legislature.

The nineteen states in category D are those in which majority control of both houses of the legislature is shared most widely and in which there is some (usually considerable) rotation of the governorship between parties. It is in these states that legislative competition is the strongest, based on the criteria of size of party delegations and division of party control. The list of strongly competitive states has increased in the last few years. In several states (such as Ohio, Illinois, New Jersey, and Michigan), the apportionment system used to make it virtually impossible for the Democratic party, with its strong urban base, to win a majority in one or both houses. Since the changes in apportionment that took place in the 1960s, there has been enough change in the balance of legislative control for these states to be considered fully competitive at the legislative level.

The competitive nature of state legislatures is one of the variables determining the importance of partisanship in the legislative process. Some degree of competition is a prerequisite. There are not likely to be any traces of partisanship in those legislatures that are in category A.1 (in Table 5.1) and very few in those classified in A.2. Partisanship is also absent or disguised as factionalism in nonpartisan states (Nebraska and formerly Minnesota). There are only a few traces of partisanship to be found in most of the states in category B. The state legislatures with the most manifestations of partisanship (as described in subsequent chapters) include some, but not all, of those listed in categories C and D in Table 5.2. Some of the states in which partisan control has been closely balanced (such as California and Nevada) have had relatively weak legislative parties. On the other hand, a few of the states in category C (such as New York and Rhode Island) have had very strong legislative parties even though one normally held the majority. In general, though, partisanship has tended to be stronger in most of the states in category D than it has been in most states in category C.

Today there is a close balance between the parties in more states than at any other time in modern history. The growth of Democratic strength in the Midwest and plains states and the Republican upsurge in the border states and the South have begun to be manifest in the legislatures. One result of this trend has been the persistence of divided government (when one party does not control the governorship and both legislative branches at the same time). Although divided government is no longer a frequent consequence of malapportionment, it often results when a minority party captures a governorship for the first time in a long period of years but lacks the strength to win both, or even one, of the legislative branches. Divided government may also occur when the members of the house or some members of the senate are elected in the middle of a governor's four-year term.

State legislatures differ from Congress because the constitutional curbs on the duration of sessions limit their effectiveness and the constitutional restrictions on the scope of their authority limit their power. On the surface, state legislatures appear to be almost-perfect replicas of Congress in terms of organization, functions of leadership and committees, and procedures. The similarities of nomenclature are deceptive, however. The roles and functions of individual leaders and legislative institutions differ widely from state to state and, as the following chapters demonstrate, only occasionally approximate those in Congress. A search for the causes of the variations in many cases leads to the differences between one-party states, in which party is a negligible factor, and two-party states, in which it is often, but not always, a factor of considerable importance.

NOTES

1. Max Farrand, *The Framing of the Constitution of the United States* (New Haven, Conn., 1913), p. 204.

2. See George B. Galloway, *History of the House of Representatives* (New York, 1961), pp. 1–4; and George H. Haynes, *The Senate of the United States,* vol. 1 (Boston, 1938), chap. 1.

3. James M. Burns, *The Deadlock of Democracy* (Englewood Cliffs, N.J., 1963), p. 17.

4. Neil MacNeil, *Forge of Democracy* (New York, 1963), pp. 23–38; and Galloway, *History of the House of Representatives,* chap. 15.

5. Haynes, *The Senate of the United States,* chap. 1.

6. William S. White, *Citadel* (New York, 1957), p. 68.

7. For a list of the sessions and their length, see the *Congressional Directory.*

8. Galloway, *History of the House of Representatives,* pp. 295–297; and U.S. Bureau of the Census, U.S. Department of Commerce, *Historical Statistics of the United States, 1789–1945* (Washington, D.C., 1949), p. 293. There are some contradictions in these two sources concerning House membership.

9. For information on unicameralism, see Belle Zeller, ed., *American State Legislatures* (New York, 1954), chap. 4; and A. C. Breckenridge, *One House for Two* (Washington, D.C., 1958).

10. Zeller, *American State Legislatures,* p. 16.

11. Duane Lockard, *The Politics of State and Local Government* (New York, 1963), p. 71.

12. Robert Dishman, *State Constitutions: The Shape of the Document* (New York, 1960), pp. 15–23.

13. Council of State Governments, *The Book of the States, 1974–1975* (Lexington, Ky., 1974), pp. 48–50.

14. Ibid., pp. 82–83.

15.   For an example of the effect of a constitutional deadline on the legislative struggle, see Thomas Flinn, *Governor Freeman and the Minnesota Budget* (University, Ala., 1961).

16.   Council of State Governments, unpublished data.

17.   Ibid., p. 68.

18.   See Zeller, *American State Legislatures,* chap. 11.

19.   Council of State Governments, *The Book of the States, 1974–1975,* p. 57.

20.   See Austin Ranney, "Parties in State Politics," in Herbert Jacob and Kenneth N. Vines, eds., *Politics in the American States* (Boston, 2d ed., 1971), chap. 3; Richard I. Hofferbert, "Classification of American State Party Systems," *Journal of Politics* 26 (1964):550–567.

CHAPTER SIX

Legislative Leadership

"Everyone knows something of leaders and leadership of various sorts, but no one knows very much. Leadership, especially in the political realm, unavoidably or by design often is suffused by an atmosphere of the mystic and the magical, and these mysteries have been little penetrated by systematic observation."[1] David B. Truman's comment is an appropriate introduction to the topic of legislative leadership; it should serve as a warning to avoid glib generalizations and the confusion of appearance with reality. Leaders are found in all legislative bodies, as they are in other organized groups. On paper, there are striking similarities in the organizational structures of legislatures, but these formal similarities mask important variations. One source of this variety is the norms developed over a period of time for the particular legislative body; these are related to legislators' expectations of the roles that leaders should play. Another source of variety is the skills and perceptions of the leaders themselves. Beyond that, actual patterns of leadership may be affected by the party balance in the legislature or by the style of executive leadership in legislative matters.

THE NATURE OF LEADERSHIP

Leadership has been studied, for the most part, by sociologists and psychologists who have been primarily interested in groups that are smaller than the average legislative body. Efforts to discover those traits of character that are endemic to leaders have led to the conclusion, generally accepted by scholars, that these traits vary with the group that is being led. The traits necessary for a successful legislative leader are not exactly the same as those required for a football coach, a business executive, or even the leader of an urban political machine. Students of leadership have begun to focus their attention not so much on personality traits as on the relationship between leader and followers within the context of a given social situation. Cecil A. Gibb defines leadership as "an interactional function of the personality and the social situation." A leader is "a member of a group on whom the group confers a certain status, and leadership describes the role by which the duties of this status are fulfilled."[2]

The requirements for successful leadership vary, even among groups as similar as American legislative bodies. One variable is the experience of the average legislator; another is the frequency and duration of the legislative sessions; and a third is the homogeneity of the legislature in terms of party and type of constituency. Moreover, as Truman points out, the requirements for successful leadership "are likely to vary through time, depending upon the internal and external circumstances in which the group is operating."[3] For example, the floor leader in Congress finds that both the necessity and the ability to initiate legislative programs are diminished when his party gains control of the White House. The power of the Speaker of the House was undermined early in the twentieth century because the incumbent proved unable to adapt to changes that had been wrought in the Republican party by the Progressive movement.

Several characteristics common to most legislatures provide the prerequisites and limitations that distinguish this brand of leadership from other forms. Although some of the duties and powers of presiding officers are clearly prescribed in legislative rules, this is not true of floor leaders and other party officials in the legislature; their sources of authority are usually vague. Both types of leaders usually have an influence broader than that which is based on formal rules. As a consequence, legislative leadership is a variable that is heavily dependent on the personal skills of the leaders. There are wide differences in the strength of sanctions available to leaders, but leaders seldom have the power to influence significantly the members' chances for renomination and reelection. For this reason, legislative leaders must rely on persuasion, tact, and bargaining; their success often depends on their ability to sense the mood of the legislature. The legislative leader seldom gives orders to anyone.

Since legislative leadership is so dependent on individual skills, it is entirely possible that legislators who hold no formal position of leadership will exercise more influence than some of the formal leaders. Robert A. Taft's influence among Republican senators was so great that the political office he held was of subsidiary importance; when he resigned as chairman of the Policy Committee to become floor leader, the locus of power simply shifted from one position to the other. Nevertheless, most legislative positions, whether party offices or committee chairmanships, carry with them both specific powers and opportunities. The ineffective legislator is not going to become influential by occupying a leadership post, but the effective legislator is likely to increase his power when he becomes a formal leader.

Truman suggests as a generally valid proposition that "the larger an organization, the more probable . . . is the convergence if not complete congruence of the 'formal' and 'informal' structures of influence and leadership." Truman believes that this results largely from the communications problem of a larger organization: the leadership is at the center of the communications network and has access to all components of the legislative system that are essential to leadership.[4] At the state level, the convergence of formal and informal leadership is likely to result from another factor: the generally high turnover of legislators and the short and infrequent sessions common in most states reduce the likelihood that legislators will be able to gain and maintain broad influence outside the formal leadership posts.

FORMAL STRUCTURE OF LEADERSHIP

Presiding Officer of the Senate

The Constitution provides that the vice-president shall be the presiding officer of the United States Senate. In fact he seldom presides except on ceremonial occasions or when a very important issue comes up on which he may have to cast a tie-breaking vote. Normally the responsibility for presiding is rotated among senators. There are forty-one states that elect a lieutenant governor, and in thirty-one of these, that official presides over the upper house of the legislature (and in Nebraska over the unicameral body). In the remaining nineteen states the presiding officer is elected by the members of the senate (including Tennessee, where the elected presiding officer holds the title of lieutenant governor). Neither the vice-president nor the lieutenant governor is regarded by legislators as a member of the legislative branch; he is an outsider, part of the executive. He is not trusted with as much power as is normally given to the presiding officer in the nineteen states where this officer is elected by members of the state senate. At the national level, the vice-president's legislative powers, other than breaking a tie on a roll call, are negligible. At the state level, the lieutenant governor, who (like the vice-president) can cast tie-breaking votes, often has to share power with an elected president pro tem or with a committee of senate leaders. One obvious reason for the weakness of the position of either the vice-president or the lieutenant governor is that he may be a member of the party that commands only a minority in the senate. In states where divided government is most common, the lieutenant governor's influence is likely to be lowest.[5]

The vice-president's most important task in the legislative process is to serve as a liaison between the president and his party in the Senate. This was a role that was performed well by Alben W. Barkley and Lyndon B. Johnson, both former floor leaders. During the first two administrations of Franklin Roosevelt, John N. Garner (the former Speaker of the House) kept the President informed about congressional opinion in both houses. On the other hand, during Roosevelt's third administration, Henry Wallace did not command the respect and did not have the rapport with the Senate that would have enabled him to serve this purpose. When the vice-president serves in a liaison capacity, he is duplicating the job of the floor leader. The latter is responsible both to the senatorial party and to the President; whereas the vice-president is responsible to neither. The lieutenant governor is in the same limbo of nonresponsibility. Aside from his routine tasks as a presiding officer, the vice-president or lieutenant governor has no *essential* part to play in the legislative process; if he succeeds in writing a bigger part for himself, it is only because his skill and advice make him valuable to the other actors in the legislative system. No vice-president was better prepared than Lyndon B. Johnson to play a major legislative part, and there were a few signs at the start of his term that he intended to do so. The negative reactions of Democratic senators and the failure of President Kennedy to use the vice-president in this fashion quickly relegated him to an intermittent backstage part in the Congress.

When the presiding officer of the state senate is elected by that body, he is usually a figure of considerable power and influence in the legislature. Not only are his formal powers likely to be greater than a lieutenant governor's, but he is often (like the Speaker) a recognized leader of the majority legislative party. In some states, the title of president pro tem is largely an honorary one given to a senior member of the senate and the only duty it involves is presiding in the lieutenant governor's absence. Frequently the floor leader, rather than the lieutenant governor or the president pro tem, is recognized as the chief of the majority legislative party. In a few states, however, the president pro tem is a powerful figure; and in some, he also holds the position of majority floor leader.

Speaker of the House

In the United States House of Representatives and in the states, the Speaker is elected directly by the members of the House; and in every legislative system, he is a figure of power. The Speaker of the house in most states is granted broad powers under the rules to appoint members to committees and to preside over the operation of the house; there are usually relatively few limitations on his freedom to exercise these powers. Comparable powers were gradually acquired by the Speaker of the United States House during the nineteenth century, but most of these were lost during the 1910–1911 revolt against Speaker Joseph Cannon. In the United States House and in two-party states, the Speaker also serves as the leader of the majority party and is selected by the majority caucus. In one-party states, he is likely to be one of the leaders in the dominant faction, usually a faction loyal to the governor. The Speaker combines many of the tasks performed by the presiding officer and the majority floor leader in the upper house. How party leadership is divided between the Speaker and the majority floor leader depends on custom and on the personal relationship between the two men.

The history of the Speaker of the United States House is a chronicle of individuals, strong and weak, in whose hands the Speaker's powers have waxed and waned. During the first two decades of the Republic, the Speaker was merely the presiding officer and, during Jefferson's administration, one of the President's lieutenants. Henry Clay, who was elected Speaker as a freshman congressman in 1811 and served intermittently until 1825, was the first to make the Speaker the leader of the majority party or faction in the House. He came to power as a leader of the war hawks faction during Madison's administration. He appointed his supporters to key committee posts, interpreted and applied the rules of the House, and insisted on the Speaker's right to participate fully in debate and voting. During the two decades before the Civil War, the Speaker's importance as a party leader declined as the slavery issue splintered the parties, making an effective majority impossible and leading to several deadlocks over the choice of a Speaker. After the Civil War, James G. Blaine, a strong Speaker in a period of congressional supremacy in Washington, helped to reestablish the Speaker as a party leader and used his authority over committee assignments as an important means of control.[6]

The Speaker's power to interpret the rules and set the precedents of the House is a major source of his authority, one which was increasingly used by several strong Speakers in the latter part of the nineteenth century, notably Samuel J. Randall, John G. Carlisle, Thomas B. Reed, and Charles F. Crisp. During this period, the Speaker gained absolute discretion in recognizing members to offer motions or to participate in debate. The Speaker began to prevent filibusters by refusing to accept motions that he considered dilatory and by counting as present members who refused to answer a quorum call. The Rules Committee was developed into the most powerful committee in the House through the use of special rules granted by the committee as the normal means of transacting legislative business. The Speaker appointed the members of that committee and chaired and controlled it. These techniques of control were refined and strengthened by Joseph Cannon, who became Speaker in 1903 and ruled with an iron hand.

The revolt of 1910–1911 resulted from an alliance of Democrats and insurgent western Republicans. It stripped the Speaker of his chairmanship and control of the Rules Committee, his power to name committee members and chairmen, and much of his discretion in recognizing members; it also established procedures for bypassing the Rules Committee and other committees. A century after Clay had demonstrated the potential power of the Speaker's office, that power once again depended more on the skill of the incumbent than on the formal prerogatives of the office. "Henry Clay had mastered the House without the benefit of the rules available to Cannon, and Speakers who followed Cannon could learn from Clay's example."[7] For fourteen years after the revolt against Cannon, the Speaker was primarily a presiding officer, and party leadership was in the hands of the floor leader. In 1925, Speaker Nicholas Longworth restored the Speaker's position as a political leader; his successors—notably Sam Rayburn, during most of the period from 1940 to 1961—demonstrated the potency of this political influence.

In Congress today, the Speaker serves both as presiding officer and as leader of the majority party, unlike the Speaker of the British House of Commons, who presides with careful neutrality and does not even vote. Several recent developments in the Democratic party have increased the influence of the Speaker (when a Democrat) over committee selections. He nominates his party's members of the Rules Committee. He chairs and appoints several members of the Democratic Policy and Steering Committee, which now nominates Democratic members and chairmen of standing committees. He is also instrumental in determining the size of committees.

Floor Leaders and Whips

The post of House majority leader did not become a distinct one until 1899, and it was not separated from the chairmanship of the Ways and Means Committee until 1919. The majority leader was appointed by the Speaker and was clearly a lieutenant of the Speaker until 1911, when he was chosen for the first time by a secret ballot of the party caucus. During the interim period of weak Speakers, the majority leader served as the party chief; but since 1925, he has served in practice as deputy party leader, with responsibility for managing the legislative program from the floor. The position of minority leader was also developed slowly, but since 1883, it has been clear that the candidate nominated for Speaker by the minority party caucus has become the minority floor leader.[8]

In the Senate, the post of floor leader evolved even more slowly. In the late nineteenth century, both parties made some use of a caucus and selected a caucus chairman who had some responsibilities for party leadership. But the most effective party leaders were not necessarily those who held such positions. The Republican party had strong leadership during the 1890s and from 1900 to 1910, but it was exercised by a small group rather than by a single leader. It was not until the period from 1911 to 1913 that the job of floor leader became a clearly recognized and permanent position in both Senate parties. The Senate majority leader has a responsibility for party leadership comparable with that of the House Speaker; at the same time, he is responsible for management of the legislative program. The minority floor leader in both houses is both the chief strategist and the spokesman for the party. There is a difference between the two senatorial parties in leadership structure. The Democratic floor leader also serves as chairman of the Policy Committee and the caucus; the Republican party, whether in the majority or the minority, divides these duties among three men, and the floor leader has not always been the most influential member of this triumvirate.[9]

Each floor leader in the Senate has a deputy leader, or party whip, to assist in managing a bill on the floor and marshaling votes for it. The much larger size of the House necessitates a more elaborate whip organization. The first party whips in the House were appointed at the turn of the century, but the use of assistant whips on a large scale was a development of the early 1930s. Today the Republicans have a seventeen-man organization, headed by a whip and three regional whips. The Democratic whip organization has twenty-one members, headed by the whip and two deputies called floor whips. Both groups are organized along regional lines, with each assistant whip responsible for one or more states. The Republican Committee on Committees in the House chooses the whip, who in turn chooses his assistants. The Democratic whip and the two floor whips are chosen jointly by the Speaker and the floor leader, but the assistant whips are selected in decentralized fashion by the deans or all members of the state delegations for which the assistant is responsible.[10]

The whips in the House

are (1) responsible for the presence of their fellow party members, but they must also (2) transmit certain information to them, (3) ascertain how they will vote on selected important pieces of legislation, and (4) guide pressure to change the minds of the recalcitrant and stiffen the wills of the wavering.[11]

In a legislative body as large as the House, it is a major task to keep track of the location of members and assure their presence on the floor for important votes. This may involve persuading members not to leave Washington or to return, arranging pairs when members must be away, and telephoning members when the time for a vote approaches. One congressman has said:

The key to effective whip action is timing. The Whip is on the Floor surveying the scene and weighing alternatives. ... He gauges the end of general debate and estimates the time when a vote is likely. If he puts out a call too soon, too urgently, many Members will assemble, take a quick look, and then begin to fade until there is a critical deficiency when the vote is taken. Yet, he can not defer too long, because a vote might come unexpectedly.[12]

The tasks of transmitting information to members and of polling members on their views are both important. One study concluded that the polls conducted by the House Democratic whips in 1962 and 1963 were usually highly accurate (80 to 95 percent correct). One of the most serious mistakes the leadership can make is to seek a vote on an issue without accurately ascertaining whether it has the votes to win. Speaker McCormack and Minority Leader Halleck made greater use of the whip organizations than their predecessors did, and the Democratic whip organization, according to Randall B. Ripley, "has become the focus of a corporate or collegial leadership in the House."[13] The Democratic whip organization, with its decentralized membership, is used more often as a two-way channel of communications; whereas the Republican whips more often attempt persuasion and pressure in dealing with members. There are enough examples of poor communications between the leadership and the rank and file in recent years to suggest that improvement in communication may be the most important task that the whip organizations can perform.

In a two-party state, floor leaders have responsibilities similar to those of floor leaders in Congress, the extent of their influence depending on the structure and cohesion of legislative parties in the state. The place of the majority leader in the party hierarchy depends on the mode of his selection (by a caucus or by the Speaker, for example) and on the extent of partisan leadership exercised by the presiding officer. In a one-party state, the floor leader is either a representative of the governor or a leader of the dominant faction in a legislative body. His position is much like a majority leader's in a two-party state, but there is usually no counterpart to the minority leader. In a few one-party states, no one consistently serves as floor leader.

TENURE AND SELECTION OF LEGISLATIVE LEADERS

In Congress and in two-party state legislatures, the Speaker is selected in the majority party caucus. The floor leaders are also normally chosen in party caucuses, although in some legislatures the Speaker selects the majority leader. The President rarely attempts to influence the choice of congressional leaders, although he may sway some votes when he does make such an attempt. There are a few states (mostly southern) in which the governor virtually appoints some legislative leaders and others in which his ability to influence the selection of leaders foreshadows the success he will have in working closely with the legislature to enact his program. More often, the governor plays little or no part. (The factors determining the executive's influence over the selection of leaders are discussed more fully in Chapter 11.) With the exception of the chief executive, outsiders have little or no influence over the choice of leaders; legislators do not perceive this to be a legitimate concern of lobbyists. Nelson W. Polsby, in describing Carl Albert's victory over Richard Bolling in the 1962 contest for House Democratic leader, emphasizes that Albert commanded greater friendship and loyalty among Democratic representatives; whereas Bolling had much greater support from liberal interest groups outside the House, including the active assistance of the AFL-CIO and the NAACP. But few congressmen were swayed by this outside pressure, and some probably resented it; the fact that the vote was conducted by secret ballot in caucus enhanced the congressmen's ability to resist this pressure.[14]

Stability of Congressional Leadership

The most obvious difference between leadership patterns at the state and national levels is that congressional leadership is more stable. Congressional leaders usually serve a longer apprenticeship, and once selected, they are rarely removed by their colleagues and usually keep their posts as long as they remain in Congress. The practice of rotating leaders after every term or two, which is common in many states, is not used for the major leadership posts in Congress. Congressional leadership has become more stable in recent decades, a trend that can be illustrated by the careers of House Speaker Sam Rayburn, Democratic Majority Leader and Speaker John McCormack, and Senate Floor Leaders Everett Dirksen and Mike Mansfield. Long tenure does not guarantee effectiveness as a legislative leader, but it suggests that the leader has the full confidence of the dominant groups in the legislature. Moreover, during a prolonged term in office, a leader, like Sam Rayburn in the United States House, can accumulate power through personal contacts, experience, and knowledge of legislative rules and techniques.[15]

Changes in leadership or attempted changes may take several forms, as shown in Table 6.1 (an adaptation of the framework used by Robert L. Peabody in his studies of congressional leadership).[16] It is rare for an incumbent in Congress to be defeated or even to be seriously challenged for reelection to his position, but in the Senate, there were such challenges in both 1969 and 1971. In 1969, Edward Kennedy successfully challenged the incumbent Democratic whip, Russell Long of Louisiana; and in 1971, Kennedy, in turn, was beaten by Robert Byrd of West Virginia. Also in 1971, Howard Baker, Jr., barely fell short in his challenge to Republican Floor Leader Hugh Scott, who had narrowly defeated Baker in 1969, after Everett Dirksen's death.

No Speaker of the United States House has been ousted (except as a consequence of a change in partisan majority) since the Civil War, and efforts to challenge the Speaker have been rare in recent years.[17] Speaker McCormack had little difficulty in defeating a challenge by Morris Udall of Arizona in 1969, even though McCormack's effectiveness as Speaker had diminished substantially by that stage in his career. No House Democratic floor leader has been removed by his party colleagues, but in recent years, the House Republican leadership has been upset on two occasions.[18] In 1959, Republican representatives replaced their veteran floor leader, Joseph W. Martin, with his deputy, Charles Halleck; in 1965, Halleck, in turn, was replaced by Gerald Ford. These changes, accomplished both times by narrow majorities in the caucus, were motivated not by liberal-conserva-

TABLE 6.1   Types of Intraparty Leadership Change

	NO CONTEST	CONTEST
No Vacancy		
Incumbent won	Status quo	
Incumbent lost	—	Unsuccessful revolt
		Successful revolt
Vacancy		
Established pattern	Routine advancement	Challenge to the
of succession		heir apparent
No established pattern	Appointment or emergence	Open competition
of succession	of a consensus choice	

tive differences in the party but by a belief among younger representatives that in the wake of the 1958 and 1964 Democratic landslides, the party needed leadership that was more aggressive and also more responsive to the less-senior congressmen.

When there is a vacancy in a major congressional leadership post, the next-ranking member in the leadership hierarchy may be chosen to fill the position, very often with little or no serious opposition. With one exception, every Speaker of the House selected since 1911 has been promoted from floor leader of his party. During the nineteenth century, it was common to choose a Speaker after only a few years of service in the House; but during the twentieth century, the average House tenure of a newly elected Speaker has been twenty-four years. Sam Rayburn was elected Speaker in 1940 after twenty-eight years in the House and four years as floor leader. John McCormack became Speaker in 1962 after thirty-three years in the House and twenty-two years as floor leader (or as whip when the Democrats were in the minority). Carl Albert moved up to the post of Speaker in 1971, twenty-four years after entering Congress and nine years after becoming majority leader.[19]

A pattern of succession has only recently become established in the choice of Senate floor leaders, and it has sometimes been challenged by a senator who was not in the line of succession. On the Democratic side, in 1949, Senator Scott Lucas was the first whip to become floor leader. When his successor, Ernest McFarland, was chosen in 1951, there was no incumbent whip. The next two Democratic floor leaders, Lyndon Johnson and Mike Mansfield, both moved up from the post of whip. On the Republican side, most of the floor leaders since 1949 have moved up either from the position of whip (Wherry, Dirksen, and Scott) or from the chairmanship of the Policy Committee (Taft and Knowland). Long tenure in the Senate seems to be becoming less necessary for election as floor leader. The average for Democratic leaders is eight years, but Lyndon Johnson was elected in 1953 after only four years in the Senate. The average for Republican leaders is fourteen years of tenure, but recent leaders have had less.[20] When Dirksen died in 1969, Hugh Scott, an eleven-year veteran serving as party whip, defeated Howard Baker, Jr., who was serving in his third year, by only five votes in the Republican caucus. An analysis of the reported votes suggests that Scott's greater seniority helped to win him several votes from senior Republicans whose ideological position was closer to that of the more conservative Baker. But it is also noteworthy that a man with only three years of senatorial experience could run such a close race for the leadership position.[21]

There is no established pattern of succession to the position of party whip in the Senate. The Republican party has had several open contests for the position in recent years, and in most of them, there has been a liberal-conservative voting alignment. Until recently, the Senate Democratic whip was usually chosen without opposition, as a matter of consensus; but in 1965, Russell Long had to defeat two opponents to win the post. Edward Kennedy's defeat of Long in 1969 was unusual because although Long (as chairman of the Finance Committee) was one of the most powerful Democrats in the Senate, Kennedy was able to make effective use of his national political strength and specifically his promises to campaign for Democratic senators who would be coming up for reelection soon. Two years later, Kennedy was ousted from his position as whip by Robert Byrd. His national political influence had been undermined by personal tragedy, but his defeat resulted primarily from the fact that he had devoted too little time to the job of being whip. Robert Byrd, who held the title of conference secretary, had been available to carry out the routine chores associated with the whip's job when Kennedy was absent; and so in 1971, a majority of his colleagues voted to give him the job.

In the House, there is no established pattern of advancement to the post of floor leader for either party. Most floor leaders have served at least twelve to eighteen years, and sometimes longer, before first being chosen as leader. Carl Albert, who became Democratic floor leader in 1962, was the first party whip to have risen to that position in many years.[22] In his successful campaign for the job of floor leader in 1971, Hale Boggs emphasized that he had served as Democratic whip since 1962. In 1973, when Boggs's death forced the Democrats to choose a new floor leader, they once again chose the party whip, Thomas O'Neill. The fact that he was chosen unanimously did not mean that promotion from the post of whip had become automatic but that he had many other assets and was widely respected by Democratic representatives. The Speaker has often had informal influence on the selection of the majority leader; Rayburn supported McCormack in 1940, and McCormack helped Albert win in 1962, but Albert remained neutral when Boggs was chosen as floor leader in 1971.[23]

The election of Hale Boggs of Louisiana as House Democratic floor leader can be used to illustrate the wide variety of factors that influence the outcome of such a race.[24] Boggs won by a comfortable majority on the second ballot after two of his four opponents withdrew. The fact that votes are cast secretly in the Democratic caucus not only makes it difficult to analyze voting patterns, but makes it difficult for candidates to build a winning coalition. Boggs's greatest advantage was that he had been party whip since 1962 and deputy whip before that. After the election his major opponent, Morris Udall, concluded that the House "apparently just insists on people getting in line, serving time. Boggs knew this, and exploited the sentiment very effectively."[25] Any party leader is in a position to do favors for other congressmen, and Boggs was able to collect political debts not only from veterans but from freshmen whom he had made a particular effort to help. As a member of the party leadership, the congressional establishment, he apparently had the support of most committee chairmen and other senior members. As a southerner with a generally liberal voting record, he was able to win most of the southern votes and also a substantial number of northern, big-city votes.

His principal opponent, Morris Udall of Arizona, had a well-organized campaign, made a serious effort to cultivate personal relationships, and tried to avoid mistakes made in the past by liberals seeking leadership posts. But he was handicapped by his close ties with the Democratic Study Group, which was seeking to reform the seniority system and other House procedures (see Chapter 7), and thus was unpopular among senior members. Udall was unable to gain support from a number of northern liberals, either because he was a westerner or because of his votes on some labor issues. Another liberal candidate, James O'Hara of Michigan, failed because the base of support of his coalition (some of the prolabor and black congressmen) was too narrow. Another also-ran, B. F. Sisk of California, tried to put together a broader coalition of northerners and southerners and failed in part because he was too liberal to satisfy the southerners and too conservative for most northerners. Perhaps the best analysis of the complicated race in 1971 came from James O'Hara:

> One, the typical Congressman doesn't really care *who* is Majority Leader as much as he wants to be with the winner. . . . Two, to the extent that most Congressmen *do* have a preference it's more likely to be based on old friendships or personal favors or dislikes than on ideology, geography, or leadership potential.[26]

Variations in State Legislative Leadership

There are great variations among the state legislatures in both the customary tenure served by leaders and the methods of selecting them. There is no obvious explanation for variations in tenure patterns. Longer tenure is not limited to either two-party or one-party legislatures. Among the two-party legislatures, the more professionalized ones (those with higher pay, better services, larger staffs, longer sessions, and more bills per session) tend to give longer tenure to their leaders, but the pattern is not a consistent one. When a particular leader serves a longer term than is usual in a state legislature, this often seems to be primarily a result of his own skill and political strength.

The variety of tenure patterns can be illustrated by reviewing the records of the house Speakers and the presidents or presidents pro tem (whichever is the top leader elected by the senate) of the senate in the fifty state legislatures from 1947 to 1976, a period of fifteen two-year terms.[27] There were six lower houses and eight upper houses in which there was a change of leadership every two years throughout the period. In most of these states the tradition of biennial rotation appears to be so strong that an incumbent normally makes no effort to serve a second term. North Dakota, Arkansas, and Florida have biennial rotation in *both* branches of the legislature.

A more common pattern of tenure is some combination of one or two terms for the leadership, which is the method followed in fourteen lower houses and fourteen upper houses. Usually this means that most leaders serve only one term but a particularly skillful leader may be able to get a second term. The legislatures in this group, where two terms are more common than a single term, include several where the governor usually determines the choice of a leader (both houses in Alabama and the lower house in Kentucky).

There are thirteen lower houses and ten senates where the usual pattern is one or two terms but where one leader since 1947 has served as many as five terms. There are another ten lower houses and ten senates where more than one leader has served from three to five terms (usually three or four terms). In both types of legislatures there seems to be no tradition of rotation; the length of a leader's tenure may be determined by his own preferences and political strength within his party or by alterations in partisan majorities in the legislature.

Finally, there are six lower houses and eight upper houses in which one leader served at least six terms out of a possible fifteen (with tenure sometimes having begun prior to 1947). For example, President Pro Tem Panzer of the Wisconsin senate served from 1947 to 1966; Speaker Curvin of the Rhode Island house served from 1941 to 1964; and Speaker Silers presided over the Mississippi house from 1944 to 1964. South Carolina provides the most dramatic example of leadership stability. In the senate, Edgar Brown served as president pro tem from 1942 to 1972 and was often described as the most powerful man in the government. In the house, Sol Blatt served as Speaker almost continuously from 1937 until 1974. The two men came from the same rural country. Obviously, when a single man served a long term in a leadership position, it is difficult to tell whether this represents a traditional pattern of leadership or simply an extraordinary individual. In several of these states, however, one long-term leader has been succeeded by another who has served at least four or five terms, an indication of a pattern.

Years of experience as a presiding officer should be a source of strength to a state legislative leader, just as it is in Congress. Shorter tenure does not guarantee weak leadership, but it is symptomatic of less independent authority for a leader. Two or four years is simply too short a time (particularly in states with biennial sessions) for a leader to develop personal bases of power or to accumulate the knowledge and experience necessary for preeminence as a legislative leader. But a leader's power and effectiveness do not depend entirely on his tenure in office; the circumstances of his election to office are equally important. If a leader has to make commitments to other legislators to get elected, the nature of these commitments may determine both the sources and the limitations of his political strength.

In a strong two-party system, the presiding officer will be selected by the majority caucus, and the majority party will normally unite behind that choice in balloting on the floor of the house or senate. William Buchanan has described the vote on choosing the presiding officer as "the indispensable glue for holding a legislative party together."[28] Even in a strongly partisan legislature, there are occasional examples of a break in party lines. In the 1975 session of the Illinois house, the Democrats were deadlocked for several weeks over the choice of a speaker because some members refused to support the candidate who had a majority of Democratic votes. Finally, on the ninety-third ballot, a number of Republican legislators defected from support of their party's candidate and helped to elect the Speaker who had most of the votes in the majority Democratic party. In both 1959 and 1961 the Illinois house chose a Democratic Speaker as a result of a combination of Democratic and Republican votes. In 1959 the winner had the support of less than half of the majority Democratic party, and in 1961 he was reelected even though his party now lacked a majority in the House. In 1965, the New York Democrats in both branches of the legislature were deadlocked for a month over the choice of presiding officers; Republicans broke the deadlock by electing Democratic leaders who had minority support within their own party.[29]

In a state with a weak party system, the candidates for leadership posts sometimes cross party lines in their search for votes. In California, for example, although the candidates for Speaker have regularly been chosen from the majority party, they have built winning coalitions by enlisting the support of members of the minority party, using committee assignments as rewards for supporters. Although the minority party could enhance its power by voting as a bloc, its members are usually divided in their support for a candidate in the majority party. When a Speaker is selected with partial support from both parties, he becomes more of a factional than a partisan leader, and both the organization and voting pattern in the legislature are likely to be factional rather than partisan.[30]

In legislatures in which it is customary for the presiding officer to step down after one or two terms, there are few occasions for anyone to run against an incumbent. Where there is no rotation policy, a long-term incumbent may be too strong to be challenged. Consequently, in most states, it is unusual for a leader to come to power by defeating the incumbent. When that does occur, the new leader may face difficult problems in unifying his party and appeasing the supporters of his predecessor.

Only a few legislative bodies have an established pattern of succession for filling vacancies. In New Jersey, there is a biennial rotation of offices, with members moving from the chairmanship of the Appropriations Committee to the post of floor leader to Speaker, after which they join the ranks of often-influential ex-Speakers. In legislatures with relatively strong party systems, it is common for the Speaker to have served as his party's floor leader; this has often been true, for example, in New York, Pennsylvania, and Wisconsin. Often the chairmanship of an important committee, such as Appropriations, Finance, or Judiciary, may be a stepping stone to the job of Speaker or of presiding officer in the senate. Seniority seems to be less important in the selection of state legislative leaders than it is in the selection of congressional leaders. Data from a number of states suggest that the length of legislative service before becoming a presiding officer or a floor leader ranges from six to sixteen years, with leaders occasionally being chosen after very short periods of service.

If there is no established pattern of selection, the choice of legislative leaders may take several forms. A candidate for a position may have enough ability and experience in other legislative jobs to win widespread support from his colleagues and discourage others from seeking the position. A small clique may select the top leaders without any open conflict, as in the Virginia senate, where a few veteran senators have held the key positions for a number of years while rotating the post of president pro tem among their number. Sometimes consensus results from the influence of political leaders outside the legislature. In several southern and border states, the governor has usually been successful in determining the choice of the presiding officer as well as his floor leaders in both houses. In such cases, the person selected has less independent authority; his effectiveness in the legislative body depends in considerable part on the skills and political strength of the governor. In some states that have strong state or local party organizations outside the legislature, the leaders of these organizations have a choice in the selection of leaders. In Illinois, for example, Mayor Daley of Chicago has influenced the choice of Democratic leaders; in New York, many legislators are also local party leaders, and their success in seeking legislative jobs may depend on their influence within the local party organization.

Open contests for legislative leadership positions are common in a number of states. In Iowa, there have been frequent contests for Speaker, with the outcome influenced by policy issues, regional factors, the role of interest groups, and the personal followings of candidates.[31] In both Wisconsin and Montana, there have been contests more often than not in the selection of the Speaker and floor leaders; and these conflicts have involved regional, urban-rural, and ideological alignments.[32] In some states, the contest for the speakership has assumed the dimensions of a political campaign, with candidates openly soliciting votes over a prolonged period. In Arkansas and Florida, the presiding officers of both houses are selected in the preceding legislative session, during which candidates for the positions seek formal pledges of support from their colleagues. In Arkansas, seniority and good fellowship are major factors in winning pledges; whereas in Florida, choice committee assignments are the usual currency of bargaining. But in both states, the effect of the system has been to maintain legislative control within a small group of old-guard members.[33] In Texas, the candidates for Speaker also start their campaigns early, seeking pledges of support not only from incumbents in the previous session but also from legislative candidates. One candidate for Speaker usually claims victory on the basis of these pledges after the primary election has been held. A winning candidate for Speaker in Texas is likely to build his coalition on the basis of ideological affinity, geographical proximity, personal friendships, and promises of committee assignments.[34]

THE POWERS OF THE PRESIDING OFFICER

The Speaker of the house and the presiding officer of the senate in the states where he is elected to this position owe much of their authority to formal powers granted in the legislative rules. The Speaker of the United States House has formal powers that are significant but, since the 1910–1911 revolt, less imposing than those of his counterparts in the states. The vice-president has little formal power as a presiding officer.

The Speaker of the United States House during the First Congress won the power to appoint committees. This power was often challenged, but it was repeatedly upheld by the House. It constituted one of the most important methods by which strong Speakers achieved control over the House until the power was taken away from the Speaker by a change in the rules in 1911 that marked the culmination of the revolt against Speaker Cannon.[35] In most states, the Speaker of the house has the authority to appoint members of the standing committees, and usually their chairmen as well; there are only three exceptions to this rule. In thirteen of the nineteen states where the presiding officer of the senate is elected by the members, he has the power to choose committees. In eleven of the states where the lieutenant governor presides, he has the power to choose committees; in seven, the president pro tem makes the selection; in the remainder, a committee or the full senate chooses the committees.[36] Changes in the senate rules regarding the lieutenant governor's authority are sometimes made when the office is won by a man who represents a party or faction different from the one that controls the senate.

The authority to choose committee members is one of the most powerful tools of leadership, and in most states, it can be exercised without the deference to seniority that is necessary in Congress. In some states, there are other kinds of limitations on the leaders' freedom to choose committees. There may be legislative norms (as there are in Montana) that require him to respect the preferences of members for assignments or to reappoint those who were on a committee previously.[37] The Speaker may have promised certain committee appointments to those who supported his campaign for the speakership. In some states, the governor takes a hand in assigning important committee chairmanships. The presiding officer often shares the responsibility for choosing majority party members with his floor leader. In many two-party legislatures, the minority party leadership submits suggestions for the minority membership of committees; and usually these suggestions are accepted by the presiding officer or other appointing authority. Those legislative leaders who are not restricted by norms or political commitments can use their authority to ensure that the most important committees are tightly controlled by men who agree with their views and are loyal to them. Examples of such leadership control can be found in a number of states, including Florida, Georgia, Arizona, and Wisconsin.[38]

A close corollary of the power to choose committee members is the authority to assign bills to committee, an authority exercised by the Speaker in forty-five states, by the presiding officer of the senate in forty-four states, and by committees in most of the remaining cases.[39] In many of these states, the presiding officer, particularly the Speaker, has wide discretion in assigning bills. In the absence of specific jurisdictional rules, he can assign bills to those committees most securely controlled by legislators who are loyal to the leadership. In some states, a majority of bills and nearly all important ones are assigned to a handful of committees, usually bearing broadly descriptive titles like Judiciary, Executive and Legislative Affairs, State Government, or Finance and Taxation. In some legislatures, the presiding officers can refer a bill to several different committees in order to minimize its chances of being reported by them all. The presiding officers in Congress have little discretionary authority because the 1946 Legislative Reorganization Act specifies the jurisdiction of congressional committees in precise detail. The subject matter of a bill may be so broad, however, that two committees have some claim to it, and the presiding officer may be able to exercise some discretion. In the United States House, the Speaker has the expert assistance of the parliamentarian in assigning bills to committee.

The Speaker of the House and occasionally the presiding officer in the senate exercise significant discretionary authority in presiding over state legislative bodies. This is not so often a matter of rules as it is one of custom and precedent and the skills of a bold presiding officer. The presiding officer in a state legislature can act more boldly and arbitrarily than would be possible for the Speaker of the United States House because his actions are less publicized; he is less bound by tradition; most rank-and-file members are not sufficiently familiar with the rules and parliamentary practice; and in some cases, his party or faction completely dominates the legislature. The presiding officer (particularly the Speaker) may be highly selective in recognizing members or arbitrary in prolonging or cutting off debate. He may affect the decision on a bill through his judgment of voice votes, his failure to recognize demands for a roll call, or even his timing in closing the voting and recording votes when a mechanical voting device is used. We have noted that legislators expect their presiding officers to be fair, and it is usually true that a successful presiding officer must retain the respect of legislators in all parties and factions. It is also true that many actions of the presiding officer which appear abrupt and arbitrary to the newcomer in the gallery may be accepted by all legislators in the interests of expediting business. Nevertheless, when the leadership is short of votes and its legislative control is endangered, the presiding officer is sometimes able to assert that control through his skill and boldness in presiding.

The Speaker of the United States House cannot be so arbitrary, but he is far from being impotent as a presiding officer. For several decades prior to the 1910–1911 revolt, the Speaker had exercised absolute discretion in recognizing members who were seeking to make motions as well as those seeking to participate in debate. Since the revolt, the Speaker's discretion in matters of recognition has been limited. Rules and customs of the House require him to recognize certain members (such as committee chairmen) who seek to make motions, and control over debate is largely handled by the member in charge of the legislation on the floor. Some discretion remains, but it is not an important source of power. Since 1890, the Speaker has had the power to refuse to entertain a motion that he considers dilatory; yet this potentially important power was never exercised by Speaker Rayburn during his long tenure.[40]

The Speaker of the United States House of Representatives has one more important power. He has the authority to interpret the rules of the House and, in so doing, to set precedents and revise the rules in important respects. He is aided in this task by the House parliamentarian, who helps him to find precedents that will justify the action he desires to take. Most of the important changes in House rules and precedents, including those enhancing the Speaker's power, have resulted from rulings by the Speaker. Neil MacNeil has said: "The Speaker's power primarily has sprung from the political nature of his office: it has been he who has applied the rules and established the precedents that have controlled and guided the House of Representatives."[41] The rulings of the Speaker can always be overruled by a majority vote of the House, but such is the Speaker's traditional authority in this area that his rulings are rarely questioned. Nicholas Longworth, who served in the late 1920s, was the last Speaker to have a decision overruled;

this happened to him twice, but the effect of the second action was to reinstate his first decision.[42]

LEADERSHIP ROLES

If effective legislative leadership is dependent on personal qualities as well as formal powers and custom, it becomes particularly important to inquire into the role of the legislative leader. How does the leader perceive his job, his relationship to the legislative party, and his responsibilities to the President or governor? In tracing the history of the Speaker of the United States House, we have shown that the powerful Speakers were those who perceived their role as being that of a party leader as well as a presiding officer. The modern Speaker in Congress and in the two-party states perceives his role in terms of party leadership.

Serving Two Masters

There is a fundamental difference between the role of a Speaker or floor leader for the administration party and that of a leader for the opposition party, a difference involving both the leader's policy-forming role and his loyalty. The opposition leader has greater freedom, which he does not necessarily use, to frame policies for his party. The leader of the administration party faces the problem of role definition. Is he the leader of the legislative party who serves as an ambassador to the chief executive, or is he the chief executive's representative in the legislature? David Truman argues that party leaders not only can but must serve two masters: "The fundamental complexity and subtlety of the role lie in the fact that the elective leaders are, and probably must be, both the President's leaders and the party's leaders." Truman admits that these requirements may not always be compatible but says that "they are generally interdependent, in the sense that representing the President provides a focus and a part of the leverage for leadership of the Congressional party, and sympathetic reflection of the problems of legislative colleagues is an essential in advancing the President's program."[43]

As Speaker, Sam Rayburn bore the brunt of winning House acceptance for many programs of Democratic administrations; and yet, at all times, he negotiated stubbornly with these administrations about the programs for which he was prepared to seek acceptance. Alben W. Barkley, who shared Rayburn's sense of responsibility to Democratic Presidents, demonstrated most dramatically the limits of this responsibility. He resigned as floor leader in protest against President Roosevelt's message vetoing a tax bill and then accepted unanimous reelection by the party caucus. Truman has pointed out that "Roosevelt's action undermined Barkley's value as the Administration's leader by treating him, implicitly, as exclusively that. Barkley's resignation and immediate reelection as majority leader restored the emphasis on his ties to his colleagues and reestablished the dual relationship, though not, apparently, in identical form."[44]

The problem of role conflict becomes more serious for a leader when there are major differences between his policy views and those of the President. In his brief months as Eisenhower's floor leader, Robert Taft demonstrated, in roughly equal parts, a willingness to use his skill and his great influence in behalf of the President's program and a determination to influence the policy content of that program. Taft's biographer says that neither Roosevelt nor Truman "had so effective a Senate leader as Eisenhower had in Taft," but he adds that Taft negotiated legislative programs with the President substantially as a coequal.[45] William Knowland, who succeeded Taft as floor leader, was frequently an effective proponent of Eisenhower's programs; but he had serious differences with the President on both the diplomatic and the legislative aspects of foreign policy. In a badly divided party, Knowland's sensitivity to senatorial opinion sometimes made him a valuable agent of compromise; but his influence in the Senate as a critic of the administration declined, in part because the conflicts involved foreign policy, a field in which the President's preeminence has usually been acknowledged by members of Congress.

The role of legislative leaders in the states varies with the governor's political effectiveness and particularly with his ability to dictate the choice of legislative leaders. Some legislative leaders, like those in Congress, serve two masters. But, in northern states like New York, where the governor dominates a strong party, and in southern states like Kentucky and Alabama, where the governor personally picks the leadership, the leaders are likely to see themselves as agents of the governor. Even in carrying out this role, they must report to the governor on the mood of the legislature and on the prospects for passing his bills; and in so doing, they may act very much like agents of the legislative majority. In those states where the leaders are elected for relatively brief terms without gubernatorial interference, they are responsible primarily to the legislative majority that chose them. In states where legislative leaders usually have longer tenure, they have an opportunity to develop their own legislative organization, which they not only serve but lead. The role of the majority leader may vary further, depending on whether he owes his being chosen to the governor, the legislative majority, or the Speaker. A leader chosen by the Speaker may operate primarily as his deputy. In a southern state, the floor leader is likely to be recognized as the governor's chief spokesman in the legislature.[46]

The Opposition Leader

The leader of the opposition party escapes this kind of role conflict because he usually owes no responsibility to the chief executive. An exception may be made for the opposition leader in Congress, particularly one leading a majority party, whose role definition may include a sense of responsibility to provide support to the President on issues of foreign policy. Lyndon Johnson and Sam Rayburn clearly felt such a sense of responsibility on issues of foreign aid, reciprocal trade, and security treaties during the Eisenhower administration. Senator Everett M. Dirksen's concept of the minority leader's role during the Johnson administration was not identical with that of either Taft or Johnson. Dirksen had developed strong rapport with Johnson while both were floor leaders, and he maintained an unusually close relationship with Johnson after he became President. Dirksen supported Johnson on several foreign-policy issues, notably the Vietnam War. Dirksen also provided support on a number of domestic issues, but only after negotiating with the President in order to get modifications in a bill or other concessions. Dirksen could not deliver the votes of all Republican senators to support a compromise worked out with the President, but he was well aware of his colleagues' viewpoints and could often provide enough votes to assure passage of bills in a form that was acceptable to both himself and Johnson.[47]

The style of opposition leadership differs in a fashion that suggests distinct differences in the role perceptions of various leaders. These differences involve their responsibility for defining party policy, a duty of the chief executive in the administration party. In the British parliamentary system, the leader of the opposition party in the House of Commons clearly has that responsibility because he is also the man who will become prime minister when and if the party wins an election. In this country, the identity of the opposition party's candidate for President is unknown in advance of the election year, but it is seldom the congressional leader.

Not since two former Speakers, James K. Polk and Henry Clay, contested the Presidency in 1844 has either party nominated a Speaker for President. Only twice since the election of William McKinley has this country had a President who had served as an important party leader in Congress, and both of these men —Lyndon Johnson and Gerald Ford—came to the Presidency by succession from the vice-presidency. At the state level, the chances of a legislative leader becoming governor are better, but still not great. In a study covering the years 1870 to 1950, Joseph A. Schlesinger found that over half of the governors had served in the legislature, one-fifth just before becoming governor, although the proportion in both cases had fallen in the later years. Only 7 percent of the governors had moved directly from a post of legislative leadership (Speaker of the House or president or president pro tem of the senate) to the governorship. The legislature, particularly legislative leadership, was most often the stepping stone to the governor's mansion in a few northeastern and southeastern states that had relatively low levels of party competition during the period studied.[48]

The contrasting perceptions with regard to the leader's role can be illustrated by the examples of Senators Robert A. Taft and Lyndon B. Johnson, two highly effective party leaders, both of whom also made serious bids for the presidential nomination. Taft, a man with sharply defined (although not doctrinaire) views on issues, sought to win the support of the Republican senatorial party for his views not through bargaining but by intellectual force. The name "Mr. Republican" that was so often applied to Taft during the Truman administration was appropriate because his viewpoints on domestic issues were broadly representative of those shared by most Republican senators and because he articulated these viewpoints more clearly and forcefully than any of his colleagues. His role was to define the party's record as an opposition party and in a few cases, such as the Taft-Hartley labor act, to enact major legislation in the face of the administration's opposition. Taft was much less successful in defining party policy on international questions, both because of his own lack of interest and experience and because the Republican party was more seriously divided on this issue.

Lyndon Johnson did not believe that he or the party could actually challenge the President's leadership or offer a comprehensive legislative program. (In 1956, he resisted demands that the party should frame its own program prior to the President's recommendations.) As a pragmatist, he was concerned with the possible, which meant finding enough common ground among Democratic (and, if necessary, Republican) senators to pass legislation. Johnson held strong views on some issues, but in contrast with Taft, he seldom served as the initiator of, or spokesman for, a policy, with a few exceptions that occurred when he began to assume the role of presidential aspirant. An example is Johnson's performance in the civil rights battles of 1957 and 1960. His own views were compatible with a "moderate" bill, and by 1960, as a possible presidential candidate, he wanted to be identified with such a bill. His role during both legislative battles was that of a negotiator and mediator. He discovered what kind of bill could be passed without a filibuster and then forced passage of the bill by warning northern senators that any stronger bill would die in a filibuster and by warning southerners at the same time that he would help to break any filibuster against the compromise bill.

Mike Mansfield, Senate Democratic floor leader from 1963 to 1976, has defined his role in more modest terms than either Taft or Johnson. During the Kennedy and Johnson administrations, Mansfield sought to expedite action on the President's legislative program; and during the Nixon and Ford administrations, he worked in behalf of programs proposed by the Democratic-controlled committees. As both administration leader and opposition leader, however, Mansfield has made few efforts either to influence the policy content of Democratic proposals or to compel his Democratic colleagues to support these proposals. According to John G. Stewart:

> This strategy of leadership rested fundamentally on Mansfield's view of the coequal status of the majority leader with all members of the senatorial party and his rejection of the notion that the party leadership assumed special responsibility for leading the senatorial party in certain directions or affecting decisively the outcome of legislative decisions.[49]

Leaders and Committees

Party leaders recognize that rank-and-file congressmen respect the views of the standing committees and particularly the members of their own party on the committees. Moreover, the committee is able to make decisions on the specific provisions of a measure before the floor leader has any opportunity to seek changes in it. Party leaders may try to influence decision-making within committees, but they proceed cautiously with any such approach, lest it arouse resentment and prove counterproductive. The chairman of a committee or the ranking minority member often commands more respect in his party with regard to the issues handled by his committee than the party leader does. Donald R. Matthews quotes one Senate floor leader as saying, "I always believed that it wasn't the leader's job to try to influence committee decisions. The leader's job is to take bills which have already been reported out of committee and placed on the Calendar and try to obtain as much party backing for them as he can."[50] Mike Mansfield has repeatedly stated his view that policy cannot be made by the floor leader or a policy committee; it can be made only in the standing committees. Other floor leaders might not have stated the position in such absolute fashion. But the independent authority of the committees imposes serious limitations on the leader's freedom. His role is not strictly that of a follower of committee decisions, but neither is it that of a commander. His role is that of negotiating quietly with the committee members and seeking to refine committee decisions when they conflict with what he thinks a party majority will accept.

This restraint is in contrast with the authority assumed by party leaders in most states. Given broad authority in appointing committee members and wide discretion in assigning bills to committee, state legislative leaders are more likely to interfere directly in committee decision-making when this appears necessary. They are more likely to have close working relationships with the chairmen of major committees; through these relationships, the leaders can exert influence without openly interfering in the work of committees.

Expectations of the Rank and File

We have described leadership roles from the viewpoint of the leaders; it is also pertinent to examine the leadership role expectations of rank-and-file legislators. Our best information on this comes from the study of four state legislatures conducted by John C. Wahlke and his associates.[51] Legislators expect the presiding officer to be fair and impartial in performing his functions, to maintain order, to follow the rules strictly, and to give individual members in both parties an opportunity to express their views. There is wide agreement among legislators that the presiding officer's role must be that of an impartial referee. In two-party states, however, a substantial (although smaller) number of legislators also expect the Speaker to play a partisan role, guiding the party program through the legislature and rallying party support of the program. Members of the majority party are more likely than those in the minority to perceive the Speaker's role in these terms. These expectations mean, of course, that the Speaker is subject to role conflict. Wahlke found that the conflict was seldom recognized by legislators, probably because some of them saw only one aspect of the Speaker's role. One legislator was articulate about the Speaker's conflict:

> He must let every member have his views considered and yet retain enough control, influence and respect so that he can rally the support when he needs it. The speaker can't be a dictator or a neutral party; he must be a blend of the two, and this is very difficult to do successfully.
> He should be fair to both sides—except in a real pinch.[52]

The same role conflict is experienced in the senate when the presiding officer is elected by a legislative majority. Where the lieutenant governor presides, this conflict is largely removed because the lieutenant governor usually has the role of the impartial referee with the president pro tem or floor leader serving as a party leader.

The floor leaders escape this conflict; legislators recognize that their role requires them to present and promote the legislative program of the majority party or of the governor (in a one-party state) or, in the case of the minority leader, to define and explain the minority party's criticisms of bills. On the other hand, some legislators, especially from states with weak party systems, stress the floor leader's responsibility to encourage full debate and avoid unnecessary partisan conflict. Some legislators emphasize the administration floor leader's responsibility to maintain liaison with the governor and other members of the administration. The actual duties of floor leaders and the structure and cohesion of legislative parties differ so widely from state to state that more studies of legislators' role perceptions are necessary in order to get a comprehensive picture of the leader's role.

STYLES AND TECHNIQUES OF LEADERSHIP

The influence that a legislative leader has depends not only on his formal powers but also on his skill and imagination in developing techniques of leadership and making the best use of the resources available to him. This is especially true of the Speaker in the United States House and the floor leaders in Congress and in the states where formal powers are limited. Truman's comments on the congressional floor leader are perceptive and can be applied to legislative leaders generally:

> A search for the substance and sources of power in the position, however, is frustrating, not because they do not exist but because they are tremendously varied and often inaccessible. One cannot draw up for this post a neat list of authorities and prerogatives that describes its power adequately if not exhaustively, as one can for a place in a tightly structured hierarchy. The sum total of influence in the role as played by any individual senator depends upon the skill with which he combines and employs the fragments of power that are available to him.[53]

What are these fragments of power, and how are they used in practice? The right to schedule legislation reported by committees for floor consideration is one of the most important powers available to the majority leader if it is employed skillfully. In the United States Senate and in some states, this power must be shared with a committee such as the Senate majority Policy Committee. In the United States House, most bills cannot be scheduled until cleared by the Rules Committee; but after that, the majority leader may still exercise discretion in determining the time of floor action. The timing of floor consideration can be crucial to the passage or defeat of a bill. The leadership may postpone action for days or weeks so that the sponsors can generate more support for a bill or develop amendments designed to overcome objections. Alternatively, a bill may be postponed in an effort to stall it until it is too late in the session for final action to be completed in both houses.[54]

The floor leader of the majority party in the United States Congress and in most state legislatures is entitled to priority of recognition from the presiding officers, and he may occasionally gain significant tactical advantages from that right. The floor leader is in a position to initiate procedural recommendations for conducting legislative business. For example, when Lyndon Johnson was majority leader, he scheduled night sessions of the Senate in order to speed up action on the most important bills and made extensive use of unanimous-consent agreements in order to place some deadlines on debate in the Senate.[55] In state legislatures in which rules usually make it easy for a majority to end debate, the floor leader can get recognition for a motion to shut off debate and sometimes also to block amendments, whenever those tactics seem necessary to get action on a bill.

One advantage enjoyed by a Speaker or floor leader is that he stands at the center of the legislative party's communications network. He is able to collect information about viewpoints and activities from the White House, the committee chairmen, and individual congressmen. Congressional leaders have often said that the leader must be able to sense the mood of the Senate or House, and this requires not merely intuition but also continuing contacts with the rank and file. The floor leader should be able to judge better than anyone else what chances a bill has for passage; he should be more sensitive than anyone else to shifts in the wind of congressional opinion. It is also important for the leader to keep the average member informed about such things as the views of the President and the plans of the leadership.[56]

It has been said that Lyndon Johnson's "greatest weapon [as majority leader] was a communications system that bordered on the psychic."[57] Johnson spent much of his time talking to other senators and relied on some of his closest associates to expand his communications network. For example, he used Hubert Humphrey as a contact man and negotiator with some of the most liberal Democrats who were cool to Johnson. Johnson also expanded the floor leader's staff partly in order to improve his network.[58] Johnson's successor, Mike Mansfield, has made less of an effort either to gather detailed information from other senators or to keep them well informed, and he gets along with a smaller staff than Johnson did. In the House, John McCormack and Carl Albert have made increased use of the whip system to gather information about viewpoints and voting intentions, but they have sometimes been criticized for not keeping rank-and-file members sufficiently well informed about legislative developments.

"Most of the time the leader is cast in the role of someone trying to help you with your problems," according to one senator interviewed by Matthews.[59] The leader can help a congressman get more votes for a pet bill; as Huitt points out, this may involve providing "a respectable vote for a senator's bill or amendment that was bound to lose—a substantial boon to a man who wants his constituents to take him seriously."[60] The leader's success in providing votes is cumulative; once he has aided a congressman on a particular measure, he can call on that congressman for help on another. Although the leaders in Congress lack the control over committee assignments enjoyed by state legislative leaders, they usually have substantial influence on them. The leader's ability to do favors extends beyond the passage of bills and committee assignments. He can provide the congressman with an important speaker for a meeting in his district, better office accommodations on Capitol Hill, assignment as a special congressional delegate to an overseas conference, assistance in getting funds for a subcommittee, and a host of other favors that make congressmen indebted to the leader. We are not suggesting that the average senator's vote on an important bill can be bought by obtaining an audience with the President for the mother of the year who comes from his state. We are suggesting that the floor leader is in a position to help congressmen and that through skillful use of these opportunities, he can create an atmosphere in which congressmen are favorably disposed to provide support for him if at all possible.[61]

There is another side to the coin. Favors that can be granted can also be withheld. In dealing with a recalcitrant member, the leader can persuade other congressmen to bury his favorite bill in committee or to vote against it or even to claim a committee assignment (on grounds of seniority) that the rebel has hoped to get for himself. Part of Lyndon Johnson's effectiveness as Democratic floor leader in the Senate was his willingness to take a tough line, to deny favors as well as to grant them. The resourceful leader, as Lyndon Johnson demonstrated, can endow the party leader's job with a power that some occupants of the post had never suspected was possible.

Every congressional leader has recognized, however, that his success depends more on persuasion and compromise than on favors and threats. House Majority Leader Carl Albert remarked: "If you can't win them by persuasion, you can't win them at all. If you whip them into line every time, by the time you reach the third vote you're through."[62] Albert studied party leadership under Speaker Rayburn, who said: "My experience with the Speakership has been that you cannot lead people by driving them. Persuasion and reason are the only ways. In that way the Speaker has power and influence in the House.[63] Lyndon Johnson, in echoing this theme, was underestimating his power but not straying far from an accurate description: "The only real power available to the leader is the power of persuasion. There is no patronage; no power to discipline; no authority to fire Senators like a President can fire his members of the Cabinet."[64]

Lyndon Johnson's techniques present the best example of persuasion in action. He used his forceful personality to argue the cause of party unity and the necessity for compromise. But he was thoroughly familiar with the views of other senators, and he was conscious of the necessity of finding face-saving ways through which senators could change their positions and facilitate compromise. Huitt has described Johnson's tactics as involving the "manipulation of the role perceptions of other senators." He tried to get senators to think as Democrats, not as liberals or conservatives. He tried to structure the legislative issues in such a way the Democrats would find it possible to vote as a bloc.[65] If Johnson was unable to persuade a senator to vote favorably, it was sometimes possible to persuade him to pair with another senator who was going to be absent, to be absent himself, or at least to avoid public statements that would dramatize the party split.

Perhaps because they had different perceptions of the floor leader's role, other Senate leaders have not tried to duplicate Johnson's success in maximizing the power inherent in the position. Stewart described Mike Mansfield's approach as follows:

> Indeed, in striking contrast to his predecessor's constant efforts to expand the power and influence of the majority leadership, Mansfield ... refrained from using even the fragments of institutionalized power at his disposal, much less did he attempt

the more difficult task of augmenting these limited resources. One could even say Mansfield deliberately abandoned recognized powers of the majority leadership.[66]

Senator Dirksen, the Republican leader during the 1960s, used the tools of persuasion more selectively than Johnson did. Perhaps in part because he led a minority party, he did not have such a passion for achieving party unity, and he left his Republican colleagues alone much of the time. When he did seek their support on an issue, he did so with such patience and respect for the other pressures facing a senator that he was often successful in winning that support. In other respects, Dirksen's tactics resembled Johnson's. "Dirksen was carefully solicitous of the needs, desires and views of his colleagues. As one senator put it, 'He knew that the art of politics is the care and feeding of egos.' He consulted frequently with members of his party, and regularly with ranking Republicans on Senate committees." Dirksen also avoided rigid stands on issues, and was skillful at adapting his views to fit those of his Republican colleagues. He was not bothered by the resulting appearance of inconsistency, and asserted, "I am a man of principle, and one of my basic principles is flexibility."[67]

It is much easier to describe the techniques used by individual leaders than to measure their effectiveness. Most likely, a leader who skillfully uses all the resources at his command can win more votes for a bill than one who is less skillful or resourceful, but this cannot be proved. Moreover, the effectiveness of a technique may depend on the partisan balance in Congress, the strategy pursued by the White House, and the substantive nature of the bill. Lewis A. Froman, Jr., and Randall B. Ripley, after studying the United States House Democratic leadership, concluded that leadership is more likely to be successful when more of the following conditions are met: the leaders are strongly committed on an issue and are accurately informed about the views of the rank and file; the issue is more procedural than substantive; the issue is not particularly visible to the public or is rather complex; congressional action is not very visible; and there are few counterpressures either from state delegations or from constituencies. In other words, many congressmen (and also state legislators) have a strong sense of party loyalty and are disposed to go along with party leaders unless the situation is such that strong counterpressures can be brought to bear on them.[68]

NOTES

1. David B. Truman, *The Congressional Party* (New York, 1959), p. 94.
2. Cecil A. Gibb, "The Principles and Traits of Leadership," *Journal of Abnormal and Social Psychology* 42 (1947):267–284; quotations at p. 284.
3. David B. Truman, *The Governmental Process* (New York, 1951), p. 190.
4. Truman, *The Congressional Party*, p. 97.
5. See Eugene C. Lee, *The Presiding Officer and Rules Committee in Legislatures of the United States* (Berkeley, Calif., 1952).
6. Useful sources on the history of the speakership are: George R. Brown, *The Leadership of Congress* (Indianapolis, Ind., 1922); George B. Galloway, *History of the House of Representatives* (New York, 1961), chaps. 4, 5, and 7; Ralph B. Harlow, *The History of Legislative Methods in the Period before 1825* (New Haven, Conn., 1917), chaps. 8, 9, and

10; Neil MacNeil, *Forge of Democracy* (New York, 1963), chaps. 3 and 4; and Randall B. Ripley, *Party Leaders in the House of Representatives* (Washington, D.C., 1967), chaps. 2 and 4.

7.   MacNeil, *Forge of Democracy,* p. 80.

8.   See Ripley, *Party Leaders in the House of Representatives,* pp. 24–32.

9.   See Randall B. Ripley, *Power in the Senate* (New York, 1969), pp. 24–33.

10.   See Randall B. Ripley, "The Party Whip Organizations in the United States House of Representatives," *American Political Science Review* 58 (1964):561–576.

11.   Ibid., p. 562.

12.   John W. Baker, ed., *Member of the House* (New York, 1962), p. 53.

13.   Ripley, "The Party Whip Organization in the United States House of Representatives," pp. 573, 574.

14.   See Nelson W. Polsby, "Two Strategies of Influence: Choosing a Majority Leader, 1962," in *New Perspectives on the House of Representatives,* 2d ed., ed. Robert L. Peabody and Nelson W. Polsby (Chicago, 1969), pp. 325–358.

15.   See Barbara Hinckley, "Congressional Leadership Selection and Support: A Comparative Analysis," *Journal of Politics* 32 (1970):268–287.

16.   Robert L. Peabody, "Party Leadership Change in the United States House of Representatives," *American Political Science Review* 61 (1967):677.

17.   For a detailed historical treatment of leadership contests and succession battles, see Garrison Nelson, "Partisan Patterns of House Leadership Change, 1791–1973" (Paper presented at the annual meeting of the American Political Science Association, 1974).

18.   Ripley, *Party Leaders in the House of Representatives,* pp. 14–15, 26–31.

19.   Ibid., pp. 14–15.

20.   Ripley, *Power in the Senate,* pp. 30–35.

21.   See Robert L. Peabody, "Senate Leadership Changes" (Paper presented at the annual meeting of the American Political Science Association, 1970), p. 17.

22.   See Ripley, *Party Leaders in the House of Representatives,* pp. 24–32.

23.   Ibid., pp. 54–57.

24.   This account of the contest is based largely on an excellent and lively study by Larry L. King, "The Road to Power in Congress," *Harper's,* June, 1971, pp. 39–63.

25.   Ibid., p. 62.

26.   Ibid., pp. 61–62.

27.   The surveys of leadership turnover and the election of Speakers are based on data in *The Book of the States* and in legislative manuals and blue books for the appropriate years.

28.   William Buchanan, *Legislative Partisanship: The Deviant Case of California* (Berkeley and Los Angeles, 1963), p. 141.

29.   For an account of the 1959 incident in Illinois, see Thomas B. Littlewood, *Bipartisan Coalition in Illinois* (New York, 1960). The 1965 deadlock in New York is described in Alan G. Hevesi, *Legislative Politics in New York* (New York, 1975), pp. 171–178.

30.   See Buchanan, *Legislative Partisanship,* pp. 139–144.

31.   See Samuel C. Patterson, ed., *Midwest Legislative Politics* (Iowa City, Iowa, 1967), p. 15.

32.   Douglas Camp Chaffey and Malcolm E. Jewell, "Selection and Tenure of State Legislative Party Leaders: A Comparative Analysis" *Journal of Politics* 34 (Nov. 1972).

33.   See Alex B. Lacy, Jr., ed., *Power in American State Legislatures* (New Orleans, La., 1967), pp. 2–3; and William G. Cornelius, *Southeastern State Legislatures* (Atlanta, 1967), p. F-1.

34.   See Clifton H. McCleskey, *The Government and Politics of Texas,* 3d ed. (Boston, 1969), pp. 132–134.

35.   See Brown, *The Leadership of Congress,* pp. 26–38, 143–171.

36.   Council of State Governments, *The Book of the States, 1974–1975* (Lexington, Ky., 1974), p. 73.

37.   See Douglas Camp Chaffey, "The Institutionalization of State Legislatures: A Comparative Study," *Western Political Quarterly* 23 (1970):185.

38.   See Cornelius, *Southeastern State Legislatures,* pp. F-1, G-2; Gordon Henderson, "Patterns of Leadership in the 1966 and 1967 Sessions of the Arizona Senate" (Paper presented at the annual meeting of the Rocky Mountain Social Science Association, 1969); and Chaffey, "The Institutionalization of Legislatures: A Comparative Study," p. 185.

39.   Council of State Governments, *The Book of the States, 1974–1975,* pp. 75–77.

40.   See George B. Galloway, *The Legislative Process in Congress* (New York, 1953), pp. 348–349.

41.   MacNeil, *Forge of Democracy,* p. 62.

42.   Ibid., p. 65.

43.   Truman, *The Congressional Party,* pp. 298, 303.

44.   Ibid., p. 306.

45.   William S. White, *The Taft Story* (New York, 1954), p. 227.

46.   For an excellent account of legislative leaders and their relations with the governor in New York, see Hevesi, *Legislative Politics in New York,* chaps. 2 and 4.

47.   See Jean E. Torcum, "Leadership: The Role and Style of Senator Everett Dirksen," in *To Be a Congressman: The Promise and the Power,* ed. Sven Groennings and Jonathan P. Hawley (Washington, D.C., 1973), pp. 185–224.

48.   See Joseph A. Schlesinger, *How They Became Governor* (East Lansing, Mich., 1957), pp. 11–15, 51–58.

49.   John G. Stewart, "Two Strategies of Leadership: Johnson and Mansfield," in *Congressional Behavior,* ed. Nelson W. Polsby (New York, 1971), p. 74. See also Andrew J. Glass, "Mike Mansfield, Majority Leader" in *Congress in Change,* ed. Norman J. Ornstein (New York, 1975), pp. 142–154.

50.   Donald R. Matthews, *U.S. Senators and Their World* (Chapel Hill, N.C., 1960), p. 126.

51.   John C. Wahlke et al., The *Legislative System* (New York, 1962), chap. 8.

52.   Ibid., p. 183.

53.   Truman, *The Congressional Party,* p. 104.

54.   See Ripley, *Party Leaders in the House of Representatives,* pp. 117–119.

55.   See Rowland Evans and Robert Novak, "The Johnson System," in *The Legislative Process in the U.S. Senate,* ed. Lawrence K. Pettit and Edward Keynes (Chicago, 1969), pp. 196–198.

56.   See Matthews, *U.S. Senators and Their World,* pp. 126–129; and Huitt, "Democratic Party Leadership in the Senate," pp. 337–339.

57.   Douglass Cater, "The Contentious Lords of the Senate," *Reporter* 16, August 1962, p. 27.

58.   See Evans and Novak, "The Johnson System," pp. 179–183, 194–196.

59.   Matthews, *U.S. Senators and Their World,* p. 127.

60.   Huitt, "Democratic Party Leadership in the Senate," p. 338.

61.   An excellent account of how strong state legislative leaders can use various kinds of favors to achieve their goals is found in Hevesi, *Legislative Politics in New York State,* chaps. 2 and 3.

62.   MacNeil, *Forge of Democracy,* p. 94.

63.   *Time,* 13 October 1961, p. 26.

64.   *U.S. News and World Report,* 27 June 1960, p. 89.

65.   See Huitt, "Democratic Party Leadership in the Senate," pp. 339–340.

66.   Stewart, "Two Strategies of Leadership: Johnson and Mansfield," p. 70.

67.   Torcum, "Leadership: The Role and Style of Senator Everett Dirksen," pp. 214, 217.

68.   See Lewis A. Froman and Randall B. Ripley, "Conditions for Party Leadership," *American Political Science Review* 59 (1965):52–63. For an effort to measure the effectiveness of leadership at the state legislative level, see Harlan Hahn, "Leadership Perceptions and Voting Behavior in a One-Party Legislative Body," *Journal of Politics* 32 (1970): 140–155.

CHAPTER SEVEN

Party, Factional,
and Informal Organization

All legislative bodies have leaders, although the roles and techniques of leadership differ from time to time and from place to place. Congress and the state legislatures use standing committees with substantive responsibilities (see Chapter 8), although they vary in importance and in methods of operation. The organizational structure of majority and minority blocs differs substantially, however, from one legislature to another and even within a single legislature over a period of years. An organ such as a rules committee or a caucus may be inconsequential in one legislature, of moderate importance in another, and the main arena for decision making in a third.

In a two-party state, the organizational structure is partisan in nature, and the cohesiveness of the party contributes to the effectiveness of party organs. In one-party states, the structure is factional in nature. In either type of legislature, the leaders usually have considerable discretion in determining what organs will be established and what tasks they will perform. The leaders regard such committees as more or less valuable tools for performing their own tasks more effectively, sharing the work load, or improving communications with rank-and-file members or with the leadership of the opposition. Often, particularly in smaller legislative bodies, the leaders prefer to rely on informal methods and make little use of such organizations. Occasionally, a legislative majority will establish a more formal structure in order to limit the authority of one man and provide a degree of collective leadership. We noted in Chapter 6 that such limitations are often placed on the power of a lieutenant governor who belongs to a party or faction different from a senatorial majority; we took note as well of the organizational changes that resulted from the revolt against a strong Speaker of the United States House early in this century.

In addition to these more formal and visible structures of party and faction, a number of informal organizations are usually found in a legislative body. Some of these are highly informal friendship cliques and social groups, and others are policy-oriented groups that may meet on a regular basis. Another significant group at the congressional level is the state delegation or the members of one party from one state. At the state level, some of the largest county delegations hold regular meetings. These groups are important and deserve to be studied because they are frequently a source of information and voting cues for legislators.

FUNCTIONS

The presiding officer has leadership responsibilities for the entire legislature, but he and the floor leaders also act as party or factional leaders. Leadership committees likewise perform functions both for the legislature as a whole and for a party or faction, and it is useful to distinguish between these two kinds of functions. *Legislative management committees* are those that function to expedite the performance of legislative tasks. They may be used to recommend rules for the legislative body, to select the membership of committees, to assign bills to committees, or to determine priorities for scheduling legislation on the floor. All are responsibilities of leadership that may be performed by one man or by a committee, and all are essential functions for a legislative body. Where committees are used for these purposes, there is no consistent relationship between the titles used and the duties performed. In two-party legislatures, the minority party is often, but not always, represented on these committees.

In a two-party legislature, there are party organizations, which vary in form and importance; in other legislatures, factional organizations are sometimes found. The most common of these organizations is a party or factional *caucus,* which may meet only at the start of a session to choose party leaders or regularly during a session to discuss or to take a stand on legislative issues. Some of the larger legislative parties also use a policy or steering committee to advise the leaders on policy and tactics. The essential function of party organizations is to provide a means of communication between the leaders and the led. For any of several reasons, the leaders may decide that such organizations are unnecessary or ineffective. The party or faction may be such a loose coalition that it lacks common purposes and agreed norms and rarely manifests cohesion in legislative voting. If so, regular meetings of caucuses or policy committees would be useless. Even in a more cohesive party or faction, there may be little use for formal organizations. If the legislative party is small, the purposes of communication may be served by less-formal devices. The styles and tactics of party leaders differ; some prefer to communicate with the rank and file through individual negotiations, an extensive whip organization, or other techniques.

In the few legislative parties where a serious effort is made to enforce party cohesion, a caucus is usually the vehicle for achieving that goal, and its decisions are frequently binding on the membership. In the larger number of legislative parties, where caucus decisions are rarely considered binding, the caucus may strengthen party cohesion by serving as a more effective source of voting cues for the members than an individual leader can. Legislators may give greater heed to party decisions arrived at after discussion in the caucus. The caucus occasionally serves a different purpose, one that causes some party leaders to avoid utilizing it: rank-and-file legislators may perceive the caucus as the best vehicle for imposing restrictions on the leaders' freedom to determine policy stands and party tactics.

LEGISLATIVE MANAGEMENT
COMMITTEES

Most legislative bodies have a rules committee, frequently chaired by the Speaker or presiding officer in the senate and consisting of legislative leaders from both parties. It usually makes recommendations on changes in the rules, a power that occasionally assumes importance. It may have administrative functions. For example, in California, the Rules Committee controls patronage, authorizes legislative expenditures, and screens resolutions creating interim committees.

Although the appointment of standing committees is normally in the hands of the presiding officer, in sixteen upper houses and three lower houses of state legislatures a committee has this function. In some other states, an informal committee may advise the presiding officer. Such a committee is usually bipartisan; frequently, it is called a committee on committees. In a few states, however, this function is performed by a committee with broader powers. In both houses of Congress, there are committees for both parties that make assignments to committees; their operations are described in Chapter 8. In four upper houses and three lower houses, the referring of bills to committee is handled by a committee instead of by the presiding officer; this, too, is normally a bipartisan committee. One of the most powerful is the Reference Committee of the Ohio house, which is authorized to eliminate frivolous or duplicate bills.[1]

Once a bill has been reported by a standing committee, the responsibility for determining priorities for consideration on the floor is usually assumed by the leadership. In many states, the majority leader makes this decision, and he is able to do so because the rules and precedents give him priority of recognition on the floor of the house. In other states, this is the responsibility of the rules committee or of a separate calendar committee, for all or part of the session. Even though such a committee is usually bipartisan, it is normally under the firm control of legislators who are members of, or loyal to, the majority leadership. The committee's power derives primarily from the fact that in the course of setting priorities, it may block action on a bill at least long enough to ensure its defeat in the hectic closing days of a session.[2]

Kentucky and Washington are examples of states in which the rules committees in both houses are used as a powerful tool of legislative leadership. Although bipartisan in makeup, they are under majority control. The leadership uses the rules committee to give priority to party measures, to block bills that they think should not have been reported by committee, and to send measures back to committee with recommendations for amendment. The powerful rules committees in both branches of the Arizona legislature are composed entirely of majority members, including leaders and (in the house) most committee chairmen. In Arizona the rules committee often makes recommendations to the majority party caucus, and its decision on a bill may reflect the sentiment expressed in the caucus; but on some occasions the rules committee either refuses to submit a bill to the caucus or ignores its recommendations. In the 1973 session of the Arizona legislature, the rules committees blocked 9 percent of all bills reported by standing committees.[3]

The importance of calendar control by a committee increases in the closing days of a session, when there is a logjam of bills; and in several states (such as Florida and South Carolina) the committee is not created or is not authorized to set priorities until the last few days of a session. In Utah a so-called Sifting Committee not only gains control of the calendar in the latter part of the session but also takes over jurisdiction of all bills that have been in standing committees, a practice that minimizes the authority of standing committees.[4] In New York the Rules Committee has the same authority, and supercedes other committees. In Iowa the Steering Committee is established to determine priorities among bills that have been reported by committees; near the end of the session it may be replaced by a Sifting Committee, which, like the one in Utah, has complete control of all bills (other than appropriations) that are on the calendar or still in standing committees.[5]

At the state level, the majority leadership normally has de facto control of priorities, either through the power of recognition or through its control of a rules committee, even though the committee is bipartisan. In Congress, there is a sharp difference in practice between the Senate and House. In the Senate, the scheduling power is in the hands of the majority floor leader and the Policy Committee. Although the internal operations of the Policy Committee are not publicized, it appears that the majority leader makes recommendations on scheduling and is rarely overruled by the Policy Committee. It is important to point out, however, that the Senate policy committees rarely block floor consideration of a bill that has been reported out by a standing committee, except in the closing days of a session when some measures must be abandoned because of the shortage of time; at that point, the scheduling function assumes its greatest importance.

United States House Rules Committee

The Rules Committee of the House has the authority to order a special rule, which is the normal method for bringing measures to the House floor unless they are privileged measures (such as appropriations bills). The Rules Committee can also limit debate and amendments through its special rule. To a far greater extent than the Senate policy committees, the House Rules Committee has used this authority to prevent, delay, or force modifications in measures that have emerged from the standing committees. In doing so, it has often acted in response to the wishes of the House leadership, but on other occasions it has acted independently. The House Rules Committee is unique in the sense that the majority leadership has not consistently had firm control over it. It is a bipartisan committee, with ten majority and five minority party members. This two-to-one majority has not guaranteed control to the Democratic leadership because a coalition of Republicans and conservative Democrats has sometimes been able to block legislation. The problem was more serious during the period from 1955 to 1973 when the chairmanship of the committee was held by strong conservatives.

The House Rules Committee developed its great power at a time when it was under the firm control of the majority leadership. Two Speakers who served during the 1890s, Thomas Reed (a Republican) and Charles Crisp (a Democrat), were the first to recognize the full value of the committee as an instrument of control by the leadership. They not only chaired the committee but appointed their top lieutenants as majority party members. They gave the committee authority to determine the legislative program of the House by developing the special rule as the regular method for handling most major legislation in the House. Under Speaker Joseph Cannon, the Rules Committee continued to grow in power and to become, in the words of Wilder H. Haines, a "sleeping giant." In the 1910 –1911 revolt against the Speaker, one of the first and most important steps taken was to remove the Speaker from the Rules Committee and deprive him of the authority to appoint its members. But the authority of the committee was not significantly reduced. Although the committee was generally responsive to majority party leadership until the late 1930s, the growth of the seniority system gave it the same independence from majority-leadership control that other committees have enjoyed, and it has often exercised that independence.[6]

Liberal Democrats at various times have followed three different strategies in trying to prevent a conservative coalition from using the Rules Committee to block legislation. The first is to make it easier to remove from the committee's jurisdiction bills that have become stalled; the second is to change the membership of the committee to make it more responsive to the Democratic majority; the third is to have the Democratic caucus issue instructions to the Democratic members on the committee. During brief periods in the past (1949–1950 and 1965–1966) the House had a rule, adopted in response to liberal pressures, that made it possible, under certain conditions, for the chairman of a committee to get a bill that had been reported by his committee brought to the floor if the Rules Committee failed to approve a special rule for it within twenty-one days. On each occasion the rule was repealed when a more conservative Congress was elected.

A more successful tactic has been to change the Rule Committee's membership. In 1961, when President Kennedy and Speaker Rayburn became concerned about Democratic programs becoming bogged down in the Rules Committee, the Speaker engineered an increase in the Committee's membership from twelve to fifteen, adding two Democrats and one Republican.[7] The proposal, which passed by only five votes, was the first step toward making the Democratic membership of the committee more responsive to majority leadership by gradually adding more liberal members. The retirement of the conservative Mississippi chairman, William Colmer, in 1973, cleared the way for a series of northern liberal chairmen in the years ahead.

A new tactic for making the Rules Committee responsive was inaugurated in 1974 when the Democratic caucus instructed Democratic members of the committee to grant a rule for a tax measure that would permit the House to vote on amendments to curb the oil depletion allowance, a tactic that was repeated for the same issue in 1975, with success. Obviously, such an approach will work only if the Democrats on the Rules Committee agree to follow instructions, as they did in 1975. The willingness of the caucus to remove committee chairmen was first demonstrated in 1975; although not applied to the Rules Committee, it was clearly a sanction that gave more weight to the instructions of the caucus.

There is no consensus among members of the Rules Committee about its responsibility to the majority party. Most liberal Democrats on the committee see it as an instrument of majority leadership. As one member put it, "The whole function is as an arm of the leadership, an arm of the majority of the majority, which is the elected leadership of the House." Republicans and some more conservative Democrats are more likely to assert that the Rules Committee should represent a consensus of thinking in the House or a bipartisan majority.[8] One leading Republican member, John Anderson, has agreed that "basically it has to be an arm of the leadership. But it can only be an arm of the leadership when there's strong leadership. When there isn't, the committee is likely to do what it's been doing—ride off in all directions."[9] Some Democrats on the committee agree that at the present time independent action by the Rules Committee is an indication that the members believe the leadership has either failed to make its wishes clear or has failed to assess accurately the mood and preferences of the House.

The Rules Committee of the House has impressive powers. Aside from private bills, noncontroversial bills approved by unanimous consent, and such privileged measures as appropriations bills, legislation that is reported by a standing committee must receive a special rule from the Rules Committee in order to get consideration in the House. The committee holds a hearing at which the leadership of the standing committee testifies; it may then grant a special rule, refuse one, or perhaps delay while it negotiates informally with the standing committee on revisions in the bill. Sometimes the committee refuses even to grant a hearing on a bill, but this tactic is seldom followed in the case of major pieces of legislation. From 1961 to 1968 the Rules Committee refused hearings for forty bills and rules for seven bills in an average Congress, but only twenty-nine of these died in committee on the average, with the rest reaching the floor through suspension of rules, unanimous consent, the twenty-one day rule (in 1965–1966), or occasionally by means of a substitute bill. During that time, approximately one-third of the bills blocked by the Rules Committee were part of the President's program.[10] Since that time, the number of hearings and rules denied by the Rules Committee has dropped sharply, however. The importance of the committee's authority cannot be measured entirely by counting the number of hearings or rules rejected, because, by delaying or threatening to deny a rule, it can force revision or modification of bills by standing committees.

The Rules Committee may grant either an open or a closed rule. The closed rule either imposes an absolute ban on amendments or permits only certain amendments or only those proposed by members of the standing committee. Closed rules, which are usually granted at the request of the House leadership or the chairman of the reporting committee, are generally reserved for such matters as tax or tariff measures, both because of their complex nature and because of their vulnerability to logrolling on the floor. With an open rule, a bill is subject to amendment by any member, who is given five minutes to speak for it.[11] The Democratic caucus has adopted a rule providing that anyone seeking a closed rule must give notice of this intention, and that if fifty or more Democrats give written notice that they wish to propose an amendment, the Democratic caucus shall meet and determine whether the proposed amendment should be allowed to be considered by the House. The Rules Committee sometimes grants a rule waiving points of order against the inclusion of legislative matters in an appropriations bill, which is usually the only occasion for appropriations bills to be channeled through the Rules Committee. The committee, in approving a special rule, always specifies the amount of time to be permitted for debate. A majority of these rules permit four hours or less of debate, and many permit only one hour. The House may always refuse to accept a rule, but such action prevents consideration of the bill on the floor. Between 1961 and 1972, only thirteen rules were defeated by the House; but in 1973 alone another thirteen were defeated, apparently because the committee was more liberal in granting rules and paid less attention than in the past to the likelihood that House members would reject the bill.[12] In most cases a proposed rule was defeated because of House opposition to the substance of the bill rather than to the terms of the rule.

PARTY ORGANIZATIONS

The most common form of party organization is the caucus. In Congress and in two-party state legislatures, each party holds a caucus to choose its leaders and its candidate for presiding officer of the senate or house. In some legislative parties, this is the only use made of the caucus; in others, the caucus meets more often and serves other purposes. Caucuses have been powerful organs of party discipline during some periods of congressional history, but congressional caucuses today seldom meet and have little influence and no authority over the rank-and-file members. A survey conducted almost two decades ago showed that in only about half of the two-party states did party caucuses meet frequently to deal with important issues and that in only a few was there a regular weekly or daily caucus meeting.[13] Since that time, increased two-party competition has prompted greater use of the caucus in some states.

Caucuses in the States

In those states where the caucus assumes some importance, it usually meets at least once a week early in the session and more often, perhaps daily, late in the session, when the legislative tempo increases. The caucus serves primarily as a communications device. It gives the leadership a chance to explain which bills are of concern to the party and to urge a particular course of action with regard to these bills. It gives the rank-and-file members a chance to express their views. If it becomes clear that the party is seriously divided, the leaders have an opportunity to revise or delay the bill and thereby to prevent the division from being transferred to the floor of the house. If the caucus demonstrates that there is substantial agreement concerning a measure, the members may be more likely to go along with it in a roll-call vote; but in most states the decisions reached in a caucus are rarely binding on the membership.

For many years the classic example of a powerful caucus was found in New Jersey, where the majority party caucus in each house met daily and decided which bills would be passed and which would die. These decisions almost always determined the fate of bills on the floor. The power of the caucus was so great that the standing committees had no significant functions and seldom met. In recent years, however, the caucuses in both houses have reduced the scope of their activities, and now take action only on a limited number of bills designated by the leaders as party policy measures. As a consequence, the committee system in the New Jersey legislature has begun to develop some independent authority.[14]

Several of the other states where the legislative caucus is important are ones where the state party organization is strong and each legislative party rests on a base of rather homogeneous constituencies; these include Pennsylvania, Connecticut, Illinois, Rhode Island, and Ohio. In Pennsylvania, "the caucus as an institution shapes the ways that committees function and it has a vital role in determining the style of floor debate." Caucuses meet at least once a week, and more often when major issues are pending. The members review the bills that are scheduled for consideration on the floor, and on a relatively small number of bills they decide to take a party position; on those issues the leadership takes a head count of the party membership, and there is some pressure on members to vote with their party unless they have a valid reason for not doing so. In Connecticut both of the senate parties hold daily caucuses in which most bills are discussed more thoroughly than they are on the floor. In the house, where the caucuses meet less regularly, their larger size makes them less useful as arenas for discussing issues, and the party leadership plays a larger role in discussion and decision making. In Illinois the Democratic party leadership uses the caucus to brief members on party policy, to plan strategy, and to line up votes; the less disciplined Republican party uses the caucus to discuss issues and determine whether there is enough consensus to develop a party position, but the caucus is very rarely used to bind the members to a position.[15] In Ohio the senate Democratic caucus meets daily and sometimes takes votes, but the house Democratic leaders seldom use the caucus.

The caucus has also developed some importance in a number of states where state party organizations have not been traditionally strong. One example is the Arizona legislature, where partisan caucuses have only recently replaced bipartisan or factional ones. There the majority party caucus meets weekly to hear the recommendations of the rules committee and to vote on whether the bills should be reported to the floor. Although most measures are handled in open session, those measures designated by the leadership as party policy issues are discussed in closed meetings of the caucus; on these party issues a vote in the caucus large enough to insure passage on the floor (a majority of all senators or representatives) is usually required before the leadership will bring the bill to the floor. In California the caucus has become a significant institution only in recent years. In the assembly Speaker Jesse Unruh, a powerful party leader, made effective use of the Democratic caucus during the 1960s, using it to discuss tactics, and, during years of a Republican administration, to develop alternatives to the governor's program. In the senate, traditionally a less partisan body, the Democratic caucus developed in the late 1960s in response to the demands of junior members and despite the foot-dragging of the leadership. In both houses the Republicans eventually followed the Democratic lead in developing caucuses.[16]

Prior to 1974, Minnesota legislators were elected on nonpartisan ballots, but the party affiliation of most members was known and caucuses have been relatively strong for a number of years. The caucuses have met weekly or more often, to discuss strategy and to take head counts on bills. In the Democratic caucus in particular, the members are expected to support the position of the caucus on those bills that the caucus designates as party measures. In 1975 the caucuses were opened to the public; as a result, there was less discussion of issues, and more decisions were made in the party steering committee with less input from the rank-and-file members. A recent study by the Citizens Conference on State Legislatures shows that in most states the party caucuses remain closed; most of the exceptions are in legislatures where the party is not very strong, including several of those in the South.[17]

In the Florida legislature, which had been exclusively Democratic for many years, the election of substantial numbers of Republicans in the mid-1960s led rapidly to the establishment of caucuses by both parties. There were brief, unsuccessful efforts in 1967 to impose binding votes on the members. Since that time, the caucuses have been used by the leadership to provide information for the members and (particularly on the Democratic side) to apply pressure on members to support the party's position on issues. In this way the caucuses appear to have contributed significantly to the development of partisan cohesion in the Florida legislature.[18]

The Congressional Caucus

Caucuses have been used in Congress intermittently since its first session, when the followers of Alexander Hamilton held meetings to reach agreement on the issues confronting Congress. When Jefferson became President in 1801, his supporters made regular use of the caucus, which became, in the words of Ralph V. Harlow, "the most noteworthy institution in Congress." Federal newspapers frequently referred in scathing terms to this institution that the Jeffersonians had borrowed from the Federalists: "The Democrats in Congress are adopting of late quite an economical plan of making laws. All business is to be settled in *caucuses* before it comes before the House; and the arguments or motives be given in *newspapers* afterwards. The federal members are to be treated as nullities." The caucus was used to determine policy as well as to select candidates for Speaker and members of committees; party caucuses during the first quarter of the nineteenth century were used to nominate presidential candidates. Under Jefferson, the caucus was a device for effecting presidential leadership; he sometimes presided at the meetings. After Henry Clay became Speaker in 1811, the House caucus became a tool of congressional leaders, under whom it remained an effective organ of party unity for several years. The caucus withered away in the years before the Civil War because sectional conflicts caused divisions within the parties and frustrated the party leadership.[19]

In the years after the Civil War, neither party had strong leadership in the Senate, and caucuses were of relatively little importance. From the mid-1880s until about 1911, the Senate Republican party (usually in the majority) was dominated by a group of particularly effective leaders who frequently used the caucus as a means of mobilizing party support. "The Republican caucus was not binding, and yet its decisions commanded obedience for party leadership was capable of enforcing discipline. Senators could no longer act with impunity unless they were willing to forgo favorable committee posts and control of the chamber proceedings."[20] The caucus met frequently to discuss legislation and to iron out differences so that the Republican senators could vote with a high degree of unity on the floor. During this period, the Senate Democratic party made some use of the caucus, but the party's minority status reduced its importance.

In the House, the caucus developed gradually in the late nineteenth century. As successive Speakers developed the authority of that office, they began to employ the party caucus once again as an effective body. Under Thomas B. Reed, for example, in the last decade of the nineteenth century, the caucus system was used to "commit members of the party, in secret and binding conference, to a party program agreed upon in advance of action in the House, and it gave to the organization a powerful weapon for the coercion of recalcitrants within the party."[21] Conformity to the decisions of the caucus became a prerequisite for getting and keeping choice committee seats.

The House Democratic party, which had taken part in the reform that stripped the Speaker of much of his power (in 1910–1911), gained a majority in 1911; and in 1913, with an increased majority, it faced the necessity of filling the power vacuum and developing the unity necessary to enact President Wilson's program. The answer of the Democratic party leadership, especially in the House, was to use the caucus as the catalyst for unity. During Wilson's first term the Democratic caucus functioned more effectively than any congressional caucus has since. It made decisions on legislative issues that were binding on Democratic members if passed by a two-thirds majority of those present and an absolute majority of the Democratic members. Democrats were permitted to avoid being bound on constitutional issues or on those which they had made a prior commitment to constituents. The caucus sometimes reached agreement on the details of a bill before it was introduced, and its approval in committee became a mere formality. At times it issued instructions to the Democratic majority on standing committees, including the Rules Committee. Moreover, Democratic members of committees often caucused to decide on positions to take in committee.[22]

In the period after World War II, little use was made of party caucuses because the congressional leaders, particularly on the Democratic side, did not consider them productive. They felt that caucuses were more likely to be divisive than unifying in their effects, and in Speaker Sam Rayburn's words, "You lose more votes than you gain." Ralph K. Huitt has explained the reason: "Party members frequently stand together for different reasons, but talking about these reasons may only open old wounds and drive them apart."[23] The party leaders preferred to work behind the scenes, without the limitations on their freedom to negotiate and to plan tactics that might be imposed by the caucus.

In more recent years the caucuses have begun to assume greater importance, partly because new leaders have had different viewpoints, and partly because rank-and-file members have demanded more caucuses in order to increase their voice in party decisions. Mike Mansfield, the Senate Democratic leader since 1961, was one of those who questioned the value of caucus meetings, but he began to make increasing use of them, and in 1971 he announced his willingness to hold a caucus whenever any Democratic senator requested one. In practice, there have been one or two Senate Democratic caucuses a month in recent years, usually at the initiative of Mansfield and the Democratic Policy Committee, but sometimes at the request of other senators. The caucus often takes votes on issues, and its decisions are announced to the press. Although the votes are not binding on the members, they appear to have some effect in establishing a party position. During the Nixon administration, for example, the Senate Democratic caucus frequently criticized President Nixon's policies in Vietnam and demanded more rapid withdrawal of American military forces. The Senate Republicans also hold occasional caucuses, which are called conferences to emphasize the nonbinding character of their decisions. The conference sometimes takes votes on issues, and its decisions are released to the press. Normally a conference is called to hear recommendations from the Republican Policy Committee, but it may be called at the request of any five senators. Because most meetings of the Policy Committee are open to all Republicans (and are held weekly), the distinction between the two groups is somewhat artificial.

In recent years the House Republican conferences have met on an average of once or twice a month, for a variety of purposes. During Republican administrations there have been briefing sessions at which administration officials explained legislative proposals and answered questions. At other sessions the Policy Committee has presented its recommendations and legislation has been discussed. Only rarely has the conference taken a vote on a major legislative issue, and, under conference rules, these votes are not binding on the members. The conferences do serve the purpose of improving communications between leaders and rank and file and giving the average member a sense of participation in party affairs.

The most significant development with respect to congressional caucuses in recent years has been the emergence of the House Democratic caucus as a major decision-making body.[24] This has occurred despite the reluctance of some Democratic leaders and largely because of the initiative of a group of liberal Democratic representatives, known as the Democratic Study Group (described later in this chapter). The starting point for revival of the caucus was the adoption in 1969 of a rule providing that the House Democratic caucus would hold regular monthly meetings and would also meet at the request of the caucus chairman, the floor leader, or any fifty members. Liberal Democrats who were interested in procedural reforms believed that frequent meetings would make possible an incremental approach to reform and would keep the issue before the caucus on a continuing basis, instead of just every two years at organizational meetings. At first this tactic appeared to be of limited effectiveness; nineteen of the twenty-seven nonorganizational caucuses held from January, 1969, to June, 1971, were adjourned because they lacked a quorum, and some representatives deliberately boycotted those at which the Vietnam war was scheduled to be discussed. In July, 1971, however, the rules were changed to ban meetings of standing committees when the caucus was scheduled to meet and to permit the caucus to discuss issues (without a vote) in the absence of a quorum. The caucus soon began to meet more regularly and to grow in importance.

It is important to understand both the scope and the limits of the House Democratic caucus's activities and power. The caucus has devoted its attention to a number of procedural reforms—many of them involving the standing committees—and to discussion of and recommendations on substantive issues. One such step was the establishment in 1973 of a Democratic Policy and Steering

Committee (discussed later in this chapter). Another was the establishment in 1970 of a committee under Representative Hansen to study problems of standing committees and seniority. A series of recommendations by the Hansen Committee, beginning in 1971, have been adopted by the caucus and have had significant effects on the committee system.

The major thrust of the procedural reforms adopted by the House Democratic caucus from 1971 to 1975 has been to erode the independent authority of committees, and particularly of committee chairmen, and to assert the authority of the caucus over Democratic members of committees. The purpose has been to reduce the ability of conservative committee members and chairmen to delay or defeat bills that have the support of a Democratic majority. The changes in the seniority system and in the operation of committees and subcommittees are discussed in more detail in subsequent chapters, but the most important changes that have resulted from the caucus decisions can be outlined briefly here.

1. *Committee organization.* Each standing committee of the House now has a caucus consisting of all of its Democratic members, which meets at the request of the chairman or a majority of its members. This caucus has authority to determine the jurisdiction and number of subcommittees, their budget and staffing, and the selection of subcommittee chairmen. All of these powers formerly belonged to the committee chairmen.

2. *Selection of committee members and chairmen.* At the start of the 1975 session, the caucus transferred authority to nominate committee members and chairmen from Democratic members of the Ways and Means Committee to the Policy and Steering Committee, which is less independent of the caucus. It also provided that the selection of subcommittee chairmen of the Appropriations Committee, as well as chairmen of all committees, would be subject to caucus ratification. In 1971 the caucus limited all members to a single subcommittee chairmanship. Beginning in 1971 the caucus took a series of steps to make the selection of committee chairmen less automatically a matter of seniority and to make it easier to challenge incumbent chairmen by requiring secret ballots on ratification of their reappointment. By 1975 this challenge to the independent authority of chairmen grew so strong that the caucus voted to oust three incumbent chairmen.

3. *Instructions to committees.* In recent years the caucus has adopted the practice of issuing instructions to Democratic members of committees. In 1974 and again in 1975 the caucus voted to instruct Democrats on the Rules Committee to permit amendments to a tax bill involving oil depletion allowances to come to a vote on the floor. In 1974 the caucus instructed the Rules Committee to delay a bill on committee reform until it had been studied by the caucus committee chaired by Representative Hansen. In 1972 the caucus instructed Democrats on the Foreign Affairs Committee to prepare and report legislation setting a date for termination of the American military involvement in Indochina. Although such instructions have been issued infrequently, they have generally been followed by Democratic members of committees. Obviously the significance of caucus instructions to committee members depends on whether they are followed. A report of the Democratic Study Group argued that Democratic committee members were obligated to follow such instructions because the caucus has complete control

over committee assignments of Democrats under long-established House norms. (The report cited only two examples of such instructions having been given by the caucus between 1924 and 1972, however.)[25] Without any doubt, the demonstrated willingness of the caucus to remove committee chairmen in 1975 has increased the likelihood that Democratic members of committees will be responsive to instructions from the caucus.

In recent years the House Democratic caucus has become a forum for discussion of a variety of substantive issues, and on a number of occasions the caucus has gone on record in support of a particular position on an issue. During the period from 1971 to 1974 the caucus endorsed a number of steps designed to end the involvement of American ground and air forces in Vietnam and Cambodia; it took stands on economic and tax questions and the Democratic party charter; and it recommended a probe of President Nixon's role in the Watergate coverup, for example.

The rules of the House Democratic caucus used to provide that on policy questions a two-thirds vote of those present and voting, if it constituted a majority of all Democratic members, would be binding on all members—although a member was exempt if a constitutional issue were involved or if he had made contrary pledges to constituents prior to his election. In fact, a binding resolution was adopted only once between 1935 and 1975, a resolution in 1971 on minority committee staffing.[26] In September, 1975, the caucus rules were revised to abolish binding resolutions on legislation, although they may still be applied to floor votes on House officers and committee chairmen. The step was taken primarily because the binding resolution, though rarely used, had become a target of criticism. At the same time the caucus voted to open to the public meetings of the caucus dealing with legislation (but not other topics) unless a majority of members voted publicly for a closed session. This change was supported by some members who had been active in the drive to open up committee meetings and also by opponents of a strong caucus, who believed that the effectiveness of the caucus would be reduced by open sessions.

A number of Republican congressmen have been critical of the revival of what they describe as "King Caucus." The abolition of binding resolutions for floor votes and the end of secret sessions on legislation remove two of the features most often criticized. A continuing source of controversy is the question of whether the caucus should instruct Democratic committee members and whether those members will obey such instructions. If that authority is used frequently, it is likely not only to weaken the committee system, but also to force action on issues before they have been thoroughly studied in committee. It seems probable that such instructions will be issued infrequently, and only when a committee has been delaying a bill or its Democratic members are clearly out of step with the caucus. The reasserted authority of the caucus is likely to have a more subtle effect, as committees respond to the wishes of Democratic representatives with greater speed in order to avoid the necessity of instructions. Even among Democrats who support a more active role for the caucus, there is no consensus about the limits of that role. Efforts to expand that role, particularly if they interfere with the authority of committees, are likely to meet with increasing resistance.

Policy Committees

State legislative leaders have made little use of policy or steering committees to plan tactics or determine party policies. The leaders frequently confer among themselves, of course, but seldom in any formal way or according to any schedule. The leaders of the administration party in both houses are likely to meet jointly with the governor. Although a number of state legislative parties include a policy or steering committee in their formal organizational structure, the practical use of such committees varies with the preferences of the leadership. In strong two-party states caucuses are more likely to assume importance than policy committees. The tasks of tactical planning, discussion, and communication of policy decisions are performed either by the caucus or by informal leadership groups; and the task of scheduling legislation is often performed by a rules committee or by the majority-party leaders.

Most congressional institutions have greater durability than their counterparts in the states, and the large size of congressional parties (compared with those in most states) creates more serious problems in communication for the leadership. For these or other reasons, policy or steering committees have assumed greater, though intermittent, importance in Congress. House Republicans used a Steering Committee in the 1920s as a strategy board to fill the gap left by the decline in importance of the Speaker. Senate Republicans used a Steering Committee intermittently beginning in the 1880s, particularly when the party had a Senate majority.

The report of the LaFollette-Monroney committee, which led to the 1946 Legislative Reorganization Act, recommended that both parties in both houses establish policy committees with paid staffs. This was not included in the Act because of opposition by leaders in the House, particularly Speaker Rayburn. The Senate, however, established policy committees with paid staffs for its parties in a 1946 appropriations act. House Republicans transformed their Steering Committee into a Policy Committee in 1949, but it did not emerge as a functioning group until Charles Halleck became Republican leader in 1959. A series of efforts by some House Democrats to establish such a body did not achieve success until 1973, when the caucus established the Democratic Policy and Steering Committee.[27]

When the LaFollette-Monroney committee recommended the establishment of policy committees in 1946, it said that their purpose should be "to formulate the over-all legislative policy of the two parties."[28] But the committees have rarely performed this function, and very few members of the committees have believed that they should. Senate Democratic Floor Leader Mansfield has consistently maintained that policy "is made in the legislative committees and is determined by a majority of the members of the committees. The policy committee, so-called, cannot go against the wishes of the legislative committees. All the policy committee can do is to expedite legislation."[29] In the case of the administration party, members of the policy committees have generally recognized the dominant policy-making role of the President. The most important function of the policy committees is probably that of communication. When a number of junior Republican representatives rebelled against the party leadership in 1959 and demanded revival of the Policy Committee, they saw it as a device for making the leadership more aware of, and more sensitive to, the viewpoints of the rank and file. According to Jones, the House Republican Policy Committee has developed into a vehicle of communication, "a device for effecting unity, not division, and there is no point in putting individual members on the spot" by demanding that they support formal decisions of the committee.[30]

The four policy committees in Congress differ both in structure and in operating style.[31] In recent years Mike Mansfield has developed the Senate Democratic Policy Committee into an important leadership body, one that works very closely with him in developing tactics for expediting passage of Democratic legislative proposals. Mansfield chairs the committee, which includes three other party leaders, six members who serve on the committee as long as they remain in the Senate, and four more members, who also serve on the Legislative Review Committee (to screen less controversial legislation). The committee meets regularly every two weeks and occasionally more often. As long as the Democratic party is in the majority, it advises the floor leader on scheduling legislation, and it may decide for tactical reasons to hold up a bill until chances for its passage have improved. The committee carries on informal negotiations in an effort to develop compromises that will be acceptable to as large a proportion of the Democratic senators as possible. On some issues the Policy Committee makes a formal recommendation, which is then transmitted to the Democratic caucus. For example, during the Nixon administration the Policy Committee adopted a large number of recommendations aimed at speeding American withdrawal from Vietnam; it has also played a significant role in developing Democratic positions on economic issues, such as taxation and energy.

Membership on the Senate Republican Policy Committee, except for a number of leaders serving ex officio, rotates among Republican senators. It often includes most of those facing reelection in the next election year. The chairman of the committee is different from the floor leader. The focus of the committee has shifted from time to time, with more effort being devoted to developing a Republican position on issues when the party does not control the White House. In recent years the Policy Committee has held a weekly luncheon to which all Republican senators are invited and which is attended by many of them; it also holds some meetings open only to its members. The luncheon meeting provides an opportunity for discussion of pending legislation and developments in committees, as well as for reports on leadership meetings in the White House during Republican administrations. Occasionally the Policy Committee makes recommendations to the conference regarding a legislative issue. Because almost half of the Republican senators are on the Policy Committee and most of its meetings are open to all, the Policy Committee does not play a very distinctive or formal role, but instead, it serves primarily as a communications vehicle. It also maintains a staff that carries out research for Republican senators.

The House Republican Policy Committee has a more elaborate structure designed to be broadly representative. In addition to the ex officio members, it includes members from each of nine geographic regions in proportion to the number of Republicans in each, a group of junior members representing those elected for the first time in each of the recent Congresses, and a number of at-large members chosen by the leadership. The Policy Committee meets every week. After bills have emerged from committee, they are discussed by the Policy Committee, and if there is substantial consensus on the issues involved, it may take a formal stand on a bill. The statement is issued to the press and sent to all members; frequently, it is discussed in a Republican conference. From 1959 through 1974 the Policy Committee issued about 300 policy statements, an average of 19 a year. In 1974, for example, the Policy Committee issued a total of 14 statements, dealing with such topics as pension reform, housing for the elderly, strip mining, election reform, and changes in House rules and House committee reform. The statements often included sharp criticism of Democratic proposals.

It is always difficult to evaluate how effective such an institution is in enhancing party unity, but Charles O. Jones concluded from a study of the committee during its first years of operation that it was the most effective of the policy committees in Congress. A study by Evelyn Schipske concluded that the policy statements issued by the committee had reflected issues where there was already broadly based consensus in the party and did not themselves have a great impact on the voting of Republican representatives. Her data show that when votes were taken on bills on which the Policy Committee had taken a stand, an average of 86 percent of the Republicans supported that position, while 46 percent of the Democrats supported it. The Republican average was fairly consistent from one Congress to another, but the Democratic level of support varied, apparently because of differences in the types of issues and the nature of the Policy Committee position. As a whole, about half of the committee's statements were in support of bills and half either opposed them completely or offered basic changes or alternatives. Sharp differences in voting between the parties tended to occur on issues where the Republican Policy Committee was in opposition to a bill.[32]

The House Democratic Policy and Steering Committee is the most recent of the policy committees to come into operation, in reality and not just on paper, and it is too early to judge how effective it will be. Like its Republican counterpart, it includes party leaders, regional representatives, and at-large members. It is chaired by the Speaker. Its most important function, acquired in 1975, is to recommend the selection of members and chairmen of standing committees. It meets about every two weeks. In 1975 it established a task force to cooperate with a similar group of Democratic senators in preparing recommendations on economic recovery and energy policies. If the House Democratic caucus continues to grow in importance, the Policy Committee may develop into an executive committee of that body, making recommendations to it and screening proposals put on the caucus agenda, but it is not yet clear whether the Policy and Screening Committee will develop such a role for itself. Its role and effectiveness, like those of other policy committees, largely depend on the leadership.

INFORMAL LEGISLATIVE ORGANIZATION

The most visible features of the internal organization of legislative bodies are the structures of leadership, party, and committee. Not so visible, but perhaps equally important to the maintenance of the legislature, are the informal, unofficial organizations, committees, or cliques with which legislators associate and within which friendship roles are enacted. In the following sections, several types of informal legislative groups are briefly discussed: state (or county) delegations, policy groups, and social groups and friendship cliques.

State Delegations

There are a number of reasons why a congressman might be expected to develop contacts with the members of his state delegation and to get information and voting cues from them. A new congressman's earliest contacts are likely to be with members of his state delegation, and he is dependent on them for help in learning his way around Congress and the bureaucracy. Members of a congressional delegation, particularly those in the same party, are likely to represent districts with similar interests and to have similar perceptions and viewpoints on issues. They also share a concern for legislation that has particular importance for their state as a whole.

Studies of voting behavior in the United States House have shown that some bipartisan state delegations have a substantial degree of cohesion, but a much higher level of cohesion is found among the members in a state delegation belonging to a single party. The level of cohesion is not consistent. Some state party delegations vote as a solid bloc on most bills; others are divided into factions, perhaps because of regional or district variations within the state. But most state party delegations have much greater unity than the political party as a whole in the House and somewhat greater unity than regional groupings of representatives, such as southern Democrats or midwestern Republicans. This suggests that the voting cohesion of state party delegations results not only from similarities of district interests and viewpoints, but also from the exchange of information and viewpoints in formal or informal meetings of delegation members.[33]

According to the data collected by Randall B. Ripley from interviews, approximately half of the state party delegations in the United States House of Representatives have regular and rather frequent meetings. In most cases, one purpose of these meetings is to seek agreement on the stand that members will take on an issue. Some party delegations, of course, consist of so few members that there is no need for anything as formal as a regular meeting. Regular meetings in larger delegations are least likely to be held if there are serious divisions among the members on policy questions. As one congressman put it, "We seldom get together. We are split all over the lot. There is little point in meeting; we could never arrive at a consensus on anything."[34]

When the members represent similar interests and viewpoints, delegation meetings are more likely to be productive. Their purpose is to provide assistance to the members but not to put pressure on them. A member of one delegation explains:

> We meet informally every ten days or so. We know the probable position of everyone. We never bind ourselves. But we do have lots of personal conversation. And there are informal efforts to get unity.[35]

One reason for a state party delegation to stick together on votes as much as possible is that the individual member may be protected from criticism if he votes along with the members of his state party. According to one experienced congressman:

> State party delegations generally vote together. They try to. . . . It is very important, in terms of re-election to vote together; if one member strays, the press and his opponents in the district will notice it. They want to be able to say that all members agreed.[36]

A state party delegation may also vote together in an effort to improve their bargaining position regarding bills that particularly affect their state. The Illinois Democratic delegation is the best example of one that deliberately tries to maintain unity for bargaining purposes.

Some state party delegations whose members represent various kinds of districts and who seldom vote together nevertheless find it useful to meet regularly. A good example is the Texas Democratic delegation, which has been meeting for weekly luncheons for the last thirty years and whose members have frequent contacts on other occasions. Even though the members disagree on many issues, such contacts improve their chances of getting good committee assignments for members of the delegation and getting federal projects for their districts. Barbara Deckard, who has studied a number of the larger state party delegations, has concluded that a high degree of interaction is likely if a large proportion of members intend to pursue a career in the House, if there is relatively low turnover among members, and if there are not sharp differences in political style among the members. She points out that any congressman needs allies to achieve his objectives, and one who comes from a large state party delegation has an advantage in gaining such allies.[37]

State party delegations serve as an important link between committees and congressmen in the communications network of the House of Representatives. The larger state party delegations make an effort to place a member on each of the standing committees that is important to the state. As one member of a large delegation said, "We have good committee spread. The man on the committee takes the lead, keeps the rest of us informed about what's going on." If a state party delegation holds regular meetings, one of the purposes is to hear analysis of pending legislation from those members who serve on the committees reporting the bills. Even if there are no regular meetings, the state party delegation may provide a framework for contacts between members and nonmembers of standing committees.[38]

In some state legislatures the county delegations representing large metropolitan counties perform functions similar to those of state delegations in Congress, on either a partisan or a bipartisan basis. They may caucus on a regular basis to discuss general legislation or bills of particular importance to their county. Many state legislatures devote much of their time to local legislation, and it is often the practice to pass such bills only if they have unanimous, or at least overwhelming, support from legislators representing the county to be affected. Consequently, legislators from such counties often find it necessary to maintain unity on local bills. They may meet as a group with local officials or even hold hearings in their home county so that interested persons can express their views.

Policy Groups

There are several organizations in Congress that are outside the formal party or committee structure but that have a definite policy focus and represent members with similar ideological viewpoints. The oldest and best known of these is the Democratic Study Group. It was formally organized by liberal Democratic representatives late in the 1959 session of Congress, the outgrowth of an informal grouping developed in the two preceding years. Like their Republican counterparts at that time, many of the younger Democratic representatives were dissatisfied with the performance of the party leadership and were frustrated by their inability to make their own voices heard by the leadership. The Democrats in this group are distinctly liberal in orientation and represent primarily urban areas in the North and West; to a greater extent than has been true of the Republican dissidents, viewpoints on policy issues have provided the best clue both to the unity of this group and to their differences with other members of the House Democratic party. Their dissatisfaction with the party leadership has resulted from the belief that it was too cautious and too willing to compromise with more conservative elements in the party. The Democrats, unlike the Republican dissidents, decided to work through a distinct organization.

Liberal Democratic representatives organized not only to make their voices more powerful but also to serve their own needs. They needed information about the substance of issues, agreement within the group on tactics, and voting cues on the many detailed provisions of legislation coming to a vote. Kenneth Kofmehl, who has studied the group's development, defines the Democratic Study Group as "an institutional response to these needs for improved communications." Obviously, the organization has no sanctions that it can impose on disloyal members; in fact, one source of its effectiveness is that its membership is voluntary and that individual congressmen can avoid interaction with the group on specific issues when they find it necessary. The members perceive the group as a service agency, providing information, facilitating prompt communications among members, and giving members a sense of identification with like-minded Democrats. The group has an executive committee and a group of task forces that concentrate on a variety of substantive questions, such as civil rights, consumer affairs, and international affairs and defense policy. It has a small professional staff to assist in the research function. The Study Group provides its members with brief fact sheets on pending legislation and produces longer booklets on major issues. It operates a whip system to alert the members to important questions that are coming to a vote on the floor. The Study Group also provides campaign materials and raises funds to support the election campaigns of its members and of liberals who are challenging Republicans in marginal districts.[39]

It is difficult to measure the impact of the Democratic Study Group, just as it is always difficult to measure the effect of legislative institutions. One study of roll-call voting has concluded that the DSG has had some success in increasing the voting turnout of its members and also enhancing their cohesion on issues of interest to the DSG. "Our findings pertaining to cohesion indicate that for the most part DSG cohesion has increased relative to that of other groups and . . . that the Democratic Study Group members are, on most issues, quite united and that they constitute a formidable bloc. The number and proportion of members comprising the cohesive core has increased rather steadily as the DSG has widened the scope of its research and communications network."[40] Perhaps more important has been the role of the DSG leadership and staff in planning the tactics and organizing the series of steps that have led to the revival of the House Democratic caucus and the erosion of independent power exercised by committees. Moreover, the DSG has provided nonincumbent Democratic candidates with funds and campaign research materials and has run orientation programs for freshman Democrats—activities that made it possible to mobilize many of the freshmen in support of the reforms adopted by the caucus.

The Wednesday Group is an organization of liberal Republican representatives that bears a limited resemblance to the Democratic Study Group. It is a much smaller group, with only twenty-nine members in 1973, and its impact has been much less. Membership is by invitation, and an effort is made to have a varied geographic representation, as well as members from most of the standing committees. The members hold weekly meetings to discuss pending legislation and other issues. It has a small staff that prepares research papers, and it occasionally sets up small study groups to explore issues in depth. Unlike the DSG, the Wednesday Group does not attempt to mobilize voting power on the floor of the House. The Wednesday Group has persisted because its members value the opportunity to exchange views and information with like-minded colleagues and because they believe the Republican party needs innovative ideas.[41]

In 1969 the nine black members of Congress organized a Black Caucus. Since that time the number of black congressmen has approximately doubled, and the Black Caucus has become more vocal and active. It has organized conferences on topics such as education for blacks and the impact of budget cuts and impoundment on programs of interest to blacks. In 1971 it held a much-publicized and long-delayed meeting with President Nixon at which it presented a list of sixty recommendations for legislative and administrative action. The Black Caucus, which is obviously handicapped by its limited size, has sometimes worked with other groups in the Congress, notably the Women's Caucus, a group that has membership overlapping that of the Black Caucus.[42]

It has been common for both Democratic and Republican freshmen to set up organizations, some of which have persisted—at least as social groups—beyond the first two years. But it has not been usual for such groups to have any particular political impact in Congress. In 1975, however, there were seventy-five freshman Democrats, constituting more than one-sixth of the House. In December, 1974, during the organizational session of Congress they met and set up an informal organization. Most significantly, they invited committee chairmen to appear before them and, in effect, explain their records and appeal for votes. The poor impression made by several chairmen in these meetings contributed to their defeat in the Democratic caucus. The meetings of the Democratic freshmen with committee chairmen symbolized most dramatically the changing norms of Congress.

Social Groups and Friendship Cliques

Legislative social groups are fairly common in Congress and also in state legislatures. The classes of entering freshman congressmen (Eighty-seventh Club, Eighty-eighth Club) and their outgrowths with broader memberships, like the Chowder and Marching, SOS, and Acorn Republican groups, illustrate the rather active social life of national representatives. The House and Senate prayer-breakfast groups, which include members of both parties, meet weekly for breakfast and prayer; and the "bonds between members of the group are unusually strong . . . often expressed in acts of legislative cooperation."[43] A study of the 1967 California legislature identified a prayer-breakfast group as one of the most important social groups. There were several luncheon groups sponsored by lobbyists and a group of brown-bag lunchers who explicitly excluded lobbyists. In addition, there were at least two discussion groups that held regular seminars throughout the session, one dealing with ghetto problems and one with fiscal affairs.[44] Clearly, some of these groups at the national and state levels have greater policy implications than others, but all offer opportunities for legislators to exchange views, gain information, and develop contacts with other legislators who may become important sources of voting cues.

Although there is much to learn about the influence of legislative friendships upon policy making, there are some clues to their importance. At least some members of Congress are convinced that the bipartisan exercises in the congressional gymnasium have policy implications. One congressman said:

> The gymnasium group is about the most influential one in the House. That isn't a joke either. Actually a lot of work is done in the gym. You can accomplish a lot on an informal, casual basis. You can discuss informally things you don't want to call a man about. One important value of the gym is that it crosses party lines. You have an opportunity to get to know better the guys in the other party.[45]

Some legislatures have fairly highly developed friendship-clique structures. A good illustration of such a structure is the 1957 session of the Wisconsin assembly, where friendship cliques were so well developed that some cliques had names familiar to the representatives. Some of these cliques had distinguishable "styles of legislative life," and there was a very marked tendency for clique members to vote together on the floor.[46] Comparative analysis of friendship choices in four other state legislatures (California, New Jersey, Ohio, and Tennessee) has indicated "that the political roles of a legislator . . . are more compelling than his social role as a friend," but "the latter does have an effect in the one chamber where we were able to test it," although "on the whole it was not large."[47]

These state and county delegations, policy groups, and less-formal groups and cliques perform important functions for the maintenance of the legislature. The friendship and social groups tend to contribute most to the socialization function, but they may also provide companionship and status reassurance. All these kinds of unofficial groups facilitate communication, which is especially important in larger legislative bodies. They provide rank-and-file legislators with channels of access to committee or party leaders and make more efficient the communication

of influence and intelligence to leaders. Again, informal legislative groups constitute cue-giving or decision-facilitating mechanisms in the legislative body, including providing members with cues about voting. Finally, these groups contribute
to legislative solidarity, facilitating the strategy of bloc voting and also permitting
representatives (from the same state, for instance) to present a united front to the
electorate.

NOTES

1.   Council of State Governments, *The Book of the States, 1974–1975* (Lexington, Ky.,
1974), pp. 74–76.
2.   Eugene C. Lee, *The Presiding Officer and Rules Committee in Legislatures of the
United States* (Berkeley, Calif., 1952), pp. 19, 23, 26, 34–36.
3.   Charles W. Wiggins, *Arizona Legislature* (Phoenix, 1974), pp. 105–108.
4.   William G. Cornelius, ed., *Southeastern State Legislatures* (Atlanta, 1967), p. F-2;
Council of State Governments, *Lawmaking in the West* (San Francisco, 1967), vol. 2, pp.
89–90.
5.   Charles W. Wiggins, *The Legislative Process in Iowa* (Ames, Iowa, 1972), pp. 48–49:
Alan G. Hevesi, *Legislative Politics in New York State* (New York, 1975), pp. 20–22.
6.   See George B. Galloway, *History of the House of Representatives* (New York, 1961),
pp. 134–155; George R. Brown, *The Leadership of Congress* (Indianapolis, Ind., 1922),
chaps. 6, 11, and 12; and Randall B. Ripley, *Party Leaders in the House of Representatives*
(Washington, D.C., 1967), pp. 18–20.
7.   Milton C. Cummings, Jr., and Robert L. Peabody, "The Decision to Enlarge the
Committee on Rules: An Analysis of the 1961 Vote," in *New Perspectives on the House
of Representatives,* 2d ed., ed. Robert L. Peabody and Nelson W. Polsby (Chicago, 1969),
pp. 253–280; and Neil MacNeil, *Forge of Democracy: The House of Representatives* (New
York, 1963), chap. 15.
8.   See Robert L. Peabody, "The Enlarged Rules Committee," in *New Perspectives on
the House of Representatives,* 1st ed., ed. Robert L. Peabody and Nelson W. Polsby
(Chicago, 1963), pp. 133–151; quotation at 148.
9.   *Congressional Quarterly Weekly Report* 32 (March 30, 1974):810.
10.   Douglas M. Fox and Charles L. Clapp, "The House Rules Committee's Agenda-
Setting Function, 1961–1968," *Journal of Politics* 32 (1970):440–443; and "The House
Rules Committee and the Programs of the Kennedy and Johnson Administrations,"
Midwest Journal of Political Science 14 (1970):667–672.
11.   James A. Robinson, *The House Rules Committee* (Indianapolis, Ind., 1963), pp.
44–47.
12.   *Congressional Quarterly Weekly Report* 32 (March 30, 1974):808.
13.   See Belle Zeller, ed., *American State Legislatures* (New York, 1954), pp. 194–197.
14.   See Eagleton Institute of Politics, *Studies of the New Jersey Legislature* (New
Brunswick, N.J., 1970), pp. 83–94; and Alan Rosenthal, "The New Jersey Legislature—
The Contemporary Shape of an Historical Institution" (Unpublished paper, May, 1975),
pp. 41–43.
15.   Sidney Wise, *The Legislative Process in Pennsylvania* (Washington, D.C., 1971),
pp. 25–38; Wayne R. Swanson, *Lawmaking in Connecticut: The General Assembly* (Washington, D.C., 1972), pp. 20–21; Samuel K. Gove and Richard J. Carlson, *An Introduction
to the Illinois General Assembly* (University of Illinois, 1974), pp. 150–152.
16.   Wiggins, *Arizona Legislature,* pp. 113–116; John Owens, E. Costantini, and L.
Weschler, *California Politics and Parties* (New York, 1970), pp. 300–307.

17. Donald Leavitt, "Changing Rules and Norms in the Minnesota Legislature" (Paper presented at the annual meeting of the Midwest Political Science Association, 1975), pp. 16–17, 32; Citizens Conference on State Legislatures, *Legislative Openness* (Kansas City, Mo., 1974), pp. 97–103.

18. Unpublished material from Douglas S. Gatlin.

19. See Ralph V. Harlow, *The History of Legislative Methods in the Period before 1825* (New Haven, Conn., 1917), pp. 143–145, 183–191, 205–206; and Galloway, *History of the House of Representatives,* pp. 128–131.

20. David J. Rothman, *Politics and Power: The United States Senate, 1869–1901* (Cambridge, Mass., 1966), p. 60.

21. Brown, *The Leadership of Congress,* p. 92.

22. Wilder H. Haines, "The Congressional Caucus of Today," *American Political Science Review* 9 (1915):696–706.

23. Ralph K. Huitt, "Democratic Party Leadership in the Senate," *American Political Science Review* 55 (1961):341; and *Congressional Record,* March 9, 1959, p. 3562.

24. For more details on the development of the House Democratic caucus, see Norman J. Ornstein, "Causes and Consequences of Congressional Change: Subcommittee Reforms in the House of Representatives, 1970–73" in *Congress in Change,* ed. Norman J. Ornstein (New York, 1975), pp. 88–114; Walter J. Oleszek, "A Perspective on the U.S. House of Representatives: Three Major Reforms" (Paper presented at the annual meeting of the Southwest Social Science Association, 1975), and *Congressional Quarterly Weekly Report* 33 (May 3, 1975):911–915.

25. Democratic Study Group, "Caucus Instruction and Binding Actions" (June 4, 1974).

26. Ibid.

27. See Hugh A. Bone, "An Introduction to the Senate Policy Committee," *American Political Science Review* 50 (1956):341–342; and Charles O. Jones, *Party and Policy-Making: The House Republican Policy Committee* (New Brunswick, N.J., 1964), chap. 2.

28. U.S. Congress, Joint Committee on the Organization of Congress, *Organization of Congress,* 79th Cong., 2d sess., 1946, Report 1011, p. 12.

29. *Congressional Record,* January 11, 1960, p. 236.

30. Jones, *Party and Policy-Making,* p. 72.

31. For the earlier history of the Senate policy committees, see Bone, "An Introduction to the Senate Policy Committees."

32. Jones, *Party and Policy-Making,* chaps. 1, 3, and 4. See also Charles O. Jones, *The Minority Party in Congress* (Boston, 1970), chap. 8; and Evelyn G. Schipske, "Policy Statements and Policy-Making: An Analysis of Congressional Response to the House Republican Policy Committee (1949–1974)" (Unpublished manuscript).

33. See David B. Truman, "The State Delegations and the Structure of Party Voting in the United States House of Representatives," *American Political Science Review* 50 (1956):1023–1045; and Arthur G. Stevens, Jr., "Informal Groups and Decision-Making in the U.S. House of Representatives" (Ph.D. diss., University of Michigan, 1970), chap. 4.

34. Ripley, *Party Leaders in the House of Representatives,* pp. 170–171. For case studies of state delegations in the United States House, see Allan Fiellin, "The Functions of Informal Groups in Legislative Institutions: A Case Study," *Journal of Politics* 24 (1962):72–91; and John H. Kessel, "The Washington Congressional Delegation," *Midwest Journal of Political Science* 8 (1964):1–21.

35. Ripley, *Party Leaders in the House of Representatives,* pp. 173.

36. Stevens, "Informal Groups and Decision-Making in the U.S. House of Representatives," p. 106.

37.   Barbara Deckard, "State Party Delegations in the United States House of Representatives—A Comparative Study of Group Cohesion," *Journal of Politics* 34 (1972): 199–220; and "State Party Delegations in the United States House of Representatives—An Analysis of Group Action," *Polity* 5 (1973):311–334.

38.   Stevens, "Informal Groups and Decision-Making in the U.S. House of Representatives," pp. 98–100; Deckard, "State Party Delegations in the U.S. House of Representatives—A Comparative Study of Group Cohesion," p. 210.

39.   See Kenneth Kofmehl, "The Institutionalization of a Voting Bloc," *Western Political Quarterly* 17 (1964):256–272; and Arthur J. Stevens, Jr., Arthur H. Miller, and Thomas E. Mann, "Mobilization of Liberal Strength in the House: 1950–1970: The Democratic Study Group," *American Political Science Review* 68 (1974):667–681.

40.   Stevens, Miller, and Mann, "Mobilization of Liberal Strength in the House," p. 68.

41.   See Sven Groennings and Jonathan P. Hawley, *To Be a Congressman: The Promise and the Power* (Washington, D.C., 1973), pp. 79–94; and Thomas P. Murphy, *The New Politics Congress* (Lexington, Mass., 1974), pp. 130–134.

42.   Murphy, *The New Politics Congress,* pp. 39–42.

43.   Clapp, *The Congressman,* p. 40.

44.   See Charles M. Price and Charles G. Bell, "Socializing California Freshman Assemblymen: The Role of Individuals and Legislative Sub-Groups," *Western Political Quarterly* 23 (1970):166–179.

45.   Clapp, *The Congressman,* p. 40.

46.   Samuel C. Patterson, "Patterns of Interpersonal Relations in a State Legislative Group: The Wisconsin Assembly," *Public Opinion Quarterly* 23 (1959):101–109.

47.   John C. Wahlke et al., *The Legislative System* (New York, 1962), p. 235.

CHAPTER EIGHT

The Committee Structure

Committees are an integral part of the legislature. They are used to facilitate the performance of significant legislative tasks, but the nature and scope of these tasks and the independent power exercised by committees vary greatly from one legislative body to another. The increasing complexity and variety of the issues that face legislatures place greater demands on the legislators' time and necessitate specialization and division of labor. This is the purpose most universally served by committees. The committee system is the best method that legislators have been able to devise to provide careful and discriminating scrutiny of proposed legislation and legislative oversight of executive agencies. The committee system is the main line of defense for congressmen and state legislators against the twentieth-century trends that threaten to turn legislative bodies into rubber stamps for the executive. The authors of the 1946 Legislative Reorganization Act were interested in enabling Congress to play a stronger role vis-à-vis the President. They sought to achieve this primarily through making the committee system more effective by streamlining the structure, clarifying the jurisdiction of each committee, improving the staffs, and permitting congressmen to concentrate more of their time on fewer committees.

The committee has other functions. It is a vital link in the communications network essential to any legislative system, the main channel used by executive agencies for conveying information and proposals to the legislature. The committee plays a part in the establishment of norms and the allocation of roles to legislators (described in Chapter 17). The committee, through its public hearings, provides a cathartic, or safety-valve, mechanism for the expression of group and individual viewpoints. Committee members, and occasionally a whole committee, often serve as representatives or spokesmen for interests more effectively than would be possible without the committee system. To the extent that legislative bodies perform adjudicative functions (settling individual grievances or investigating crimes), this work is usually done in committee.

The two most important functions of legislative committees in the larger political system are the making of decisions with regard to legislation and the authorization and oversight of administrative actions. It is in the exercise of these two functions that there is the greatest variety among legislative bodies. If legislators frequently follow the advice of committees, this means that the most important legislative decisions are usually made in committees, that legislative power is decentralized. If the committees are effective in administrative oversight, the executive may have to take its cues in policy making from these committees rather than from laws passed by the whole legislature. In both cases, the committees become the primary source of legislative leadership.

In the preceding chapters, we have described another source of leadership: the political parties or factions that are found in most legislative bodies. There is an inherent contradiction between party and committee leadership. Party leadership is centralized; committee leadership is decentralized. Where committees are strong and independent, party leadership is weak. Where party leadership is strong, the committees are either weak or simply agents of the party leaders.

In the British House of Commons, where the political parties are strong and unified, the committees are relatively weak. The standing committees are large; they lack continuing jurisdiction over specific substantive areas; and they have a fluctuating membership. They are not sources of power but vehicles for detailed work. One authority, Herman Finer, has given this description:

> Committees are utterly subordinate to the whole House in their status and role. They do not possess the power of life and death over bills such as is enjoyed by the committees of the U.S. Congress or even Continental legislatures. They are lowly handmaidens to help clean up amendments, and their work is sandwiched in between Second Reading of an *already formulated* bill and Report (to the House) and Third Reading, when their work will be reviewed.[1]

Party leaders have resisted efforts to increase the role of committees in the House of Commons because they realize that this would undermine party control and create barriers to the smooth and orderly approval of legislation proposed by the ruling party.

In contrast, the committees of Congress are strong, proud, and independent. Some of them date back to the early days of the Republic. The jurisdiction of each committee in the two houses is carefully defined in the standing rules, which were made more explicit by the 1946 Legislative Reorganization Act. Each committee jealously guards its jurisdictional prerogatives. The senior members of committees have often served twenty years or more, long enough to have become experts in the field, well able to handle the complexities of modern legislation, and capable of holding their own in encounters with officials of the executive departments. Each committee determines its own rules and operating procedures, giving the chairman more or less power as it sees fit. The committees determine which bills will be reported out and which will be buried in obscurity, and congressional rules and traditions offer only the narrowest of opportunities for a congressional majority to extricate a bill that has been buried in committee. Favorable committee recommendations are not always followed on the floor of Congress, but the greater the strength of committee support for legislation, the greater its chances for passage.

The weakness of the party system in Congress results directly, although not entirely, from the independent strength of committees. Although the majority party has proportionate majorities in each committee, party lines are often crossed in the voting within committee. Party leaders have great difficulty persuading members to follow their wishes with regard to bills in committee when the views of these committee members are substantially different. The seniority system used in selecting committee chairmen frequently promotes to the chairmanship a man who is out of step with the opinion of his party with respect to the issues under his jurisdiction.

The congressional committee system is duplicated at the state level in form but not usually in substance. The committees in state legislatures bear subject-matter titles similar to those in Congress, but jurisdictional rules and traditions are weaker. Legislative leaders may assign most of the important bills, whatever their subject, to a few dependable committees. State legislative committees do not have the time and the staff for a careful, expert scrutiny of bills. Most legislatures lack a strong seniority system; consequently, the committees lack the hard core of veteran members, independent of party control, who can make a committee both expert and independently powerful.

The fact that state legislative committees are usually not independent centers of power does not mean that their role is insignificant. They may provide the means for the dominant faction or party to control the legislative process through the party leaders who chair the important committees and the loyal party majorities on these committees. In other states, the committee role may be a more perfunctory one, as the members concern themselves with technical details and perfecting amendments to a bill. In most states, there is strong party or factional leadership in the legislature, and the committee system is designed not to conflict with that leadership.

There are three factors that provide clues to the function of committees. Each will bear some analysis. The first is simply the committee structure in legislative bodies. The second is the method of choosing committee members and chairmen. The third is the internal structure of committees, including the role of the chairman and the part played by subcommittees.

THE STRUCTURE OF COMMITTEES

Congress

The three major categories of congressional committees are: *standing,* or permanent, committees; *special,* or select, committees; and *joint* committees representing both houses. Conference committees, used to adjust Senate-House differences over the terms of a bill that has passed both houses, are ad hoc groups selected from the standing committees that had original jurisdiction over the bill in both houses.

The standing committees are the most important because of their permanence and because, as a rule, they are the only ones that can report bills. In its earliest sessions, Congress relied primarily on a large variety of select committees, but these gradually declined in importance during the nineteenth century. The first standing committees were established in 1789; by 1822, there were fifteen standing committees in the Senate and nineteen in the House. Many of these have persisted in name and function to the present. The number of congressional committees proliferated, reaching a total of seventy-four in the Senate and sixty-one in the House by the early 1920s. Both houses made drastic cuts in the number of committees (the Senate in 1922 and the House in 1927).[2]

When the Joint Committee on the Organization of Congress met in 1945 to study congressional reform, it decided that the number of committees (thirty-three in the Senate and forty-eight in the House) was still too large. Congressmen, particularly members of the Senate, often found it impossible to attend meetings of all their committees (sometimes two or three at one time), to say nothing about devoting careful attention to the work of each. Some senators were on as many as ten committees. The large number of committees hampered the effort to provide better and larger staffs for all. The proliferation of committees had created jurisdictional disputes and inequitable work loads. The 1946 Legislative Reorganization Act cut the number of committees in each house by more than half. The reduction was difficult because it meant not only abolition of forty-seven chairmanships but also thwarting of the ambitions of countless other members who lost high seniority posts on vanishing committees. (It was facilitated by the turnover in majority party control that also occurred in 1947.)[3] The accomplishment of committee reorganization in the face of these obstacles showed that most congressmen believed it was a prerequisite to strengthening congressional committees. Since 1946 each house has added some standing committees, raising the total to eighteen in the Senate and twenty-two in the House (see Table 8.1).

During the Ninety-third Congress a special House committee chaired by Richard Bolling conducted a thorough study of House committees, and issued a report recommending fundamental changes in committee jurisdiction. The purpose was to modernize and rationalize the subject-matter responsibilities of committees. The committee found, for example, that sixteen different committees handled aspects of the energy problem. The recommendations of Bolling's committee aroused strong opposition because they would have diminished the power of some of the most important committees and their chairmen. The House rejected the Bolling committee report, and instead adopted a substitute proposal, drafted by a committee of the Democratic caucus, that made much less significant changes in the jurisdiction and structure of House committees.

Select, or special, committees of Congress are temporary, lasting only during the life of the Congress in which they were created. Their function is normally one of study and investigation, and with occasional exceptions, they do not have the power to report bills to the Senate or the House. As originally drafted, the Legislative Reorganization Act of 1946 banned the use of select committees. The Senate approved that version of the bill, but in the House, this prohibition was removed.

The select committees in the House have four major purposes: (1) to serve interest groups that feel they lack access to standing committees, (2) to serve individual congressmen or make use of their particular talents, (3) to evade standing committees when circumstances make it necessary, and (4) to perform specific duties in areas of overlapping committee jurisdiction. In the Senate, a Select Committee on Small Business, which clearly serves a particular economic interest, has become a perennial committee, although theoretically it is still a

TABLE 8.1   Standing Committees in Congress

SENATE	HOUSE
Foreign Relations	Rules
Finance	Ways and Means
Appropriations	Appropriations
Judiciary	International Relations
Armed Services	Armed Services
Commerce	Interstate and Foreign Commerce
Agriculture and Forestry	Judiciary
Interior and Insular Affairs	Agriculture
Labor and Public Welfare	District of Columbia
Banking, Housing, and Urban Affairs	Public Works and Transportation
Public Works	Education and Labor
Rules and Administration	House Administration
Government Operations	Government Operations
Post Office and Civil Service	Interior and Insular Affairs
District of Columbia	Banking, Currency, and Housing
	Merchant Marine and Fisheries
	Post Office and Civil Service
Aeronautical and Space Sciences	Veterans' Affairs
Veterans' Affairs	
Budget	
	Science and Technology
	Standards of Official Conduct
	Budget
	Small Business

NOTE: The committees are listed in the order of preference among the members of Congress, based on data concerning transfers to and from the committees from the Eighty-first to the Ninetieth Congresses. The committees at the end in each column are more recently established, and data on their preference ranking are not available.
SOURCE: George Goodwin, Jr., *The Little Legislatures: Committees of Congress* (Amherst, Mass., 1970), pp. 114–115.

select one. The space committees in both houses started out as select committees and later became standing committees designed to deal with a new field that overlapped existing committees. The Senate now has a Select Committee on Standards and Conduct that parallels the standing committee in the House.[4]

Since select committees cannot normally report legislation to Congress, what part can they play in the legislative system? Sometimes their recommendations lead to legislation. When this occurs, it is not because the select committees themselves are powerful. On occasion, however, the leaders of the committee do have the power and prestige necessary to win support in the standing committees and on the floor of both houses for legislation that has had its genesis in a select committee. In addition to its legislative role, the select committee may have an educational, promotional, or representative role, serving to lay the groundwork for long-run legislative objectives. The role of select committees in Congress might be compared with that of third parties in a two-party system. They serve individual or group interests that are not being served by the standing committee structure; sometimes, they promote causes so effectively that the standing committees must give attention to them. Despite their persistence on the congressional scene, however, they have neither displaced nor challenged the dominant position of standing committees in the structure of Congress.

Congress has not made extensive use of joint committees or joint action by the standing committees. It is often argued that joint hearings would save the time of administration witnesses, but occasional experiments with such hearings have convinced members of both houses that this technique minimizes the chance that each congressman has for raising questions because the joint committees are so large. Moreover, House members feel handicapped in joint hearings with senators, who have greater prestige. Although the professional staffs of the committees often cooperate and exchange information, the use of joint staffs is discouraged because one committee or the other might have its control over the staff diluted. Whatever the advantages of conducting committee activities jointly, these are obviously outweighed by the spirit of bicameralism, the jealously guarded prerogatives of the two houses, and the significant differences in attitudes, operating procedures, and vested interests of Senate and House members.

The few existing joint committees of Congress resemble the select committees in their powers and purposes. They do not have the power to report bills to the Senate and the House. They are used primarily to carry out studies and investigations or to supervise the work of administrative agencies. The Joint Economic Committee, for example, holds extensive hearings and makes recommendations to Congress on the President's annual economic report. The Joint Committee on Internal Revenue Taxation is composed of senior members from the taxing committees in the Senate and the House and provides a vehicle for them to coordinate activities and supervise a staff of taxation experts. Several other joint committees (such as Printing, Library, and Disposition of Executive Papers) perform primarily housekeeping functions.

A unique example of a joint committee with power equal to or greater than that of most standing committees is the Joint Committee on Atomic Energy. This is the only joint committee that is authorized to report legislation. Its most important activities have been nonlegislative: supervising the atomic energy program and goading the administration into developing that program along the lines set by the committee. In this field, the committee has been unusually vigorous and effective. Senator Henry M. Jackson has claimed that "in the case of certain vital policy decisions the urging from the Joint Committee has played so powerful a role that it can be said the Committee made the decisions, with the advice and consent of the executive branch."[5] The Joint Committee, established by the 1946 Atomic Energy Act, draws some of its power from specific provisions of that act (with 1954 amendments), which give it complete jurisdiction over atomic energy legislation, authority to make "continuing studies" of the atomic energy field and to make use of facilities of the executive department in its investigations, and the right to "be fully and currently informed" with regard to all activities of pertinent executive agencies. Moreover, the joint nature of its organization has given the committee stronger bargaining power with the administration and greater influence in Congress.[6]

State Legislatures

There has been a trend in the states toward the reduction in, and rationalization of, committees, as shown in Table 8.2. The purpose of these changes has been to

TABLE 8.2   Committees in State Legislatures

NUMBER OF STANDING COMMITTEES	NUMBER OF STATES			
	House		Senate	
	1946	1973	1946	1973
10 or fewer	0	9	0	14
11–20	2	22	8	26
21–30	9	13	15	8
31–50	27	4	22	1
51–70	9	0	3	0

SOURCES: Council of State Governments, *The Book of the States, 1964–1965* (Chicago, 1964), p. 40; and *The Book of the States, 1974–1975* (Lexington, Ky., 1974), p. 74

reduce the number of committee assignments, eliminate committees that handled little legislation, and balance the work load among committees. Unlike Congress, many state legislatures still operate in a procedural jungle when it comes to committee jurisdiction over bills. Legislative leaders frequently make it a practice to assign most of the important bills to a few committees dominated by members loyal to them. This is one reason why imbalances in committee work loads remain in many legislatures.

Connecticut uses joint committees exclusively, and Maine, Massachusetts, Pennsylvania, and California make extensive use of them. (Connecticut is excluded from Table 8.2, and Maine and Massachusetts are among the states with ten or fewer regular committees in each house.) Most other states make only occasional use of joint committees. The joint committee permits more careful consideration of bills without duplication of effort, offers better opportunities for hearings, and makes feasible more staff assistance. Joint committees might not appear feasible when different parties control the two houses, but in Connecticut, where this situation has frequently prevailed, the rules permit either senate or house members to report separately to their chambers if joint approval in a committee proves impossible. The success of the experiment in a few states has not led to any rapid adoption of the practice by other legislatures.

CHOICE OF COMMITTEE MEMBERS AND CHAIRMEN

The best clue to the part played by committees in a legislative system is the technique used to choose and to retain or to replace committee members. When a legislative body is under tight control by party or factional leaders, these leaders will choose the members of key committees and even replace them with more loyal members if necessary. If power is decentralized, however, the committees may become the loci of power, and the members may have secured tenure on the committees.

In legislatures with two effective parties, the partisan makeup of committees approximates the proportions found in the house as a whole, and the chairman is normally a member of the majority party. In Congress, this formula is adhered to closely. In the House, however, the Rules Committee usually has a two to one ratio. In state legislatures, even where both parties are strong, the formula is likely to be less exact; the majority party often has more than its share of seats on the more powerful committees.

In state legislatures in which parties are weak or in which a single party dominates, party membership may have little to do with committee assignments and the choice of chairmen. In California, where legislative parties have developed slowly, the majority party has held a majority on all committees but has not held all the chairmanships.[7] The habit of giving occasional chairmanships to the minority Republican party in Arizona ended when the minority contingent in the house grew to greater numerical importance.[8] In some southern legislatures in which the Republican party is beginning to develop modest legislative strength, the Democratic leadership has been reluctant to provide a share of seats on the most important committees. In Kentucky, it was not until 1968, during a Republican administration, that the minority Republican party gained a proportionate voice on all the legislative committees.

We have already noted the inherent contradiction between party and committee leadership. Where the majority party leadership is strong, it must achieve its purposes in one of two ways: either by minimizing the importance of committees in the legislative process or by controlling membership on the committees. It may combine these techniques by bypassing some committees and assigning important bills to those committees that it controls.

State Legislative Committees

In most state legislatures, seniority is only one of several factors that affect the selection of committee members and chairmen. In seeking choice committee assignments, freshmen may be handicapped, but they are not so completely excluded as their counterparts in Congress. Although chairmanships are more likely to go to experienced legislators, there are only a few states in which committee chairmen have an assurance of continuity in their positions comparable to that enjoyed until very recently by chairmen in Congress. One reason for the smaller importance of seniority is the much higher turnover rate in state legislatures. When a legislature has a large proportion of freshmen, there is likely to be room for some of them on even the most important committees. Because of short legislative terms and a tendency to move from one committee to another, relatively few members stay on a single committee long enough for a core of stable, experienced members to develop.

There are distinct differences among the legislatures, however, in the weight given to seniority, either formally or informally. In state legislatures that are dominated by strong party or factional leadership, the leaders are careful to choose committee members and chairmen who will be loyal to the party or faction and its leadership. They usually concentrate their attention on the major committees that will be handling the most important pieces of legislation. In addition to the criterion of loyalty, the leadership is concerned with such characteristics as competence, experience in the subject matter, the maintenance of geographic balance, and an effort to satisfy members' wishes when possible. Once the major appointments have been determined, the leadership may be willing to follow the preference of legislators almost entirely with regard to other committee assignments.

In one strong-party state, Pennsylvania, the leadership is primarily concerned with choosing chairmen, because they usually dominate committees. The leaders seek men of demonstrated ability and loyalty, but they must also maintain regional balance and recognize the claims of large-county delegations to some chairmanships. Seniority plays a part in the selection because the more senior members have had a greater opportunity to demonstrate legislative skills and because seniority often provides a standard for balancing the claims of rival county delegations, but seniority is never followed blindly.[9] A recent comparative study of committee chairman selection in eight states (based on a survey of chairmen) showed that in the three having the strongest party systems—New York, Indiana, and Wisconsin—individual expertise appeared to be the most important criterion in the selection process. In all three, however, a majority of the chairmen were the most senior members of their committees, and seniority was evaluated as a more important criterion than in the other states. In these three states the leaders are not bound by rigid seniority rules, but they often select reliable senior members for chairmanships and may use seniority as a device for minimizing intraparty conflict.[10]

In states where legislative parties are strong, the party leadership is able to replace the chairman of an important committee at the start of a new session if his voting record or incompetence has made him a liability. Chairmen are not protected by seniority, and the leadership is not bound to follow a seniority rule in selecting a new chairman. This is the most important difference between such state legislatures and the norms that have prevailed in Congress until recently. Because the leaders have a wide range of choice and because of the high rate of legislative turnover, it is not unusual for a legislator to be appointed chairman of a committee he has never served on.

In legislatures where parties are less important, the Speaker or senate president may make committee assignments primarily on the basis of a legislator's loyalty to him or to the coalition or faction that he heads. Sometimes the dominant coalition represents identifiable regions or interests; in other cases it may be little more than a personal faction organized by the presiding officer. Particularly in the latter case, the presiding officer may have promised committee posts to win the votes necessary for his selection. Iowa and Arizona are examples of states in which there is often a contest for the Speakership, and the Speaker is likely to choose committee chairmen and members of key committees in part on the basis of commitments made during that contest. Alabama and Florida are examples of states in which a major factor in the selection of chairmen is loyalty to the presiding officer or dominant faction; seniority plays a very limited part.[11]

In the California assembly the Speaker usually wins election by putting together a bipartisan coalition; he rewards the members of that coalition with chairmanships and memberships on key committees. For many years partisanship was muted in both houses of the California legislature. Despite the development of stronger legislative parties in the assembly in the 1960s, the Speaker has continued to rely on bipartisan support, partly because the partisan balance has usually been very close. The minority party has usually been given chairmanships and/or a majority of seats on some of the less important committees. Although freshmen have rarely been chairmen, seniority has not been an important factor in determining the most important assignments.[12]

Although the governor is likely to have an indirect influence on major committee assignments in some strong-party states, the best examples of gubernatorial domination have occurred in legislatures controlled by one party. Kentucky and Tennessee are states in which the legislative leaders, who have usually been selected in accord with the governor's wishes, have generally consulted with him carefully in the selection of committee chairmen.

There are a few states in which formal rules or informal procedures give priority to seniority, either in the assignment of members to committees or in the selection of chairmen, or both. Seniority is the major factor in assigning committee seats in North Dakota, New Mexico, Virginia, the Washington senate, the Arkansas house, and the South Carolina senate. Nebraska uses a system of regional caucuses to select members, with each region entitled to a certain number, but conflicts within these caucuses are usually settled on the basis of seniority. In the Texas lower house, although the Speaker has the authority to choose the chairmen and new members of committees, he has no power to remove committee members who served in the previous session (except on the Rules and Administration committees). The effect of this rule, adopted in 1967, permitting members to remain on committees, was to limit the bargaining power of persons campaigning for the office of Speaker. In the Montana house there are informal norms requiring the Speaker to reappoint those members of major committees who desire reappointment.[13]

Seniority is used for the selection of chairmen in Arkansas. In North Dakota there is no formal seniority rule but most committees are chaired by members of the majority party with high legislative seniority. The Virginia legislature and the South Carolina senate are exceptional not only because seniority is important in choosing chairmen but also because there is an unusually high degree of stability in committee memberships and chairmanships. Seniority is also a factor in the Nebraska legislature, but since 1973 the chairmen have been chosen by all members of the legislature in a secret ballot, a procedure that encourages bargaining and puts a premium on individual skills and prestige. A study of the Minnesota lower house has concluded that the most important factors in the selection of chairmen are seniority in the house and in the legislature as a whole and committee seniority, although party loyalty is a factor of some importance, especially for a few key committees.[14]

For many years in the California senate, legislative seniority was the major factor used in assigning chairmanships and seats on the most important committees, and no consideration was given to party affiliation. In the 1959 session, for example, the Republicans had only thirteen seats out of forty, but ten of these Republicans were among the most senior senators, so Republicans got half of the twenty chairmanships. In 1967 a large turnover following reapportionment resulted in only eighteen members returning to the senate, not enough to chair twenty-two committees, but the remaining chairmanships were filled by former members of the assembly on the basis of their seniority in that branch. The decision of the bipartisan Rules Committee, chaired by the president pro tem, to adhere strictly to seniority was challenged by junior members of both parties, many of whom felt that the majority party should always control at least a majority of chairmanships. The conflict intensified during the 1967–1969 period when the president pro tem, a conservative Democrat, held his post despite a Republican gain of a majority of seats. The replacement of the president pro tem in the middle of a session, followed by other leadership changes within a short period, led to the collapse of the strict seniority system. Both partisanship and loyalty to the presiding officer have assumed greater importance in the selection of chairmen and members on major committees.[15]

On most state legislative committees the rate of turnover is high and the number of members having many years of experience is low. We pointed out in Chapter 3 that in most legislatures between one-fourth and one-half of the members are freshmen; the average for all states is about one-third. Obviously the higher the rate of turnover in legislative members, the higher the rate of turnover on committees will be. In addition, a substantial proportion of members who get reelected change committees, either at their own request or because the leadership wants to make changes. In those states where the seniority principle is established by written rules or informal norms, there is likely to be more stability in committee membership and also in chairmanships. The most thorough study of reappointment and turnover in committees, covering twelve states for a period of fourteen years, has been done by Porter and Leuthold.[16] There are no obvious reasons for the variations that they found among the states (see Table 8.3). None of these states has a rigid seniority system. Two states where we have indicated that seniority is relatively important—New York and Wisconsin—are at the top and near the bottom, respectively, of the ranking of percentage of reelected members who are reappointed. In California loyalty to the Speaker is important, and committee stability might be lower in periods having frequent changes in the Speakership. The rate of reappointment in Texas (at the bottom of the table) may have increased after 1967 when the rule was changed to permit members who wished to keep their committee seats.

Porter and Leuthold suggest several reasons for variations in the turnover rate among reelected members. They found that in four states—Wisconsin, Michigan, California, and New York—the rate of turnover was much higher when there was a change in party control of the legislature between two sessions, but in the remaining states where such change occurred it made little difference. One reason for this in Wisconsin and New York was that in those states majority party members regularly got more committee assignments than did those in the minority party. In all of the states the more senior members were more likely to be reappointed to the same committee than were more junior members. The authors of this study also found that there was more stability on the most important committees, presumably because members would be unlikely to take the initiative in shifting to other committees.[17]

There is also evidence from a number of states to show that relatively few chairmen chair the same committee for long periods of time; it is quite common

TABLE 8.3   Reappointment and Turnover of State Legislative Committee Members in the Lower Houses of Twelve States, 1958–1971

STATE	PERCENTAGE OF ALL MEMBERS REAPPOINTED TO SAME COMMITTEE IN NEXT SESSION	PERCENTAGE OF ALL MEMBERS WHO WERE REELECTED	PERCENTAGE OF REELECTED MEMBERS REAPPOINTED TO SAME COMMITTEE*
New York	49	71	75
California	49	76	70
West Virginia	34	54	69
Mississippi†	28	42	68
Ohio	39	63	63
Michigan	45	74	63
Nevada	32	59	56
Wyoming	34	62	55
Maryland†	24	48	55
Wisconsin	32	68	48
Utah	20	48	43
Texas	26	68	39

*In the states where committees were reorganized between sessions, the calculations in this column exclude cases where a committee was abolished and no equivalent committee was available for appointment to.

†Mississippi and Maryland legislators are elected for four year terms, and these calculations are made every four years in these states, although in Maryland appointments are changed every two years.

SOURCE: H. Owen Porter and David A. Leuthold, "Acquiring Legislative Expertise: Appointments to Standing Committees in the States" (paper prepared for the 1974 annual meeting of the American Political Science Association).

in state legislatures for a chairman of one committee to shift to chairing another committee in the next session; a person who has never belonged to a committee before, or even a freshman, may become chairman of a committee. Such practices are either rare or completely unknown in Congress, where members reach the chairmanship only after long experience on a committee. A committee chairman often holds that position for many years, and only occasionally shifts to another chairmanship if he becomes the senior member of a more powerful committee. These generalizations can be substantiated with data collected in a number of states. For example:

In years with no shift of party control, over half of the committees in Iowa have new chairmen.

Over a long period of time, half of the chairmen of important committees in the Texas lower house had never served on the committee and only one-tenth had been on it for more than one term.

Nearly half of the chairmanships in the Rhode Island legislature (under one-party domination) change every two years.

A study of turnover of chairmanships of the major revenue and appropriations committees in all legislatures shows that these committees (which we would expect to have more stability than less important ones) averaged two and a half different chairmen over a six-year (three-term) period.[18]

Selection of Congressional Committee Members

Because congressional committees play central roles in the decision-making structure and because membership stability on committees is high, it is particularly important to understand how committee assignments are made. Although more senior congressmen have an advantage in getting the more desirable assignments, a number of factors other than seniority affect the choice of committee members. We will first explain what factors lead members to seek particular committees, then describe the mechanism for selecting members, and finally examine the criteria used in selecting members.

All freshman congressmen submit their requests for assignments, and all returning congressmen have an opportunity at the beginning of each Congress to request transfers to other committees. The new congressman's degree of success in getting on a desirable committee may have an important impact on his career, although subsequent opportunities to change committees provide him with chances to overcome initial mistakes or failures. Richard Fenno, who has queried many congressmen about their reasons for seeking particular committees, has concluded that there are three major motivations at work:

1. The desire to help their constituents and thereby improve the chances for reelection;
2. The desire to exercise influence within the House;
3. An interest in helping to formulate public policy in certain fields.[19]

The committee assignment that a member seeks depends on his motivation. Fenno, who was studying six House committees (and their Senate counterparts), found that members of the Interior committees in both branches believed that their membership would help their state. A member of the House Interior Committee said, "I was attracted to it, very frankly, because it's a bread and butter committee for my state." A senator on the Interior Committee said:

> I wanted Interior because I come from a Western state and the Committee deals with matters like dams, parks, recreation, mines, public lands—all especially important to the so-called public lands states. Everything I can get from the committee —big dams, mining, outdoor recreation, parks—helps me back home.[20]

Fenno found that members of the House Appropriations and Ways and Means committees emphasized the power and prestige of these committees as reasons for joining them. Membership on such committees increases a congressman's influence over other members; this may also enhance his ability to serve the interest of his constituents by putting him in a position to bargain with congressmen on other committees. Members of the Senate Appropriations Committee, who have larger constituencies than representatives, often see it as a way of serving state interests:

> When you've got a fast-growing state with millions of people, you've got a lot of eggs in the appropriations basket—military installations, flood control, urban renewal, rivers and harbors, reclamation, agricultural research, and so forth.[21]

Finally, members of the House Education and Labor and the International Relations committees (and their Senate counterparts) are primarily motivated by policy goals and by their interest in these topics; they recognize that such committees offer fewer opportunities for serving constituency interests.

The best systematic data on the preferences of freshman congressmen come from the requests that they submit for assignments. These are available for Democratic representatives for the Eighty-sixth, Eighty-seventh, and Ninetieth Congresses, and they illustrate how the requests of freshman congressmen vary according to the types of districts they represent. Rural members from the West and Midwest have been most likely to seek membership on the Interior Committee; rural members in general have sought the Public Works Committee; urban members have given priority to the Banking, Currency and Housing Committee and the Interstate and Foreign Commerce Committee; those from farm areas have sought the Agriculture Committee.[22]

If we combine the data on all requests and on first choice requests by freshman Democrats, we find that the most popular committees in the House are Banking, Currency and Housing and Interstate and Foreign Commerce, followed in approximate order by International Relations, Armed Services, Public Works, Judiciary, and Interior and Insular Affairs. This is not the same as the rank order of committee preferences based on transfers to and from committees (see Table 8.1 and discussion below). This is partly because freshmen recognize that they have little chance to get on the three most prestigious committees—Rules, Ways and Means, and Appropriations. They concentrate their requests on the committees that rank in the middle range in terms of prestige. In other words, the requests by congressmen reflect not only their preferences but also their perceptions about what is realistic. Similarly there are indications that members specify a smaller number of requests when they are the only member from a state requesting a particular assignment and they have reason to believe that their state will be able to fill that vacancy (perhaps because the state had previously held a seat on the committee in question).[23]

A congressman may seek a change in his committee assignments after his freshman term either because his interests and priorities have changed or because his increased seniority has enhanced his chances for getting on one of the most prestigious committees. A congressman who shifts committees gives up his seniority on the old and starts at the bottom of the seniority ladder of the new committee. For this reason most changes occur relatively early in a congressman's career. A variety of studies of House committees have provided the following pattern of committee transfers:

In each Congress about one-tenth of the returning members shift committees. More than a third of those changing have served only one term; about three-quarters have served three terms or less.

Over half of those shifting have served only one term on the committee they are leaving, and 85 percent have served three terms or less on it.

The members most likely to shift are those whose initial assignments were limited to lower-prestige committees.

Members who have accumulated more than one term of seniority on a committee are willing to make a change only to get on one of the most prestigious committees: Ways and Means, Rules, Appropriations, International Relations, and Armed Services.[24]

Several studies of House committee transfers have produced rankings of committee desirability, taking into account such factors as: transfers to and from committees, the amount of committee seniority surrendered to shift to another committee, and preference requests of those seeking a change.[25] The different criteria have produced differences in ranking, but the position of the top committees remains approximately the same, and similar to that in Table 8.1. Ways and Means, Appropriations, and the much smaller Rules Committee are ones that members very rarely leave and that they are willing to join even at the cost of giving up several terms on another. (These are also the only exclusive committees; under House rules a member of one of these cannot serve on any other committee.) International Relations and Armed Services rank next; they rarely lose a member except to one of the top three. Commerce and Judiciary rank next in the preference order of transfers.

We do not have such detailed data available on the preference requests or actual transfers of senators. From the viewpoint of senators seeking assignments, it is worth noting that the number of vacancies at any time is much smaller than in the House. Because senators can have more assignments than House members, and because there are proportionally greater opportunities to chair subcommittees, the costs of shifting from one committee to another may be less in the Senate than they are in the House. In other words, a senator may have to wait longer to get a very prestigious assignment, but when it finally becomes available, he may be able to take it with a smaller cost because he can retain other important committee posts.

The procedures, as well as the criteria, for selecting committee members have been changing; both types of changes have had the result of reducing the importance of seniority and increasing the influence of party leaders on the selection process. Until 1975 the Democratic members of the Ways and Means Committee served as that party's committee for selecting members of House committees. Because that committee was made up primarily of senior members, who relied heavily on the advice of the senior members of state delegations, the norm of seniority tended to be important in the selection process. In 1975 the Democratic caucus transferred this authority to a Policy and Steering Committee, which is chaired by the Speaker and includes several party leaders, some members appointed by the Speaker, and some members elected regionally. Given its composition, it seems certain to be more responsive to the wishes of the party leadership than the Ways and Means members were. In the past the Democratic leaders intervened on behalf of particular candidates or to fill particular vacancies, but did not consistently participate in the selection process. The Speaker also recommends to the caucus nominees for the Rules Committee. The state delegations continue to make recommendations to the committee, and settle conflicting claims among their members. The Democratic caucus has continued the practice established in 1971 of reviewing committee action and making the final decisions on committee assignments.

The selection process for House Republicans has remained stable in recent years. The Republican Committee on Committees is composed of one member from each state with Republican congressmen, normally the senior member from that state; each member has a number of votes equal to the number of Republican representatives from his state. The actual work of this group is delegated to a subcommittee, normally dominated by the states with the most Republican representatives, where the same voting pattern prevails. The consequence is to give Republicans from such states as New York, New Jersey, Pennsylvania, Ohio, Illinois, Michigan, and California a dominant voice in choosing committee members. Although these are heavily metropolitan and industrial states, the senior Republican members from them are likely to represent the more rural areas of the states. Republican party leaders appear to have some influence over committee assignments, but it is exercised with a cautious restraint and is clearly less direct than the influence of their Democratic counterparts.[26]

Influence over committee assignments is important to party leaders not only because they can affect the balance of power on committees (and thus their output) but also because they can reward cooperative members with good assignments. The party leaders (particularly in the majority party) can increase the available rewards by initiating increases in the size of committees. Louis Westefield has collected data showing that from 1947 (when committees were reorganized) to 1971 there was a 30 percent increase in the total number of committee seats, not including additions resulting from new committees. Moreover, the increases were concentrated among the more desirable committees. The only committees that were not enlarged significantly during that period were the least popular ones and one major committee—Ways and Means—which was increased in 1975.[27]

Both party committees sometimes consult the senior members of their party on the committees where vacancies exist. In the past it has appeared that these members have had what amounted to a virtual veto power over new members.[28] As one congressman described the process:

> I don't see how the Committee on Committees could have the nerve to ram somebody down the throat of a committee chairman or ranking member who doesn't want that candidate. It would be natural to consult with your top man on the committee, and unless some unusual issue is at stake, his wishes would be adhered to.[29]

In the Senate procedures for choosing committee members are less formal, perhaps because of the smaller task involved; and there are considerable differences between the parties in their methods of selection. Each party has a committee on committees. The Democrats call this group the Steering Committee. The Democratic floor leader selects the Steering Committee and chairs it; its members continue to serve as long as they remain in the Senate. The Republican party leaders select the chairman and members of their Committee on Committees, most of whom (other than the chairman) serve only two-year terms. Both party conferences approve the selection of these committees, normally in routine fashion.[30]

When he served as Senate Democratic leader, Lyndon Johnson played an active role in the selection of committee members. At the start of his term he persuaded his party to approve a new selection policy that gave less weight to seniority and guaranteed that each freshman senator would have a seat on at least one major committee. This reduction in reliance on seniority had the effect of giving greater discretion to the Steering Committee, and its leader, Lyndon Johnson. According to John G. Stewart:

> Johnson also viewed each committee assignment as an opportunity for augmenting his personal resources for bargaining and negotiation on other issues. A desirable assignment could reward a senator for past support and assistance, or, more likely, establish a fund of credit to be drawn upon in the future.[31]

To maintain his influence over the selection process, Johnson was also careful to select new members of the Steering Committee who would support him; the result was an increase in the conservative and southern influence on that committee. In contrast, Mike Mansfield has consciously avoided efforts to dominate the Steering Committee or force specific choices on it. After he became floor leader, Mansfield slowly and deliberately expanded the size of the Steering Committee to nineteen members, choosing senators who made it broadly representative of the geographical and ideological wings of the party. As a result the criticism of the selection process that had frequently been voiced by liberals during the Johnson era gradually died away.

What criteria are used in assigning members to committees, particularly when there are conflicting demands for filling vacancies on the most desirable committees? It is possible to describe the most important criteria and cite some of the results of quantitative research, but the process is too complex to make possible any precise formula for predicting how vacancies will be filled. Seniority is still an important factor in committee assignments in both houses, but it is rarely the only factor taken into consideration. One congressman has aptly summarized its importance: "Seniority may control if all other things are equal. But other things usually are not equal. Sometimes you begin to think seniority is little more than a device to fall back on when it is convenient to do so."[32] Seniority is particularly important in selection to the most prestigious committees. The record shows that members chosen for the top committees average more years of service at the time of selection than those chosen for less important committees.[33] One study of House Democratic selections has shown that when there is a conflict between a freshman and a nonfreshman for a particular committee position, the nonfreshman wins almost four times out of five, and this proportion is even higher in contests for the most prestigious committees. It is also apparent that when two or more members of a state delegation want to fill the same committee vacancy, the more senior member usually gets the support of his state delegation and wins the seat.[34] Obviously when the choices must be made among competing freshmen or among other members having the same amount of seniority, other factors must be considered.

Particularly in making appointments to the top three committees in the House, the selection committees seek congressmen who have shown themselves to be "responsible," a term more often used than defined, which suggests a congressman who is moderate and reasonable in his approach to issues, who contributes his share to the less-publicized committee chores, who works well with the leadership and other congressmen, and who recognizes and accepts the congressional norms. There is some evidence to suggest that among nonfreshman Democratic representatives those with a stronger voting record of party loyalty will get better assignments than those with a weaker record, particularly if party leaders take an active part in filling the vacancy. Fenno asserts that party orthodoxy is particularly important in filling both Democratic and Republican vacancies on the Ways and Means Committee and Republican vacancies on the Appropriations Committee. The selection committees try to give members assignments that will improve their chances for reelection, but studies of committee assignments and electoral margins have failed to provide any evidence that members from marginal districts are consistently given better assignments. On the contrary, in the case of the top three House committees, there seems to be an effort to avoid members from marginal districts who might be particularly vulnerable to pressures from their constituents.[35]

State party delegations play an important though unpublicized role in filling vacancies on House committees. A freshman congressman is heavily dependent on the more senior members of his state party delegation for advice in determining which committees to apply for and for support of his application. Some state party delegations rely almost entirely on seniority in determining which member should be supported for a vacancy, while others try to select someone who meets the expectations of the party's committee on committees. The Texas Democratic delegation, for example, regularly follows the seniority rules in endorsing candidates for vacancies, and as a result some of its more conservative nominees have lost out to members from other state delegations. Once a delegation decides on its candidate for a vacancy, all members of the delegation are expected to do what they can to help the candidate succeed.[36] The larger state delegations try to keep a member on all of the important committees and on all committees that deal with issues of particular concern to that state. Some of the larger state party delegations have succeeded in establishing a claim to seats on particular committees, so that when their member on that committee leaves the House they can replace him with another from their delegation. One study of House committee assignments from 1947 through 1968 led to the conclusions that specific state party delegations had maintained a hold on 38 percent of all the committee seats during that period, with even higher percentages applying to the most prestigious committees and those directly related to constituencies, such as Agriculture.[37]

There have been fewer studies of the committee selection process in the Senate, and it is more difficult to generalize about that process because of the much smaller number of vacancies filled in each Congress. In a year with little turnover a newly elected senator may have a very limited range of choices for committee assignment. When a vacancy occurs on one of the most important committees, such as Foreign Relations, Finance, Appropriations, or Judiciary, a contest along ideological lines sometimes develops between nonfreshman senators. In 1975, for example, Democratic liberals worked hard and persuaded the Steering Committee to choose a liberal rather than a highly conservative southerner to fill a vacancy on the closely balanced Judiciary Committee; they also persuaded the committee not to expand the Judiciary Committee to include both. In addition, Senate liberals succeeded in strengthening the liberal membership on two other committees—Armed Services and Finance, which they felt to be under conservative domination.

Although seniority is only one factor in determining committee assignments, it is, with rare exceptions, the only factor considered in determining retention on a committee. If a party's majority drops and it loses seats on a committee, the members with the least committee seniority are dropped. Once a congressman has gained a place on a committee, the party leadership is unable to use the threat of removal to influence the congressman's vote. The power of the leadership to remove a committee member, which is so important in many states, has fallen into disuse since the days of the strong House Speakers like Joseph Cannon. Congressmen are usually able to bolt their party in a presidential election (in the sense of actively supporting the other candidate) without risking their places on committees, so long as they do not leave the party.

In modern times, there have been very few examples of congressmen being deprived of seniority rank on a committee. These have usually resulted from the member's support of an opposing party's presidential candidate during a campaign, but only a small proportion of such mavericks have lost their seniority. The last such example in the Senate occurred in 1925, when Robert La Follette and three senators who had supported his presidential campaign on the Progressive ticket were deprived of chairmanships and/or seniority rank on their committees. In 1965, the House Democratic caucus punished two Goldwater supporters, John Bell Williams and Albert W. Watson, by dropping them to the bottom of their committees; and a similar sanction was applied in 1969 against another Democrat, John Rarick, who had supported the candidacy of George Wallace in the 1968 campaign. In 1953, when Senator Wayne Morse left the Republican party to become an independent, he discovered that he had lost his seats on two major committees and had been relegated to minor ones. Because of a very narrow two-party balance in the Senate at that time, neither party was willing to let Morse have one of its seats on a major committee. Morse suffered because he had declared himself an *independent;* the bipartisan norms for committee assignments leave little room for independents.[38] In 1965, when Senator Strom Thurmond shifted directly from the Democratic to the Republican party, he was able to retain one of his major committee assignments with a high rank on that committee.

Seniority and Congressional Committee Chairmanships

The principle of seniority in the choice of committee chairmen was established in the Senate during the last quarter of the nineteenth century and in the House during the second decade of this century.[39] The seniority principle was based on tradition, not on written rules, but it was rigidly followed, with very rare exceptions, until 1975 when a dramatic revolt broke out in the House Democratic caucus. Under the seniority principle, when a vacancy occurs in a chairmanship, it is filled by the member of the majority party who has been on the committee for the longest time. If a member is eligible to chair two committees, he must take his choice of one; the next ranking member chairs the other. The senator or representative of the majority party who stays on a committee long enough will eventually become chairman of it, and the time it takes is a matter of luck, depending on the death, retirement, or electoral defeat of those ahead of him on the seniority ladder in the committee. The seniority principle also guaranteed that committee chairmen would remain in office as long as they remained in the Senate or House and their party held a majority. The congressional party leadership, unlike its counterparts in most state legislatures, was unable to remove a chairman, even if he was in fundamental disagreement with the party leadership and a majority of the party on the major issues under the jurisdiction of his committee. From 1925 to 1975, no committee chairmen in the Senate and few if any in the House had been removed, even at the start of a new session, as long as their party retained its majority.[40] (In 1967, House Democrats decided to remove Adam Clayton Powell as chairman of the Education and Labor Committee, but this action was superseded by a decision of the House to expel him from Congress.)

In January, 1975, the House Democratic caucus replaced three committee chairmen and accepted the resignation of a fourth. (These were, incidentally, four of the five representatives with the longest seniority in the House.) This turnover did not eliminate seniority as a major factor in the selection of chairmen, but it did end, once and for all, the rigid adherence to seniority as the sole criterion for selecting chairmen and keeping them in power. Sudden and unexpected as it was, the revolt had been foreshadowed by procedural changes that were initiated in 1971 in both the House and Senate; these changes made it simple to replace a chairman or ranking minority member if a majority of representatives or senators in his party decided to do so.

In 1971 both the Democratic and Republican caucuses in the House adopted rules specifying that the Committee on Committees did not have to follow seniority in nominating chairmen or ranking minority members. The Republican rules provided for an automatic secret vote in caucus on each nominee; Democratic rules, as modified in 1973, provided for a secret caucus vote at the request of one-fifth of the members, but it soon became the practice to have secret ballots on all nominees for chairman. Secret ballots, of course, protect members from possible reprisal if an effort to remove an incumbent chairman fails. No chairman was ousted as a result of the votes taken by the Democratic caucus in 1971 and 1973, but in 1975 the results were different. That year the Steering and Policy Committee recommended two changes in chairmanships. The Democratic caucus eventually agreed with one of these recommendations, replacing eighty-one-year-old Wright Patman as chairman of the Banking, Currency and Housing Committee with Henry Reuss, who had been only the fourth-ranking Democrat on the committee. The caucus also replaced the veteran chairmen of the Agriculture and Armed Services committees, contrary to the recommendations of the Steering and Policy Committee. These sweeping changes in chairmanships coincided with the resignation as chairman of the Ways and Means Committee of Wilbur Mills, perhaps the most powerful and respected House chairman, whose bizarre personal behavior led to overwhelming pressures on him to step down.

In the Senate, where most Democrats chair subcommittees, there has been much less criticism of committee chairmen, and no serious effort has been made to replace incumbent chairmen. But both parties in the Senate adopted procedural rules, similar to those in the House, to facilitate challenges to existing chairmen or ranking members. Senate Democrats have adopted a procedure under which a secret vote will be held on any chairman nominated by the Steering Committee if 20 percent of the Democratic senators (also acting in secret) request it. The procedure makes it possible to challenge a chairman without risking retribution. In 1973 Senate Republicans adopted a procedure under which the ranking member on each committee would be elected by the Republicans on that committee —a procedure that has not yet led to the replacement of any Republicans who hold committee rank by virtue of seniority.

It is important to understand what impact the seniority system for committee chairmen has had on Congress and what the implications are of the recent erosion of that system. The most obvious consequence of the seniority system is that most committee chairmen are older than the average member, although a stereotype of doddering, senile chairmen would not be accurate. In 1975 the average age of chairmen was the same in both branches—sixty-three, while the average senator was fifty-five and a half, and the average representative was fifty. In Congress as a whole 23 percent of the chairmen were seventy or over and 73 percent were sixty or over.

Perhaps more significant is the fact that long terms of service, particularly in the House, are required to reach a chairmanship. Data compiled by Barbara Hinckley show that during the period from 1947 to 1966, the median years of service in the Senate required to become a chairman or ranking minority member were ten for Democrats and seven for Republicans; in the House the figures were sixteen years for Democrats and twelve for Republicans.[41] In 1975, sixteen of the eighteen Senate chairmen had served at least sixteen years in that body, and seventeen of twenty-two House chairmen had served at least twenty years. Long congressional service is no guarantee of a chairmanship or ranking minority position. In 1975 there were twenty-six Democratic representatives who had served at least twenty years and were not chairmen (not including the Speaker and the four ex-chairmen). Long-term members who do not become chairmen are likely to have shifted committees after several terms on one committee, or are unlucky enough to be in line behind committee members who are very healthy and represent safe districts. The erosion that has occurred in the seniority system is not likely to result in the selection of much younger, less experienced chairmen. If the most senior member is not chosen as chairman, the post is likely to go to someone who ranks near the top of the committee seniority list.

A more significant and more complicated consequence of seniority is the effect it has had in giving certain types of states or districts a disproportionate share of committee chairmen, particularly among Democrats, who have controlled Congress most of the time since the New Deal.[42] For many years southern Democrats have held more than their share of committee chairmanships in both the Senate and House. Now the southern share of chairmanships has begun to decline, largely because of the delayed effect of changes in the regional composition of the Democratic congressional parties. From 1947 through 1968 an average of 60 percent of the Democratic chairmen in each branch came from the South.[43] There were two reasons for this southern advantage. Before the New Deal the Democratic congressional delegation was predominantly southern. Gradually the proportion of northern Democratic congressmen increased, but as late as 1951 roughly half of the Democratic senators and representatives came from the South. Because of the seniority system, the distribution of chairmanships reflects the regional balance in the congressional party fifteen to twenty years earlier. The second reason for the southern advantage is that congressmen from safe seats and districts are more likely to be reelected repeatedly than those from marginal ones. Southern senators and representatives have been able to win reelection very easily until the most recent elections. Although some northern Democratic representatives came from relatively safe districts in large cities, Democratic senators from the large northern states faced much more competition. Data compiled by Goodwin show that in the period from 1947 to 1968, 67 percent of the Senate Democratic chairmen and 91 percent of the House Democratic chairmen had won their latest election by over 60 percent of the vote, and most of these states and districts had presumably been safe for long periods of time.[44]

The regional distribution of chairmanships is now changing, and will change even more drastically in the years ahead. The growth of the Republican party in the South, the death or retirement of some veteran southern chairmen, and the ability of a number of northern Democratic senators and representatives to develop long tenure are factors that have all combined to change the regional pattern of chairmanships. In 1975, 33 percent of the chairmen in the Senate were southerners; the replacement of incumbent chairmen in the House reduced the proportion of southerners from 64 to 45 percent. More significant, perhaps, is the fact that, particularly in the Senate, nonsoutherners hold many of the ranking positions immediately behind southern chairmen who are likely to retire in a few years. In 1975 five of the six most senior Democratic senators were southerners, but only six of the thirty-four most senior ones were from the South. Before long the South is likely to be underrepresented in Senate chairmanships. In the House thirteen of the sixteen most senior Democrats were Southerners, but only about half of the top fifty were.[45]

The decline in the proportion of southern chairmen that is occurring has obvious implications for the policy output of committees because southern congressmen, particularly the more senior ones, tend to be more conservative than other Democratic congressmen. Goodwin's data for 1947 through 1968 show that Democratic chairmen in both houses were less likely to vote with their party and less likely to support the programs of Democratic Presidents than the average Democrat was and that they were much less likely to vote with their party and support the President than Democratic floor leaders were.[46] Most of the Democratic senators who have recently won chairmanships or who are likely to succeed to them soon belong to the liberal wing of the party. Many of the northern representatives who have become, or are in line to become, chairmen represent urban constituencies that expect them to take a liberal stand on most issues.

Perhaps the most important consequence of the seniority system was that it guaranteed the independence of committee chairmen. Despite the fact that he disagreed with a majority of his party on issues pertinent to his committee or blocked bills in the committee that party leaders were supporting, the chairman could not be removed from his position by either the party leaders or a majority of his party's members. Although the 1975 revolt of Democratic congressmen against the seniority system directly affected only four chairmen, it had a powerful impact on all House committee chairmen. It meant that in the future a chairman who was arbitrary or dictatorial in handling committee business, or one who was simply inept, or whose views were much more conservative than his colleagues on issues his committee handled would run a serious risk of being removed. These factors had all contributed to the ousting of one or more chairmen in 1975. Those chairmen who had been confirmed in their posts, but with a significant opposition vote, had particular reason to be concerned. Almost immediately there were signs that committee chairmen were running their committees less arbitrarily and more democratically, and that they were more responsive to pressures for prompt and favorable action on legislation that was part of the party's program. To understand more fully the impact of changes in the seniority system and other recent developments, we must examine carefully the role played by the chairmen of House and Senate committees.

INSIDE THE COMMITTEES

The Chairman

On almost all congressional committees, the chairman is the most important and influential member. His influence depends in part on his formal powers, which have been curtailed in recent years in the House, and in part on his skill in developing personal and political bases of support, a skill that obviously varies from one chairman to another. We should begin by noting some significant differences between chairmen in the two branches of Congress. In the Senate most of the committees are organized into subcommittees, nearly every Democrat chairs at least one subcommittee, and many of the powers normally exercised by the chairmen are delegated to subcommittee chairmen. Consequently the chairmen of senatorial committees, though usually very influential, seldom dominate their committees as completely as some House chairmen have done in the past. Until very recently, some House chairmen ruled their committees with an iron hand and either refused to use subcommittees or maintained tight control over them. During the 1960s several House committees adopted rules designed to limit the authority and discretion of the chairmen. Then in 1973 the Democratic caucus established a Democratic caucus on each House committee, which was given much of the authority over subcommittees that had previously been exercised by the chairman. The seniority reforms in 1975 further inhibited the House chairmen in their efforts to dominate their committees.[47]

The power exercised by a chairman of a committee, or a subcommittee, has a number of bases.[48] Although most committees provide in their rules for a fixed meeting time, the chairman has considerable control over scheduling both hearings and working sessions of the committee. He determines the amount of time allocated for hearings on a bill. He presides at the meetings of his committee and controls its agenda. A determined chairman, with at least the tacit support of some members, can delay hearings indefinitely, and can also prevent a member from gaining a vote on a bill for many weeks by refusing to recognize him in meetings, bringing up other bills, ruling motions out of order, adjourning regular meetings early, and refusing to schedule extra meetings.[49] The chairman exercises some control over the committee's resources. For many years the chairmen in both houses selected the committee staff, assigned it to subcommittees, controlled the budget and determined how it would be allocated among subcommittees. Recent changes have given members of Senate committees more control over staff and have guaranteed adequate staff and budgets to House subcommittees. When a bill is reported to the floor, the chairman either manages the bill or appoints the floor manager. If the bill goes to a conference committee, the chairman normally serves on it and also selects the other members to serve on it. In the exercise of his authority, the chairman is in a position to do favors for individual members of his committee, helping them get action on their bills, providing staff assistance, and authorizing trips abroad for deserving members.

The effectiveness of a committee chairman depends not only on the formal prerogatives of his office but also on his skills in developing political and personal bases of power.[50] In the committees, knowledge is power, and the chairman often has more information and understanding about the measures coming before his committee than anyone else. The chairman, particularly in the House, devotes nearly all of his time to the work of his committee. Senators, on the other hand, have so many responsibilities and subcommittee assignments that the subcommittee chairman dominates the hearings and becomes *the* expert on the issues before his subcommittee. The knowledge and experience of the chairman force administration officials appearing before his committee to respect his views, and these qualities command attention when the bill reaches the floor of the House or Senate. During Wilbur Mills' long tenure as chairman of the House Ways and Means Committee, he was recognized as the leading tax expert in Washington, and other members of his committee relied heavily on his knowledge and judgment.

The committee chairman also has the advantage of long experience in working with the other members of the committee. This is important because, in the last analysis, the chairman's effectiveness depends on his ability to keep the support and confidence of his colleagues on the committee. Despite his large share of formal power, a chairman cannot single-handedly report a bill to the floor, nor can he indefinitely delay a bill if a majority of the committee is determined to pass it. Chairmen differ, of course, in their leadership skill and in the extent to which they try to influence the work of the committee and its subcommittees. The most successful chairman is not one who uses power arbitrarily but one who uses his formal and informal resources skillfully to build consensus on the committee and who is sensitive to the wishes of committee members. One member said of the former chairman of the House Interior Committee, "Aspinall is probably as good a chairman as you'll find. He dominates the committee in a fair way."[51] The author of a study of Wilbur Mills during his chairmanship of the Ways and Means

Committee concluded: "The decisions of the Committee are shaped and articulated by Mills, but if his word comes close to being law in the Committee, it is because he has listened well to the words of others."[52]

The chairman's influence also depends on the degree of ideological and interest cohesion or division on the committee. The sharper the divisions within the committee, the more difficult the chairman's job and the more important it is for him to be aligned with the majority coalition if he is going to be effective. Mills gained influence from the fact that he held a pivotal position between the liberal and conservative blocs on the committee, and this enabled him to vote with a majority on most of those occasions when it was not possible to reach consensus on an issue. Mills' successor, Al Ullman, had greater difficulty in winning support for compromise proposals in part because the committee was divided more sharply along ideological lines following the addition of a large number of Democratic members, most of them quite liberal. The House Education and Labor Committee is deeply divided along ideological lines, and its members are very policy oriented. As Fenno has pointed out, the committee "has no protective norms, no tradition of deference to its chairman to shield him from intolerance of his policy"; instead it has "harsh rules of policy combat." As a consequence, two of the previous chairmen (preceding Carl Perkins, the incumbent) eventually had much of their power stripped away by a coalition within the committee.[53]

Subcommittees

A major decentralizing force in Congress, and one that weakens the authority of committee chairmen, is the growing use of subcommittees.[54] With a few exceptions (including several small committees and the new budget committees), all committees in the Senate and House are divided into subcommittees. The House rule requiring most committees to have subcommittees was adopted in 1975 and had the major effect of requiring the powerful Ways and Means Committee to establish subcommittees for the first time in many years. In 1975 there were almost 300 subcommittees, 139 in the Senate, 146 in the House, and 14 related to joint committees. (These figures include a few special subcommittees and subcommittees of select committees.)[55]

One effect of the extensive use of subcommittees is to increase the degree of specialization in Congress; members tend to concentrate their attention on some or all of their own subcommittees and to pay little attention to the issues being considered by other subcommittees within their committee. Another consequence of using subcommittees, particularly in the Senate, is to increase the pressure of time on members, who frequently discover that two or more of their subcommittees are meeting at the same time. In 1975 the Senate Judiciary Committee had fifteen members, and fifteen subcommittees—the largest number in the Senate. Most Democratic members found it necessary to chair one or two of these subcommittees while serving on at least five others, not to mention their assignments on other committees.

There are several reasons for the growing use of subcommittees, which have doubled in number since 1947. The need for greater specialization than the committee structure permits is the most obvious one. Subcommittees allow Congress to cope with the variety and complexity of governmental problems and permit individual congressmen to concentrate their time and attention on fewer subjects. In the case of the appropriations committees, the use of subcommittees is virtually essential if congressmen are to give careful scrutiny to the budget requests of all departments. Some of the factors that caused the creation of select committees also lead to the establishment of subcommittees. They provide convenient channels of access for both pressure groups and governmental agencies. They make it possible to give attention to detailed technical problems, such as improvements in judicial machinery, state taxation of interstate commerce, oceanography, and space sciences. Perhaps more important, they give experienced, able congressmen a chance to gain prestige and pursue their interests as subcommittee chairmen.

Recent changes instituted by the House Democratic caucus have provided more diversified leadership and considerably greater autonomy for the subcommittees in that branch. In the past, most committee chairmen had followed the principle of awarding subcommittee chairmanships to the senior majority members of the committee, a practice that frequently led to situations where a member chaired two or more subcommittees on one or more committees.[56] In 1971 the House Democratic caucus revised its rules to specify that no congressman could be chairman of more than one subcommittee in the House. The reform had several immediate effects in 1971: there were twenty-nine new subcommittee chairmen, sixteen of them as a result of the reform; the new chairmen were much less senior than those whom they replaced; on several committees—Banking and Currency, Judiciary, and Foreign Affairs—the new subcommittee chairmen were considerably more liberal than the men they replaced. By 1973 there were another twenty-four new subcommittee chairmen, partly as a result of the reform, and they also tended to be less senior and more liberal than those they replaced.[57]

The other major change instituted by the House Democratic caucus was the adoption in 1973 of a so-called "Subcommittee Bill of Rights," designed to give the subcommittees more autonomy, subject only to decisions of a Democratic caucus on each full committee. The new rules provided that at the start of each Congress, the Democratic members of each committee should meet for the following purposes:

1. To vote for subcommittee chairmen under a procedure permitting each member to bid for a chairmanship in order of his seniority on the committee (or on a subcommittee, if the committee caucus prefers that formula). Chairmen of Appropriations subcommittees, however, would be confirmed by the entire Democratic caucus.
2. To vote for subcommittee members, under procedures giving members a chance to retain some previous assignments and some choice in new ones.
3. To determine the number of subcommittees and the jurisdiction of each. Moreover, each subcommittee would be entitled to an adequate budget and to at least one staff member, subject to the overall control of the Democratic caucus on the committee.[58]

These changes in the rules governing House subcommittees have made it impossible for committee chairmen to dominate subcommittees, to manipulate them, or to ignore them, as some chairmen had done in the past. There remain some differences among both House and Senate committees in the degree of autonomy exercised by subcommittees, and the extent to which members concentrate on their own subcommittees and are willing to accept the decisions made in other subcommittees when they report to the full committee. We will discuss these committee norms affecting subcommittees in Chapter 17.

In recent years there have been at least twice as many subcommittees in the Senate as there were Democratic senators available to chair them, and as a result most Democrats chair at least one or two. In the Ninety-fourth Congress (1975) only five Democrats (all first-year senators) had no subcommittee chairmanships. Most Senate committees followed the committee seniority principle (with minor exceptions) in allocating subcommittee chairmanships. The wide diffusion of subcommittee chairmanships in the Senate has important political implications. It has contributed to a distribution of power that Randall B. Ripley has described as neither centralization nor decentralization but rather individualism.[59] Senators (unlike representatives) do not have to wait for many years before they become recognized as specialists and have a substantial impact on legislation. Minority senators, though unable to chair subcommittees, gain the advantages of specializing in the work of a few subcommittees. Members of either party who are considered to be mavericks share in the opportunity to chair committees or become minority member specialists. An imaginative subcommittee chairman can use his position to attract public attention through hearings and through his sponsorship of legislative measures, and he is strategically placed to facilitate the passage of such measures in the Senate. Although senators often complain about their multiple subcommittee memberships, the system suits the individual needs of most senators very well, and it is likely to persist, in part for that reason.

State Legislative Committees

The whole fabric of the committee system in the states makes it difficult for the committees to be tightly run citadels of power. There are only a few states, such as North Carolina, in which subcommittees are used extensively; elsewhere, there appears to be no need for such structural complexity. There is a large turnover in committee membership in every session, which makes it difficult to develop widely accepted norms and traditions for committee operation or to accumulate a core of members who are experts on the subject matter with which the committee deals. Expert knowledge comes less from committee experience than from the custom of putting legislators with specific occupational or professional experience on appropriate committees. Lawyers are assigned to the judiciary committee, insurance men to the insurance committee, and farmers to the agriculture committee. Not only does this create obvious problems concerning conflicts of interests, but it may turn the committee into an arena for competing interest groups, each of which is directly represented on the committee.

Early in this chapter we described the high rate of turnover of committee chairmanships found in most state legislatures. It is unusual for a member to serve on the same committee for many terms before becoming chairman, and not many chairmen continue to serve in that capacity on the same committee for long periods of time. Committee chairmen are unlikely to be powerful figures in the legislative system when some of them have had little legislative experience and many of them have had little experience on their own committees. In some states with strong legislative leadership, the major committee chairmanships go to veteran legislators who are loyal to the leadership, but these men are likely to advance rather rapidly to more important committee and party assignments rather than to retain a specific chairmanship for many sessions. These chairmen are usually powerful, not because of their established reputation as subject-matter experts, but because they are skilled and trusted leaders of the majority party or faction.

It is true, however, that many of the recent innovations in state legislatures have been designed to increase the importance and effectiveness of committees. In Chapter 5 we described the growth of interim committees in a number of states. In those states where the regular session committees continue to meet during the interim (instead of special ones being established), the power of these committees and their chances of developing stronger norms and cohesion are enhanced. The level of activity and degree of effectiveness of committees during the interim may depend very heavily on the initiative provided by the chairman. Both interim committees and longer sessions that allow committees more time to operate increase the opportunities for committee members to develop an expertise on the topics that come before their committee.

NOTES

1. Herman Finer, *Governments of Greater European Powers* (New York, 1956), p. 116.

2. For the history of congressional committees, see George B. Galloway, *The Legislative Process in Congress* (New York, 1953), pp. 276–278; Randall B. Ripley, *Power in the Senate* (New York, 1969), pp. 47–48; and George Goodwin, Jr., *The Little Legislatures: Committees of Congress* (Amherst, Mass., 1970), chap. 1.

3. See Goodwin, *The Little Legislatures,* pp. 18–24.

4. See V. Stanley Vardys, "Select Committees of the House of Representatives," *Midwest Journal of Political Science* 6 (1962):247–265; and Dale Vinyard, "Congressional Committees on Small Business," *Midwest Journal of Political Science* 10 (1966):364–377.

5. Henry M. Jackson, "Congress and the Atom," *Annals of the American Academy of Political and Social Science* 290 (November 1953):77.

6. See Harold P. Green and Alan Rosenthal, *Government of the Atom* (New York, 1963), pp. 25–30, 79–103.

7. See William C. Johnson, "The Political Party System in the 1959–1960 California Legislature" (Master's thesis, University of California, 1960), pp. 40–43.

8. See Dean E. Mann, "The Legislative Committee System in Arizona," *Western Political Quarterly* 14 (1961):925–941.

9. See Kenneth T. Palmer, "The Legislative Committee System in Pennsylvania" (Ph.D. diss., Pennsylvania State University, 1964), pp. 19–35.

10. Corey Rosen, "Seniority and the Selection of Committee Chairmen in American State Legislatures" (Paper presented at the annual meeting of the Midwest Political Association, 1975).

11. Ibid.; Charles W. Wiggins, *Arizona Legislature* (Phoenix, 1974), pp. 34–41; Charles W. Wiggins, *The Legislative Process in Iowa* (Ames, Iowa, 1972), pp. 38–39.

12. Alvin D. Sokolow and Richard W. Brandsma, "Partisanship and Seniority in Legislative Committee Assignments: California After Reapportionment," *Western Political Quarterly* 24 (1971):527–539; Joel M. Fisher, C. M. Price, and C. G. Bell, *The Legislative Process in California* (Washington, D.C., 1973), pp. 50–57.

13. See James Herndon, "Legislative Politics in North Dakota," in *Minnesota-Dakotas Assembly: Background Papers,* pp. 1–13; Susanne A. Stoiber, ed., *Legislative Politics in the Rocky Mountain West* (Boulder, Colo., 1967), p. 54; Alex B. Lacy, Jr., ed., *Power in American State Legislatures* (New Orleans, La., 1967), pp. 3–4; William G. Cornelius, ed., *Southeastern State Legislatures* (Atlanta, 1967), p. S-5; Douglas C. Chaffey, "The Institutionalization of State Legislatures," *Western Political Quarterly* 23 (1970):184–188; Douglas Bothun and John Comer, "Correlates of Committee Assignments in the Nebraska Unicameral" (Paper presented at the annual meeting of the Midwest Political Science Association, 1975).

14. Lacy, *Power in American State Legislatures,* pp. 3–4; Herndon, "Legislative Politics in North Dakota," pp. 1–3; Chaffey, "The Institutionalization of State Legislatures," pp. 184–188; Cornelius, *Southeastern State Legislatures,* p. S-5; Bothun and Comer, "Correlates of Committee Assignments in the Nebraska Unicameral"; Donald Leavitt, "Changing Rules and Norms in the Minnesota Legislature" (Paper presented at the annual meeting of the Midwest Political Science Association, 1975), pp. 17–26.

15. Sokolow and Brandsma, "Partisanship and Seniority in Legislative Committee Assignments: California After Reapportionment"; Fisher, Price, and Bell, *The Legislative Process in California,* pp. 50–57.

16. H. Owen Porter and David A. Leuthold, "Acquiring Legislative Expertise: Appointments to Standing Committees in the States" (Paper presented at the annual meeting of the American Political Science Association, 1974).

17. Ibid.

18. Alan Rosenthal, *Legislative Performance in the States: Explorations of Committee Behavior* (New York, 1974), pp. 174–178.

19. Richard F. Fenno, Jr., *Congressmen in Committees* (Boston, 1973), chap. 1.

20. Ibid., pp. 6, 140.

21. Ibid., p. 143.

22. David W. Rohde and Kenneth A. Shepsle, "Democratic Committee Assignments in the House of Representatives: Strategic Aspects of a Social Choice Process," *American Political Science Review* 67 (1973):889–905.

23. Ibid.

24. Malcolm E. Jewell and Chu Chi-hung, "Membership Movement and Committee Attractiveness in the U.S. House of Representatives, 1963–1971," *American Journal of Political Science* 18 (1974):433–441; Charles S. Bullock, III, "Committee Transfers in the United States House of Representatives," *Journal of Politics* 35 (1973):85–120.

25. Jewell and Chi-hung, "Membership Movement and Committee Attractiveness in the U.S. House of Representatives"; unpublished data from Kenneth A. Shepsle.

26. For a fuller description, see Nicholas A. Masters, "House Committee Assignments," *American Political Science Review* 55 (1961):345–357.

27. Louis P. Westefield, "Majority Party Leadership and the Committee System in the House of Representatives," *American Political Science Review* 68 (1974):1593–1604.

28. There have been some exceptions to this policy, however, notably on the House Armed Services Committee while Hebert was chairman.

29. Charles L. Clapp, *The Congressman: His Work as He Sees It* (Washington, D.C., 1963), p. 194.

30.   See Goodwin, *The Little Legislatures,* pp. 83–86; and Ripley, *Power in the Senate,* pp. 132–139.

31.   John G. Stewart, "Two Strategies of Leadership: Johnson and Mansfield," in *Congressional Behavior,* ed. Nelson W. Polsby (New York, 1971), p. 64. Stewart provides details on the contrasting attitude of Mansfield.

32.   Clapp, *The Congressman,* p. 200.

33.   Fenno, *Congressmen in Committees,* p. 19.

34.   Christopher H. Achen and John S. Stolarek, "The Resolution of Congressional Committee Assignment Contests: Factors Influencing the Democratic Committee on Committees" (Paper presented at the annual meeting of the American Political Science Association, 1974); Rohde and Shepsle, "Democratic Committee Assignments in the House of Representatives," p. 899.

35.   Fenno, *Congressmen in Committees,* pp. 20–26; Achen and Stolarek, "The Resolution of Congressional Committee Assignment Contests"; Rohde and Shepsle, "Democratic Committee Assignments in the House of Representatives," p. 904; Charles S. Bullock, III, "Freshmen Committee Assignments and Re-election to the United States House of Representatives," *American Political Science Review* 66 (1972):996–1007.

36.   Barbara Deckard, "State Party Delegations in the United States House of Representatives—An Analysis of Group Action," *Polity* 5 (1973):312–334.

37.   Charles S. Bullock, III, "The Influence of State Party Delegations on House Committee Assignments," *Midwest Journal of Political Science* 15 (1971):525–546.

38.   See Ralph K. Huitt, "The Morse Committee Assignment Controversy: A Study in Senate Norms," *American Political Science Review* 51 (1957):313–329.

39.   See Nelson W. Polsby, M. Gallaher, and B. S. Rundquist, "The Growth of the Seniority System in the U.S. House of Representatives," *American Political Science Review* 63 (1969):787–807; and Ripley, *Power in the Senate,* pp. 42–47.

40.   See Huitt, "The Morse Committee Assignment Controversy," pp. 313–329; and Goodwin, *The Little Legislatures,* pp. 95–97.

41.   Barbara Hinckley, *The Seniority System in Congress* (Bloomington, Ind., 1971), pp. 20–29, 31, 126.

42.   For a further discussion of the consequences of seniority, see Barbara Hinckley, *The Seniority System in Congress;* and "Seniority in the Committee Leadership Selection of Congress," *Midwest Journal of Political Science* 13 (1969):613–630.

43.   Goodwin, *The Little Legislatures,* p. 127. The South is defined here as the eleven Confederate states plus Kentucky and Oklahoma.

44.   Ibid., p. 131.

45.   See also Norman J. Ornstein and David W. Rohde, "Seniority and Future Power in Congress," in *Congress in Change,* ed., Norman J. Ornstein (New York, 1975), pp. 72–87.

46.   Goodwin, *The Little Legislatures,* pp. 133–135.

47.   See Norman J. Ornstein, "Causes and Consequences of Congressional Change: Subcommittee Reforms in the House of Representatives, 1970–73," in *Congress in Change,* ed. Ornstein, pp. 88–114.

48.   See Goodwin, *The Little Legislatures,* pp. 136–142; Ripley, *Power in the Senate,* pp. 110–124; and Fenno, *Congressmen in Committees,* pp. 114–137.

49.   The chairman's ability to control committee procedure is well illustrated in Howard E. Shuman, "Senate Rules and the Civil Rights Bill: A Case Study," *American Political Science Review* 51 (1957):961–962.

50.   Fenno has an excellent analysis of the informal aspects of leadership exercised by the chairmen of the six committees he studied in depth, in *Congressmen in Committees,* pp. 114–137.

51.   Ibid., p. 118.

52.   John F. Manley, "Wilbur Mills: A Study in Congressional Influence," *American Political Science Review* 63 (1969):442–464, quotation at 464.

53.   Fenno, *Congressmen in Committees,* pp. 132, 127.

54.   For a detailed discussion of subcommittees, see Goodwin, *The Little Legislatures,* pp. 45–63.

55.   For a complete list of subcommittees and their members, see *Congressional Quarterly Weekly Report* 33 (May 17, 1975): Supplement.

56.   Thomas R. Wolanin, "Committee Seniority and the Choice of House Subcommittee Chairmen: 80th–91st Congresses," *Journal of Politics* 36 (1974):687–702.

57.   Ornstein, "Causes and Consequences of Congressional Change."

58.   "Standing Rules and Manual of the House Democratic Caucus" (February, 1975).

59.   Ripley, *Power in the Senate,* pp. 11–13, 152–154.

CHAPTER NINE

The Legislative Bureaucracy

The scope, magnitude, and complexity of modern governmental activities have dictated increasing specialization and division of labor in legislative systems. The most clearly manifest by-product of legislative specialization has been the development since the late nineteenth century of staff operations to make available to congressmen and state legislators personnel who are able to assist them in the performance of their tasks. Legislative bureaucrats play functionally significant roles in the legislative system. At the clerical level, the staff facilitates the integrative function of the legislative system insofar as the members' or committees' staffs are involved in office-management operations, particularly those related to communication with interest-group representatives, constituents, or officials of the administration. Technical and research staff operations may contribute to the management of conflicts, to the extent that controversial issues can be converted into matters of expert knowledge. The availability of staff to congressmen and state legislators tends to increase the capacity of the legislature to be independent of the executive. One of the purposes of the provision in the Legislative Reorganization Act of 1946 for increased member and committee staffs was to diminish the practice of borrowing staff from executive agencies, a policy that had tended to make congressional committees dependent upon these agencies for facts and interpretation. Finally, staffs provide a source of independence for legislative committees from centralized political control by the party leadership. The relatively small staff facilities for most state legislative committees is one factor that helps to account for the weakness of committees at that level.

It should not be assumed that legislative bureaucrats are nothing but neutral servants who unerringly supply the legislature with indisputably objective evidence. The staff members are inexorably involved in the political struggle within the legislative system, and their role behavior may have fundamental policy implications.[1] The legislator often prefers knowledge that supports his preconceptions, and the staffman himself is not devoid of political values that he may wish to see implemented by the legislature. Thus, the staff may contribute to the development and crystallization of legislative conflict, and it may be directly involved in negotiations and bargaining among the conflicting interests that are focused upon particular issues.

TYPES OF LEGISLATIVE STAFFS

In general, there are two broad types of legislative staffs for American legislatures: the *housekeeping* staff and the *specialist,* or *professional,* staff. The housekeeping staff performs clerical, secretarial, and service tasks of a relatively routine kind. The overwhelming preponderance of clerks and other staff assistance for Congress and the state legislatures has been occupied with records, schedules of witnesses for committees, clerical detail, general housekeeping duties of office supply and management, mail, services for constituents, and other routine work. Since the beginning of legislative operations, legislators in the United States have recognized the necessity for such routine assistance because of the importance of maintaining records of proceedings. The growth in the numbers of housekeeping staff people is related to the increasing complexity of legislative work. Congressional committees began to employ full-time clerks when the House Ways and Means Committee and the Senate Finance Committee first obtained regular appropriations for such assistance in 1856, although some clerical assistance for congressional committees was made available on a temporary basis as far back as the late eighteenth century.[2] Clerical services for state legislators probably was largely a late-nineteenth-century development, and even today, anything like adequate clerical assistance for legislators is provided only in a minority of states.[3]

The specialist staff performs policy-related tasks, although their degree of involvement in policy may vary a great deal. The specialist staff may be characterized in terms of several subtypes: research, bill-drafting, investigating, subject-matter expert, political.

Research Staff

The research man gathers data and other information. His work may vary from routine collections of information (looking up references in the legislative library or tabulating simple information) to major research investigations. Research-staff operations have been institutionalized at the congressional level in the Congressional Research Service of the Library of Congress, an agency that was created in 1914. (Until 1970, it was called the Legislative Reference Service.) At the state level, institutionalized research operations may be associated with the legislative councils, which now exist in thirty-eight states, or with state legislative reference services. The first permanent legislative reference library was created in Wisconsin in 1901.[4]

Bill-drafting Staff

Bill drafters provide technical services to legislators in the preparation of legislation. The bill-drafting service for Congress is the Office of Legislative Council, established in 1918. The New York and Wisconsin state legislatures created bill-drafting assistance at the turn of the century, and this service is now available to legislators in every state.

Investigating Staff

Experts in the arts and sciences of investigation are essential to the modern congressional investigating committee. The importance of a staff to a congressional committee is probably increased when

> the chief function of that committee is the making of investigations by means of public hearings. Unless such hearings are planned with great care, the background of the subject under investigation thoroughly explored, and the potential contribution of each witness carefully estimated, an investigation is apt to prove aimless and fruitless.[5]

Lawyers and accountants are particularly needed by investigating committees. Although trained investigators on loan from the executive branch have been, and are still, used by congressional committees, and such committees frequently work in cooperation with executive investigating agencies (such as the Federal Bureau of Investigation), the tendency has been for committees to rely more and more on their own staffs.[6] Investigating staffs are much less available to state legislative committees, although there have been some notable cases of their use at the state level.[7]

Subject-matter Experts

Traditionally, experts on taxation, social security, procurements, education, mental health, and other subjects have been used by Congress and the state legislatures on a temporary loan basis from executive agencies or have been in the employ of interest groups and associations concerned with particular subject-matter areas. Increasingly, Congress and especially congressional committees have acquired their own expert staffs; this has been particularly true since the passage of the Legislative Reorganization Act of 1946. Economists, accountants, lawyers with a specialist expertise, natural and physical scientists, and political scientists are among those now found in considerable numbers among the professional staffs of Congress.

In the 1970s, state legislatures have expanded their permanent expert staffs in a dramatic way. While a number of state legislatures have had some central research staff (legislative reference bureau or legislative council staff) for a relatively long period of time, beginning in the late 1960s the legislatures began to acquire more specialized staffs (e.g., for fiscal research and policy analysis) both managed centrally by joint legislative management committees and assigned directly to substantive legislative committees.[8]

Political Staff

Some staff operations are almost exclusively political and require personnel with political expertise. The legislative strategist, the ghost writer of political speeches and books, and the political campaigner are found on the staffs of senators and representatives and sometimes even on committee staffs.

INDIVIDUAL MEMBERS' STAFFS

There was a time when almost all state legislators' offices were their desks in the legislative chambers, and they had no individual staff assistance. In regard to facilities and staff, the state legislatures have been modernized enormously since the late 1960s. By 1971, some legislators were provided office space in twenty-six states, and secretarial assistance was provided to legislators in all but five states.[9] In the two largest states, New York and California, the legislatures have come to have relatively large staffs. By 1974, the California legislature provided about $22 million to employ a total of 1,875 clerical and professional staff personnel for legislators and committees; the total number of legislative employees had grown to as many as 1,429 in New York by the 1972 session.[10] But the substantial staffing of individual legislative offices is largely a congressional phenomenon.

The staffing of congressional offices varies a great deal from one office to another. From the funds available for individual congressional offices (still archaically referred to as "clerk hire" allowances), members may organize their staffs as they see fit and hire the staff personnel they choose. In the United States House of Representatives, members' individual office staffs average about twelve persons. According to Donald G. Tacheron and Morris K. Udall:

> During the first session of the 91st Congress, according to information prepared for a House Appropriations subcommittee, about three-fifths of the members employed ten or more persons. Somewhat more than a quarter of the members employed eight or nine persons, and forty-four employed fewer than eight persons.[11]

The staffs of United States Senators are considerably larger than those of House members. In the Ninety-fourth Congress, Senate members' staffs averaged twenty-four people, with twenty senators having staffs of more than thirty employees. In the main, senators from the most populous states have the larger staffs: Senator John V. Tunney (D-Calif.) had fifty-six staff assistants, and Senator Alan Cranston (D-Calif.) had fifty-five; Senator Jacob K. Javits (R-N.Y.) had fifty-one aides, Senator James L. Buckley (R-Cons.-N.Y.), forty-five; both Republican senators from Pennsylvania, Richard S. Schweiker and Hugh Scott, had forty-seven assistants.[12]

The activities of the congressional office staff are varied, but in general, members' own staff people devote most of their time and energy to servicing and nursing the constituency. As John S. Saloma's inventories of activities in congressional offices show, representatives themselves spend two-thirds of their time on legislative activities—on the House floor, in committee, doing legislative research, and so forth. In contrast, the members' staffs devote their time largely to constituency service and support activities—handling casework, answering mail, meeting with constituents, and the like.[13] Table 9.1 shows the proportions of time during an average week that office personnel devote to various activities. More than two-fifths of the time of the average congressional office is invested in the mailbags; strictly legislative support activities are engaged in only about 14 percent of the time.

There are many variations in the staff organization of the aides of individual

TABLE 9.1 Activities of a Congressional Office Staff (In percentages)

ACTIVITY	TOTAL STAFF WORK IN AN AVERAGE WEEK DEVOTED TO THE ACTIVITY
With the member in committee	1
Handling constituent problems (casework)	19
Visiting with constituents in Washington	6
With lobbyists and special-interest groups	2
Press work, radio, and television	6
Writing speech drafts, floor remarks	5
Legislative research, bill drafting	6
Pressure and opinion mail	16
Opinion ballots (preprinted by organizations)	2
Requests for information	7
Letters of congratulation, condolence	4
Other correspondence	12
Mailing government publications	4
Other miscellaneous activities	9
Total	99

SOURCE: John S. Saloma III, *Congress and the New Politics* (Boston, 1969), p. 185.

members of Congress. Generally, the staffs of members of the House of Representatives are small enough for the congressman to have a relatively close working relationship with each aide on a personal basis. Senate members' staffs vary more in size and are more likely to be bureaucratized. Donald R. Matthews describes the types of Senate staff organization that have been observed:

> It is possible to distinguish between two types of Senate offices, the bureaucratic and the individualistic. While very few offices are pure examples of either, most offices can be easily classified as tending toward one or the other. In the bureaucratic offices, the senator has delegated considerable non-routine responsibilities to his staff, established a fairly clearcut division of labor and chain of command. The administrative assistant is really a "senator, junior grade," and under his direction other members of the staff specialize in such things as legislative research and speechwriting, answering the mail, press relations, or patronage matters. At the opposite end of the spectrum are the individualistic offices, "vest pocket" operations in which the senator has delegated only routine tasks and in which the staff has little influence and less authority. In these offices, a division of labor is relatively amorphous—"everyone does a little bit of everything in this office"—and the administrative assistant's job is reduced to that of a "paper shuffler."[14]

The role of senators' staffs in policy making varies between individualistic and bureaucratic offices. In bureaucratic contexts, the staff serves as the important communications link between the senator and other members, lobbyists, newspapermen, executive officials, and constituents; in individualistic offices, the policy role of the staff is much reduced, and there is a tendency for the senator himself to handle all important matters.

HOUSEKEEPING STAFFS

No treatment of legislative staff organization would be adequate without some consideration of the staffs of the legislative houses themselves. These aides constitute an important part of the housekeeping staff for legislatures and usually include the Clerk of the House, the Sergeant at Arms, the Parliamentarian, and a variety of other officers. Unfortunately, there are no systematic data by means of which to generalize extensively about such aides, but it is clear that they may facilitate the performance of legislative tasks, ease the adjustment of legislators to the legislative system, and influence legislative policy-making. Congressional housekeeping staffs are substantial in size and varied in function. In the Ninety-fourth Congress, for instance, the Secretary of the Senate had thirty-nine staff employees, and the Sergeant at Arms had eleven aides not including the police department, recording studio, telephone and telegraph facilities, and other administrative services which he supervised. On the House side, the Clerk's Office contained thirty-six staff members, the Sergeant at Arms had fourteen assistants, and the Doorkeeper had seventeen staff aides.[15]

At the state level, the staff assistance for the legislative houses is much less elaborate, and ordinarily the clerks of the house and senate are the key figures. They are the chief administrative officers of the houses and in many states serve over a long period of years. Perhaps largely because of their typically long tenure of service for essentially amateur legislative bodies, these clerks can come to have substantial influence on state legislation.[16]

GROWTH AND UTILIZATION OF CONGRESSIONAL COMMITTEE STAFFS[17]

Development of Staffs

In the early days of the Republic, congressional committees had no staffs, and probably needed none. The first congressional committee staffman appears to have been employed by a secret committee of the Continental Congress. But this was a temporary and unusual assignment. Congressional committees took a half-century to become well established, and it was not until the House Ways and Means Committee hired a full-time clerk in 1856 that some kind of committee staffing became anything like a regular affair. Other major congressional committees acquired clerical help over the latter half of the nineteenth century. The use of professional staff, as opposed to strictly clerical assistance, dates from about the mid-1920s; in 1924, the first comprehensive legislative pay act authorizing appropriations for all committee employees was passed.[18] Professional staffing for all committees became fully established with the passage of the Legislative Reorganization Act of 1946, which authorized each committee to hire four professional staff aides and six clerks. The Legislative Reorganization Act of 1970 increased basic committee staff allowances from four to six professional staff members. These staff limitations do not apply to the appropriations committees. The 1976 appropriations bill for legislative branch spending substantially increased staff allowances, providing additional staff assistance for senators to help them with committee work.[19]

Until the end of World War II, committee staff personnel were, in the main, chosen on a patronage basis and served only while their patron, usually the committee chairman, was in office. There were a few exceptions to this. The appropriations committees had clerks who, although recruited on a patronage basis, became expert and served under several chairmen; and the House Foreign Affairs Committee had the same staff administrator from 1939 to 1970.[20] The conditions of congressional committee staffing as of the immediate postwar years were succinctly summarized by former Congressman Jerry Voorhis:

> As for the regular committees, which constitute the very heart of the work of Congress, their entire staff consisted of one or two clerks and a "messenger." These people were always appointed by the chairman and they were almost always people from his own district who had been politically active on his behalf. But they were not even supposed to be trained for the work of advising a congressional committee regarding its legislative work. The most minor bureau in the Department of Agriculture had on its staff a dozen people far more highly trained, far better informed, and considerably better paid than anyone on the staff of the Committee on Agriculture of the House or Senate.[21]

Since 1946, committee staffs have become much more professionalized. Although political considerations sometimes are involved, most staff personnel are appointed because of their competence. Tenure in staff positions is now secure in most committees, and salaries are competitive with those of executive agencies.

Committee staffs have grown fairly steadily in size since the reorganization act was passed (see Figure 9.1). In 1947, House committees employed about 222 persons; staff size reached 848 employees in 1973. Senate committee staffs have grown from about 340 persons in 1952 to more than 600 in the 1970s. Of course, many of the employees of congressional committees are secretarial or clerical personnel. But the professional staffs have grown very markedly since 1946. Table 9.2 shows the sizes of the professional staffs of the House and Senate for the years 1948, 1952, and 1967. The 1946 Reorganization Act authorized 60 professional staff appointees for Senate standing committees and 76 for House committees. Additional permanent and temporary employees have been added for the appropriations committees, which were exempted from the act, and by special authoriz-

TABLE 9.2   Sizes of Congressional Committee Professional Staffs, 1948, 1952, and 1967

YEAR	HOUSE	SENATE
1948	51	42
1952	126	137
1967	269	319

SOURCES: Gladys M. Kammerer, "The Record of Congress in Committee Staffing," *American Political Science Review* 55 (December 1951): 1130; George B. Galloway, *The Legislative Process in Congress* (New York, 1953), pp. 412–413; and U.S. Congress, *Congressional Record* (daily), 1967, 90th Cong., 1st sess., pp. H1488–H1498, S2313.

FIGURE 9.1   House Committee Staff Personnel, 1947–1967

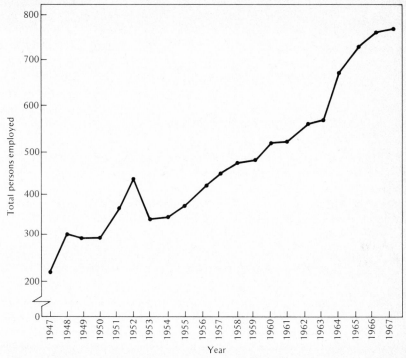

SOURCES: Margaret Fennell, Susan S. Koppel, and John S. Gosnell, *Statistical Study on the Staffing of Committees of the House of Representatives* (Washington, D.C., 1963); U.S., Congress, *Congressional Record,* 88th Cong., 2d sess., 1964, pt. 1, pp. 1179–1188; *Congressional Record* (daily), 89th Cong., 1st sess., 1965, pp. 1619–1628; *Congressional Record* (daily), 89th Cong., 2d sess., 1966, pp. 830–839; *Congressional Record* (daily), 90th Cong., 1st sess., 1967, pp. H1488–H1498.

NOTE: The unusual increase in the size of committee staffs during the second session of the Eighty-second Congress occurred because of extraordinary subcommittee investigations of the Justice Department (Judiciary) and the administration of the internal revenue laws (Ways and Means), as well as an unusually large but temporary staff increase in the Public Works Committee.

ing resolutions that the committees have brought to their respective houses for approval.

Increases in staff activity are reflected very directly in steady increases in committee expenditures for inquiries and investigations. The Eighty-fourth Congress authorized the expenditure of nearly $7 million for this purpose, although less than $4.8 million was actually expended. By the Eighty-ninth Congress, more than $12 million was authorized, and nearly $9.6 million was spent for investigations and inquiries.

Congress has become an increasingly complex institution. Although the number of standing committees was reduced in 1946 from eighty-one to thirty-four, this streamlining has been followed by a rather remarkable increase in the number of subcommittees. The tendency has been to staff these subcommittees, either separately or from increased full committee staffs, by special authorizations beyond those provided in the 1946 legislation. Thus, increased committee staffing, both in terms of personnel and money, follows the increased complexity of Congress as an institution and the increasing work load that the institution processes.

Utilization of Committee Staffs

Congressional committee staffs as they are now constituted are heavily utilized by committee and subcommittee chairmen and ranking minority members. The relationships between staff personnel and committee leaders generally are persistent, regular, and close. However, committee staff time is utilized also by the general congressional membership, lobbyists, and officials in executive agencies. Brief comments about each of these users of committee staffs will indicate the kinds of outside constraints on staffs that are operating in the congressional system.

Committee staffs are utilized by members of the Congress in general, although the evidence is mounting that such utilization is not of highest rank or of major significance. The best available data indicate that on the average, only about 12 percent of congressional effort for legislative research, about 21 percent of the effort invested in preparation for committee meetings and hearings, and less than 9 percent of effort directed to the preparation for floor debate and voting involved committee staffs.

The data in Table 9.3 are based upon an analysis of interview responses from a sample of 160 members of the House of Representatives. They suggest that for the House as a whole, committee staff effort ranks third in importance of the work agencies analyzed for members' legislative research and preparation for floor debate and second for preparation for committee sessions.[22] Republicans and Democrats do not differ significantly in committee staff utilization, but members with high committee rank make much heavier use of committee staffs than those

TABLE 9.3   Sources of Legislative Effort by Congressmen (In percentages)

| | LEGISLATIVE ACTIVITY | | |
WORK DONE BY	Legislative Research	Preparation for Committee Meetings and Hearings	Preparation for Floor Debate
Member himself	30.2	61.3	59.6
Members' office staffs	45.6	15.4	28.2
Committee staffs	11.7	20.9	8.7
Legislative reference service	9.0	1.4	2.8
Executive agency staffs	3.3	—	—
Other	0.2	1.0	0.7
Total	100.0	100.0	100.0

SOURCES: John S. Saloma III, "The Job of a Congressman: Some Perspectives on Time and Information" (unpublished paper, 1967), p. 34; preliminary analyses of these data appear in Donald G. Tacheron and Morris K. Udall, *The Job of the Congressman* (Indianapolis, Ind., 1966), pp. 280–288; and Mary McInnis, ed., *We Propose: A Modern Congress* (New York, 1966), pp. 290–291.

with low seniority do. In addition, committee chairmen and ranking minority members exhibit about the same extent of committee staff utilization.

The evidence for the utilization of congressional committee staffs by executive agencies is much more tenuous. It is clear that especially with the increasing development of stable, professional committee staffs since 1946, executive agencies have come to pay a great deal of attention to some committee staffs and to rely heavily upon them for help. Agency officials maintain very close contact with committee staff personnel, and much of the field, or network, of legislative-executive relations is filled with daily interactions between committee and agency staffs. Agency staffs maintain contact with committee staffs for their own purposes, largely out of needs for anticipatory intelligence. The agency's success in congressional hearings may depend upon effective anticipation of committee staff interests and concerns, since committee staff concerns tend to be, or to become, committee member concerns. Thus, it has been pointed out:

> Continuity in legislative staffing has brought about a close relationship between committee staffs and career executives. Sometimes the career staffs of the two branches maintain contacts without specific participation by members of committees or by the politically appointed executives in the agencies. These relations gradually develop into meaningful bonds; they provide a line of communication that often has a marked bearing on the environment of the executive.[23]

Richard F. Fenno has observed firsthand the closeness of these relationships for interactions between the appropriations committees and agency budget personnel. He has shown that "the subcommittee clerk on the one hand and the departmental budget officer or bureau officer on the other hand constitute the day-to-day linkage between the legislative and executive branches in appropriations matters."[24] Two executive agency budget officers described their relationships with Appropriations Committee staffs to Fenno in the following terms:

> [Departmental budget officer] I'm on close personal relationships with the members of the Committee's staff. During the working season [prior to the hearings] we're in constant contact, daily and on weekends, here or at home . . . we want to be sure they talk about important things and don't go running off into unimportant areas. Or, if there are going to be important questions coming up, we want to know what they are. The Committee staff will tell us. And that's good. It's much better to be prepared than to say, "I don't know, I'll look it up."[25]

> [Bureau budget officer] We have very friendly relations with the clerk . . . [he] will call us and tell us that Congressman X is worried about this or that program so we can be ready for it in the hearing. They help us to have a more fruitful hearing in that way. Or, they may ask us for additional data on something . . . that will help them out in understanding our program. Then they may be able to explain it to the congressman better than we can. The congressmen don't read our justifications very thoroughly—and I sympathize with them—but the clerks do. If we can help them in answering their questions, they may sell our program for us. They will sit in the hearings handing questions to the congressmen, and if we have given them information their questions will be more understandable.[26]

A great deal of committee staff time is involved in information exchange and negotiations with agency staff personnel. These interactions require a major part of the time of some congressional staff personnel, and it is also clear that staff-to-staff relations involve reciprocal staff utilization.

Lobbyists consume some committee staff time, although probably less than is suggested by the conventional wisdom about pressure politics. The extent of actual lobbyist–committee staff contact has not been measured carefully, but it is known that Washington lobbyists tend to prefer committee staff contacts to contacts with congressmen, their personal staffs, or executive agency staffs. Data gathered by Lester W. Milbrath for 114 Washington lobbyists are shown in Table 9.4. He reports that "committee staff persons were selected as important (first or second choice) contacts by 61 per cent of the respondents," but that "executive agency staff persons were selected by 49 per cent, and members of Congress by 42 per cent."[27] Furthermore, lobbyists prefer congressional staff personnel over other agencies as sources of inside information. Milbrath suggests that lobbyists prefer committee staff contacts because staff personnel are more accessible, because they are more expert in subject matter, and because information is more likely to be forthcoming from them.

Our major concern is with committee utilization of committee professional staffs. The preponderant loyalties of committee staff personnel are to their committees and their leaders. They work in the committee rooms. For most, the work is hard and demanding. And they work in a very special kind of institution. What are the capabilities of congressional staffs in this institution? What constraints impinge upon their roles and behavior?

CAPABILITIES OF COMMITTEE STAFFS

The American legislative institution, especially the Congress, provides an organizational setting in which professional staff personnel have significant performance capabilities; but in addition, the organizational context constrains or limits their behavior in important ways. Some explication of these capabilities and constraints can contribute to understanding the character of the American legislature. On the capabilities side, congressional committee professional staffs gather intelligence and contribute to the integration of the legislature. They can partake in policy innovation, and they have considerable general influence. The most visible capability of committee staffs involves the intelligence function of Congress. Staffmen are facts-and-figures men, and for a great deal of their working time, they are engaged in processing information and supplying it to committee members.

Again, committee staffs contribute to the integration of committees and subcommittees, to intercameral integration, and to legislative-executive integration. In his richly detailed picture of the House Appropriations Committee, Fenno shows that committee staffs tend to be tightly knit groups, working closely together, often doing one another's work, and frequently close socially; and these highly integrated staffs eliminate a potential source of committee disintegration.[28] Furthermore, committee staffs contribute to intercameral integration in the extent to which the staffs in one house are in close contact with staff members of

TABLE 9.4   Lobbyist Contacts and Preferred Information Sources (In percentages)

CONTACTS AND SOURCES	BEST CONTACT OR SOURCE	SECOND-BEST CONTACT OR SOURCE
Locus for contacts		
Members of Congress	22.8	14.9
Staff assistant to members	6.1	9.6
Congressional committee staffs	24.6	28.9
Executive agency staffs	23.7	19.3
Other	10.5	0.9
No response	12.3	26.3
Total	100.0	99.9
Sources of inside information		
Members of Congress	20.2	14.9
Congressional staffs	28.9	24.6
Executive agency staffs	14.0	15.8
Journalists	3.5	2.6
Other lobbyists	6.1	5.3
Other	14.0	13.2
No response	13.2	23.7
Total	99.9	100.1

SOURCE: Lester W. Milbrath, *The Washington Lobbyists* (Chicago, 1963), pp. 266–268.

the parallel committee in the other house; a great deal of the coordination between the House and the Senate actually is effected through such staff relationships. Finally, committee staffs facilitate integration of the legislature and executive through the close relations between staff people and agency and department personnel.

Committee staff personnel occupy strategic locations in the congressional power structure and have very considerable actual and potential influence on public policy. Some committee staffs are more innovative than others, and on these committees, staff members may be about as likely as committee members themselves to initiate legislation. But beyond policy innovations, staff people have a great deal of general influence over public policy. They gather and analyze much of the information upon which policy is based; they plan and to a very large extent execute public hearings and investigations; and they draft legislation and committee reports that not only justify committee recommendations of bills but contain sanctionable policy in themselves. But although a knowledge of the influence of committee staffs is of great importance in achieving an understanding of the congressional process, it is equally important to learn what the real limitations on the exercise of staff influences are. At this stage in the study of the ways in which Congress works, more can probably be learned about its operation by focusing upon the ways behavior is constrained than by elaborating the potential influence that can be exerted there.

CONSTRAINTS ON COMMITTEE STAFFS

A variety of biases in the congressional institution affect the behavior of committee professional staffs. These biases, or constraints, may be seen as limitations on staff capabilities, real or potential, brought about by the institutional environment. Constraints are associated with group norms, committee leadership, staff organization, partisanship, isolation, and specialization. This analysis is illustrated with the comments of staff members themselves, obtained by Patterson in interviews with a sizable number of committee staff personnel in 1965 and 1966. Focusing upon these sources of constraint will indicate in some important ways the manner in which Congress as an institution molds and shapes the behavior of the staff personnel who work within it.

Legislative Norms

Committee staff members tend to adopt the goal orientations dominant among members of the committees for which they work. Thus, staff members of the House Appropriations Committee tend to accept the budget-cutting and treasury-guarding orientation of the committee, and members of the Senate Appropriations Committee staff tend to accept its appellate orientation. The normative integration of committees varies fairly widely, and thus, accepted goal orientations vary on the part of committee staffs. However, it is possible to generalize about widely shared normative standards generally reflected by staff personnel. The most salient of these norms are limited advocacy, loyalty to the chairman, deference, anonymity, specialization, and limited partisanship.

The staff norm of limited advocacy implies that the staffman will not press his own policy position too far, that he should be sensitive to limitations on the presentation of his own conclusions and proposals. A number of comments from staff professionals reflected this. One House Science and Astronautics staffman said:

> The Chairmen and subcommittee chairmen do their homework well, but they do ask for the opinion of the staff on policy matters. And, the staff does make recommendations without being asked to do so. But if a staff man makes a proposal or objects to a Committee decision, and the Committee disagrees, the staff man is expected to forget it.[29]

The game of anticipating committee member antagonism or rejection and of limiting advocacy accordingly is a delicate one. On the Senate side, a staff member from the Senate Aeronautical and Space Sciences Committee discussed this problem:

> In hearings, I do most of the questioning; in executive sessions, the Senators do most of the talking and I do most of the explaining. I sometimes feel between the devil and the deep blue sea. I try to stay out of serious disagreements between senators, and just provide information. But, on a number of occasions, I've argued for something that none of the Senators were prepared to accept. I remember once Senator Anderson admonished me jokingly that I didn't have to argue so vehemently for the agency.

A staff member of the Senate Subcommittee on Education pointed out that "if you can't persuade a member to your own policy position, you lay out the alternatives and you've got to be as objective as you possibly can." And a very highly regarded staff member of the Senate Armed Services Committee observed that "the job of the staff is to be objective, restrained, and not doctrinaire. The staff is expected to play down individual policy preferences. The more restrained the staff is, the more likely it is to be influential."

The norm of loyalty to the chairman is very crucial to the structure of congressional committee staffs, and here the sanctions for failure are likely to be immediate and terminal. Most committees delegate staff appointment to the chairman alone, and he is clearly the major figure in the staffman's employment relationship. In a variety of ways, interviewed staff members reflected their loyalty to the chairman. A Senate staffman said, "It's hard to draw the line between what the Senator thinks and what I think." The prototypical manifestation of the norm of loyalty is the so-called chairman's man who is appointed by, and obediently serves, the chairman first and foremost. This trusted chairman's man serves on the staff of the Veterans' Affairs Committee:

> My basic job is to enhance the prestige of the Chairman. My job is that of ensuring that Congressman Teague is the No. 1 man in the country on veterans' affairs; that the final decisions on veterans' affairs are made by the staff and the Chairman, and not by the White House or by private groups. . . . In executive sessions, it sometimes boils down to the staff and the Chairman against the rest of the Committee. . . . When the Chairman of the Committee on Science and Astronautics retires, I hope to become a member of that staff, and to help make Mr. Teague No. 1 in space!

The norm of deference to congressmen is very strong and is often reflected by staff comments about how staff members must "be on tap, and not on top," that they must not "try to run the show," or that "you must remember that staff is staff, and members are members." A staff member of the House Education and Labor Committee, a committee particularly sensitive to staff deference, accounted for the high staff turnover on the committee in terms of successive violations of this norm:

> One person brought in by Mr. Powell as education counsel began to think she was too important. She referred to bills as her own bills, rather than the members', and she antagonized members; so Powell had me fire her. . . . One of the three labor chiefs lasted only two weeks. He committed the crime of going around to committee members announcing he was the new labor chief ready to take charge; their response to Powell was, "Who the hell is this?" Powell ordered me to fire him.

The norm of anonymity is equally powerful and probably more difficult than others for staff members to live with. This norm is strongly reflected in the House Appropriations Committee, as Fenno has shown.[30] Anonymity is fiercely protected by members of this staff, but it is also an important part of the expectations of other committee staffs. One staff member of an appropriations subcommittee remarked about anonymity: "You have to be anonymous to be effective. Congressman Passman is Mr. Foreign Aid; you can't have me being Mr. Foreign Aid." Another appropriations subcommittee staff member said: "A staff man has to be anonymous. He can't have any axe to grind. He can't have any politics. I try to be objective. I could staff anything." Some staff members are reluctant to take a prominent place in public committee activities for fear of violating the anonymity norm:

> [House Agriculture Committee staff man] The members increasingly ask my opinion on policy, since I've been around here so long. I was reluctant at first, but when they asked for my judgment I had to give it. At full Committee hearings, I try to keep out of asking questions. I suggest questions to the Chairman, and sometimes ask some myself, but I like not to. In executive sessions I talk more than I like, and it's a close line in give and take there.

> [House Appropriations Subcommittee staff man] The staff man should stay in the background, and not become identified with particular policies, but this is not always easy to do. For instance, if the staff man asks a lot of questions in hearings it tends to take the glow off members, and you tend to become identified with particular policies.

> [House Armed Services staff man] The acting Chairman asks me or one of the other staff men to ask questions in hearings. I don't like this very much. To me it makes the staff too prominent. In the role of the questioner, the staff man has to be very careful not to get any publicity, or to overstep his place.

One Senate committee, the Committee on Foreign Relations, has clearly stated written rules against staff publicity:

> Members of the staff must not accept public speaking engagements or write for publication in the field of foreign relations without specific advance permission from the chief of staff or, in this case, from the Chairman. In any event, such public statements should avoid the expression of personal views and should not contain predictions of future, or interpretations of past, Committee action.[31]

Anonymity is not easy, nor is it always comfortable. Staff members who come to have great expertise naturally desire recognition. Often they are praised by committee members, and sometimes this occurs on the floor of the House or the Senate. But expertise encourages expression, and the rules prohibit public staff prominence. This can sometimes lead to frustration. In an interview, one Senate staffman painfully but pridefully recounted his authorship of several law review articles published under the names of senators. At bar association meetings, he has been asked why he has not published his ideas in the law reviews. He has, but none of his peers in the legal profession know it. A Senate staff member from the Committee on Labor and Public Welfare said:

> I practiced law for ten years before coming to work for the Committee, and I feel that in my practice I was better able to deal with people directly, to do direct service for people, whereas on the Committee this is impersonal. The impersonality and anonymity of the work is disturbing to me.

And a staff member from an appropriations subcommittee of the House said:

> A staff man has to be a eunuch politically, and totally anonymous. If he can't do that, he won't last. The most frustrating part of the job is that a lot of work comes

to nothing. You build a case, and do a lot of writing about something that is not politically feasible. A lot of good ideas go down the drain.

For a full discussion of partisanship and specialization as structural biases in the congressional environment, see the sections "Partisanship" and "Specialization." In this context, specialization and limited partisanship operate as normative expectations for committee staff members. In general, committee staff people are expected to specialize and develop a subject-matter expertise. The confidence that committee members have in the staff is dependent upon their demonstrated expertness. As one House Veterans' Affairs Committee staffman put it: "One unwritten rule of the game has to do with competence. Members have a lot at stake, and must be able to trust the staff. In this relation, the staffman gets only about one major mistake. This tends to make the staff fairly conservative."

Although clearly some committees are more partisan than others in the manner in which the decision-making process operates, a very wide range of committee activity is nonpartisan. Further, there does exist the general expectation of limited partisanship, even though there is considerable slippage in the implementation of this expectation. The most widely respected staffmen are the most nonpartisan ones, and the performance capability of the staff is highly associated with nonpartisan decision-making climates. A large number of professional staff people report working for members of both parties; some have served under both Republican and Democratic chairmen; and many report writing both majority and minority views for committee reports on bills. Fenno has pointed to the very nonpartisan character of the staff of the House Appropriations Committee. The same is true of a number of other congressional committees, including Ways and Means, Science and Astronautics, Armed Services, International Relations, and Interior and Insular Affairs; Appropriations and Foreign Relations on the Senate side; and the Joint Committee on Atomic Energy, the Joint Committee on Internal Revenue Taxation, and the Joint Economic Committee.[32]

Committee Leadership

The performance of a congressional committee staff is very much dependent upon the committee or subcommittee chairman and to some extent upon the ranking minority leaders. In addition to loyalty to the chairman, the staff must learn to anticipate the reactions of the chairman and behave accordingly. In the words of a House subcommittee staff member, "You have to be able to anticipate what the Chairman and members want, and you can't check with them too often to cover yourself because then they get annoyed at being bothered all the time. You have to develop a feel for the members, and this takes time." The chairman is the key figure in the world of the staffman, and sensing what he wants is a major part of the game.

On the whole, House staff people are in greater proximity to the chairman than Senate staff people are, and thus, Senate staffs are more likely to have to get their cues for behavior from the chairman indirectly—through the senator's office staff, from memorandums, or on the telephone. This more distant relationship between senators and Senate staffs seems to lend itself to indecision and inactivity in staffs whose chairman is very busy and perhaps concentrating his energies on the work of other committees or subcommittees.

When a hiatus develops between a committee or subcommittee staff director or major staff assistant and the chairman, the consequences are disastrous for staff performance. Three situations of this sort existed in House committees during the Eighty-ninth Congress. The glaring case is that of the Committee on Education and Labor under the aegis of Chairman Powell. Conditions were chaotic as a result of the lack of trust between Mr. Powell and the professional staff. A similarly anomic condition could be found on the Select Subcommittee on Labor, where the staffman realized he didn't have the confidence of the acting chairman and could not figure out why, where no real use was made of the staffman, and where he hardly saw the chairman over a period of several months. Finally, lack of mutual confidence between Chairman Bonner and the staff of the Committee on Merchant Marine and Fisheries weakened the effectiveness of that staff and made life miserable for some staff members.

On most committees of the House and Senate, either staff appointments are made outright by the full committee chairman or the subcommittee chairmen or, when staff directors are involved in the appointment process, the chairmen clear appointments. The House and Senate committees on foreign affairs and the Joint Committee on Atomic Energy utilize personnel subcommittees for staff appointments. There are three brief comments that can be made about staff appointments. First, most committees have not experienced much turnover among professional staff personnel, so that the appointment process is not frequently invoked. Second, most professional staff appointments are made on the basis of competence and not primarily on the basis of partisan considerations. The House Appropriations Committee is an excellent example of merit recruitment. During the Eighty-fifth Congress, Chairman Cannon made a rare statement on the House floor about Appropriations Committee staff appointments:

> Of the 50 members of the staff accredited to the Committee on Appropriations, I have appointed all but 6. I have not known at the time of appointment—and I do not know today—to what political party, to what church or to what fraternal organizations a single one of the 50 belong, and may I say further, Mr. Chairman, that none of them are from my congressional district, or from my own State. I have never exercised personal political preference in the appointment of any of them.[33]

Third, some staff members are appointed on a patronage basis, but they have a very marked tendency to "go professional." In the case of committees that have both staff director and a chief clerk, the latter is most likely to be a political appointment; and it is common on Senate committee staffs for there to be a chairman's man appointed on a political basis. But it should be reiterated that the biases of the system tend to press even political appointees in the direction of professionalism.

Staff Organization

Staff organization varies widely in detail.[34] In general, three patterns of staff organization can be found in congressional committees. These three patterns are

depicted in Figure 9.2. But the patterns in Figure 9.2 do not reflect some important variants. Some committees have independent subcommittee staffs appointed
by subcommittee chairmen (in the House, Public Works, Merchant Marine and
Fisheries, Government Operations, Education and Labor; in the Senate, Labor
and Public Welfare, Government Operations, Appropriations). Type I Senate
committees frequently have a chairman's man, who serves as an adjunct to the
chairman and is independent of the rest of the staff. Still, the three types portray
the main parameters of staff organization. The hierarchical Type I staff is one in
which the chairman's staff contacts are mainly through the staff director, who
commands both clerical and professional staff personnel. These staffs are easier
to explain in terms of organizational relationships, and staff members of these
committees were better able to describe the organizational structure. These Type
I staff arrangements probably promote staff performance. The staff director of the
Senate Government Operations Committee described his organization in a way
that suggests this. He related that under Senator Aiken's chairmanship, the
responsibilities of the staff director and the chief clerk were separate, but that
when Senator McClellan became chairman, Aiken recommended that this not
be continued—not "to create positions for two prima donnas who argue all the
time over what is who's job"—and staff supervision was given to one staff
director.

The Type II staff is one in which the committee or subcommittee chairman
deals with all the professional staff on pretty much an equal footing, with the staff
director or chief clerk (use of titles varies) directing the clerical staff. This arrangement is more demanding for the committee or subcommittee chairman, and tends
to be utilized where the professional staff is small.

The Type III staff involves dual leadership, with a staff director supervising the
professional staff and a chief clerk directing the clerical staff. This kind of organizational structure works reasonably well in some committees but seems exces-
sively prone to tension between the two staff leaders. This situation arises
especially when the staff director is a professional and the chief clerk is a political
appointee. Staff performance tends to suffer when the staff director and the chief
clerk are at loggerheads.

FIGURE 9.2   Patterns of Staff Organization

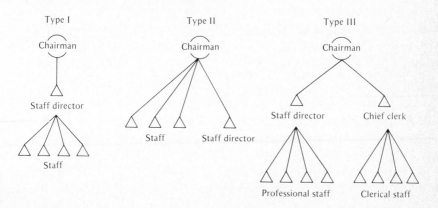

Even where committees regularly do business through standing subcommittees, there is a tendency, especially on the House side, to maintain full-committee control over the staff. Staff may then be temporarily assigned to subcommittees. This organizational strategy helps the full-committee chairman to maintain control of subcommittees and their chairmen, and it serves to facilitate staff integration and coordination as well.

Partisanship

The partisan aspect of congressional committee staffing has received more attention inside and outside Congress than any other. Although the Legislative Reorganization Act of 1946 did not contemplate it, a number of committees and subcommittees have designated certain staff positions as belonging to the minority members. In some cases, these members of the staff are officed separately; and in most of these cases, the minority staff is appointed by the ranking minority member of the committee or subcommittee.[35] The Legislative Reorganization Act of 1970 provided that two of six professional staff members may be chosen by minority party committee members if this is requested by a majority of the minority members of a committee. To the degree committee staffs are structured in partisan terms, such structures are relevant to consideration of congressional constraints on staffing.

We have already pointed to the strength of the committee staff norm of limited partisanship. Staff assistance for members of the minority party may go far beyond the numbers explicitly designated as minority staff. The problem is not really one of availability. For instance, the House Committee on Armed Services has had no staff members designated as minority staff; but a chief counsel who directed the staff for many years was appointed to the staff by a Republican chairman. A longtime general counsel of the House Agriculture Committee was appointed in 1947 by a Republican chairman. An executive director of the House Science and Astronautics Committee staff was first a Republican appointee of the Armed Services Committee staff. And a chief clerk and staff director of the Senate Committee on Government Operations got his appointment on the recommendation of the ranking Republican senator. Although the ranking Republican on the House District of Columbia Committee picks the minority clerk, this designation is entirely nominal, and this staff member works as a regular member of the staff. One committee counsel was a nominal Republican, and a clerk, although a registered Democrat, regularly voted Republican. The ranking Republican on the House Merchant Marine and Fisheries Committee wanted a staffman assigned to the minority, and selected for this position a man already on the staff who was known to be a Democrat. Other examples abound.

Some committees (such as House and Senate Armed Services, House Science and Astronautics, Interior and Insular Affairs, Ways and Means, and Senate Foreign Relations) have had no minority staff and have been entirely nonpartisan. The staff has served all members of the committee. Other committees (such as House Merchant Marine and Fisheries, International Relations, and Agriculture, and Senate Astronautical and Space Sciences, Government Operations, Appropriations, and Rules and Administration) have had staffs directed to serve all committee members, but minority staffs have been designated as special contacts for Republicans. Still other committees have very separate minority staffs. The separate minority staff may work more or less closely with the majority staff; or they may be closed out of the majority staff operations completely. A House Public Works Committee staff member said, "They participate in the work of the staff, but perhaps are somewhat slighted in the sense that they are often kept informed rather than participating from the beginning." The staff of House Interstate and Foreign Commerce is very nonpartisan, but there is a staffman for the minority who works entirely apart from the regular staff; "he works exclusively with the minority, although minority members do not work exclusively with him." Arrangements are essentially the same in the House Government Operations, Judiciary, and Appropriations staffs. In the case of Appropriations, the minority staff is housed in a different building; and because it is virtually the private staff of the ranking minority member, it is not considered a part of the committee's professional staff. House Education and Labor, Senate Labor and Public Welfare, and House Banking and Currency exemplify the type of committee where the staff is not really available to the minority committee members. For instance, the chief clerk and staff director of one of these staffs said, "The minority staff is completely segregated, and only minimally kept informed. . . . Minority members of the Committee deal exclusively with the minority staff; they don't ask for help from the majority staff. . . . I have no dealings with minority congressmen."

Most staff members attribute nonpartisanship in staff operations to nonpartisan decision-making behavior on the part of committees themselves. The House and Senate committees dealing with education, labor, and welfare legislation, which is obviously very controversial, have difficulty developing nonpartisan professional staffs. Staff operations are clearly impaired. Where committees handling relatively nonpartisan legislation are concerned, minority staffs may be a hindrance to staff operations. For instance, one staffman for a subcommittee of the Senate Committee on Appropriations pointed out:

> There is a minority man assigned to this subcommittee. We don't work at cross-purposes, but he doesn't help me much. Actually, he is some trouble, because when Republicans ask him questions he usually has to ask me. It takes up my time, and the members had just as well ask me directly. The subcommittee almost never divides along party lines; we've had minority views once in thirteen years.

On the whole, Republicans tend to use the regular staff of committees on which they serve and minority staffs (where they are designated) on committees of which they are not members. In 1965, 149 House Republicans were asked by the staff of the Republican Task Force on Congressional Reform and Minority Staffing: "At any time this year, have you requested additional staff for yourself or on behalf of other minority members of the committee and been turned down?" The answer of 71.8 percent was no, and it was clear that some of those reporting yes had actually been turned down by the ranking minority member of the committee.

Isolation

Congressional committees are independent and autonomous little legislatures. In each house, committee staffs tend to be very much isolated from one another; and where committees have independent subcommittees, their staffs often are isolated, too. Although degrees of contact and coordination vary, on the whole, each House committee staff has little to do with other committees' staffs; the same is true in the Senate. Committee staff isolation probably is less consequential for collaboration and coordination in the Senate because of the high incidence of overlapping committee leadership. For example, Senator Russell of Georgia was for many years chairman of the Armed Services Committee and also chairman of the Appropriations Subcommittee on Department of Defense. He chaired one committee to authorize defense funds and another to approve frequently held joint hearings.

Most staff members report very little contact with staff people on other committees or subcommittees. More intercameral contact is reported than intracameral contact, although across the board, there is not much of either. The most isolated House committees have been Veterans' Affairs and Internal Security.

Staff isolation is a result of the balkanization of Congress into highly institutionalized committees. It is reinforced by the structure of committee prestige, institutional jealousies, and intercameral hostilities. Staff loyalties and identifications are committee-specific. At the same time, committee structures are divisions of labor that encourage subject-matter expertise, and specialization itself seems to support and reinforce committee staff isolation. Of course, staff isolation tends to produce duplication and ignorance in intelligence efforts; it works against congressional integration but tends to facilitate committee integration; and it probably increases staff influence. Policy innovation in a narrow sense may be facilitated by staff isolation, but one suspects that innovation of far-reaching consequences is made rather unlikely.

Specialization

Committee staffing is very highly specialized, and as has been pointed out, specialization is a part of the normative mandate of the committee structure. Specialization encourages staff isolation, but it is strongly associated with staff influence, integration, and innovation. Staff members invariably describe their jobs in specialist terms, and even staff directors tend to stress their subject-matter expertise more than their general management activities in describing their jobs. Of course, specialization varies, and there is some generalist-specialist tension in the staff system. The structural problem of specialization can best be illustrated by looking at the staff of the House Appropriations Committee. In this staff, attempts have been made to develop generality and interchangeability of specialist competence. Although the committee has standing subcommittees with fixed subject-matter jurisdictions and a permanent staff assigned to them, the staff director has sought to rotate the staff. Also, he has attempted to assign two different subcommittee staffmen to a bill, one with major responsibility and the other as backup man. This has not been very successful. In practice, subcommittee staffmen seldom have time to work as backup men on the parts of the appropriations legislation being processed by other subcommittees. Rotation of staff has not worked well either. As the staff director said, "I would like to rotate the subcommittee people more, but the subcommittee chairmen get too attached to them. When this was tried a few years ago, the subcommittee chairmen went up in smoke."

State Legislative Staffing

Until the late 1960s, the bulk of the staff services available to members of the state legislatures was contained in the research arms of the legislative council organizations, which operate in forty-four states.[36] As the state legislatures have come to enlarge their staffs for leaders, members, and committees, significant changes have occurred in the nature of staff assistance provided and in the coordination of staff services. In many states, the legislative councils—committees of legislators serving in the interim between regular legislative sessions—have undertaken the performance both of centralized research assistance and the management and coordination of the multitude of new staff offices. In some states where there is no legislative council, and in Florida and Connecticut where the legislative councils were abolished, management or coordinating committees have been created. The common tasks performed by these committees have come to include "preparation of the legislative budget, employment of personnel, establishment of pay plans and job descriptions, procurement of supplies and equipment, and general coordination of the various service agencies."[37]

The increased staff facilities for state legislative leaders and committees, brought about by escalation of needs for research and policy analysis, have meant that the legislative councils, once the only major legislative research agencies, are now, in at least one-fourth of the states, only one among several offices undertaking research and policy analysis for the legislatures. Current practices of state legislative staffing may be summarized as follows:

> There appear to be two basic patterns by which committees are being staffed in the State Legislatures, regardless of whether partisan or nonpartisan staffs are utilized. Committee chairmen are either permitted to hire their own staff, or staff is assigned from some central agency. The central agency may be a joint management committee, the legislative council, the leader's office, or a caucus staff. ... The use of a central agency to provide committee staff is thought to result in better coordination of work and better management of the time of staff in peak and slack periods. Permitting committee chairmen to control the selection of staff, on the other hand, is believed to make staff more responsive to the committee's needs.[38]

The growth of staff assistance for state legislatures has not increased the kinds of services provided to legislators as much as it has improved the capacity of staffs to provide services that have long been available in more modest ways.

One arena in which the state legislatures have exhibited a particularly strong tendency for staff development is that of analysis and review of the state budget. Only nineteen state legislatures had fiscal analysis staffs in 1956, but that number had grown to thirty in 1965, and now all but two states (Kentucky and Wyoming) have some kind of full-time, permanent fiscal staff. Also, staffs to assist in legislative oversight of state programs and spending have developed to the point that, although fewer than ten states had legislative auditors in 1951, about thirty-three states had such staffs by 1973. In addition, revenue- and program-review staffs are becoming more prevalent in the legislatures.[39] The extensiveness of fiscal analysis staffing in the large, urban states is suggested by the fact that in 1974 nearly sixty professional staff aides worked for the fiscal analyst organization in California, and a similar organization for the New York legislature consisted of thirty-four majority staff members and fourteen minority staff assistants. These are the larger fiscal analysis staffs; the average such staff was ten in 1974.[40]

The organizational structure of state legislative staffs can be characterized in terms of the degree to which they are partisan, the extent of central management of staff services, and the number of staff agencies. Although these criteria do not exhaust the possible bases for classifying staff organization, their use leads to five distinctive types of legislative staffing in the states:[41]

1. *Nonpartisan, centrally managed, one or two agency Legislatures.* The States with the largest staffs which fall in this category are probably Ohio and Kentucky. Most of the smaller States with only one or two small staff agencies, such as Delaware and North Dakota, also fall in this category. Numerically, this category is the largest.

2. *Nonpartisan, centrally managed, multiple agency Legislatures.* Most of the States with management committees, such as Connecticut and Florida, belong in this category. This type of system is rapidly gaining in popularity.

3. *Nonpartisan, decentralized, multiple agency Legislatures.* Michigan and Wisconsin are probably the best examples of this category (with the specific proviso that caucus staffs are excluded).

4. *Partisan, centrally managed, multiple agency Legislatures.* The only striking example of this is the New York Senate where the leadership office serves as central coordinator and controller of a number of "unofficial" offices which serve the Senate, in addition to controlling the amount of money allocated to individual senators for staff.

5. *Partisan, decentralized, multiple agency Legislatures.* The Legislature which best represents this category is, of course, the U.S. Congress. Among the States, Illinois and Pennsylvania are by far the leading examples of this type of organization.

It is clear that state legislative staffs will continue to grow in size and complexity. These rudimentary types only begin to explore questions of staff organization, role, recruitment, and operation. Inasmuch as very little effort has been made to analyze and evaluate these staffs, much is yet to be learned about staff organization and behavior in the state legislatures.

NOTES

1. For example, Norman Meller, "The Policy Position of Legislative Service Agencies," *Western Political Quarterly* 5 (1952):109–123; and Max M. Kampelman, "The Legislative Bureaucracy: Its Response to Political Change, 1953," *Journal of Politics* 16 (1954):539–550.

2. See Kenneth Kofmehl, *Professional Staffs of Congress* (West Lafayette, Ind., 1962), p. 3; and Lauros G. McConachie, *Congressional Committees* (New York, 1898), p. 65.

3. See Belle Zeller, ed., *American State Legislatures* (New York, 1954), pp. 156–159.

4. In this and succeeding paragraphs, references to staff development are drawn from George B. Galloway, *The Legislative Process in Congress* (New York, 1953), pp. 407–425; Zeller, *American State Legislatures,* pp. 124–162; Council of State Governments, *The Book of the States, 1964–1965* (Chicago, 1964), pp. 67–83; and *The Book of the States, 1970– 1971* (Lexington, Ky., 1970), pp. 59–62.

5. Robert K. Carr, *The House Committee on Un-American Activities* (Ithaca, N.Y., 1952), pp. 247–270; quotation at pp. 247–248.

6. See M. Nelson McGeary, *The Development of Congressional Investigative Power* (New York, 1940), pp. 59–66.

7. For example, Vern Countryman, *Un-American Activities in the State of Washington* (Ithaca, N.Y., 1951), p. 22; and Edward L. Barrett, *The Tenney Committee* (Ithaca, N.Y., 1951), pp. 18–19

8. Karl T. Kurtz, "The State Legislatures," *The Book of the States, 1974–1975* (Lexington, Ky., 1974), pp. 60–65.

9. Council of State Governments, *American State Legislatures: Their Structures and Procedures* (Lexington, Ky., 1971), pp. 29–32, 47.

10. Dennis Dorch, "Legislature's $25 Million Staff: How Much Is Spent for Politics," *California Journal* 5 (1974):271–272; Alan P. Balutis, "Legislative Staffing: A View from the States," paper presented at the 1974 Annual Meeting of the American Political Science Association, p. 5.

11. Donald G. Tacheron and Morris K. Udall, *The Job of the Congressman* (Indianapolis, Ind., 2d ed., 1970), pp. 46–47.

12. Charles B. Brownson, comp., *1975 Congressional Staff Directory* (Washington, D.C., 1975), pp. 125–152.

13. John S. Saloma III, *Congress and the New Politics* (Boston, 1969), pp. 183–189.

14. Donald R. Matthews, *U.S. Senators and Their World* (Chapel Hill, N.C., 1960), pp. 83–84.

15. Brownson, *1975 Congressional Staff Directory,* pp. 123–124, 244–246.

16. For example, Charles D. Hounshell, *The Legislative Process in Virginia* (Charlottesville, Va., 1951), pp. 8–9; see also Council of State Governments, *The Offices of Legislative Clerks and Secretaries in the States* (Chicago, 1957).

17. This section and the remaining sections on congressional committee staffs are drawn directly from Samuel C. Patterson, "Congressional Committee Professional Staffing: Capabilities and Constraints," in *Legislatures in Developmental Perspective,* ed. Allan Kornberg and Lloyd Musolf (Durham, N.C., 1970), pp. 391–428. Copyright 1970 by Duke University Press. Used by permission. See also Samuel C. Patterson, "The Professional Staffs of Congressional Committees," *Administrative Science Quarterly* 15 (1970):22–37.

18. Early in 1776, the secret committee of correspondence and the secret committee, later to be the Foreign Affairs and Commerce committees, employed Silas Deane, a former member of Congress, to engage in some dealings with French agents. See Edmund C. Burnett, *The Continental Congress* (New York, 1964), pp. 118–119; Lindsay Rogers, "The Staffing of Congress," *Political Science Quarterly* 56 (1941):1–22; Charles L. Clapp, *The Congressman: His Work as He Sees It* (Washington, D.C., 1963), pp. 254–255; Galloway, *The Legislative Process in Congress,* pp. 410–414; and McConachie, *Congressional Committees,* pp. 65–66, 170–171, 293–294.

19. See Gladys M. Kammerer, "The Record of Congress in Committee Staffing," *American Political Science Review* 55 (1951):1126–1136; and Max M. Kampelman, "The Legislative Bureaucracy: Its Response to Political Change, 1953"; and *Congressional Quarterly Weekly Report* 33 (July 26, 1975):1625–1626.

20. Joseph P. Harris, *Congressional Control of Administration* (Washington, D.C.,

1964), pp. 72–73; and Holbert N. Carroll, *The House of Representatives and Foreign Affairs* (Pittsburgh, 1958), pp. 102–109.

21.   Jerry Voorhis, *Confessions of a Congressman* (Garden City, N.Y., 1947), p. 296.

22.   See also Lowell H. Hattery and Susan Hotheimer, "The Legislator's Source of Expert Information," *Public Opinion Quarterly* 18 (1954):300–303.

23.   Marver H. Bernstein, *The Job of the Federal Executive* (Washington, D.C., 1958), p. 109.

24.   Richard F. Fenno, Jr., *The Power of the Purse* (Boston, 1966), p. 304. For a relevant analysis of the staff of the Joint Committee on Atomic Energy, see Harold P. Green and Alan Rosenthal, *Government of the Atom* (New York, 1963), pp. 65–114.

25.   Fenno, *The Power of the Purse,* pp. 304–305.

26.   Ibid., p. 305.

27.   Lester W. Milbrath, *The Washington Lobbyists* (Chicago, 1963), pp. 267–270.

28.   Fenno, *The Power of the Purse,* pp. 149–155, 182–188, 206–207. For an analysis of the role of the staff of a joint committee in intercameral integration, see John F. Manley, "Congressional Staff and Public Policy-Making: The Joint Committee on Internal Revenue Taxation," *Journal of Politics* 30 (1968):1046–1067.

29.   This quotation and quotations hereafter not otherwise identified are from Patterson's interviews, originally reported in Kornberg and Musolf, *Legislatures in Developmental Perspective,* pp. 412–428.

30.   As Fenno points out, only one member of the large Appropriations Committee staff lists his biography in the *Congressional Staff Directory.* See Fenno, *The Power of the Purse,* p. 184; and Charles B. Brownson, comp., *1967 Congressional Staff Directory* (Washington, D.C., 1967).

31.   From a Senate Committee on Foreign Relations memorandum entitled "Report of the Subcommittee on Staff Problems on General Staff Problems, of Feb. 10, 1958, as Adopted by the Committee on March 4, 1958," dated March 4, 1958, p. 3.

32.   Fenno, *The Power of the Purse,* pp. 184–185. See also John F. Manley, "The House Committee on Ways and Means: Conflict Management in a Congressional Committee," *American Political Science Review* 59 (1965):927–939; and for a sharp contrast, see Fenno's comments on the House Committee on Education and Labor in Frank J. Munger and Richard F. Fenno, Jr., *National Politics and Federal Aid to Education* (Syracuse, N.Y., 1962), pp. 106–136. On the Joint Committee on Atomic Energy, see Green and Rosenthal, *Government of the Atom,* pp. 65–66.

33.   U.S., Congress, *Congressional Record* (daily), 85th Cong., 1st sess., p. 6319.

34.   For further organizational details, see Kofmehl, *Professional Staffs of Congress,* pp. 37–51.

35.   See James D. Cochrane, "Partisan Aspects of Congressional Committee Staffing," *Western Political Quarterly* 17 (1964):338–348; and Kofmehl, *Professional Staffs of Congress,* pp. 52–69.

36.   For an analysis of these developments see William J. Siffin, *The Legislative Council in the American States* (Bloomington, Ind., 1959).

37.   Kurtz, "The State Legislatures," *The Book of the States, 1974–1975,* p. 61.

38.   Ibid., p. 62.

39.   Council of State Governments, *State Legislative Appropriations Process* (Lexington, Ky., 1975), p. 25. For an analysis of the work of the fiscal analysis staff of the California legislature, see D. Jay Doubleday, *Legislative Review of the Budget in California* (Berkeley, 1967). Also, see Alan Rosenthal, *Legislative Performance in the States* (New York, 1974), pp. 146–165, for a treatment of the work of the Fiscal Bureau of the Wisconsin legislature.

40.   Council of State Governments, *State Legislative Appropriations Process,* pp. 26–27, 67.

41.   Kurtz, "The State Legislatures," *The Book of the States, 1974–1975,* p. 64. Reprinted from *The Book of the States, 1974–75,* by permission of the Council of State Governments, Iron Works Pike, Lexington, Kentucky 40511.

CHAPTER TEN

Legislative Procedures and Their Effects

Formal rules and procedures are among the most important functional requisites of a legislative body. Together with the informal rules of the game (discussed in Chapter 14), they constitute the primary means of normative regulation for legislators. It is difficult to imagine a legislature or any other organization existing and functioning for long without clearly defined rules. The importance of rules should be obvious to anyone who has attended a meeting in which the leading participants lacked knowledge of, or agreement on, procedural rules and has watched it degenerate into chaos. It may be helpful to distinguish between the rules that help a group to maintain its existence and those that help it to achieve its goals. In addition, certain rules are part of the strategy of political conflict and may be viewed as serving the aims of particular groups, whether majorities or minorities.

FUNCTIONS OF RULES

Fundamental to the existence of the legislature are rules that ensure stability, order, and predictability; for example, rules that establish a regular order of business and assure orderly debate, as well as some of the organizational rules found in state constitutions. Several groups of rules can be related to the legislature's purpose as a lawmaking institution and not merely to the maintenance of its existence. Certain rules ensure the public and orderly consideration of bills; for example, the rules, often found in state constitutions, which require that bills be printed and read three times and that roll calls be recorded on the passage of all bills. Many rules serve to expedite legislative business; for example, the use of voice votes or standing votes, the handling of noncontroversial measures through unanimous-consent procedures, and the suspension of rules by an extraordinary majority. In legislatures where the committee system is important, rules and practices safeguard the prerogatives of the committee; these include rules on committee jurisdiction and rules and practices that discourage discharging bills from committee. The maintenance of strong committees is considered in many legislatures to be requisite for a high level of specialized competence, which, in turn, is essential for legislative independence from the executive.

A careful examination of those rules that are functional for some group within the legislature (rather than for the legislature as a whole) reveals much about that particular legislature. Changes in rules are significant chapters in the history of a legislative body. Some rules serve the interests of a majority or its leadership. Rules that give the majority leadership control over the committee jurisdiction on bills or over the timetable on the floor of the house are designed for this purpose. Other examples are rules that permit a majority to cut off debate or to prevent the consideration of amendments. Other rules serve the interests of a minority. Such rules may, of course, serve any minority that wants to delay or prevent action; but more particularly, they benefit a minority party, faction, or regional grouping. Among these are rules that permit unlimited debate or that make it difficult to limit debate, as well as rules that require an extraordinary majority to transact certain kinds of business. Rules that affect timing are particularly important because the entire legislative process is a race against time; rules that facilitate delaying tactics are among the most valuable weapons available to a minority. If a group with minority status in the legislature has effective control over a committee (as sometimes happens in Congress), rules designed to safeguard the committee's prerogatives and thus serve a legislative function may also serve the minority's interests.

SOURCES AND HISTORY

The rules and precedents in Congress constitute a large, detailed, and complex body of information.[1] The Constitution provides broad authority for congressional rule-making: "Each House may determine the rules of its proceedings." The Senate and House have each adopted rules, which are printed in the manuals of the two branches. The Legislative Reorganization Acts of 1946 and 1970 provided for changes in the rules of both houses but included provisions recognizing the right of either house to make changes in its rules on its own authority. Both houses make use of a manual prepared by Thomas Jefferson when he was serving as vice-president. In addition, the rulings of the presiding officers of both houses have established precedents that affect the procedures to be followed. The rulings of the Speaker of the House, which have been more extensive and detailed, have been compiled in a multivolume publication.[2] Both houses have official parliamentarians whose responsibility it is to supply the presiding officer and individual members with advice and information concerning interpretation of the rules and pertinent precedents.

There is a significant difference between the two houses with regard to the status of rules. In the House, the rules are adopted at the beginning of each Congress, at which time the old rules may be readopted or modified; occasionally, changes have been made during the life of a Congress. The Senate, however, is a continuing body in the sense that only about one-third of its members are elected or reelected prior to the opening of each Congress. Consequently, the Senate does not follow the practice of formally readopting the rules of the previous Congress. The rules may be modified, and efforts to change them are often made at the start of a new Congress, but the Senate is at all times bound by its previous rules. This is true even though all legislative business is considered *de novo* in the Senate, as well as in the House, at the start of a new Congress.

A history of changes in the rules of the House is a significant chapter in the history of the House; in particular, it throws light on the conflict between majority and minority interests. Throughout the first hundred years of its existence, the House operated under rules that made it possible for a minority to delay and obstruct action on legislative matters. Little by little, changes in the rules enhanced the power of the majority and reduced that of the minority. These changes were often initiated by the Speaker; those Speakers who viewed their role as that of a party leader were the most aggressive in initiating changes that would serve the interests of the majority party. Often, the changes initiated by the Speaker were consolidated through formal changes in the rules. In 1811, in an atmosphere of deadlock and division over foreign affairs, the House adopted the previous-question motion to permit cutting off debate. This proved inadequate to prevent filibusters, and during the 1840s, the House adopted a one-hour limit for speeches and a five-minute rule for discussion of amendments. Basic revisions of the rules in 1860 and 1880 brought greater order and efficiency to the House but did not substantially enhance majority power.[3]

It was Speaker Thomas Reed who initiated the devices that provided the majority with its modern control over the business of the House. By the simple device of counting as present members who were in the chamber but who refused to answer quorum calls, Reed eliminated the "disappearing quorum" as an effective tool of obstruction for the minority. He also declared his intention to reject any motions that were clearly dilatory in purpose. Reed's bold initiatives were promptly written into the House rules in 1890. Reed and Speaker Charles Crisp developed the special rule as the normal method of handling controversial legislation on the floor. Since special rules were the province of the Rules Committee, which was tightly controlled by the Speaker, this was an important technique of majority leadership. The famous revolution of 1910–1911 against Speaker Cannon, who had followed Reed and enlarged upon his techniques for control, stripped the Speaker of much of his power over the machinery of the House. The revolt and the subsequent development of the seniority principle made the committees independent of majority leadership. But the rules for procedure on the floor of the House that had been developed late in the nineteenth century remained in effect. House procedures today serve primarily majority interests and leave little room for minority obstruction and little time for discussion and the proposal of amendments by individuals.

The rules of state legislatures, unlike those of Congress, are prescribed in some detail by constitutions. As we indicated in Chapter 5, these constitutional provisions sometimes impose serious limitations on the legislature's ability to adapt its procedures to its needs, but many of the constitutional requirements are ignored or evaded in practice. State legislative bodies develop formal rules that are usually adopted with little change at the start of a session. Legislative procedure varies in particulars from state to state, but there are many similarities, often the result of the historical practice of copying the rules of a neighboring state or the rules of Congress. The variations reflect differences in environment and customs that have developed independently in the various states. What is lacking in most state legislatures is a body of precedents, either in written form or in the memories of veteran members, having to do with the detailed interpretation of the written rules. In the absence of detailed precedents, and with few members in most bodies who have a wealth of experience or parliamentary knowledge, the leadership usually can, if it chooses, run the legislature in an arbitrary fashion, with little regard to procedural niceties. Rules are a significant factor at the state legislative level, and a careful examination of them may provide useful clues to the power structure that has produced them. But in most state legislatures, the rules are more flexible, less binding, and less comprehensive than in Congress; consequently, written rules provide an imperfect guide to legislative practice.

PROCEDURES CONCERNING BILLS AND COMMITTEES

In the United States House of Representatives and in some state houses, a member may introduce a bill simply by sending it to the Speaker's desk. In the United States Senate and most state senates, the member must announce publicly that he is introducing a bill, and it must be read by title, a time-consuming chore in some legislatures. To expedite business and to prevent the crowding of the calendar late in the session, most states set a deadline on the introduction of bills for several days or weeks before the date provided by law for termination of the session. The purpose of such deadlines is often evaded, however, either by the introduction of skeleton bills, which may include only the title, or by the quite normal practice of consenting to late introduction by extraordinary majorities.

In Congress, there are detailed rules concerning committee jurisdiction that leave little discretion to the presiding officer in the matter of referring bills to committee and thus protect the committees' authority over particular categories of bills. In the states, the presiding officer or occasionally a committee normally exercises broad discretion in referring bills and is consequently able to send important bills to dependable committees either to ensure that they will be reported favorably or to guarantee that they will be buried (in what are often referred to as "graveyard" committees).

In recent years Congress has adopted several rules that provide more uniform procedures than in the past for the internal operation of committees. These include requirements that, with rare exceptions, committee hearings and working sessions and also conference committees be open to the public, and that all votes taken in committees be recorded. There has also been an increase in the frequency of and publicity concerning committee hearings in state legislatures. (These developments are covered more fully in Chapter 17.)

Procedure and practice with regard to the method of removing a bill from further consideration by a committee illustrate something about the importance of committees in the legislative system. Several states require committees to report out all bills, a requirement often evaded in practice. The rules of most legislatures include a provision for discharging a committee from further consideration of a bill. In about half of the states, this requires a simple majority of those voting; and in the rest, a larger vote is needed. In most states, the procedure is rarely used. This often results from a legislative norm with regard to the judgment and authority of committees, but in some states, it means that the same majority party or group whose votes are necessary to a successful discharge motion has firm control over at least the most important committees.

Both branches of Congress have adopted procedures for drawing bills out of committees through discharge motions. These procedures have seldom been effective, except occasionally as threats, for two reasons: the procedures are difficult to effect and relatively easy to obstruct, and congressional norms discourage members from interfering with committee authority over bills. Taken together, the procedures and the norms have the effect of protecting the authority of committees, including the House Rules Committee, except in extraordinary circumstances. The discharge procedure is a safety valve, but a remarkably weak one. Since the action or inaction of committees often conflicts with the wishes of the majority leadership, it might be expected that the leaders would encourage use of the discharge procedure. In reality, congressional leaders have usually been reluctant to encourage the use of this device because it is one over which they have little control and, perhaps, because many of them are also senior members of committees. The House discharge rule, in fact, was first adopted in 1910 as part of the revolt against the strong leadership of Speaker Cannon.

The House discharge rule provides that a petition to discharge a committee from further consideration of a bill must be signed by a majority of House members. Passage of a bill, of course, requires only a majority of those voting; and during several periods prior to 1935, the required number for discharge was less, either 145 or 150. The discharge motion may apply to any bill that has been in a committee for thirty days or in the Rules Committee for seven days. Once a majority have signed the petition, it is placed on the Discharge Calendar, where it must remain for seven days, whereupon any member who signed the petition may call it up for consideration by the House, but only on the second or fourth Monday of each month. If the House votes favorably, then the bill is considered immediately.[4] The procedure in the Senate appears on the surface to be simpler, but it is just as difficult to effect. Any senator may introduce a discharge petition, on which the Senate may vote the following day; if the vote is favorable, the Senate may start consideration of the bill the next day. This is a simple procedure for a bill that is relatively noncontroversial or has overwhelming support, but bills that are trapped in committee are likely to be highly controversial. A determined opposition group can prevent use of the discharge procedure because debate in the Senate is virtually unlimited and because the procedures for discharge and a vote on the bill require four separate motions, each of which is debatable. This procedure is not, for example, a practical way of getting a civil rights bill out of a hostile committee.[5]

Statistical summaries show that from 1947 to 1973, there were 146 discharge petitions filed in the House, but only 9 bills were discharged from committees and passed the House. Since the House first adopted a discharge procedure in 1910, only two bills that were brought to the floor under this procedure have become law: the Fair Labor Standards Act of 1938 and the Postal Pay Act of 1960. Motions to discharge Senate committees from considering bills have been even less successful; between 1789 and 1966, there were only fourteen discharge motions filed in the Senate; only six of these were successful, and only one became law.[6] But the discharge procedure, particularly in the House, has a utility that is not measurable in the number of discharged bills. When the signatures on a discharge petition begin to approach a majority, a committee may decide to jump before it is pushed and report the desired bill to the House. Congressmen also sometimes sign a discharge petition to satisfy constituents or interest groups, with the assurance that not enough signatures will be collected to force action.

The Civil Rights Acts of 1957, 1960, and 1964 were passed despite the opposition of the Senate Judiciary Committee and without use of the cumbersome discharge procedure. In 1957, after passage of the bill in the House, proponents took advantage of a little-used rule that permitted a bill received from the House to be placed directly on the calendar if anyone objected to its consideration in committee; the Senate overruled a point of order by Senator Russell of Georgia, who argued that other rules made referral of the bill to committee mandatory. The same procedure was used in 1964. In 1960, under similar circumstances, the leaders of the Senate succeeded in sending the civil rights bill that had been already passed by the House to the Judiciary Committee with binding instructions to report it back within five days.

Other procedures exist for bypassing the House Rules Committee, but they are little used in practice. *Calendar Wednesday* is the name of a procedure, adopted in 1909, under which committees may be called upon in turn alphabetically each Wednesday and given an opportunity to present bills that are not privileged and have not cleared the Rules Committee. This procedure is rarely used because it is awkward and out of line with normal procedures in the House. It has occasionally been used in an attempt to pass a controversial measure trapped in the Rules Committee. One weakness in this procedure when it is applied to a measure as controversial as civil rights legislation is that chairmen of committees having alphabetical priority can introduce bills approved by their committees as a delaying device if they are hostile to the controversial bill in question. During the period from 1949 to 1952, Calendar Wednesday was used to bring twenty-two bills to the floor of the House; but since that time, the procedure has fallen into disuse. Between 1953 and 1967, the committees were called on a total of only six Wednesdays, and only three bills were called up by committees. The last time a bill was passed by this procedure was in 1960.[7]

Another device for bypassing the Rules Committee is a motion for suspension of the rules, which is in order on the first and third Mondays. A bill taken up under such a motion cannot be amended and requires a two-thirds vote. Consequently, it is seldom a feasible device for passing highly controversial legislation, although it has been used with success for less controversial matters. The number of bills and resolutions passed under suspension of rules in recent years has often been as high as 75 to 100.[8]

PROCEDURES TO EXPEDITE NONCONTROVERSIAL LEGISLATION

Legislatures handle a large quantity of noncontroversial bills and have devised procedures for passing them expeditiously once they have been screened by committees. In the United States House, this is accomplished by placing bills on special calendars. Bills that are on the House Calendar (public bills) or the Union Calendar (money bills) may be placed by a congressman on the Unanimous Consent Calendar. On the first and third Mondays, the bills on this calendar are reported by title; and if there is no objection, they are passed one by one, without the formality of a vote. A single objection is enough to prevent passage, and the bill will be reported out again on the next call of the calendar. If three congressmen then oppose passage, the bill is dropped from the calendar for the remainder of the session; if not, it is passed. Each party assigns to a small group of its members the task of reviewing bills on the Consent Calendar and raising objections when necessary. Between 200 and 300 bills are passed by this method each year. All private bills (such as private claims, land bills, and immigration matters) are placed on a Private Calendar after review by subcommittees of the Judiciary Committee and are considered in a similar manner. A private bill will be sent back to committee if there are two or more objections from the floor, but the committee may include such a bill in an onnibus bill, which is considered on the Private Calendar by majority vote. The House usually passes between 300 and 500 bills a year on the Private Calendar. Although the Legislative Reorganization Act of 1946 reduced the number of private bills by prohibiting legislation on certain subjects, private legislation still constitutes a drain on congressional time, made tolerable only because the careful review by subcommittees of the Judiciary Committee makes it possible for the Private Calendar to be handled in cursory fashion.[9]

The Senate achieves the same objective of expediting noncontroversial bills in simpler fashion. These bills are not placed on special calendars or considered on specific days; instead, approximately twice a month, there is a call of the calendar that makes possible quick action on noncontroversial bills, both public and private. Both parties have committees to raise objections to bills so considered. This procedure is sometimes carried out under a unanimous-consent agreement for passage of bills without objection; at other times, the procedure permits these bills to be passed by a majority vote, but this technique is not used for important, controversial matters. The Senate carries out much of its business under unanimous agreements, and as a consequence, it does not follow such rigid and complicated procedures as are common in the House.

In the states, procedural rules vary but are seldom as detailed as those in the House. A mass of noncontroversial legislation is considered and passed expeditiously, but it is not usually passed by unanimous-consent procedures, although unanimous votes are common. In some states, constitutional requirements for roll calls on the final passage of all bills, although not always rigidly adhered to, are an impediment to rapid action. Some states have a special calendar for local bills, and whether or not this procedure is followed, local bills are often handled in the way that private bills are handled at the national level. In many state legislatures, approval is given without question or dissent to any purely local bill that has the support of any and all legislators from the county concerned; conversely, legislatures usually hesitate to act if this unanimity among the local legislators involved is lacking.

CONTROL OVER AGENDA

As we have said, in most legislative bodies, procedural rules and practice make it difficult to place a bill on the agenda for consideration until it has been reported favorably by a committee. How is priority determined among the bills that have been so reported? Routine, noncontroversial bills are usually handled quickly in the order in which they were reported. In the United States House, more important legislation, unless it has a privileged status (like appropriations and revenue measures), must receive a special order from the Rules Committee; in some state legislatures, the rules committee has similar authority, at least in the closing days of the session. (See Chapter 7 for a description of the operations of rules committees at both levels.) It is the majority leadership that determines priorities among bills that have survived screening by committees and, where this requirement is applicable, by rules committees. In the United States Senate, the majority leader consults with his Policy Committee before setting priorities. In Congress, the majority leadership is careful to give advance notice to the minority party about the schedule of major business, but this practice is not followed consistently in the states. The authority of the majority leader to make the final determination of priorities, limited though it may be by prior committee decisions, rests less on formal rules than it does on customary procedure, particularly on the common practice of giving priority of recognition to the floor leader. Thus, although the rules of a state legislature may appear to give any legislator the right to move that a bill be called up for consideration, in practice the Speaker may recognize only the floor leader for that purpose, which gives him a power that may be far-reaching but entirely a matter of custom and precedent.

LIMITATION OF DEBATE

No procedural rules are more important to a legislative body than those that govern debate. Strict rules not only expedite business but serve the purposes of the majority; rules that are broadly permissive serve minority interests and sometimes, as in the United States Senate, make certain kinds of legislation almost impossible. A series of changes in the rules of the United States House during the nineteenth century transformed it from an ineffective body in which the majority was frequently frustrated to one in which business was conducted with great efficiency, if little deliberation. The most fundamental of these rules for stopping debate is the *previous question,* which was adopted in 1811, a nondebatable motion to bring about a vote immediately on a pending motion or bill. Since that time, the House has developed a series of procedures that drastically limit debate: debate must be pertinent to the issue; no one may speak for more than an hour; and only five minutes are permitted for the proponents of an amendment and five minutes for its opponents. More significantly, most important legislation is considered under a special rule adopted by the Rules Committee that limits the time for debate prior to amendment. More than three-fourths of the bills considered under this procedure are allotted either one or two hours for debate; only a small minority of highly important bills receive more than four hours. The time is evenly divided between proponents and opponents and is allotted to individual congressmen by managers on each side.[10]

The practice in most state legislatures is to apply strict limits to debate. A study made two decades ago showed that in nearly every lower house and in about three-fourths of the upper houses, the rules provided for the previous-question motion, in many cases by a simple majority vote. In some cases, a brief amount of time was provided for debate after the previous question had been moved. Many legislatures limited the length of time a member could speak as well as the number of times he was permitted to speak on a bill (usually once or twice).[11] Filibusters are rare in state legislatures, but they are not unknown in states where the rules for limiting debate are ineffective or can be evaded. Constitutional limitations on the length of legislative sessions sometimes play into the hands of those who are using debate in an effort to block legislation.

The United States Senate is the citadel of unlimited debate in this country. The rules of the Senate do not provide for a previous-question motion; debate can be limited only voluntarily or through approval of a cloture motion by three-fifths of the total membership (sixty senators). Debate is frequently controlled in the Senate by a unanimous-consent agreement. When the leadership has determined that there is consensus in the Senate on concluding debate, it will usually seek such agreement to vote at a given time and date; often the last few hours prior to a vote are divided equally between supporters and opponents. Since 1964 the Senate rules have provided that for a given period each day all debate must be germane to the pending bill or amendments, a departure from long-established practice.

The Senate adopted a cloture rule for the first time in 1917, after a filibuster had prevented passage of President Wilson's proposal for arming United States merchant ships, prior to this country's entry into the war. There have been several changes in the majority required to end debate. For most of the period since its adoption, the rule required a two-thirds vote, though during most of the 1950s it was two-thirds of the total membership. The present rule specifies that if sixteen senators sign a cloture petition a vote will be taken, and cloture may be imposed by three-fifths of the total membership. To end debate on proposed changes in the Senate rules, however, two-thirds of those present and voting must approve cloture. The present rule was adopted in 1975 as a compromise, after reformers had battled for several weeks in an effort to reduce the voting requirement from two-thirds to three-fifths of those present and voting. Past experience suggests that the most recent change will not make it much easier to pass cloture motions except on issues important enough to bring all or almost all senators to the floor for a vote.

In recent years there has been a major increase in the frequency of efforts to cut off debate through cloture motions; there has also been an increase in the number of successful cloture motions, as Table 10.1 shows. In the first decade after the cloture rule was adopted, it was used successfully on several occasions, but from 1928 through 1961 there were no successful cloture motions and very few efforts to impose cloture. The breakthrough in the use of cloture came during the 1960s, when three of the four successful cloture motions involved civil rights bills. More remarkable has been the use of cloture during the 1970s. From 1971

TABLE 10.1   Cloture Votes in the U.S. Senate, 1919–1974

YEARS	NUMBER OF CLOTURE VOTES TAKEN	NUMBER OF BILLS ON WHICH CLOTURE VOTES TAKEN	NUMBER OF SUCCESSFUL CLOTURE VOTES
1919–1927	10	10	4
1928–1961	14	12	0
1962–1970	25	16	4
1971–1974	51	23	13
TOTAL	100	61	21

SOURCE: *Congressional Quarterly Weekly Report* 33 (March 1, 1975):452.

through 1974 there were more cloture votes taken than during the entire period from 1919 to 1970, and there were successful motions on almost half of the bills under consideration. (There were often several cloture votes on a single bill.)[12]

Although the filibuster remains an important procedural weapon, it is obvious that senators are much more willing than in the past to use cloture to cut off debate and to facilitate passage of legislation that they favor. At one time most southern senators were unwilling to use cloture, even for a bill that they favored, because they believed that the filibuster was an essential weapon against civil rights bills. But the successful use of cloture motions to pass civil rights bills has changed the situation. The filibuster is now a technique that may be used by any bloc of senators who believe that an issue is important enough to justify delaying Senate business. It has been used by conservative opponents against several civil rights bills, the reform of the cloture rule, a constitutional amendment to abolish the electoral college, and a bill to permit public financing of election campaigns. Liberals have filibustered against a bill to delay state legislative reapportionment under court orders, appropriations to continue development of the supersonic transport plane, a renewal of the draft, and an anti–school-busing bill. Both liberals and conservatives have filibustered against approval of appointments to the Supreme Court. Just as the filibuster may be used by opponents representing any ideological viewpoint or interest, any group of supporters of legislation may support cloture motions. Despite this fact, it is the liberal senators who have made periodic efforts to amend the Senate cloture rules to make it easier to shut off debate, and it is the conservatives who have opposed these efforts.

When the opponents of a bill decide to resort to a filibuster, they have one or more strategic objectives, as noted by Edward Keynes: "(1) The actors may use a filibuster simply to talk a measure to death; (2) they may use the tactic of extended debate primarily to bargain for changes in the proposed legislation; (3) the actors may use a filibuster to focus public attention on their struggle." According to Keynes, "the size of the minority is important in determining which of these three objectives will be pursued."[13] If there are enough minority votes to prevent cloture, a bill can be defeated by a filibuster. If the minority is very small, prolonged debate can only attract public attention and make political capital of the issue. If the coalition is medium-sized, the threat of prolonging a filibuster may force a bill's supporters to make compromises and accept amendments to the bill. The timing of a filibuster is also important. Late in the session, a filibuster becomes a more potent weapon, particularly for bargaining purposes, because a number of important bills are usually awaiting passage at that stage.

PROCEDURES REGARDING VOTING

Normally, before a vote is taken on passage of a bill, there is an opportunity for members to offer amendments. This is always the practice in the United States Senate, but in the House it is possible for the Rules Committee to limit amendments by adopting a closed rule. The closed rule may prohibit any amendments, or it may limit amendments to those that cover certain topics or those offered by the standing committee that reported the bill. Closed rules, which are used on less than one-tenth of the measures considered, are applied most often to revenue measures and other highly complex legislation. Their purpose is to avoid amendments that serve purely local interests, which would result in logrolling tactics, or to avoid revisions that might have a chaotic effect on a particularly complicated measure.[14] They also serve, of course, to force the House to accept the committee's version of the bill on a take-it-or-leave-it basis. In 1973 the House Democratic caucus adopted a new rule that restricts the freedom of the Rules Committee to adopt closed rules. If fifty members of the caucus initiate such a request, the caucus may vote to instruct Democrats on the Rules Committee to provide that specific amendments can be voted on when they get to the floor of the House, and this tactic has been used successfully on several occasions.

In some state legislatures the previous-question motion is often used not merely to halt debate but also to prevent the introduction and consideration of amendments. Where this is the practice, the motion is a powerful tool in that it permits the majority party or faction to force the minority into a take-it-or-leave-it position and denies them even the chance of publicizing proposed revisions in the bill.

When a vote is taken on amendments, those prepared by members of the committee normally have priority. In the Senate it is frequently the practice to take a number of roll calls on proposed amendments prior to a vote on final passage of the bill. The United States House follows a different procedure for consideration of amendments; it is known as the committee of the whole. When the House is sitting as the committee of the whole, the Speaker selects someone else to preside, and a quorum of only 100 members instead of a majority of the House is required. Proposed amendments are briefly debated and then voted on. When the committee of the whole completes its work and reports the results to the House, a single vote is taken to accept all of the amendments that have been adopted, although members may request a vote on individual amendments. But if an amendment has been defeated in the committee of the whole, it cannot be resurrected in the House.[15]

Prior to 1971 no recorded votes were taken in the committee of the whole; as a consequence, it was impossible to determine how representatives voted on most amendments, including all of those defeated in the committee of the whole. The 1970 Legislative Reorganization Act, however, provided that at the request of one-fifth of a quorum of the committee of the whole (only twenty members), a record would be kept of those voting. One consequence of this change was a dramatic increase in the number of recorded votes, by almost 50 percent, in the 1971 and 1972 sessions. There was a further increase in 1973 when the House installed an electronic voting machine that greatly speeded up the process of recorded voting. A second consequence of recording votes on amendments in the committee of the whole was to increase the participation of representatives in those votes, from an average of 190 in 1970 to an average of 373 in 1971.[16]

One significant difference between Senate and House rules has to do with the nature of amendments that are permitted. In the House and in the committee of the whole, an amendment must be germane to the bill and to the part of the bill being amended. The presiding officer has the authority to exclude from consideration amendments that he regards as not germane, and although his ruling is subject to appeal, the House rarely overrules the presiding officer. In the Senate, on the other hand, there is no requirement that amendments be germane. For example, amendments pertaining to civil rights have sometimes been offered in the Senate on bills dealing with entirely different subjects, such as education.

The rules regarding voting on amendments, which are substantially the same in the two branches of Congress, are highly technical; on occasion, however, they may have a significant effect on the outcome of votes. After an amendment is offered, it is in order to offer a substitute for it, as well as an amendment both to the original amendment and to the substitute. So-called third-degree amendments, an amendment to the amendment to the amendment, are not permitted. When votes are taken, the voting follows a strict order: first, the amendment to the amendment, then the amendment to the substitute, the substitute, and finally the original amendment. A case study of the 1957 civil rights bill shows that this inflexible rule had the effect of making it difficult for liberal senators to carry out an effective voting strategy. They were forced to vote on modifying a section of the bill before a vote was taken on eliminating that section. After amendments to a section of a bill have been considered, no separate vote is taken on that section of the bill.[17] William H. Riker has demonstrated that these voting rules sometimes have the effect of compelling the Senate or the House to order its preferences in a nonrational way, principally because there is no vote on the section of a bill to which two or more amendments have been considered.[18]

In addition to amendments, certain other motions may be made before a vote is taken on the bill itself. A motion to recommit a bill to committee is normally an indirect but effective way of killing it. Sometimes the motion will include instructions to the committee to make certain, often fundamental, changes in the bill; but such a motion is usually a method of demonstrating the nature of one's objection to a bill rather than a motion made with the expectation that the committee will act accordingly. A motion to table a bill is in effect a motion to kill the bill; since that motion is not debatable, it is a quick method of eliminating a bill without debate if there is majority sentiment against it. In the Senate, it can also be used to table an amendment without debate; this is not feasible in the House, however, where the result of such a motion is to table the bill along with the amendment. The sponsor of a bill or an amendment will frequently ask for a quorum call in order to get members to the floor prior to a roll-call vote.

Quorum calls are sometimes used as a delaying device (especially in the United States House, where they take half an hour) either by opponents of a measure or by a legislative tactician who needs more time to round up additional supporters for a vote.

In most legislative bodies, voice votes are commonly used to determine the wishes of the majority unless a more exact count is dictated by the closeness of the vote, the desire of the members, or constitutional requirements. A standing vote is sometimes used when the voice vote leaves doubt about the number on each side. The United States House (because of its large size) frequently achieves greater precision with a teller vote, in which the members are counted as they file past the teller. A roll call may be demanded by one-fifth of those present in the Senate or the House. In the states, there are wide variations in the number of members needed to force a roll call, but a majority of the states require roll calls on final passage of all bills. In this latter category of states particularly, it is sometimes common practice to use some technique as a shortcut in calling the roll on noncontroversial measures (perhaps combining the roll calls on several bills or recording as favorable all those who do not indicate otherwise). A mechanical voting device is used in three-fourths of the lower houses and one-fourth of the upper houses; this makes it possible to have roll calls whenever they are necessary or requested, without using shortcuts. A common practice in Congress is the use of *pairing,* a technique by which a member who has to be absent is paired with another member (either present or absent) who intends to vote on the opposite side of a question. Such pairs may apply to specific issues or may be general pairs, agreed on by two members who usually oppose each other in their votes, to be effective whenever one or both are absent.

When the roll is called in Congress or in a state legislature, it is possible for a member who was absent or who did not vote to have his vote recorded at the end of the roll call but before the result is announced. It is also possible for a member to change his vote before the result is announced, and where a mechanical device is used, he can change his vote at any time until the vote is recorded. These procedural rules are used by party leaders to assist in their efforts to corral votes. If a member is reluctant, for whatever reason, to support his party's position, he may withhold his vote to the end of the roll in order to see whether the vote is close and what difference his vote will make. The leadership may occasionally persuade a member to change his vote if the change will be decisive for a partisan victory and may even keep a few unrecorded votes or vote changes in reserve in order to counter similar strategy on the part of the opposition. The presiding officer may exercise some discretion in delaying the announcement of a vote to facilitate such changes.[19] The rules in Congress and in some states permit a motion to reconsider a vote by which a motion has been passed or defeated; often only one such motion to reconsider may be made, and it must be made within a day or two. To prevent reconsideration of a close vote, those who have won may move immediately to reconsider the vote and to table the motion to reconsider; this provides a quick way of eliminating the possibility of later reconsideration.

NOTES

1.   The best recent description of congressional rules is found in Lewis A. Froman, Jr., *The Congressional Process* (Boston, 1967).

2.   Asher C. Hinds and Clarence A. Cannon, *Precedents of the House of Representatives* (Washington, D.C., 1907), vols. 1–5; and *Precedents of the House of Representatives* (Washington, D.C., 1935–1941), vols. 6–11.

3.   Good sources on the history of the House rules are: George B. Galloway, *History of the House of Representatives* (New York, 1961), chap. 5; Neil MacNeil, *Forge of Democracy* (New York, 1963), chaps. 3 and 4; and Floyd M. Riddick, *The United States Congress: Organization and Procedure* (Manassas, Va., 1949).

4.   See Froman, *The Congressional Process,* pp. 90–93.

5.   See Howard E. Shuman, "Senate Rules and the Civil Rights Bill: A Case Study," *American Political Science Review* 51 (1957):963–964.

6.   James A. Robinson, *The House Rules Committee* (Indianapolis, Ind., 1963), p. 6; George Goodwin, Jr., *The Little Legislatures: Committees of Congress* (Amherst, Mass., 1970), pp. 220–221; Froman, *The Congressional Process,* p. 131; and *Congressional Quarterly Weekly Report* 32 (March 16, 1974):702.

7.   Robinson, *The House Rules Committee,* pp. 8–9; Riddick, *The United States Congress,* pp. 257–262; Froman, *The Congressional Process,* p. 96; and *Congressional Quarterly Weekly Report* 32 (February 9, 1974):319.

8.   Robinson, *The House Rules Committee,* pp. 5–8.

9.   Ibid., p. 5; Riddick, *The United States Congress,* pp. 228–235; and Froman, *The Congressional Process,* pp. 44–48.

10.   See Robinson, *The House Rules Committee,* pp. 43–45; and Riddick, *The United States Congress,* pp. 308–310.

11.   See Belle Zeller, ed., *American State Legislatures* (New York, 1954), pp. 112–114.

12.   *Congressional Quarterly Weekly Report* 33 (March 1, 1975):452.

13.   Edward Keynes, "The Senate Rules and the Dirksen Amendment," in *The Legislative Process in the U.S. Senate,* ed. Lawrence K. Pettit and Edward Keynes (Chicago, 1969), p. 142.

14.   See Robinson, *The House Rules Committee,* pp. 43–46.

15.   Although the parliamentary rules used by the House make it possible for the House to vote on amendments rejected in the committee of the whole, the House Rules Committee generally establishes rules for consideration of measures that make this impossible. See Froman, *The Congressional Process,* pp. 83–84.

16.   Congressional Quarterly, *Congress and the Nation, 1969–1972,* III:378, 383.

17.   See Riddick, *The United States Congress,* pp. 313–314; and Shuman, "Senate Rules and the Civil Rights Bill," pp. 971–972.

18.   William H. Riker, "The Paradox of Voting and Congressional Rules for Voting on Amendments," *American Political Science Review* 52 (1958):349–366.

19.   See MacNeil, *Forge of Democracy,* chap. 13.

Participants in the Legislative Process

part IV

In the two preceding parts of this book, we have examined the recruitment process for American legislators and its product, and we have described the structures of legislative institutions in the United States. But the borders of American legislative systems go far beyond the legislatures themselves, encompassing a wide variety of other individuals and institutions playing roles related to legislative action. Our analysis of legislative systems must take into account these other participants. We have chosen to give attention in Part IV to three sets of participants who are particularly relevant to American legislative activity: the executive, lobbyists, and constituents.

Although the chief executive is not a part of the legislative branch, he plays a central role in the legislative process. The President sets the agenda for Congress, provides almost all the important business, and today customarily engages in one legislative foray after another. His legislative role can easily be exaggerated, but it cannot be ignored. The governor's legislative role varies considerably from state to state, but in every state, he is at least a significant participant in legislative action.

Lobbyists, the spokesmen for private-interest groups and associations, play representative roles in the legislative system. They speak for constituents who make up the organized social, political, professional, ethnic, economic, and religious interests in American society.

Private-interest groups and associations have long been recognized as important elements in the American political process. The organizational and propaganda activities of the major American pressure groups have been studied extensively. Usually these groups are analyzed in some sense in terms of their relationships with legislatures, but often their access to political power has been vaguely implied rather than examined specifically. We think that an analysis of interest-group politics vis-à-vis legislatures is most useful if the focus is upon the groups' representatives: the lobbyists. The AFL-CIO does not lobby in Congress; rather, individuals who represent the AFL-CIO and whose roles can be identified do. Congressmen do not react to, or interact with, the American Farm Bureau Federation (AFBF) as an organization, although they may have some diffuse image of that entity. Individuals who play roles as congressmen interact with other individuals who play roles as representatives of the AFBF. Therefore, our analytical focus is upon lobbyists, and this focus is consistent with the conceptual orientation outlined in Chapter 1.

In principle, it should be possible to identify those representatives of interest groups and agents of the executive branch who play roles in the legislative system. Constituent participants constitute a much more ambiguous category, and the boundary lines of the legislative system in regard to constituents are very complex and difficult to draw. Still, some constituents do play roles related to legislative action, and American legislators tend to respond to relevant constituents. They certainly are important participants in the legislative process. Because an American legislator's response to his constituents clearly constitutes an important factor in his own role definition, we think it is essential to stress the legislator's reaction to his constituency and to interchanges of communication between legislator and constituents.

CHAPTER ELEVEN

The Executive as a Legislative Leader

The United States Constitution is specific in its vesting of "all legislative powers herein granted" in the two houses of Congress. Similar provisions are found in state constitutions. Despite these clear constitutional assignments of legislative power, it has become customary to refer to the President or governor not merely as a partner in the legislative process but as the chief legislator. Students will look in vain for amendments to the United States Constitution that expand the President's role in the legislative process. The only amendment affecting his power, the Twenty-second, restricts the President by limiting him to two terms. The grants of legislative authority to the President in the Constitution are few but important: he shall make legislative recommendations to Congress; he may call special sessions; and he has the power to veto legislation (subject to overriding by a two-thirds vote in the Congress).

The case of the governor is different. It is possible to trace the trends in state constitutions that have enhanced his power in legislative affairs. Under early state constitutions, the governor had a short term, exercised minimum powers, and was heavily dependent on the legislature. In the words of William H. Young, "The American governorship was conceived in mistrust, and born in a strait jacket, the creature of revolutionary assemblies."[1] During the Jacksonian period, popular election of the governor became universal, the term of office was extended, and the veto became common. Later on in the nineteenth century, the proliferation of elected officials and boards and commissions reduced the governor's control over the executive branch and consequently his influence with the legislature. In the early years of the twentieth century, constitutional and statutory changes enhanced the governor's power, transforming him, in the words of Leslie Lipson, "from figurehead to leader." In many states, his term was increased to four years, and the item veto became more common. Programs to reorganize the state administrative structure and the development of the executive budget system, paralleling trends at the national level, strengthened not only the governor's administrative control but also his ability to influence legislative developments.[2]

The emergence of the chief executive as chief legislator at both the national and the state levels has been caused primarily by other factors. The growing demands on government and the growing complexity of these demands have increasingly forced the executive to take the initiative in the development of a legislative program. These trends did not evolve automatically; they were the product of strong executives with bold concepts of their responsibilities. The history of national government is the history of rivalry and shifts in the locus of power between President and Congress. Thomas Jefferson used many of the techniques of leadership that were duplicated or attempted a century or more later. He chose legislative leaders and made them responsible to him, used the party caucus effectively, drafted bills, and persuaded supporters to run for Congress. Under his successors, the reins of leadership shifted to congressional leaders such as Henry Clay and John C. Calhoun. Although Andrew Jackson used the veto and patronage powers with unprecedented vigor, neither he nor other presidents before the Civil War exercised such direct leadership of Congress as Jefferson had. Lincoln battled with Congress throughout the Civil War and accomplished some of his major objectives through bypassing it; the conflict was renewed during the next administration and came to a climax in the impeachment proceedings against Andrew Johnson. The remainder of the nineteenth century was characterized by congressional supremacy. The stronger presidents resisted attempted congressional encroachments on presidential power, but they did not work effectively to enact legislative measures.[3]

Three twentieth-century presidents (the two Roosevelts and Wilson) enabled the President to become the chief legislator. Each of these men came to Washington with experience in the states, where they had transformed the image of the governor into that of a leader with broad legislative, as well as administrative, responsibilities. Theodore Roosevelt started the practice of initiating a wide range of legislative proposals in messages to Congress, and Wilson dramatized his legislative recommendations by appearing personally before Congress to deliver them. Bills were drafted in the executive departments and forwarded without fanfare to Congress. Roosevelt and Wilson did not merely propose legislation; they recognized the need, in Clinton Rossiter's words, "to push politely but relentlessly" for enactment of their proposals, and they did so by writing letters to members of Congress, conferring with congressional leaders, and delegating members of the cabinet to lobby in caucuses and in the corridors of the Capitol.[4]

The men who set the precedents of strong gubernatorial leadership during the early years of the twentieth century were found primarily in the industrial states: Alfred E. Smith and Franklin Roosevelt in New York, Woodrow Wilson in New Jersey, Frank Lowden in Illinois, and Robert La Follette in Wisconsin. These were men who recognized that new demands were being placed on government in the larger states and that the governor must take the initiative to accomplish needed reforms. Most of them initiated statutory or constitutional changes to strengthen the tools at the governor's command. It was Lowden (1917–1921) who reorganized the executive branch in Illinois to make the most of the agencies of government directly responsible to him, and it was Smith who established the executive budget system in New York in 1927. Both reforms were widely copied in other states, and both strengthened not only the governor's control over the executive branch but also his influence in legislative matters.

The most important changes wrought by these governors, however, were political rather than constitutional. They appeared in person before the legislature to present programs that became increasingly specific over the years. They used the veto, the special session, and messages to the legislature boldly and skillfully. Above all, they mobilized public support with radio speeches, press conferences, and speaking tours across the state. They capitalized on the public demand for social reforms and on the tarnished image of the legislatures to force legislative approval of at least some of their major proposals. They transformed the governor into a legislative leader, a public figure highly visible to the voters. The precedents set by a few have been followed, with varying degrees of success, by scores of less famous governors in a majority of the states.

CONSTITUTIONAL SOURCES OF POWER

Legislative Recommendations

"He shall from time to time give to the Congress information of the state of the Union, and recommend to their consideration such measures as he shall judge necessary and expedient." Here, in Article II, Section 3 of the Constitution, is the constitutional base for the President's proposals to Congress. The executive initiation of legislation has become the accepted norm in our political system. Since Eisenhower's administration, it has been common for the President to present Congress with a comprehensive legislative program. The annual State of the Union message may be used to outline the legislative program, and it is usually followed by a series of messages dealing with major legislative proposals.

Legislative recommendations emerge from individual departments and are sent to the President far in advance of presentation to Congress. Just as departmental budgets must be cut to avoid overcommitting the government's fiscal resources, legislative recommendations must be screened to avoid overcommitting the President's political resources. The White House staff and the Office of Management and Budget play a part in this screening effort, but the final decision, like that on the budget, must be made by the President. When the session is drawing to a close, the President may tell his legislative leaders which items he considers "must" legislation; with this step, the process of selection becomes more difficult and more crucial.

Thus institutionalized, presidential initiative has become a permanent feature of the legislative process. This does not mean that most legislative proposals originate in the mind of the President or within the confines of the White House. Many come from governmental agencies, interest groups, or members of Congress. Particularly in recent years, with Democratic control of Congress and Republican control of the White House, a substantial proportion of legislative proposals have actually originated in the halls of Congress. What the President does is to determine priorities and focus attention and pressure on high-priority measures. Moreover, when the President assigns a low priority to a measure, or actively opposes it, the chances for passage of that proposal are seriously diminished. Once the President has committed his prestige to certain proposals, he must choose how best to use the resources of his office to advance his legislative program. In any session, the President is able to win enactment of only a part of his program, but few major pieces of legislation win without his active support.

State constitutions provide governors with a comparable mandate to make legislative recommendations. The process by which a governor prepares a legislative program has not been studied extensively, but it appears to replicate the process at the national level on a smaller and less complex scale.[5] State agencies have myriad suggestions for legislation. Some of these deal with noncontroversial matters and do not need gubernatorial support. In at least a few states, some agencies have enough influence in the legislature to operate independently. But generally, state agencies seek to gain a place for their major bills on the governor's list of recommendations because this enhances the prospects for passage.

The governor, like the President, must determine priorities and provide direction to a legislature that is dealing with masses of bills, many of which are trivial. In states where the governor can depend on the loyal voting support of some legislators, this support applies primarily to legislation publicly advocated in gubernatorial messages. Even in states where party or factional alignments are weaker, there is often a strong disposition to support the governor's program whenever possible. Whatever the strength of its support, the governor's program becomes the focus of attention.

The Veto

The constitutional right to veto is a powerful negative weapon for both President and governor. The President has ten days in which to return a bill to Congress with his objections to it spelled out; a two-thirds vote in each house is necessary to override his veto. After Congress has adjourned, the President may exercise the *pocket veto* by simply failing to sign a bill within ten days. Comparable provisions for the veto are found in the constitution of every state except North Carolina. There are variations among the states in the size of the legislative majority needed to override a veto. In most states, it is either two-thirds of all elected members or two-thirds of those voting; several states specify either a majority or three-fifths of the elected membership.[6]

The veto is a powerful presidential weapon because it is seldom reversed. A President can almost always rally more than one-third of the members of one or both houses of Congress to his support. The success record for vetoes is impressive. From Washington through Nixon, Presidents have vetoed 2,293 bills, and only seventy-nine of the vetoes (about 3 percent) have been overridden. One study of historical patterns shows that presidents who have been elected by large margins and those who face a Congress controlled by the opposition party are more likely to veto bills, and also more likely than others to be overridden.[7] Grover Cleveland was the first President to veto many bills. His 584 vetoes in two terms was more than twice as many as the vetoes by all of his predecessors combined. It was Franklin Roosevelt, with 635 vetoes (nine of them overridden), who established the veto as a significant tool of the modern presidency. The success record of recent presidents is impressive. Eisenhower lost only two vetoes (out of 181) despite having a Democratic Congress three-fourths of the time; and neither Kennedy (twenty-one vetoes) nor Johnson (thirty vetoes) had any overridden.[8]

The veto has become even more important lately because of the frequent conflicts over legislation between Republican presidents and Democratic majorities in Congress. The number of Nixon's vetoes (forty-three) was not very large, but they covered some major pieces of legislation, and six of them were overridden. During Gerald Ford's first fourteen months in office, the veto rate sharply increased; he vetoed thirty-nine, and seven were overridden. In 1975 the congressional Democrats were frustrated by the fact that, despite their lopsided margin in both houses, they could not usually maintain enough cohesion to override vetoes of important bills, such as those dealing with strip mining, emergency job relief, farm prices, and oil import fees.

A recent study of twenty-six states showed that the average governor vetoed about three bills during a session.[9] On the average, only 1 or 2 percent of the gubernatorial vetoes throughout the country are overridden in a year; most of these are likely to be in a few states where governors are locked in partisan or factional struggles with a legislative majority. In some states the veto has become so invulnerable that there is rarely any effort to override it.[10] There are states in which the governor's veto is, in effect, unchallenged because, with a high proportion of bills being passed in the closing days of the session, many vetoes come after adjournment.

The veto is essentially a negative weapon, but a skillful executive may use it positively to force improvements in a bill. In four states (Alabama, Virginia, Massachusetts, and New Jersey), the governor has the power of executive amendment, the option of returning the bill to the legislature with amendments, which the legislature may adopt or reject. The Washington governor has the power to veto any section of a bill or even any words or phrases in it.[11] In forty-three states, the governor has the item veto on appropriations bills. He can eliminate an item in an appropriations bill, and in eight of the states he can reduce the amount of a particular item.[12] This permits him to exclude unwanted sections to the budget without the risk of vetoing a whole appropriations bill. Although the President lacks an item veto for appropriations, recent presidents have increasingly used their authority to impound funds voted by Congress, a step that has caused sharp conflicts between the two branches and led to congressional legislation enabling Congress to override an impoundment of funds. (For further discussion of impoundment, see Chapter 18.)

Special Sessions

The President has the power to call special sessions of Congress. This power has been used on occasion to meet particular emergencies; it has often been used as a political weapon to focus attention on presidential programs. In all states, the governor has the power to call special sessions. In three-fifths of the states, this power is exclusively his; and in one-third of the states, the governor alone can determine the subject matter of such a session. At the state level, the special session assumes greater importance because regular sessions are fewer and usually shorter. The threat of a special session may be a powerful device for gaining action sought by the governor, just as the threat of the veto may block bills and amendments he opposes.

Term of Office

Most of the constitutional powers possessed by the governor do not vary significantly from state to state. All governors may propose legislation. All but one may exercise the veto, and the variations in requirements for overriding it make little difference. All governors can call special sessions. There are significant constitutional differences in the governor's control over various components of the executive branch (discussed in the section "Diversity and Coordination in the Executive Branch"). One remaining difference of great importance is in the governor's term. There are nineteen states in which the governor has a four-year term of office with no limit on reelection and nineteen other states where he is limited to two consecutive four-year terms. In the remaining twelve states, the limitations of the governor's term constitute a serious obstacle to his effectiveness as chief legislator. In eight states, mostly southern, he has a four-year term but cannot be reelected. This reduces the governor's legislative effectiveness during the second half of his term and makes it difficult for him to build a political base in the legislature, particularly in one-party states. In four states, the governor has a two-year term but no limit on the number of successive terms possible.[13] The two-year term gives the governor a minimum of time to build legislative support and to develop a legislative record before he must face the voters again. One of the most important recent trends in constitutional revision has been to lengthen the governor's term and remove the restrictions on successive terms. The number of states in which the governor has a four-year term and can serve at least two consecutive terms increased from thirteen to thirty-eight between 1955 and 1975. Only three states elect the governor and all legislators simultaneously for four years. The four-year governor normally faces the prospect of midterm elections for half the senate and all the house members, although in a few states, all senators are elected during the gubernatorial election. At the national level, the Twenty-second Amendment, by limiting the President to two terms, was widely believed to have weakened his effectiveness as a legislative leader during the closing years of his second term. President Eisenhower cast some doubt on this theory because he seemed to many observers to be a more aggressive leader during his last two years in office. Until more presidents have completed second terms, the effects of the third-term ban will remain uncertain.

LEADERSHIP OF PUBLIC OPINION

Every recent President or governor who has been effective as a legislative leader has brought the force of public opinion to bear on the legislative body on behalf of his proposals. When the President wishes to, he can command newspaper headlines and television time in order to capture the attention of the nation in a way that no member of Congress can duplicate. A governor's impact on public opinion is far less but still exceeds that of legislators. In an age when the processes of government are complex and confusing to the average citizen, the chief executive of nation or state has visibility. The tools of public relations are available to any chief executive; it is his skill in using them that determines their effectiveness.

The press conference provides an example of how rapidly the innovations of strong presidents (like Franklin Roosevelt) become institutionalized in an age when each President needs to utilize fully the resources of his office. The press conference has become a permanent institution, but the style has been affected by the personality of the President and by technological change. A small, almost intimate affair under Roosevelt, it gradually became larger and more formal; it was televised under Eisenhower and shown live under Kennedy. Lyndon Johnson, more accessible to the press than any President since Franklin Roosevelt, varied the format from occasional large-scale conferences on television to informal and impromptu ones in such locations as his Texas ranch and the White House grounds.[14] Nixon held fewer conferences than his recent predecessors, but used a variety of other communications techniques, including talks outside Washington to media representatives from particular regions. Ford increased the use of press conferences, and changed the format by permitting a reporter to ask a follow-up question in an effort to make the conferences less disjointed in terms of subject matter. At the state level, the press conference remains a small, informal affair, comparable to that devised by Roosevelt during his term as governor and carried by him to Washington. Some governors meet daily with the press.

The advent of television has given the chief executive an opportunity for direct, intimate contact with the American people. Franklin Roosevelt first recognized the value of radio as a means for communicating directly with the people. No President since has equaled Roosevelt's skill in personalized mass communications, but each has used radio and television in an effort to make his policies and legislative proposals understandable and acceptable to the public, and to criticize the actions and inactions of Congress. The President also uses radio and television for many other purposes, such as a report on a trip abroad or an international or domestic crisis.

Examples of the use of the electronic media to promote legislation include Lyndon Johnson's dramatic personal appeal to Congress for his voting rights bill in 1965, which was televised and scheduled in prime evening time. In 1970, President Nixon used television to explain to the public why he was vetoing an education appropriations bill that exceeded his request. In May, 1975, Gerald Ford used television to defend his energy program and to goad Congress into action on this problem, dramatizing his point by tearing the pages off a calendar:

> Now what did the Congress do in February about energy? Congress did nothing. ... What did the Congress do in March? ... in April? Congress did nothing. ... So, what has Congress done in May about energy? Congress did nothing and went home for a 10-day recess.

Nixon's extensive use of television led to demands by Democratic leaders for equal time to reply. But even when the networks granted such time, it is very unlikely that those who enunciated Democratic proposals on television attracted as much attention as Nixon had done. During the Kennedy administration, the Republican congressional leaders, Everett Dirksen and Charles Halleck, staged periodic televised press conferences (popularly known as the "Ev and Charlie Show"). These conferences attracted little attention from press reporters, networks, or the public, not because the principals were inept or untelegenic, but because the task of competing with the President is so difficult.[15]

Since Wilson's time, and particularly since Roosevelt's time, presidents have gone to the country on speaking tours designed to dramatize their legislative programs through personal endorsement. Although the President may speak directly to only a few thousand, these trips are important because some of the talks are made to opinion leaders and others are delivered in sections of the country where the presence of the chief executive attracts attention and interest. Moreover, these talks are reported by the national press and television networks and are occasionally telecast live. The President makes great use of the vice-president to speak for him throughout the country, and some of these speeches deal with the legislative program. Vice-President Agnew, for example, spoke to a number of state legislatures and meetings of local officials in support of President Nixon's revenue-sharing bills.

The governor, although he attracts less attention, has the chance to be seen and heard in person by a larger proportion of his constituents. Some governors have weekly television reports or newspaper columns, and all have a multitude of invitations to dedicate highways, address graduating classes, and adorn state conventions. The governor can use these occasions to polish platitudes or to extol the virtues of the town where he speaks; he can also use them to generate public support for his legislative program.

The President and the governors of two-party states also influence public opinion by serving as party spokesmen. During the election campaign, they define the issues and make the commitments that form the basis for their legislative programs. An incumbent chief executive, the party nominee, or one who seems likely to win nomination (depending on the timing and function of a convention) usually has a dominant voice in determining the content of the platform; the candidate who has not been able to dictate the platform can largely ignore it in his campaign. Voters who consider themselves Democrats may not agree with a Democratic governor's pronouncements, but they are likely to identify these as party policy. Studies of voting behavior have shown a tendency for voters to approve many of the policy positions taken by the leader of the party with which they identify. The governor, as a party leader, speaks not only to loyal members of the legislative party but, with some effectiveness, to loyal and attentive voters as well, despite the vast public ignorance on most issues. The fact that the opposition party never has an undisputed leader, except during election campaigns, reduces the impact of the opposition leadership on public opinion.

These techniques for influencing opinion assume importance because legislators have some sensitivity to public opinion. If these techniques work perfectly, the chief executive will not only influence the thinking of the voters but will so impress them with the importance of an issue that they will deluge their legislators with demands to support the chief executive's program. To the extent that the legislator is sensitive to constituent opinion, he will then vote as the executive wishes. The many legislative successes of chief executives suggest that this model sometimes corresponds to reality, but the many examples of executive failure and legislative deadlock are proof that the model does not always work in this fashion. Why not? What weaknesses undermine the chief executive's control over the legislature through public opinion?

Although the President has a great advantage over any congressman in gaining access to the news media, he has to compete with every other source of news, from home-run hitters to movie starlets, in attracting public attention. The average citizen has only the most casual interest in the problems of politics and government, which he often finds complex, boring, and irrelevant to his personal life. The President cannot get and keep an audience simply by appearing before the television cameras. Richard E. Neustadt has said of the President:

> He has to ride events to gain attention. Most members of his public grow attentive only as they grow concerned with what may happen in their lives. . . . Without a real-life happening to hoist it into view, a piece of presidential news, much like the man's own voice, is likely to be lost amidst the noises and distractions of the day.[16]

In time of obvious crisis—for example, the attack on Pearl Harbor or the discovery of missile bases in Cuba—the President commands attention. The President's legislative program seldom has enough intrinsic interest to attract such attention. An intensive campaign for a legislative measure, highlighted by a major television address, will have an impact, but not if it becomes a weekly feature. The President may decide that it is unrealistic to try to focus public attention on more than two or three measures during one session of Congress. In competing for public attention, the governor faces greater obstacles than the President. He is a less important figure and deals with problems that attract less attention. Except for desegregation crises in a few southern states, it is difficult to think of recent state issues that would enable a governor to attract full public attention. The governor may devote a large proportion of his time to explaining his legislative program and still wonder whether anyone is listening.

The success of the President's program depends not only on the public's support for it but also on the President's prestige. Neustadt points out that congressmen, as well as the other actors on the Washington scene, are dependent in varying degrees on public support and are consequently interested in gauging the President's prestige. This prestige can be measured roughly by the public-opinion polls, but it remains a vague thing, "a jumble of imprecise impressions held by relatively inattentive men."[17] The President's prestige may affect the success of his legislative program, but the effect is a subtle, unmeasurable one. One reason for this is that there seems to be little connection between the President's prestige and public understanding of and support for his legislative program. This was the finding of polls conducted during Kennedy's administration, and it was also true during the New Deal. The public liked the President but was apathetic or hostile to important parts of his program.[18] If a chief executive's prestige is not necessarily an asset to his program, and if his campaigns for public support often founder on apathy and ignorance about issues, perhaps he can seldom do more than generate public confidence, a willingness to give him and his program a chance. To focus this general support on specific measures, the executive must exercise political leadership in his direct dealings with legislators.

POLITICAL LEADERSHIP

The executive and the legislature are separate branches of government, independent in their electoral bases and distinct in the functions each performs. The division of power in our constitutional system breeds conflict, but the part played by the modern executive in the legislative process requires cooperation between the two branches. We have described how chief executives have used the formal powers of their office and their leadership of public opinion to advance their legislative proposals, but the legislative branch retains the power to delay, amend, or defeat those proposals. It is also possible for the chief executive to block measures initiated by the legislative branch. In the words of Gary Orfield:

> It is vital to realize that the making of national domestic policy takes place in a context of genuinely divided power, and that the Congress as well as the President possesses both the ability to initiate and the power to veto major policy changes. ... The Nixon period clearly shows that the modern Presidency can be quite as efficient an engine of negative social policy as was Congress during the earlier progressive Administrations.[19]

Congress not only plays a major role in initiating legislation, particularly during conservative administrations, but it has an important voice in determining priorities for spending on established domestic programs through the appropriations process.

It has become common to describe the President as the "chief legislator," but some students of the Presidency consider that to be an exaggeration. Gallagher says, "It is a paper title. Congress legislates, and, except in rare instances, the President has little to say about it."[20] Koenig argues that "the reality is less impressive than this grandiose title suggests," and explains why:

> No function of the President is more beset with uncertainty, is more vulnerable to breakdowns, and is more readily the victim of the will and whim of individuals whose outlooks and responsibilities tend to be different from his own than his duty to lead in legislation. Nowhere else in the Presidential enterprise is there found a greater gap between what the Chief Executive wants to do, what he promises to the electorate in his contest for the office, and what he can do in bringing Congress to enact the laws that alone can give effect to the party program of the previous campaign. In no other major nation is the program of a head of government more susceptible to rebuff in the legislature, to delay and crippling amendment, to absolute, uncompromising rejection. The President runs an obstacle course on Capitol Hill that other heads of government would find strange and even incredible.[21]

The chief executive cannot compel legislative support. He must persuade legislators by skillfully using the informal techniques of political leadership. Though a President or governor is often referred to as the leader of his party, he cannot automatically command the loyalty of his legislative party. As Neustadt has said, "What the Constitution separates our political parties do not combine. The parties are themselves composed of separated organizations sharing public authority."[22] In earlier chapters, we have explored the leadership structure of legislative bodies and found that in Congress and in some state legislatures, this structure provides the basis for a significant degree of party cohesion. In Chapter 16 we shall summarize the evidence from research showing that in many legislative bodies party alignments appear frequently on roll calls, in part because of the different constituency bases of the two parties. In this chapter we will discuss the contribution of the chief executive to party cohesion and the available means of political leadership where party loyalties are weak.

At the national level in recent years, executive-legislative relations have frequently been characterized by deadlock. Democratic presidents have often had great difficulty in getting important parts of their legislative programs adopted, despite Democratic majorities in Congress. These failures have obviously reflected a lack of party cohesion, as well as the decentralized congressional decision-making structure and the independence of committees. On the other hand, party cohesion has been strong enough so that Democratic majorities in Congress have often rejected the recommendations of Republican presidents and have often seen their bills vetoed by the President. Congress is perfectly capable of defeating presidential programs, and the President has often demonstrated his ability to veto congressional bills and make the veto stick. The system seems well designed to produce deadlock more often than it produces legislation on the most controversial and complex issues facing the country. Whether the system produces deadlock or positive results depends to a large extent on the political environment.

Political Environment

In Chapter 5 we described the two-party pattern in Congress and the various levels of party competition found in state legislatures. The political environment in which a President or a governor must work obviously affects his strategy of leadership. One aspect of this environment is the balance of partisan strength in the legislature; another is the historical pattern of party competition in the legislature.

If the chief executive's party is relatively cohesive and responsive to his leadership, it makes a great deal of difference whether or not his party holds a majority in both legislative branches. If it lacks a majority in one or both branches, the chief executive must adjust his tactics; he must temper overtly partisan appeals, rely more heavily on public opinion, distribute patronage to both parties, and constantly base his tactics on the necessity of ultimate compromise with the opposition party. He must be effective as both a partisan and a bipartisan leader.

Democratic presidents since Roosevelt have had Democratic majorities in both houses of Congress (except for Truman's Eightieth Congress), but Republican presidents have not fared so well. Eisenhower had a Republican Congress for only the first two of his eight years in office; Nixon faced Democratic majorities throughout his term; Ford inherited a Democratic majority that was increased following the 1974 election. No state that has had some alternation in party control of the governorship has completely avoided divided government in recent years. If the five southern states with complete Democratic control (listed in Table 5.1) and the two states with nonpartisan legislatures are excluded, the picture of the incidence of divided government becomes clearer. In the period from 1961 to 1976 in these forty-three states, Republican governors had to face opposition party control of one or both legislative houses 55 percent of the time, and Democratic governors encountered this situation 38 percent of the time. Divided government has been a more common occurrence for Republican governors in recent years because that party won governorships in a number of states (primarily southern and border) with long histories of Democratic control of the legislature. There are only a few states, such as New Hampshire, Vermont, and Kansas, where the Democrats have frequently won the governorship but not the legislature. Other causes of divided government appear to affect both parties equally.

If the chief executive's party has a legislative majority, its size also has an important effect on his tactics and his prospects for success. The larger his party's majority in Congress, the bolder the President can be in trying to enact his program and the less he has to compromise with members of the opposition party or critics within his own party. Moreover, the size of the President's own electoral margin has an important psychological effect on executive-legislative relations. The importance of both the congressional and presidential margins is illustrated by the contrast between President Kennedy's dealings with Congress and those of Lyndon Johnson, particularly after Johnson's 1964 election. Kennedy was elected by the narrowest of margins, and although he had Democratic margins of 80 to 90 in the House and approximately two-to-one in the Senate during the two Congresses, a substantial number of southern Democrats were unsympathetic to liberal programs. Kennedy was acutely conscious of the narrowness of his margin and his lack of any meaningful mandate, and he proceeded very cautiously in his legislative program, trying to avoid issues, such as civil rights bills, that would crack the fragile Democratic majority. Many of the controversial measures that he did seek to enact, such as medicare and aid to education, ran into trouble. By contrast, Lyndon Johnson was elected in 1964 by a landslide, and in that election the Democrats won a huge 155-vote margin in the House, while holding their two-to-one Senate majority. Johnson, who was determined to make an impressive legislative record, pressed vigorously for an ambitious legislative program, and Congress passed a long string of Great Society measures, many of which had been on the legislative agenda for years.[23]

The historical pattern of party competition is probably even more important to the chief executive than the exact party ratios in the legislature. In Congress and in some state legislatures, there is a long-established tradition of competition between two relatively strong legislative parties. Under these conditions, the members of his legislative party are likely to have a sense of loyalty to the chief executive and a predisposition to give sympathetic consideration to his legislative program. Members of the legislative party have a stake in the success of the chief executive's program; some of them may believe that their reelection is dependent upon his victory at the polls. The chief executive is recognized as the party leader. A tradition of two-party competition is conducive to a norm of partisanship in the legislature, although it is no guarantee of consistently high cohesion in roll-call voting.

There are a number of states, particularly in the South, where two-party legislative competition is not rooted in history but has just begun to emerge in recent sessions. In state legislatures that have been dominated by a single party, partisan norms have been weak or nonexistent. Under these conditions, the governor cannot depend on partisan loyalties or a tradition of high cohesion; he must build a personal following from scratch in a new legislature. This is particularly difficult for those southern governors who cannot serve a second consecutive term. Legislators are unlikely to link their political fortune with the governor. Nothing the governor does is likely to help or hurt the legislator at the polls, and both of them realize it. On the other hand, the governor in a state dominated by one party has some often-neglected advantages. Normally there is no group of legislators with the organizational structure or motivation to play the part of an opposition faction consistently. Opposition blocs that have been formed on one issue fade away with the next. In contrast with a two-party legislature, there is no group whose regular business it is to oppose the governor's program. This helps to explain the seeming ease with which some southern governors have been able to enact their legislative programs.

The Chief Executive and the Party Organization

Control over a strong party organization outside the legislature may be an asset to the chief executive who is seeking to enact a legislative program. At the state level, strong, well-organized parties are found more often in the industrial states of the East and Midwest, where party machines remain potent in some of the metropolitan centers. Party organization is weaker in the West, where party loyalties and local organizations are weaker. Although he wears the mantle of party leader, a governor does not automatically inherit de facto control of a strong party organization. Rhode Island and Connecticut are examples of states in which governors have often been able to use the party organization to advance their legislative programs. Mayor Richard Daley's firm control over the Democratic organization in Chicago extends to the party's legislators from Cook County and provides a Democratic governor with a large bloc of votes that he can count on as long as he maintains good relations with the mayor. A governor who wins nomination by defeating an entrenched organization may be handicapped in trying to control that organization during his term.

Party leadership presents a different kind of challenge to the President because the federal nature of the national party structure makes impossible the tight control that some governors exercise over state parties. Modern presidents have recognized the need to exert some type of influence over the national party. Franklin Roosevelt played a larger part in state politics than any subsequent President. He used patronage to support one faction or another in state parties. He supported some progressive Republican and independent candidates, even against Democrats. He was primarily concerned with strengthening his own prospects for reelection, rather than with the long-run goal of reshaping the state Democratic parties or establishing a centralized national party.[24] President Eisenhower lacked the continuing interest in politics necessary to have any impact on the Republican party at the state level. Both John Kennedy and Lyndon Johnson were masters of party politics, and both occasionally dabbled in state political affairs, but neither was willing or able to devote the time and attention necessary to establishing a greater national party authority.

The crux of the problem is congressional nominations. The classic example of a public effort by a President to unseat his party's congressmen in a primary is Franklin Roosevelt's attempted purge in 1938, and the failure of the purge partly explains why no President since has followed his example. Roosevelt endorsed several incumbent Democratic senators, but his real break with tradition came when he campaigned against several incumbent Democrats. The incumbents endorsed by Roosevelt won, but so did those whom he opposed. The venture entered the history books as a complete failure. Roosevelt undertook the purge without any clear idea about either objectives or tactics, and the campaign was poorly managed from start to finish.

Recent presidents have avoided public intervention in primaries but have occasionally tried to influence nominations by methods that do not entail a risk to their political prestige or arouse the resentment of voters. There are examples from the administrations of Kennedy, Johnson, and Nixon of presidential efforts to protect an incumbent from primary competition and also efforts to recruit and assist strong candidates to run against incumbents in the opposite party. But examples of even quiet efforts to purge a member of the President's party are rare. The best-known recent example occurred in 1970 when the Republican administration (notably Vice-President Agnew) attacked a Republican senator from New York, Charles Goodell, who was seeking reelection, and gave tacit support to a Conservative party candidate, James L. Buckley, who was elected. Goodell had been a vigorous critic of the President's Vietnam policy. Although this was a significant victory for President Nixon, he found it necessary after the election to assure liberal Republican senators that similar purges were not planned for the 1972 election. In both presidential and midterm election campaigns, recent presidents have given increasingly direct support and endorsement to members of their congressional ticket. The President's time for personal campaigning is limited, and he can be selective about the candidates whom he actively assists. It is difficult to measure how much effect personal campaigning by a President has on the outcome of a congressional race. As a technique for building congressional support for a President's program, selective assistance in the campaign may have potential value, but there is little evidence of its systematic use by a President.

The governor of a state might be expected to have greater opportunities to influence legislative nominations than a President. In several states, such as New York and Connecticut, where local party organizations can usually control legislative nominations, state party leaders have sometimes persuaded local party leaders to deny renomination to a legislator who failed to support the governor's program. This sanction is seldom used, but its potential for use may be an important asset for the governor. In states where the direct primary cannot be controlled by local organizations, it is rare to find the governor openly involved in legislative nominations. Most governors seem to fear that the probable risks of intervention would outweigh the possible gains. They probably believe that the reaction of voters would range from hostile to apathetic and that they could not find enough local allies to make endorsements effective. The failure of a gubernatorial purge is a virtual guarantee that the legislators who were intended victims will be hostile at the next session of the legislature.

The Chief Executive and the Legislative Leadership

In dealing directly with Congress, the President must rely primarily on his party's leaders, as David B. Truman has explained:

Relations with the leaders of the Congressional party can be supplemented, as they often have been, but no substitutes have appeared on which he can rely with equal confidence. To the degree that the mechanism of the Congressional party is relied upon, however, it must be taken as it is, with the leaders it has produced. For a President to attempt to act directly as the leader of the Congressional party almost certainly would be to destroy, for the time being, this valuable, if variable, governing instrument.[25]

Donald R. Matthews lists several practical reasons for the President's dependence on these leaders: he lacks the time and detailed knowledge for personal leadership; he is interested in the total legislative program and therefore can deal more effectively with the party leaders, who are generalists, than with committee chairmen and other specialists; he can minimize his personal involvement in possible legislative defeat and reserve his direct intervention for major crises. Moreover, "if the Senate party leaders lose their prestige and effectiveness—and this they will certainly do, if they are perceived merely as presidential messenger boys—the president and his program are in serious trouble."[26] Finally, party leaders, who stand at the center of the congressional communications network, are better informed and better able to judge the political climate and the prospects for legislation than anyone else on Capitol Hill.

The regular channel for communications with the congressional party leadership is the weekly meeting, which has become another presidential institution since Franklin Roosevelt started the practice. The vice-president, Senate floor leader, House Speaker (if a member of the President's party), House Floor Leader, and frequently party whips attend, along with committee chairmen or other important congressmen who may be invited on an ad hoc basis. Regular meetings minimize the chances for misunderstanding and may help to create a sense of rapport between the President and his party leaders. Whether this happens depends on the skill and candor of the participants and the degree of mutual trust that has developed among them.

The governor's relationship to his legislative leaders is similar but not identical. He runs the risk of damaging their effectiveness if he bypasses them or ignores them too often, and he is dependent on their knowledge and advice concerning the legislative system. He can devote more time than the President to legislative matters, however, particularly during the rather brief periods when the major legislative decisions are being made. In addition to meeting as often as every day with his leaders, the governor may hold more conferences with individual legislators than the President would normally attempt. Although he may be bypassing the leadership, often the governor is simply using his prestige and persuasive powers to implement strategy that has been agreed upon with the leadership. The relationship between governor and legislative leaders is a variable one, dependent on the influence that the governor has over their selection.

If the President or governor must usually live with and work through his legislative leaders, it is important to determine whether and how he can affect their choice. This depends to a considerable extent on the tradition of leadership stability or turnover in the legislature. In Chapter 6, we pointed out that in Congress and in some state legislatures, leaders frequently hold office as long as they retain their legislative seats; in other legislatures, there is a tradition of short tenure or rotation of office. Where there is a tradition of stable leadership, it is most difficult for the chief executive to remove an established leader. Over a period of years, the Speaker of the house or presiding officer of the senate can often develop a secure base of political support based on personal loyalty and the favors he has done for individual legislators. As a legislative leader develops tenure, he becomes not only more difficult to replace but more powerful. The Mississippi house Speaker served in that post for twenty-two years; "during that time his influence developed and increased to the point that executive influence with members of that body could be exercised only if channeled through the presiding officer."[27]

Recent presidents have not tried to defeat the House Speaker or the floor leaders, no matter how serious their policy differences might be. During Eisenhower's administration, Senate Republican Floor Leader William Knowland frequently disagreed with him on major questions of foreign policy. Knowland spoke for at least a substantial minority of senators, and the President knew that he could not make any effort to displace him as floor leader without risking a bitter split in the party and, quite probably, a humiliating defeat. Although Lyndon Johnson deeply resented congressional criticism of his Vietnam policies, he made no effort to oust one of the most prominent critics, Mike Mansfield, from his post as Senate Democratic Floor Leader; but he provided quiet support for a firm defender of those policies, Speaker John McCormack, when many Democratic representatives thought that McCormack ought to retire. The only recent White House effort to remove an incumbent congressional leader occurred in 1973, at the start of the second Nixon administration, when Robert Haldeman, Nixon's top assistant, called Senate Minority Leader Hugh Scott to announce that the White House had decided that he was ineffective and must be replaced. The maneuver turned out to be as ineffective as it was clumsy and arrogant; a few days later Scott was reelected by his Senate colleagues with little difficulty.[28]

When leadership posts are vacated because of a retirement or the custom of rotation, the governor may have an opportunity to influence the choice of a successor. His success or failure in exercising that influence may be an indication of his probable effectiveness in legislative leadership. A recent Republican governor of Illinois who faced a Democratic majority was even able to determine which of two Democrats would become Speaker of the house by swinging Republican votes to the candidate who would work more closely with him. His Democratic successor was able to secure the reelection of the same Democratic Speaker, despite a narrow Republican majority in the house, by swaying a few Republican legislators.[29]

The governor has traditionally been able to choose the presiding officers as well as the floor leaders in several southern states, including Alabama, Louisiana, Arkansas, and Kentucky. These leaders often consult the governor on the choice of major committee members. In Alabama, the governor's choices are almost always accepted without question by the legislators, and the designated leaders are expected to remain loyal to the governor. In Louisiana, the governor often publicly announces his choice for Speaker of the house, although his control in the senate depends on his relations with the lieutenant governor. Governor Faubus, during his long term as governor of Arkansas, depended heavily on the support of legislators whom he had been able to place in the major positions of leadership. In Kentucky, both Democratic and Republican governors have usually been able to dictate the selection of leaders in their party. In Texas, the governor has to be more cautious about intervention because a public endorsement is likely to arouse legislative hostility.[30]

Presidents have seldom tried to exercise much influence in the choice of a new leader even after the death or retirement of the incumbent. Thomas Jefferson played a larger part in the choice of leaders, and in their removal, than most modern presidents. Franklin Roosevelt took no open part in the choice of party leaders, and if he played a more subtle role, it seems to have been largely lost to history. He may have provided quiet support for Rayburn's election as majority leader in 1937. That same year, when a bitter fight developed for the Senate leadership post, Roosevelt sent Alben Barkley a public letter that was interpreted as an endorsement, and more importantly, he worked behind the scenes to swing senators to Barkley's support. Barkley won by a single vote. Neither Truman nor Eisenhower seems to have tried to influence the choice of new leaders. After Senator Taft's death, Eisenhower told his cabinet members to remain neutral and asked them to avoid even the expression of personal views about a successor; he believed that a policy of nonintervention was essential to maintaining smooth relations with Congress.[31]

The situation faced by President Kennedy after Speaker Rayburn's death in 1961 illustrates and summarizes the dilemma of the President. Leadership positions, particularly in the House, are often inherited. Although John McCormack, for a variety of reasons, was not Kennedy's choice for Speaker, the sentiment among House Democrats so strongly supported rewarding the veteran floor leader that it would have been foolhardy for Kennedy to oppose him. The contest for majority leader (and heir apparent to the speakership) was between two men, Carl Albert and Richard Bolling, each of whom was friendly to the administration. Nelson W. Polsby has neatly summarized the President's thinking:

> To intervene in behalf of one friend would have meant sacrificing another. For the White House to intervene and lose would have been disastrous for its prestige and legislative program. To intervene and win would have been more satisfactory, but still would have involved (aside from the making of enemies) great exertion, the distribution of indulgences and "cashing in" on favors owed, all of which could otherwise be employed to improve the chances for passage of controversial reciprocal trade, medical aid, tax reform, and education bills.[32]

Contact with Rank-and-File Legislators

Every recent President has used his persuasive powers directly on rank-and-file congressmen. Usually this has been done on the advice or with the approval of the congressional leadership, although occasionally press reports suggest that the President is bypassing the leadership. Sometimes, the contacts have been in the nature of White House briefings on the virtues of an important legislative measure; and on other occasions, the President has made his appeal on the basis of personal or party loyalty. Woodrow Wilson conferred frequently with congressmen both at the Capitol and at the White House. Calvin Coolidge's frequent breakfasts for congressmen had little impact because they were social events totally devoid of substantive discussion. Arthur M. Schlesinger reports that Franklin Roosevelt "spent long hours, in his office and over the telephone, persuading, ressuring, mollifying, and disciplining individual senators and congressmen." Roosevelt estimated that he averaged three to four hours a day on congressional relations during a session.[33] Since World War II, the other demands of the Presidency have reduced the time available for presidential liaison. Eisenhower started his administration with Coolidge-like social luncheons for congressmen and in later years made only occasional use of direct appeals to congressmen for support of legislation. Kennedy was more active but had neither the time nor the inclination to duplicate Roosevelt's personal role in legislative liaison. Lyndon Johnson relied heavily on personal persuasion, through telephone calls and visits of congressmen to the White House, to advance his legislative program during the early years of his term; but these efforts declined in the later years because his time and attention were increasingly devoted to the Vietnam War.[34] Richard Nixon was criticized for not being accessible enough to congressmen and also for not being persuasive enough in selling his program when he did meet congressmen.

The pressures of time have forced recent presidents to rely increasingly on staff members for maintaining contacts with members of Congress. An effective staff makes it possible for the President to conserve both his time and his prestige for crucial occasions. Wilson used liaison men on a quiet, informal basis; Franklin Roosevelt used them more frequently and more openly, but still in an informal, unstructured fashion. The practice grew during Truman's administration, and during the Eisenhower administration, the White House staff became more institutionalized, with responsibility for legislative liaison delegated to specific members of the staff. This organizational pattern has been followed by Eisenhower's successors, but there have been variations in practice from one administration to the next. Under Eisenhower, liaison was a low-pressure operation, with considerable attention being devoted to providing services for congressmen and their constituents. Kennedy's congressional liaison chief, Lawrence O'Brien, was given greater authority than Eisenhower had given his aides, and he concentrated his attention on the legislative program, although he did not neglect service performance and patronage. Under O'Brien's leadership, the activities of the legislative liaison officers of all departments and agencies were coordinated in the White House for the first time. This was accomplished by means of periodic meetings and written reports. O'Brien also worked closely with private lobbyists whose organizations were supporting the President's program. O'Brien's skills were recognized by President Johnson, who kept him in charge of legislative liaison during the early years of his administration. During the Kennedy and Johnson administrations, the White House liaison office mushroomed "into a service agency devoted to the care and feeding of Congressmen—arranging White House tours for constituents, helping to handle constituent problems with governmental agencies, providing Congressmen with autographed photos of the President."[35]

At the start of the Nixon administration, an attempt was made to reduce the scope of liaison office activities, and particularly its service functions, but the effort was not successful because of congressional demands for such services. Although the liaison office during the Nixon administration was staffed by experienced men, they did not have the authority that Kennedy and Johnson had given to O'Brien, and their efforts were frequently undermined by higher ranking staff members, particularly presidential assistants Robert Haldeman and John Ehrlichman. They tended to view Congress as "an awkward and obnoxious obstacle, a hostile foreign power," and their arrogance in personal dealings had the effect of unnecessarily alienating the members of Congress. Periodic efforts were made to strengthen the congressional liaison staff in order to improve relations with Congress. With this purpose in mind, in 1971 Nixon selected Clark MacGregor, a ten-year Republican veteran of Congress, to head the staff. MacGregor promptly instructed his staff to wear buttons that said, "I Care about Congress," and undertook more serious efforts to bridge the gap between Congress and the White House, but with little success. The start of the Ford administration signaled a new effort at more harmonious congressional relations, and demonstrated again that the success of the liaison staff depends heavily on the attitude toward Congress shown by the President and his top aides.[36]

White House staff members responsible for liaison have come to be accepted by the congressional leadership and the rank and file because they perform a variety of useful tasks and maintain a communications network between Congress and the White House more effectively than the busy President could do by himself. Although congressmen may resent pressure from the White House, they rely on the staff members for information about legislative matters and for services to constituents that the White House can provide. It should be recognized that however great their skill, staff members have no political power or authority of their own; they have only what the President delegates to them. One of Lawrence O'Brien's major assets was that Kennedy gave him extensive authority not only to do favors for congressmen but also to negotiate substantive compromises in legislative proposals. O'Brien has described his unusual authority in these terms:

> For the first time, someone from the White House could sit in the Speaker's office with the congressional leadership and be recognized as a spokesman for the President. You weren't an errand boy or a head-counter, you had the authority to speak for the President.[37]

Despite O'Brien's skills, many parts of Kennedy's legislative program were defeated or delayed, and Johnson had serious difficulties with Congress except during the Eighty-ninth Congress, when his party had lopsided majorities in both houses. There are many obstacles in Congress to any President's legislative program, and no staff system can be expected to overcome them all. But George Reedy, who served on Johnson's staff, has suggested that the staff system fails to keep the President in touch with the viewpoints of congressmen. Reedy argues:

> A President does not have available to him methods of gauging the intensity of the opposition—something that any politician must have in order to be successful. He

lives in an environment where it is not possible to make valid, intuitive judgments about just how angry people will become and about what must be done to blunt their opposition without losing sight of his objective.

Of course, he finds out soon enough once his proposal becomes public. The legislative liaison staff is quite efficient at determining such things once a message has hit the floor of Congress. By that time, it is too late. The President's positions are solidified.[38]

A governor, with fewer demands on his time, can devote more personal attention to legislators than the President. Most governors also depend on staff assistance for this purpose, and in a few of the larger states, there is a specific staff member assigned to legislative matters. Occasionally, employees of state agencies may be borrowed for legislative liaison. Members of his staff represent the governor at committee meetings and caucuses, keep track of important bills in the legislative mill, service the requests of legislators, and generally duplicate the work of the White House staff. The governor personally attends caucus meetings in some states, and in some, it is not unusual for him to testify at committee meetings. Some governors may be found on the floor of the legislature lobbying for a bill or watching a roll-call vote. In Louisiana, where Governors Huey Long and Earl Long established the precedent of frequent floor appearances, Governor McKeithen visited one or both legislative chambers on more than a dozen occasions during the 1966 session, even though he had loudspeakers and electric voting boards in his office that enabled him to follow the debate and voting from there.[39]

Most governors devote many hours, particularly during the closing days of the session, to face-to-face meetings with legislators, individually or in small groups. There are several reasons why governors use this technique. They may be able to win votes of individual legislators because of their bargaining skill or because of personal loyalties or political alliances. Another important reason is that many legislators expect it. They are flattered by the personal attention, and they want the opportunity to negotiate directly with the governor rather than dealing with intermediaries. Legislators tend to be critical of governors who are remote and inaccessible.

Patronage

One of the tools of presidential leadership that is, of necessity, usually handled at the staff level is *patronage,* which can be usefully defined to include not only jobs but all the assistance the executive can provide for members of the legislative body. Job patronage is of limited value to the President for several reasons. A small proportion of federal jobs are outside of civil service, and the most important of these must be filled largely on the basis of the availability of skilled personnel. On many local positions, the President must be guided by congressmen and local politicians; in filling these local slots, particularly, the President is likely to alienate as many politicians as he pleases. Most jobs must be filled at the start of the administration, which leaves few jobs to be used for day-to-day bargaining. Job patronage can be a liability if mishandled or an asset if handled skillfully, but it has declined in importance as compared with other forms of patronage. The President can add local projects to his legislative program—the dams, parks, hospitals, river improvements, and reclamation projects that mean much more to a district than jobs that would benefit only a handful. Military installations may be even more important to the district's economy. The Kennedy administration perfected another patronage device: permitting a congressman to make the announcement about any development of particular interest to his district, thus creating the impression that the congressman was instrumental in obtaining it, even if it was a defense contract awarded without regard to patronage considerations. The President can lend his presence or that of other top officials for election campaigns or a variety of speaking engagements, or he can meet or otherwise honor the congressman's constituents.

The President's patronage resources are varied but not unlimited, and he encounters a multitude of patronage demands in his efforts to advance a comprehensive legislative program. He may also encounter resentment if his tactics in dispensing patronage appear petty, threatening, or vengeful to congressmen. The President and his staff must be misers, spending patronage carefully to gain the maximum benefits. They must bargain with congressmen, who are usually skilled bargainers, and they must compete with congressmen who have patronage to dispense, such as the key members on appropriations committees. They must not alienate loyal congressmen by dispensing all the patronage to the waverers. They must handle patronage as a centralized operation in order to avoid contradictory commitments; in the Kennedy administration, this was done under the White House assistant for congressional liaison. Finally, and most important, because the supply of patronage always falls short of demand, the President and his staff must make hard decisions about priorities: which bills are most important, and which congressmen are keys to passage of these bills.[40]

In dealing with legislators, the average governor relies on patronage to a greater extent than the President does. In fact, the average governor is a myth; variations in patronage are among the major reasons why governors vary in legislative influence. In more than half the states, there is a general civil service system; and in some states, the system is so comprehensive that only a few hundred jobs are available as patronage. In some states, elected officials can make a large proportion of the patronage appointments independent of the governor; in other states, the governor has extensive powers to fill local vacancies. Most of the major industrial states have general civil service systems, although some have several thousand patronage jobs available for the governor. The patronage opportunities seem to be greatest in the South, although these states vary widely in the scope of the governor's control over major departments. Some governors have access to jobs with interest groups or with contractors who seek favor with the state.

The governor also can offer a wide variety of services and favors to the legislator's district. State funds are available to build new roads and bridges, to improve the old ones, and to build or improve a variety of other facilities, such as parks, hospitals, and community colleges. These projects are important to legislators because their constituents are usually far more interested in a new road or project for the district than in any aspect of the legislator's voting record. Highways are a particularly valuable form of patronage, although in some states the governor is unable to control the distribution of highway funds. The governor may be inhibited by federal requirements, expert advice, or campaign promises from locating state projects in the districts of favored legislators; but in most states, the governor retains some discretion and therefore some bargaining power. Another form of patronage is the awarding of state contracts, whether for highway work, the supply of state liquor stores, the purchase of textbooks, the insurance of state buildings, or the bonding of state employees. Most contracts for these purposes must be let through competitive bidding, but in most states, some types of contracts are exempt from these regulations, and too often there are ways of avoiding or manipulating the legal provisions to favor a certain company. These forms of patronage often go to politicians who have provided assistance in campaigns, but some may be available for the friends or supporters of legislators.[41]

Some of the patronage at the state level goes directly to legislators and their families. In those states that still permit dual office-holding, loyal legislators may expect to receive a remunerative position, at least between sessions. Legislators associated with legal, insurance, and other firms sometimes do business with the state. Because the state legislator (unlike the congressman) is a part-time representative with a full-time, long-term interest in some other profession or occupation, he is more receptive than the congressman to patronage offers that benefit him personally.

Often patronage may be distributed without any quid pro quo or support for specific bills. Most of the bargains that are made never become public, but occasionally they are obvious to even the casual observer. During a recent session of the Kentucky house, a majority adopted an amendment to the governor's sales tax bill that would have reduced the available revenue. Members of the governor's staff got to work, and the next day, a majority of members voted to reconsider their action and defeat the amendment. One of the members provided a clue to the persuasive tactics of the governor's office when he announced that he was changing his vote because his district was heavily dependent on a number of state projects that might be reduced or eliminated if the governor's tax bill were amended. Governor Faubus of Arkansas was more direct in his approach, in 1965, when he asked a special session of the Arkansas legislature to support a package of road bills that would affect construction in every district of the state. He warned:

> If you are in opposition and vote against each and all of these proposals designed to furnish the people of Arkansas an adequate highway system, then it must be assumed that you have all the highway improvements which are needed in your county or district.[42]

DIVERSITY AND COORDINATION IN THE EXECUTIVE BRANCH

The chief executive is the most powerful, but far from the only, member of the executive branch who has an influence on the legislative process. The other agencies in the executive branch may be an asset or a liability to the chief legislator. At the state level, the governor's leadership of the executive branch is dependent on widely varying degrees of political and constitutional authority. The President has constitutional authority that would be envied by many governors, but this does not guarantee his control over the vast bureaucracy.

The attention devoted by the departments to all kinds of congressional requests suggests a belief by the departments that such attention will help to secure congressional support for their legislative programs and budget requests. On a smaller scale, state agencies follow the same pattern of behavior for the same reason. It is worth emphasizing that once the departments have built up a fund of credit and good will in the legislative body, they may draw on this fund in support of their legislative objectives, whether these coincide with or contradict the chief executive's legislative program.

In addition, the agencies bear most of the burden of defending and promoting a legislative program. They are responsible for drafting a bill and carrying on the negotiations with interest groups on the terms of the bills. Spokesmen for the agencies testify before committees in support of legislation and before appropriations subcommittees in defense of their budgets and the record of the agency. The skill with which this testimony is presented is one of the important factors in the success of the program. Furthermore, top officials in the agencies lobby on behalf of their programs as persuasively and ubiquitously as possible. In sheer manpower, agency heads outnumber the chief executive, and agency assistants and liaison men outnumber those assigned to the chief executive. The President may pick a high administrative official largely because of his skill and popularity in dealing with Congress—for example, Cordell Hull in Roosevelt's administration, George Marshall in Truman's administration, and Douglas Dillon in Kennedy's administration. A cabinet member who has lost support in Congress can become a serious liability, as Truman discovered with respect to Dean Acheson and Henry Wallace.

Although it is often said that the chief executive initiates legislative programs, the actual initiative usually comes from the agencies, which have far more detailed knowledge about the fields in which legislation may be needed. The typical pattern is for the agency to prepare a bill and send it to the chief executive, together with whatever budget request may be required, in the hope that the bill will become part of his legislative program. The President's role in the legislative process has become so persuasive that his failure to support a bill not only seriously handicaps it but often places the agency in the position of appearing to disregard the President's wishes if it persists in seeking congressional support. At the state level, where a much wider variety of minor bills are prepared by the agencies, the governor's unwillingness to endorse a measure often leaves the agency free to seek legislative support without any inhibitions.

The legislative activities of government agencies, although not a new phenomenon, have recently grown in importance and become more centralized in each agency. The major agencies of national government have a "chief lobbyist," who usually bears the formal title of "assistant to the secretary for legislative liaison." He is responsible for directing the handling of congressional requests for service and information. He acts as the political adviser to the department head and keeps him informed about congressional attitudes. He engages in lobbying, trying to coordinate his tactics with those of liaison men in the White House and to gain maximum White House support for his department's legislative program. Not the least of his job is to coordinate legislative liaison within the department. The bureaus within departments often advance their own parochial purposes by developing rapport with congressmen and congressional committees. The task of the agency liaison man is to reverse this trend toward decentralization without alienating members of Congress or destroying the advantages of the rapport developed by subordinate members of the bureaucracy. Agency liaison men are usually men with political and congressional experience, and some of them have largely succeeded in channeling liaison activity through their offices. Yet these officials, like their counterparts in the White House, lack personal authority and can be no more effective than their political chief.[43]

There are many specific reasons why agencies sometimes fail to work in harmony with the chief executive in support of his legislative program. The fundamental reason is that government comprises a vast array of interests. Each agency serves a different purpose, and many of them serve or represent interests outside of government. In pursuit of this purpose, and in service to these interests, each develops certain policies and viewpoints. One reason why these policies come into conflict is that they cost money and consequently represent competing claims on the budget. In addition, they represent the conflicting interests, domestic and foreign, that this government serves. There will inevitably be differences of opinion among agency heads over budgetary priorities, as well as, for example, conflicts between diplomats and military leaders over disarmament or between those responsible for developing power resources and those concerned with conservation of natural resources. These conflicts are not merely the result of bureaucratic rivalry and empire building, although these factors may contribute to dissension; they are inevitable in modern representative government.

The head of an agency in Washington must serve three masters in addition to the President. He must espouse as effectively as possible the viewpoints, developed by his subordinates, that have become departmental policy; he must serve interest groups, which are a source of his department's power; and he must serve Congress, particularly the congressional committees that review his budgetary requests and his legislative program. It is not surprising that agency heads sometimes resolve these conflicts by giving less than full support to the President's program.

The President has to be cautious about disciplining the agency or antagonizing its interest-group and congressional allies. He may need these allies to help enact a bill on which he and the agency are in accord; the agency's allies are often his. He may remove the head of the agency as a last resort, but this may be a costly move if it antagonizes these powerful allies.

At the state level, there are examples of both greater and lesser control by the chief executive. The weakness of the legislative committee system and the absence of vast bureaucratic power centers comparable with the Pentagon or the Agriculture Department diminish the resistance of alliances to the governor's legislative program. On the other hand, in some states, the governor's direct authority and his power of removal extend to so few of the state agencies that his ability to generate administrative support for his legislative program is seriously handicapped. The administrative reorganization movement of the last few decades has undoubtedly strengthened the governor's position both as an executive and as a legislative leader, but it has left some areas of state government virtually untouched. The proliferation of elected officials extends to most states. Over half the states have six to nine elected officials in addition to the governor, and only eight states have three or less. The governor, particularly if he represents the traditional minority party, may find most of these offices controlled by the other party. In some states, particularly southern states where the governor is limited to a single four-year term, other officials are free of this restriction and are frequently reelected for several terms. In some states, the governor's authority over many appointed officials is limited by overlapping terms of board members and restrictions on removal without cause, a procedure that is cumbersome and difficult.

The chief executive has devised institutional techniques for controlling the executive branch, principally the executive budget. Under the federal budget act, passed in 1921, the President was authorized for the first time to present a single budget to Congress and was provided with the Budget Bureau to assist in the task. In keeping with this, the Senate and House centralized their appropriations functions in single committees. Within a few years, during the economy-minded Coolidge administration, the Budget Bureau was given authority to make recommendations to the President on the budgetary implications of all departmental proposals concerning legislation. The Budget Bureau developed elaborate procedures for reviewing departmental budgets and repeatedly cut these budgets, although the final determination has remained the President's.[44]

The executive budget, inaugurated by Alfred E. Smith and made effective by Franklin Roosevelt in New York late in the 1920s, has become a standard practice in most states. There are a few states in which the budget is prepared by a board, on which the governor has a single vote, and a few others in which the governor's role in budget-making is overshadowed by that of a legislative agency. In the vast majority of states, the governor's authority over the budget, coupled with the item veto, provides his most effective control over administrative agencies, including those over which he lacks complete appointment and removal power. Agencies are seldom able to gain legislative restoration of funds that have been eliminated in the presidential or gubernatorial budgets.

The President's control over legislative recommendations of the departments has become institutionalized through the Budget Bureau. This development, described in detail by Neustadt, was started in 1934 by President Roosevelt, who recognized the importance of blocking agency support of bills that conflicted with his policies and also of making explicit which measures had his endorsement. In Roosevelt's words, "If I make every bill that the Government is interested in *must* legislation, it is going to complicate things . . . very much." This central clearance was designed to coordinate policy and not merely, like earlier procedures, to control the costs of proposed legislation. Since Roosevelt's time the clearance procedures have varied with personalities and circumstances, but they have gradually become part of the institutionalized Presidency. Clearance is carried out by personnel in the Budget Bureau, working closely with the White House staff. Neustadt, in explaining the development and survival of central clearance, emphasizes its value to the agencies: "Most measures of most agencies face an uncertain future in the legislative process. Whatever clearance brings by way of support, even acquiescence, from President and Budget Bureau, from other agencies, and, implicitly, their clientele, may help to reduce hazards, strengthen prospects in Congress." Central clearance provides a service to Congress, a dependable source of information about the administration's stand on issues. Some congressional committees, as a matter of routine, request the Budget Bureau's evaluation of all bills that they consider. Neustadt concludes that central clearance serves both agencies and congressmen without restricting their freedom to maneuver and that it makes both groups conscious of presidential authority.

> The vitality of central clearance lies in the fact that it can satisfy, at once, both these conditions. The President, as he may choose, gains ample opportunities to make known his desires. But Congress and the agencies are not compelled to notice. And he, meanwhile, retains the right to alter course, or change his mind.[45]

The chief executive has constitutional and institutional resources for executive leadership that are valuable at the national level and variable in the states. His executive and legislative leadership are interdependent, and both are dependent on his public prestige and his skill in interpersonal relationships with administrators and legislators. The tasks of a chief executive who would lead, as Neustadt has vividly shown in his *Presidential Power,* require the imaginative conservation and utilization of all the resources of the office in order to maximize a power that is, essentially, the power to persuade.

NOTES

1. William H. Young, "The Development of the Governorship," *State Government* 31 (1958):178.

2. See Leslie Lipson, *The American Governor from Figurehead to Leader* (Chicago, 1939).

3. See Wilfred E. Binkley, *President and Congress* (New York, 1962); and George B. Galloway, *History of the House of Representatives* (New York, 1961), chap. 15. There is an excellent description of Thomas Jefferson's techniques of legislative leadership in Ralph B. Harlow, *The History of Legislative Methods in the Period before 1825* (New Haven, Conn., 1917), chap. 10.

4. Clinton Rossiter, *The American Presidency* (New York, 1960), chaps. 3 and 4; and Binkley, *President and Congress,* chaps. 10 and 11.

5. See Roy D. Morey, *Politics and Legislation: The Office of Governor in Arizona* (Tucson, Ariz., 1965).

6. See Council of State Governments, *The Book of the States, 1974–1975* (Lexington, Ky., 1974), pp. 80–81.

7. Jong R. Lee, "Presidential Vetoes from Washington to Nixon," *Journal of Politics* 37 (1975):522–546.

8. For data on the number of vetoes by each President, see *Congressional Quarterly Weekly Report* 33 (December 7, 1974):3281.

9. Sarah P. McCally, "The Governor and His Legislative Party," *American Political Science Review* 60 (1966):923–942.

10. See Frank W. Prescott, "The Executive Veto in American States," *Western Political Quarterly* 3 (1950):97–111.

11. Ernest H. Campell, ed., *The State Legislatures of Alaska, Oregon and Washington* (Seattle, Wash., 1966), p. 54.

12. Council of State Governments, *The Book of the States, 1974–1975,* pp. 80–81.

13. Ibid., p. 147.

14. See Elmer E. Cornwell, Jr., *Presidential Leadership of Public Opinion* (Bloomington, Ind., 1965), chaps. 7 and 8.

15. Ibid., pp. 288–289.

16. Richard E. Neustadt, *Presidential Power* (New York, 1960), pp. 105, 102.

17. Ibid., p. 87.

18. See James M. Burns, *Roosevelt: The Lion and the Fox* (New York, 1956), pp. 338–339.

19. Gary Orfield, *Congressional Power: Congress and Social Change* (New York, 1975). p. 325.

20. Hugh G. Gallagher, "Presidents, Congress, and the Legislative Functions," in *The Presidency Reappraised,* ed., Rexford G. Tugwell and Thomas E. Cronin (New York, 1974), p. 232.

21. Louis W. Koenig, *The Chief Executive,* 3d ed. (New York, 1975), p. 150.

22. Neustadt, *Presidential Power,* p. 33.

23. See Erwin C. Hargrove, *The Power of the Modern Presidency* (New York, 1974), pp. 205–219.

24. James M. Burns, *The Deadlock of Democracy* (Englewood Cliffs, N.J., 1963), pp. 104–106, 130–136, 156–176.

25. David B. Truman, *The Congressional Party* (New York, 1959), p. 298.

26. Donald R. Matthews, *U.S. Senators and Their World* (Chapel Hill, N.C., 1960), pp. 142–143.

27. Alex B. Lacy, Jr., ed., *Power in American State Legislatures* (New Orleans, La., 1967), p. 111.

28. Dan Rather and Gary Paul Gates, *The Palace Guard* (New York, 1974), pp. 302–303.

29. See Thomas B. Littlewood, *Bipartisan Coalition in Illinois* (New York, 1960).

30. See Lacy, *Power in American State Legislatures,* p. 24; and Gene F. Tarver, "A Comparative Study of Gubernatorial Roles in Four Southern States" (Ph.D. diss., University of Kentucky, 1971), pp. 73–74.

31. See Burns, *Roosevelt,* p. 309; and Robert J. Donovan, *Eisenhower: The Inside Story* (New York, 1956), p. 112.

32. Nelson W. Polsby, "Two Strategies of Influence: Choosing a Majority Leader, 1962," in *New Perspectives on the House of Representatives,* 2d ed., ed. Robert L. Peabody and Nelson W. Polsby (Chicago, 1969), p. 347.

33. Arthur M. Schlesinger, Jr., *The Age of Roosevelt,* vol. 2, *The Coming of the New Deal* (Boston, 1959), p. 554.

34. See Rowland Evans and Robert Novak, *Lyndon B. Johnson: The Exercise of Power* (New York, 1966), chap. 17.

35. See Patrick Anderson, *The Presidents' Men* (Garden City, N.Y., 1969), pp. 302–310; Abraham Holtzman, *Legislative Liaison: Executive Leadership in Congress* (Chicago, 1970), chap. 9; Rowland Evans and Robert D. Novak, *Nixon in the White House* (New York, 1972), pp. 105, 109, 378–379.

36. Evans and Novak, *Nixon in the White House,* pp. 109, 378–379.

37. Anderson, *The Presidents' Men,* p. 307.

38. George E. Reedy, *The Twilight of the Presidency* (New York, 1970), p. 83.

39. See Tarver, "A Comparative Study of Gubernatorial Roles in Four Southern States," pp. 88–90, 113–121.

40.   See Stanley Kelley, Jr., "Presidential Legislative Leadership: The Use of Patronage" (Paper presented at the annual meeting of the American Political Science Association, 1962).

41.   See Coleman B. Ransone, Jr., *The Office of Governor in the South* (University, Ala., 1951), pp. 88–96; and Robert Highsaw, "Southern Governor—Challenge to the Strong Executive Theme," *Public Administration Review* 19 (1959):7–11.

42.   Lacy, *Power in American State Legislatures*, p. 24.

43.   See Holtzman, *Legislative Liaison.*

44.   President Nixon reorganized the Executive Office and changed the name of the Budget Bureau to the Office of Management and Budget.

45.   Richard E. Neustadt, "Presidency and Legislation: The Growth of Central Clearance," *American Political Science Review* 48 (1954):641–672, especially 650, 670–671.

CHAPTER TWELVE

The Lobbyists

American society is characterized by a multiplicity of private groups and associations that are more or less integrated into the political system. Because of the constitutional structure of the American governments, with their multifarious focal points of political decision making, and because of the fragmented and decentralized nature of the American political party system, private groups and associations tend to participate in the process of public policy making through representatives of their own, distinct from those who are elected or appointed to public office.[1] These representatives are usually called *lobbyists*. The term is a rather flexible one; it is sometimes used to refer to anyone who seeks to influence governmental decisions, including those of administrative agencies and courts. But its descriptive utility will best be maintained if we limit its inclusiveness to those representatives of private groups and associations who stimulate and transmit communication to a governmental decision-maker in the hope of influencing his decision.[2] Here we are interested in representational communications directed toward American legislators.

The lobbyist plays a functional role in the American legislative system. He contributes to the maintenance of the legislative system by virtue of his key location in its communications structure. The lobbyist provides one of the important links between organized constituents and legislators, and communications flow in both directions (from organized group via lobbyist to legislator, and from legislator via lobbyist to organized group). This "two-step" flow of information is probably prerequisite to the maintenance of the American legislative system. In addition, the lobbyist's participation in the legislative system facilitates its contribution to the polity. The lobbyist's role is fundamental to both the crystallization and the resolution of political conflict and the integration of the polity. He represents demands on the legislative system from organized citizens; he participates in the negotiation processes leading to their satisfaction; and his involvement in decisional processes facilitates support in the polity for public policy.

Lobbyists occupy a variety of positions vis-à-vis the groups or associations that they represent. Some are full-time employees of their organizations, directing or working in Washington offices or serving as executive directors of associations. There are others (e.g., many of those who are Washington representatives of corporations) who are in the position of endeavoring to justify political activities to companies whose interests are mainly directed elsewhere. And there are many lawyers and public relations professionals in both national and state capitals who have salaries or retainers from several organizations.

HOW MANY LOBBYISTS?

One means of determining the number of lobbyists at the national and state levels of government is to consider those who register under national and state lobby-registration laws. Although in all probability not all the individuals who should be regarded as lobbyists are required to register in those jurisdictions where such statutes exist, and although not all states have such enactments, it is possible to get a rough approximation of the extent of lobbying activity in this manner. The Federal Regulation of Lobbying Act of 1946, passed by Congress as part of the Legislative Reorganization Act, requires the registration of names and spending reports of anybody who "solicits, collects or receives money or any other thing of value to be used principally to aid in . . . the passage or defeat of any legislation by the Congress of the United States." Supreme Court interpretation of the statute has limited its application only to those who engage in direct communication with members of Congress; several large national associations have not registered on the claim that they are not engaged in direct lobbying. The number of lobbyists who are not registered because of the limited application of the act is not known. However, most of those who are actively engaged in lobbying probably register with the Clerk of the House and the Secretary of the Senate. The rather ambiguous interpretation of the law makes it safer to register in order to avoid possible penalties. Also, probably quite a high percentage of persons who register under the act never actually do any lobbying.[3] Rather, they merely monitor congressional activities for their employers. Under the federal law, about 600 organizations and law firms, and about 400 individuals, registered during 1974.[4]

State lobby-regulation laws vary a great deal, although as of 1975, forty-six states required the registration of lobbyists, and thirty-four required the filing of expense statements. In some states, the law requires the lobbyists who are registered to wear identification badges; in some others, lobbyists are required to carry identification cards issued to them by the Clerk upon registration.[5]

The number of lobbyists registered at the state level varies considerably from state to state. Table 12.1 indicates the number of lobbyist organizations and individuals registered in 1973. State lobbyists range in number from as few as 13 in Mississippi to as many as 1,394 in Florida; the median number is about 200. Obviously, the interstate variations can be accounted for, at least to some extent, by differences in population size, urbanization, industrialization, and political complexity. Nevertheless, a major source of interstate variation in lobby registrations must occur because of differences in state lobby-registration laws. In many states, the law is patterned after the Federal Regulation of Lobbying Act of 1946, but there are important differences in the legal status of lobbying. Lobbying is prohibited by law in Louisiana, insofar as it is conducted privately or secretly, and criminal penalties are provided for those found to be "guilty of lobbying."

TABLE 12.1   Lobbyist Registrations in 1973

LEGISLATURE	NUMBER OF GROUPS AND INDIVIDUALS REGISTERED
Alabama	143
Alaska	72
Arizona	319
Arkansas	285
California	552
Colorado	198
Connecticut	201
Delaware	63
Florida	1,394
Georgia	276
Hawaii	*
Idaho	*
Illinois	355
Indiana	324
Iowa	428
Kansas	263
Kentucky	164
Louisiana	*
Maine	167
Maryland	145
Massachusetts	133
Michigan	208
Minnesota	1,254
Mississippi	13
Missouri	254
Montana	245
Nebraska	246
Nevada	*
New Hampshire	98
New Jersey	145
New Mexico	171
New York	136
North Carolina	123
North Dakota	227
Ohio	328
Oklahoma	103
Oregon	247
Pennsylvania	338
Rhode Island	94
South Carolina	63
South Dakota	94
Tennessee	197
Texas	1,052
Utah	*
Vermont	63
Virginia	158
Washington	365
West Virginia	*
Wisconsin	437
Wyoming	17
U.S. Congress	1,120

*Registration not required.

SOURCE: *Directory of Registered Federal and State Lobbyists* (Orange, N.J., 1973), pp. 1–525.

Some state lobby laws limit the registration requirements to those who receive compensation for lobbying or who are employed to lobby, while in other states all persons who attempt to influence legislation are required to register, whether they are compensated for doing so or not. Some states, like Iowa and Oregon, specifically require state government employees to register as lobbyists if they seek to influence legislation; in other states, such as Pennsylvania and Texas, state and local government employees are exempt from the lobby registration requirements. In many states all persons who lobby must register, but a number of states exempt "occasional" lobbyists—those who, for only one day, "merely appear before a committee in an individual capacity," lobby on an "isolated basis," or simply furnish information. In Wisconsin and Montana, lobbyists are required not only to register, but also to pay a fee and secure a license. In Texas, church lobbyists are exempted from registering. The lobbying laws in a few states, such as New Hampshire and South Carolina, apply only to those who act in a "representative capacity," or to those who "employ any person to act as counsel or agent." Penalties for violation of the lobby-registration requirements also vary considerably. Although in most states violation is a misdemeanor, Michigan and Indiana statutes make violation a felony, and in several states (Minnesota, Florida, Alabama, and Arizona) the penalty for violation is limited to censure, reprimand, or prohibition from appearing before legislative committees or otherwise engaging in lobbying activities. No penalties for violation are provided in some states— Connecticut, Colorado, Arkansas, Delaware, and Iowa.[6]

Numerically, business groups and associations are more extensively represented in Washington and in the states than other types of interest groups. Data for the states are fragmentary, but it is possible to show comparisons among groups and organizations registered in Washington and nineteen states (see Table 12.2).[7] Insofar as national lobbyists are concerned, the percentage of business groups out of the total number of groups registered is considerably less than the aggregate numerical presence of business lobbyists. A study of a random sample of lobbyists registered with the Clerk of the United States House of Representatives during the first two quarters of 1956 showed that nearly 61 percent of those registered represented business groups, the largest component of which were spokesmen for small trade associations (about 40 percent of the total). Only 16 percent of the lobbyists represented labor organizations; only 5 percent represented farm organizations; and the remainder were scattered among a variety of organizational types.[8] There are some comparable analyses for lobbyists at the state level. Studies of lobbyists for various years in Oklahoma, Illinois, and Kentucky indicate that the proportions of lobbyists in those states were distributed in about the same way as the groups they represented.[9] It is likely that at the state level, organizations will tend to be represented by only one or two lobbyists.

Lobbying involves the expenditure of money for salaries, travel, research, public relations materials, entertainment, and the like. At the national level, reported lobbying expenditures reached $9.7 million by 1973, which is not a large amount, comparatively speaking. However, the reported figures probably represent only minimums because of the ambiguous nature of the reporting requirements of the lobbying act. Lobbyist spending varies greatly from state to state,

TABLE 12.2 Types of Organizations with Registered Lobbyists (In percentages)

LEGISLATURE	YEAR	TYPE OF ORGANIZATION						TOTAL	NUMBER
		Business	Labor	Farm	Professional	Governmental, Citizens	Other		
U.S. Congress	1969	53	11	6	6	22	2	100	269
California	1964	52	11	2	5	17	14	101	432
Connecticut	1964	71	5	1	6	10	7	100	175
Florida	1964	47	20	2	6	12	13	100	439
Illinois	1963	48	11	3	15	16	7	100	280
Indiana	1964	50	10	2	7	16	15	100	136
Iowa	1964	47	9	3	5	24	12	100	204
Kansas	1964	49	10	3	5	19	14	100	41
Kentucky	1964	58	19	2	12	9	0	100	57
Maine	1964	56	9	3	5	18	9	100	165
Michigan	1964	55	8	2	12	19	3	99	322
Montana	1964	54	14	4	4	15	8	99	180
Nebraska	1964	49	5	5	9	18	14	100	150
New York	1964	74	8	1	8	6	4	101	174
Ohio	1964	60	15	1	12	8	4	100	173
Oklahoma	1961	42	16	14	7	14	7	100	56
Pennsylvania	1964	63	10	1	12	11	2	99	243
Rhode Island	1964	55	17	2	8	7	12	101	60
South Dakota	1964	63	5	5	9	13	4	99	92
Virginia	1964	81	8	4	2	1	4	100	107

SOURCES: *Congressional Quarterly Weekly Report* 28 (July 13, 1970), p. 81; and Patterson, "The Role of the Lobbyist: The Case of Oklahoma," p. 1970; Harmon Zeigler, "Interest Groups in the States," in *Politics in the American States*, ed. Herbert Jacob and Kenneth N. Vines (Boston, 1965), p. 110. Data for Illinois and Kentucky come from unpublished studies by Ronald D. Hedlund and Malcolm E. Jewell.

ranging in some years of the 1960s from as high as $1 million in California to well below $100,000 in Alaska, Kentucky, Maryland, North Carolina, Virginia, and Ohio. There is also considerable interstate variation in the expenditures of business, labor, and farm groups, although the evidence available indicates that business groups, including trade associations, corporations, construction, and communications firms, and loan, banking, and insurance companies, far outstrip other state lobby groups in their expenditures.[10] Again, in all likelihood, these figures reflect only bare minimums of expenditure. Although accurate spending data for political-interest groups are not available, and although the figures reported here are probably low estimates, lobbying expenses are much lower than the folklore of American politics would suggest.

THE RECRUITMENT OF LOBBYISTS

There is now fairly abundant evidence that lobbyists do not differ substantially from legislators in their social and political backgrounds. Both kinds of political actors are recruited from among essentially the same strata of the population. Based on detailed studies conducted in Massachusetts, North Carolina, Oregon, and Utah in 1966 and in Iowa in 1967, it can be shown that legislators and lobbyists are very similar in their levels of income and education, in their occupational status, in the degree of politicization in their early family environments, and in their adult political experiences.[11] However, it is clear that the roles of lobbyist and legislator are not interchangeable. For instance, in general, the prelegislative political experience of state legislators has been in local political office; whereas lobbyists tend to be recruited more notably from among those who served in state-level political offices. Furthermore, although the conventional wisdom is to the contrary, few legislators become lobbyists, and few lobbyists become legislators. Former congressmen sometimes become lobbyists, but this is rather rare. Lester W. Milbrath found that less than 3 percent of the Washington lobbyists he interviewed had ever served in Congress. Studies of lobbyists at the state level have demonstrated that the proportion of lobbyists who have served in the legislature seldom exceeds 10 percent.[12]

Where lobbyists and legislators do differ substantially is in the recruitment to their respective political roles. Only a few lobbyists in the national capital

can be said to have an over-all career pattern in lobbying. Even if careers in association work, which includes more than lobbying activities, are considered to be lobbying careers, less than one-fourth of the respondents have had over-all careers in lobbying. Those who have had predominantly lobbying careers received their training in a variety of professions.[13]

Educational institutions do not provide training programs for lobbyists, and careers in lobbying are not those to which Americans usually aspire from an early age. Most men become involved in lobbying later in life, after a career in another field. Harmon Zeigler and Michael A. Baer, in their analysis of interviews with legislators and lobbyists in four states, were able to show that legislators' entry into their political role was largely purposive, having either propelled themselves into politics or been explicitly recruited to the legislature. Lobbyists were found to be "drifters," not likely to have entered this occupation out of predetermined choice.[14]

Lobbying is a fairly intense form of political activity, and it might be expected that lobbyists would be active in partisan politics. Most lobbyists are affiliated with one of the two major political parties, although the differences indicated in Table 12.3 are very interesting. Washington lobbyists were about evenly split in party preference; Oklahoma lobbyists were overwhelmingly Democratic at a time when their state legislature was also predominantly Democratic; Michigan, Iowa, and Illinois lobbyists were mostly Republicans in legislative settings that were fairly heavily Republican; and Nebraska lobbyists were largely Republicans in a Republican state with a nonpartisan legislature. There may be factors in lobbyist recruitment that result in the selection of lobbyists in a way that reflects the dominant political atmosphere of the system into which they are recruited. And if legislators and lobbyists are more alike than different in basic partisan orientation, interaction between them is very likely to be facilitated.

Insofar as the evidence permits generalization, lobbyists are not particularly active in politics. Milbrath found that among Washington lobbyists in the mid-1950s, nearly half had never been active in party politics, and only a fourth were active at the time they were interviewed. Few had been candidates for public office, and less than 10 percent had held party office. Less than a third had ever made a contribution to party funds, although 42 percent had assisted in the raising of political funds. In data gathered in Iowa, where comparisons between lobbyists and other political leaders are possible, it can be shown that although lobbyists certainly reflected a highly politicized group, they engaged in ordinary political activities to a lesser degree than legislators, party leaders, or attentive constituents (see Table 12.4). It seems likely that strong party attachments, which might be indicated by the holding of a party office or a campaign for public office, "can be impediments to lobbyists who work with people in both parties."[15] Walter D. DeVries asked his sample of Michigan lobbyists: "Do you find it

TABLE 12.3 Lobbyists' Political Party Affiliations (In percentages)

PARTY	U.S. 1956	OKLA. 1961	MICH. 1959	ILL. 1963	NEB. 1967	IOWA 1967
Democratic	46	77	3	30	32	26
Republican	48	9	58	55	62	61
Independent	6	7	15	10	3	9
Not classifiable	—	7	24	5	3	3
Total	100	100	100	100	100	99

SOURCES: W. D. DeVries, "The Michigan Lobbyist: A Study in the Bases and Perceptions of Effectiveness" (Ph.D. diss., Michigan State University, 1960), p. 67; Ronald D. Hedlund and Samuel C. Patterson, "Personal Attributes, Political Orientations, and Occupational Perspectives of Lobbyists: The Case of Illinois," *Iowa Business Digest* 37 (1966):7; Bernard D. Kolasa, "Lobbying in the Nonpartisan Environment: The Case of Nebraska," *Western Political Quarterly* 14 (1971):68; Lester W. Milbrath, *The Washington Lobbyists* (Chicago, 1963), p. 77; Patterson, "The Role of the Lobbyist: The Case of Oklahoma," p. 78; and Iowa Legislative Research Project, University of Iowa.

TABLE 12.4   Comparison of Political Activities Among Iowa Political Leaders (In percentages)

POLITICAL ACTIVITY	LOBBYISTS	LEGIS-LATORS	PARTY LEADERS	ATTENTIVE CONSTITUENTS
Made financial contribution	81	97	100	92
Attended party meeting	76	96	100	82
Served as party convention delegate	40	83	100	62
Campaigned for other candidates	70	86	98	77
Helped plan campaign strategy	46	77	93	69
Held a formal party leadership position	34	54	100	50

SOURCE: Samuel C. Patterson and G. R. Boynton, "Legislative Recruitment in a Civic Culture," *Social Science Quarterly* 50 (1969):250.

necessary to work both sides of the aisle on most issues?" A total of 85 percent responded with a "yes" or "sometimes." Among Illinois lobbyists interviewed in 1963, 83 percent reported working "always" or "frequently" with both Democratic and Republican legislators.[16]

Much has been said in the popular and even the scholarly literature of pressure-group politics about the personality orientations and characteristics of lobbyists. Thurlow Weed, a prominent nineteenth-century politician whose reputation as a lobbyist was well deserved, is referred to by his biographer as a "wizard" and a "Lucifer," and it is clear that his political successes stemmed partly from his commanding personality.[17] Lobbyists have been described as "snake-oil men" or "pernicious sugar men."[18] The personalities and motivations of lobbyists have been caricatured more often than they have been adequately described and analyzed.

The available evidence about the personality characteristics of lobbyists is meager indeed. For example, evidence from a study of a sample of Washington lobbyists fails to support any hypothesis of the uniqueness of lobbyists in personality terms. The limited data suggest that "lobbyists do not seem to have personalities very different from the general population and certainly not much different from persons in other political skill groups."[19] Lobbyists are sometimes portrayed as conniving, devious, and unprincipled men; but there is no general evidence of this. On the contrary, the evidence does suggest that lobbyists do not, as a group, have unusual personality characteristics. Furthermore, they tend to think of lobbying as an honorable career in which they are likely to stay, and their motivations for entry into lobbying as a career do not appear to reflect particularly pernicious values.[20]

THE ROLE OF THE LOBBYIST

We referred in Chapter 1 to the importance of role allocation in the maintenance of legislative systems. The lobbyist is a distinctive actor in the legislative system, and he plays a representative role, just as the legislator does. Whereas the role of the legislator tends to be diffuse and susceptible to conflicting expectations by relevant reference groups, the role of the lobbyist tends to be more specific. The "extensive internal conflict which the legislator experiences is virtually non-existent" for lobbyists.[21] The principal function of the lobbyist in the political system is to provide an essential connecting link between actors in official legislative roles and interest-group hierarchies in the society.

The role of the lobbyist, like other political roles, is likely to be played in somewhat different forms by different actors. That is to say, in playing the lobbyist role, individuals give that role various orientations. Five distinct lobbyist role orientations can be identified for analysis here: the contact man, the campaign organizer, the informant, the watchdog, and the strategist.

The Contact Man

The contact man plays a classic role as a lobbyist. He is the legislative representative who conceives his job to be that of making crucial contacts with the members of the legislative group. He devotes his time and energies to walking the legislative halls, visiting legislators, collaring them in the halls, establishing relationships with administrative assistants and others of the legislators' staffs, cultivating key legislators on a friendship basis, and developing contacts on the staffs of critical legislative committees. The contact man is gregarious; he likes to talk about the mundane routine of the legislative process; he concerns himself with the details. The contact man believes that the legislative goals of his organization can best be achieved through personal influence and personal contact with legislators. When faced with a legislative problem for his group, the lobbyist with a contact-man orientation is likely to propose as the solution personally contacting as many members of the legislative body as possible and directly presenting the interest group's case.

All lobbyists may make contacts with legislators, but the contact man is a lobbyist for whom this is the primary or most salient orientation. There are important differences in the ubiquity with which this role is played, differences between national and state legislative systems and differences among groups. At the national level, the complexity of legislative life has made contact work relatively impractical, and Washington lobbyists reported spending relatively little time in face-to-face contacting.[22] A lobbyist before Congress is likely to spend more time in face-to-face contact in the early stages of his career and then simply maintain his contacts by letter or telephone, although fence-mending personal calls are usually required to maintain continuous contact.[23]

Although Washington lobbyists reported spending relatively little of their time in direct contact work, more than 80 percent said they preferred direct methods, even though they were not able to employ them extensively.[24] Contact work is probably much more pervasive at the state level, where access to legislators is easier. Lobbyists in Oklahoma and Michigan emphasized this role; 54 percent of the Oklahoma lobbyists and 76 percent of the Michigan lobbyists could be classified as contact men. Zeigler and Baer found that a high proportion of lobbyists in the four states they investigated were contact men, ranging from 54 percent in Oregon to 30 percent in Massachusetts. Furthermore, they found that over-whelming proportions of lobbyists spent most of their time engaging in direct communication with legislators.[25] The Washington lobbyist is much more likely to make his contacts through "intermediaries" (congressmen's friends, associates, and constituents) than the state lobbyist is. At the state level, the contact man is likely to be more effective and to spend more time in lobbying activities than lobbyists with primarily different orientations.

The contact-man orientation is taken variously by lobbyists, depending upon the kinds of organizations they represent. This role orientation is predominant among lobbyists for labor organizations.[26] Among the lobbyists for business associations and companies, however, this orientation is much more uncom-mon.[27] It is clear that "representatives of organizations with high power at the polls spend more time with members of Congress than do representatives of organizations with little power." Thus groups vary in terms of the contact-man orientation of their lobbyists.[28]

Contact operations are not, of course, indiscriminate. The contact man is likely to have his most persistent and regular contacts with friendly legislators, those who share at least a considerable proportion of the group's views. Again, where leadership is very strong and concentrated in the legislature, legislative leaders are much more likely than rank-and-file members to be objects of contact work. Where party organization is strong within the legislature, contact activities tend to be concentrated upon the party leaders. In a highly partisan legislature like the Connecticut senate, for example, some interest-group spokesmen have limited contact mainly to party leaders, even when voting margins for the group's propos-als were slim.[29] In Michigan, where party leadership has been relatively strong, only 39 percent of the lobbyists reported attempts to establish contacts with *all* legislators.[30] Where legislative leadership is more diffuse, it has been found that leaders and nonleaders do not differ much in interaction with lobbyists.[31] In Washington, maintaining contacts with 535 members of Congress is an unman-ageable task for an individual lobbyist except at the most rudimentary level of communication. The large national lobbying organizations divide the labor so that each lobbyist has a limited number of members assigned to him for contact purposes.

The Campaign Organizer

The campaign organizer's conception of his role as a lobbyist is different from the contact man's conception. Although he may make some contacts, this is not, for him, the important part of his job. He conceives his job to be that of organizing mass grass-roots support for his organization's legislative program. He believes that his most important contacts are with leaders in the field and with rank-and-file members of his organization. He feels that the most effective lobbying for his group's program is achieved by demonstrating mass support for that program among the members of his organization "back home" who are the legislators' constituents. When a problem in legislative strategy is raised, the campaign organizer's solution is to map out a nationwide or statewide campaign from the grass roots, utilizing television and radio programs, fact sheets on specific legisla-tion for workers in the field, millions of leaflets for field distribution, delegations to the capitol, and letters to legislators. He sees the value of personal contact but regards it as merely routine and by no means the most significant part of his own job. As one Washington lobbyist put it:

> I'm convinced that the grass-roots support is the important thing rather than my contacts. I know this from my experience on the Hill where I have been on the receiving end. I can go up and explain the technical end of the thing, but it's the grass roots that lets the member of Congress know who is behind it. I would give 75 percent to the grass roots.[32]

The campaign organizer is more likely to be a Washington lobbyist than a lobbyist at the state level, although there are several case studies that describe the work of such lobbyists in their efforts to secure state legislation.[33]

The Informant

The informant is a lobbyist who conveys information to legislators without necessarily advocating a particular position or program. He may lobby only by testimony, presenting information in his area of expertise to a legislative committee. He differs from the contact man in that his lobbying is often public and his contacts are frequently collective rather than individual. He may simply provide informational services for legislators. One Washington lobbyist, speaking of his congressman friends, said, "I will use my friends to get information for me; they are always calling me up about things I ought to know; but I will not ask favors of them. You can lose friends if you keep imposing on them."[34] The informant is not a particularly numerous genre. In Oklahoma, only 12 percent of the lobbyists could be classified as informants; and in Michigan, only 21 percent could be classified roughly in the same way.

The Watchdog

This is the lobbyist who conceives of his job as that of scrutinizing closely the legislative calendars and watching legislative activity carefully, usually from a distance. His job is to be alert to developments in the legislative system that might affect his client group. Whenever legislation that affects his employer is proposed or introduced, his job is to signal his group so that it can attempt to bring pressure on legislators. He is a listening post for his organization, staked out in the capital to keep alert to developments that might affect his client. In performing this role, he may seldom enter the legislative halls or talk to individual members; he may never leave his office downtown in the capital city. One Oklahoma lobbyist described his job in watchdog terms:

> We attempt to keep our people informed about the merits of all legislation which has a direct effect on our business, as well as all legislation which has any effect on the state economy, and general interest. My member associations are kept informed on current legislative proposals via a legislative bulletin, and we make use of special bulletins and special committee actions when we wish to directly render an opinion concerning any act or prospective act.

The watchdog orientation was characteristic of about one-fourth of Oklahoma lobbyists in 1961, and it has been reported in other states among company, oil, and church lobbyists.[35]

The Strategist

A few lobbyists specialize in the formulation and development of legislative strategy; thus, their orientation with regard to lobbying is a strategy-formulating one. The strategist plans legislative campaigns to be executed by other lobbyists. He may advise other lobbyists concerning legislative strategy and thus act as a "lobbyist's lobbyist." These lobbyists are rare, and little data about them are available. Only three of the hundred-odd lobbyists in Washington interviewed by Milbrath could be classified as strategists, and his is virtually the only study of this type.

> Such men must have an impressive array of talents: they must be exceptionally intelligent and perceptive; they must have an accurate and broad grasp of the political and governmental system; they must have intimate and detailed knowledge of the formal and informal rules of the policy-making process; and, perhaps most important, they must know the habits of thinking, quirks of mind, and patterns of action of the major players in the drama that they attempt to influence. With such requirements, it is not surprising that strategist-lobbyists are few.[36]

These role orientations are not mutually exclusive. A contact man plans strategy; a campaign organizer makes contacts; both alert their groups to action and convey factual information. These are analytically distinct orientations in the sense that it is possible to type lobbyist roles in terms of the primacy and saliency of the lobbyist's approach to his job.

THE TECHNIQUES OF LOBBYING

The literature of pressure-group research is filled with descriptions of the tactics of organized groups.[37] We shall limit our focus in this chapter to the specific techniques used by lobbyists. We already have indicated the extent to which Washington lobbyists engage in direct communication with congressmen. Although they spend relatively little time in direct communication, and although there has been a shift from direct to indirect means of communication, Washington lobbyists continue to rate "personal presentation of viewpoints" highest as the most effective technique of lobbying. As Table 12.5 shows, lobbyists in the four states studied by Zeigler and Baer also exhibit substantial similarity in their preference for direct-contact techniques. Furthermore, these investigators have shown that lobbyists consider the personal presentation of arguments to be a more effective technique; whereas legislators are more inclined to regard presentation of research results as more effective.[38] In general, in both Milbrath's research on Washington lobbyists and the Zeigler and Baer study of lobbyists in four states, lobbyists regarded direct-contact methods as most effective, indirect contacts as next most effective, and wining and dining legislators as least effective. In all

TABLE 12.5 Lobbyists' Ratings of Techniques

TECHNIQUE	MASS.	N.C.	ORE.	UTAH	WASHING-TON, D.C.
Direct communication					
Personal presentation of viewpoints	6.6	6.7	6.9	6.4	6.7
Presenting research results	5.8	5.4	6.0	5.5	5.8
Testifying at hearings	5.6	5.3	5.7	5.0	5.2
Communication through intermediaries					
Contact by constituents	3.2	5.4	4.3	5.0	4.7
Contact by a close friend	2.5	4.2	3.7	4.0	3.0
Letter-writing campaign	3.4	4.0	4.0	4.0	3.7
Public relations campaign	3.7	4.6	4.0	4.6	3.5
Publicizing voting records	2.2	1.4	2.0	2.4	1.7
Methods of keeping channels open					
Entertaining legislators	1.3	2.5	2.2	3.0	1.4
Giving a party	1.0	1.8	1.6	2.3	1.1
Campaign contributions	2.0	2.4	2.5	3.3	1.6
Bribery	0.1	1.2	0.2	0.3	0.1
Mean for all techniques	3.0	3.5	3.5	3.7	3.2

NOTE: Ratings of effectiveness on a scale from 0 (ineffective) to 8 (effective).
SOURCES: Milbrath, *The Washington Lobbyists*, pp. 392–393; and Harmon Zeigler and Michael A. Baer, *Lobbying: Interaction and Influence in American State Legislatures* (Belmont, Calif., 1969), p. 176. Milbrath's responses were originally coded from 0 to 10 and have been recoded to make them compatible with the Zeigler-Baer data.

settings where the matter has been subjected to any kind of careful inquiry, unethical lobbying techniques such as bribery were found to be regarded as very ineffective relative to other techniques. If it is the conventional wisdom that entertaining and bribing legislators are thought by American lobbyists to be effective persuasive methods, the evidence is heavily against it.

The use of different lobbying techniques does vary among lobbying groups. For instance, organizations with mass memberships (such as labor and farm organizations) are likely to rate letter campaigns higher than other groups do. Again, as Zeigler and Baer have shown, "business lobbyists give a substantially higher rating to direct, personal communication than do labor lobbyists" at the state level. "Business lobbyists, whose direct access to legislators is more easily achieved, attribute a greater effectiveness to direct communication. The labor lobbyist's inability to achieve direct communication necessitates his reliance upon the second category of communications, the use of intermediaries."[39]

Entertaining and party-giving were rated higher by state lobbyists than by Washington lobbyists. In all probability, there is more lobbyist entertaining of legislators at the state level. State legislators are away from their hometowns and from their homes and families when the legislature is in session. Few can afford to set up housekeeping in the capital city. Thus, the state legislator is more likely to need and to seek entertainment of the sort the lobbyist may provide. At the same time, state legislators may be much more sensitive about the practice of lobbyist-provided entertainment than congressmen are. Among Wisconsin legislators, for example, it had always been regarded as proper for a member to accept meals and drinks from lobbyists, although some did not accept such favors on principle. Many Wisconsin legislators thought of this practice as a legitimate supplement to their low income or as acceptable among friends. Until 1957, this had been an accepted practice for many years. But some Wisconsin legislators got bad reputations by abusing this relationship with lobbyists. These moochers solicited favors from lobbyists; they might go to a restaurant with their friends, order a meal, and then afterward see a lobbyist sitting at another table and take their checks to him. They might insist that a lobbyist take them and their friends out for an evening on the town. These moochers (few in number, to be sure) took advantage of lobbyists and put them in an uncomfortable position. Some lobbyists refused to have anything to do with the moocher-legislators, but others felt that they had to cater to their demands for fear of losing crucial votes. In 1957, the Wisconsin legislature passed a law prohibiting lobbyists from buying meals or drinks for legislators. Few legislators privately believed in this enactment, but it passed the legislature because members were persuaded that it would improve their public relations image.[40] It is not known to what extent lobbyists become ensnared in the entertainment dilemma, but the Wisconsin experience may be a deterrent to the use of entertaining as a lobbying technique in other states. An Oklahoma lobbyist suggested a similar lobbying problem in that state: "Too many of our representatives are out for the dollar that is flowing around the capitol building. I was 'touched' a number of times in regard to our own bill." Certainly, in a state where entertaining is restricted by law, it is not likely to be rated as a very effective technique by lobbyists.

Contributing money to a legislator's campaign for election is considered by many groups to be a way of acquiring access for their lobbyists. For instance, during the 1972 congressional elections, milk-industry groups contributed more than $1.3 million to House and Senate candidates. The American Medical Association contributed over $850,000; the National Association of Manufacturers more than $440,000; the AFL-CIO about $1.2 million; and a banking group about $200,000.[41] Reporting of interest group campaign expenditures was made much more thorough and detailed by the enactment of the Federal Election Campaign Act of 1971, which contained provisions eliciting more comprehensive reporting of interest-group contributions to congressional campaigns in 1974. Preelection reports in 1974 indicated that groups had spent about $13 million in campaign contributions, more than was reported to have been spent in the entire 1970 election campaigns.[42]

Partly as a reaction to the large campaign contributions of economic interest groups, and partly to engage in lobbying activities designed to bring about more strict regulation of lobbying activities in general, so-called "public interest" lobbying became a prominent technique in the late 1960s and 1970s. New interest groups, epitomized by Common Cause, Ralph Nader's consumer lobby, and environmental groups, sought to balance the influence of the large economic interests. Such groups have sought to get consumer-protection legislation enacted, to mobilize citizens in support of more comprehensive regulation of elections and lobbying activities, to bring about legislative reform, and to achieve the enactment of legislation protecting the environment, alleviating urban problems, assuring equal rights and opportunities, providing criminal justice, and dealing with a host of social problems. The tactics of such "public interest" lobbying have emphasized citizen involvement, constituency influence over legislators, public endorsement of specific candidates rather than direct financial contributions, and utilization of media campaigns to publicize and dramatize social, political, and economic problems and to promote the "public interest" solution.[43]

THE LEGISLATORS' RESPONSE TO LOBBYING

As a general proposition, American legislators tend to view lobbyists and lobbying as making significant contributions to the effective operation of the legislative process. One congressman expressed these attitudes about lobbying, which are widely shared among his colleagues:

A lot of people seem to think that lobbying is a bad thing. I think that is one misconception which still needs to be corrected as far as the general public is concerned. Lobbying is an essential part of representative government, and it needs to be encouraged and appreciated. [Lobbyists] are frequently a source of information. If they come to your offices and explain a program or factors contributing to the need for legislation, you get a better understanding of the problems and the answers to them. If you have your independence, and I think we all do, they can teach you what an issue is all about, and you can make your own decision. There can be bad lobbying technique, of course, but basically lobbying is a good thing.[44]

A state legislator explained:

Lobbyists are a vital part of the legislative process. Without them to explain, you couldn't get a clear picture of the situation. They can study and present the issues concisely—the average legislator has no time or inclination to do it, and wouldn't understand bills or issues without them. A professional lobbyist in ten minutes can explain what it would take a member two hours to wade through just reading bills. Both sides come around to you, so you can balance off all one-sided presentations (and they're all one-sided). A definite function is performed by lobbyists.[45]

In general, legislators react most favorably toward lobbyists in terms of the measure of public sentiment and the information, research, and support the lobbyist can provide, rather than in terms of pressures or assertions of demands.

American legislators are, on the whole, well aware of the presence of political-interest groups and are able to discriminate among them concerning their relative influence. Evidence at the state legislative level suggests that legislators' perceptions of relative group influence in the legislative process vary somewhat in different states. For example, in 1960, Indiana legislators were asked which were the "most powerful" lobbying organizations in the state. The results are summarized in Figure 12.1. The configuration of relative group influence perceived by state legislators in other states does not follow the Indiana pattern exactly, although labor, business, teacher, and governmental groups tend to have the highest perceived influence in the states for which data are available.[46] Business interests tend to be most salient for legislators at the state level, with educational

FIGURE 12.1   Indiana Legislators' Perceptions of "Most Powerful" Groups

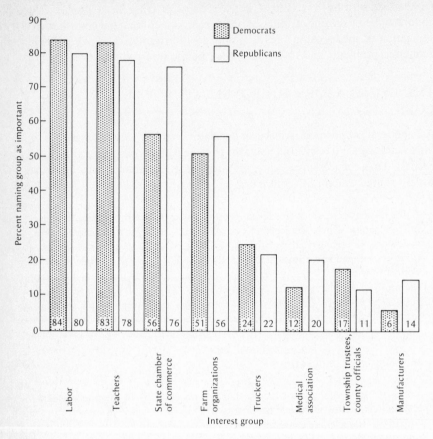

NOTE: Number of Republicans interviewed was 82; number of Democrats interviewed was 55.

SOURCE: Kenneth Janda et al., *Legislative Politics in Indiana* (Bloomington, Ind., 1961), p. 18.

interests second and labor interests third. That agricultural interests are not pronouncedly salient for state legislators in Indiana, Ohio, New Jersey, California, and Tennessee may be due to the more direct representation of farmers by the legislators themselves, especially in the more predominantly agricultural states (such as Tennessee).

Figure 12.2 indicates the reasons given by Democratic and Republican Indiana legislators for their rankings of relative interest-group influence. They tend to associate the interest group's political influence more with its claim to be represented or with its general political power (electoral influence, organization, financial resources) than with its lobbying activities in the legislative arena itself. These general findings for Indiana legislators are supported by analyses of legislators' perceptions of group influence in California, Tennessee, Ohio, and New Jersey. Table 12.6 summarizes the combined findings for these four states, indicating the categories of reasons that legislators gave for the power of specific groups. That state legislators rank reasons involving the interest group's usefulness to

TABLE 12.6 Reasons for Interest-Group Power Given by Legislators in California, Tennessee, Ohio, and New Jersey (In percentages)

LEGISLATORS' REASONS	INTEREST GROUPS				
	Agricultural	Business	Labor	Professional	Governmental
Representational Claims (Size, prestige, potential electoral influence)	43	19	34	44	39
Informational utility (facts, knowledge, research)	6	5	3	4	8
Lobbying activity (entertainment, favors, skill, experience, money)	9	41	20	7	20
Extralegislative political activity or power (organization activity, publicity, campaign activity, letter-writing campaigns)	40	30	40	41	30
Other reasons	2	5	3	4	3
Total	100	100	100	100	100
Number	87	464	188	367	88

SOURCE: John C. Wahlke et al., *The Legislative System* (New York, 1962), pp. 334–335.

FIGURE 12.2   Indiana Legislators' Perceptions of Reasons for Interest-Groups' Power

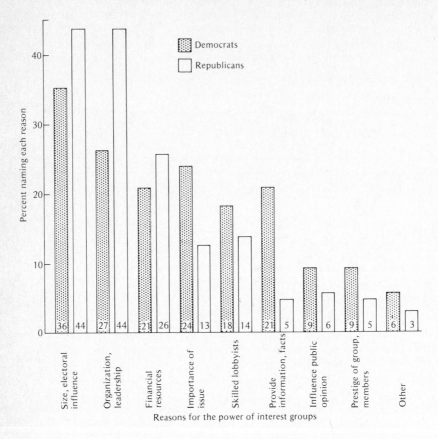

NOTE: Number of Republicans interviewed was 62; number of Democrats interviewed was 33.

SOURCE: Janda et al., *Legislative Politics in Indiana*, p. 18.

the legislature relatively low suggests that "the most powerful groups appear to legislators to be external forces, posing problems for the legislature to deal with, and not agencies intimately associated with the legislature in the business of lawmaking."[47]

These findings suggest the rather low visibility of lobbyists in the perspective of the American legislator. Legislators are familiar with organized interest groups and perceive them as differing in legislative influence. Perceived group power is likely to be focused mainly in terms of the general representational claims and external influence potential of the groups. The lobbyist is likely to be less visible than the group itself. An analysis that supports this hypothesis comes from interviews with members of the 1951 session of the Vermont legislature. During the course of the interviews, legislators were asked if they could identify the leading groups in Vermont politics, their lobbyists, and the issues in which these groups were interested. The principal findings of this study of the visibility to

TABLE 12.7 Vermont Legislators Able to Identify Organized Groups, Their Lobbyists, and Issues of Interest to Them (In percentages)

QUESTION	LEGISLATORS ABLE TO RECOGNIZE		
	Farm Bureau	AIV	AFL-CIO
Group itself	100	63	78
Lobbyist	70	40	38
More than one issue	60	30	30

SOURCE: Oliver Garceau and Corinne Silverman, "A Pressure Group and the Pressured: A Case Report," *American Political Science Review* 48 (1954):685.

legislators of groups, lobbyists, and issues are presented in Table 12.7. It is particularly striking to note that 30 percent of the Vermont legislators could not identify the Farm Bureau lobbyist even though he had been its president and lobbyist for a generation, and that only about one-third of the legislators could identify the lobbyists for the Associated Industries of Vermont (AIV) or for the state AFL-CIO. Legislators most oriented to programs and policies as the focus of legislative activities were best able to identify lobbyists and organized groups' issues; whereas for the legislators least able to perceive the factional informal substructure of the 1951 session, lobbyists and issues were least visible.[48]

The salience and visibility of lobbyists to legislators are likely to be affected as well by the relationship between legislator and lobbyist. Lobbyists who are the close personal friends of legislators or lobbyists for organized interests with which the legislator identifies are less likely to be identified as lobbyists than group representatives who speak for interests inimical or hostile to those of the legislator. For instance, a Washington labor-union lobbyist said:

One time during the minimum wage battle, Senator _____ began to weaken on the $1.00 minimum. Someone had touched his sympathy with a picture of what the bill would do to the sawmills of the South. He told me that he was contemplating making an exception in their case. I said, "_____ (first name), if you even hint that you might back down from your previous position, this place will be swarming with lobbyists!" "Lobbyists," he said, looking around him, "I don't see any lobbyists around here." Then he realized that I was one and laughed. Hell, we don't think of ourselves as *lobbyists!*[49]

Although lobbying is a widely accepted practice in the American legislative system, and although lobbyists are actors in it who are generally acceptable to American legislators, legislators vary in their orientation to lobbying activity by organized groups. Some legislators have relatively substantial knowledge about interest-group activity and have a friendly attitude toward it. Legislators who fit this type have been called *facilitators.* The moochers to whom we referred earlier in this chapter are facilitators of one kind (perhaps overfacilitators). A second type of legislator either has no strong effective orientation toward organized groups or has a very low level of knowledge about them; legislators of this type have been called *neutrals.* Finally, legislators may be relatively knowledgeable about organized-group activity and have a hostile attitude toward it. These legislators have been named *resisters* in their lobbying orientation.

Interviews with legislators in California, Ohio, New Jersey, and Tennessee indicate that a substantial majority are of the facilitator or the neutral type, although, on the average, about one-fourth can be classified as resisters.[50] But resisters were found to be relatively less well educated than other legislators, relatively less experienced in legislative work, and characterized by a lower sense of legislative efficacy. The facilitators were found to be more sensitive to the complexity and multiplicity of interest-group politics and seemed to play a more important part in the process of accommodation of conflicting interests. Furthermore, facilitators appeared more often to be uncommitted to either probusiness or prolabor interests; whereas resisters were more often committed legislators. Among the ranks of resisters are those who tend to be committed to one set of interests and hostile to others. Facilitators, on the other hand, are more responsive to lobbying activities of a diverse kind and tend to be brokers of competing interests.

The American legislator is not to be viewed realistically as the pawn of contending forces. The legislator may influence the lobbyist as much as the lobbyist influences him. Legislator-lobbyist relationships are reciprocal. But in this relationship, the legislator is more likely to have the upper hand. He is often quite free to refuse to cooperate with lobbyists, without fear of electoral retaliation. Again, legislators may influence lobbyists by virtue of their friendly relations (the friendship ploy). Donald R. Matthews points out that "friendship with a lobbyist can be as beneficial to a senator as to a lobbyist" because "it makes the lobbyist indebted to him, more sensitive to his political problems, less willing to apply 'pressure,' a more trustworthy ally."[51] And furthermore, legislators who deal with lobbyists as a part of the nature of legislative life build up credit with lobbyists just as much as lobbyists build up credit with legislators, and legislators may influence lobbyists by calling in that credit. Finally, lobbyists are always susceptible to legislative attack; they are very vulnerable to legislative investigation and exposure, and "their public reputation is so low that public attack is bound to be damaging."[52] Lobbying is a part of the conflict-management process; it is an aspect of legislative bargaining, negotiation, and compromise. The legislator-lobbyist relationship is not a one-way street.

To the extent that it is possible to talk meaningfully about lobbying in rather general terms, it is fair to say that lobbying in American legislative systems is not very effective in the sense of conventional popular conceptions of the shrewdness and manipulative ability of lobbyists. Lobbying activity is, in the main, directed at legislators who sympathize with the policy positions of the group or groups involved; lobbyists depend very substantially on their friends, those who sympathize with their cause. Much of lobbying involves the reinforcement and activation of sympathetic legislators, rather than the conversion of legislators from one policy position to another.

Assessments of lobbying effectiveness involve all the unresolved problems of the measurement of influence. It is thus necessary to rely perforce upon crude and impressionistic evaluations of lobbying effectiveness. Impressions will differ where varying criteria of effectiveness are employed. The sensationalist muckraking literature is not very helpful in an assessment of lobbying effectiveness. There is both historical and contemporary evidence for lobbying effectiveness, just as there is evidence of ineptitude in lobbying efforts. Some of the most effective lobbying in the recent history of the Congress has been done by the railroad brotherhoods, the oil and gas interests, and the National Rifle Association, and these lobbying efforts have been relatively narrow in scope.[53] On the other hand, there is reliable evidence that even large and important organized groups, such as business associations or labor unions, are often quite inept and ineffective in their lobbying efforts on crucial issues.[54] The key to successful lobbying in the postwar world has clearly been to communicate to policy-makers in the legislative body accurate parameters of popular sentiment.

NOTES

1.   See Harmon Zeigler, *Interest Groups in American Society* (Englewood Cliffs, N.J., 1964); David B. Truman, *The Governmental Process,* 2d ed. (New York, 1971), especially pp. xvii–xlviii; and Donald C. Blaisdell, *American Democracy Under Pressure* (New York, 1957).

2.   See Lester W. Milbrath, *The Washington Lobbyists* (Chicago, 1963), p. 8.

3.   See *United States* v. *Harriss,* 347 U.S. 612 (1954). See also Congressional Quarterly, *The Washington Lobby* (Washington, D.C., 1971); and Lewis A. Dexter, *How Organizations Are Represented in Washington* (Indianapolis, Ind., 1969).

4.   *Congressional Quarterly Weekly Report* 33 (January 25, 1975), Index:63–68; and *Congressional Quarterly Weekly Report* 32 (July 27, 1974):1947–1955.

5.   See Belle Zeller, "Regulation of Pressure Groups and Lobbyists," *Annals of the American Academy of Political and Social Science* 319 (1958):94–103. See also Edgar Lane, *Lobbying and the Law* (Berkeley and Los Angeles, 1964).

6.   A compilation of state lobbying laws is available in the *Directory of Registered Federal and State Lobbyists* (Orange, N.J., 1973), pp. 529–611.

7.   See Charles D. Hounshell, *The Legislative Process in Virginia* (Charlottesville, Va., 1951), p. 45; and William C. Havard and Loren P. Beth, *The Politics of Mis-representation: Rural-Urban Conflict in the Florida Legislature* (Baton Rouge, La., 1962), pp. 220–225.

8.   Milbrath, *The Washington Lobbyists,* p. 31.

9.   Samuel C. Patterson, "The Role of the Lobbyist: The Case of Oklahoma," *Journal of Politics* 25 (1963):81.

10.   See Lane, *Lobbying and the Law,* pp. 141–152.

11.   See Harmon Zeigler and Michael A. Baer, *Lobbying: Interaction and Influence in American State Legislatures* (Belmont, Calif., 1969), pp. 38–59; and Samuel C. Patterson and G. R. Boynton, "Legislative Recruitment in a Civic Culture," *Social Science Quarterly* 50 (1969):243–263.

12.   In 1966, about 5 percent of the lobbyists in Massachusetts, North Carolina, Oregon, and Utah had been legislators. In 1961, 12 percent of the Oklahoma lobbyists had served in the legislature. Interchangeability between legislative and lobbyist roles has been found to be relatively higher in Nebraska. See Bernard D. Kolasa, "Lobbying in the Nonpartisan Environment: The Case of Nebraska," *Western Political Quarterly* 24 (1971): 69.

13.   Milbrath, *The Washington Lobbyists,* p. 72.

14.   Zeigler and Baer, *Lobbying,* pp. 46–48.

15.   Lester W. Milbrath, "The Political Party Activity of Washington Lobbyists," *Journal of Politics* 20 (1958):346.

16. Walter D. DeVries, "The Michigan Lobbyist: A Study in the Bases and Perceptions of Effectiveness" (Ph.D. diss., Michigan State University, 1960), p. 203; and Ronald D. Hedlund and Samuel C. Patterson, "Personal Attributes, Political Orientations, and Occupational Perspectives of Lobbyists: The Case of Illinois," *Iowa Business Digest* 37 (1966):7.

17. Glyndon G. Van Deusen, *Thurlow Weed: Wizard of the Lobby* (Boston, 1947).

18. See Kenneth G. Crawford, *The Pressure Boys* (New York, 1939).

19. Milbrath, *The Washington Lobbyists,* p. 107.

20. Ibid., p. 136; De Vries, "The Michigan Lobbyist: A Study in Bases and Perceptions of Effectiveness," pp. 133–134; and Zeigler and Baer, *Lobbying,* pp. 70–74.

21. Robert E. Lane, "Notes on the Theory of the Lobby," *Western Political Quarterly* 2 (1949):155; see E. Pendleton Herring, *Group Representation Before Congress* (Baltimore, 1929), pp. 28–29.

22. See Milbrath, *The Washington Lobbyists,* pp. 116–119.

23. See Donald R. Matthews, *U.S. Senators and Their World* (Chapel Hill, N.C., 1960), pp. 180–181.

24. Milbrath, *The Washington Lobbyists,* p. 212.

25. DeVries, "The Michigan Lobbyist: A Study in Bases and Perceptions of Effectiveness," pp. 97–99; Patterson, "The Role of the Lobbyist: The Case of Oklahoma," p. 85; and Zeigler and Baer, *Lobbying,* pp. 13, 79.

26. See Samuel C. Patterson, "The Role of the Labor Lobbyist" (Paper presented at the annual meeting of the American Political Science Association, 1962); and *Labor Lobbying and Labor Reform: The Passage of the Landrum-Griffin Act* (Indianapolis, Ind., 1966).

27. See Paul W. Cherington and Ralph L. Gillen, *The Business Representative in Washington* (Washington, D.C., 1962), pp. 45–70; and Raymond A. Bauer, Ithiel de Sola Pool, and Lewis A. Dexter, *American Business and Public Policy: The Politics of Foreign Trade* (New York, 1963), pp. 350–357.

28. Milbrath, *The Washington Lobbyists,* p. 119.

29. See Duane Lockard, *New England State Politics* (Princeton, N.J., 1959), p. 288.

30. DeVries, "The Michigan Lobbyist: A Study in the Bases and Perceptions of Effectiveness," p. 199.

31. See Zeigler and Baer, *Lobbying,* pp. 144–145.

32. Milbrath, *The Washington Lobbyists,* pp. 238–239.

33. For a description of activities at the national level, see Edith T. Carper, *Lobbying and the Natural Gas Bill* (University, Ala., 1962); for a description of activities at the state level, see Rae F. Still, *The Gilmer-Aiken Bills: A Study in the Legislative Process* (Austin, Tex., 1950).

34. Milbrath, *The Washington Lobbyists,* p. 165.

35. See Gilbert Y. Steiner and Samuel K. Gove, *Legislative Politics in Illinois* (Urbana, Ill., 1960), p. 47; Cherington and Gillen, *The Business Representative in Washington,* pp. 47–48; Robert Engler, *The Politics of Oil* (New York, 1961), p. 378; and Luke E. Ebersole, *Church Lobbying in the Nation's Capital* (New York, 1951), pp. 76–77. The quotation comes from unpublished interviews with Oklahoma lobbyists; see Samuel C. Patterson, "The Role of the Lobbyist: The Case of Oklahoma," *Journal of Politics* 25 (1963):72–92.

36. Milbrath, *The Washington Lobbyists,* pp. 167–168.

37. See Truman, *The Governmental Process,* pp. 213–498.

38. See Milbrath, *The Washington Lobbyists,* pp. 162–294. See also DeVries, "The Michigan Lobbyist: A Study in the Bases and Perceptions of Effectiveness," p. 147; and Lester W. Milbrath, "Lobbying as a Communication Process," *Public Opinion Quarterly* 14 (1961):463, 465–466.

39.   Zeigler and Baer, *Lobbying,* pp. 181–182.

40.   Samuel C. Patterson, "The Role of the Deviant in the State Legislative System: The Wisconsin Assembly," *Western Political Quarterly* 14 (1961):463, 465–466.

41.   Randall B. Ripley, *Congress: Process and Policy* (New York, 1975), p. 209.

42.   *Congressional Quarterly Weekly Report* 32 (September 28, 1974):2583–2586.

43.   Thomas P. Murphy, *The New Politics Congress* (Lexington, Mass., 1974), pp. 139–153. For a case study indicating some of the limitations of "public interest" lobbying, see Bruce Ian Oppenheimer, *Oil and the Congressional Process* (Lexington, Mass., 1974), pp. 112–117.

44.   Charles L. Clapp, *The Congressman: His Work as He Sees It* (Washington, D.C., 1963), pp. 162–163.

45.   John C. Wahlke et al., *The Legislative System* (New York, 1962), p. 338.

46.   Ibid., pp. 314–316. For a useful discussion of school lobbying, see Nicholas A. Masters, Robert H. Salisbury, and Thomas H. Eliot, *State Politics and the Public Schools* (New York, 1964).

47.   Wahlke et al., *The Legislative System,* p. 335.

48.   See Oliver Garceau and Corinne Silverman, "A Pressure Group and the Pressured: A Case Report," *American Political Science Review* 48 (1954):685–686.

49.   Matthews, *U.S. Senators and Their World,* p. 178.

50.   See John C. Wahlke et al., "American State Legislators' Role Orientations Toward Pressure Groups," *Journal of Politics* 22 (1960):203–227.

51.   Matthews, *U.S. Senators and Their World,* p. 189.

52.   Ibid., p. 190.

53.   See Carper, *Lobbying and the Natural Gas Bill,* pp. 36–38; and Engler, *The Politics of Oil,* pp. 372–394.

54.   The ineptitude of lobbying operations in congressional controversies over foreign-trade legislation is particularly stressed in Bauer, Pool, and Dexter, *American Business and Public Policy,* pp. 323–399.

CHAPTER THIRTEEN

The Legislator
and His Constituents

In Chapters 11 and 12, we described the importance of lobbyists and executive agents as participants in the legislative process. In this chapter, we shall deal with the constituent as a participant, indicating some of the problems of legislator response to constituent participation, and suggesting some of the occupational role strains created for the legislator by his constituents. Here our treatment must, of necessity, be in rather general terms; we deal specifically with constituency effects on the voting behavior of legislators in Chapter 16.

It has become a part of the common lore of the legislative way of life that a legislator, to survive politically, must maintain constant, persistent, favorable, and perhaps even obsequious relations with his constituents. In reality, the conventional wisdom is, as usual, both right and wrong. Legislators in the United States are deeply concerned, sometimes even obsessed, with their image among their constituents; but constituents do not, on the whole, reciprocate with commensurate concern about their legislators. A theory of representation adequate to describe and explain legislator-constituent relationships in the real world cannot rely upon the existence of highly attentive constituents who, as a body, watch the work of their legislators closely.

CONSTITUENTS AND THE SALIENCY OF LEGISLATORS

Since the 1930s, sample surveys and public-opinion polls have supplied substantial data about constituents (voters) in the United States. Our purpose here is not to develop these data; they are treated at length in numerous studies of the electorate.[1] It is more pertinent in this context to summarize this knowledge about the cognitive orientations of constituents toward their legislators. The simple fact is that constituents have relatively little knowledge about their legislators. National surveys conducted by the American Institute of Public Opinion (AIPO) have consistently shown the low level of saliency of legislators for American adults. In 1945, a representative sample of the adult population was asked: "Do you happen to know the names of the two United States Senators from this state?" Only 35 percent of the sample correctly named both of their senators, and

22 percent could name only one. In 1954, a similar query was put to an adult sample, and only 31 percent were able to identify both of their senators.[2] Levels of awareness of congressmen appear to be increasing. In 1947, the AIPO asked its sample: "Can you remember off-hand the name of the United States Congressman from your district?" Only 38 percent were able to do so correctly. By 1965, 43 percent could name their congressman. Two Gallup surveys in 1970 indicated that 53 percent knew the name of their congressman, but a 1973 Harris survey showed that only 46 percent could correctly name their representative in Congress, and only 41 percent could identify that representative's political party affiliation. In 1973, 59 percent of Americans could give the correct name of one United States senator, and 39 percent could name both senators from their state.

If the cognitive hurdle is lowered somewhat, it is possible to indicate to what extent constituents know how many senators and representatives they have. For instance, in 1945, 55 percent of the adults interviewed were able to state the correct number of United States senators from each state, although in 1954, only 49 percent were able to do so. In 1954, only 11 percent of the AIPO sample were able to answer correctly when asked: "How many states will elect members of the House of Representatives this fall? how many will not?" In 1973, 8 percent of Americans could not describe the composition of Congress as including the Senate and House of Representatives, and 20 percent expressed the belief that Congress included the Supreme Court.

Following the congressional elections in 1958, the Survey Research Center interviewed a sample of constituents living in a sample of 116 congressional districts. It was found, among other things, that only 47 percent correctly attributed control of the Eighty-fifth Congress to the Democrats. Beyond that, "of the people who lived in districts where the House seat was contested in 1958, 59 percent—well over half—said that they had neither read nor heard anything about either candidate for Congress, and less than 1 in 5 felt that they knew something about both candidates."[3] Eliminating nonvoters from this analysis does not improve the saliency of congressmen very much; 46 percent of those who went to the polls in 1958 admitted that they had done so without having read or heard anything about either candidate. The incumbent congressman is more visible than his opponent. In districts where there was a contest in 1958, 39 percent of the constituents sampled knew something about the congressman; only 20 percent reported knowing anything about his opponent.

If the saliency of American congressmen and senators is relatively low, constituents are more aware of congressional *activity,* at least of the more dramatic sort. There are occasions when popular awareness of congressional activity reaches rather impressive levels. But public awareness of dramatic congressional activities that involve questions of public policy cannot be taken to mean that constituents evaluate their legislators primarily in policy terms. In Gallup surveys taken in 1965 and 1970, only a fifth of the national sample reported knowing anything about how their congressman voted on any major bills. The 1958 Survey Research Center interviews with constituents in 116 congressional districts led to the following conclusions about the image of the congressman that constituents reflect:

> Our constituent interviews indicate that the popular image of the Congressman is almost barren of policy content. A long series of open-ended questions asked of those who said they had any information about the Representative produced mainly a collection of diffuse evaluative judgments: he is a good man, he is experienced, he knows the problems, he has done a good job, and the like. Beyond this, the Congressman's image consisted of a mixed bag of impressions, some of them wildly improbable, about ethnicity, the attractiveness of family, specific services to the district and other facts in the candidate's background. By the most reasonable count, references to current legislative issues comprised not more than a thirtieth part of what the constituents had to say about their Congressman.[4]

Constituents are not, generally speaking, particularly aware of the issue positions of their legislators, and they tend to evaluate legislators more in terms of nonissue factors that are only remotely related to policy orientation.

The saliency of legislators for constituents is a variable of very great interest, but woefully little is known about the correlates or determinants of saliency. It is, however, very clear that there is a generally low level of saliency among constituents regarding Congress. It seems very likely that state legislators are less visible to their constituents than congressmen are. A 1967 Gallup poll showed that only 28 percent of Americans knew who their state senator was, and only 24 percent knew their representative in the lower house of the state legislature.[5] Here are some comments from interviews with state legislators that indicate their impressions of their saliency with their own constituents:

> There isn't much interest in my county. The local newspaper gives me the only indication as to how my constituents feel. I think I'd say they were disinterested. If they are not affected by the legislation, they don't care. Sometimes someone will tell them to come up here and tell me how to vote on a certain bill, but they don't know what the bill is about. They are pitifully ignorant of how you spend state money. People often fight for legislation, like education, that would hurt the county taxwise. Thirty PTA women once came to see me about education. I explained to them my position, but they don't know and don't care.

> I don't think my constituents have the slightest idea of what the legislature is for. They're very poorly informed, speaking in general terms, of course. There are always the people who are close to you and they come to ask questions, so they know a little more, but there is just too much apathy on the part of the rank and file. Constituents have the impression that we're in session all the time and are surprised to learn that we have only one session every two years. This is because they see Congress news all year. I am thought of like a representative in Washington. People ask me to support federal bills, and ten to one, ask me, "How are things in Washington?"[6]

Well over half the legislators in California, Ohio, New Jersey, and Tennessee who were asked about their constituents characterized them as uninformed about the legislature or the work of the legislator.

The American legislator is not generally very visible to his constituents, even to those who go to the polls to vote for him; and the American constituent is poorly informed about the identity of his legislator, the work of his legislature, and the policy position of his representative. But these things are not true of all constituents. There are attentive publics in every legislator's constituency, and he responds to them. The legislator may endeavor to widen the attentiveness of his constituents, or he may attempt to restrict it, but he does respond to it. He communicates with some of his constituents, and they with him. Although these attentive constituents have a variable impact upon the legislator's policy position (described in Chapter 16), he does organize his work around them.

LEGISLATOR-CONSTITUENT COMMUNICATION

Most state legislators are in almost constant touch with at least some of their constituents. They live with their constituents, earn their living among them, and in many cases, were born and raised within easy distance of most of them. The legislative session is relatively brief, and even during the session, they are home for part of the week. Their communication with their constituents is largely that of personal contact on a fairly continuous basis. There are, of course, some exceptions to these generalizations. A few rural state legislators represent geographically enormous districts where constituents are so scattered that contact is difficult to maintain. The urban legislator elected at large in a metropolitan county may, like the Los Angeles state senator, have millions of constituents, more than most congressmen have. The state legislator elected from a district within a metropolitan center may have difficulty maintaining contact with his constituents when, for example, not even the press, which covers the entire metropolitan area, is very accessible to him. Although there is very little detailed information available concerning the communications practices of state legislators, it can be assumed that they tend to be informal. The full complexity of the routinized and formalized mechanisms of legislator-constituent communication are discovered by examining these mechanisms as they are used by a remote and professionalized legislative body like the Congress.

Congressmen, like state legislators, apparently rely most heavily upon personal contact as a source of information from their constituents, with the mail, newspapers, party organization, and opinion polls (among the factors considered in Table 13.1) taking on importance in that order. As often happens, what is most impor-

TABLE 13.1   Extent of Reliance upon Various Communication Channels by Congressmen from 116 Districts, 1958 (In percentages)

EXTENT OF RELIANCE	SOURCE OF INFORMATION				
	Personal Contact	Mail	Newspapers	Party Organization	Opinion Polls
A great deal	62	25	5	8	6
Quite a bit	19	30	27	10	7
Some	8	23	24	15	11
Not much	8	19	29	28	15
None	2	3	15	39	61

SOURCE: Warren E. Miller, "Policy Preferences of Congressional Candidates and Constituents" (Paper presented at the annual meeting of the American Political Science Association, 1961).

tant is least understood. Almost nothing is known about the nature of personal contacts between legislators and constituents in any systematic way. Personal contacts are intensified during the legislators' campaigns for election, and constituents come to Washington (or to the state capitals) in considerable numbers to see their representatives. Congressmen and senators from districts near Washington are particularly likely to have a high degree of interpersonal contacts with constituents. A congressman from southern Maryland or northern Virginia may see constituents daily and in fairly large numbers. They come to his office in downtown Washington, or they call him on the telephone. Similarly, congressmen are frequently in their district offices (the best illustration of this being the New York City members of the so-called Tuesday–Thursday Club, who spend midweek in Washington and the rest of the week in their city offices), where they hold forth for constituents. In recent years, increases in allowances for congressional staff and facilities have made it possible for members of Congress to maintain district or state offices to facilitate regular contacts with constituents. In addition, Congress has increased appropriations for members' travel to their states and districts, so that the legislative branch appropriations bill, for instance, provided House members with twenty-six free trips home for the 1976 fiscal year. Beyond that, many members return to their districts at their own expense, and spend every weekend in their district offices.

The Mail

Although personal contact with constituents is apparently the channel of legislator-constituent communication most relied upon, the most regular and pervasive is the mail. The revolution in mass political letter-writing that occurred in the 1930s had a tremendous effect upon congressional mail. According to reports in the *New York Times,* incoming congressional mail reached 50,000 pieces daily in early 1934, and by February of the following year, 40,000 pieces had gone to the Senate alone. The *Times* reported estimates by congressmen that their mail in 1946 had risen 100 percent over the last prewar session, and in 1954, the Senate postmaster estimated incoming mail at 25 percent higher than it had been the preceding year.[7] It has been estimated that the House post office handled nearly 23 million pieces of incoming mail in 1962.[8] Senator Hubert Humphrey's experience illustrates the increasing mail load: "In my first year in the Senate—1949 —an average of 150 letters were received each day. Today (April 1963), the daily average is between 800 and 1,000 letters."[9] In more recent years, the volume of mail to and from Congress has escalated enormously. The Postal Service has estimated that it processed 190 million pieces of mail sent from Congress in 1970 at a cost of $11.2 million, and that the 1976 volume would be 322 million pieces of mail at a cost of $46.1 million. A 1973 Harris survey indicated that 74 percent of Americans reported having received a mailing or letter from their congressman and 59 percent reported receiving mail from their senator.[10]

At the same time, the percentage of a congressman's or a senator's constituents who write is small, although probably growing. Various polls over the past thirty years indicate that the percentage of Americans saying that they had at some time written or wired their congressman, senator, or other public official has seldom risen above 15 percent, and the overwhelming majority of letters written come from a very small proportion of adult Americans.[11] The constituents from whom a member of Congress receives mail are not likely to constitute a representative sample of opinions in his constituency. Letter writers differ significantly from the general population in occupational status, education, and level of political activity. Metropolitan legislators receive disproportionately more mail than their brethren from rural districts because people who live in urban areas are more inclined to be letter writers.[12] On some issues, so few constituents may write that legislators get virtually no guidance from the mail about constituency opinions.

As a result, congressional mail is not likely to be a good estimate of public opinion in a legislator's constituency. For instance, business leaders are more likely than others to write their congressmen. In a study of foreign-trade legislation, a sample of business leaders selected from the heads of firms with more than 100 employees was questioned about writing congressmen. The investigation revealed that:

> three-fourths of our sample said that at some time they had communicated with Congress on some issue other than foreign-trade policy. By size of firm the percentages were 88 (large), 79 (medium), and 71 (small). By a large margin, the heads of business organizations are more inclined than the average citizen to act on the assumption that one writes his representative or senator on matters of public policy in which he is concerned.[13]

There are some pieces of evidence on specific issues of the inaccuracy of the mail as an estimate of public opinion.[14] A legislator who relies heavily on the mail as a channel of communications with his constituents and who is not aware of the potential distortions it can represent may be bewildered by adverse reactions.

Massive letter-writing campaigns, often inspired by pressure groups, have varying effects under different conditions. If mail is demonstrably inspired, it may be heavily discounted by the legislator. If a legislator is unaccustomed to getting large amounts of mail from his constituents, a massive influx of mail may influence his behavior considerably. Thus, southern congressmen, who get less mail than their colleagues from northern states, were heavily influenced by the large amount of constituent mail on foreign-trade legislation in 1955, much of it inspired by the American Cotton Manufacturers Institute.[15] Furthermore, the extent of constituent interest in and support for a legislative proposal may be highly overestimated by legislators if the influx of mail is great. For instance, sensitivity among United States senators to the Bricker amendment issue appears to have been primarily the result of the large amount of mail they received, especially during 1954, even though polls indicated very little general public interest in this issue.[16]

Congressional mail is very diverse in tone, subject matter, quality, and content. A sizable proportion of the mail is *junk*—press releases, printed materials, magazines, and other printed propaganda material. In addition, members receive a considerable amount of *fan* mail—requests for autographs or photographs. This kind of mail is increasing in volume. Again, a relatively small but regular volume of *crank* and *crayon* mail is received by congressmen. A letter addressed in crayon is quickly spotted and (unless it is from a child) is likely to have been written by a constituent who is living in an institution where sharp pencils are not permitted. The crank mail is often annoying to congressmen and their staffs, although some of it is unwittingly witty. A constituent once wrote to Senator Bartlett (D-Alaska): "I voted for you 3 times and I think you are wonderful. Please send me $900 at once so I can buy an ice box and repaint my car. P.S. The 3 times I voted for you were in the election of 1946."[17] Another wrote Congressman Arends (R-Ill.): "I understand that you have free mailing privileges. I am sending you all my Christmas cards. Would you be good enough to drop them in the mail for me?" A young man once wrote to Senator Chaves (D-N.M.): "Although I'm not through school yet, I'm interested in a Political Career. By a slight oversight and through no fault of my own, my Father and Mother were never married. Some people tell me Congress is just the place for me. What do you think?" Although the amount of junk, fan, and crank mail varies in volume from time to time and from member to member, it has been estimated that on the average, about a fourth of the congressional mail is of these kinds.[18]

Another large category of congressional mail is *inspired* or *stimulated* by private interests, public officials, lobby organizations, and the like. On the average, a substantial proportion of the congressional mail is inspired, perhaps as much as a fourth of it. However, on some occasions and with regard to specific issues, the proportion of inspired mail is much higher. During congressional consideration of reciprocal-trade legislation in 1954, it has been estimated that 40 percent of the protectionist mail was stimulated by the Westinghouse, Dow, Monsanto, and Pittsburgh Plate Glass companies and that three-fourths of the antiprotectionist mail was inspired by the League of Women Voters.[19] Inspired mail is usually easy to identify because of the similarity of the messages. But what is stimulated mail is not always easy to define; the voluminous mail in 1959 during congressional consideration of labor-reform legislation (the Landrum-Griffin Act) was overwhelmingly inspired by the labor unions, the trade associations, corporations, the President, Robert Kennedy, and Jack Paar, host of the Tonight Show on television, as well as by congressmen themselves.

Between one-third and one-half of the congressional mail relates stories of distress, asks for redress of grievances, or requests help. This *case* and *issue* mail is various, including requests for information or for statements of the congressman's viewpoint, as well as for help with administrative agencies or for the introduction of private legislation. The case mail involves regular intervention by members of Congress in the administrative process and requires members to develop established relationships with administrative agencies. A considerable amount of executive branch time is consumed in the processing of case mail to congressmen, and some members believe that it is in this process that Congress most effectively engages in surveillance, or oversight, of the administration.[20]

In addition to the evidence in Table 13.1, there is overwhelming testimony in the comments of senators and representatives concerning the importance of the mail, and most of them insist that every letter from a constituent must be answered.[21] A good illustration of the importance of the mail for members of Congress is provided by congressional action on foreign-trade legislation in the mid-1950s:

Despite the fact that, on issue after issue, the mail has been shown to be not representative—in 1954–1955 it was about ten-to-one protectionist—and despite the fact that there is no reason to suspect that letter-writing on any given issue has any relationship to voting or political influence, the mail is nevertheless seen as the voice of the district or state. As is to be expected, many congressmen and senators run counter to the mail in obedience to dictates of conscience, party, or committee; but, when they do so, many of them appear to think that they are defying something very significant.[22]

Beyond this, it was found that

the mail is the congressman's main source of information on foreign-trade policy. Whenever we asked a congressman if he had heard anything about foreign-trade policy, he almost inevitably answered in terms of mail. We cannot say whether this is true of other issues, but it is our distinct impression that congressmen are far more conscious of what the mail says about foreign-trade legislation than they are about any other exposition of foreign-trade matters.[23]

So significant is the mail to members of Congress that they tend to inspire a considerable amount of mail themselves:

Once a congressman becomes accustomed to a heavy mail, he tends to worry if it drops off. So important does he regard mail to his success that he actively seeks it. The special mailings to particular groups, for example, constitute an important means by which legislators try to stimulate correspondence with residents of their districts.[24]

In their campaigns, members of Congress often urge voters to write them. Congressmen frequently initiate correspondence with constituents by mailing letters of condolence or congratulation to persons whose names are culled from the columns of local newspapers. Over 90 percent of the members of Congress send newsletters to the residents of their districts or states (the franking privilege permits them to do this at public expense), and the newsletters often contain explicit invitations to reply. The legislator's mailing list may be his most prized and closely guarded possession.[25]

Why is the mail given a position of such importance? The best answer to this question is found in an article by Lewis Dexter:

In the first place, members of their staffs spend an enormous amount of time on mail. And having invested that time on it, they like to feel that it means something.

Second, a great deal of the time Congressmen operate in a pretty complete vacuum so far as the voters of their district go. Most people seem to know what they are supposed to do (if even in some cases merely so that they can protest or revolt). The mail gives a sense that one is doing something that excites large numbers of people.

Third, . . . many Congressmen are irritated and annoyed because they come to Washington expecting to do and be something important; and because of the complexity of government and the seniority system they find they are hampered and shut off from effective action at every turn. Granted this rather general exasperation, handling mail is almost the only thing on which a Congressman finds himself quite free; he can write any sort of letters he likes without let or hindrance from anybody. Thus letter writing becomes a disproportionately significant aspect of his job, for it represents the freedom and importance that he thought he would find when he got to Washington (but rarely does).

Fourth, most Congressmen genuinely treasure the right of petition and the opportunity of the individual citizen to complain about mistreatment. This right has great importance on many issues where bureaucrats mistreat individuals or overlook individual rights.

Fifth, whether realistically or not, some Congressmen actually believe and many others like to feel that on any issue of national significance, rational communication between them and any constituent is possible. For this reason they spend a quite irrational amount of time on correspondence that is essentially academic in the sense that it is fairly clear that no political or legislative purpose is really served by the time they give it.[26]

Congressional Polls

The use of polling methods to get estimates of the views of constituents has increased markedly since World War II. Although only about one-fourth of the congressmen interviewed in 1958 indicated that they relied upon opinion polls (see Table 13.1), some members of Congress apparently give much more than the average weight to polls. In the mid-1950s, 15 percent of the members of the House of Representatives indicated that they had used constituency polls; by 1961 this proportion had increased to 30 percent; and by 1970, 74 percent reported taking constituency polls.[27] The relatively greater attention given to polls by some members is indicated in the comments of one congressman:

> Since people more often write letters when they are against something, mail can be a useful reflection of the intensity and degree of organization of the opposition to a particular issue. *But I would put greater—though also limited—trust in polls and surveys.* Most useful, I think, are the views of my friends and associates in the district. And I place great stock in the impressions I have received myself from many years in public life.[28] (italics added)

A study of the delegation of representatives from one state (Washington) indicates that congressmen from that state attach a great deal more than the average importance to their polls.[29]

Congressional polling of constituents ordinarily involves staff personnel in the congressman's office in preparing and mailing a questionnaire to each constituent on the mailing list, which usually includes a disproportionate number of the congressman's avid supporters. Some congressmen have sought to develop more-or-less refined sampling methods for their polls; in other cases, members have persuaded district newspapers to run their questionnaires, urging readers to return them to the congressman. In any event, the sampling problems involved in the polling done by most congressmen are enormous, and the representative adequacy of most congressional polls is, at best, unknown. Still, some members claim to rely heavily upon them, referring to the poll results as indicating "definite trends in the thinking of the people of the district."[30] Generally, when question-naires are used, thousands are mailed to district residents, and thousands are returned. Processing these returns makes for very substantial staff effort, but the large numbers may serve to convince congressmen who use polls that the results are representative of constituent opinions.

Another source of difficulty in congressional polling stems from the questions asked. Because the polling device may be used for public relations or campaign purposes or to reinforce the congressman's own preconceptions, as well as to get information, biased or distorted questions are often asked. In addition, congres-sional polls often include questions that call for a quite unreasonable amount of knowledge on the part of the ordinary citizen. Illustrations of these two difficulties in survey questions can be found in a 1962 poll by a New York congressman. He asked one biased question: "Do you believe that United States and free world policies have been that of vacillation, conciliation, appeasement, and retreat?" Of those constituents who replied, 79 percent said "Yes." He also asked a question that called for a very great deal of technical information: "Admiral Rickover states our Navy is technologically obsolete. Do you favor equipping naval vessels with ICBM's for ICBM mobility and dispersal advantages?" About 90 percent who replied said "Yes."[31]

The mails and polling do not, of course, exhaust the channels of communica-tion between legislator and constituent. A legislator is very often a public relations man, and he may pay a great deal of attention to the press in his district, county, or state. Both national and state legislators have the newspapers, especially the weekly press, at their disposal as a potential channel of communication with constituents; and legislators often utilize the press as a means of gauging public sentiment. Furthermore, radio and television broadcasting of reports to the peo-ple has become common legislative practice. In spite of his low visibility to his constituents in general, the American legislator is substantially concerned with his communications to and from them.

In the face of their relatively low saliency among constituents, the concern of American legislators with constituency communications and their representative image is, in a sense, contradictory. This can be explained, in part, by the tendency of legislators to overestimate their public visibility. The constituents with whom the legislator has contacts personally, through the mail, or via the communica-tions media are not likely to be representative of the adult population of his district as a whole, or even of the voting population. The legislator is likely to perceive his constituents, not as atomized, but as organized into groups or blocs. His contacts are with group leaders or with constituents who are more politically active and informed than the average citizen.

But the legislator's concern with constituency opinion, even though he may realize that he is not very visible to many of his constituents, has a sound basis in the electoral facts of life. In the first place, the degree of party regularity in the voting behavior of his constituents is substantial. The legislator "starts with a stratum of hardened party voters, and if the stratum is broad enough he can have a measurable influence on his chance of survival simply by attracting a small additional element of the electorate—or by not losing a larger one."[32] The legis-lator's communications with constituents and his legislative record may have a substantial bearing on his success at the polls, even though most of his constituents are not aware of his record and are only marginally aware of his existence. In the second place, the nomination process itself involves a meaningful, although less tangible, kind of electoral sanction, where "the customary norms of the constituency which must be met if a person is to be 'available' as a candidate limit the field to those candidates with broad views consonant with those of the district."[33] Finally, the image of the legislator is not created for all constituents by way of direct communication; rather, the legislator's image is filtered through agents acting as intermediaries between legislator and constituent—the news media, interest groups, ethnic groups, and party organizations. Although the legislator's own response, in terms of his perception of constituency expectations, may not be directly reflected to his constituents, it may affect the cues given to them by these intermediaries.

There are also intangible cultural factors in the consonance of outlook between legislators and constituents, to the extent that such agreement exists. The legislator tends to respond to his constituency in the way he organizes his work and represents himself to "his people," even though they may know little about him or his record and even though he may have little evidence of their opinions through external communication. The legislator may have very reliable intuitions about his constituents because he shares their cultural values, and he may respond in their terms "without any conscious interchange of ideas or beliefs."[34]

The legislative office in America is a response-oriented institution. Its principal response is to the constituency. We shall refer to the sum total of behavior patterns associated with the legislative office—the responses of representative and staff—as the *institutionalized legislator*.

THE INSTITUTIONALIZED LEGISLATOR

Legislative service is not a leisurely way of life. In general, legislators are harried men; they ordinarily have more work to do than they can do thoroughly in the time available. The legislative work load has increased substantially since the 1930s, although errand-running or service activities occupy a large share of the time of the legislator's office.[35] These increases in the burden of legislative work have given rise to the institutionalized legislator. The institutionalization of the legislative office can be seen as varying from the lonely state legislator who, virtually without staff assistance of any kind, performs by himself as best he can both service and legislative work to the United States senator with a highly organized office and staff of forty or fifty assistants and secretaries. The complex institution that is known to the outside world as "Senator Javits" is, merely to cite one example, a highly organized administrative apparatus.

The legislative office, especially at the national level, has become fairly highly bureaucratized. The state legislative office is more individualistic and less highly organized, although this varies from state to state. Bureaucratic tendencies not unlike those observable for congressmen have developed noticeably in an increasing number of states. And in most states, the offices of presiding officers and committee chairmen are relatively highly organized.

The office of a member of Congress is largely occupied with constituent-service activities. "Most congressional offices," writes a student of the House of Representatives, "are more concerned with activities not strictly legislative in character than they are with legislative ones." Although "representatives generally assign as much of the extra legislative work as possible to their staff," still "constituent-oriented activities usually occupy the major portion of their own time."[36] Most of the work of a congressman's office is performed in the District of Columbia, ordinarily with inadequate physical facilities, but most, if not all, members maintain offices in their own districts as well. In 1975, House members were authorized to maintain as many as three district offices, either located in federal buildings or, if acceptable office space in government facilities is not available, through the rental of private offices. Congressmen were authorized to spend a rental allowance of up to $7,200, and allocated $15,000 for office equipment and furniture for district offices.[37] Even so, the facilities available to a congressman are seldom adequate to meet the demands placed upon the office. According to one congressman:

> It is true that we just don't have much time to legislate around here ... all this nonlegislative work which our office gets means that I don't get any help from anybody there on research or speeches or things like that. My staff is busy taking care of constituent matters, case work, and such things. My press man helps some on political speeches but not very much. It would be helpful to have someone who could assist me in carrying out my legislative role.[38]

Senate offices are larger than those in the House office buildings, and some are the fastest-growing bureaucracies in Washington. A fairly typical Senate office has been described in the following way:

> One walks in the door and there is a receptionist, eager to have you sign the guest book, to give you a gallery visitor's card and a tourist's map of Washington, to talk about "home." In the same narrow room, decorated with pictures of the state's industries and tourist attractions, are three or four other girls ... typing and answering the constantly ringing telephone. Next door, in another room or two there are more typists, the senator's administrative assistant, a legislative assistant or two, and perhaps an executive secretary. Beyond this, a tranquil oasis amid the noise and clutter of the "outer" and "working" rooms, is the senator's private office.[39]

House and Senate offices seem fairly similar in appearance, but in actuality there are considerable variations among them. Members of Congress are free, within the limitations of space and their office-expense and clerk-hire allowances, to organize their offices as they wish. No two offices are quite the same, and staff members with the same titles may have different duties and responsibilities. On the House side:

> There is no clear pattern in office organization, particularly where the duties of the top assistant are concerned. Some first assistants perform little more than routine responsibilities; others are in every sense advisers and assistants. As one congressman said, "I think every office is run differently and shaped after the personality of the congressman."[40]

Donald R. Matthews argues that "the way a senator staffs and organizes his office," reveals "a great deal about him as a man, what his problems and preoccupations are, and how he defines his role."[41]

The most time-consuming activity of the legislative office is the processing of the mail. Most members of Congress answer all mail from their districts or states, and some answer all letters whether they are from constituents or not. The regular constituent issue mail is divided into those that can be answered by use of one of the standard form letters and those that the congressman or senator ought to see. The case mail is usually handled by an assistant who specializes in its processing; in Senate offices where more than one case-mail expert is employed, there may be area specialists: one for veterans' cases, one for social security, another for immigration cases. Most of the routine mail can be answered with form letters, a process that is described accurately in the following commentary about one Senate office where

> about five hundred letters daily are opened, classified, and tabulated by some half-dozen staff members. They decide which letters can be answered with form replies, which need the attention of one of the Senator's assistants, and which few the Senator must see himself. (He once said that if he had to see more than 4 percent of his mail, his staff wasn't doing its job.) His form replies have, in general, been drafted by an assistant, but approved by the Senator. They have been transcribed onto player-piano-like rolls which operate electric typewriters, so that a typist need type only the address and the salutation and turn the machine loose to finish the letter. This is done in one of the rooms which house a pool of automatic typewriters in the basement of the Old Senate Office Building. When the letter and envelope have been completed, an automatic pen traces the Senator's signature, in ink, from a matrix cut from an authentic signature. So the constituent back home gets what appears to be a letter dictated and addressed to him personally, and signed by the Senator. In fact, the Senator never saw either the constituent's incoming letter or his reply. He will, however, see a monthly tabulation of letters received.[42]

Members of the House of Representatives are more likely to read their mail than senators because it is a more manageable job, and some regard reading their own mail as an important aspect of maintaining constituency contact. But in many House offices, it is impossible for members to read more than a few selected letters, and the use of the automatic typewriter and signature machine is increasing, a sign of the bureaucratic times.

But the fact that the processing of congressional mail is more bureaucratic than it used to be does not mean that congressmen are any less concerned about it. Being unable to read it all worries some congressmen; they begin to feel they are losing touch. One congressman's comments reflected this source of anxiety with regard to his case mail:

> Unless you retain a fairly direct interest in the so-called routine case work you may find the staff takes it too much in stride, without realizing that for the individual involved it is a matter of great importance. I sometimes find an irritated letter from a constituent saying, "Why haven't you been able to help me?" or "Why haven't I gotten an answer?" Had I known about those cases perhaps I would have been

able to accelerate them more than the staff did. So, I always find myself looking over their shoulder saying, "What is this case?" and asking them to put anything unusual on my desk.[43]

It would be a mistake if the impression were left that legislative life is a kind of Hobbesian nightmare. Legislators often complain about the meager political awareness of their constituents, and congressmen, in particular, about the tremendous burden of nonlegislative work upon which they must concentrate most of their time. But generally speaking, the service activities are accepted by congressmen as part of their job; and for those employed in a legislative office, life is never dull or unduly exasperating. The excitement of legislative politics comes from being in the swim, even if the main arena is some distance off.

CONSTITUENTS' SUPPORT FOR THE LEGISLATURE

We have seen that the American legislator is quite highly attuned to his constituency and that at the same time, substantial proportions of constituents exhibit very low levels of saliency vis-à-vis the legislature or their representative. These empirical realities create great difficulties in interpretation when representative-constituent relationships are thought of exclusively in terms of public policies. If a system of representation requires that both representatives and constituents deal with one another in policy-oriented terms, then the American evidence suggests that both exhibit serious deficiencies. Observations that focus exclusively upon the input of policy demands and the presumed response of representatives to such demands are not, however, likely to account adequately for legislator-constituent relationships.[44]

Constituents provide support for the legislature both in the specific senses of voting in legislative elections, casting their vote for particular candidates, or evaluating the general performance of a particular legislative session, and in the diffuse sense of supporting the legislative body as an institutionalized component of the regime (see Chapter 1). Support for the legislature in a particular constituency may be substantially independent of policy-demand considerations. Diffuse support for legislative institutions in the United States is comparatively high. Congress and state legislatures constitute important representative symbols for most Americans; there are no significant efforts reflected either in political movements or public sentiments to make fundamental changes in the structure or character of legislative representation in the United States.

Specific support for American legislatures appears to fluctuate quite a bit over time, although rather little is known about the causes or consequences of these perturbations. If performance evaluation is used as an indicator of specific legislative support, it is possible to make crude assertions about changes in specific support for the national legislature. Figure 13.1 arrays data for recent years and shows that approval of congressional general performance increased from 1963 to 1965 and then quite regularly declined to a point at which, by 1971, only about a fourth of Americans could approve congressional performance. (The data are taken from Harris surveys in which respondents were asked: "How would you rate the job Congress did in [year]—excellent, pretty good, only fair, or poor?") It certainly is not easy to interpret these fluctuations in specific support for Congress in exclusively policy-related terms, although the temporary increase in congressional support in the early 1960s may be accounted for, in part, by the very active role of Congress in inaugurating and enacting sweeping new legislation during that period. But the decline in congressional support since 1965 is difficult to explain. That support for congressional performance and approval of the job being done by the President may be associated is suggested to some extent by comparing public approval of both (percentages of Americans who approve of the job the President has done are also shown in Figure 13.1), but it seems clear that approval of the President and positive evaluation of Congress do not necessarily occur simultaneously.

Generalized, or diffuse, public support for Congress has not been analyzed with particular care. Both the Gallup poll and the Harris survey have asked national samples over the past few years how much respect or confidence people have in Congress and in other institutions. The alarmist headlines produced by the results of some of these polls undoubtedly exaggerate the case, although the evidence does seem to indicate a decline in public confidence in, or support for, Congress and just about all other public institutions. In spite of the decline in confidence, the best evidence does show relatively high levels of public confidence in Congress, permitting the assertion that confidence in Congress as an institution is considerably higher than the level of approval of its performance. As Table 13.2 indicates, 68 percent of a national sample interviewed in 1974 exhibited at least "a fair amount" of confidence in Congress (in response to the question, "How much trust and confidence do you have at the present in the legislative branch, consisting of the U.S. Senate and the House of Representatives?"). That proportion represented virtually no change from responses to the same question in 1972.

FIGURE 13.1   Specific Support for the President and Congress, 1963–1975

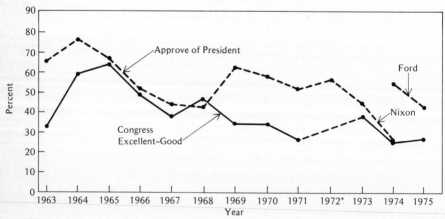

*Congressional support data not available for 1972.

SOURCES: Harris Survey and Gallup Poll.

TABLE 13.2   Diffuse Support for Congress (In percentages)

DEGREE OF TRUST AND CONFIDENCE	1972			1974		
	Con-gress	Presi-dent	Courts	Con-gress	Presi-dent	Courts
A great deal	14	27	17	12	13	17
A fair amount	58	49	49	56	29	54
Not very much	23	18	23	24	36	20
None at all	2	5	7	5	19	5
Don't know	3	1	4	3	3	4
Total	100	100	100	100	100	100
Number		1,806			1,865	

SOURCE: Data for 1972 are from William Watts and Lloyd A. Free, *State of the Nation* (New York, 1973), p. 240; data for 1974 are from William Watts and Lloyd A. Free, *State of the Nation* 1974 (Washington, D.C., 1974), p. 73. Both of these studies are based upon surveys conducted by the Gallup organization.

Table 13.2 also shows the very large drop in confidence in the chief executive precipitated by the Watergate affair and the discrediting of President Nixon.

Research conducted in Iowa in 1966–1967 makes it possible to examine support for a state legislature. G. R. Boynton, Samuel C. Patterson, and Ronald D. Hedlund conducted extensive interviews in that state, gathering data on attitudes toward the state legislature from the general public, attentive constituents, party leaders, lobbyists, and legislators themselves (discussed in Chapter 4).[45] They were asked to evaluate the performance of the legislature; their responses are shown in Table 13.3. It can be noted that their evaluations fall very heavily in the middle categories ("good job" and "fair job") and that differences between those in the mass public and those in politically elite groups are not very great. However, in the Iowa study it was found that evaluation of the performance of a particular legislative session was highly affected by the political party identification of the constituents; Republicans rated a Republican-controlled session highly, and Democrats rated a Democratic-controlled session highly. So it does appear that at least under the conditions existing in Iowa, constituents evaluate

TABLE 13.3   Specific Support for the Iowa Legislature in the Mass Public and Among Political Elites, 1966–1967 (In percentages)

SPECIFIC LEGISLATIVE SUPPORT	MASS PUBLIC	PARTY LEADERS	LOBBYISTS	ATTENTIVE CONSTITUENTS
Excellent job	4.8	5.0	2.2	7.3
Good job	49.9	53.2	54.4	61.5
Fair job	41.2	33.4	33.3	25.0
Poor job	4.0	8.4	10.0	6.3
Total*	99.9	100.0	100.0	100.1
Number	931	91	96	479

*Excludes respondents who had no opinion.
SOURCE: Samuel C. Patterson, Ronald D. Hedlund, and G.R. Boynton, *Representatives and Represented* (New York, 1975), p. 51.

the specific performance of their legislature very much through the tinted specta-
cles of their partisan attachments.

Evaluations of the performance of state legislatures based on sample surveys
have been conducted in a number of states in recent years, and especially during
1968 in connection with the Comparative State Elections Project headquartered
at the University of North Carolina at Chapel Hill. The results of such studies,
shown in Table 13.4, indicate that evaluations of legislative performance varied
considerably from state to state when citizens in thirteen states were interviewed
in the fall of 1968. And, the table also shows the substantial variations that can
occur within states, illustrated by the figures for Minnesota and Iowa. In some
states—Alabama, North Carolina, South Dakota, Ohio, and Minnesota in 1968,
and Iowa in 1966—about half or more of the states' citizens expressed approval
of the legislatures' performances. Nevertheless, on the whole, these legislative

TABLE 13.4 Specific Support for Legislatures in Fourteen States

| STATE | YEAR | PERFORMANCE EVALUATION* | | |
		Percent Who Approve	Percent Who Disapprove	Percent Who Had No Opinion
Massachusetts	1968	32	57	12
New York	1968	29	56	15
Pennsylvania	1968	40	50	11
Illinois	1968	44	46	9
Minnesota	1965	26	44	30
	1968	49	41	10
	1971	19	56	25
	1973	37	51	12
	1974	35	48	17
Iowa	1959	28	48	24
	1963	25	60	15
	1965	28	53	19
	1966	51	42	7
	1967	20	64	16
	1968	48	33	19
	1969	22	53	25
	1972	29	29	42
Ohio	1968	55	34	12
South Dakota	1968	49	43	8
California	1968	33	51	16
Florida	1968	37	50	13
North Carolina	1968	51	36	13
Texas	1968	46	42	12
Alabama	1968	52	31	14
Louisiana	1968	47	43	11
National U.S. Sample	1968	41	41	18

*The usual question asked is, "In general, how would you rate the job the state legislature has
done . . . excellent, pretty good, only fair, or poor?" In this table, "approve" includes excellent
and pretty good ratings; "disapprove" includes fair and poor.

SOURCES: Except for Iowa, the 1968 percentages are from Merle Black, David M. Kovenock,
and William C. Reynolds, *Political Attitudes in the Nation and the States* (Chapel Hill, N.C.,
1974), p. 186; Iowa data come from surveys conducted by the Iowa Poll, reported in news
releases for the *Des Moines Register and Tribune;* Minnesota data are from news releases of the
Minnesota Poll for the *Minneapolis Tribune.*

ratings indicate considerable dissatisfaction with the state legislatures, in some cases very one-sidedly so.

It may be that an important reason for negative evaluation of legislative performance is the belief that legislators waste time. When Minnesotans were asked in 1965 why they disapproved of the legislature's performance, a third indicated the belief that legislators wasted time and did not get enough done. Iowans interviewed in 1968 were asked whether they thought the legislature made good use of its time or wasted it; 59 percent indicated they thought the legislature wasted time, taking too much time deciding issues and spending their time on trivial, unimportant things.[46] At the same time, individual legislators tend to be more favorably rated than the legislature as a whole. At least that is the implication of results of the Minnesota Poll in 1971, when Minnesotans were asked, "Do you have any idea what kind of job your representative in the Minnesota House of Representatives did this year? Did he do a good job or a poor one?" Less than a third of the respondents knew what kind of a job their representative did, but of those who did, 42 percent rated his performance as excellent, 33 percent as fair, and 23 percent as poor.[47] Inasmuch as less than a fifth of Minnesotans had rated the whole legislature as excellent or good, it seems that disapproval of the performance of the legislative body does not necessarily devolve upon individual legislators.

Diffuse support for the legislature on the part of its constituents is difficult to measure, since in doing so, it is necessary to get beneath the evaluation of a particular legislative session to probe the underlying reservoir of good will in the constituency directed to the legislature as an institution. Such an attempt was made in the Iowa study, in the course of extensive interviewing. Diffuse legislative support was measured by asking respondents to what extent they were predisposed to comply with laws enacted by their state legislature and whether or not they favored fundamental change in the legislative power structure or the power of the legislature in relation to other agencies. This research made it possible to construct a diffuse legislative-support score for each respondent in the study. One of the distinctive findings of the analysis was that at least in this one state, underlying support for the legislative institution increased markedly across the social and political structure of a state's population; constituents with high socioeconomic status and those who were in the politically active subculture exhibited the highest levels of support for the legislature. Figure 13.2 depicts the increase in legislative support that occurred in Iowa across different levels of political strata. The profound influence on variations in legislative support of socioeconomic status and political involvement persisted even when other possible factors (such as urban or rural residence) were taken into account. Also, racial differences could not be investigated in Iowa because of the very small percentage of racial minorities in the population. Furthermore, because there was no way to make comparisons, it was not certain whether Iowa was relatively high or low in the general level of legislative support among constituents.

In 1968, some of the basic data for this investigation were replicated in surveys in thirteen additional states. With this evidence, it was possible to locate states roughly in terms of general levels of legislative support and to explore some causes of variations in support, such as urbanism or racial differences. Statewide mean

FIGURE 13.2   Diffuse Support for the Legislature in Iowa Political Strata

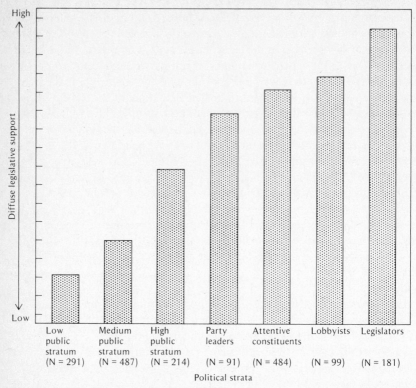

SOURCE: Samuel C. Patterson, Ronald D. Hedlund, and G. R. Boynton, *Representatives and Represented* (New York, 1975), p. 69.

support scores were constructed from interviews with 500 to 600 respondents in these states. The Iowa, California, and Minnesota legislatures ranked highest in public support; Ohio, Texas, Massachusetts, Pennsylvania, Illinois, Florida, North Carolina, and New York were in the middle; Louisiana, South Dakota, and Alabama ranked lowest. Variations from state to state in the relative level of support for the state legislature cannot be explored in detail here, but there are two interesting relationships that could not be developed adequately in the otherwise more elaborate and complex collection of data for Iowa: urban-rural differences in a metropolitanized state (New York) and racial differences in a southern state with a large black population (Alabama).

In the Iowa analysis of citizens' support for the legislature, there were no significant differences in degree of support between those living in cities, those in towns, or those on the farm. The same is true in other states, including California. Here it is not possible to develop the variety of effects of the milieu in which people live on their support for the legislature, but the case of New York is one in which levels of support for the state legislature vary quite substantially between those who live in the metropolis and those who live in small communities and on farms. Although there is no direct evidence that definitively accounts for the rural-urban differences, the conflict between New York City (where most of the "large city" respondents live) and the rest of the state appears to be reflected here fairly directly.[48] New York City dwellers may represent a generally alienated population, or they may identify themselves with the city political system and regard the legislature in Albany as "the enemy." Support for the legislature in New York is relatively low on a statewide basis mainly because of the low level of support for it among residents of the largest cities and suburbs.

In Alabama, urban-rural differences are of no great consequence—the distinctly low level of support for the legislature is relatively evenly spread among residents of cities, towns, and farms. What is most interesting about Alabama is the way in which racial differences combine with both socioeconomic status and political participation to produce variations in support. In Alabama, there is almost no correlation for the whole population between differences in socioeconomic status and support or between variations in political activism and support. High-status, highly politically involved Alabamians are not significantly more supportive than those lower in the social and political strata. What is more, the average levels of support are about the same among blacks and whites. However, socioeconomic and political stratification work quite differently in influencing the support levels of blacks and whites. These differences are depicted in Figure 13.3. When blacks and whites are analyzed separately, the relationships between both socioeconomic status and political participation and diffuse legislative support are, for the whites, comparable with those in the Iowa study (although the relationships are somewhat weaker: correlations are .19 for political involvement and .18 for socioeconomic status for Alabama whites). But for blacks, these two factors work in the opposite direction (correlations are −.19 for political participation and −.28 for socioeconomic status for blacks). In general, the higher Alabama whites are in the social strata and the more politically active they are, the higher their degree of support for the legislature. But social and political life in Alabama is such that for blacks, the opposite is the case. The higher the black's location in the social and political strata, the lower the tendency to support the legislature.

Although Americans usually do not give their state legislature's performance high ratings, a very supportive orientation toward the legislature as an institution is part of the American's sentiments of legitimacy toward the regime. Even citizens of a state who think the last session of the legislature did a poor job are very likely to support the legislature as an appropriate institution for enacting the laws. This kind of basic support for the legislative institution is especially marked in states that are highly competitive politically—where open conflict and partisan competitiveness help to stimulate and legitimize the legislative process. And, legislative support is generally greatest among citizens who are the most politically active and knowledgeable. Paradoxical as it may seem, Americans tend to be very supportive of the legislature as an institution, and, at the same time, often quite prone to react to its imperfections whenever it meets. If the immediate constituency environment of the legislator seems hostile to him, he may take some comfort in knowing that while the legislature may be disapproved of in practice, it is overwhelmingly supported in principle!

There is much to be learned about the structure and correlates of constituents' attitudes and predispositions with regard to their representatives. We have illustrated only some of the possibilities for analysis and indicated only some of the

FIGURE 13.3 Diffuse Support for the Alabama Legislature Among Blacks and Whites by Political Participation and Socioeconomic Status

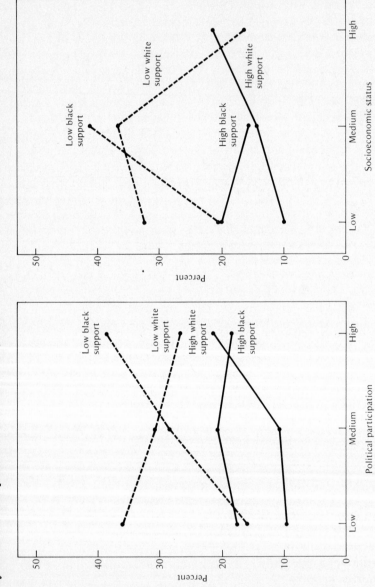

complexities of comparative research in this realm. The American legislator is, for reasons explored in many places in this book, able to function independently of his constituents in many respects. His office and the legislature in which he serves have become highly institutionalized. Constituents at large do affect the behavior of representatives, and legislators do pay attention to their constituents. But the nexus between the two is a complicated matter, indeed. American legislatures appear to generate very substantial support for the institution in their constituencies, although such support certainly varies among states and probably over time, as well. These variations are most likely not extraordinary, although the full consequences of intersystem differences in constituent support are not known.

NOTES

1. See, for example, Angus Campbell et al., *The American Voter* (New York, 1960); and William N. McPhee and William A. Glaser, eds., *Public Opinion and Congressional Elections* (New York, 1962).

2. The figures in this and the following paragraph can be found, developed in greater detail, in Hazel Gaudet Erskine, "The Polls: Textbook Knowledge," *Public Opinion Quarterly* 27 (1963):137–138; *Gallup Political Index* 5 (1965):18; and *Gallup Opinion Index* 64 (1967):10.

3. Donald E. Stokes and Warren E. Miller, "Party Government and the Saliency of Congress," *Public Opinion Quarterly* 26 (1962):540.

4. Ibid., pp. 542–543.

5. *Gallup Opinion Index* 20 (1967):17–19. See also Morris Showel, "Political Consciousness and Attitudes in the State of Washington," *Public Opinion Quarterly* 17 (1953): 394–400.

6. John C. Wahlke et al., *The Legislative System* (New York, 1962), pp. 296 and 301–302.

7. Leila A. Sussmann, *Dear FDR: A Study of Political Letter-writing* (Totowa, N.J., 1963), p. 12.

8. Charles L. Clapp, *The Congressman: His Work as He Sees It* (Washington, D.C., 1963), p. 69.

9. Hubert H. Humphrey, "Modernizing Congress," *AFL-CIO American Federationist* (April 1963):2.

10. Estimates of congressional mail are reported in the *Congressional Quarterly Weekly Report* 33 (May 24, 1975):1116. The 1973 Harris survey results are from U.S. Senate, Committee on Government Operations, *Confidence and Concern: Citizens View American Government*, Part 2 (Washington, D.C., 1973), p. 373.

11. Sussmann, *Dear FDR*, p. 134. Also, see Robert S. Erikson and Norman R. Luttbeg, *American Public Opinion: Its Origins, Content, and Impact* (New York, 1973), p. 273.

12. An analysis of some of the general characteristics of letter writers and non–letter writers is in ibid., pp. 135–138.

13. Raymond A. Bauer, Ithiel de Sola Pool, and Lewis A. Dexter, *American Business and Public Policy: The Politics of Foreign Trade* (New York, 1963), p. 201.

14. See, for example, Sussmann, *Dear FDR*, pp. 76–77; Rowena Wyant, "Voting Via the Senate Mailbag," *Public Opinion Quarterly* 5 (1941):359–383; L. E. Gleeck, "96 Congressmen Make Up Their Minds," *Public Opinion Quarterly* 4 (1940):3–24; and Robert A. Dahl, *Congress and Foreign Policy* (New York, 1950), pp. 34–35.

15. Bauer, Pool, and Dexter, *American Business and Public Policy*, pp. 359–361.

16. Malcolm E. Jewell, *Senatorial Politics and Foreign Policy* (Lexington, Ky., 1962), pp. 182–183.

17. The letters are reproduced in Juliet Lowell, *Dear Mr. Congressman* (New York 1948), pp. 12, 23, 38.

18. See Ellen Davis, "Don't Write Your Congressman, Unless . . . ," *Harper's,* June 1961, p. 13.

19. Bauer, Pool, and Dexter, *American Business and Public Policy,* p. 439.

20. See Donald R. Matthews, *U.S. Senators and Their World* (Chapel Hill, N.C., 1960), p. 225; and Clapp, *The Congressman,* pp. 75–84.

21. See Matthews, *U.S. Senators and Their World,* pp. 219–220; Clapp, *The Congressman,* pp. 73–74; Jerry Voorhis, *Confessions of a Congressman* (Garden City, N.Y., 1947), pp. 40–54; Al Toffler, "How Congressmen Make Up Their Minds," *Redbook,* February 1962, p. 129.

22. Bauer, Pool, and Dexter, *American Business and Public Policy,* p. 438.

23. Ibid., p. 436.

24. Clapp, *The Congressman,* p. 74.

25. Clapp, *The Congressman,* p. 89. For examples of outstanding congressional newsletters, see John W. Baker, ed., *Member of the House: Letters of a Congressman by Clem Miller* (New York, 1962), and Robert L. Peabody, ed., *Education of a Congressman: The Newsletters of Morris K. Udall* (Indianapolis, 1972).

26. Lewis A. Dexter, "What Do Congressmen Hear: The Mail," *Public Opinion Quarterly* 20 (1956):18.

27. Carl Hawver, "The Congressman and His Public Opinion Poll," *Public Opinion Quarterly* 18 (1954):125; and *The Congressman's Conception of His Role* (Washington, D.C., 1963), p. 102. See also Erikson and Luttbeg, *American Public Opinion,* p. 268.

28. Davis, "Don't Write Your Congressman, Unless . . . ," p. 20.

29. See John H. Kessel, "The Washington Congressional Delegation," *Midwest Journal of Political Science* 8 (1964):1–21.

30. Comment made by Representative Tom V. Moorehead (R-Ohio); see U.S., Congress, *Congressional Record* (daily), Appendix, 1962, p. A4033. For an analysis of one congressman's polling, see Frank V. Cantwell, "The Congressional Poll—Six Years' Experience," *Public Opinion Quarterly* 18 (1954):130–135.

31. See U.S., Congress, *Congressional Record* (daily), Appendix, 1962, p. A2789. See also Richard A. Brody and Edward R. Tufte, "Constituent-Congressional Communications on Fallout Shelters: The Congressional Polls," *Journal of Communication* 14 (1964): 34–49. For an extended analysis of congressional polling methods, including sampling and questionnaire construction, see Leonard A. Marascuilo and Harriett Amster, "Survey of 1961–1962 Congressional Polls," *Public Opinion Quarterly* 28 (1964):497–506; and Hawver, *The Congressman's Conception of His Role,* pp. 195–211.

32. Warren E. Miller and Donald E. Stokes, "Constituency Influence in Congress," *American Political Science Review* 57 (1963):55.

33. V. O. Key, Jr., *Public Opinion and American Democracy* (New York, 1961), p. 497.

34. Harold F. Gosnell, *Democracy: The Threshold of Freedom* (New York, 1948), pp. 137–138. For evidence that winners in legislative elections tend to have higher estimates of the civic competence of constituents than losers do, see John W. Kingdon, "Politicians' Beliefs About Voters," *American Political Science Review* 61 (1967):137–145.

35. Several descriptions of a day in the life of a legislator are available in the literature. For example, see Stephen K. Bailey and Howard D. Samuel, *Congress at Work* (New York, 1952), pp. 96–135; Baker, *Member of the House,* pp. 66–68; Matthews, *U.S. Senators and Their World,* pp. 80–81; and Voorhis, *Confessions of a Congressman,* pp. 291–301.

36. Clapp, *The Congressman,* pp. 51–52.

37. See the discussion in Donald G. Tacheron and Morris K. Udall, *The Job of the Congressman,* 2d ed. (Indianapolis, 1970), pp. 56–59.

38. Ibid., p. 61.

39. Matthews, *U.S. Senators and Their World,* p. 83.

40. Clapp, *The Congressman,* p. 63.

41. Matthews, *U.S. Senators and Their World,* pp. 83–84.

42. Davis, "Don't Write Your Congressman, Unless . . . ," p. 14.

43. Quoted in Clapp, *The Congressman,* p. 74. For a discussion of congressional case work see Sven Groennings and J. P. Hawley, eds., *To Be a Congressman: The Promise and the Power* (Washington, D.C., 1973), pp. 53–72.

44. See John C. Wahlke, "Policy Demands and System Support: The Role of the Represented," *British Journal of Political Science* 1 (1971):270–290.

45. The results of Iowa Legislative Research Project are reported in G. R. Boynton, Samuel C. Patterson, and Ronald D. Hedlund, "The Structure of Public Support for Legislative Institutions," *Midwest Journal of Political Science* 12 (1968):163–173; Samuel C. Patterson, G. R. Boynton, and Ronald D. Hedlund, "Perceptions and Expectations of the Legislature and Support for It," *American Journal of Sociology* 75 (1969):62–76; G. R. Boynton, Samuel C. Patterson, and Ronald D. Hedlund, "The Missing Links in Legislative Politics: Attentive Constituents," *Journal of Politics* 31(1969):700–721; Samuel C. Patterson, John C. Wahlke, and G. R. Boynton, "Dimensions of Support in Legislative Systems," in *Legislatures in Comparative Perspective,* ed. Allan Kornberg (New York, 1972); and Samuel C. Patterson, Ronald D. Hedlund, and G. R. Boynton, *Representatives and Represented: Bases of Support for the American Legislatures* (New York, 1975).

46. Press release of the Minnesota Poll, *Minnesota Tribune,* July 11, 1965; Independent Research Associates, Inc., "A Study of Voters' Opinions of State Legislatures: Iowa," prepared for the Citizens Conference on State Legislatures (July 1968), pp. 6–7.

47. Press release of the Minnesota Poll, *Minneapolis Tribune,* September 16, 1971.

48. See, for instance, the discussion of city-state relations in Wallace S. Sayre and Herbert Kaufman, *Governing New York City* (New York, 1965).

The Legislature as a Social System

part V

It has now become rather commonplace to observe that a legislative body, like other human groups, is a social system in the sense that it is characterized by widely shared standards of proper conduct, or norms; that each position in the legislative structure has associated with it expectations about the behavior of the people who occupy these positions; and that these expectations about positions, or roles, are interlocking in an interactional system. In the subsequent chapters, we deal with the observed norms of Congress and state legislatures and with the network of those roles that seem to be most notable in American legislatures. In principle, these analyses could be enlarged to include all the elements of the legislative system, but the accumulated research is limited primarily to the legislatures themselves.

To begin to understand and explain the legislative policy-making process, it is necessary to learn about the context, or setting, in which policy is or is not made. The unwritten rules of the legislative game must be understood to make sense out of the things that legislators do and say (or fail to do and say), to assess the situational limitations or possibilities for public policy, and to be aware of the strategic implications of the norms of the legislature in the use of written rules or formal organization. The ability to explain legislative behavior depends, among other things, upon an understanding of how legislators perceive their jobs and how those with whom they interact expect them to behave.

CHAPTER FOURTEEN

Legislative Norms

Every human group or institution develops within a context of normative standards of proper conduct that the participants uphold. The *norms*—those widely held expectations of what members must do, should do, or ought to do in particular circumstances, the violation of which leads to some kind of sanction or punishment—are acutely significant in political subsystems as highly stylized and institutionalized as legislative systems are.[1] Legislative norms are, in some particulars, so highly authoritative, persistent, stable, formalized, and legitimate that they are elaborately codified and come to constitute the written rules of legislative bodies. Otherwise, standards of proper conduct in legislative settings may be informal and unwritten, but they are not necessarily less authoritative or sanctioned. Thus, we may speak of the norms of legislative systems in terms of their relative formality or, in a sense, of their visibility. Table 14.1 provides an illustration of the manner in which legislative norms may be classified in terms of their visibility; it indicates an intermediate category that has analytical virtue when this crude typology is applied to certain American legislatures, such as the United States Senate. Highly formalized legislative norms (the written rules of procedure, standing orders, precedents, and rulings of the chair) are so commonplace and so highly visible to the most casual observer of legislative life that they are seldom treated as norms. Although discussion of the written rules clearly belongs in any general analysis of legislative norms, they are so independently significant for any understanding of legislative decision-making that we have treated them separately in Chapter 10. Our concern in this chapter will, therefore, be restricted to the so-called unwritten rules of the game, the informal norms that, along with the written rules, are associated with the control, consensus-building, socialization, and cognitive functions that maintain the legislative system.

It is possible to describe and illustrate the most notable norms that have been observed to operate in congressional and state legislative systems, and it is also possible to cite examples of the application of sanctions under some circumstances. But contemporary legislative research does not provide data with which the development of legislative norms can be examined systematically. And we know of no data that can be synthesized in order to arrive at a thorough explanation of policy effects.

TABLE 14.1   Typology of Legislative Norms

DEGREE OF FORMALITY OR VISIBILITY	DESCRIPTION	U.S. SENATE
High	Highly formalized, written rules	Rules and standing orders of the Senate, committee rules, precedents, rulings of the chair
Intermediate	Well-established, traditional unwritten rules	Senatorial courtesy, seniority rule
Low	Informal, unwritten rules	Apprenticeship, specialization, courtesy, reciprocity, institutional patriotism, and so forth

THE PROFESSIONAL AND THE AMATEUR LEGISLATURE

Legislative norms can be expected to vary in terms of their formality or visibility; they can also be expected to vary in terms of the degree of institutionalization of the legislature. The more permanent and professionalized the legislative institution, the more likely it is that the norms of the legislative system (or of any other social system, presumably) will be more highly structured, more highly traditionalized and legitimized, more authoritative, more strongly institutionalized, more widely and intensely accepted, and probably more rigidly and overtly enforced. At least in a limited way, it adds to the perspective of legislative norms to contrast the professional and the amateur legislature in terms of descriptive normative differentiation. Table 14.2 indicates the kind of comparison being suggested. Where the legislature itself is highly professionalized, its normative underpinnings are likely to be more highly structured, consistent, and sanctioned than would be expected in the case of a more amateur legislature. This distinction between professional and amateur legislatures corresponds roughly to the differ-

TABLE 14.2   Normative Differences in Professional and Amateur Legislatures

	PROFESSIONAL	AMATEUR
Characteristics	High status, meets regularly, lengthy sessions, well established, legitimate, has relatively high public respect and esteem, long history, relatively well-integrated, highly formalized, stable, complexly organized	Low status, meets periodically or irregularly, brief sessions, less well established, relatively low public esteem, brief or cloudy history, fewer traditions, relatively disintegrated, informal, unstable, simply organized
Norms	Coherent and congruent, highly structured, pervasive, highly institutionalized, widely and intensely accepted, well established, regular, automatic sanctions	Contradictory, incoherent, unstructured, erratic, only moderately institutionalized, unevenly recognized and accepted, erratic application of sanctions

ences between Congress and many state legislatures. Congressional norms are likely to be more highly developed than those prevalent in the legislatures of the states. As Lester W. Milbrath has written in a different context: "The policy-making process in the state capitals is more informal; there is less structure, less rigid adherence to rules, and less permanent record-keeping. There also seems to be less personal commitment by the actors to the success of the system and to the building of long-range personal reputations."[2]

UNWRITTEN RULES: CONGRESS

Traditional Norms

Two congressional norms that are highly visible are those of *senatorial courtesy* and *seniority*. The former applies to the Senate in its constitutional role of giving its "advice and consent" to presidential nominations for federal appointments and has been practiced since the Washington administration.

> The custom of senatorial courtesy is the sanction by which a majority of the Senate may require the President to nominate the candidate proposed by the senator or senators from the state in which the office is located, provided they belong to the same party as that of the President.[3]

For example, if the President nominates a person to serve as a federal judge in Illinois, and an Illinois senator of the President's political party declares that person to be "personally obnoxious" to him, the Senate will not ordinarily con-firm the appointment. The objecting senator may be expected by his colleagues to present reasons for his objections, but this has not always been required. In fact, the person nominated by the President may not be disliked by the objecting senator; he may simply prefer or may have recommended someone else. Thus, in 1951, the Senate rejected two nominations for judgeships in Illinois because Senator Douglas "stated that the manner of their selection was personally obnox-ious to him."[4] Douglas had recommended other men for these posts, which recommendations President Truman had not followed; and Douglas thought that his candidates were more worthy. But the norm of senatorial courtesy is not absolute. It is interlaced with other senatorial norms, and it has not always been successfully invoked. Joseph P. Harris suggests the interdependence of senatorial courtesy and other Senate norms when he outlines the standards of the Senate for invoking it:

> In passing upon a personal objection of senators to a nomination, the Senate takes into account the standing of the senator, as well as the grounds of his objection, and whether the office is one located within the state of the senator or is a national office. When the Senate has declined to honor an objection it is usually due to the fact that the objecting senator is not in good standing with his colleagues. . . . A senator who has not shown the usual courtesies to his colleagues may be denied the courtesy of the Senate.[5]

Senatorial courtesy is seldom invoked, but this is because senators are almost invariably consulted in the nominating process and virtually make federal appointments of some judges and administrators in the lower levels of administration in the federal field service. Thus, senatorial courtesy, although an unwritten rule, has modified those provisions of Article II of the Constitution that provide the appointing powers of the President.

The seniority rule applies most directly to the selection of committee chairmen, a process that we have described in detail in Chapter 8. However, its congressional application is much wider than the selection of committee chairmen, and it pervades the whole life of the Congress. Members of the House and the Senate are ranked according to the length of their uninterrupted service. For senators, the ranking commences on the opening day of the Congress to which they are first elected. Senators elected or appointed to fill an unexpired term begin to accrue seniority on the day their state governor certifies their appointment or, if they are elected, on the day the senator takes the oath of office, provided the Senate is in session. House procedure is much the same except that for some purposes, House members receive more credit for nonconsecutive service (i.e., representatives with three nonconsecutive terms are ranked above those with two consecutive terms).[6] Seniority in the respective houses of Congress confers status upon a member that affects much of his legislative life and especially the perquisites available to him. Office space is assigned on a seniority basis; seating at official dinners is based upon seniority; and committee assignments are usually, if not always, made on the basis of seniority.[7] "In no other place," writes George B. Galloway, "does seniority or length of service carry so much weight as it does in the Congress of the United States."[8]

Informal Rules

Closely related to the seniority norm is the norm of *apprenticeship*. When this norm is operating, new legislators are expected to exercise restraint in their participation in debate, to show respect for their elders, and to perform some of the more unexciting legislative chores, such as presiding over floor debate in the United States Senate. Roland Young has pointed out in regard to the Congress of the 1950s:

> New members continually identify themselves in a remarkably short time with what might be called the congressional point of view, but the period of full maturation, when the politician becomes also a seasoned legislator trusted fully by his colleagues, may require several years. Until relatively recently, the Senate expected a new member to remain sedately quiet for most of his first term in office, but with the greater number of Senators who serve for a single term, this practice is no longer followed. In both Houses, new members are tested and trained before they are given major responsibilities and before their words carry weight.[9]

At one time, new members of both houses were expected not to participate in legislative debate at all, to be seen but not heard. "Don't try to go too fast," Speaker Rayburn used to tell new members. "Learn your job. Don't ever talk until you know what you're talking about. .... If you want to get along, go along."[10]

Freshmen who ignore this advice—and some do—irritate their peers and are often the subject of sanctions. "He talks too much" is a description often heard in connection with a few members. At times these men cannot understand why they are passed over for assignments for which they are intellectually prepared. The blunt truth is that colleagues do not wish to see them get ahead or to work with them, despite their qualifications.[11]

Until the 1960s, expectations regarding apprenticeship were very real to freshman congressmen. Although the sanctions for deviation were unevenly applied and, in any event, were not likely to be severe, the pressures toward conformity with the apprenticeship norm were very pronounced.[12] An illustration from the Senate is the case of William Proxmire (D-Wis.). Proxmire's accommodation to the apprenticeship norm is described by Ralph K. Huitt as follows:

Throughout the spring of 1958, for roughly half his first session in the Senate, Proxmire strove earnestly to be a model freshman senator. He worked hard on his committees and took care of his constituents. He accepted cheerfully a mammoth portion of the burden of freshmen of the majority party, presiding over the Senate. He did much more than his share; an unofficial tabulation midway in the session showed that he had sat in the chair longer than anyone else and about sixteen times as long as Vice President Nixon. ...

But Proxmire had not satisfactorily answered the question that mattered most to him: How much could he talk on the floor? Ordinary prudence, as well as Senate practice, counsel a neophyte to bide his time before exercising very freely his undoubted right to speak at any time. But to a man like Proxmire the life of the Senate is the debate on the floor. Not to be there and participate is to deny himself equal membership in the Senate. Proxmire said of a freshman colleague who seldom spoke: "He might as well not be a senator!"

Nevertheless he forbore, trying to find socially acceptable ways to take some part. The "morning hour," that period at the beginning of each day when senators introduce bills and insert material in the *Congressional Record*, seemed safe enough so he quickly became a regular contributor to the *Record*. He entered colloquies on the floor only when specifically invited to do so by senior members. He cautiously scheduled his first major speech for the day before the Easter recess when most members would be gone, having been assured that this was an appropriate time for a freshman to talk. ...

But almost as if he could not help himself, Proxmire became steadily more active in debate until he was one of the busiest men on the floor. Then came the first warnings that he was "talking too much." The warnings were characteristic of the operations of the Senate. None of them was direct. They came in friendly tips: someone heard an unnamed person say it; the report was passed on to a Proxmire staff man for what it was worth. Or a very senior senator in the chair would pointedly overlook Proxmire standing at his desk, to recognize other members ahead of him out of turn.

Proxmire retired, brooding, to his office. He was puzzled and frustrated. He believed that he *had* exercised great restraint. He had kept his speeches short, except when asked by a party floor man to help kill time.[13]

Proxmire's immediate reaction to the cues that he was thought to be violating the apprenticeship norm was to withdraw entirely from debate; however, his retirement was brief. He decided not to worry about his Senate influence and to talk whenever he chose to do so. He then pursued a variety of issues in Senate debate, including mutual security, social security improvement, the Lake Michigan water-diversion bill, and the Democratic Senate leadership itself. Although his behavior was widely disapproved, his deviation was tolerated by a Senate that was predisposed to apply severe sanctions only in the most outrageous cases.

However pressing the apprenticeship norm was on congressional freshmen up through the 1950s, as a generalized expectation for appropriate congressional behavior it had collapsed by the 1970s. Beginning with the congressional election of 1958, a new generation of men and women was elected to the House and Senate —younger people, more northerners, less conservative. Accordingly, the House and Senate came to have a different atmosphere, one much more receptive to the voices and activism of new members. The dominance in the House, and even more so in the Senate, of a small group of older, conservative, and largely southern senior members quickly eroded and finally evanesced. Congressional leadership came into the hands of members (like Speaker Carl Albert, D-Okla., and Senate Majority Leader Mike Mansfield, D-Mont.) more receptive and responsive to freshman congressmen and senators. By 1969, Herbert Asher found that, based upon interviews with thirty freshmen and sixty-five incumbent House members, "almost half of the nonfreshmen sample flatly denied the necessity of serving an apprenticeship, and if the qualified disagreements are added to this figure, almost two-thirds of the incumbents rejected apprenticeship. . . ."[14] After five months' experience, well over half the freshmen rejected the need to serve an apprenticeship.

About the same story can be told of the Senate. In a recent study involving interviews with forty-seven senators, members were asked whether a period of apprenticeship was still expected of freshmen, and only two thought it was. One senior Republican said:

> At the time when I came, a man who was very junior . . . served as an apprentice to the senior members. . . . That is all gone now, of course, and the freshmen usually come in as highly vocal young men.

And senior senators, many themselves elected in 1958 and thereafter, actually have been encouraging new senators to participate actively from the beginning, so that a junior Democrat could say, ". . . all the communications suggest 'get involved, offer amendments, make speeches. The Senate has changed, we're all equals, you should act accordingly.' "[15]

Two of the norms of the Congress have to do with the nature of the task load of the legislative bodies. One prescribes concentration by the member upon *legislative work*; the other prescribes *specialization*. Donald R. Matthews points out that "the Senate folkways . . . prescribe that a senator place first priority upon being a *legislator*."[16] A member of the House is often "told that the committee system is the core of the legislative process and that the best way to attract the favorable attention of his colleagues is to participate wholeheartedly in his committee work," where "he should develop a specialty and concentrate on it, playing down other interests he may have that fall within the jurisdiction of other committees."[17] A member of Congress is expected to devote his major efforts to legislative tasks and to give secondary priority to personal advancement or publicity. This emphasis upon the work load of the legislature produces the commonplace disparity between "inside" and "outside" prestige; some of the most respected and effective legislators, with high inside prestige, are little known outside the institution. As Harry S Truman once observed, "the real business of the Senate was carried on by unassuming and conscientious men, not by those who managed to get the most publicity."[18]

Specialization of tasks is probably essential in a modern legislative body, which has a limited amount of time and a complexity of tasks to perform. A member is expected to specialize in the relatively few matters that are of particular importance to his state or district or that are immediately connected with his own committee work so that he can speak as an expert on those subjects. Specialization may be a more powerful norm in the United States House than in the Senate. It does seem clear that House members (more than senators) are required to develop expertise in a single subject-matter specialty in order to be maximally effective. Such expertise enhances the influence and effectiveness of the member; when he speaks in debate, he is listened to because he is regarded as an authority. And although the specialization norm may have become more important in the last forty years, it has been important for a much longer time. It is said, for instance, that Representative Nelson Dingley (R-Maine) advised Champ Clark (D-Mo.) to specialize if he wished to "make a great name for himself in Congress." Himself a specialist on tariff legislation, Dingley advised:

> I have been in Congress for many years and I have watched and studied men as they have come and gone. . . . If a man be a specialist on a subject, if he knows more than the ordinary congressman knows or can hope to learn by mere dabbling, then he can compel Congress to listen to him, and he rises to be a power. That is the secret of success here.[19]

Two additional congressional norms are associated with the manner in which legislative business is conducted: *interpersonal courtesy* and *reciprocity*. Interpersonal courtesy among legislators helps to resolve conflict in an atmosphere relatively free from invective and personal attacks upon members. Representatives and senators are forbidden by the formal rules from questioning the motives of another member, criticizing another state, or making reference to members of the other chamber. Members address their remarks in debate to the chair—to "Mr. Speaker" or to "Mr. President"—rather than to another legislator. Impersonality in reference to other members is adhered to so that members do not refer to one another by name; rather, a representative refers to the "gentleman from New York," and a senator refers to the "senior senator from Rhode Island." A congressman may engage in mudslinging in his campaign, but not on the floor of the House. As one House member put it, "we acknowledge that a person does a little bit of demagoguery with his people, but snow is for the folks."[20] Interpersonal courtesy makes it possible for competitors to cooperate.

Reciprocity is so fundamental a part of the American legislative process that we can scarcely do it justice in a few sentences. It is pervasive in the congressional system and may take the form of personal exchange of assistance or favors, compromise and negotiation over the provisions of legislation, or logrolling (trading of votes). Members are expected to play the game of exchange and mutual aid, especially where the immediate concerns of their own constituents are not directly involved. Much reciprocal behavior is both private and subtle, but it cannot be doubted that it is there. In referring to his colleagues, for example, a House member observed:

When one of them votes with you on something in which you're interested, it is pretty tough to turn him down when he comes to you later and wants some assistance on a matter of importance to him. There is a great deal of logrolling in Congress, and it's not going to be changed. It is particularly apparent on a close vote. Now I vote against any farm bill despite the fact that members who would like my support on those bills often support me on other things. People know my stand on the farm situation, and they just don't bother trying to get me to go along. This doesn't affect our relationship on other things, however, I think most of us recognize a cardinal rule in the House and that is that you don't ask a member to support you if such support is going to be going against his district or against a particular project in which he happens to be interested. We all respect one another's views on those matters.[21]

Legislative reciprocity emerges most visibly when the Congress considers public works appropriations bills and other pork-barrel legislation. Perhaps the operation (as well as the frustrations) of reciprocity in the life of the Senate is best illustrated by the candid reflections of Senator Paul Douglas (D-Ill.). When the public works bill was considered in 1956, Douglas said:

This bill is built up out of a whole system of mutual accommodations in which the favors are widely distributed, with the implicit promise that no one will kick over the applecart; that if Senators do not object to the bill as a whole, they will "get theirs." It is a process, if I may use an inelegant expression, of mutual backscratching and mutual logrolling.

Any member who tries to buck the system is only confronted with an impossible amount of work in trying to ascertain the relative merits of a given project; and any member who does ascertain them and who feels convinced that he is correct is unable to get an individual project turned down because the Senators from the State in which the project is located, and thus is benefiting, naturally will oppose any objection to the project; and the other members of the Senate will feel that they must support the Senators in question, because if they do not do so, similar appropriations for their own states at some time likely will be called into question.[22]

It is important to stress that not all legislation enacted by the House and the Senate is the result of such implicit bargaining or such pervasive reciprocity. Furthermore, it is an understatement to say that knowledge of the place and impact of reciprocity on decisional processes in Congress is incomplete. At the same time, it is clear that congressmen widely share expectations that representatives ought to behave in these terms.

A further consideration of congressional norms leads to expectations about *institutional patriotism*. Members of Congress are expected to have an emotional attachment to the institution and in particular to the house of which they are members. House members tend to regard themselves as the "real" representatives of the people and more responsive to their needs than senators; they tend to hold to the Protestant ethic of work and to believe that they are harder working than members of the Senate; they tend to regard senators as too publicity-seeking and the Senate as too "clubbish."[23]

If the members of the House of Representatives are prone to express their chauvinism in terms of relatively invidious comparisons with senators, members of the Senate are likely to express their institutional patriotism in much more sweeping ways. Senators are inclined to refer to the Senate as "the greatest deliberative body in the world," and they are certainly expected to believe it. A senator is expected to champion the Senate, to respect it, and to honor it. The most celebrated illustration of the application of sanctions by the Senate for the violation of its norms is that of the late Senator Joseph McCarthy (R-Wis.), who, as chairman of the Permanent Subcommittee on Investigations of the Committee on Government Operations, engaged in a Communist witch hunt during 1953–1954 that focused mainly upon the Department of State and the United States Army. In December, 1954, the Senate voted to censure McCarthy for his conduct. But the Senate did not censure his browbeating of witnesses before his subcommittee, indiscriminately accusing people of being Communists and traitors, or even abusing the investigatory powers of Congress. McCarthy was censured and his power was deflated because he attacked the integrity of the Senate itself. The language of the censure resolution, in a certain sense, permits the Senate to explain itself:

SECTION I: Resolved, that the Senator from Wisconsin, Mr. McCarthy, failed to cooperate with the Subcommittee on Privileges and Elections of the Senate Committee on Rules and Administration in clearing up matters referred to that subcommittee which concerned his conduct as a Senator, and *affected the honor of the Senate* and instead, repeatedly abused the members who were trying to carry out assigned duties, thereby obstructing the constitutional processes of the Senate, and that the conduct of the Senator from Wisconsin, Mr. McCarthy, is *contrary to Senatorial traditions* and is hereby condemned.

SECTION II: The Senator from Wisconsin (Mr. McCarthy) in writing to the chairman of the Select Committee to study censure charges (Mr. Watkins) after the Select Committee had issued its report and before the report was presented to the Senate charging three members of the Select Committee with "deliberate deception" and "fraud" for failure to disqualify themselves; in stating to the press on November 4, 1954 that the special Senate session that was to begin November 8, 1954 was a "lynch party"; in repeatedly describing this special Senate session as a "lynch bee" in a nationwide television-radio show on November 7, 1954; in stating to the public press on November 13, 1954 that the chairman of the Select Committee (Mr. Watkins) was guilty of "the most unusual, the most cowardly thing I've heard of" and stating further: "I expected he would be afraid to answer the questions but didn't think he'd be stupid enough to make a public statement"; and in characterizing the said committee as the "unwitting handmaiden," "involuntary agent," and "attorneys in fact" of the Communist Party and in charging that the said committee in writing its report "imitated Communist methods—that it distorted, misrepresented, and omitted, in its effort to manufacture a plausible rationalization" in support of its recommendations to the Senate, which characterizations and charges were contained in a statement released to the press and inserted in the *Congressional Record* of November 10, 1954, *acted contrary to Senatorial ethics and tended to bring the Senate into dishonor and disrepute,* to obstruct the constitutional processes of the Senate, and to impair its dignity; and such conduct is hereby condemned.[24] (italics added)

But the censure of McCarthy for a failure of loyalty to the Senate meant much more than the terse language of the resolution suggests. Politically, he was effectually stripped of power in the Senate; he was ignored; he was given the silent treatment, almost the severest sanction a group can apply to one of its members.[25]

A final congressional norm that deserves some mention in this analysis has to do with the loyalty of members of Congress to their political party. The party norm is not clear-cut and unambiguous in the American Congress. The congressman is subjected to a variety of pressures in his decision-making behavior, some of which may be conflicting; political party pressures (either strategic or psychological) are difficult to sort out from the maze of pressures he feels. Furthermore, when the outcomes of congressional votes are certain, party pressures may not be pressed strongly. Thus, although there are among congressmen widely shared expectations that members ought to support their party, the machinery for the implementation of such expectations is not particularly well developed, and severe sanctions are seldom applied for violating expectations of party loyalty. Even when members of the United States Senate have failed to support or have actively opposed their party's presidential candidate in a national election, seldom have such sanctions as deprivation of committee assignment been imposed.[26] But a great deal more is known about the party voting of legislators than about how partisan norms are invoked; we fully synthesize party-voting data for legislators in Chapter 16.

Conformity to Norms

It is clear that normative rules of conduct exist in American legislative systems. The norms described here deal explicitly with the legislative institution itself, but presumably more thorough research would reveal norms that regulate conduct more widely in American legislative systems, including the behavior of newspapermen, lobbyists, bureaucrats, and so forth. Of course, the norms existing within the legislative body are not universally accepted by all legislators, nor are they consistently adhered to, but the available knowledge of the correlates of normative conformity is very limited. Matthews, in his study of the "folkways" of the United States Senate, explored the effects of four factors that influence conformity to Senate norms: previous training and experience, political ambitions, constituency problems, and political ideology. His data support the hypothesis that the recruitment function affects normative conformity so that those senators "elected relatively early in life with considerable political experience seem to conform most readily and often," whereas "amateur politicians, men who have entered politics relatively late in life after distinguished business and professional careers, have the hardest time of all."[27] State legislators and judges who moved to the Senate seemed to conform most; whereas former state governors and former federal executives in the Senate were less likely to accept the norms of the Senate. (The measures of conformity used by Matthews were frequency of floor speaking and an index of specialization based upon the number of bills a senator introduced that were referred to the two committees receiving the greatest number of his bills.) Furthermore, Matthews's data suggest that senators with political ambitions beyond the Senate (such as the Presidency) are less likely to conform to the institutional norms and that senators elected from competitive two-party or complex urban-industrial constituencies are more likely to deviate from the norms. Finally, Senate liberals are more likely to be nonconformists than conservatives are. These findings comport with the status of the norms themselves; they tend to support, reinforce, and buttress the status quo in the legislative body. Since rural, conservative, and safe-district senators are overrepresented in the Senate and have set many of its norms, liberal senators who face electoral insecurity are most likely to seek to upset the status quo. But at least with respect to the success senators have in getting their bills passed, Matthews's data show that conformity to Senate norms is related to "legislative effectiveness."[28]

Conformity to congressional norms is seldom obtained by overt threats of sanction or by the formal application of sanctions to deviant legislators. The sanctions that support congressional norms are not fully understood or documented by adequate research, but the pressures to normative conformity are impressive. A few illustrations of the formal application of sanctions (such as the McCarthy censure) are available, and a variety of informal sanctions are known to exist. Congressmen may get interpersonal cues from other members that indicate disapproval of violations of the rules of the game. *Selective inattention,* manifested by personal avoidance, exaggerated inattention in debate, or ignoring suggestions and requests, constitutes an observable sanction for normative violations. *Process sanctions* are known to have been applied to legislators, as in instances where bills are mysteriously "misplaced," neglected, or ignored. Although a member who persistently violates the norms is very likely to be tolerated, his behavior is not likely to be regarded as legitimate.

STATE LEGISLATIVE NORMS

The norms we have discussed with respect to Congress—senatorial courtesy, seniority, apprenticeship, legislative work, specialization, interpersonal courtesy, reciprocity, institutional patriotism, and party loyalty—are certainly applicable to any discussion of the unwritten rules of the state legislative game. An inventory of the normative expectations of legislators in five states (California, New Jersey, Ohio, Tennessee, and Wisconsin) indicates that in these states, there exists a wide range of expected behavior. The interview responses of these states' legislators were coded into a total of forty-two categories, based upon asking legislators to name the " 'rules of the game' that a member must observe to hold the respect and cooperation of his fellow members."[29] These categories were:

1. Performance of obligations
2. Respect for other members' legislative rights
3. Impersonality
4. Self-restraint in debate
5. Courtesy
6. Openness of aims
7. Modesty
8. Integrity
9. Independence of judgment
10. Personal virtue
11. Decisiveness
12. Unselfish service
13. Advance notice of changed stand
14. Openness in opposition
15. Sociability
16. Conciliation
17. Agency for party or administration
18. Restraint in opposition
19. Application
20. Respect for other members' political rights
21. Objectivity
22. Agency for legislative party
23. Gracefulness in defeat
24. Ability and intelligence
25. Non-venality
26. Restraint in bill-introduction
27. Maintenance of confidences
28. Avoidance of trickery
29. Apprenticeship
30. Caution in commitments
31. Commitment to job
32. Institutional patriotism
33. Respect for opposition groups
34. Negotiation
35. Limits to negotiation
36. Seniority
37. Acceptance of committee system
38. Self-restraint in goals
39. Senatorial courtesy
40. Compliance with group
41. Limits to partisanship
42. Abstinence from dilatory actions

The parallels between congressional and state legislative norms suggest the wide generality of the legislative way of life in the United States. Yet the more transient, more temporary, less stable, less professionalized character of state legislatures provides, in general terms, a more flexible group life than is true of the Congress.

Because Congress is more highly institutionalized than state legislatures (or certainly most of them), its norms tend to be more *institution-oriented*. Although institution-oriented norms (such as seniority, legislative work, apprenticeship, institutional patriotism, and specialization) are not alien to the state legislative system, they are apparently far less salient for state legislators (in the sense of being important rules of the game). The norms of the American state legislatures appear to be more *individual-oriented*. The standards of proper individual conduct that are widely accepted in our society—simple honesty, trustworthiness, respect for others, sociability, openness, and sportsmanship—are given preeminence as state legislative norms and are probably given greater emphasis and held with greater intensity in the state legislative setting than among the general population. The pioneering research of John C. Wahlke and his associates found that the rules of the game most frequently mentioned by state legislators were those involving performance of personal obligations and commitments, respect for other members' legislative rights, and impersonality, including observance of the golden rule.[30]

The most frequently mentioned normative expectation among state legislators in four states (California, New Jersey, Ohio, and Wisconsin) and the third most frequently mentioned expectation in another (Tennessee) was *performance of obligations*. State legislators overwhelmingly expect their colleagues to keep their word and abide by their commitments. This expectation of reliability is illustrated in the comments of a Wisconsin legislator: "Keeping your word is an unwritten law among assemblymen. You vote the way you say you will or you explain why you changed your mind. You just don't double-cross people."

Almost as important among legislators in these states are standards of fairness and helpfulness in playing the legislative game: *reciprocity*. State legislators expect that members of the legislature will support the local bills of others, respect a member's amendments to his own bill, and refrain from unnecessarily objecting to another member's local bill before legislative committees. The norm of *interpersonal courtesy* has special importance in state legislative systems. As one state legislator said:

> You have to have respect for other people's opinions and refrain from personal abuse. I mean you have to exhibit a spirit of cooperation regardless of party or urban-rural residence. You might even vote with the other group when you think they are right. Also, give constructive criticism—don't tear a bill down just because it was introduced by a certain party or individual. Don't make fun of ridiculous measures either, or ridicule witnesses when they come before committee. You have to hear everybody and not abuse or hurt anybody's feelings.[31]

The original exploratory research conducted by Wahlke and his associates involved asking legislators to indicate what the unwritten rules of the game were in their legislatures. Subsequent studies based upon this exploratory work have inquired of legislators to what extent they agreed or disagreed that certain norms were extant. In one such study, Donald Leavitt interviewed house and senate members of the Minnesota legislature in 1974–1975. In general, he found stronger acceptance of individual-oriented norms than of institution-oriented ones. Here are some illustrations of the levels of agreement among Minnesota legislators to expectations about their personal conduct:

Honesty in explaining bills 90%
Keep tight rein on temper 90%
Considerate of members of opposing party 91%
Never divulge confidential information 86%
Be graceful in defeat 85%
Respect presiding officer 78%
Self-restraint in debate on bills 76%

In another study of state legislative norms, Samuel Kirkpatrick and Lelan McLemore interviewed 90 percent of the members of the 1972 Oklahoma house and senate; 88 percent of the house members and 85 percent of the senators responded that a legislator should never deal in personalities in remarks on the floor of the legislative chamber. Finally, Ronald D. Hedlund drew upon interviews with members of the 1965 and 1967 sessions of the Iowa legislature to show that 84 percent of the 1965 Iowa house members and 98 percent of the 1967 legislators believed that it was highly inappropriate for legislators to deal in personalities in debate, and that well over 90 percent of the Iowa legislators in both sessions emphasized the importance of sociability and friendliness among members. In both the Oklahoma and Iowa studies, such individual-oriented expectations generally far exceeded agreement on institution-oriented norms.[32]

Interstate Variations and Change

We have contrasted state legislatures with the Congress, but this should not imply that there are not important differences in norm structure from one state legislature to another. Each state legislature operates within its own political system and is embedded in its own political culture. In the early work on legislative norms, it became clear that in the relatively competitive two-party states of Wisconsin, Ohio, and New Jersey, party norms were much more frequently salient for legislators than they were in factional, nonpartisan, or one-party states (approximated by conditions in California and Tennessee in the late 1950s). The more recent studies in Iowa, Minnesota, and Oklahoma suggest variations among states in commitments to party norms as well. Very large majorities of Iowa legislators in 1965 and 1967 accepted as a norm that members should follow party leadership when decisions were made in party caucuses (see Table 14.3). Only 54 percent of the 1974–1975 Minnesota legislators indicated that they thought it was important for a member to support the decisions of his or her party caucus; in even

TABLE 14.3 Norms of the Iowa Legislature, 1965 and 1967 (In percentages)

NORMATIVE EXPECTATION	LEVEL OF ACCEPTANCE		
	1965 House of Representatives	1967 House of Representatives	1967 Senate
1. Campaigning against incumbent legislator in his district	52.6	21.5	21.1
2. Being known as a spokesman for special interest group	23.5	9.8	5.4
3. Seeking publicity from the press to look good for people back home	56.4	5.7	7.0
4. Dealing in personalities in debate or remarks made on floor of chamber	15.7	2.4	1.8
5. Standing by commitments even after a change of heart	96.0	38.5	37.5
6. Concealing real purpose of bill or purposely overlooking some portion in order to assure passage	87.2	2.4	3.5
7. Serving apprenticeship period at beginning of first term	55.6	61.0	42.4
8. Following decisions of party, particularly when made in caucus	79.3	69.4	85.7
9. Making compromises with opposition and settling for less than believe necessary	82.4	25.2	45.6
10. Voting with opposition party bad thing to do	68.4	81.7	78.9
11. Talking on subjects before legislature when not completely informed a mistake	91.1	100.0	96.5
12. Being known among legislators as "loner" and not having much to do with them outside chamber not desirable	91.0	97.6	94.7
13. Giving first priority to reelection in all actions as a legislator	64.0	2.4	5.3
14. Being entertained by lobbyists	97.1	35.0	37.5

SOURCE: Ronald D. Hedlund, "Legislative Norms and Legislative Behavior: Functional Requisite Analysis and State Legislatures" (Paper presented at the 1973 annual meeting of the Midwest Political Science Association), pp. 12–13.

sharper contrast, only about 40 percent of Oklahoma legislators in 1972 said they thought members should usually follow the party leadership.

But however real interstate variations in legislative norms may be in regard to such matters as partisan loyalty and solidarity, the more interesting thrust of the few recent studies is on changing patterns of normative expectations in the legislatures. Donald Leavitt's study of the Minnesota legislature, for instance, strongly suggests that there have been substantial changes in norms in that body: legislators much more strongly emphasize the norm of specialization than they had previously, the norms restraining issue conflict have eroded substantially, and the reciprocity norm has virtually disappeared. Compared with previous sessions, the 1974–1975 Minnesota legislators emphasized expectations about the openness of the legislative deliberations and the efficacy of party and issue conflict over principles of public policy; they eschewed compromise of principle, reciprocity, restraint on parliamentary maneuvering, vociferous opposition, and deference to committees and their chairmen.[33]

Ronald D. Hedlund's study of two successive sessions of the Iowa legislature (1965 and 1967) provides an opportunity to observe normative changes in a legislature by making direct comparisons. An example of his findings is given in Table 14.3. The expectations of 1967 Iowa legislators, compared with those in the 1965 session, gave much greater emphasis to conflict and opposition politics, openness of legislative consideration of issues, and the primacy of the merits of issues rather than that of reelection success. For example, the unwritten rule that legislators could appropriately make "compromises with the opposition which settle for less than they believe necessary" was acceptable to 82 percent of the 1965 legislators, but rejected by three-fourths of the 1967 representatives and well over half the senators in the 1967 session.

Another important source of interstate variability in normative emphasis may be those expectations that have to do with the behavior of lobbyists. We noted in Chapter 12 that American legislators tend to view lobbyists as playing functional roles in the legislative system, although there are variations from state to state in the proportions of legislators who have a positive image of lobbying. Presumably, lobbying norms exist in all American legislative systems, although little is known of the range of such expectations. Lobbying norms appear to include expectations related to the entertainment of legislators by lobbyists. A study of the 1957 Wisconsin legislature revealed legislators' expectations about the behavior of other legislators in their relationships with lobbyists:

> [The] norms of the Assembly prescribed that it was permissible for a member to accept meals and drinks from lobbyists. There were a number of members who did not do so because of personal convictions, but most members agreed that such behavior was all right for others if they wished to do so. However, "chiseling" or "mooching" from lobbyists violated the norms of the Assembly. It was all right if a lobbyist invited a member to lunch, but a member who mooched from a lobbyist was an "outlaw."[34]

But expectations about appropriate behavior vis-à-vis lobbyists may well be among state legislative norms most likely to have undergone changes in recent years, as these legislatures have become more professionalized and more conscious of citizens' disapproval of illicit lobbying activities. For instance, 97 percent of the 1965 Iowa legislators indicated that being entertained by lobbyists was acceptable behavior for members; but, in contrast, for about two-thirds of the 1967 Iowa legislators this practice was not acceptable.

The shifting patterns of norm acceptance exhibited in Hedlund's Iowa study (reflected in Table 14.3) are not easy to account for. The number of shifts from 1965 to 1967 do indicate the degree of volatility of norms in a state legislature with high turnover of membership. Although the Democrats controlled the 1965 house and the Republicans the 1967 house, there were few party differences in the acceptance of norms, and one party's adherents did not change more than the other's. A considerably more probing inquiry than is available at the present time is needed to plumb the extent and causes of changes in state legislative norms over time.

Sanctions

State legislators are quite conscious of a variety of sanctions that may be imposed upon a member who violates the rules of the game. Although punishment is seldom so severe that it involves virtual expulsion (as was essentially the result of the McCarthy censure by the United States Senate), the sanctions, though subtle, are severe enough to be salient to legislators. For example, legislators who deviate from the party norm may be subjected to attempts by the party to purge them at the polls, or violators may be relieved of their committee chairmanships. Legislators interviewed by Wahlke and his associates had no difficulty in delineating the ways in which the norms were enforced; most of them made reference to obstruction of their bills, ostracism, and mistrust as the probable consequences of nonconformity.[35] But beyond specific sanctions recognized by legislators, the rules of the game are significant because they are both widely accepted and regarded as functional for the legislative system. The norms of American legislatures are not catechisms that legislators can recite by rote, slogans suitable for framing to be hung on the legislator's office wall, or pious platitudes about good behavior. Enforcement of the rules of the game may be variable, but it is real. At the same time, sanctions seldom need to be applied, and the really remarkable conformity to legislative norms would "seem to be obtained not primarily through members' fear of such punishment but through their general acceptance of the functional utility of the rules for enabling the group to do what a legislature is expected to do."[36]

The unwritten rules of the game in a legislative system must be understood in order to comprehend fully the written rules that may be invoked, who may invoke them, and under what circumstances. This point is particularly well illustrated from the few studies extant of state legislative norms. It is clear, for instance, that in the states studied, the rules permit objection to unanimous-consent requests, but the unwritten rules almost invariably prohibit such objection. Rules regulating debate may be vitiated by informal norms. The rules of procedure in the Wisconsin assembly contain a straightforward provision for moving the previous question to end debate, but a norm intensely held among members for many years prohibited invoking the rule under any circumstances.

The functional contributions of legislative norms are significant, even though they are unmeasured (and perhaps unmeasurable). The norms contribute to the socialization function, providing new members with cues by which they can shape their behavior along appropriate lines. They support the control and consensus-building functions of the legislative system by advancing the group solidarity and cohesion without which the system could not function, promoting the predictability of the behavior of legislators within the system, limiting the channeling of conflict, and expediting legislative business. They provide an important element in the culture of the system and thus contribute to cognitive sharing, making it possible for members to operate on similar premises, to share meanings, to see things in about the same ways.

In this chapter, we have dealt with the expectations of proper conduct by legislators in general. There are other norms in a human system that are concerned with specific locations that people occupy in the system. Those legislative norms that are focused on, relate to, and describe specific positions in the legislative structure constitute *roles;* these special kinds of norms are examined in Chapter 15.

NOTES

1. See George C. Homans, *The Human Group* (London, 1951), pp. 124–125.
2. Lester W. Milbrath, *The Washington Lobbyists* (Chicago, 1963), p. 302.
3. Joseph P. Harris, "The Courtesy of the Senate," *Political Science Quarterly* 67 (1952):39.
4. George B. Galloway, *The Legislative Process in Congress* (New York, 1953), p. 577.
5. Harris, "The Courtesy of the Senate," p. 51.
6. See George Goodwin, Jr., "The Seniority System in Congress," *American Political Science Review* 53 (1959):413.
7. Galloway, *The Legislative Process in Congress,* pp. 367–368.
8. Ibid., p. 367.
9. Roland Young, *The American Congress* (New York, 1958), pp. 62–63.
10. Neil MacNeil, *Forge of Democracy* (New York, 1963), p. 129.
11. Charles L. Clapp, *The Congressman: His Work as He Sees It* (Washington, D.C., 1963), p. 11.
12. Jerry Voorhis, *Confessions of a Congressman* (Garden City, N.Y., 1947), pp. 28–29.
13. Ralph K. Huitt, "The Outsider in the Senate: An Alternative Role," *American Political Science Review* 55 (1961):568–569.
14. Herbert B. Asher, "The Learning of Legislative Norms," *American Political Science Review* 67 (1973):508–509.
15. David W. Rhode, Norman J. Ornstein, and Robert L. Peabody, "Political Change and Legislative Norms in the United States Senate" (Paper presented at the 1974 annual meeting of the American Political Science Association), pp. 35–36.
16. Donald R. Matthews, "The Folkways of the United States Senate: Conformity to Group Norms and Legislative Effectiveness," *American Political Science Review* 53 (1959):1067.
17. Clapp, *The Congressman,* p. 12.
18. Quoted in Matthews, "The Folkways of the United States Senate: Conformity to Group Norms and Legislative Effectiveness," p. 1067.
19. Quoted in MacNeil, *Forge of Democracy,* p. 130.
20. Clapp, *The Congressman,* p. 13.
21. Ibid., pp. 180–181. For a discussion of reciprocity in the congressional committee context, see Richard F. Fenno, Jr., "The House Appropriations Committee as a Political System: The Problem of Integration," *American Political Science Review* 56 (1962):316–319.
22. Quoted in Matthews, "The Folkways of the United States Senate: Conformity to Group Norms and Legislative Effectiveness," p. 1072. For a detailed analysis of legislative processes exhibiting the reciprocity norm, see John A. Ferejohn, *Pork Barrel Politics: Rivers and Harbors Legislation, 1947–1968* (Stanford, 1974).
23. See Clapp, *The Congressman,* p. 35.
24. Quoted in Richard H. Rovere, *Senator Joe McCarthy* (Cleveland, 1960), pp. 229–230.
25. For impressions of the effects of the censure upon Senator McCarthy's prestige, status, and physical and mental health, see Rovere, *Senator Joe McCarthy,* pp. 239–248; and William S. White, *Citadel: The Story of the U.S. Senate* (New York, 1956), p. 133.

26.   See Ralph K. Huitt, "The Morse Committee Assignment Controversy: A Study in Senate Norms," *American Political Science Review* 51 (1957):313–329.

27.   Matthews, "The Folkways of the United States Senate: Conformity to Group Norms and Legislative Effectiveness," p. 1088.

28.   Ibid., pp. 1085–1086. See also, Charles M. Price and Charles G. Bell, "The Rules of the Game: Political Fact or Academic Fancy?" *Journal of Politics* 32 (1970):839–855.

29.   John C. Wahlke et al., *The Legislative System* (New York, 1962), pp. 143, 146–147.

30.   Ibid., p. 144. Also, see F. Ted Hebert and Lelan E. McLemore, "Character and Structure of Legislative Norms: Operationalizing the Norm Concept in the Legislative Setting," *American Journal of Political Science* 17 (1973):506–527.

31.   Ibid., pp. 144–145.

32.   The studies referred to in this paragraph are only reported at the present time in unpublished papers. See Donald Leavitt, "Changing Rules and Norms in the Minnesota Legislature" (Paper presented at the 1975 annual meeting of the Midwest Political Science Association), especially p. 28; Samuel A. Kirkpatrick and Lelan McLemore, "Evaluative and Perceptual Dimensions of Legislative Norms: An Analysis of Congruence and Conflict" (Paper presented at the 1975 annual meeting of the Midwest Political Science Association), especially p. 14; Ronald D. Hedlund, "Legislative Norms and Legislative Behavior: Functional Requisite Analysis and State Legislatures" (Revised paper originally presented at the 1973 annual meeting of the Midwest Political Science Association), pp. 12–13.

33.   Donald Leavitt, "Changing Rules and Norms in the Minnesota Legislature," pp. 27–35.

34.   Samuel C. Patterson, "The Role of the Deviant in the State Legislative System: The Wisconsin Assembly," *Western Political Quarterly* 14 (1961):463.

35.   Wahlke et al., *The Legislative System,* p. 154.

36.   Ibid., p. 168.

CHAPTER FIFTEEN

Legislative Role Orientations

Throughout this book, our conceptualization of the activity, action, and behavior that goes on within the fluid boundaries of American legislative systems has been somewhat eclectic because we recognize that a variety of scientifically and politically relevant factors contribute to the understanding of legislative situations. We have examined (and will examine in the remaining chapters) the legislature as a lawmaking or policy-making institution, but we have also sought to show that it is inadequate and incomplete to consider the legislative system solely in instrumental terms (as a sort of policy-making factory). We have eschewed the policy-making approach because, among other reasons, a considerable amount of politically relevant representational behavior occurs in legislative systems that is not immediately or directly related to specific policy outcomes, and because even where policy outcomes are considered, more fundamental than the policy processes themselves are those behavioral conditions that affect the policy configuration of a legislative system.

One set of behavioral conditions that we regard as most important involves the legislative norms and the ways in which those norms are focused around specific locations in the structure of the legislative system, thus constituting expectations about the behavior of individuals there. We have defined *role* in Chapter 1 as consisting of a pattern of reciprocal expectations of proper conduct among those who occupy positions in the structure of the legislative system. An exhaustive description of the role structure of a legislative system would involve a complete map of the interactions among participants and a definitive analysis of the sum total of behavioral expectations that participants share about each system position. Legislative behavior research has by no means provided adequate empirical data for such a complete description. But it is possible to enter into the role structure of American legislative systems at least to the extent of examining *some* of the variations in the legislative role.

The norms of the larger society, as well as those operating in the legislature itself, define the generalized role of the American legislator. However, the American legislative system is an open society in the sense that within the framework of a rudimentary consensus, considerable flexibility is possible in the legislator's definition of his job. In this chapter, we will be concerned with the role *orientations* of congressmen and state legislators, that is, the patterns of variability that have been observed in the role conceptions of American legislators. In earlier chapters, we have used role as an interpretive concept; here, we synthesize research that bears directly upon legislative role systems.

All this sounds very promising, but in fact our claims are modest. As the reader will discover, the emphasis of our analysis rests more on the importance of the subject than on any plethora of empirical material. The data available to us are uneven, and the analysis of available evidence is somewhat inconclusive.

A LEGISLATIVE ROLE MODEL

Since role theory of legislative behavior has been adequately developed, our analysis can proceed tentatively around a model of legislative role orientations of the sort depicted in Figure 15.1, which takes the perspective of the legislator and attempts to show the major components of role orientation for him. The legislator is placed in the context of a legislative input-output scheme in which the input into the system is the demands made, the expectations held, and the support and resources provided by constituency, interest group, party, and the bureaucratic components of the system. The output is shown as decisions (action on bills and resolutions), policies (including formulations of goals and means not necessarily enacted into law), and services. To make the model more complete, the feedback from output to input is indicated.

This model suggests eight categories of orientation for the legislative role. Although it draws very heavily upon the study of the role structure of four state legislatures, it is a useful, if not entirely satisfactory, conceptualization for the analysis of both congressional and state legislative roles.[1] The specific role orientations depicted in Figure 15.1 can be described briefly as follows:

1. CONSTITUENCY ROLE ORIENTATIONS: orientations in which the geographic entity of the constituency is the focus of representation.
    a. *District-oriented* (or *state-oriented*). The legislator conceives his job explicitly as that of sponsoring and supporting legislation for the benefit of the constituency from which he is elected.
    b. *State-oriented* (or *nation-oriented*). The legislator overcomes the parochial interests of county, district, or state and conceives his job in terms of the general policy; the state legislator concerns himself more with broad state policy as opposed to the narrower interests of his county or district; the congressman concerns himself more with national programs and policies than with his district or state.
    c. *District-state-oriented* (or *district-nation-, state-nation-oriented*). The legislator gives analytically undifferentiated weight to the interests of his own constituency and of the larger political system.

2. INTEREST-GROUP ROLE ORIENTATIONS: orientations of the legislator toward political-interest groups.
    a. *Facilitators.* Legislators who are knowledgeable about group activity and have a friendly attitude toward pressure groups.

FIGURE 15.1 Legislative Role Orientations

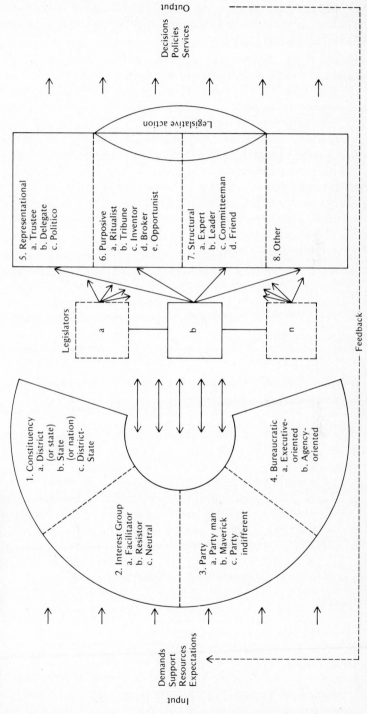

    b. *Resisters.* Legislators who are knowledgeable about group activity and have a hostile attitude toward it.

    c. *Neutrals.* Legislators who have little knowledge of pressure-group activity or no strong attitudes toward it, either favorable or unfavorable.

3. PARTY ROLE ORIENTATIONS: the legislator's conception of his job as a member of the political party to which he belongs.

    a. *Party Man.* The legislator who conceives of his job as supporting the program of his party or its leaders, regardless of his own judgments or the consequences of party loyalty.

    b. *Maverick.* The legislator who sees his job as taking a course independent of partisan programs or leadership and who votes with the other party with some regularity.

    c. *Party Indifferent.* The legislator who eschews partisan considerations, who conceives his job after his election to be that of representing all citizens regardless of party; for him, party has little salience.

4. BUREAUCRATIC ROLE ORIENTATIONS: orientations of the legislator toward the executive (governor, President) or toward the administrative apparatus.

    a. *Executive-oriented.* The legislator who sees his job as that of spokesman for the executive officer in the legislative body, who considers his job to be that of introducing the governor's or President's program, defending the executive's bills, and seeking their passage, and who may defend the executive generally; or the legislator who sees his job as opposing the executive.

    b. *Agency-oriented.* The legislator who sees his job as that of spokesman for, or opponent of, some governmental administrative agency.

5. REPRESENTATIONAL ROLE ORIENTATIONS: the orientation the legislator takes with regard to the way in which decisions are to be made, regardless of whether his focus of representation is district, political party, interest group, administrative agency, or a combination of these.

    a. *Trustee.* The representative who sees himself as a free agent, required to make decisions according to principles, conviction, and conscience.

    b. *Delegate.* The legislator who thinks that his decisions ought not to be premised upon his own independent judgment but that he ought to consult his constituents, accept their instructions, or even follow their mandate when it may differ from his own convictions.

    c. *Politico.* The legislator who expresses both trustee and delegate role orientations.

6. PURPOSIVE ROLE ORIENTATIONS: the legislator's orientation to the purposes and processes of the legislative institution.

    a. *Ritualist.* The legislator whose concept of his role involves the technical routines of legislative work: committee work, rules and procedures, progress of bills, and so forth.

b. *Tribune.* The legislator who conceives his job as that of discovering popular feelings and desires, defending popular interests, or advocating popular demands.

c. *Inventor.* The legislator who sees his major tasks as those related to the creation, formulation, and initiation of public policy.

d. *Broker.* The legislator who conceives his job in terms of compromising, arbitrating, coordinating, and integrating conflicting demands and interests within the legislative body.

e. *Opportunist.* The legislator who accepts only the bare minimum of expectations about the legislative role and uses his legislative office to play essentially nonlegislative roles.

7. STRUCTURAL ROLE ORIENTATIONS: the orientation of the legislator toward other critical legislative roles (experts, leaders) or to critical structural features of the legislative institution (committees, informal groups, or cliques).

a. *Expert.* The legislator who regards himself, and is regarded by others, as having special subject-matter expertise.

b. *Leader.* The legislator who performs integrative and directional functions, who gives cues to others for their behavior; this includes occupants of official leadership positions (speaker, floor leaders, whips, committee chairmen), and informal leaders.

c. *Committeeman.* The legislator whose conception of his job is as a member of a legislative committee or subcommittee.

d. *Friend.* The legislator whose role conception includes interpersonal relations vis-à-vis his legislative friends and companions.

The legislature is a role *system* in the sense that roles are interrelated in a network. In principle, the legislative system as a whole can be viewed as a role system in which the roles of legislators, lobbyists, constituents, administrative officials, party leaders, the executive, and perhaps other relevant actors are interrelated. Our model focuses only upon the legislator's role and deals with it in terms of his role orientations. This restriction in practice is called for by the limited empirical evidence now available. But within these limitations, it is possible to view the legislative role system through the interpenetration of role orientations. A legislator's *role-set* may consist of a variety of combinations of orientations; thus, a representative may be a district-oriented–facilitator–delegate–broker–tribune and perhaps also an anti-agency-oriented–expert–maverick. In actual, ongoing legislative institutions, a variety of combinations of role orientations are possible in principle and are observable empirically.

CONSTITUENCY ROLE ORIENTATIONS

It certainly seems safe to say that a substantial proportion of American legislators, both national and state, are oriented toward the geographic territory within which they are elected and feel responsible for the interests of their districts. In the congressman's scheme of values, says George B. Galloway, "the interests of the district come first, of his state second, and of the nation third."[2] Of course, a representative may identify his district's interests and the state or national interests as synonymous, but the extent to which congressmen select one area focus over another is impressive. One congressman expressed the district-oriented focus in an almost classic way:

> My first duty is to get reelected. I'm here to represent my district. . . . This is part of my actual belief as to the function of a congressman. . . . What is good for the majority of districts is good for the country. What snarls up the system is these so-called statesmen—congressmen who vote for what they think is the country's interest . . . let the Senators do that. . . . They're paid to be statesmen; we [members of the House] aren't.[3]

The incompleteness of the communications between congressman and constituent (noted in Chapter 13) does not obviate the predominant district orientation that characterizes members of the Congress. Given the nature of the legislative recruitment function, with its distinctively local orientation, the orientation of congressmen to their own districts is probably not surprising. The systematic evidence is somewhat limited, but Roger H. Davidson did interview a systematic sample of the members of the United States House of Representatives in 1963–1964. His evidence indicated that of the eighty-seven congressmen he questioned, 42 percent could be categorized as having a "district-dominant" orientation; 28 percent could be classified as "nation-dominant"; and 23 percent combined both national and district orientations.[4]

Investigations of the constituency role orientations of American state legislators indicate the generality of district-oriented focuses in American legislative systems. As one Wisconsin legislator put it: "An assemblyman's job is representing his county or district. He should serve the interests which are most important in that county. His task is to determine what the major interests in the county are, and then see how proposed legislation would affect those interests."[5] Interviews with members of a number of state legislatures provide some systematic evidence about the pervasiveness of district orientations among them.[6] Although the quality of this evidence is uneven, the data indicate fairly wide variations among states in the extent of local-district versus system-wide legislative orientations. In the four states where Wahlke and his associates interviewed almost all the legislators in 1957, the proportion of district-oriented legislators exceeded the proportion of state-oriented members in every case. In California, the district-oriented members made up 35 percent of all legislators; in New Jersey, 27 percent; in Ohio, 28 percent; and in Tennessee, 21 percent. The proportion of state-oriented members ranged from 9 percent in Tennessee to 20 percent in California. Analysis of interview data from the membership of the 1965 Iowa legislature indicated an even split: 35 percent were classified as district-oriented and 35 percent as state-oriented. Studies of the legislators in Wisconsin, Pennsylvania, and North Carolina suggest a considerably higher proportion of district-oriented legislators in those states. In Samuel C. Patterson's study of the 1957 Wisconsin legislature, as many as 70 percent of the members were categorized as district-oriented. Frank J. Sorauf found that among Pennsylvania legislators in 1958, 35 percent of the Democrats and 56 percent of the Republicans could be characterized as district-oriented. Donald P. Sprengel identified 65 percent of the 1965 North Carolina legislature as district-oriented. At the other extreme, Elmer E. Cornwell and his associates found that although 21 percent of the members of the 1969 Rhode Island legislature were district-oriented, more than double that proportion (47 percent) were state-oriented. These interstate variations in constituency role orientations are not easy to explain, although they may be better understood in terms of interstate differences in political culture. For instance, in Pennsylvania, a substantial amount of localism in state politics based on a tradition of party fragmentation may help to explain why a sizable proportion of its legislators in the late 1950s were district-oriented. In Wisconsin, political independence is a well-established norm, and there is some evidence to suggest its special legislative impact.[7]

In every state, and in Congress as well, there are legislators whose area focus is broader. In all the studies referred to in the preceding paragraph, a considerable proportion of the legislators could be said to be something more than narrow parochialists. Of the congressmen interviewed by Davidson, 51 percent indicated that their constituency role orientation included something beyond the narrow representation of their own bailiwick. Although the proportions vary considerably, state legislators do, in some significant number, show signs of representational interests that are wider than those of their own constituencies. Wherever the question has been analyzed, legislators have been found who think of themselves as representing both their own constituents and the larger constituency of the state or nation. One state legislator said:

> Well, I consider the state legislature to be like a board of directors of a great state on the same plane as in a large corporation. I feel the legislator has two basic responsibilities—to represent their own section, but beyond that to exercise judgment in representing all the people of the state.[8]

And a congressman described his constituency role orientation by asserting: "My job is to serve the best interests of my district as well as the best interests of the nation. There is no conflict here, because whatever is good for a segment of the country is good for the whole."[9] At the same time, Wahlke and his associates concluded that such so-called district-state legislators may reflect only a minor dose of cosmopolitanism, that "these hyphenated legislators may more resemble district-oriented than state-oriented respondents in attitudes and behavior."[10]

The area focus of the legislative role is likely to have a relationship to the political milieu in which the legislator is elected. Representatives from politically competitive districts should be more district-oriented than those from safe districts; whereas legislators elected from one-party districts should be more state-oriented (or nation-oriented, in the case of congressmen). This set of expected relationships between political environment and role conception is borne out for congressmen and for representatives in California, New Jersey, Ohio, and Wisconsin; in none of these states is the relationship simply an artifact of rural-urban differences in the political competitiveness of legislative districts.[11]

The constituency role orientations of legislators are closely tied to certain of the service outputs of the legislative system, in particular to errand-boy and educational activities. In Chapter 13 we noted some of the errand-boy activities of congressmen in handling case mail, and although such activities do prevail in state legislatures, they are perhaps less important there than in Washington. Similarly, educational activities are more notable at the congressional level. Speeches, newspaper columns, newsletters, and other communications devices are common for the performance of these educational activities. The newsletter is perhaps the most widely used. About 90 percent of the members of Congress send newsletters to constituents, and these newsletters increasingly have an educational purpose.[12] District-oriented legislators (among state legislators, at any rate) are more likely to engage in these service activities than state-oriented legislators are.[13]

INTEREST-GROUP ROLE ORIENTATIONS

In Chapter 12, we discussed the role orientations of lobbyists and suggested the legislators' role responses to interest groups. The data that fulfill the facilitator, neutral, and resister conceptualizations are based on interviews with legislators in California, New Jersey, Ohio, Tennessee, and Iowa and with a small sample of United States congressmen.[14] These data indicate that in the relatively pluralistic states of California, New Jersey, and Ohio, where pressure politics is fairly highly developed, about two-fifths of the legislators take the facilitator orientation, about one-fifth take the resister orientation, and the remainder are neutrals. In Iowa in 1965, 29 percent of the representatives were facilitators, 12 percent were resisters, and the remainder were neutrals. More than three-fourths of the Tennessee legislators were either neutrals or resisters, which suggests both that the absence of partisanship does not necessarily increase the importance or salience of interest-group politics for legislators and that underdeveloped pluralistic group life, along with negative legislator attitudes toward interest-group activity, may provide a political culture that lessens the importance of pressure-group politics for legislators.[15] Davidson found that 29 percent of congressmen were facilitators, a fifth were resisters, and half were neutrals, with House Democrats more likely to be resisters and Republicans more likely to be facilitators.

PARTY ROLE ORIENTATIONS

In Chapter 16, we will deal in some detail with the party voting behavior of American legislators. But the party attachments of legislators can be viewed in terms of their normative expectations about conformity to party. Orientations toward political parties are ambiguous in American politics, and it is not always clear whether legislators, in verbalizing their expectations about partisan behavior, are referring to the legislative or the extralegislative parties. The legislative party in Congress "appears to extend little beyond the survival of the group as a scheduling device and as a means of allocating instrumental rewards such as committee assignments."[16] But as David B. Truman has suggested:

Even these seem in many instances to be contingent upon the satisfaction of norms deriving from elsewhere in the political system, upon the reconciliation of the legislator's multiple group memberships. Yet the norms do seem at times to include more than procedural functions. When the competing demands of loyalties outside the legislative party are not dominant, the norms of the legislative party apparently can reach into areas of significant substantive policy.[17]

Without minimizing the importance of party orientations in the Congress, it must be pointed out that the scope of party orientations may vary considerably among members, even when they are party-oriented. The fragmentation and localism of American party organization make the congressional district a rather autonomous unit in the party structure. Legislators who have the same party label may respond to their party in different ways because the scope of their focus is their district party rather than the national party. And when the congressman owes his election to a well-organized, well-disciplined district party organization, he may even be relatively free from national party and other pressures.

Indeed, there is considerable reason to believe that a strong local party organization either insulates him or screens out the conflicting pressures so that he finds it easier to clarify and vote his personal convictions. Professional party men tend to be reluctant to tell each other how to do their jobs. Contrariwise, when the district party organization is inchoate, factional, and the incumbent is highly dependent upon his own personal organization, he is much more exposed to conflicting group demands and to claims placed upon him by personal-financial and friendly sources of support.[18]

Party-oriented legislators who conceptualize their roles in terms of the legislative party may conceive of the legislative party in different ways. Differences in the meaning of party orientation can be observed not only in different legislatures but also within the same legislative body. Party-oriented legislators who were members of the 1952 session of the Massachusetts legislature fell into three categories in terms of the meanings they gave to party: (1) those who saw party as a vehicle for the advancement of class or ideological forces, (2) those who defined party issues by the activity of the party leaders, and (3) those who were principally oriented to the party program.[19] Differences between Republicans and Democrats in their party orientations were not significant among Massachusetts legislators, although Avery Leiserson found that Republican congressmen were somewhat more party-oriented than Democrats (on the strength of interviews with a small sample of members of the United States House of Representatives).[20]

The party man is the legislator who votes with his party and supports his party's program. As a party man in the Wisconsin assembly put it: "It's absolutely necessary for a member to vote with his party on party platform bills. It's your bible, and if you don't want to belong to that religion, you should get another bible."[21] The party man gives great weight to party in orienting his behavior; he supports the party leadership; he may support the legislative party even when the party position is at variance with his own preferences. But his party expectations do not necessarily require blind loyalty to party. Studies of state legislators' party orientations indicate that party men may deviate from the decisions of party caucuses if they do so within the party framework and explain their problems to party colleagues (usually at the caucus). The most generally acceptable reason for departing from party loyalty among party men arises when the legislator believes that the interests of his district require him to act contrary to a party position. But in partisan state legislatures, few representatives are likely to perceive significant differences between party role expectations and the interests of their district. For instance, among party-oriented Republicans in the Wisconsin assembly, more than three-fourths said that conflicts between the interests of their party and the interests of their districts were "infrequent."[22]

Among state legislators, the extent of party role orientations varies greatly. Obviously, such orientations are not meaningful in nonpartisan or one-party legislatures. In states such as Wisconsin, New Jersey, Ohio, and Massachusetts, party role orientations have great importance, and expectancies related to party are frequent. It may be expected that party role behavior will be more intensely and widely expected as partisan competition increases in the legislature. In states like California, where the legislature has undergone a change from nonpartisan to partisan, party-oriented role-playing appears to be increasingly expected. But the data are not conclusive; Sorauf found a relatively low incidence of party-oriented expectations in the highly partisan Pennsylvania legislature.[23]

Party role orientations are clearly affected by the majority-minority status of the legislative party. A legislative party with a large majority may tolerate more deviation from party positions than one that is functioning under circumstances where the margins between parties are close. Again, the minority party member may exhibit very limited party role orientation, as is illustrated by the following comments by two Democratic members of the Wisconsin assembly:

The Democrats are in the minority, so the only thing we can do is hold them on the line—we have to hold them to the manual.

A minority member should try to get his party's program through. But when you're in the minority, you have a hell of a time getting anything through, except pointing up what's wrong with the majority party.[24]

The indifferent legislator is one who eschews partisan expectations about his behavior, who serves in a legislature where partisan expectations are not relevant, or who endeavors to rise above party. Presumably, legislators in nonpartisan and one-party state legislatures could be said to be indifferent with respect to their party role orientations. But even in partisan legislatures, some members may be indifferents. For example, one Wisconsin legislator said: "I never listen to anything that goes on in caucus. Everybody in caucus speaks for his own selfish interest in their district." Sometimes the hopelessness of minority status appears to be the basis for the indifferent orientation. In Wisconsin, some Democrats defined their roles in a way that minimized their partisan obligations and maximized cooperation with the Republican majority.

A minority member can't get anything passed if you become a red-hot party man. They don't hold it against our floor leader or assistant floor leader; that's their job. But if any other member gets violently partisan he's in trouble. They won't let him pass any legislation. It's better to have a record of accomplishment.

Another Wisconsin legislator illustrated the indifferent who rises above party:

> I was elected to the Assembly on a party vehicle, but after the election an assembly-man represents all the people of his district and should conduct his job on a nonpartisan basis. There have to be two parties, but I supported beneficial Republican legislation. If you can't get your bill passed you support a similar Republican bill. There should be closer harmony between the parties on bills that benefit the people.[25]

Interviews with a sample of congressmen indicated that about one-fifth of them were partisan indifferents.[26] The indifferent role orientation hangs between the party man and the maverick. He may or may not vote consistently with his party on party issues, but he does not attach great importance to partisan expectations.

The maverick regularly and persistently deviates from the position of his party; he takes an independent course; he has a reputation for deviancy and independence from party; and other members expect him to behave that way. Senators Wayne Morse (D-Oreg.) and William Proxmire (D-Wis.) are good examples of mavericks in the United States Senate, where mavericks have not been at all unusual. Among the United States representatives studied by Davidson in 1963–1964, 19 percent were classified as mavericks.[27] Maverick role expectations have not been widely characteristic in American state legislatures. Of the members of the four state legislatures studied by Wahlke and his associates, half or more did not make reference to maverick orientations. The percentages of these legislators referring to mavericks in their legislatures were:

Tennessee	6
New Jersey	30
California	39
Ohio	50

But in a state like Wisconsin, where political independence in the legislature is supported by norms in the wider political community, maverick orientations are much more notable and more widely expected. Almost all the Republicans in the 1957 session of the Wisconsin assembly recognized and identified a maverick role.

Intralegislative variations in party role orientations are related both to the majority-minority status of the legislative party and to the degree of electoral competition in legislative districts. The strength and flexibility of the party role tend to be greater where the legislative party is the majority and lesser for minority party members. Mavericks tend to be elected from districts that are atypical of their party or from districts where electoral margins are close. But interstate variations in party role orientations are more complex, involving important differences between states in their political environments or cultures. A partisan political culture might be defined as one in which party conflicts are perceived as highly relevant and important, where emotional involvement in and attachment to party are significant, and where political actors evaluate positively party influence in policy-making. Since these kinds of attitudes and beliefs about partisanship vary from state to state, the political cultures in which legislatures act are clearly varied. Attitudes toward, and presumably enactment of, party roles will tend to vary in terms of the partisan political culture; one correlation analysis among the factors suggested here has provided support for the proposition that "the more a legislature's political culture is party-oriented, the more likely will legislators look on the role of the party man as a positive asset of his total legislative position."[28]

BUREAUCRATIC ROLE ORIENTATIONS

Legislators may be executive-oriented or agency-oriented (or both) with reference to the executive branch of government. In state legislatures, the governor's man is a common role orientation, although it may take various forms and have varied results. In some states, especially those of the South and Southwest, the state governors have often been in a position to designate their legislative leaders, who occupy the official leadership positions in the legislature.[29] But these relationships are not always stable. In California, for instance, the floor leader had been considered the governor's spokesman in the Progressive days, but this practice was abandoned in the 1920s. Thereafter, in the individualistic and relatively nonpartisan California assembly, the chairman of the Ways and Means Committee came to be recognized as the spokesman for the governor, and the majority floor leader came to represent the institutionalization of opposition to the governor.[30] The highly atomized legislative politics of Florida has tended to make gubernatorially oriented legislative roles untenable, and the governor is often required to bargain individually with legislators.[31] Of course, executive-oriented roles are more general in American legislatures and go beyond those who are gubernatorial spokesmen to include any legislator who defines his job in terms of executive leadership. Legislators who take their cues from the governor and whose role expectations are executive-oriented are fairly common in partisan legislatures, where the governor shares the same party identification as the legislative majority, as well as in nonpartisan or one-party legislatures, where the governor is the dominant legislative leader.[32]

In Congress and in a few state legislatures, executive-oriented roles are patterned institutionally, so that it is possible to describe the legislative role structure crudely in terms of "administration supporters" and the "loyal opposition." But executive-legislator interaction in the Congress is much more complex and ambiguous than it is in most states. In Congress, official and informal leadership roles are very unlikely to be played by different individuals, and the President is usually required to rely upon his party's congressional leaders, even though their loyalties and orientations tend to be directed toward the legislative institution. Although "the fundamental complexity and subtlety of the role lie in the fact that the elective leaders are, and probably must be, both the president's leaders and the party's leaders," congressional leaders are usually disposed to "play down their spokesmanship for the President."[33]

In addition to executive orientation, American legislators may be agency-oriented. Their formal legislative positions, the nature of their constituencies, or their substantive legislative interests may lead them to orient their jobs toward a specific administrative agency or set of agencies. Legislative committee structure and norms of specialization frequently facilitate agency orientation, especially among congressmen. Some members of Congress, typically those who have served for many years, know certain administrative agencies or departments intimately and frequently have had more experience with them than the agency heads themselves. These members may come to take very personal interests in agency operations and have great influence upon agency policy.[34]

The relationships between legislators and bureaucrats, although persistent (especially in the case of congressmen) and often mutually agreeable, tend to be characterized by suspicion, jealousy, and hostility. "The role of the legislator versus the bureaucrat is an old one," Ralph K. Huitt has observed, "rooted in an institutional jealousy never hard to arouse."[35] And the tensions in legislator-agency relationships may be quite impersonal, as was reflected, for example, in the exchange between Senator Robert A. Taft and Chester Bowles (who was director of economic stabilization) during hearings before the Senate Committee on Banking and Currency on the question of price controls after World War II. Taft told Bowles:

> I don't distinguish you from the administration. The administration has one policy; you are the Director of Economic Stabilization. What your particular views are makes no difference to me. You are carrying on the policies of the administration. When I say "You" I should be more explicit. I mean the administration. I am not attacking you personally on it, or anything of the sort. I am criticizing your analysis of the situation which is only affected by administration policy; not what you personally think. That makes no difference to me.[36]

The resentments and hostilities of legislators toward administrators are often reflected in the context of committee or subcommittee hearings. Although "there is seldom the element of direct challenge to the personal status of the legislator, ... the authoritative and self-assured way in which the administrator disposes of his own knowledge and the legislator's questions can ... become a source of uneasiness" because "the administrator deals self-confidently with a matter which the legislator does not always grasp with the same measure of self-confidence."[37]

Tensions between legislators and administrators are very well illustrated by J. Leiper Freeman's analysis of the relationships between bureaucrats in the Bureau of Indian Affairs and congressional committees, especially the House and Senate Committees on Indian Affairs. He concluded that:

> The committee member's role, in which he is expected to choose wisely among policy alternatives as well as to represent his local constituency, tends to create blocks against his receptivity to the views of bureau leaders, despite their often alleged superior technical knowledge. The committee member frequently feels a strong urge to protect his status as the lawmaker in the face of bureaucratic challenge. Consequently, the committee member often prefers information and suggestions about policy from sources other than bureau leaders and their allies. Furthermore, he may frequently play something less than a neutral role in the deliberations within the sub-system by giving encouragement to non-bureau spokesmen. Certainly, even if the committee member does not feel especially sensitive about his status relative to that of bureaucrats on occasions in which the committee member's interests lie counter to the bureau leader's, he may find it convenient to

pretend that the bureaucrat is attempting to preempt the legislative function and to lay claim to a superiority of knowledge that is based on theory rather than on practicality.[38]

Members of Congress have, and must virtually cultivate, regular and personal relationships with bureaucrats. Their need for information is enormous, and administrative agencies often provide the only expertise available. The frequent recourse to personal intervention with administrative agencies on behalf of constituents "has greater consequences than the maintenance of a sensitive attachment of the legislator to his audible constituency. . . . It fosters in him a particular attitude of personal expectancy toward the bureaucracy and toward the individual administrator."[39] James A. Robinson has estimated that 75 percent of the members of the House and Senate discuss some topic with the Department of State each week, and most of these communications concern the representatives' constituents. In interviewing a sample of congressmen, Robinson investigated the association between approval of State Department foreign policy and various aspects of the communications linkage between congressmen and the department. He found that

> statistically significant relations do not exist between Congressmen's satisfaction with the way the Department of State handles requests from constituents and satisfaction with foreign policy. . . . Significant relations are observed between satisfaction with other aspects of the communications network linking Congress and the Department and foreign policy. These include the Department's record for answering requests for policy information, volunteering information to Congress, and perception of the weight of Congressional opinion in the Department's formulation of policy.[40]

REPRESENTATIONAL ROLE ORIENTATIONS

Legislators' role orientations may differ in terms of their style of representation. The trustee sees himself as a free agent, premising his decision-making behavior upon what he considers morally right and just, and following the dictates of his judgment and conscience. John F. Kennedy, when he was still a United States senator from Massachusetts, once articulated a trustee conceptualization of the legislative role. He said:

> The voters selected us . . . because they had confidence in our judgment and our ability to exercise that judgment from a position where we could determine what were their own best interests, as a part of the nation's interests. This may mean that we must on occasion lead, inform, correct and sometimes even ignore constituent opinion, if we are to exercise fully that judgment for which we were elected.[41]

In the same vein, a state legislator clearly set forth the trustee orientation when he explained his conception of the legislator's job: "I have never subscribed to the theory that I'm here to reflect the views of my constituents. I'm here to vote as

I see it. You can't vote by what you think the constituents' thinking is. You don't know what that thinking is."[42]

But surely a substantial proportion of American legislators are inclined to a non-Burkean formulation of the legislative role. The delegate thinks of his job in terms of reflecting constituent opinion. There are many illustrations of this role orientation; here are two expressions of it from Wisconsin legislators:

> I regard myself as the servant of the people, not their master. Whether I believe in something or not, I go along with the people in my district when I'm voting on legislation. Daylight saving is a good example. I was personally opposed to it, but the people in my district wanted it, so I voted for it.

> My duty is to go to Madison and vote the way the people in my district want me to, whether I personally agree with it or not. I'm not going to Madison to do what I want, but what the people want.[43]

The politico is an intermediate type, the legislator who is sometimes a trustee, sometimes a delegate, or who reconciles both orientations. One state legislator who appeared to combine both trustee and delegate orientations said:

> There is a line of demarcation between what they want at home and what you think is good for them. I haven't been too disturbed by that yet but it could become a major problem. I don't think I could ever settle just where the line is. It is too flexible. Each piece of legislation must be considered individually to determine it.[44]

It is possible to compare the representational role orientations of legislators in nine states and of the United States House members; such a comparison is made in Table 15.1. These data present numerous anomalies. Wahlke and his associates argue, apparently ex post facto, that legislators ought to be found to be predominantly trustees because the business of government has become so complicated and technical that people are neither capable of nor interested in giving their representatives instructions. But it might be argued that legislators are increasingly able to get their constituents' opinions, given rapid transportation and communication, polls, and the like. Certainly governmental life is simpler in Tennessee than in California, New Jersey, or Ohio; and yet 81 percent of the Tennessee legislators were found to be trustees.

Wahlke and his associates found a relatively low proportion of delegates in California, New Jersey, Ohio, and Tennessee. Yet in the Wisconsin assembly, two-thirds of the legislators were delegates; and a preponderance of Pennsylvania and North Carolina representatives were delegates. The complications of modern government are not likely to have been less serious in Wisconsin and Pennsylvania than in the states Wahlke and his associates studied. We can at present offer no rationale to reconcile these anomalies in the data except to say that the findings for Wisconsin, North Carolina, and Pennsylvania cast grave doubt upon the conclusion that "the trustee role is the easiest and the delegate role the most difficult to take."[45] But Table 15.1 does demonstrate the empirical possibility of categorizing legislators analytically in terms of the stylistic dimension of representation.

TABLE 15.1 Distribution of Representational Role Orientations (In percentages)

REPRESENTATIONAL ROLE ORIENTATION	CALIF. (1957)	N.J. (1957)	OHIO (1957)	TENN. (1957)	WIS. (1957)	PA. (1957)	N.C. (1965)	IOWA (1967)	MICH. (1967)	U.S. HOUSE (1963–1964)
Trustee	55	61	56	81	21	33	38	51	37	28
Politico	25	22	29	13	4	27	5	23	31	46
Delegate	20	17	15	6	66	39	57	24	33	23
Not classifiable	–	–	–	–	9	1	–	2	–	3
Total	100	100	100	100	100	100	100	100	101	100
Number	49	54	114	78	89	106	100	181	95	87

SOURCES: Roger H. Davidson, *The Role of the Congressman* (New York, 1969), p. 117; Patterson's study of the 1957 Wisconsin assembly and the 1967 Iowa House of Representatives; Frank J. Sorauf, *Party and Representation* (New York, 1963), p. 124; John W. Soule, "The Influence of Political Socialization, Interpersonal Values, and Differential Recruitment Patterns on Legislative Adaptation: The Michigan House of Representatives" (Ph.D. diss., University of Kentucky, 1967), p. 212; Donald P. Sprengel, "Legislative Perceptions of Gubernatorial Power in North Carolina" (Ph.D. diss., University of North Carolina, 1966), p. 55; and John C. Wahlke et al., *The Legislative System* (New York, 1962), p. 281.

PURPOSIVE ROLE ORIENTATIONS

One cannot observe the floor action of an American legislature without being impressed with the importance of the *process*—the rules of procedure, the steps in the passage of legislation, the importance of committee work, and the ritual of floor debate and action. In some legislatures, particularly the amateur state legislative bodies, there are members who are very minimally adapted to the legislative role. They may be process-oriented only to the extent of sitting in the audience, hardly participating at all; they are simply spectators. Others' purposive orientations may be more to their private occupational and career ambitions than to legislative processes. These members may use legislative office primarily to advertise their private occupations. They are advertisers, lacking both the commitment to legislative work and the patience to master legislative skills. Still other members may be minimally adapted to the legislative role in terms of their general reluctance to enact it fully. The reluctant finds the legislature populated by strangers with backgrounds and values different from his own; he finds the pace of legislative processes suspiciously swift; and he may be baffled, confused, and discomfited by the complicated processes of lawmaking.[46] Legislators whose adaptation to the legislative process is more fully developed are likely to have a fairly wide range of role orientations.

In state legislatures, a high proportion of representatives undoubtedly orient their jobs with regard to decision-making in terms of the legislative rituals; they are ritualists. Perhaps the leading example of a ritualist in the United States House of Representatives was H. R. Gross (R-Iowa), whose only important claim to fame in the House was his mastery and skillful use of the rules of procedure, especially his objections to unanimous-consent requests, to obstruct legislation and frustrate the leadership. Clearly, the legislative body would be immobilized if a large proportion of the membership were not oriented toward the mechanics of the legislative process.

Other orientations toward legislative purposes are important, too. Some legislators approach their tasks as advocates and defenders of popular wishes, needs, and desires: the tribunes. Others are innovators and creators of policy directions or programs: the inventors. Still others mediate and negotiate conflicting interests: the brokers. Many legislators play a combination of these roles.

A careful study of these analytical role types conducted in California, New Jersey, Ohio, and Tennessee indicated that the ritualist orientation was most common in these states. The broker orientation was taken by more than one-fourth of the legislators in New Jersey, Ohio, and California; but it was less important in Tennessee, where, presumably, interest-group conflict is not so complex. Tribune and inventor orientations were found to be most important in New Jersey, where, at the time, party control of the legislature and the governorship was divided and where, therefore, greater expressions of legislative initiative were to be expected.[47]

Quite similar results were obtained in research on 119 members of the Iowa house in 1965. Ronald D. Hedlund found that about a third (32 percent) of the legislators conceptualized their purposive role as that of ritualist. About 29 percent identified themselves as brokers; 24 percent, as tribunes; and 13 percent, as inventors.[48] However, the sample evidence for United States congressmen presents a different picture at the national level. Of the congressmen Davidson interviewed in 1963–1964, 47 percent were categorized as tribunes and 41 percent as ritualists. Inventors and brokers were few in number (7 percent and 4 percent, respectively). Davidson believes that a difference between Congress and state legislatures should be expected:

> It seems reasonable to argue that in comparison with state legislators, Representatives perceive themselves more visible to their constituents and devote more time to dealing with constituency problems. Representatives no doubt sense that communications media have made their voters more aware of certain national issues and more apt to turn to them for help in resolving problems. . . . State legislators, in contrast: undoubtedly receive less mail, have less office contact, and typically have no staff help in dealing with district affairs.[49]

STRUCTURAL ROLE ORIENTATIONS

The roles of committee members and legislative leaders are discussed in Chapter 17 and Chapter 6, respectively. Readers interested in these roles should turn to the relevant sections of those chapters.

The role of the expert is a particularly important and functional role orientation, given the increasing specialization of American legislatures and the significance of specialization in the normative systems of these bodies. Although the committee structures of legislatures provide the basis for the organization of legislative specialization, some legislators have reputations for, and respond to expectations about, specialization in particular policy arenas. With regard to Congress, the role of expert is familiar. Well-known Senate experts, such as Fulbright (D-Ark.), on foreign affairs; Morse (D-Oreg.), on labor law; Javits (R-N.Y.), on legal matters; and Monroney (D-Okla.), on legislative reorganization, and less familiar House specialists, such as Vinson (D-Ga.), on defense; Fogarty (D-R.I.) on medical research; Kilday (D-Tex.), on military regulations; Mills (D-Ark.), on taxation; and Judd (R-Minn.), on Asian policy, have testified to the expert role in the Congress.

Attributions of, and expectations about, expertise in state legislatures are no less important, although the state legislative expert is perhaps less visible to the ordinary citizen. Considerable consensus among legislators who have been interviewed systematically suggest the functional importance of the expert in the state legislature.[50] The subject-matter fields of legal problems, taxation, education, agriculture, conservation, labor, and local government tend to be those with which state legislative experts deal most.

The expert role carries with it considerable responsibility. "There is the feeling that the legislator-expert should play a dual role, responsible in some degree to his colleagues."[51] As one of the experts in the Wisconsin assembly put it: "I am very careful when I take a stand on bills to make sure that my vote is absolutely right and based on my very best judgment, because people respect my experience and I know they follow my vote. It is a very great responsibility."[52]

State legislative experts tend to base their expertise upon their extralegislative occupational experience more than upon other factors; whereas congressmen may be more likely to develop expertise in areas other than those that might be expected on the basis of their occupational experience. Finally, although partisan considerations are involved in expectations about experts, these representatives tend to have reputations for special knowledge that cross party lines.

ROLE INTERRELATIONSHIPS AND CONFLICT

The role orientations of American legislators are interrelated, and it is likely that some kinds of orientations go naturally together. Thus, representational and constituency role orientations are, in a sense, complementary. The district-oriented legislator is more likely to take the delegate orientation than state-oriented or state-district-oriented representatives are; and the state-oriented legislator is more likely to take the trustee orientation than other legislators are. The data for state legislators confirm these expected combinations of role orientations. Wahlke and his associates found this to be the case in California, New Jersey, Ohio, and Tennessee. The data in Table 15.2 illustrate these findings for Wisconsin and for the United States House of Representatives.[53] A complete map of the role structure of the legislative body would include an analysis of the interpenetrations of each type of role orientation with all the others. An attempt at such an analysis with partial data has been made for the four legislatures studied by Wahlke and his associates. Their analysis suggests that "through the use of nonconventional analytical categories, in our case derived from a role analysis of legislators, we can describe the structure of a legislative chamber, not as it is embodied in rules and bylaws, . . . but as it represents a system of action."[54]

At the same time, the legislative role is particularly susceptible to conflicting expectations. Many a legislator has been torn between the demands of his constituents, political-interest groups, and party leaders. Role-conflict resolution is a social-psychological process about which rather little is known, but it is possible in legislative settings to observe behavior from which the existence of such a process can be inferred.[55] Perhaps the problems of Silvio O. Conte (R-Mass.) will serve as an adequate illustration of the occupational role strains that can be experienced by a congressman:

> When I returned to my district office there were long and loud complaints that I was spending too much time there and should be in Washington. Then when I didn't make it for several weeks, others said, "Who does that guy think he is? We only see him during elections."
>
> When I came home shortly after being sworn in, driving my old car, they were upset because it looked like something farmers use to haul trash. But, by gosh, when I bought a new one, they were sure the lobbyists had gotten to me already.
>
> The first time I came home wearing an old suit people said, "Look at him! Just an old bum." Yet when I bought a new suit, I heard, "He's gone high-hat with that Ivy League suit of his."
>
> One Sunday I missed church because I was tied up talking with constituents and some people said that being down in Washington had made an atheist of me. Several weeks later, when I was again back home and did get to church, they said, "Why that pious fraud! He's just trying to dig up votes!"[56]

TABLE 15.2 Constituency and Representational Role Orientations (In percentages)

REPRESENTATIONAL ROLE ORIENTATION	WISCONSIN ASSEMBLY (1957)			U.S. HOUSE OF REPRESENTATIVES (1963–1964)		
	District-oriented	State-district-oriented	State-oriented	District-oriented	State-district-oriented	Nation-oriented
Trustee	13	34	53	6	11	0
Delegate	74	56	47	55	21	45
Politico	5	10	0	39	68	55
Not classified	8	0	0	0	0	0
Total	100	100	100	100	100	100
Number	62	9	15	33	19	29

SOURCES: Patterson's study of the 1957 Wisconsin assembly; and Roger H. Davidson, *The Role of the Congressman* (New York, 1969), p. 126.

We do not wish to minimize the importance of role conflict in legislatures or to make light of the difficulties, tensions, and agonies that individual legislators may experience in resolving conflicting expectations about how they should perform their jobs. On the other hand, some legislative role conflicts are probably fairly easily resolved, in at least two respects. First, the legislative process involves a multiplicity of decisional points, and the legislator can be guided by different orientations at different times. Charles O. Jones's analysis of members of the House Agriculture Committee suggests how congressmen may resolve conflicting demands by taking different role orientations serially:

> The representative on the House Agriculture Committee can view his composite role retrospectively as one in which he has taken several separate actions to make up a total pattern in regard to the omnibus farm legislation. He also can recognize that on different occasions he felt differing demands upon him in his several capacities, as a member of a party, a representative of a constituency, a member of a committee, of a Congress, of interest groups, etc. He was able to reconcile, compromise or avoid some of the inherent conflicts in these demands, at least in part, because of the multiple action points.[57]

Second, a very common kind of potential legislative role conflict—that between constituency expectations and demands as opposed to others—is probably quite easily resolved by American legislators by simply deferring to constituency demands. American legislators probably do not often perceive constituency versus state or national differences or constituency versus party differences as very salient ones, but even when they do, they are likely to opt for the constituency expectations.[58]

CITIZENS' EXPECTATIONS

The little evidence there is about the perceptions and idealizations of constituents with regard to the role of their representative is indicative of both consensus and ambiguity. With respect to the purposive roles of national representatives, there appears to be very broad consensus between congressmen's role definitions and the expectations of the general public about the representative role. In 1968, Davidson acquired interview data for a national population sample of about 2,500 respondents. He asked them to articulate what they thought their congressman should do as an elected representative and found that their responses could be classified according to the same purposive role types as the responses of the legislators themselves (in his 1963–1964 survey). His results are depicted in Table 15.3, which shows distributions of role orientations for citizens and congressmen for the purposive categories. Although public expectations appear to lean more heavily on the side of the inventor role than the orientations of representatives do, in general it could be said that citizens and representatives are in substantial agreement on the broad orientation that a congressman ought to take toward his role. Of his findings, Davidson says:

TABLE 15.3 Purposive Role Orientations as Perceived by Congressmen and Citizens (In percentages)

PURPOSIVE ROLE	U. S. CONGRESSMEN (1963–1964)	GENERAL PUBLIC (1968)
Tribune	47	41
Ritualist	41	32
Inventor	7	15
Broker	4	2
Other	1	11
Total	100	101
Number	87	2,532

SOURCE: Roger H. Davidson, "Public Prescriptions for the Job of Congressman," *Midwest Journal of Political Science* 14 (1970): 654.

> The Tribune role is so commonly expressed that it must be interpreted as a cultural norm for legislative performance, a collective specification as to what individuals think is proper. . . . The vast majority of citizens probably lack the knowledge or the inclination to convert this norm into an overt sanction. Yet the norm emits strong and unambiguous signals, and upon occasion sanctions may be imposed against an errant legislator who defies his constituents on a particularly salient issue, or who seems to have gotten "out of touch."[59]

Whether such sanctions are, in fact, invoked is problematic, but it does seem correct to think of public attitudes toward the purposive roles of American legislators as constituting an important element in the distinctive cultural parameters that help to mold and shape legislative behavior in the American context.

When it comes to more specific prescriptions of the way in which a representative ought to perform his job, the fragmentary evidence from which generalizations must be made suggests great ambiguity in public expectations about the legislative role. Carl D. McMurray and Malcolm B. Parsons interviewed a small sample of citizens of Florida in 1962, asking them (among other things) whether a congressman or state legislator "should find out what his district wants and always vote accordingly," or whether he "should decide what he thinks is best, and always vote accordingly, even if it is not what his district wants." Thus, the trustee and delegate orientations were juxtaposed in perhaps unrealistically sharp focus for this sample of Florida constituents. In any event, 47 percent of the respondents clearly favored the delegate role and opposed the trustee role, and 18 percent favored the trustee and opposed the delegate. But a total of 35 percent of the respondents either favored or opposed *both*. What expectations for their representative the 10 percent of the respondents who opposed both orientations might have had is difficult to imagine, but the 25 percent of the respondents who felt their legislator could be both trustee and delegate may have harbored the most realistic perceptions of the possibilities in the legislative role.[60] Unfortunately, there are no comparable data for Florida legislators, and the interstate variations in the distributions of representational roles are so great (see Table 15.1) that interpretation of these results is not easy to make.

THE UTILITY OF ROLE ANALYSIS[61]

Mapping patterns of legislative role orientations is a useful exercise in at least two different ways. First, it is possible to learn a great deal in a descriptive way about the legislature as an institution by identifying the matrix of representative roles played by its members and to come to see how the normative political expectations in the political system and in the legislative institution itself are reflected in the orientations legislators have toward their jobs as elected representatives. Second, role analysis of a legislative system makes it possible to identify who may legitimately make demands on legislators and the range of demands that they may legitimately make. If the norms of the legislative system are specific and widely accepted, all the participants may recognize what the bounds of legitimacy are. For example, if one of the legislative norms is a high degree of party loyalty, it might be unthinkable for an outside group to ask a legislator to vote against his party; such a demand would be widely regarded as an illegitimate one. If the system is not so well integrated and norms are less pervasive, legislators may have different viewpoints about what is legitimate. Research at the state level has shown that some, but not most, legislators would exclude lobbyists or certain categories of lobbyists from the ranks of those who can legitimately make demands on them.

At the same time, it is important to recognize the substantial limitations on legislative role analysis, at least insofar as the presently existing evidence is concerned. As role analyses for an increasing number of American legislatures accumulate, it becomes clear that the correlates of variations in legislators' role orientations are by no means stable from one system to another. Several scholars have explored the sources of roles in legislatures at the national and state levels. Their findings (summarized in Table 15.4) show how many variables are associated with differences in roles, and how much these variables differ in importance from one legislature to another. Because representational roles have received the most study, our analysis focuses on them. In addition to a variety of state legislative studies and research on Congress, Table 15.4 includes the entry "Metropolitan," which refers to an analysis of data gathered in 1967 from 141 legislators in nine metropolitan counties in seven states.

The correlates listed in Table 15.4 demonstrate the contradictory character of findings, especially with regard to educational background, career goals, seniority, ideology, and partisan competitiveness of districts. For other correlates of role orientations, either no statistically significant relationships have been discovered or evidence is based upon investigation in only one state. These bivariate relationships have their limitations, since it is impossible to be sure what effect other variables may have on them; but it seems clear enough that both with respect to personal background characteristics and attributes of legislative districts, the evidence concerning possible sources of legislative roles is fragmentary and sometimes contradictory.

In addition to asking how variations in the role orientations legislators take can be accounted for, it may be helpful to ask how useful role analysis might be in explaining the actual behavior of representatives. If findings about the former

TABLE 15.4 Correlates of Representational Roles

FINDINGS CONCERNING REPRESENTATIONAL ROLE	STUDY	CORRE- LATION	LEVEL OF STATISTICAL SIGNIFICANCE
Psychological factors			
1. Legislators with a low faith in people are more likely to be trustees.	Iowa	0.08	0.01
2. Legislators who place a high value on exercising leadership are more likely to be trustees.	Michigan (1967)	0.34	0.01
Political socialization			
1. Legislators who were introduced to politics after adolescence and before entering politics are more likely to be delegates.	Iowa	0.06	0.05
2. Legislators who were socialized as adults are more likely to be trustees.	Four states	0.17	
Education			
1. Legislators with a higher level of education are more likely to be trustees.	Michigan (1967)	0.36	0.01
	California	0.37	0.05
	Metropolitan	0.45	0.01
2. There is little relationship between education and representational role.	Iowa	0.04	n.s
	Congress	*	n.s
	Indiana	*	n.s.
Occupation			
1. Legislators having a higher-status occupation are more likely to be trustees.	Iowa	0.17	n.s.
	Metropolitan	0.19	n.s.
2. There is little relationship between occupational status and representational role.	Congress	*	n.s.
	Indiana	*	n.s.
Career goals			
1. Legislators with higher career aspirations are more likely to be trustees.	Michigan (1967)	0.25	0.05
2. There is little relationship between career goals and representational role.	Iowa	0.07	n.s.
Ideology			
1. Legislators with stronger ideological views are more likely to be trustees.	Metropolitan	0.12	n.s.
2. More conservative legislators are more likely to be trustees.	Metropolitan	0.13	n.s.
3. There is little relationship between ideology and representational role.	Indiana	*	n.s.
Legislative seniority			
1. Legislators with longer legislative tenure are more likely to be trustees.	Congress	0.39	0.01
2. There is little relationship between seniority and representational role.	Iowa	0.06	n.s.
	Michigan (1967)	*	n.s.
	Pennsylvania	*	*
	Metropolitan	0.02	n.s.

TABLE 15.4 (continued)

FINDINGS CONCERNING REPRESENTATIONAL ROLE	STUDY	CORRE-LATION	LEVEL OF STATISTICAL SIGNIFICANCE
Party and campaign experience			
1. Legislators with more service in party organizations are more likely to be delegates.	Pennsylvania	*	*
2. Legislators who have been active in party organizations are more likely to be trustees.	California	0.35	0.05
3. Legislators who have been more active in campaigns are more likely to be trustees.	California	0.60	0.05
Level of party competition			
1. Legislators from competitive districts are more likely to be delegates.	Congress	0.51	0.01
	Michigan (1967)	0.15	n.s.
2. There is little relationship between competition and representational role.	Metropolitan	0.07	n.s.
3. There is little relationship between per-ceived competition and representational role.	Indiana	*	n.s.
Metropolitan versus rural districts			
1. Metropolitan legislators are more likely to be trustees.	Michigan (1961)	0.22	n.s.
2. There is little relationship between met-ropolitan status of district and representa-tional role.	Iowa	0.00	n.s.
	Congress	0.00	n.s.
	Indiana	*	n.s.
Form of districting			
1. In metropolitan counties, legislators elected at large, rather than by district, are more likely to be trustees.	Metropolitan	0.17	n.s.
Homogeneity of district			
1. Legislators who perceive their district as having many kinds of people are more likely to be trustees.	Iowa	0.54	0.05

*Relationships tested, but comparable statistics not reported.
n.s.: Not significant.
SOURCE: Malcolm E. Jewell, "Attitudinal Determinants of Legislative Behavior: The Utility of Role Analysis," in *Legislatures in Developmental Perspective,* ed. Allan Kornberg and Lloyd D. Musolf (Durham, N.C., 1970), pp. 474–475, 481. Copyright 1970, by Duke University Press.

have been inconclusive, the latter has been subjected to hardly any careful inquiry. It is useful to know a legislator's role orientations because they indicate something about the importance or priority he gives to various demands. In other words, it is possible to tell to what extent a legislator shares the expectations that others have concerning the way he should perform his job. These expectations include not only the explicit and overt demands of others but also norms that the legislator has internalized, such as a strong sense of party loyalty. A specific role orientation means a predisposition or inclination to act in a particular way; it indicates a probability, not a certainty, about voting or any other action.[62] With enough information about the legislator's role orientations, it should be possible to predict more accurately how he will respond to demands, that is, how he will vote or otherwise act as a representative. Although some effect of role orientations on legislative voting has been demonstrated, the evidence is meager, indeed.[63]

The utility of role analysis for explaining other forms of legislative behavior has seldom been explored, perhaps because political scientists have focused so much of their attention on the dependent variable of voting. At an earlier stage in the passage of legislation (when a bill is in committee), the decisions of legislators are sometimes veiled in secrecy and are more difficult to study. According to Richard F. Fenno's study, committee norms may be pervasive enough so that there is little difference among congressmen in their roles as committee members. Jones's study of the Agriculture Committee shows that in some committees, partisan and interest-group demands undermine the effectiveness of committee norms and lead members to assume a variety of roles.[64] But studies are lacking showing how the behavior of committee members is influenced by their roles.

Legislative output includes more than the passage of bills, and consequently, the behavior of legislators in other areas of decision making needs to be explained. Legislative output includes, among other things, the oversight of executive agencies and the satisfaction of constituent requests, sometimes described as errand-running. How a legislator deals with any client, whether executive agency, lobbyist, or constituent, presumably depends on his client role concepts. In some cases, legislative norms may be so clear and widely accepted that there is little room for differences in legislative roles. For example, congressional norms (and appropriations for staffing) clearly require members to service the needs of constituents, whether this means sending them a booklet on baby care or finding out why a veteran has not received his pension.

In other cases, legislative norms may be less explicit, and variations in roles may provide some clues to behavior. A number of years ago, Huitt used the concept of role to describe various patterns of behavior among members of congressional committees reviewing the policies and actions of executive agencies.[65] Congressmen use committee hearings to prosecute or defend an agency, to promote the cause of an interest group seeking policy changes, or to force an agency to deal more favorably with a constituent. There has been relatively little attention to congressional oversight of the executive, and Huitt's illustration of the utility of role analysis in this area has not been followed up.

There are differences in the specific steps legislators take to keep in touch with their constituents. A small but increasing minority (particularly at the congressional level) conduct polls. Some pay more attention than others to mail on legislative issues; some make greater efforts to attend meetings in their district; and some use election campaigns as an opportunity to determine constituent attitudes. Some legislators make a great effort, through speeches, newsletters, and radio or television appearances, to influence the thinking of constituents. It is very possible that the extent and nature of legislative efforts to maintain contacts with constituents have a significant impact on the level of public support for the legislature. Consequently, it is important to understand what motivates legislators to devote more or less attention to constituency contacts, and role analysis may be expected to provide some clues to the answer. It may be expected, for example, that delegates would take more steps to determine the views of constituents on issues and that trustees would be more interested in making constituents understand and accept their views.

Legislators differ in their day-to-day relationships with lobbyists. Some are relatively accessible; some are hard to see; and others appear to be suspicious and even hostile. When a legislator shares some common interest with a lobbyist, he must decide how closely to cooperate with him in a legislative campaign, whether to accept the lobbyist's advice on tactical questions, and whether to serve as spokesman for the interest group on the floor. The legislator may, of course, be influenced by factors such as personal friendship for the lobbyist, but his choices are likely to be shaped by his underlying attitudes about the legitimacy of the group's claims and the propriety of a legislator's working so closely with a lobbyist.

Legislative analysts have sometimes used the role concept to describe a member's own expectations regarding his career and his purpose in the legislature. If his reasons for coming to the legislature—what he hopes to achieve, what he perceives as his duty (all of which might be called purposive roles)—are understood, it may be possible to arrive at a better explanation of his decisions about seeking to play a more active and influential part in the legislature and about seeking reelection or election to some other office. James D. Barber has shown that the motivations for entering the legislature and the intention of serving several terms help to explain the types and extent of activities in the legislature.[66] It may be argued that career motivations and plans for legislative service are not properly described as roles because they are not primarily shaped by either the norms of the legislative system or the expectations of others in the system. Career motivations and plans result principally from a legislator's own choices, but they may be of fundamental importance in his definition of the responsibilities of his job.

NOTES

1. The scheme that follows adheres closely to that of John C. Wahlke et al., *The Legislative System* (New York, 1962), pp. 170–413. See also David Easton, "An Approach to the Analysis of Political Systems," *World Politics* 9 (1956–1957): 383–400; and Gabriel A. Almond, "Comparative Political Systems," *Journal of Politics* 18 (1956):391–409.

2. George B. Galloway, *The Legislative Process in Congress* (New York, 1953), p. 374.

3. Lewis A. Dexter, "The Representative and His District," *Human Organization* 16 (1957):3. See also Raymond A. Bauer, Ithiel de Sola Pool, and Lewis A. Dexter, *American*

Business and Public Policy: The Politics of Foreign Trade (New York, 1963), pp. 403–432, 445.

4.   Roger H. Davidson, *The Role of the Congressman* (New York, 1969), pp. 122–123.

5.   From Samuel C. Patterson's unpublished study of the 1957 session of the Wisconsin assembly. For additional illustrations, see Wahlke et al., *The Legislative System,* pp. 289–290.

6.   The studies referred to here include: Elmer E. Cornwell, Jr. et al., *The Rhode Island General Assembly* (Washington, D.C., 1970), p. 32; Heinz Eulau et al., "The Role of the Representative: Some Empirical Observations on the Theory of Edmund Burke," *American Political Science Review* 53 (1959):753; Ronald D. Hedlund, "Legislative Socialization and Role Orientations: A Study of the Iowa Legislature" (Ph.D. diss., University of Iowa, 1967), p. 56; Frank J. Sorauf, *Party and Representation* (New York, 1963), p. 124; and Donald P. Sprengel, "Legislative Perceptions of Gubernatorial Power in North Carolina" (Ph.D. diss., University of North Carolina, 1966), p. 53.

7.   See, for example, Wilder W. Crane, Jr., "Do Representatives Represent?" *Journal of Politics* 22 (1960):295–299.

8.   Wahlke et al., *The Legislative System,* p. 290.

9.   Davidson, *The Role of the Congressman,* p. 123.

10.   Ibid., p. 291.

11.   The data for California, New Jersey, and Ohio appear in Wahlke et al., *The Legislative System,* pp. 292–293. See also, Davidson, *The Role of the Congressman,* p. 128.

12.   See Charles L. Clapp, *The Congressman: His Work as He Sees It* (Washington, D.C., 1963), pp. 89, 100. For a good illustration of a series of congressional newsletters with a primarily educational purpose, see John W. Baker, ed., *Member of the House: Letters of a Congressman by Clem Miller* (New York, 1962), pp. 1–140.

13.   See Wahlke et al., *The Legislative System,* pp. 304–308.

14.   Ibid., pp. 323–342; John C. Wahlke et al., "American State Legislators' Role Orientations Toward Pressure Groups," *Journal of Politics* 22 (1960):203–227; Samuel C. Patterson, "The Role of the Deviant in the State Legislative System: The Wisconsin Assembly," *Western Political Quarterly* 14 (1961):465–466; Hedlund, "Legislative Socialization and Role Orientation: A Study of the Iowa Legislature," p. 58; and Davidson, *The Role of the Congressman,* p. 166.

15.   For a study that deals with facilitator, resister, and neutral orientations in the Wisconsin assembly with regard to branch-banking legislation, see Wilder W. Crane, Jr., "A Test of Effectiveness of Interest-group Pressures on Legislators," *Southwestern Social Science Quarterly* 41 (1960):335–340. See also Henry Teune, "Legislative Attitudes Toward Interest Groups," *Midwest Journal of Political Science* 11 (1967):489–504.

16.   David B. Truman, "The State Delegations and the Structure of Party Voting in the United States House of Representatives," *American Political Science Review* 50 (1956):1045.

17.   Ibid., p. 1045. See also David B. Truman, *The Congressional Party: A Case Study* (New York, 1959).

18.   Avery Leiserson, "National Party Organization and Congressional Districts," *Western Political Quarterly* 16 (1963):643.

19.   See Corinne Silverman, "The Legislators' View of the Legislative Process," *Public Opinion Quarterly* 18 (1954):184–188.

20.   Leiserson, "National Party Organization and Congressional Districts," p. 647. See also Davidson, *The Role of the Congressman,* p. 150.

21.   Patterson, "The Role of the Deviant in the State Legislative System: The Wisconsin Assembly," p. 462.

22. Ibid., p. 468. See also Sorauf, *Party and Representation*, p. 125.

23. Sorauf, *Party and Representation*, p. 124.

24. From Patterson's unpublished study of the 1957 Wisconsin assembly.

25. Ibid.

26. Davidson, *The Role of the Congressman*, p. 150.

27. Ibid., p. 150.

28. Wahlke et al., *The Legislative System*, p. 371.

29. For a good example, see Hallie Farmer, *The Legislative Process in Alabama* (University, Ala., 1949), p. 168.

30. William Buchanan, *Legislative Partisanship: The Deviant Case of California* (Berkeley and Los Angeles, 1963), p. 91.

31. William C. Havard and Loren P. Beth, *The Politics of Mis-representation: Rural-Urban Conflict in the Florida Legislature* (Baton Rouge, La., 1962), pp. 196, 202.

32. For example, see Oliver Garceau and Corinne Silverman, "A Pressure Group and the Pressured: A Case Report," *American Political Science Review* 48 (1954):672–681; and George A. Bell and Evelyn L. Wentworth, *The Legislative Process in Maryland* (College Park, Md., 1958), p. 26.

33. Truman, *The Congressional Party*, pp. 298–300.

34. For a good illustration, see Rowland Evans, Jr., "The Sixth Sense of Carl Vinson," *The Reporter*, 12 April 1962, pp. 25–30.

35. Ralph K. Huitt, "The Congressional Committee: A Case Study," *American Political Science Review* 48 (1954):349.

36. Ibid., pp. 345–346.

37. Edward A Shils, "The Legislator and His Environment," *University of Chicago Law Review* 18 (1951):577. Surely a leading example would be Congressman Otto Passman (D-La.). See Rowland Evans, Jr., "Louisiana's Passman: The Scourge of Foreign Aid," *Harper's*, January 1962, pp. 78–83.

38. J. Leiper Freeman, *The Political Process: Executive Bureau–Legislative Committee Relations* (Garden City, N.Y., 1955), p. 67.

39. Shils, "The Legislator and His Environment," p. 573.

40. James A. Robinson, *Congress and Foreign Policy-making* (Homewood, Ill., 1962), pp. 189–190.

41. Irwin J. Schulman, "The Case Against the 'Fireside Chat,' " *New York Times Magazine*, 14 June 1964, p. 70.

42. Wahlke et al., *The Legislative System*, p. 275.

43. Patterson's unpublished study.

44. Wahlke et al., *The Legislative System*, p. 279.

45. Ibid., p. 286. See also Charles G. Bell and Charles M. Price, "Pre-legislative Sources of Representational Roles," *Midwest Journal of Political Science* 13 (1969):254–270.

46. James D. Barber provides a lucid development of these orientations in his analysis of freshman Connecticut legislators, *The Lawmakers: Recruitment and Adaptation to Legislative Life* (New Haven, Conn., 1965).

47. Wahlke et al., *The Legislative System*, pp. 245–266. A somewhat similar formulation can be found in Garceau and Silverman, "A Pressure Group and the Pressured: A Case Report," pp. 682–689, where some purposive orientations are characterized as "policy-oriented," "program-oriented," "faction-oriented," and "non-generalizers."

48. Hedlund, "Legislative Socialization and Role Orientation: A Study of the Iowa Legislature," p. 51.

49. Davidson, *The Role of the Congressman*, p. 81.

50. Wahlke et al., *The Legislative System,* pp. 193–215. See also Wayne L. Francis, "Influence and Interaction in a State Legislative Body," *American Political Science Review,* 56 (1962):953–960.

51. Ibid., p. 209.

52. Patterson's unpublished study.

53. Wahlke et al., *The Legislative System,* p. 396.

54. Ibid., p. 423.

55. See William C. Mitchell, "Occupational Role Strains: The American Elective Public Official," *Administrative Science Quarterly* 3 (1958):210–228.

56. *Washington Post and Times Herald,* 5 April 1959, pp. E1–E2.

57. Charles O. Jones, "Representation in Congress: The Case of the House Agriculture Committee," *American Political Science Review* 55 (1961):367. For a comment along similar lines with reference to Pennsylvania legislators, see Sorauf, *Party and Representation,* p. 126.

58. This statement is illustrated for congressmen on the foreign-trade issue in Bauer, Pool, and Dexter, *American Business and Public Policy,* pp. 444–450. See also Davidson, *The Role of the Congressman,* pp. 70–76, 177–179, 188–190.

59. Roger H. Davidson, "Public Prescriptions for the Job of Congressman," *Midwest Journal of Political Science* 14 (1970):655.

60. Carl D. McMurray and Malcolm B. Parsons, "Public Attitudes Toward the Representational Roles of Legislators and Judges," *Midwest Journal of Political Science* 9 (1965):177.

61. This section draws upon, and to some extent quotes directly from, Malcolm E. Jewell, "Attitudinal Determinants of Legislative Behavior: The Utility of Role Analysis," in *Legislatures in Developmental Perspective,* ed. A. Kornberg and L. D. Musolf (Durham, N.C., Duke University Press 1970), pp. 460–500.

62. See Wayne L. Francis, "The Role Concept in Legislatures: A Probability Model and a Note on Cognitive Structure," *Journal of Politics* 27 (1965):567–585.

63. See LeRoy C. Ferguson and Bernard W. Klein, "An Attempt to Correlate the Voting Records of Legislators with Attitudes Toward Party," *Public Opinion Quarterly* 31 (1967):422–426 and Sorauf, *Party and Representation,* p. 140.

64. Richard F. Fenno, Jr., "The House Appropriations Committee as a Political System: The Problem of Integration," *American Political Science Review* 56 (1962):310–324; and Jones, "Representation in Congress: The Case of the House Agriculture Committee," pp. 358–367.

65. Huitt, "The Congressional Committee: A Case Study," pp. 340–365.

66. Barber, *The Lawmakers.*

The Legislature in Action

part VI

Most of this volume has been devoted to analyzing the factors that affect legislative decision making: the selection of legislators; their roles; the legislative structure, norms, and power distribution; and the impact of outside groups on the legislative process. Now we focus our attention on the output of the legislative process and on the interaction of that process with the administrative and judicial processes.

The best technique for evaluating the decisions recorded on the floor of the legislature is an analysis of roll calls. Most important and controversial issues that reach the floor are tested in roll calls, and these provide data that are precise and susceptible to measurement and analysis through relatively sophisticated techniques. These techniques give evidence of role behavior that sheds light on legislative roles. When votes are taken, the groups that serve as potential sources of voting cues range widely through the legislative system, as we have noted. Under what circumstances does each group become salient for the legislator? When he is subjected to conflicting pressures, how are these conflicts resolved? Some of the answers can be found in an examination of roll calls.

Many legislative decisions are reached in committees, where the process of decision making is sometimes out of public view. But information is becoming more available about the sources and effects of committee norms, the factors contributing to committee cohesion and influence, and the ways in which decisions are reached. Committees not only make preliminary decisions on bills, but also provide the best mechanism for oversight of the executive through control of appropriations, investigations, and other forms of continuing regulation. Whether legislative oversight of the executive is effective depends in part on the adequacy of staff and the level of expert knowledge found in the committee; in both respects congressional committees have a large advantage over those in state legislatures. At the national level the controversies over impoundment of funds and the budgetary process, as well as the Watergate scandal, have focused attention on the need for more effective oversight.

The relationships between the legislative and judicial institutions in this country are complex and can be covered only briefly in a study of the legislative process. Because of their ability to interpret laws and to override those that appear to violate the Constitution, the courts provide an alternative arena for groups seeking to change legislative output and to significantly affect the environment in which the legislative branch operates. To illustrate the influence of the judiciary, we will study in some detail how the courts have established new standards for apportionment and thereby fundamentally changed legislative composition. It is also important to recognize that legislative bodies have several means by which they may influence judicial decisions or even limit the scope of judicial power—even though these methods are used sparingly.

CHAPTER SIXTEEN

Legislative Voting Behavior

"The yeas and nays have been ordered. The clerk will call the roll." The clerk begins to read the names of senators. Bells ring in the chamber and throughout the Senate office buildings. Members come hurrying into the chamber. Party leaders anxiously check off names as the roll call proceeds. Visitors in the gallery sense an air of excitement and suspense as the roll call nears the end with the outcome still in doubt. The scene is repeated in the House chamber where (as in many state legislatures) it is possible for spectators to watch the drama being enacted electronically, as the lights on the scoreboard switch back and forth as members cast or change their votes. Are the drama and excitement real, or is this simply the formal ratification of agreements negotiated behind the scenes in committees or in meetings of the leadership? Does a study of roll-call voting reveal anything that is not already obvious from the other aspects of the legislative process that we have discussed?

We have said that resolving conflicts is one of the important legislative functions, and we have emphasized the decisional aspect of this function. The decisions embodied in bills are the most important legislative output. The roll call is a significant, but not always decisive, step in the decision-making process. At one of the earlier stages in the legislative process, negative decisions may have precluded a roll-call vote, or a positive decision, such as committee approval of a noncontroversial measure, may have assured consensus and unanimity in the vote. At an earlier stage, the bill may have become a party issue, and the size and cohesion of the party majority may assure passage on the floor. Unanimous and one-sided votes are common, especially in those states that have a roll call on every bill. But in any legislative body, there will be some issues that remain in doubt until the vote has been taken on the floor. Whether the vote is close or one-sided, whether or not preliminary decisions have foreshadowed the outcome, the vote on the floor is an essential part of reaching decisions on bills.

Beyond this, the roll call is of interest because of what it reveals about the legislator. If he is forced to choose among the competing demands of his constituents, his party leadership, and his committee colleagues, he may resolve the conflict by playing different roles in public and private. His public role, at least, stands revealed by the nature of his vote; and it is largely on the basis of this vote

380 THE LEGISLATURE IN ACTION

that he will be judged by most of those who are making demands on him. Whether his vote represents an agonizing choice or follows inevitably from past actions, it is an important act from the viewpoint of the legislator.

In Congress, a roll-call vote is taken only when the motion being voted on concerns a controversial or highly important matter; consequently, the roll calls represent a record of the principal congressional actions. In the states, however, the constitution often requires a roll call on final passage of every bill; the usual consequence is that a large proportion, sometimes as many as 90 percent, of the roll calls are unanimous or nearly unanimous. Analysis of roll calls that approach or achieve unanimity is of little value because the record does not reveal any differences among the legislators. They may be voting together for different reasons, and these differences may be significant, but this possibility is not demonstrated by the roll-call statistics. Unanimity on a roll call usually means that legislators are taking their voting cues from the same sources or from sources who are in agreement. Before a bill reaches the floor, it has been screened, carefully or perfunctorily, by a committee and by the majority leadership and perhaps by the minority leadership as well. When the majority floor leader calls up a measure and no objection is raised by the minority leader or anyone else, the legislator recognizes that the bill is acceptable to the committee and to his leadership, two of the main sources of his voting cues. If he has no reason to believe that the measure will arouse criticism in his district and has no personal objection to it, the legislator can be expected to vote favorably.

Most bills on which voting is unanimous can be described as noncontroversial. If the issue arouses controversy, one or more of the groups that are sources of voting cues is likely to raise an objection with enough force to guarantee dissenting votes. A few of the bills that pass with little dissent are matters of great controversy, perhaps even of serious conflict among interests or between parties. In these cases, the controversial points are negotiated and settled in committee or at some other point prior to action on the floor. These decisions are fully as important as those that are recorded in roll calls, but there is no way of measuring them in the sense in which roll-call votes can be measured. By excluding unanimous votes from analysis, we are excluding many trivial issues and a few important ones, just as we are excluding negative decisions that prevent an issue from coming to a vote. We are including those votes that provide some clue to the conflicting forces and pressures at work in the legislative system.

Roll-call statistics can reveal *how* legislators vote. They can show how often Republicans vote together, or southerners, or Catholic members, or representatives of urban constituencies. The roll calls cannot explain *why* legislators vote that way. Does Congressman Brown support the federal aid to education bill because he is a Democrat, because he represents a low-income urban constituency, because he is a former high school teacher, or because a close friend is sponsoring the measure? It is impossible to *prove* causal relationships from roll-call statistics. But roll-call statistics do provide hard, measurable evidence that may be added to other sources of knowledge about the legislative system to provide the basis for judgments about the importance of party, constituency, and other sources of voting cues.

PARTY AS A REFERENCE GROUP

Studies of roll-call voting in Congress and in some of the two-party state legislatures have shown that on nonunanimous roll calls, the voting follows party lines more often than it follows sectional, urban-rural, or other factors that have been tested. Occasionally, the voting pattern on a particular roll call can be better explained by some factor other than party, but voting follows party lines more or less perfectly on the largest proportion of roll calls. This statistical fact suggests the strong possibility that the party is an important source of voting cues, a reference group (a group to whose norms the actor refers for his behavior). But there are other possible explanations for the prominence of party alignments in voting. If a high proportion of the Democrats who support federal aid to education represent northern urban constituencies, are most of these congressmen using the constituency as their only reference group? Behind the mask of a party vote, is there some other factor—constituency, region, personal conviction—that actually explains the vote?

To bolster the statistical evidence for describing the party as an important reference group, it is necessary to recall other evidence about the party. Congress and many state legislatures are organized along party lines; caucuses are active in some states; friendship groups tend to be intraparty more than interparty; and partisan leaders in both the executive and legislative branches apply rewards and sanctions primarily to members of their own party. Legislators frequently say that they prefer to go along with the party whenever possible. As Donald R. Matthews has said in describing the United States Senate, "Party 'discipline' may be weak, but party 'identification' is strong."[1] On many issues, the pressure for conformity to a party position is immediate and direct; whereas constituency pressures are often distant, vague, ill informed, and contradictory. There is ample evidence to bear out the assumption that where statistics demonstrate that party alignments are frequent, party is an important reference group. In fact, the symptoms of party identification and activity are most apparent in those states with a high level of party alignment on roll calls; where both kinds of evidence are strong, the party can be described as a source of voting cues, a reference group.

PARTY VOTING IN STATE LEGISLATURES

In this section, we will describe the variations that are found in the levels of party cohesion in various legislative bodies, and we will try to explain some of the reasons for these variations. Later in the chapter, we will analyze some of the most important forces, both within the legislature and outside it, that serve as additional reference groups for members on roll-call votes. Some of these have the effect of reinforcing party alignments, and others diminish the effect of party on voting.

Techniques of Measurement

Political scientists have applied a wide variety of statistical techniques, often very complex, to the analysis of roll-call techniques. Fortunately (from the student's viewpoint), the best techniques for comparative purposes are relatively simple. The measures described here and used in Table 16.1 have been used frequently enough to provide data on a number of legislatures. Because unanimous and nearly unanimous votes indicate very little about the forces affecting voting, the data in Table 16.1 exclude unanimous roll calls and in most cases exclude roll calls with a small number of dissenters (usually under 10 percent).

One measurement that most clearly shows the contrast between the voting records of two parties is the *index of difference*, which is simply the difference between the percentage of Yea (or Nay) votes cast by one party and the percentage of Yea (or Nay) votes cast by the other. The larger the figure, the greater the difference between the two parties. (Some studies of legislative voting refer to an "index of likeness," which is simply the index of difference subtracted from 100.) Another index that is very simple and widely used is the percentage of roll calls on which a majority of Democrats vote against a majority of Republicans. This provides a rough measure of the frequency with which roll calls provoke a different response from Democrats and Republicans, but it fails to measure how great these differences are or how cohesive either party is.

The most common measure of party unity is the *index of cohesion*. If all the members of a party (excluding absentees) vote the same way, the index is 100; if three-quarters vote one way, the index is 50; if they are evenly divided, the index is 0. The index of cohesion may be found by subtracting the percentage in the minority from that in the majority in a party. Table 16.1 presents data from several states on the percentage of roll calls on which the parties were opposed, and the average index of cohesion for a party. Table 16.1 includes only the average index of cohesion for roll calls with the two parties in opposition (whenever those data were available) because we are primarily interested in party cohesion under that condition.

Contrasts Between Urban and Rural States

It is clear from Table 16.1 that there are substantial differences among the states in the extent of party voting and that it is most common in some of the more urbanized and industrialized two-party states in the Northeast and Midwest, although even in these areas, there is no uniformity in the patterns of voting. Party alignments are weaker and less frequent in the border and western states and, generally, in states that have lower levels of urbanization and industrialization. The correlation between urbanization-industrialization and party voting in the legislature is far from perfect, but it is strong enough to raise questions about the causal relationships that may exist. In states with high party voting, each of the parties is likely to be relatively homogeneous in its composition. The Democratic party draws its electoral strength from the metropolitan centers and particularly from labor groups, racial and ethnic minorities, Catholic voters, and persons with below-average incomes. The Republican vote is in the higher-income sections of the metropolis, the towns and cities, and some of the farm areas. This is the familiar political pattern in the industrial North that grew out of the New Deal realignment. The operation of the single-member district system (and multimember districts, in the absence of proportional representation) creates an even sharper polarization of party strength. Republican voters in the metropolitan areas (particularly in multimember districts) and rural Democratic voters are underrepresented in the legislatures. The result of this polarization is that each legislative party is quite homogeneous in the constituencies represented by its members. There is a maximum of opportunity for agreement on issues within each party and a minimum of likelihood that legislators will be torn between loyalty to the legislative party and loyalty to the constituency.

In the states with lower levels of urbanization and industrialization, both parties are likely to draw a substantial proportion of their support from rural areas, with the specific centers of support being based on traditional party loyalties. There are a few metropolitan centers, and even in these, the Democrats may not consistently predominate. Both parties usually have more diverse constituencies and consequently legislative party cohesion is more difficult to achieve. The parties are less likely to have a programmatic base. Legislators are more likely to be elected because of their personal ability and experience or because of voting traditions in the areas than because of the programs their party stands for.

The Effects of Party Competition

The level of competition between the two legislative parties also has an effect on the frequency of party voting and the strength of party cohesion, but the effect is neither direct nor simple to explain. An absolute prerequisite for party voting is the existence of two parties in the legislature. When a single party consistently has a monopoly or an overwhelming majority of legislative seats, the party is not a reference group for legislative voting. If the minority consistently holds no more than 10 or 15 percent of the legislative seats, it has little incentive to achieve cohesion in voting; and as a consequence, the members of the majority party see little need to maintain voting cohesion. Moreover, a majority party that controls nearly all the legislative seats may have to represent such a wide variety of interests in the state that it is difficult for it to maintain cohesion. (For these reasons, state legislatures under complete one-party control are excluded from Table 16.1.)

The states included in Table 16.1 that have had the strongest party alignments on roll calls are generally ones that have had strong statewide party competition for a long time (such as most of the northeastern and midwestern states), but several of these (including New York and Michigan) had a long record of Republican majorities in one or both legislative houses prior to the reapportionment of the mid-1960s. The states with relatively weak party alignments on roll calls include several (such as Kentucky) with legislatures that until recently have been dominated by one party, but they also include several (such as Montana and Oregon) with close partisan balances in the legislature over a number of years. During a period of transition in a legislature from one-party dominance to close two-party competition, the minority party is likely to begin voting as a bloc more frequently as it gains a larger proportion of seats, and the old majority party may be forced to unify in self-defense. Consequently, the proportion of roll calls on

TABLE 16.1 Party Voting in Selected State Legislatures on Nonunanimous Roll Calls

STATE	INDEX OF DIFFERENCE		PERCENTAGE OF ROLL CALLS WITH MAJORITY OF BOTH PARTIES OPPOSED		AVERAGE INDEX OF COHESION (MEDIAN SESSION)—BOTH PARTIES OPPOSED*				YEARS
					Senate		House		
	Senate	House	Senate	House	D	R	D	R	
Penna.	75		82	29	82	90			1959
N.Y.	65		70		76	88			1959
Mass.	63		74	72	78	77	53	73	1959(S); 1965(H)
Del.	63		62	51	84	87			1959
Ohio			74	61	84	83	61	66	1959–1969
Mich.	52		56		85	73			1962
W. Va.	63	65	53		61	67			1959, 1969
Calif.	43	38	43	46	64	40	59	37	1967–1969
Vt.			59	62					1963–1972
Wash.	45		50		60	78			1959
Iowa	44		49	55	79	70	72	70	1965–1974
Ind.	44		51		65	68			1959
Ill.	41		27		75	63			1959
S.D.	40		44		67	67			1959
N.H.			62		63	38			1959
Kans.	37	30	35	73	49	82	49	29	1959(S); 1953–1957(H)
Ky.	34		39		51	59			1960
Fla.	36		45		58	55			1967, 1971
Mo.	33		35		49	63			1959
Okla.	32	26	35		53	64	53	63	1967, 1971(S); 1970(H)

N.D.	30				83	52			1965, 1973
Oreg.	28				53	59			1959, 1967, 1973
Idaho	28	27			58	53			1959, 1967, 1973
Mont.	29	37			54	56			1959
Wyom.	26	24			65	51			1967, 1973
Utah			20	8	60	52	70	65	1965
N.M.			20	24	42	53	65	57	1951–1959(S); 1951, 1953, 1957, 1963(H)

*For the following states, the average index of cohesion is for all roll calls and not just those with the parties opposed: Kansas House, Vermont, Florida, Oklahoma, North Dakota, Oregon (1967 and 1973), Idaho (1967 and 1973), and Wyoming.

NOTE: In all states, unanimous votes are excluded; in most states roll calls with less than 10 percent voting in the minority are also excluded. In the years column, S and H indicate only Senate and only House.

SOURCES: All data on state senates in 1959 (and for Kentucky in 1960) come from Hugh L. LeBlanc, "Voting in State Senates: Party and Constituency Influences," Midwest Journal of Political Science 13 (1969):33–57. Data for Florida, Oklahoma, North Dakota, Wyoming, and (except for 1959) for Oregon and Idaho come from E. Lee Bernick, "The Role of the Governor in the Legislative Process: A Comparative State Analysis" (Paper prepared for the 1975 annual meeting of the American Political Science Association). Data for other states comes from these individual studies: R. S. Friedman and S. L. Stokes, "The Role of Constitution-Maker as Representative," Midwest Journal of Political Science 9 (1965):164 (Michigan); John G. Grumm, "Party Responsibility in the Kansas Legislature" (Paper presented at the Wichita Conference on Politics, April, 1959); Frank J. Sorauf, Party and Representation (New York, 1963), pp. 136–137 (Pennsylvania house); Frank M. Bryan, Yankee Politics in Rural Vermont (Hanover, N.H., 1974), chap. 4; Bruce Robeck, "Legislative Partisanship, Constituency and Reapportionment: The Case of California" (unpublished manuscript); Dennis Kellogg and Charles W. Wiggins, "Party Voting in the Sixty-fifth Iowa General Assembly" in State Legislative Innovation, ed. James A. Robinson (New York, 1973), pp. 272–274; JeDon Emenhiser, "Utah's Legislative Politics" in Legislative Politics in the Rocky Mountain West, ed. Susanne A. Stoiber (Boulder, Col., 1967), p. 96; Sheldon Goldman, Roll Call Behavior in the Massachusetts House of Representatives (Amherst, Mass., 1968), p. 40; Jack E. Holmes, Politics in New Mexico (Albuquerque, N.M., 1967), pp. 279–281.

which the parties take opposite sides will increase. If the minority party elects a governor, whether or not it wins a legislative majority, its members are likely to provide the new governor with united support for the major parts of his program, and the opposition party is likely to vote against the governor on at least some parts of his program.

This was the pattern that occurred in the Kansas lower house during the late 1950s; the Democratic party became more cohesive, and there were more party conflicts as the Democratic party grew from an ineffective minority to a strong minority and a Democratic administration came to power.[2] In Tennessee, as the Republican minority grew in size during the 1960s, there was an increase in the proportion of issues affected by partisan voting, even before a Republican governor was elected.[3] In Iowa, during the 1950s, the proportion of roll calls on which the parties clashed increased, Democratic cohesion increased, and there was a more gradual growth of Republican legislative cohesion. These trends coincided roughly with the growth of Democratic strength in the legislature; and party conflict reached a high point in the 1965 session when the Democrats for the first time controlled the governorship and both houses.[4] A similar pattern can be found in Vermont, where the legislature was once overwhelmingly Republican. During the mid-1960s, aided by reapportionment, the Democrats won a larger proportion of legislative seats, though falling short of a majority; more importantly, they elected a governor for six years. The result was an increase in Democratic party cohesion and in the index of party difference.[5]

In both Iowa and Vermont, the Democratic gains in the legislature during the 1960s resulted partly from reapportionment, which benefited parties with an urban base. To some extent the Democrats gained by winning seats in traditionally Republican rural and small-town areas, a development that made the party's constituency base less homogeneous and therefore limited the potential for high party cohesion. Frank Bryan, in his study of Vermont, points out that increased party cohesion in that state did not result from any greater homogeneity in party constituencies. Based on the Vermont experience, he suggests that "in the formative stages in intralegislative party competition, causal responsibility does not reside in any linkage between district and party, but rather in a minority upstart party which, reinforced by an historically unique breakthrough at the polls, seeks to push its own policies through the legislative system, causing the reverberations that produce party cohesion."[6] It is noteworthy that in both Vermont and Iowa there have been drops in Democratic party cohesion at the end of Democratic administrations (though not back to the previous low levels), and Republican cohesion has grown during periods of Republican administrations.

Patterson has studied seating patterns in legislative chambers and concluded that a seating arrangement based on party not only is a sign of partisanship but also reinforces partisanship because it facilitates communication among members of the same party. He found that in Iowa, for example, during the late 1950s and 1960s seating arrangements in the legislature were based increasingly on party membership, a trend that roughly coincided with increased partisanship in roll-call voting.[7]

The Impact of State Party Systems

The frequency of party voting and the levels of cohesion may be affected not only by characteristics of the legislative parties but also by the nature of the party system found in the state as a whole. Some of the states that have a high level of legislative party voting appear to be characterized by issue-oriented party systems. Duane Lockard attributes party cohesion in the Connecticut legislative parties to the ideological similarities within each party: the Democrats are generally liberal, and the Republicans are generally conservative.[8] States with issue-oriented parties include New York, with its Democratic heritage of Smith, Roosevelt, and Lehman; Michigan, with its parties sharply oriented, the Democrats toward labor and the Republicans toward business; and Rhode Island, where the Democratic party is heavily committed to the labor and welfare policies of union interests. In these and other states, the two parties are likely to draw their votes from the same interests that the national parties do in the North. The two parties in such a state appear to stand for different things, at least in the minds of some voters; they are not merely benefiting from traditional voting habits.

It is necessary to be extremely cautious, however, in attributing party cohesion to the issue orientation of parties. Voting-behavior research has shown that few voters have clear perceptions of the issues for which the two national parties stand; even fewer have any clear ideological attachment to a party. They are more likely to perceive a party in terms of the groups or classes that are allied with it or that benefit from its programs.[9] Perceptions of issues at the state level are probably even weaker. In states where the most perceptive observer finds it hard to define the issues that separate the parties, it is clear that this factor is an obstacle to party cohesion. Where there appear to be differences in the issue orientation of parties, this fact is primarily important as a symptom of the differences in constituency interests represented by the two parties. Frank J. Sorauf's analysis of the Pennsylvania parties is pertinent and broadly applicable:

> So, the parties achieve an indirect responsibility to an inarticulate ideology—the common interests and goals of the similar constituencies from which they draw their most loyal partisans. It is in the support of this inarticulate ideology and the gubernatorial program, rather than in that of a spelled-out party program, that this party discipline is used. The legislative party merely mobilizes the cohesive party vote from among its basically non-ideological ranks.[10]

Some of the states with a high level of party voting are among those with the strongest state and local party organizations in the country; these include several of the most urbanized states of the Northeast. Strong local party organizations may result in a highly cohesive party delegation from a particular county in the legislature, but the local party is likely to take an interest in only a small proportion of legislative issues. If a strong state party organization is to have any direct effect on the cohesion of the legislative party, it must be able to dispense rewards and sanctions; for the state organization to affect a legislator's chances for renomination, it must apply pressure to the local organizations that control or influence nominations. But because most local parties have little interest in state issues, only the most extreme pressure from a state party organization is likely to compel them to discipline a maverick legislator.[11] The state party that is out of power does not have any means to exert such pressure. Whether the administration party seeks to do this is largely dependent on the governor, and we have seen (in Chapter 11) that the governor seldom finds the party organization to be a valuable tool of legislative leadership and seldom wants to take the risks involved in trying to block a legislator's renomination. Strong party organization and cohesive legislative parties may coincide because of a common cause, such as homogeneous parties growing out of urban-rural polarization, but there are relatively few states where party organization directly enhances legislative party cohesion.

A study of the New York legislature suggests another reason why there is stronger legislative party cohesion in some of the states that have strong state and local party organizations:

> It is brought about by the fact that the legislators bring certain political values with them from their local party organizations to the legislature. As Stuart Witt has pointed out, the legislator has been born within the party atmosphere of the local political arena and bred on basic political values, such as strong leadership, intraparty bargaining and compromise, all of them enveloped with the strongest and highest value, that of partisanship. As he enters the arena of lawmaking, he discovers that essentially the same values prevail there as well. . . . It is no hardship for him at all to accept strong legislative leadership for he had dealt with, and profited from, strong local party leadership. . . . He arrives in Albany as a trained party regular and almost automatically joins his colleagues who consider conformity as the highest party value.[12]

Among the two-party states, legislative systems vary widely with respect to the importance of party voting. The most common attribute of legislatures with strong party alignments in voting is the presence of parties that are highly homogeneous as a result of the urban-rural or socioeconomic polarization of constituencies. In many of these states, the parties may be very loosely described as issue-oriented, and the state party organizations are often strong. It is usually difficult, however, to demonstrate a direct impact of either factor on legislative party cohesion. In the legislatures where such aspects of the party system are conducive to party voting, party regularity becomes one of the legislative norms. The new legislator quickly learns that when the party takes a position on certain issues, a degree of conformity is required. In Chapter 15, we showed that different legislators interpret their roles, including the party role, differently. Where party regularity is a widely accepted norm, the party role is accepted by more legislators, and party homogeneity reduces the role conflict between party and constituency. In these states, party regularity can best be understood not as a discipline, but as a custom or habit. The legislator becomes accustomed to the party as a reference group. He "goes along" with the party and "follows the leadership" unless "pressure from constituents is heavy" or he has "strong personal convictions."[13] The function of the caucus or other leadership devices in this environment is largely one of efficient communication: to make it clear to the legislator when the party has taken a particular stand on an issue, and to reinforce (rather than to enforce) the norm of conformity to the party's position.

PARTY VOTING IN CONGRESS

We have asserted that roll-call votes in Congress follow party lines more often than they follow any other alignment. Party cohesion is much weaker in Congress, however, than it is in the British House of Commons or in most national parliaments in Europe. We pointed out in Chapter 2 that the proportion of roll calls with most Republicans voting against most Democrats is substantially lower in the United States House today than it was in the latter part of the nineteenth century. Perhaps the best way to put congressional voting into perspective is to compare it with voting in the state legislatures described in the previous section. Most measurements of party voting show that Congress ranks near or somewhat below the middle of the two-party states. In any comparison of roll calls in Congress and in state legislatures, it should be kept in mind that Congress deals with a small number of bills and does not require roll calls on the final passage of all of them; most congressional roll calls are on the more important and controversial issues.

Variations in the Level of Party Voting

The most complete data on congressional voting since World War II has been compiled by the *Congressional Quarterly,* the source of most of the data in Table 16.2. The table shows considerable variation from year to year in the proportion of roll calls on which the two parties have taken opposite sides, probably partly because those issues most likely to create party votes generate more roll calls in some years than in others. Generally, the two parties have opposed each other on from one-third to one-half of the roll calls. In most years from 1953 to 1968 the index of difference fluctuated between 25 and 40, with a median of 30 in the Senate and 34.5 in the House.[14] By these two measures of party alignment, both branches of Congress would rank about two-thirds of the way from the top in the list of states in Table 16.1. (If nearly unanimous roll calls were excluded from the congressional data in order to make a more accurate comparison with state legislatures, partisan voting in Congress would rank somewhat higher.)

Both indexes suggest that party voting has been declining in Congress. The index of difference was lower during the Eisenhower administration than it had been during the Truman years (not shown in the table). After a slight increase under Kennedy, it fell during the Johnson administration. In most years interparty differences were slightly greater in the House than in the Senate. The proportion of votes on which the parties were in conflict has declined in the Senate since reaching a high point (50 percent) during the Kennedy years, while in the House there has been a greater decline (from an average of almost one-half during the Eisenhower and Kennedy years to only one-third during the Nixon administration).

The *Congressional Quarterly* measures the "party unity score" of each member by calculating the percentage of times he votes with his party on those roll calls on which the two parties are opposed, thus producing a measure of party cohesion that is the average party unity score. (Under this method, failure to vote lowers the party unity score.) Table 16.2 shows that there has been a gradual decline in average party loyalty, which has affected both parties in both houses. Among

TABLE 16.2 Partisanship in Congressional Roll Calls, 1955–1974

YEAR	INDEX OF DIFFERENCE		PERCENTAGE OF ROLL CALLS WITH TWO PARTIES IN OPPOSITION		AVERAGE PERCENTAGE OF VOTES WITH PARTY WHEN TWO PARTIES IN OPPOSITION*			
					Senate		House	
	Senate	House	Senate	House	D	R	D	R
1955	27	31	30	41	72	75	72	69
1956	38	32	53	44	71	72	70	70
1957	31	39	36	59	66	69	70	67
1958	32	27	44	40	71	64	66	65
1959	34	46	48	55	67	72	79	77
1960	26	33	37	53	60	64	65	70
1961	40	39	62	50	69	68	72	74
1962	35	34	41	46	65	64	70	70
1963	35	39	47	49	66	67	73	74
1964	27	39	36	55	61	65	69	71
1965	28	36	42	52	63	68	70	71
1966	31	29	50	41	57	63	62	68
1967	23	27	35	36	60	65	67	69
1968	21	23	32	35	51	60	59	64
1969			36	31	63	63	61	62
1970			35	27	55	56	58	60
1971			42	38	64	63	61	67
1972			36	27	57	61	58	66
1973			40	42	69	64	68	68
1974			44	29	63	59	62	63
Averages								
1955–1960	31	35	41	49	68	69	70	70
1961–1963	37	37	50	48	67	66	72	73
1964–1968	26	31	39	44	58	64	65	69
1969–1974			38	32	62	61	61	64

*This is the average percentage of times a congressman voted in agreement with his party out of the total number of roll calls on which the two parties were opposed.
SOURCES: Congressional Quarterly, *Congressional Quarterly Almanac*, vols. 11–30 (Washington, D.C., 1955–1974). The index of difference is from Duncan MacRae, Jr., *Issues and Parties in Legislative Voting* (New York, 1970), p. 204.

Democrats, the decline occurred first in the Senate, where party unity was consistently lower than in the House from 1959 through 1968; but throughout the Nixon administration there was little difference between the two branches. Among Republicans the decline in unity also occurred first in the Senate; from 1959 through 1974 Republican senators were almost always less unified than representatives. Democratic senators were less unified than Republican senators during the Johnson administration. Democratic representatives were less unified than Republicans in the Johnson and early Nixon years. One of the most consistent relationships found in Table 16.2 is that with very few exceptions both parties in both houses of Congress had lower cohesion in the second session of each Congress than they had in the first session. There is no obvious reason for this trend; it may reflect increasing conflicts between party and constituency as the election approached, although the drop was as great in the Senate (where only one-third of the members faced election) as it was in the House. It should be kept in mind that these data provide only a partial picture of party unity, because they apply only to those issues on which a majority of Democrats oppose a majority of Republicans.

Factionalism within the Parties

Party alignments are more fluid and party cohesion is weaker in Congress than is the case in most of the legislatures in the urban states of the Northeast and Midwest. Stronger party cohesion might be expected in Congress because of the long history of close two-party balance and the strength of partisan norms. But both parties in Congress represent a much greater diversity of constituencies than is the case of the most cohesive state legislative parties, and this diversity limits the possibilities for high congressional party cohesion.

There are a number of ways to describe and measure factions within the two parties, but the simplest and most commonly used delineation is a regional one. Within the Democratic party, the fundamental split is between southern and nonsouthern congressmen. It would be a mistake to assume that either the southern or the northern bloc within the Democratic party is a monolithic one, but the voting patterns of the two groups are distinctly different. On about three-fourths of the votes that split the Democratic party along North-South lines there has been what is usually called a *conservative coalition* of southern Democrats and Republicans voting against northern Democrats. The conservative coalition is one of the most significant features of congressional voting because it frequently undermines Democratic majorities in the Senate and the House. When the minority Republican party is successful in defeating the majority Democrats on a roll call, it is usually because of this alliance with some of the southern Democrats.

The conservative coalition had its origins late in the Roosevelt administration, when southern congressmen were becoming disillusioned with the New Deal because its programs were increasingly responsive to urban and labor interests. According to Key, the conservative coalition began to appear in the House on a significant number of roll calls (almost 10 percent) in 1937, and it increased in the 1940s. A detailed analysis by Margolis shows that the conservative coalition emerged as a powerful force in the Senate in 1943, and was present on at least

20 percent of the roll calls during the 1943–1948 period. The Margolis data also show that the conservative coalition won over 90 percent of the roll calls on which it appeared in the Senate from 1945 through 1958, a much higher record of success than in more recent years.[15]

Since 1959 the *Congressional Quarterly* has compiled data on the frequency with which the conservative coalition has appeared on roll calls in both houses, and its rate of success.[16] These data are summarized in Figure 16.1 (a and b). (In these calculations, Kentucky and Oklahoma are included along with the eleven traditional southern states.) Several conclusions can be drawn from the data:

The proportion of conservative coalition roll calls is generally higher in the Senate than in the House.

The conservative coalition appeared more often in both branches during the Johnson and Nixon administrations than it usually had in the past.

The success rate of the conservative coalition has fluctuated sharply. It was particularly high during Nixon's first term; it was at a low point, particularly in the House, after the 1964 election, when northern Democrats had a large numerical advantage—one of the few times when the conservative coalition won less than half of the roll calls. At times the conservative coalition has been much more successful in the Senate; at other times it has done much better in the House.

Even though there are a number of liberal Democratic congressmen in the South (including several black representatives), the gap between northern and southern Democrats in both houses has been steadily widening. The decline in Democratic party unity scores noted earlier (on roll calls when the two parties are opposed) is, in the Senate, almost entirely the result of increased southern defections; in the House party loyalty has dropped faster and more consistently among southerners than among other Democrats. The North-South Democratic split, which once was centered on a few issues, such as civil rights, now includes a wider variety of issues and occurs on well over half of the roll calls on which there are substantial divisions within Congress.[17]

There is also evidence of an increasing split within the ranks of Republican congressmen, although the geographical lines are not so clear as in the Democratic party. The more liberal wing of the Republican party includes most of the senators and some of the representatives from the northeastern and midwestern states. Those Republicans who most consistently support the conservative coalition include most of the increasing numbers being elected from the South, many from the West, and a number of House members from the Midwest and Northeast. The drop in Republican party unity scores in the Senate can be attributed almost entirely to increasing defections among eastern Republicans, while in the House the greatest defections have occurred among eastern and midwestern Republicans, particularly from urban areas. The growing split within the Republican congressional party has produced an alignment that appears on an increasing proportion of roll calls: northern Democrats and eastern Republicans against southern Democrats and noneastern Republicans. Barbara Deckard surveyed the more controversial roll calls in the House (those with high turnout and a minority vote of at least 20 percent) and found that from 1959–1960 to 1969–1970 the

FIGURE 16.1a   Percentage of Roll Calls in the U.S. Senate on Which the Conservative Coalition Appeared and Percentage of Roll Calls on Which It Won

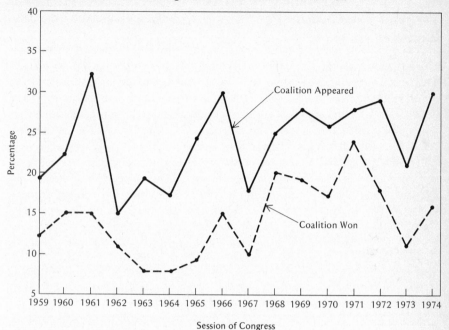

SOURCE: Congressional Quarterly, *Congressional Quarterly Almanac*, vols. 15–30.

FIGURE 16.1b   Percentage of Roll Calls in the U.S. House on Which the Conservative Coalition Appeared and Percentage of Roll Calls on Which It Won

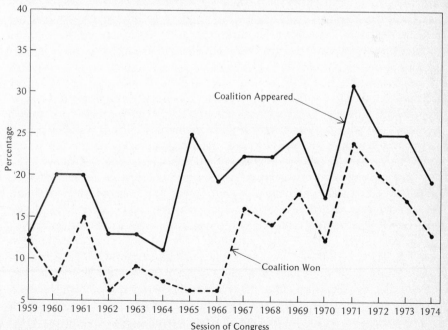

SOURCE: Congressional Quarterly, *Congressional Quarterly Almanac*, vols. 15–30.

proportion of roll calls on which eastern and noneastern Republicans took opposite stands increased from 14 to 31 percent.[18] It is obvious that the Republican congressional party, like the Democratic one, represents constituencies and interests that frequently come into conflict on the issues facing Congress.

The cautious student of congressional voting hesitates to attach great importance to such imperfect patterns of regional blocs. Truman has described geographic cleavages in a legislative party as "a symptom whose origins are multiple and complex and are not readily susceptible to isolation and rating except in general terms." He warns that regional variations may be "less geographic than demographic, reflecting rural-urban differences."[19] But the regional variations in voting are not merely a reflection of urban-rural differences. Several studies have indicated that regional differences persist when urban-rural factors are held constant, particularly in the House, where the size of and variation in districts make such manipulation possible. Northern urban Democrats have a more liberal voting record than southern urban Democrats; the same distinction applies to northern and southern rural Democrats.[20] We will explore the differences between the various kinds of districts more fully later in the chapter when we examine the influence of district characteristics on individual congressmen. It is clear that regional splits within the congressional parties are particularly likely to occur on certain types of issues, just as certain issues, particularly at the state level, are likely to cause party alignments. To understand both partisanship and intraparty divisions, we must look more closely at the issue content of legislation.

PARTISAN ISSUES

An examination of the issues that arise in legislative bodies shows distinct differences between those that are most likely, and those least likely, to produce partisan alignments, a contrast that is sharpest at the state legislative level. Even in states with high party cohesion, a substantial number of bills produce roll calls, sometimes sharply divided, on which party appears to have no effect. Whether party cohesion is high or low in a state, party alignments are more likely to appear on issues that fit into one of three categories: (1) issues involving the prestige and fundamental programs of the administration, (2) social and economic issues that are associated with the liberal-conservative dichotomy of viewpoints on which major interest groups are likely to have taken conflicting stands, and (3) issues involving the special interests of the state or legislative parties.[21]

In Congress the contrast between partisan and nonpartisan issues is not so sharp. Congress deals less frequently with issues that concern only local and special interests, the type of issues that are most likely to be nonpartisan at the state level. A substantial proportion of congressional roll calls (at least half) involve bills on which the President has taken a stand and/or bills pertaining to liberal-conservative issues or issues affecting major interest groups. On such issues there are likely to be appreciable differences between the voting of Democrats and Republicans. On the other hand, many of these issues create conflicts between party and constituency and produce regional or factional splits within one or both of the parties. One reason for looking at congressional issues is to identify those that have contributed to the decline in party voting that we have noted.

Administration Issues

In state legislatures the administration party is more likely to unite on measures that involve the governor's prestige; for political reasons, the opposition party is also more likely to unite on such issues. In most states the governor is likely to commit his prestige to the support of, or in opposition to, only a small percentage of the bills in the legislature, while remaining neutral on most others, even on some advocated by his administrative agencies. The governor normally takes a stand, for example, on virtually all taxation and appropriation bills, confirmation of his appointments, and most measures that directly affect the administration of state government. Studies covering a large number of states show that these issues consistently rank near the top in the categories of issues producing party alignments. It is also probable that many of the social and economic measures (discussed later in this chapter) that produce party alignments are those on which the governor takes a stand. In states with high party cohesion and an active governor, the governor's stand on an issue becomes the signal for party conflict, and the absence of such a stand makes party conflict unlikely. Even in states with lower party cohesion, the governor's program may generate more partisan conflict than most other issues.

Two recent comparative state studies have examined voting patterns on bills that were part of the governor's program. Bernick studied seven states where the legislature has been generally dominated by one party and where there has not been a high level of partisan voting in the legislature. He looked at two sessions (in the late 1960s and early 1970s) in each state. He found that, in each of these states, in one or both sessions there was substantially higher interparty conflict on bills that were part of the governor's program or that he clearly opposed than there was on other bills. One or both parties was usually more cohesive on the bills on which the governor had taken a stand; in a slight majority of sessions the governor's party was more cohesive than the opposition party on such bills.[22]

A second study, by Morehouse, analyzes voting on bills in the governor's program for the 1971 session in twenty states, ranging from strong two-party to one-party-dominated legislatures. It is designed to explain why some governors are more successful than others in getting their bills passed and particularly why some get greater support from their own party. It shows that interparty conflict is much higher in the competitive two-party states. In almost all of the states the governor's party is more united in support of his program than the opposition party is united against it. A governor is more likely to have high support from his own party if his political strength is great (as measured by his primary vote, particularly that following the session), if his formal powers are substantial, and also if his party does not have too large a majority in the legislature.[23]

The President probably takes a stand on more issues than most governors, and his impact on voting is similar to that of the governor. Because the President is a party leader, his stand on an issue often has a positive influence on the votes cast by members of his party. Members of the opposition party may be influenced favorably by the President's stand because he is the President or unfavorably because he is the leader of the other party. Support for the President in both parties may vary depending on his popularity, his skill in dealing with Congress, and other factors. Support for the President over a period of years has been calculated by the *Congressional Quarterly,* and the data are summarized in Table 16.3, which shows the percentage of times the President won on roll calls on which he took a stand and the percentage of times members of each party supported him. (In this table, the failure to vote lowers a member's presidential-support score.) The data on percentages of presidential victories are also presented in Figure 16.2, in order to provide a more graphic picture of changes over time.

The most obvious conclusion we can draw from the data is that from 1955 to 1974 the Democratic presidents were usually more successful than Republican presidents in getting what they wanted from Congress, which always had a Democratic majority. Eisenhower's success generally fell during his administration, hitting a low point in the 1959 session. (Its high point, not shown in the table, was during the 1953–1954 session, when there was a narrow Republican majority in Congress.) The highest levels of presidential support occurred during the Kennedy and early Johnson years; in the later Johnson years there was a drop, particularly in the Senate. Nixon's success rate was much higher in the House than in the Senate from 1970 through 1972, but it was low in both branches in 1973 and 1974; Ford did not make any immediate gain during his first months in office.[24]

The presidential success rate can be explained by two factors: the support rate in each party and the ratio of Democrats to Republicans in the Senate and House.

FIGURE 16.2   Percentage of Roll Calls in Senate and House Won by President

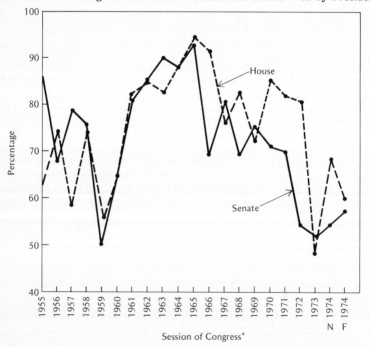

Session of Congress*

*N and F stand for Nixon and Ford

SOURCE: Congressional Quarterly, *Congressional Quarterly Almanac,* vols. 11–30.

TABLE 16.3 Congressional Support for President's Position on Roll-call Votes

	SENATE							HOUSE						
	Party Balance		Percentage of Roll Calls Won by President	Average Percentage of Votes in Support of President				Party Balance		Percentage of Roll Calls Won by President	Average Percentage of Votes in Support of President			
				Administration Party		Opposition Party					Administration Party		Opposition Party	
YEAR	D	R		D	R	D	R	D	R		D	R	D	R
1955	48	47	85		72	56		232	203	63		60	53	
1956	48	47	68		72	39		232	203	74		72	52	
1957	49	47	79		69	51		234	201	58		54	49	
1958	49	47	76		67	44		234	201	74		58	55	
1959	66	34	50		72	38		283	154	55		68	40	
1960	66	34	65		66	43		283	154	65		59	44	
1961	64	36	81	65			36	263	174	83	73			37
1962	64	36	86	63			39	263	174	85	72			42
1963	68	32	90	63			44	258	176	83	72			32
1964	68	32	88	61			45	258	176	88	74			38
1965	67	33	93	64			48	295	140	94	74			41
1966	67	33	69	57			43	295	140	91	63			37
1967	64	36	81	61			53	248	187	76	69			46
1968	64	36	69	48			47	248	187	83	64			51
1969	57	43	75		66	47		243	192	72		57	48	
1970	57	43	71		60	45		243	192	85		66	53	
1971	55	45	70		64	40		255	180	82		72	47	
1972	55	45	54		66	44		255	180	81		64	47	
1973	57	43	52		61	37		243	192	48		62	35	
1974N	57	43	54		57	39		243	192	68		65	46	
1974F	57	43	57		55	39		243	192	59		51	41	

NOTE: The figures for the party balance do not take into account changes resulting from deaths and resignations during a Congress. The average percentage of votes in support of the President is based on the total roll calls on which the President took a stand, and consequently, the failure to vote lowers the average percentage. 1974N and 1974F are Nixon and Ford.

SOURCE: Congressional Quarterly, *Congressional Quarterly Almanac*, vols. 11–30.

In most sessions the average presidential support rate in the administration party has been between 57 and 74 percent; in the opposition it has usually ranged from 37 to 53 percent. This means, of course, that the President can seldom depend on the votes of just his own party to win; he needs and can usually get substantial support from the opposition party. Changes in the success record for a particular President may result from changes in the level of support in one or both parties, but are more substantially affected by changes in the party balance in Congress. For example, the sharp drop in President Eisenhower's batting average in the 1959 and 1960 sessions was caused partly by a drop in Democratic support, but it was due primarily to a very large increase in Democratic majorities in both houses in the 1958 election. The high point of presidential success, in 1965, followed the 1964 Democratic landslide that produced an unusually large Democratic majority in the House. The sharp drop in Johnson's success rate in the Senate during his later years resulted from a drop in support by Democratic senators (which reached a record low of 48 percent in 1968); the more modest drop in the House resulted primarily from a smaller Democratic majority following the 1966 election. From 1970 through 1972 Nixon was more successful in the House than in the Senate, primarily because he had greater support from both parties in the House. His poorer record in 1973 and 1974 apparently resulted from a loss of Democratic support in both houses (particularly in 1973) and from a loss of Republican support in the Senate.

It is useful to distinguish between presidential support on foreign policy and domestic issues. Even though the number of foreign policy roll calls is usually small, these are likely to be particularly important from the President's point of view. Perhaps the best way to measure the impact of the President on foreign policy roll calls is to look at the changes in the voting record of the two congressional parties when there is a change from a Democratic to a Republican administration, or vice versa. The Eisenhower administration resulted in more Republican support and less Democratic support for foreign commitments than had been true under Truman.[25] Aage Clausen has demonstrated that Democrats gave much more support to the President's program of foreign commitments under Johnson and Kennedy than they had during the Eisenhower administration, while Republicans were much less supportive than they had been. The Nixon administration produced greatly increased Republican support and much lower Democratic support. Many northern Democrats and many east and west coast Republicans supported these foreign commitments rather consistently under all administrations. It was those members of both parties who had the greatest doubt about the policies (southern Democrats and interior Republicans) who were most likely to shift their votes in response to the leadership of a President of their party. Clausen has argued that the President has greater impact on congressional voting in foreign policy because he is able to change the votes of many members of his party. In the domestic field, where members of Congress are more likely to stick to established positions (based on their own viewpoints and their constituency), members tend to support the President when his policy coincides with their own position, but they are unlikely to shift position in response to the President's wishes.[26]

Although the President's impact on the members of his party may be greatest in the area of foreign policy, this does not mean that voting on foreign policy can be explained strictly in terms of partisan loyalty to a President. The President can never command complete support from his own party. During the early Eisenhower years, many Republican representatives, who had criticized Truman's foreign aid programs, were slow in responding to Eisenhower's endorsement of the same programs. Lyndon Johnson's support from Democratic senators was eroded by the controversy over Vietnam. At the same time it is true that presidents have often received more support from the opposition party on foreign policy issues than on domestic programs. Many Democrats, particularly northerners, supported the foreign programs of the Eisenhower administration, which had been inherited from President Truman. Presidents Kennedy and Johnson won considerable support from Republican senators, in particular, for their foreign programs. Both the authority and prestige that the President normally enjoys in foreign affairs and the continuity of foreign policy from one administration to the next have contributed to a situation in which the President is able to swing a substantial number of votes in his own party while holding the support of many opposition congressmen. It is too early to tell how seriously the President's influence in foreign affairs has been eroded by the new spirit of congressional independence, manifested in congressional voting on such issues as the War Powers Act, the ban on bombing in Cambodia, and the arms embargo to Turkey.[27]

Social and Economic Issues

A second broad category of issues that often produce party alignments is social and economic issues that affect major interest groups in the country. This includes such issues as health, education, and welfare services; civil rights; the control of the economy; some environmental issues; labor legislation; and measures to regulate business.

We would expect such issues to produce partisan alignments in those states (primarily the heavily urban and industrial ones) where the two parties have established records and made commitments on these issues in order to win votes from major interests in the state. Moreover, in these states, each legislative party represents a distinct and fairly homogeneous group of constituencies, with interests that would be expected to come into conflict on such issues. In most of the states that have been surveyed in voting studies, roll calls on labor issues are among the most partisan ones faced by the legislature, ranking right behind taxation and appropriations measures. Among the other issues that frequently rank high in partisanship are welfare, education, health, civil rights, and environmental issues. None of these issues consistently produces partisan alignments; whether this occurs in a particular state is likely to depend on the role played by the governor and the commitments that each party has previously made on the issue.

These same categories of issues are likely to produce partisan alignments in Congress for the same reason: the national parties have established records and made commitments on these issues in order to win voter support. The congressional parties, however, represent constituencies that are far more heterogeneous than those of state legislative parties. Many of these issues are certain to generate conflicting viewpoints from the diverse constituencies in the congressional party, thereby weakening party cohesion. Several recent studies enable us to define with greater precision those issues on which party cohesion is relatively high and the nature of intraparty divisions that occur on issues with lower cohesion. They also make it possible to spot trends, to determine which types of issues are contributing to the erosion of party cohesion. The major categories of social and economic issues we will use are those defined by Clausen in his studies of Congress from 1953 to 1972.[28]

Government Management. The clearest and most consistent divisions between Democrats and Republicans have occurred on roll calls in this category, which includes the management of the economy, regulation of business, public power, development and preservation of natural resources, and taxation and fiscal policy. On such issues there is an almost ideological division between Democrats and Republicans about the proper role of the federal government. Even in this area, however, there has been some erosion of party cohesion in the late 1960s and early 1970s, particularly among southern Democrats and eastern, urban Republicans, and particularly on bills involving conflicts between industrial development and environmental protection.

Social Welfare. This area includes bills on the regulation of labor, public housing, urban affairs, and education. On these issues voting has been influenced both by party and by constituency. The Democrats have traditionally supported federal programs in these areas, and Republicans have either opposed them or tried to reduce their scope and cost. Democrats have supported, and Republicans have opposed, the policies of unions regarding labor relations. The Democrats who have not followed the party position have been those from southern and rural districts whose constituents either did not need or want the programs; dissident Republicans came from metropolitan districts where there was most support for such programs. Although partisan cohesion is relatively high on traditional social welfare programs that stem from the New Deal, cohesion in both parties has been eroded in recent years on such measures as the "war on poverty" and related programs.

Agricultural Assistance. For many years there has been a rather strong partisan alignment on agricultural issues, with Democrats much more willing than Republicans to support farm subsidies and production controls. There have been some deviations in both parties related to constituency interest in (or opposition to) farm programs. In recent years, however, a new dimension of farm policy has arisen: the issue of limiting federal subsidies to large corporate farm enterprises. On this issue party alignments are much weaker, with the Democrats in particular split along urban-rural lines.

Civil Liberties and Rights. On these issues the divisions within both political parties are so great that they cannot be considered partisan issues. The split within the Democratic party along North-South lines is well known and long established; it is very rare for a majority of northern Democrats and of southern Democrats to vote on the same side of any controversial roll call. There has also been increasing evidence of a split within the Republican party along regional and urban-rural lines on these issues. There is also evidence, in the House only, of a more conservative shift on these issues by both Democrats and Republicans, particularly on the issue of school busing, which has produced a large number of roll calls. In general we can conclude that this is one issue on which constituent opinion is so strong, and both parties have such diverse constituencies, that party is not effective as a unifying force.

The issue dimensions of partisan voting in Congress have been explored at great length by political scientists, and it is neither possible nor necessary to review the findings in any greater detail here. But several conclusions are worth reiterating:

Partisan alignments and cohesion are much stronger on some social and economic issues than on others.

Party cohesion on a particular category of issues, such as agriculture or welfare, may shift substantially over a period of several years because of changes in the specific types of bills on the congressional agenda.

Party cohesion tends to be strongest on those issues where the parties have distinctly different, well-understood positions, often dating back to the New Deal period.

Party cohesion is weak, and often growing weaker, on newer issues that arouse strong viewpoints at the constituent level, issues on which both parties' constituencies are sharply divided.

Party-interest Issues

William J. Keefe concluded from a study of Illinois and Pennsylvania that: "A large number of party conflicts develop on issues the primary concern of which is the party organization, not the public. The party, in this sense, is a pressure group."[29] The number of such issues in Congress is small because the national parties are weak and are seldom directly affected by congressional legislation. However, in recent years bills to provide stricter regulation of, and federal subsidies for, campaign financing have produced a high level of party conflict. In most states a number of different kinds of issues affect the parties at the legislative, statewide, and local levels. There is often some overlap between these issues and issues involving the prestige and authority of the governor; an example would be a bill affecting civil service. Some of the measures in which the parties have a strong interest, such as election legislation, also have important public consequences; frequently, however, the issues in dispute are of concern only, or primarily, to the politicians.

Several studies have shown that the issue that most consistently produces partisan voting is legislation affecting elections. Other types of issues that directly affect the parties are often not so easily recognizable as, for example, economic and social issues. The party may have an interest in the patronage implications of a bill to transfer functions from one unit of local government to another, to reorganize a state agency, or to increase the number of judges in a district court. In his study of two states, Keefe found that party interests were most often revealed in bills designed to protect or enhance the status of one party, to jeopardize that of the other, to embarrass state or local administrations controlled by the opposite party, to secure favorable election laws, to offset electoral defeats in state governments, and to increase access to all forms of patronage.[30] When such issues attract little attention from either the general public or interest groups, it is easy to understand why the party becomes the only important reference group for the legislator.

A closely related area that often produces very high party cohesion is roll calls on matters of legislative organization, such as the election of the Speaker and the adoption or amendment of legislative rules. When legislative or congressional reapportionment legislation is perceived as giving an advantage to one party or the other, highly cohesive partisan voting can be expected. Often, however, the political parties compromise on apportionment bills, and the opposition comes from members of both parties who believe that their districts are being hurt by reapportionment.

VOTING IN ONE-PARTY LEGISLATURES: AN UNFILLED VACUUM

In those state legislatures that are completely dominated by a single party, the party is not a source of voting cues. The constituency remains a reference group of intermittent importance; lobbyists remain eager to provide advice; and legislators frequently turn to other legislators for voting cues. But there is no substitute for party. Only rarely does any factional grouping demonstrate voting cohesion on a significant number of roll calls, and even more rarely does such a faction retain its identity and cohesion beyond a single session of the legislature.

In many one-party states, the governor is the most visible source of voting cues. Those measures that have his endorsement have the best chance of passage, and those that he opposes face serious obstacles to achieving a legislative majority. The governor often has no dependable, cohesive faction to support his program, nor does he face a cohesive opposition. In his effort to win votes for his program, he is entirely dependent on his skill in using the resources of his office (described in Chapter 11). In some one-party states, these resources are sufficient to assure the governor of legislative support for the major bills in his program. In a few states, a bifactional system has appeared at times in the legislature as a result of the personality and program of the governor. Examples in the past could be found in Louisiana and Kentucky. The opposition faction has rarely been strong enough to overcome the advantage of power enjoyed by the governor. Moreover, the factional alignment has seldom been durable enough to survive from one administration to the next. Prior to reapportionment and the growth of a Republican minority, however, the Florida senate had a rather stable and cohesive factional system along urban-rural and regional lines.[31] A study of the 1961 and 1967 sessions of the one-party Alabama legislature concluded that "neither factional nor gubernatorial alignments . . . were able to provide an institutionalized source of continuous voting cues to the degree that parties in competitive legislatures provided this source." Moreover, "urban-rural divisions do not serve as the basis for continuous voting alignments over a wide range of policy categories," but are limited to a few issues, such as alcoholic beverages and apportionment.[32]

Samuel C. Patterson's study of the 1959 session of the Oklahoma house provides a good example of the variety and fluidity of voting patterns in a state with neither strong parties nor factions. The voting pattern of individual legislators was consistent enough to permit the creation of seven scales, pertaining to the governor's program, labor and welfare, schools, campaigns and elections, public morals, appropriations, and taxation. But rank-order correlation analysis showed that these scales represented independent and largely unrelated dimensions of voting behavior; only the governor's program scale was associated to any extent with the others. On most, but not all, scales, metropolitan legislators voted differently from other members. Patterson's conclusions would apply to many other one-party states: "In the absence of party as a reference group, the legislator is likely, consciously or unconsciously, to respond to different pressures in different voting areas."[33]

A detailed study of the nonpartisan Nebraska legislature by Susan Welch showed that in the 1959 and 1969 sessions only one-third to one-fourth of the roll calls could be fitted into any scale (which required a minimum of four roll calls). In other words, the voting patterns were highly fragmented. For some of those roll calls that did scale, urban-rural (or industrial-nonindustrial) constituency alignments appeared. In the absence of party leadership and organization and partisan norms, the party identification of legislators had very little effect on roll-call voting.[34]

THE LEGISLATOR AND HIS DISTRICT

Up to this point in our analysis of roll-call voting, we have concentrated on major patterns of voting in legislative bodies, particularly the evidence of party alignments and (in Congress) intraparty blocks. Now we turn to an examination of the forces influencing the votes of individual legislators. What factors determine how frequently a legislator votes with his party on party-line roll calls? Whose advice does he follow on roll calls on which the party has not taken a stand? What reference groups other than party are salient to legislators? Under what conditions do they become salient?

In Chapter 15, we discussed the variety of roles played by legislators, many of them pertinent to voting decisions. A legislator's perception of his role may make him particularly loyal to his party, sensitive to the needs of his constituency, or responsive to the demands of a particular interest group, for example. Likewise, the President or governor, a legislative committee, a state or local delegation, or some other grouping may be a significant reference group for the legislator on some issues. The average legislator does not self-consciously choose one or another role, but every legislator is aware of his need to make choices and to maintain some kind of balance among the pressures exerted on him from time to time. Not all legislators make the same choice or give the same priority to a particular reference group, and consequently there are differences in legislators' role perceptions and in the factors influencing their voting decisions.

Despite the attention that political scientists have given to legislative roles, there is very little evidence to show how role orientations affect voting behavior. One study of four states showed that legislators whose role orientation was one of party loyalty were more likely to support the party on roll calls in four houses and less likely to support the party in two houses; in two houses, party role seemed to have little effect on voting.[35] There are several reasons why it is difficult to predict voting from a knowledge of a legislator's role orientations. When a legislator is classified as a party loyalist or a maverick, a delegate or a trustee, he is being stereotyped in a fashion that may oversimplify or distort his actual attitudes and values. Moreover, a role orientation should be considered as a statement of probability rather than a rigid prediction about behavior. This means that some legislators are more strongly committed than others to a particular role orientation and that some will not always act in accord with a role orientation if contradictory pressures become too intense.

A role orientation is a way of describing a legislator's attitude toward the expectations or demands of others. To predict how he will vote on a bill, it is necessary to know not only his attitudes toward these demands but also whether he perceives that such demands are being made regarding the bill. A party loyalist's vote may be predictable on many roll calls, but the legislative party does not take any stand on many of the issues that come to a vote, even in states where party discipline is strong. On many issues, the legislator looks in vain to his constituency for voting cues: "I don't know how my constituents see things. I don't have a crystal ball that tells me how my constituents feel." "You can't vote by what you think the constituents' thinking is. You don't know what that thinking is."[36]

If a legislator faces role conflict, it may be particularly difficult for him to decide how to vote; and for that reason, it is difficult to predict how he will vote from a knowledge of his role orientation. Of course, the fact that some of his potential reference groups may remain silent helps to reduce the role conflict perceived by a legislator. Moreover, conflict between a legislator's views and those of his constituents is reduced by the fact that he is a product of his district, often a lifelong resident. As one Pennsylvania legislator said, "A man usually agrees with his district, since he's one of them and typical of them."[37] As political scientists develop a deeper understanding of legislative roles, they will learn more about how legislators resolve role conflicts and how legislative behavior is affected by role perceptions, but it is unlikely that they will be able to predict roll-call voting with much precision from a knowledge of role orientations.

District Characteristics—Concepts

We want to know how a legislator's votes are affected by various characteristics of his district. Under what conditions will he be responsive to demands of certain groups in his district and, as a consequence, vote against the position taken by most members of his legislative party? Put another way, we are asking whether party loyalists and mavericks in the legislature can be distinguished by certain characteristics of their constituencies. There has been a substantial amount of research done on this question, some of which we will summarize in the next section. Unfortunately, some of the research findings are contradictory, and some are not supported by firm evidence. The study of this question has been hampered by a lack of conceptual clarity. Before summarizing the research findings, therefore, we need to try to clarify how districts are classified and how these categories might be expected to affect voting. We will concentrate on three types of classification for districts: their homogeneity/heterogeneity, their typicalness, and the safe or marginal character of elections in the district. Districts can be ranked along a continuum on any of these characteristics, or can be divided into two or more categories, such as safe and marginal, for convenience of analysis. We will begin with the first two types of classification and their effect on voting, before turning to the more difficult question of election margins.[38]

If a district is relatively homogeneous in its socioeconomic character, there is likely to be a minimum of conflicting interests and viewpoints on those legislative issues that attract attention in the district. On such issues, the legislator is likely to know what constituent opinion is and to follow it if constituents feel strongly. If the district is heterogeneous in character (such as a mixture of urban and rural, or suburban and central city), there are likely to be sharp conflicts of interest and viewpoint on some issues, and when this happens the legislators must make difficult choices about which position to take, based perhaps on which groups or interests are larger or better organized or whose support he needs to win reelection.

When we refer to a district as being typical, we mean that it is similar in socioeconomic characteristics to the majority of districts represented by that party and different from those represented by the other party. If most metropolitan districts in a state are Democratic and most small-town and rural ones are Republican, a Democrat from a metropolitan area would have a typical district; one from a rural area would have an untypical district. We would expect that representatives from typical districts would usually vote with their party because they would not be cross-pressured; those from untypical districts would sometimes have to choose between party and constituency. This follows logically from our findings earlier in the chapter that the most homogeneous parties are likely to be most cohesive. Obviously, if the two legislative parties represent highly heterogeneous and indistinguishable constituencies, there would be no such thing as typical and untypical districts, and few party positions that a member could be loyal or disloyal to.

Now we want to combine the concepts of homogeneity and typicalness and see how they might affect voting. Figure 16.3 is designed to show how frequently various categories of districts appear in combination at the congressional and the state legislative levels. (For the time being we can ignore the bottom bar in each diagram.) The bars in the diagram are divided to show roughly what proportion of districts are in each category (based on our impressions, not any firm data). For example, compared with congressional districts, a larger proportion of state legislative districts are rather homogeneous (because most of them are smaller).

In two-party state legislatures most of the districts that are homogeneous are also typical. (In a state where the Democratic party is heavily urban, it would be difficult for a Democrat to win in an overwhelmingly rural district.) A member representing a homogeneous, typical district rarely experiences party-constituency conflict over issues. However, at the congressional level, the two parties represent a much wider variety of districts, and we use the term *typical* to refer to the characteristics of a majority of districts (but far from all of them). There

FIGURE 16.3.   Legislative Districts Categorized by Homogeneity, Typicalness, and Electoral Margin

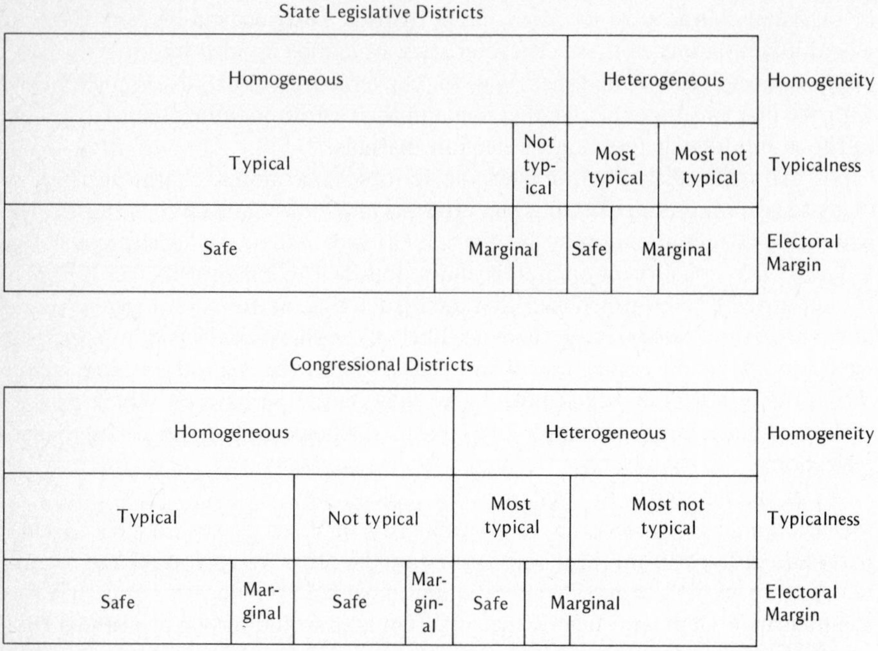

State Legislative Districts

Homogeneous			Heterogeneous		Homogeneity
Typical		Not typical	Most typical	Most not typical	Typicalness
Safe	Marginal		Safe	Marginal	Electoral Margin

Congressional Districts

Homogeneous			Heterogeneous		Homogeneity
Typical	Not typical	Most typical		Most not typical	Typicalness
Safe / Marginal	Safe / Marginal	Safe	Marginal		Electoral Margin

are many congressmen representing homogeneous, untypical districts—for example, the Democrats from rural and small-town southern districts. Such members frequently experience conflict between constituency and party, and on issues of great interest to the district, members usually vote with the constituency.

The situation in heterogeneous districts is more complex. By definition such districts are not completely typical. An example might be a suburban district in a state where the Democrats usually represent the central city and the Republicans the rural and small-town areas; another example would be a congressional district encompassing a medium-sized city and several rural counties. We have suggested that congressmen are more likely than state legislators to have such districts. At least for analytical purposes, we can divide the heterogeneous districts into those where a majority of the voters are typical or untypical; the larger the proportion of untypical voters, the greater the conflicts faced by the legislator. But in any heterogeneous district, at least some issues are likely to provoke conflicts within the district.

How does the legislator handle conflicting demands by constituents, and how does he decide which group, if any, should influence his vote? Keep in mind that his decisions are based on his *perceptions* of the views and attributes of groups, and these perceptions may or may not be accurate. Also it should be remembered that to win reelection, he does not need 100 percent of the vote, and so he does not have to satisfy every interest or group. In making his decision he will pay attention to the size, cohesion, and political power of the groups making conflicting demands. He will also take into account his past and future dependence on the group for votes. A legislator is likely to be cautious about trying to expand his political base by shifting his past position on an issue because he runs the risk of alienating previous political supporters. A shift in position away from the stand taken by his party may be particularly risky if it would alienate the political activists in his party whose help he needs in organizing and financing his next campaign. He may be sensitive to the perceived interests of particular groups in his district even if they are not making demands on him concerning an issue. The legislator is concerned that a future opponent may arouse these groups or interests by attacking the stand that he has taken. Finally, in a heterogeneous district it is possible that groups that are interested in an issue may appear to be evenly divided, or so unimportant, that the legislator can ignore the constituency and vote with his party (or with some other group in the legislature).

The third way of classifying districts is according to their electoral record—whether they are safe or marginal. Political scientists who have tried to study the effects of electoral margins on voting have produced both theories and findings that are contradictory. In our efforts at clarification, let us begin by looking at the bottom bars in Figure 16.3, which estimate what types of districts are more likely to be safe or marginal. Most of the homogeneous, typical districts are safe for one party; but the margin should have no effect on voting because the member rarely faces conflicts between party and constituency. The homogeneous, untypical districts (mostly southern Democratic congressional districts) are also normally safe. It is the heterogeneous districts that are most likely to have narrow electoral margins. Only veteran legislators who have built a strong political base are likely to have safe seats. As we have already noted, the congressman or state legislator faces difficult choices on some issues in a heterogeneous district.

The most common theory advanced by political scientists about electoral margins has been that members representing marginal seats have to be very sensitive to demands of constituents, and so will more often rebel against their party. But empirical research has failed to show consistently that the safety/marginality of districts has such an effect on voting above and beyond what might be caused by the homogeneity or typicality of districts. From what we have said it should be clear why the electoral margin, by itself, is of little importance in explaining voting. In homogeneous districts the legislator has no problems, even if his margin is small. In heterogeneous districts, the member has difficult choices on those issues that stir up (usually conflicting) constituent interests. If that member has a close electoral margin, or perceives it to be close (which is more pertinent), this fact may increase his anxieties or give him an ulcer, but it does not help us to predict whether or not he will abandon his party or follow any other particular course. The choice he makes will be determined by the factors we have already discussed—his electoral strategy, his perceptions of groups and interests in the district, his previous commitments to them.

District Characteristics—Research Findings

Political scientists studying district characteristics that affect voting in legislatures have failed to distinguish between heterogeneous and homogeneous districts, but they have measured differences between typical and untypical districts.

Several studies of individual states, including Massachusetts, Pennsylvania, and Ohio, have shown that, at least in the lower house of those legislatures, members who represent districts more typical of their party vote more consistently with their party. The correlation between an individual member's party loyalty and his district's characteristics should logically be higher in states where the legislative parties represent two distinctly different, homogeneous sets of constituencies. A study of the California senate from 1957 to 1969 showed that the correlation between party loyalty and constituency characteristics increased sharply after reapportionment, which drastically increased urban representation and changed the constituency base of both parties.[39]

The most comprehensive study of the effect of state legislative constituencies on party loyalty is LeBlanc's study of the 1959–1960 session of twenty-three state senates. He tested the influence of various socioeconomic characteristics of districts and found that they varied in importance from state to state, with ethnic and racial factors most often being related to party loyalty in legislative voting. In almost all the state senates some combination of constituency characteristics appeared to affect partisan voting of legislators. He did not attempt to measure directly the typical/untypical character of districts, but he did find that interparty conflict in voting (the index of difference) was greatest in states where constituency characteristics had the greatest effect on party loyalty.[40]

In Congress, the division between northern and southern Democrats demonstrates that there is some relationship between constituencies and party voting in Congress. Southern Democratic congressmen, many of them representing rural constituencies, tend to have lower records of party loyalty than northern Democrats, often from urban districts, who constitute a majority within the congressional party. How does the thesis linking typical districts with loyal party voting stand up under a more rigorous analysis at the congressional level? A number of studies, covering both branches of Congress during different time periods, have measured the effect of constituency on voting.[41] At the risk of oversimplifying, it can be concluded from these studies that constituency does affect congressional voting but that the effect is much more substantial on some issues than on others.

It is clear that Democratic congressmen from northern metropolitan districts vote with the party more frequently than those from southern rural districts, but it is also apparent that there are differences in voting patterns among northern Democrats and among southern Democrats that are related to constituency. The most loyal northern Democrats are likely to represent districts in metropolitan areas with a high proportion of foreign-born or nonwhite population, many blue-collar workers, and below-average levels of income. Because relatively few northern Democrats do not have a high record of party loyalty, the relationship between party voting and constituency variables is not as strong as it is for two other groups—southern Democrats and Republicans. In the case of southern Democrats, those with voting records least loyal to the Democratic party are likely to come from rural areas, particularly those with large black populations. There is some evidence that Republican congressmen who represent lower-income blue-collar districts in urban areas are less likely to support the party than the Republicans from higher-income suburban districts or rural–small-town districts. In general, the studies that have demonstrated a stronger impact of constituency variables on party voting are those that have measured a larger number of such variables. Most of the studies of congressional constituencies have concentrated on the House, where districts are usually more homogeneous, but a recent study of the Senate has concluded that constituencies have a substantial effect on the voting of most senators.[42]

Almost every study of congressional voting has demonstrated that the influence of constituency varies with the issue. We emphasized this point earlier in the discussion of social and economic issues, and the evidence does not need to be repeated. Of all the issues faced by congressmen, they are most likely to be sensitive to constituency views on issues related to civil rights. Several studies have emphasized the importance of constituency viewpoints on agricultural and also welfare issues.[43] Several studies have suggested that foreign policy questions are among those least likely to be affected by constituency, but Rieselbach's study of foreign aid and foreign trade votes showed that congressmen with isolationist records were more likely to come from constituencies that were rural and below average in socioeconomic status.[44]

Most studies of constituency influence are based on data concerning the characteristics of districts rather than directly on the views of constituents. One exception to this was a study conducted in 1958 by the Survey Research Center of the University of Michigan that provided data for 116 House districts on four factors: (1) the attitudes of constituents, (2) the attitudes of the congressman, (3) the congressman's perception of his constituents' attitudes, and (4) the congressman's voting record.[45] The study showed that constituency influence was greatest on civil rights issues; the congressman had a very accurate perception of constituents' attitudes and was very likely to vote in accordance with this perception. He was least likely to follow constituents' views on foreign policy questions. More broadly, the study led to the conclusion that constituency influence on a congressman will be greatest when he has a clear and accurate perception of constituency opinion. That is most likely to occur on issues of greatest interest to constituents and in districts that are more homogeneous and where, consequently, constituents are more likely to be in agreement.

A number of studies at both the state legislative and the congressional levels have sought to determine whether a legislator's record of party loyalty is affected by the size of his electoral margin. The results have been contradictory and inconclusive, partly because of methodological problems and partly because—as we explained in the previous section—there is no clear theoretical reason why we should be able to explain how a legislator will vote by knowing whether his electoral margin was large or small. Nevertheless, it should be noted that studies of several states (California, Pennsylvania, Massachusetts, and Wisconsin) and LeBlanc's multistate study have provided some evidence for the theory that party loyalty is weaker in the case of legislators who come from unsafe districts.[46]

There is considerably stronger evidence, from both congressional and state legislative studies, suggesting that a legislator is more likely to support the legislative program of a President or governor if the chief executive has won a large vote (or a larger vote than the legislator) in his district.[47] This relationship may apply to members of the chief executive's own party or (in some studies) to members of both parties. One multistate study indicated that the governor's primary vote in the district was related to the legislator's support of the governor, while another focused on the governor's general election vote. Several of the studies show that the legislator's record of party loyalty or support for the chief executive is related at least as strongly to the President's or governor's vote in the subsequent election as it is to his vote in the preceding election. This finding suggests that legislators may be making estimates about the chief executive's future popularity in their district and not merely reading past election returns. It also undermines the simple explanation that legislators regard the vote for a President or governor as a mandate to vote for his programs.

The explanation for the relationship between a legislator's voting record and the votes cast for the President or governor in his district is probably complex and multifaceted. Presumably, legislators are aware of the votes cast in their district for other candidates, and some of them may perceive a large vote for the chief executive as a measure of his political strength and/or the popularity of his programs. Moreover, in those districts where there is strong political support for a President or governor, there are likely to be both general public attitudes and specific organized groups that are supportive of the chief executive's policies— and the legislator will be aware of this. Finally, we may conclude that this relationship is likely to be stronger in those elections and those districts where the vote for President or governor is issue-oriented and not simply based on party loyalty.[48]

SOURCES OF VOTING CUES WITHIN THE LEGISLATURE

A review of the literature on constituencies leads to the conclusion that much of the variation in individual patterns of voting and party loyalty cannot be explained by any socioeconomic or electoral data in the district. The reason is that a legislator often has to vote on issues that do not have any particular effect on the interests of his district and that have not provoked any noticeable expression of viewpoints from the district. Under these conditions, if the legislator has not made up his mind on a bill, he can be expected to turn to others for advice, often to other members of the legislature. In previous chapters, we have discussed some of the most common sources of voting cues in the legislature: party leaders, policy committees and caucuses, state or county delegations, and committees. Over a period of years, particularly at the congressional level, a member develops close personal relationships with a number of his colleagues, particularly those on his committee and in his delegation; and he comes to respect the opinions of those whom he recognizes as specialists on particular subjects. For these reasons, sources of voting cues within the legislative body may be more important than sources in the legislator's district, even on some bills that affect the interests of important groups in the district.

During the course of a session, a congressman or state legislator must make a decision about a large number and variety of bills. Unless the bill directly affects his district, has come before one of his committees, or relates to some field in which he has specialized knowledge, he is likely to be poorly informed about the bill and proposed amendments that come to a vote. He has very little time to collect information about the bill from sources that he considers trustworthy, and this is another important reason why he is likely to turn to other legislators. He can get information from them immediately, and he knows which colleagues he can trust. For these reasons, Donald R. Matthews and James A. Stimson suggest the following hypothesis about congressional decision making:

> When a member is confronted with the necessity of casting a roll-call vote on a complex issue about which he knows very little, he searches for cues provided by trusted colleagues who—because of their formal position in the legislature or policy specialization—have more information than he does and with whom he would probably agree if he had the time and information to make an independent decision. Cue-givers need not be individuals. When overwhelming majorities of groups which the member respects and trusts—the whole House, the members of his party or state delegation, for example—vote the same way the member is likely to accept their collective judgment as his own.[49]

John Kingdon emphasizes similar points in his study *Congressmen's Voting Decisions.* Congressmen need usable information "which takes into account the political as well as the policy implications of voting decisions." They are pressured for time and "must confine their searches for information only to the most routine and easily available sources." He concludes, "Trusted colleagues within the House, sensitive to their fellow congressman's information needs, generally meet those requirements quite nicely." If the colleagues whose advice he trusts are in agreement on an issue, the member has no difficulty in making a decision; if they are not in complete agreement, he tries to determine if there is some lower level of consensus that can provide a basis for his vote.[50] Interviews with congressmen suggest that: "The foremost criteria for selecting whom to consult among fellow congressmen are the informant's agreement with one's own point of view, and expertise; the latter being defined as membership on the committee that considered the bill."[51]

On the basis of their interviews with members of the House, Matthews and Stimson conclude that the cue-taking process occurs in several stages, as intermediaries frequently pass on advice and suggestions from those who are the initial cue-givers. The most important sources of initial cues are the members, and particularly the leaders of committees and subcommittees because of their recognized expertise on particular issues. Another initial source is party leaders, whose importance sometimes results from the fact that they speak for the President. Party leaders also play a role in disseminating information from committees. Another important intermediary source of voting cues are the various policy-oriented groups in the House, such as the Democratic Study Group and the Republican Wednesday Club, which we described in Chapter 7. Congressmen also frequently say that they get voting cues from their state party delegation. These are particularly important intermediary groups when the delegation is large enough to have members on a substantial number of committees who can report on the policy positions developed in those committees. As we explained previously (Chapter 7), a congressman is likely to turn to members of his state party delegation not only because they are convenient and familiar sources of advice but also because they are likely to have similar viewpoints and interests.[52]

There have been several efforts to measure the impact of various types of cue-givers in Congress through roll-call studies. Using a simulation model of decision making in the House, Shapiro concluded that other members from a congressman's state were particularly influential.[53] Similarly, Matthews and Stimson, relying on a simulation model of the House, concluded that "the consistently most important single cue-giver in both parties is the member's state delegation."[54] They also stressed the importance of party leaders and the chairman and ranking member of committees. Jackson's study of senatorial voting indicates that both Democratic and Republican leaders were important cue-givers but that Democratic leaders had little influence on southern Democrats. Leading members of the reporting committees (not always the chairman or ranking minority member) often provided cues for northern Democratic and Republican senators.[55]

Several studies have emphasized the high degree of consistency in patterns of cue giving. In other words, many congressmen became accustomed to turning to the same sources for advice and information, whatever the subject matter of the roll call. The primary sources of cues (such as committees) may vary, of course, depending on the expert information that is needed. But one advantage of certain intermediary groups, like a state party delegation or the Democratic Study Group, is that it can be a dependable source of guidance on a wide variety of issues.[56]

State legislators may be even more dependent than congressmen on information and advice from fellow legislators. They are less likely to be familiar with issues or to be aware of strong constituent interests, at least on a large proportion of issues. Patterns of cue taking presumably vary from state to state, but a study by Uslaner and Weber, based on a large sample of legislators in all states in 1974, gives us some perspective on the most common sources of voting cues. Legislators said they most often sought the advice of personal friends in the legislature. Ranked immediately below that group were: legislators who were recognized as specialists in policy areas, interest groups, committee chairmen or ranking minority members, legislators of the same party from the same or an adjoining district, and legislative party leaders.[57] A more detailed study of cue taking in the Michigan legislature by Porter showed that legislators reported that when they needed advice on legislation they were not well informed about, they most often turned to other legislators whom they considered knowledgeable in the field, and whose judgment they respected. That study also showed that for some important policy areas there may be few if any recognized experts in the legislature, a problem that is common to most legislatures where there is considerable turnover in membership and in committee membership.[58] Where voting cues on some issues within the legislature are inadequate, members may be more heavily dependent on advice from outside sources, such as the governor, administrative agencies, and interest groups.

NOTES

1. Donald R. Matthews, *U.S. Senators and Their World* (Chapel Hill, N.C., 1960), p. 123.
2. John G. Grumm, "Party Responsibility in the Kansas Legislature" (Paper pre-

sented at the Wichita Conference on Politics, 1959); and "A Factor Analysis of Legislative Behavior," *Midwest Journal of Political Science* 7 (1963):336–356.

3.   Glen T. Broach, "A Comparative Dimensional Analysis of Partisan and Urban-Rural Voting in State Legislatures," *Journal of Politics* 34 (1972):905–921.

4.   Charles W. Wiggins, "Party Politics in the Iowa Legislature," *Midwest Journal of Political Science* 11 (1967):86–97; and Dennis Kellogg and Charles W. Wiggins, "Party Voting in the Sixty-Fifth Iowa General Assembly" (Iowa City, 1975).

5.   Frank M. Bryan, *Yankee Politics in Rural Vermont* (Hanover, N.H., 1974), chap. 4.

6.   Ibid., p. 196.

7.   Samuel C. Patterson, "Party Opposition in the Legislature: The Ecology of Legislative Institutionalization," *Polity* 4 (1972):344–366.

8.   Duane Lockard, *New England State Politics* (Princeton, N.J., 1959), pp. 291–292.

9.   See, for example, Angus Campbell et al., *The American Voter* (New York, 1960), chap. 10.

10.   Frank J. Sorauf, *Party and Representation* (New York, 1963), p. 151.

11.   Ibid., p. 146; for similar comments on Ohio, see Thomas A. Flinn, "Party Representation in the States," *American Political Science Review* 58 (1964):61.

12.   Alan G. Hevesi, *Legislative Politics in New York State* (New York, 1975), p. 171. Hevesi is citing the conclusions of Stuart Witt, in "The Legislative-Local Party Linkage in New York State" (Ph.D. dissertation, Syracuse University, 1967), pp. 246–255.

13.   John C. Wahlke et al., *The Legislative System* (New York, 1962), pp. 362–363.

14.   See Duncan MacRae, Jr., *Issues and Parties in Legislative Voting* (New York, 1970), p. 204.

15.   V. O. Key, Jr., *Southern Politics in State and Nation* (New York, 1950), p. 375; Joel Margolis, "The Conservative Coalition in the United States Senate, 1933–1968" (Paper prepared for the annual meeting of the American Political Science Association, 1972). See also W. Wayne Shannon, *Party, Constituency, and Congressional Voting* (Baton Rouge, 1968), pp. 95–107.

16.   Congressional Quarterly, *Congressional Quarterly Almanac,* vols. 15–30.

17.   See Leonard G. Ritt, "Partisan Realignment: The View from Congress" (Paper prepared for the annual meeting of the American Political Science Association, 1974); Barbara Deckard, "Political Upheaval and Congressional Voting" (Paper prepared for the annual meeting of the Midwest Political Science Association, 1975).

18.   Ritt, "Partisan Realignment: The View from Congress"; Deckard, "Political Upheaval and Congressional Voting," table 1.

19.   David B. Truman, *The Congressional Party* (New York, 1959), p. 78.

20.   See Shannon, *Party, Constituency, and Congressional Voting;* Julius Turner, *Party and Constituency: Pressures on Congress,* rev. ed., Edward V. Schneier, Jr. (Baltimore, 1970), chaps. 4–7; Duncan MacRae, Jr., *Dimensions of Congressional Voting* (Berkeley, Calif., 1958), chap. 3.

21.   The conclusions about partisan issues in the sta es are based primarily on four multistate studies: Malcolm E. Jewell, "Party Voting in American State Legislatures," *American Political Science Review* 49 (1955):773–791; Wayne L. Francis, *Legislative Issues in the Fifty States* (Chicago, 1967), p. 22; Hugh L. LeBlanc, "Voting in State Senates: Party and Constituency Influences," *Midwest Journal of Political Science* 13 (1969):40–44; Broach, "A Comparative Dimensional Analysis of Partisan and Urban-Rural Voting in State Legislatures." See also Wiggins, "Party Politics in the Iowa Legislature."

22.   E. Lee Bernick, "The Role of the Governor in the Legislative Process: A Comparative State Analysis" (Paper prepared for the annual meeting of the American Political

Science Association, 1975). The seven states are: Florida, Idaho, North Dakota, Oklahoma, Oregon, Vermont, and Wyoming.

23. Sarah McCally Morehouse, "The Impact of the Governor on Legislative Policy Output" (Paper prepared for the annual meeting of the American Political Science Association, 1975).

24. For further discussion, see Joseph Cooper and Gary Bombardier, "Presidential Leadership and Party Success," *Journal of Politics* 30 (1968):1012–1027.

25. See Mark Kesselman, "Presidential Leadership in Congress on Foreign Policy," *Midwest Journal of Political Science* 5 (1961):284–289; Malcolm E. Jewell, *Senatorial Politics and Foreign Policy* (Lexington, Ky., 1962), chaps. 1–3.

26. Aage R. Clausen, *How Congressmen Decide* (New York, 1973), chap. 8.

27. See Leroy N. Rieselbach, *The Roots of Isolationism* (Indianapolis, Ind., 1966), chap. 2.

28. The analysis of these issues is based on: Clausen, *How Congressmen Decide;* Clausen and C. E. Van Horn, "Policy Trends in Congress and Partisan Realignment" (Paper prepared for the annual meeting of the American Political Science Association, 1974); Deckard, "Political Upheaval and Congressional Voting."

29. William J. Keefe, "Comparative Study of the Role of Political Parties in State Legislatures," *Western Political Quarterly* 9 (1956):726–742.

30. Ibid.

31. Malcolm B. Parsons, "Quasi-partisan Conflict in a One-party Legislative System: The Florida Senate, 1947–1961," *American Political Science Review* 56 (1962):605–614.

32. Broach, "A Comparative Dimensional Analysis of Partisan and Urban-Rural Voting in State Legislatures," pp. 917–918, 921.

33. Samuel C. Patterson, "Dimensions of Voting Behavior in a One-party State Legislature," *Public Opinion Quarterly* 26 (1962):185–200; quotation at 200.

34. Susan Welch and Eric H. Carlson, "The Impact of Party on Voting in a Nonpartisan Legislature," *American Political Science Review* 67 (1973):854–867.

35. See LeRoy C. Ferguson and Bernard W. Klein, "An Attempt to Correlate the Voting Records of Legislators with Attitudes Toward Party," *Public Opinion Quarterly* 31 (1967):422–426.

36. Wahlke et al., *The Legislative System,* p. 296.

37. Sorauf, *Party and Representation,* p. 124.

38. The theoretical framework outlined in this section is based in part on Morris P. Fiorina's excellent analysis, *Representation, Roll Calls, and Constituencies* (Lexington, Mass., 1974).

39. Duncan MacRae, Jr., "The Relation Between Roll Call Votes and Constituencies in the Massachusetts House of Representatives," *American Political Science Review* 46 (1952):1046–1055; Sorauf, *Party and Representation,* p. 142; Thomas R. Dye, "A Comparison of Constituency Influences in the Upper and Lower Chambers of a State Legislature," *Western Political Quarterly* 14 (1961):473–480; Flinn, "Party Responsibility in the States," pp. 61–66; Bruce W. Robeck, "Legislative Partisanship, Constituency and Malapportionment: The Case of California," *American Political Science Review* 66 (1972):1234–1245.

40. LeBlanc, "Voting in State Senates: Party and Constituency Influences," pp. 33–57.

41. Lewis A. Froman, Jr., *Congressmen and Their Constituencies* (Chicago, 1963), chaps. 7 and 9; Shannon, *Party, Constituency and Congressional Voting,* chaps. 6 and 7; David R. Mayhew, *Party Loyalty Among Congressmen* (Cambridge, Mass., 1966); Turner, *Party and Constituency,* chap. 8; MacRae, *Dimensions of Congressional Voting,* chap. 3; Clausen, *How Congressmen Decide,* chap. 6.

42. John E. Jackson, *Constituencies and Leaders in Congress* (Cambridge, Mass., 1974).

43.   MacRae, *Dimensions of Congressional Voting,* chap. 3; J. Roland Pennock, "Party and Constituency in Postwar Agricultural Price-Support Legislation," *Journal of Politics* 17 (1956):167–210; Aage Clausen and R. B. Cheney, "A Comparative Analysis of Senate-House Voting on Economic and Welfare Policy, 1953–1964," *American Political Science Review* 64 (1970):138–152, at 145.

44.   Rieselbach, *The Roots of Isolationism,* chap. 5.

45.   Warren E. Miller and Donald E. Stokes, "Constituency Influence in Congress," *American Political Science Review* 57 (1963):45–46; Warren E. Miller, "Policy Preferences of Congressional Candidates and Constituents" (Paper presented at the 1961 annual meeting of the American Political Science Association).

46.   Robeck, "Legislative Partisanship, Constituency and Reapportionment"; Sorauf, *Party and Representation,* p. 141; Dye, "A Comparison of Constituency Influences in the Upper and Lower Chambers of a State Legislature," p. 477; Pertti Pesonen, "Close and Safe Elections in Massachusetts," *Midwest Journal of Political Science* 7 (1963):54–70; Samuel C. Patterson, "The Role of the Deviant in the State Legislative System: The Wisconsin Assembly," *Western Political Quarterly* 14 (1961):467–468; Flinn, "Party Responsibility in the States," pp. 66–69; John Grumm, "The Systematic Analysis of Blocs in the Study of Legislative Behavior," *Western Political Quarterly* 18 (1965):350–363; LeBlanc, "Voting in State Senates: Party and Constituency Influences."

47.   LeBlanc, "Voting in State Senates: Party and Constituency Influences"; Robeck, "Legislative Partisanship, Constituency and Reapportionment"; Marvin G. Weinbaum and Dennis R. Judd, "In Search of a Mandated Congress," *Midwest Journal of Political Science* 14 (1970):276–302; Sarah McNally Morehouse, "The State Political Party and the Policy-Making Process," *American Political Science Review* 67 (1973):55–72; George Edwards, "Presidential Influence in the U.S. House of Representatives" (Paper presented at the annual meeting of the American Political Science Association, 1974): J. Vincent Buck, "Presidential Coattails and Congressional Loyalty," *Midwest Journal of Political Science* 16 (1972):460–472.

48.   Clausen and Van Horn, "Policy Trends in Congress and Partisan Realignment."

49.   *Yeas and Nays: Normal Decision-Making in the U.S. House of Representatives* (New York, 1975), p. 45.

50.   John W. Kingdon, *Congressmen's Voting Decisions* (New York, 1973), p. 227.

51.   Ibid., p. 101.

52.   Matthews and Stimson, *Yeas and Nays,* chap. 5.

53.   Michael J. Shapiro, "The House and the Federal Role: A Computer Simulation of Roll-Call Voting," *American Political Science Review* 62 (1968):494–517.

54.   Donald R. Matthews and James A. Stimson, "Decision-Making by U.S. Representatives: A Preliminary Model," in *Political Decision-Making,* ed. S. Sidney Ulmer (New York, 1970), pp. 14–43, quotation at p. 31.

55.   Jackson, *Constituencies and Leaders in Congress,* chaps. 4 and 7.

56.   Aage Clausen has measured the effect of state party delegations on voting in the House, and has discussed the problem of isolating and explaining this variable in "State Party Influences on Congressional Policy Decision," *Midwest Journal of Political Science* 16 (1972):77–101.

57.   Eric M. Uslaner and Ronald E. Weber, "Partisan Cues and Legislative Decision Making in the American States" (Paper presented at the annual meeting of the Midwest Political Science Association, 1975).

58.   H. Owen Porter, "Legislative Experts and Outsiders: The Two-Step Flow of Communication," *Journal of Politics* 36 (1974):703–730.

CHAPTER SEVENTEEN

Legislative Committees at Work

Visitors to the Senate or the House who do not see their congressman on the floor are usually told that he is in a committee meeting, where the real work goes on. The press of varied and complex legislative business forces both Congress and state legislatures to delegate a large share of the decision making to committees. In Chapter 8, we described the function of committees in the legislative system, their organizational structure, and the techniques used for choosing members. In this chapter, we shall examine their operation and their methods of reaching decisions on legislation. With rare exceptions, it is the practice to refer all bills and resolutions to a committee after introduction in the first house and, after passage there, to repeat the process in the second house.

In most committees, a bill will first be assigned to one of several subcommittees. Where subcommittees are used, the hearings are conducted and the significant decisions made at that level; approval by the full committee is usually a matter of routine. We shall examine four stages of committee (or subcommittee) action and influence. (1) In the hearing, the committee members play a variety of roles other than that of a neutral judge. (2) In the mark-up session, decisions are made about how to amend the bill and whether to report it; we are concerned with the factors that tend to produce (or reduce) consensus regarding these decisions. (3) When the bill is considered on the floor, a number of variables determine how much weight the committee's recommendations will have. (4) After a bill has passed both houses in different versions, a conference committee, chosen from members of the original Senate and House committees, often has wide latitude in determining the final contents of the bill.

THE HEARINGS

The Purpose of Congressional Hearings

A hearing is usually necessary before a congressional committee will vote on a bill. Approval of a bill without a hearing is rare; on the other hand, there is no guarantee that a bill will receive a hearing. This initial decision on the bill is primarily in the hands of the committee or subcommittee chairman, although he may be persuaded by pressure from other members. It is at this stage that many bills are given a quiet burial because of their trivial or unrealistic nature, because the chairman judges that they will not engender enough support for serious consideration in Congress, because of the overwhelmingly negative pressure of interest groups, or because the committee or its chairman is hostile to the bills. The decision to hold hearings on a bill indicates that it is going to receive serious consideration because the committee members are interested in it or because they believe the interest of outside groups is sufficient to warrant a hearing.

Hearings serve several purposes, recognition of which facilitates an understanding of the various roles that committee members play. The hearings provide an opportunity for interested groups and individuals to present their viewpoints and their versions of the facts to a committee. This is by no means the only route of access that interest groups have to Congress, but it is the open, formal, direct route. Hearings provide the committee with one of its best means of obtaining information. One of the committee's functions is fact finding. This does not mean that committee members are necessarily impartial, but usually they are interested in gaining information, even if it is only to reinforce their preconceptions. Sometimes, the need for information is great enough to justify a broad investigation of the whole problem, perhaps lasting for months; whereas on other occasions, the study is limited to the specific provisions and immediate implications of a bill. In either case, the fact-finding role is pervasive for committees.

Because committee members are not merely neutral judges, they sometimes use the hearings for another purpose: to develop support for, or opposition to, a bill. The chairman may accomplish this purpose by the timing of the hearings, the selection and priority of witnesses, and the use made of staff resources during the hearings. Other members may use friendly or hostile questions to witnesses in order to achieve the same end. The purpose of these maneuvers may be the narrow one of persuading undecided committee members, or it may be the broader one of generating public interest and support that will impress Congress as a whole. When the committee chairman solicits testimony from a long series of distinguished witnesses or schedules a prolonged and highly publicized investigation, his purpose is usually to attract attention to a problem and to inform the public and Congress about the viewpoint he supports. Also, as Congressman Clem Miller once explained, "Many times, the hearings seem to be *pro forma,* just going through the motions, with the key decisions already made. They resemble a large verbal orchestration, as a 'record' is carefully shaped under the vigilant gavel of the chairman."[1]

The Setting

The stage for committee hearings is usually set by the chairman, whose decisions may affect the outcome by affording a significant advantage to one side or the other. The chairman who is trying to enhance the chances of a bill may decide that hearings should start quickly or else should be postponed until group support can be organized. He may hold prolonged hearings in order to develop public and congressional interest and support, or he may decide that brief, little-publicized hearings will be more effective because they arouse less opposition.[2]

In recent years there has been a dramatic increase in the proportion both of congressional committee hearings and of working, or mark-up, sessions that are open to the public. Rules adopted by the House in 1973 and by the Senate in 1975 generally provide that both types of sessions will be open unless the members of the committee vote in public to close a particular session and that this can be done only for a particular reason, such as the discussion of national security issues or of charges that might be harmful to an individual. Prior to 1973 about 40 percent of all committee sessions were closed. In the Ninety-third Congress (1973–1974) only 9 percent of committee meetings were closed in the House, but the figure was 25 percent in the Senate, which had not yet adopted the rule for open meetings. In 1975, only 3 percent of Committee meetings in the House and 15 percent in the Senate were closed.[3] It is now the practice to open nearly all Senate and House hearings to the public, except for those involving national security issues and some in which charges are made against individuals.

The chairman schedules the witnesses. Although the committee can sometimes hear all who want to testify, this is usually impossible in the case of major pieces of controversial legislation. Then the chairman may make choices that are not always impartial. But the chairman's power is not merely negative; he may recruit witnesses who support his point of view on legislation. On sharply divisive issues, a committee sometimes splits up the hearing time equally between supporters and opponents, giving two members of the committee supervision over the witnesses on each side. When the hearings take on an investigatory nature and the committee surveys a broad area of concern, the staff plays a more important role, subject to the chairman's direction, in recruiting witnesses, questioning them, producing evidence, and even carrying out extensive investigations of its own as a prelude to the hearings.

One aspect of the hearings over which the chairman has no control is the presence of committee members. Congressional hearings are normally held in the morning, when the Senate and House are not in session. But there are many other demands on a congressman's time. Other committees or subcommittees of which he is a member may be meeting simultaneously. Occasionally, he finds it necessary to testify before another committee. There are unavoidable meetings with constituents, conferences with other congressmen on legislative strategy, and appointments with government officials in order to serve the needs of constituents. The result is that there is rarely full attendance at a hearing; often only a small fraction of the committee members are present, and witnesses become accustomed to seeing congressmen wandering in and out of the hearings. One of the chores of an effective lobbyist is to make sure that some committee members who are sympathetic to his cause will be present to support his testimony with friendly questions.

Normally, a witness is given a chance to make a prepared statement first, although there is no guarantee that he will not be interrupted by questions. When a large number of committee members are present, protocol requires that members be permitted to ask questions in order of seniority. This may leave the junior member with little to say. In smaller hearings, the questioning is likely to be more informal. On occasion, staff members may ask most of the questions or may supply the committee members with questions to use during the hearing.

The Roles of Committee Members

Committee members assume a variety of roles that reflect a variety of views about what is expected of them by constituents, pressure groups, and fellow congressmen, among others. As Ralph K. Huitt has said, "The congressional role probably is most usefully conceived not as a single role but as a multiplicity of roles, defined for the congressman by the varying expectations of the groups which he represents or with which he identifies."[4] The most obvious clues to these roles can be found in the committee hearings, particularly at the congressional level, where hearings are frequent and well publicized. An identification of these roles demonstrates why committee members selcom act as impartial judges at hearings; outside groups usually have a claim on their loyalties.

Sometimes the committee member interprets his role in national terms. One example of this is the *administration loyalist.* He cooperates closely with administration witnesses, feeding them questions that advance their argument, but he sharply challenges witnesses who are critical of the administration. One of the handicaps faced by any administration is that it cannot automatically depend on having a loyal supporter at every committee hearing, although there will frequently be some member or members playing this role. On issues of foreign policy, a member of the opposition party may assume this role, as Senator Vandenberg did in guiding the hearings on the Marshall Plan in 1947. Bernard C. Cohen describes the role played by senators of both parties during hearings of the Senate Foreign Relations Committee on the Japanese peace treaty in 1952:

> There appeared to be an implicit set of ground rules agreed to by almost everybody according to which no questions likely to prove embarrassing would be asked. Most of the questions, in fact, seemed to be set up in such a way as to give Mr. Dulles [who had negotiated the treaty and was the key witness] excellent opportunities to make his major points, and he always cheerfully obliged. . . .
>
> Sometimes the questions which the Senators asked of Administration witnesses inadvertently led into areas of controversy, exposing for a moment the still-raw nerve ends of a policy dispute. Generally, when this happened, the line of questioning was brought to a quick close, before the real substance of the disagreement was drawn into public view.[5]

A natural counterpart to the administration loyalist is the *opposition spokesman,* which is likewise a role not played consistently by most congressmen. Senator Robert A. Taft is perhaps the best example of a congressman who assumed this role in most committee hearings. In a study of the 1946 hearings on price control, Huitt found that most congressmen were concerned with the effects of price control on particular interests and constituents, but for Senator Taft "the price control contest was simply one round in a continuing battle with the Administration."[6]

Congressmen very often assume more parochial committee roles. Most of the major pressure groups have at least one *advocate* on the committees that concern them most. He serves as a source of information, a prompter during the hearings, and a spokesman in the closed sessions. The congressman's loyalty may be based on personal conviction or association, agreement on specific policy objectives, political alliance, or campaign contributions. A congressman working in alliance with a lobbyist who is giving testimony may work out in advance a series of questions that will help the lobbyist or may warn him about the kinds of questions he may expect from hostile members of the committee. Just as some congressmen serve as advocates for an interest group, others serve as *critics.* In 1955, when the spokesman for the Vigilant Women for the Bricker Amendment testified before a Judiciary subcommittee, Senator Bricker, naturally enough, congratulated the women on their fine work, but Senator Kefauver suggested that the organization should have registered with Congress as a group engaged in lobbying.

A closely related role is that of *representative* of a local constituent interest, organized or unorganized. In his study of price-control hearings, Huitt uses the example of Senator McFarland of Arizona, who showed great interest in subsidies for lead, zinc, and copper industries important to his state and guided the testimony of witnesses for those industries, but who showed little interest in other aspects of the hearing. A congressman may, in fact, seldom appear at hearings until the subject matter touches on constituent interests. Huitt points out that when these regional or local interests are involved, the congressmen are likely to be better informed than when they are dealing with broader issues.[7] Sometimes the make-up of a committee guarantees that most attention will be focused on local interests. Charles O. Jones has described the make-up of commodity subcommittees of the House Agriculture Committee, which are composed to a large extent of members from a constituency where that particular commodity (corn, cotton, or peanuts, for example) is important.[8]

Sometimes the congressman is representing not a general constituency interest but a particular constituent, perhaps a businessman; this might be called the *errand boy* role. During the price-control hearings cited by Huitt, Senator Capehart wanted information for several constituents about pricing policies on trousers; Senator Hickenlooper wanted to secure records about quotas and prices for meat; and Senator Tobey wanted to know why one of his constituents was not permitted by the government to fabricate lumber that he had logged himself.[9] This is an important role, one assumed on some occasions by nearly all congressmen who are seeking public redress for bureaucratic mistreatment of their constituents. Behind the scenes, the congressman may use his committee position to get a favor for an important business constituent or for the broader purpose of getting projects and benefits for his district.

In addition to the broader national roles and the interest and constituency roles already described, some congressmen play roles that derive peculiarly from their position on a committee. Every congressman with a few years of committee experience becomes an expert on some topic. Although this is a role played by many, the *expert* is the member who subordinates other roles to this one, who takes great pride in displaying to administration witnesses his superior knowledge and proficiency in the techniques of government.

One role is particularly associated with investigating committees, but it is popular enough to emerge at almost any point in a hearing: the *prosecutor.* The congressman may be interrogating an evasive bureaucrat, an erring labor leader, an unrepentant Communist, or simply a presidential appointee who is lacking in humility. The role of prosecutor comes easily to the many congressmen who are former lawyers. It is a natural role for committee members, who are traditionally suspicious of administrative officials and are sometimes frustrated by the difficulty of penetrating to the depths of the complex process by which policies are made and administered in Washington.

Hearings in State Committees

In some state legislatures, committee hearings are a rarity; at the other extreme, a few states require hearings on all bills. The variation in practice is wide, but generally speaking, committee hearings play a smaller role in the legislative process in most states than they play in Congress. There are several reasons for this. The shortage of time is an important obstacle, particularly in legislatures where most of the important controversial legislation is referred to a few committees or in states where the session is limited to two or three months. The large number of committee assignments for each member sometimes reduces attendance at those hearings that are held. The lack of a professional staff makes it difficult or impossible for most legislators to be prepared to question witnesses who appear at the hearings.

Often the absence of hearings can be explained simply by the absence of witnesses. In contrast with most congressional legislation, a large proportion of the bills considered by state legislatures deal with issues of trivial, technical, or local importance, issues unlikely to stir much public interest. It is not surprising that no one requests a chance to be heard before a committee on many such bills. In a number of states, it is the practice to hold a hearing whenever there is a demand for it; in most cases, there is no demand. In some states, however, an observer cannot escape the suspicion that committees discourage persons and groups from appearing at hearings by failing to publicize the time and place of such hearings or by avoiding the holding of hearings so regularly that interested citizens are led to believe that they do not have any chance to testify. A recent study by the Citizens Conference on State Legislatures showed that most state legislatures now have some standard procedure for giving public notice of committee hearings, although most do not routinely give more than one or two days of advance notice. Announcements are posted in the capitol building, are usually announced to the press, and are sometimes mailed to interested groups and individuals.[10] In some states, particularly where interim committees are used, hearings are held on important issues in various parts of the state to encourage testimony by a wider variety of groups.

Variations in the frequency and importance of committee hearings result in part from differences in the independent authority exercised by committees. The states where hearings not only are frequent but also have a significant impact on the decision-making process are primarily those in which legislative parties are weak, such as New Hampshire, Tennessee, California, and Oregon. Another example is Nebraska, where procedural rules assure that adequate publicity and time will be provided for committee hearings. There are a number of other states where hearings are held regularly on important bills or upon request, but these hearings are usually *pro forma* affairs, serving only the purpose of permitting interest groups to be heard and to put their views on record. New York, where adequate notice is given for joint hearings held on major bills, and Connecticut, which also makes frequent use of joint hearings, are states in which the crucial decisions are nevertheless more often made by the party leadership or in caucus than by the committee. In Illinois, hearings are always held if the sponsor of the bill requests it; if he does not, the bill dies a quiet death. Illinois committee hearings are usually brief, informal affairs at which testimony is heard quickly, a minimum of questions are asked, and a quick vote is taken. Illinois committees usually give routine approval to bills and leave the question of their passage to the party leadership.

In some states where partisan or factional leadership is particularly strong, committees seldom hold hearings, except perhaps on appropriations bills or highly controversial measures. In both Pennsylvania and New Jersey the committee chairmen serve as agents of the party leadership and the caucus. In Pennsylvania committees infrequently hold hearings, although on some controversial issues there have been lengthy hearings that have contributed substantially to the resolution of issues and the passage of bills. More often the chairman consults informally with some or all of the interest groups affected by a bill. In New Jersey, where a few years ago there was an average of only twenty public hearings a year, the committees are becoming more active but hearings are still the exception rather than the rule. Infrequent and poorly publicized hearings are also the rule in a few states that lack strong party or factional leadership.[11]

In states where committees are primarily tools of the legislative leaders, it may be assumed that most committee members play the role of loyalist. The role of pressure-group advocate is a familiar one in many legislative committees, and it is enhanced by the frequent practice of weighting a committee heavily with members who have a personal interest in the subjects under the committee's jurisdiction. The role of expert is often combined with that of advocate. It may be difficult to find unbiased experts for state legislative committees, since most members have a primary profession that overshadows their legislative career. On an insurance committee, for example, there will be a number of members who are considered experts because that is their profession, but these legislators cannot separate their expert knowledge from their advocacy of the viewpoints held by the insurance profession. Under these conditions, lobbyists are likely to have unusually easy access to the committee; and in some committees, lobbying by outsiders is unnecessary because of the work already being done by insiders. This becomes a more serious problem when the committee deals with regulatory legislation, such as banking, insurance, or the liquor business.

DECISION MAKING IN COMMITTEES

Working Sessions

If the real work of Congress is conducted in committees, the real work of committees can be said to occur when the hearings are over and the committee undertakes the task of reaching decisions on the content of proposed bills. In the past, there have been serious gaps in our knowledge about committee decision making because these working sessions were conducted in secret. The most significant aspect of the trend toward open committee meetings has been the shift from having all working sessions in private to having most of them in public. It is too early to say what effects this change will have on how the decisions are made. It is clear that all interested groups will be able to observe the decision-making process first hand, while in the past only a few outsiders—usually government agency representatives—could attend sessions, and lobbyists had to depend on their contacts with committee members to find out what was happening. It is also possible that in open meetings, committee procedures will be somewhat more formal and more decisions will be reached by taking votes and fewer by informal consensus.

These working sessions are often referred to as mark-up sessions, because proposed bills are rewritten and amended by the committee. The bill is read section by section, with the committee discussing any suggested changes and reaching decisions on them. As the details are ironed out, only a few of the best-informed members of the committee are likely to be active, including the chairman and the ranking minority member on the committee or subcommittee. In the Senate appropriations subcommittees, the chairman and ranking minority member usually get together for an informal planning and bargaining session before the subcommittee meets to mark up the bill.[12] The committee staff also plays a very important advisory role in the mark-up stage of committee action. This stage may take several weeks if the committee is dealing with a thorough revision of the tax code or some equally technical subject. In other cases, the whole process may only take a few hours. Sometimes the committee is dealing with a single bill; but more often it has a variety of bills and revised drafts, and its first decision must be to determine which one offers the best starting point.

The decisions that are made during the mark-up sessions are of vital importance for two reasons: they usually determine the detailed contents of the bill passed by that house, and they may determine whether or not the bill passes. Decisions made in a subcommittee concerning the detailed contents of a bill are seldom reversed in the full committee. On the floor of the House, no more than a few amendments are likely to be offered and even fewer passed; some bills reach the floor under rules prohibiting any amendments. The Senate is likely to make more revisions in the bills that come from its committees, but most provisions of the bill are usually left unchanged.

If the committee members accurately reflect or anticipate congressional attitudes on an issue, their revisions may clear the way for passage of a bill that would have been doomed in its original version. By limiting the scope, paring the cost, or adding provisions sought by particular interests, the committee may effectively pacify potential opponents. If the committee members are out of step with a congressional majority, their revisions may inadvertently doom a bill. In 1953, Senator John Bricker introduced a constitutional amendment affecting the conduct of foreign policy. It had sixty-four cosponsors, enough to guarantee passage by the necessary two-thirds vote if none was lost. The Judiciary Committee, where isolationist sentiment was disproportionately strong, added provisions that made the amendment much more restrictive. The result was to scare off several cosponsors and to stir up strong enough opposition both in the administration and in the Senate to defeat the proposal by a single vote, even though the Judiciary

Committee's additions had been eliminated before the final vote.

If the committee decides against reporting the bill, its decision is almost always final. Although the rules of both houses make it possible for a bill to be extricated from committee and brought to the floor by a majority of the congressmen, the procedure is seldom used, both because it is cumbersome in practice (see Chapter 10) and because congressional norms dictate respect for the authority of committees. The committee's decision to report the bill may be made unanimously or by a divided vote. The committee usually makes a written report explaining its recommendation, and the nature of any division within the committee becomes apparent only if the minority chooses to file a dissenting report. On rare occasions, the committee may report a bill without any recommendation concerning its passage, but congressional committees (unlike those in some states) do not report a bill with negative recommendations.

Congressional Committee Unity and Diversity

In Chapter 1, we discussed the concept of legislative bodies as systems and as subsystems within larger political systems. A congressional committee is, of course, an important subsystem in Congress. The norms of the committee are shaped in part by the larger unit, Congress; and its purposes are closely related to those of Congress in the sense that most committee decisions have effect only when ratified by Congress. Congressional committees have a group life of their own, with traditions, objectives, and norms growing out of a long history and a high degree of independence.

Like any political group, the congressional committee has certain common objectives and elements of diversity. The primary objective of the committee may be defined as maximizing its power and influence in order to get its decisions accepted by Congress. Richard F. Fenno, Jr., who has made a pioneering analysis of the committee as a system, defines the task of maximizing internal unity and minimizing diversity as *integration.* Integration becomes possible when the broad common objectives are translated into a degree of consensus on the substantive policy goals of the committee and effective committee norms with regard to its operating methods.[13]

Any congressional committee has many sources of diversity. One potential source is subcommittees, which operate as subsystems within the committee, with their own traditions, objectives, and norms that may be in conflict with those of the committee. Every committee is divided into Democratic and Republican members, another potential source of great diversity. Not only are the purposes of the two party groups likely to differ, but the members of each have strong ties with members of Congress outside the committee who may not share the committee's norms. There are other sources of diversity present from time to time in most committees. Some members have deep loyalties to a region, a state, a constituency. Some share the views of pressure groups with regard to the issues facing the committee. Members have conflicting philosophies of government that are related but not limited to the conflicts between Democratic and Republican programs. Another conflict smoldering below the surface in some committees is that between veteran members of both parties and the relative newcomers.

These sources of diversity account for the variety of roles (already described) that become apparent in committee hearings. In fact, committee members have two kinds of loyalties, reflected in two kinds of roles. There is a loyalty to the committee, which requires that the congressman's role be based on the norms set by the committee. There is also a loyalty to outsiders (the various constituencies of party, state, and interest group), which requires the congressional role of advocate for such a group. Actually, this role conflict experienced by the committee member is no different from that experienced by all members of the congressional system. It may be said that integration in a committee depends on its success in substituting one role for another.

The formula for successful committee integration is easily expressed: that which unites the committee must be more important than that which divides it. To begin with, there must be consensus in the committee concerning its major purposes. Fenno, who has cited the House Appropriations Committee as a model of integration, has described the agreed purpose of that committee as being *"to guard the Federal Treasury,"* a purpose that the committee members agree implies "the task of *cutting whatever budget estimates are submitted."* This is not merely a cliché but an apt description of the major purpose underlying the committee's activities and accepted by all or nearly all its members. The words of committee members underline the strength of this norm: "It's a tradition in the Appropriations Committee to cut." "You're grounded in it. . . . It's ingrained in you from the time you get on the Committee." Fenno suggests that consensus of purpose in this particular committee is facilitated by the fact that the members are dealing with money decisions, which can always be compromised at some dollars-and-cents level, rather than with policy decisions, which are not only more difficult to compromise but also force members into specific and inescapable public commitments. The character of the committee may facilitate the growth and survival of committee norms. The Appropriations Committee is one of the most attractive in the House. Members who join it have already had some House experience; they are chosen in part because they have already made an impression as responsible legislators who conform to the norms of the legislative process. Once on it, they stay; the committee has unusual stability of membership.[14]

There are several factors that determine how active and autonomous subcommittees are, and the most important of these is the attitude of the committee chairman. In the past some House committee chairmen succeeded in avoiding subcommittees altogether, and others used subcommittees without fixed jurisdictions and controlled the assignment of bills to them. As we noted in Chapter 8, the rules in the House now require the use of subcommittees in most committees, give the majority caucus on each committee the power to set committee jurisdictions, and permit a bill to be held in the full committee only by a vote of the committee. In the Senate, although most committees use subcommittees, some of the chairmen have assigned most bills to subcommittees and others have kept bills at the committee level if they were particularly interested in them or lacked confidence in the subcommittee that would normally handle them. Where subcommittees are used for most or all bills, there are considerable differences among the committees in the extent to which the decisions of the subcommittees are accepted by the full committee, differences related to committee norms and to the extent of agreement or disagreement among members on questions of ideology and policy.

The House Appropriations Committee is probably the best example of a committee with strong subcommittees, yet one that is also well integrated. Fenno has described the norms that serve this purpose. The members usually specialize in only one of the few subcommittees on which they serve; they normally accept the recommendations of each subcommittee without dissent; and members of a subcommittee generally support its recommendations before the full subcommittee. If these principles of specialization, reciprocity, and subcommittee unity can be maintained, a high level of committee integration is possible within the framework of powerful subcommittees. This may appear to be a paradox, but in the eyes of committee members, it is not a contradiction. They argue that the common goal of cutting the budget can be accomplished skillfully and carefully only if each subcommittee is given wide latitude and if its recommendations are accepted by the committee.[15] The House Interior Committee and the Senate Labor and Public Welfare Committee are two others on which the subcommittees exercise a large degree of autonomy, and the members of the committee generally accept the recommendations of their subcommittees, though they differ from the House Appropriations Committee in that a much larger proportion of the members serve on each subcommittee and therefore it is easier to combine integration and decentralization.[16]

Another pattern of subcommittee power is found in the House Education and Labor Committee, where a high degree of authority is given to the subcommittees, but their recommendations are frequently challenged in the full committee. Fenno quotes a member of the committee:

> The members of the subcommittee always have the first crack at the legislation they report. They explain it and they are allowed to talk first. Then everyone pitches in. We question the subcommittee, we crossexamine the subcommittee, and they'd damn well better be able to answer the questions. . . . Very few pieces of legislation get through the full committee the way they come out of subcommittee. Maybe a few noncontroversial bills, but not the major ones. They are all amended in full committee. Sometimes I wonder why we have subcommittees at all.[17]

The basis of this committee norm is probably the fact that the issues the committee handles are generally ones on which the liberal-conservative battle lines are drawn, and most members have strong convictions and often strong commitments to support certain interests.

There are other congressional committees on which the subcommittee pattern does not quite fit either of these models. The Senate Judiciary Committee has a large number of subcommittees with a large measure of autonomy, and most bills reported by these subcommittees are accepted by the full committee. But the Judiciary Committee is deeply divided along ideological lines, and the outcome of battles on controversial issues may not be the same in the full committee that it is in the subcommittee. The Senate Appropriations Committee, out of necessity, delegates a large measure of autonomy to its subcommittees, but unlike members of the House Appropriations Committee (who usually serve on only two or three subcommittees), the Senate members serve on five or six of the thirteen subcommittees. Another pattern is found in the Senate Commerce Committee, where the chairman is willing to give subcommittees a great deal of freedom in handling some bills, but keeps a large proportion of them for consideration only at the full-committee level. Finally, the Senate and House Foreign Relations and International Relations committees use subcommittees extensively for information-gathering purposes, but consider most legislation at the full-committee level.[18] The pattern of subcommittee use on any of these committees may change, of course, with changes in the chairmanship or in the wishes of the membership. The trend, particularly in the House, seems to be toward greater autonomy for subcommittees, but this does not guarantee committee acceptance of subcommittee decisions on controversial issues.

Political parties have greater potential as a disruptive force than subcommittees. Party loyalty is a strong force in Congress. As a subsystem of Congress, the committees cannot escape politics. Each committee member has ties to party colleagues outside the committee. The partisan make-up of each committee is based on that of the parent body. But if committee integration is to have any meaning, partisan influences must be minimized. Democrats and Republicans seldom operate as cohesive blocs within a committee, but the extent of partisanship varies substantially from one committee to another. To understand the various patterns of partisanship, we need to examine some of these committees more carefully, particularly in the House.

Partisanship may arise, and may be measured, at several stages in the committee decision-making process, as illustrated in Table 17.1. Partisanship may be pervasive throughout the deliberations of a committee; it may be reflected in the

TABLE 17.1 Levels of Partisanship on the More Important Committees of the U.S. House of Representatives

LEVEL OF PARTISANSHIP	DELIBERATIVE STAGE	COMMITTEE REPORTS	VOTES BY MEM-BERS ON FLOOR ON COMMITTEE BILLS
High	Education & Labor Agriculture Public Works	Public Works Ways and Means Education & Labor	Education & Labor Agriculture Public Works Ways and Means
Medium	Ways and Means International Relations Post Office Interior	Interior Post Office International Relations	Appropriations Banking & Currency Judiciary Post Office Interior
Low	Appropriations	Appropriations	Armed Services International Relations

SOURCE: Data in first and second column come from Richard F. Fenno, Jr., *Congressmen in Committees* (Boston, 1973), pp. 83–94; James T. Murphy, "Political Parties and the Pork-barrel: Party Conflict and Cooperation in House Public Works Committee Decision Making," *American Political Science Review* 68 (1974):169–185; Charles O. Jones, "The Role of the Congressional Subcommittee," *Midwest Journal of Political Science* 6 (1962):327–344. Data in the third column, for a larger number of committees, come from James W. Dyson and John W. Soule, "Congressional Committee Behavior on Roll Call Votes: The U.S. House of Representatives, 1955–64," *Midwest Journal of Political Science* 14 (1970):626–647.

majority and minority reports filed by the committee; and it may be measured by calculating how committee members vote on bills reported by the committee when they come to the floor. Until 1971 the votes taken in committees were not made public, and the best way of measuring partisanship was to look at how the members voted on roll-call votes on the floor, on the assumption that most members would be consistent in their voting in committee and on the floor. Dyson and Soule used this technique to study levels of unity and partisanship for House committees from 1955 to 1964. They found that the most unified committees were likely to be those on which a majority of Democratic members and a majority of Republicans agreed and also those on which the Democrats had a high level of cohesion. Table 17.1 shows the levels of partisanship in these votes for the more important House committees.[19]

Fenno has calculated, for a smaller number of committees over a similar time period (1955–1966), the proportion of committee reports on major legislation on which there was a majority report primarily by members of one party and a minority report by members of the other (Table 17.1, second column). In general, the level of partisanship at this stage is similar to that in voting on the floor. (The low level of partisanship in Appropriations Committee reports is somewhat deceptive because there is a strong committee norm against filing minority reports.)[20]

The estimates of partisanship in the deliberative stage have to be somewhat impressionistic, based on studies of committees by Fenno and others. Fenno points out an important distinction between partisanship in deliberations and in the final reports of committees, using two committees as an illustration:

> Ways and Means members limit the play of partisanship to the final stages of decision making and do most of their work in a nonpartisan atmosphere. Education and Labor proceeds, at all stages, in an atmosphere charged with partisanship. The two committees are, therefore, as different in their decision-making styles as they are similar in their voting splits.[21]

There are several reasons why partisanship is a more pervasive force in some committees than in others. Some committees deal with a larger proportion of issues on which party stands are sharply defined and on which there are few neutrals; these issues often involve the role of government in economic affairs, the welfare state, and the vital interests of major pressure groups that are aligned with the parties. On these issues most congressmen are deeply committed to their constituencies. Partisanship may also be affected by the personal styles of the committee chairman and ranking minority member, the goals of individual members, committee norms, and the prestige and level of turnover on the committee.[22]

The Education and Labor Committee is one of the most thoroughly partisan committees in the House. It deals with highly controversial issues on which party and interest-group differences are sharply defined. The member who represents a district where labor unions are strong must be sensitive to the views of organized labor, and most northern Democrats find themselves more or less in this position. The committee lacks the prestige, stability of membership, and traditions that might lead to a norm of nonpartisanship. According to Fenno, the "operational decision rule for both party contingents is to do battle with one another. And they have achieved a consensus on this basic strategic premise: *to prosecute policy partisanship.*"[23] The only breaks in party alignment occur because of the strong policy or interest-group commitments of particular members. When the Democrats have large majorities, the crucial decisions are likely to be made in caucuses of Democratic members.

The House Agriculture Committee is an example of a committee in which party lines are strong, largely because the committee deals with price-support programs for specific commodities, and "the Republicans and Democrats have constituency interests in different commodities," as a study by Jones has shown. He points out that "the sectional character of American party strength results in Republican and Democratic commodities. Cotton, rice, and tobacco are Democratic commodities; wheat, corn, and small grains are Republican commodities." This not only makes it difficult to achieve bipartisan agreement; it also makes it difficult to achieve committee integration. There are subcommittees for each of the major commodities, and the partisan-tinged competition among the various commodity programs makes it difficult to achieve either subcommittee unity or committee acceptance of proposals made by a majority of a subcommittee. One aspect of the problem is that a subcommittee dealing with a commodity of the greatest interest to Republicans, such as wheat, has a majority of Democrats (when the Democrats control Congress). The difficulty that Congress has had in passing agricultural legislation is in no small part a result of the identity between party and commodity that makes it difficult for the Agriculture Committee to unite behind agricultural bills.[24]

The House Public Works Committee deals with a variety of issues on which Democrats usually oppose Republicans: aid to economically depressed areas, public versus private power, federal versus state responsibility for handling water pollution, and more generally the role of the federal government in the economy. The parties usually agree on the allocation of funds for public works programs that are national in scope but disagree on projects that primarily aid districts represented by members of one party. Moreover, the committee lacks the prestige and membership stability that might contribute to norms of nonpartisanship. Instead there is a norm of partisanship; members are expected to vote with their party and to support projects that serve the interests of their party colleagues on the committee.[25]

The House Ways and Means Committee deals with some of the most controversial and partisan issues facing Congress, but it has been able to develop a norm of "restrained partisanship," according to John F. Manley: "Ways and Means is neither racked by partisanship nor dominated by nonpartisanship; conflict and consensus coexist within the Committee and the balance between them varies chiefly with the nature and intensity of the external demands which are made on the committee."[26] How this works in practice is described by a close observer of the committee, quoted by Manley:

[It is a] partisan committee in the sense that you get a lot of partisan voting. But while you get a lot of partisan votes the members discuss the bills in a nonpartisan way. It's a very *harmonious* committee, the members work very well and harmoniously together.[27]

Fenno suggests that the committee makes a deliberate effort to restrain partisanship because the "members want influence in the House, a goal that forces an internal concern for their reputation in the House and for winning on the House floor."[28] During his many years as chairman, Wilbur Mills worked closely with the ranking minority member and tried to develop as much bipartisan support as possible for measures reported by the committee. There is some doubt about whether the committee will be able to maintain the restraints on its partisanship with a new chairman and with a much larger committee, including more liberal Democratic members.

The House Appropriations Committee, like Ways and Means, is a very prestigious committee whose members minimize partisanship in part because of their concern for maximizing their influence in the House. As we have already noted the committee is a highly integrated one with well-established norms, one of which is to curb partisanship as much as possible. One member described the committee in these words:

> But on this Committee there are no Democrats or Republicans. There's harmony. There's no two-party system on Appropriations. In full Committee, the chairman of the subcommittee gets up and then the ranking minority member of the subcommittee. And they say what a good job the other has done. They scratch each other's backs. There's never any dissent.[29]

The chairman and ranking minority members of the committee and its subcommittees have traditionally worked closely together, trying to work out compromises to avoid partisan splits and the filing of minority reports. Although the committee deals with questions of vital importance to both parties and interest groups, members of the committee find it relatively easy to support compromises because they are not committed to any particular level of government spending for any specific program.

Diversity in State Committees

Everything that we have said about state legislative committees in this chapter and in Chapter 8 should have made it clear why such committees are usually poorly integrated, why they seldom have definable norms affecting the members. The committees, in most legislatures, have not developed a set of norms and customs or agreed on objectives over a period of years, nor do they have a stable membership to perpetuate patterns of action over a prolonged period. Members come and go rapidly on most state committees, and few serve for more than four or six years. In the short run, the committees do not have time enough for studies of legislation that might bring about committee consensus strong enough to override partisan, interest-group, or local loyalties of members.

Some state legislative committees serve as the agents of the majority leadership, partisan or factional in the legislature, and these are usually sharply divided along partisan or factional lines, with the majority being very responsive to the legislative leadership. In some one-party states the most important committees are similarly responsive to the governor. Where partisan or factional leadership is less, the committee members are more likely to be swayed by the demands of their local constituency or pressure groups. In any case, if the committee is poorly integrated and lacks well-recognized norms, the role of committee members will be determined by the expectations of one or another group outside the committee.

Alan Rosenthal has defined five criteria by which to measure the performance of legislative committees in the evaluation and passage of legislation:

1. Referral of legislation: What proportion of bills are referred to committee? (A related question is whether bills are regularly referred to committees having clearly defined jurisdiction over them.)
2. Screening of legislation: What proportion of bills does the committee refuse to report favorably?
3. Shaping of legislation: What proportion of the bills that it favorably reports does the committee amend?
4. Passage of legislation: What proportion of the bills that a committee favorably reports are considered on the floor, are not amended (contrary to committee wishes), and are passed?
5. Study of issues: Does the committee have a chance to study issues and develop legislation during the interim between sessions?[30]

The first three of these criteria are directly related to the decision-making process in state committees. In states where committees are subservient to party or factional leadership, committees may sometimes be bypassed entirely, and they are expected to report bills desired by the leadership promptly and with few, if any, changes. It is possible, of course, that the leadership will use committees to block proposed bills as well as to report them. The fact that a particular committee fails to report out a substantial proportion of bills does not prove that is exercising independent authority. Nor are these criteria necessarily measures of the *quality* of committee performance. A statistical analysis cannot tell us whether the committee is acting wisely in its choice of bills to report or to block or whether its amendments have the effect of improving or worsening bills. The criteria, at best, suggest the minimum requirements for effective committees.

No efforts have been made to collect comprehensive data from the fifty states to determine how well the committees meet these requirements. Rosenthal relied on evaluations from experienced observers in each state to classify committee systems, and using the criteria listed above, concluded that fourteen legislatures have committees that perform well, sixteen have a medium level of performance, and twenty perform poorly. He found that better committee performance occurred in states having a high level of institutional capacity and in states where political power was not too heavily centralized. Most of the states with stronger committees are ones that have not had a tradition of strong legislative parties (states such as Arizona, California, Iowa, Minnesota, Oklahoma, and Washington). The states with a poor level of committee performance include most of those with very strong legislative parties (such as Connecticut, Illinois, Massachusetts, Michigan, New Jersey, New York, Pennsylvania, and Rhode Island), but also some one-party and weak-party states.[31] A much more extensive study of legislative committee systems is necessary before we can describe and explain patterns of committee performance and power with more confidence.

However effective or weak the decision-making processes may be in committees, they are becoming increasingly visible to the public. A recent study by the Citizens Conference on State Legislatures has shown that an increasing number of states have laws requiring that all or most committee meetings (and not just hearings) be open to the public. As of 1974, almost half of the states (twenty-two) had such laws, and twenty-one other legislatures had rules requiring open committee meetings for some or all committees. A few states have all meetings closed, and several more regularly conduct committee votes in secret.[32]

COMMITTEE INFLUENCE ON THE FLOOR

The purpose of efforts to achieve unity in a committee is to maximize its influence on the floor in order to gain passage of bills in the form recommended by the committee. It is difficult to measure the impact of committee voting on the floor, in part because it is not always possible to determine when committee members are leading congressional opinion and when they are reflecting it. (Unanimous passage of a bill after unanimous committee approval would seem to be a perfect example of strong committee influence, but it might simply mean that the bill involved a noncontroversial issue.) There is reason to believe that some committees are more successful than others on the floor of the Senate and the House. There are a number of possible explanations for this. It might be expected that the more united committees or those with the highest prestige would be more successful or simply that committees handling the least controversial legislation had the best batting average on the floor.

Studies of the Senate and the House provide some explanations for committee success. Both measure committee unity in terms of the voting record of committee members on the floor. Matthews, in his study of the Senate during the Eighty-fourth Congress, found that the degree of committee unity was closely related to committee success on the floor. All motions on the floor concerning a bill were passed when they were supported by 80 percent or more of the members of the committee reporting the bill. There was a 90 percent chance that motions would pass if supported by 60 to 79 percent of the committee members. Below that level of committee support, the proportion of motions that passed dropped quickly. If 20 to 40 percent supported it, there was less than a 20 percent chance of passage; if support went below 20 percent, no motions were passed. Matthews also found that the Senate committees with the greatest prestige had greater success on the floor. Whereas the highest-prestige committees had the greatest internal unity and also the greatest agreement with a majority of the Senate, the interest committees (such as Agriculture, Labor and Public Welfare, and Banking and Currency), which ranked in the middle in terms of attractiveness, had the least unity but were second only to the high-prestige committees in their success on the floor.[33]

Dyson and Soule, in their study of the House from 1955 to 1964, found that as a whole, the committees were successful on 90 percent of the motions; that is, a majority of the House voted with a majority of the committee members on 90 percent of the motions concerning bills reported by the committees. The study found that there was no relationship between the attractiveness of a House committee and its record of success. There was a close relationship between committee unity and success on the floor, and this relationship was based on interparty agreement and Democratic party cohesion in the committee. A majority of Democrats and a majority of Republicans on the committee agreed on 61 percent of the roll calls, and the committees were successful on 95 percent of such roll calls. When there was a split between the parties on the committee, the success record was 84 percent if the majority Democratic membership maintained enough unity to prevail in the committee but only 75 percent if the Democrats were so divided that the Republican position determined the committee's recommendations.[34]

The Dyson-Soule study shows that the success rate among the committees varied from 82 to 100 percent. The most successful ones included several dealing with small numbers of noncontroversial issues (including Internal Security and Merchant Marine and Fisheries) but also several major committees handling a large number of bills (International Relations, Armed Services, and Ways and Means). Although the House Appropriations Committee had an 86 percent record of success, this was one of the lowest rankings, and the number of its defeats was by far the largest because there were a large number of roll calls on its bills. (For the 1947 to 1962 period, Fenno found that 90 percent of that committee's recommendations were adopted by the House without change.) Other committees with a relatively low record of success included Education and Labor and Agriculture. It is clear that some, but not all, of the most successful committees had nonpartisan norms and practices, while the least successful ones included some of the more partisan ones.[35]

Committee integration requires the subordination of partisanship, but voting on the floor of Congress is substantially affected by party. Democrats in Congress often look upon the Democratic members of a committee as the party's leaders with regard to the issues handled by that committee; the same is true for Republicans. If most Democrats and most Republicans on a committee have approved a bill, it is likely to pass that house of Congress with strong bipartisan support. If a bill is reported from committee with majority and minority reports closely following party lines, the stage is set for a struggle between the parties on the floor of Congress. The degree of committee unity significantly affects the floor action not merely because congressmen defer to committee members as specialists but also because they regard them as their party's specialists. In this sense, committee members have an additional role to play, that of party specialists.

It is entirely possible that the recommendations of Democratic members on a particular committee might have greater impact on their party colleagues than the recommendations (whether the same or different) of Republican members on their colleagues, either because of greater unity among the committee Democrats or because Democratic congressmen have greater respect for the views of the committee members of their own party. (On other committees, of course, Republicans might be more influential.) Murphy, in his study of the House Public Works Committee, found a very high correlation between the votes of Democrats on the committee and other Democrats on roll calls involving major committee bills; the correlation on the Republican side was substantial but somewhat lower, suggesting that Republicans were slightly less likely to look to Republican committee members for voting cues.[36]

In Chapter 7, we discussed the importance of state delegations in the House communications network. Individual congressmen often take voting cues from members of their state delegation who are on the committee that handled the bill under consideration. Some state delegations hold regular meetings at which members report on legislation that has been studied by their committee. There is some evidence that members of a state party delegation are more likely to support the position of that party's membership on the committee reporting a particular bill if the state party delegation has a member on that committee. This is particularly true if the groups represent similar viewpoints (such as an Illinois Democratic delegation and a predominantly northern Democratic membership on a committee).[37]

The fact that a committee is successful in getting its bills adopted on the floor without change suggests that the committee is influential, but it may also mean that the committee is particularly skillful in estimating what the entire House membership will accept in shaping a bill along those lines and/or that the committee members are a good cross-section of the full House. In the case of the most successful committees, all these factors are probably at work. Fenno and Manley, who have studied the House Ways and Means Committee, both concluded that the committee exercises a great deal of influence over the House and at the same time it is sensitive to viewpoints in the House. Fenno quotes former Chairman Mills as saying that the committee's responsiveness to House attitudes occurs "because our committee is a cross-section of the membership of the House," and he quotes an experienced observer as follows:

> The Ways and Means Committee is attuned to the temper of the House. They are sensitive to the feelings of House members—as sensitive as an adolescent girl.[38]

Murphy believes that the Public Works Committee is particularly likely to influence the House membership on those issues and bills that are new, in contrast to the renewal of ongoing programs.[39]

Because state legislative committees lack the prestige, resources, and experience of congressional committees, their recommendations would not be expected to carry comparable weight on the floor of the legislature. Whether this is true, however, depends on the influence of alternate sources of leadership. In most state legislatures, committee decisions on killing legislation are final. Rarely are successful efforts made on the floor to discharge a bill from committee. In some states, the rules require committees to report out all bills (a rule sometimes evaded in practice); and in a few other states (such as New Hampshire and Illinois), the committees customarily report out all bills. If there is neither strong partisan nor strong factional leadership, the legislators may be dependent on the leadership of committees. This may be less a result of the committees' institutional strength than of the respect that certain committee chairmen and members command as experts on substantive fields. The Montana house is an example of a legislature with strong committees. The rules of the house give priority to amendments recommended by the committee, and legislative norms discourage amendments from the floor. The party leaders in that state are generally expected to defer to the committees, and the committee chairmen carry a lot of weight in the caucus and on the floor.[40]

In states where there is strong partisan or factional leadership, the committees have less independent influence on legislative decisions concerning major legislation. They may serve as agents of the majority leadership, reporting, revising, or burying bills in accord with the wishes of that leadership. In Arizona, where the committees are carefully controlled by the dominant faction, they "play a critical role in the legislative process," and very few bills reported out by committees fail to pass on the floor.[41] In other states (such as Illinois, Pennsylvania, and New Jersey), the committees may almost completely surrender their responsibilities to the caucus or party leadership. In Illinois, the committee is "of scant importance" as an "independent determinant of the fate of legislative proposals." In Pennsylvania, the committees "are creatures of a disciplined and cohesive majority political party," and their reports carry weight only because they are in accord with the views of the majority caucus. Committee chairmen in Pennsylvania sometimes release tentative reports on bills in order to determine consensus in the caucus. In New Jersey, the caucus determines which bills should be reported from committee. Where partisan or factional leadership is so strong, the committees may retain some authority and influence over the fate of minor bills that do not interest the majority leadership. The Pennsylvania committees make independent decisions "only on items which do not deeply involve the interests of major groups in or outside of the Assembly."[42]

CONFERENCE COMMITTEES

When a bill passes the Senate and the House in different versions and neither house is willing to accept the other's bill, a conference committee is used to adjust the differences. This device, patterned after the conference committee used in the British Parliament as early as the sixteenth century, was first adopted by Congress during the early days of its first session in 1789. The rules and precedents surrounding the conference committee evolved gradually, but by 1852, the major governing principles had become well established.[43] The conference committee plays a powerful role in the legislative process because its reports are not subject to amendment and are usually accepted by both houses. To avoid deadlock in a bicameral system, there must be some locus for final decisions, some group charged with reconciling differences. In Congress, this is the part played by the conference committee, an ad hoc body consisting of senior members from the Senate and House committees that originally reported the bill. Although minor differences between the Senate and House versions of bills are sometimes reconciled without resort to the committee, the more important and complex the bill, the greater is the need for a conference committee. In the Eightieth to the Ninetieth Congresses, there were 1,381 conferences held successfully on the 8,777 public laws enacted. (There were 78 other bills that died in conference after being passed by both houses.)[44]

Tactical Considerations

A conference committee becomes necessary whenever the house that first passed a bill refuses to accept the amendments adopted by the second house. If the differences are trivial, the first house will probably accept the amendments to expedite matters. On major bills, it is often taken for granted that a conference will be necessary. There are occasions, however, when congressional leaders will try to avoid a conference despite major differences between Senate and House bills. In the closing days of the session, sponsors of a measure may fear that the delay caused by conference action would be fatal or that opponents of the bill would be strong enough in the conference committee or on the floor to defeat it if given another chance. Democratic leaders blocked a conference committee on the 1957 civil rights bill, for example, because they were afraid that if the concessions made to southerners in the Senate were eliminated in conference, the bill would be destroyed by filibuster in the Senate. Republican leaders, including President Eisenhower, wanted a stronger bill and wanted specifically the elimination of the jury-trial amendment for contempt cases. A compromise involving minimum changes in the Senate bill was finally engineered by leaders of both parties without resort to a conference committee.

Since conference committees are usually required for major legislation, many tactical decisions on the floor of the Senate and the House are made in anticipation of developments in the conference committee. For example, the floor leader for a bill often faces a dilemma when an influential member of the Senate or House offers an amendment that the leader considers damaging but not destructive. If he opposes the amendment, he runs the risk of precipitating a floor fight and perhaps losing votes for the bill itself. He may decide to accept the amendment without a vote and work for its elimination in the conference committee. One of the factors that determines the outcome of conference committee deliberations is the presence or absence of recorded votes in either house on specific amendments. Consequently, the sponsor of an amendment, if he is reasonably sure of strong support, may ask for a roll-call vote to record the strength of that support. The same logic may require that a roll-call vote be avoided. The House Appropriations Committee has often made deep cuts in the appropriations for foreign aid. Unless they were quite sure that they had the votes to raise the figure, Democratic leaders have often avoided a roll call on that issue, anticipating that the Senate would increase the appropriation and that a better result could be obtained in the conference committee in the absence of recorded votes in the House. Another consequence of the reliance on conference committees is that in the appropriations process, one committee will make deeper cuts and the other larger restorations of funds because both realize that the final figure will be a compromise. The same tactic of starting the bargaining process prior to the conference committee is also applied to other legislation. The sponsors of a bill or the leadership in one house will seek the adoption of amendments likely to be unacceptable in the other house in order to use these as pawns in the bargaining process. Even the threat of a filibuster by senators against an amendment adopted by the House may be used as a bargaining weapon by Senate conferees.

Choice of Participants

Members of conference committees are formally chosen by the presiding officers in both houses, but they always follow the advice of the chairmen of the committees that handled the bill, and the chairmen usually consult the ranking minority members concerning minority appointments. In recognizing the members of conference committees, the chairmen usually choose only the senior members of both parties, frequently themselves serving on committees for major bills. If a bill was handled first in a subcommittee, its senior members will usually be designated to serve. Data compiled by David J. Vogler for all conferences in the Seventy-ninth, Eightieth, Eighty-third, Eighty-eighth, and Eighty-ninth Congresses show that seniority, either in the committee or in the subcommittee, was the major criterion used in the selection of 83 percent of the Senate delegations and 81 percent of the House delegations to conference committees. In 88 percent of those cases where a bill had originally been handled in a subcommittee, seniority within the subcommittee rather than seniority within the full committee was followed (with little distinction between the two houses). In the Senate, Democratic chairmen were more likely than Republican chairmen to follow seniority; and in both houses, Democrats were more likely to follow subcommittee rather than committee seniority if subcommittees had handled the bill.[45]

Because Senate subcommittees are smaller and most junior senators serve as chairman or ranking member of one or more subcommittees, assignments on conference committees are more evenly divided among senators than among representatives. During the Eighty-ninth Congress, only three senators but 44 percent of the representatives had no conference committee assignment; in the Eighty-sixth to the Ninetieth Congresses, roughly half of the senators participated in six or more conferences per Congress, but the proportion of representatives with that much participation varied from 5 to 14 percent, depending on the Congress.[46]

Theoretically, the members of a conference committee should represent the viewpoints of each house as accurately as possible in order to defend those viewpoints in the conference committee. It is possible, however, that a majority of the senators or representatives on the committee will be persons who either voted against the bill or voted against one or more of the amendments in dispute between the two houses. Under these conditions there is a risk that the conferees of one house will surrender without a fight to the demands of the other house. This occurred in 1970 when the Senate voted to delete from an appropriations bill a House appropriation of $290 million for the controversial supersonic transport plane. Four of the seven Senate conferees had opposed the amendment to eliminate the appropriation for the plane, and the conference agreed to an appropriation of $210 million for it. In that case the Senate balked at approving the conference report, a filibuster occurred, and eventually a new conference committee was appointed that agreed to a lower level of funding.[47]

Critics of the selection process are particularly concerned that the senior members of committees are likely to be more conservative than the average member of Congress or of the committee that reported the bill being considered in conference. The problem is reduced when the senior members of subcommittees are selected because, particularly in the Senate, they are less senior and perhaps less conservative and because they may have greater interest in defending the version of the bill that was drafted in the subcommittee. A study by Vogler suggests that when seniority is not followed in selecting conferees, the effect is usually to increase the proportion of conference committee members supporting the bill.[48] In 1974 the House adopted a rule requiring that a majority of the conferees appointed must be members "who generally supported the House position," and placing responsibility for enforcement on the Speaker.[49] It is not yet clear what the effects of this change will be.

Exercise of Power

Until 1974, conference committees almost always met in secret, a fact that made it difficult for political scientists to study the decision-making process, and left lobbyists and other congressmen unaware of the factors that led to particular outcomes. This secrecy enhanced the aura of conference committee omnipotence. In 1974 twelve conference committees opened their meetings to the public, an experiment that was evidently judged to be successful. In 1975 the Senate and House voted that all conference committees would be open unless either the Senate or House conferees voted in public for closed meetings, the procedure that has also been adopted for other committee meetings.[50] Whether the decision-making process will operate any differently in public, or whether compromises on most difficult issues will be worked out in informal, secret meetings remains to be seen.

The chairmen and ranking minority members who represent each house are likely to be the most influential members of the conference committee, perhaps more powerful than they are in their own committee or subcommittee. Skillful, determined leaders can guide a conference committee, often with great effectiveness. Occasionally the floor leaders of one or both parties will intervene in conference deliberations, usually in an effort to end a deadlock, although the committee leaders are jealous of their prerogatives and do not often welcome such intervention.

Members of the committee staffs regularly participate in conference committee deliberations, and experts from the government departments concerned with the bill usually attend. The advice of government officials may carry more weight during conference meetings than at earlier stages in the legislative process. They can make clear the agency priorities when there are differences between the two houses in the level of appropriations for a program. If an amendment has been introduced and passed on the floor in one house that will have damaging consequences, perhaps not foreseen by its sponsor, government officials can probably get it removed in the conference committee.

Occasionally, the President intervenes in conference committee deliberations on the advice of White House staff members, departmental officials, or legislative leaders. Intervention may take the form of letters (publicized or private), telephone calls, or perhaps meetings with the conference committee or its leaders at the White House. In recent years publicized letters to conference committees handling foreign aid bills have become almost a routine tool of presidential influence.

Although outside influences are often important, the reins of power are held by the conference committee members. If politics is the art of the possible and the essence of the legislative process is compromise, then the conference committee is the epitome of legislative politics. Nowhere in the legislative process are congressional skills—skills born of experience, knowledge, and patient attention to the specialized demands of committee work—put to a greater test. Formal votes in conference are relatively rare; each provision must be acceptable to a majority of conferees from each house. The conference usually proceeds informally, relying on consensus whenever possible. The conference may be a matter of minutes or of weeks. Some controversies are minor and easily settled; often a simple trade will give each side the provisions it values most. Appropriations bills are particularly negotiable because the level of funds is easily adjustable and because, as a last resort, the conferees can usually compromise at the halfway point. In some cases, however, one house has completely rewritten the bill passed by the other, or there are a few points of profound difference between the bills, perhaps on emotionally charged or politically explosive issues.

Conferees may debate the substance of the points in controversy, but one of their major tactics is to persuade their colleagues that one house feels more strongly about an issue than the other house and should be permitted to have its way. This is often the reason why the floor managers of bills will either seek or avoid a recorded vote. Sometimes, when a conference is pending, one house or the other will vote to "instruct" its conferees to insist on a particular provision in dispute, although the conferees are not bound by this. Sometimes, as a bargaining tactic after conference sessions have started, the conferees for one house will take the issue back to the floor to get a vote supporting and insisting on a specific provision (particularly if there has been no previous separate vote on that provision). Occasionally, the conferees from one house will ask those from the other house to obtain such a vote to give the former an excuse for receding from their stand on the issue. Since the conferees must justify to their own house the reasons for concessions (sometimes in broad terms, sometimes in detail), such a face-saving device may be necessary.

The Senate and the House meet on equal terms in the conference, although on rare occasions, the threat of a Senate filibuster may strengthen the hand of Senate conferees. Vogler's study of conference committees in five Congresses selected between 1945 and 1966 shows that the outcome was favorable to the Senate's position 65 percent of the time and favorable to the House only 35 percent of the time (not including a small proportion of conferences in which the result was evenly balanced). The percentages varied from one Congress to another, but the Senate had an advantage in each of the five.[51] Similarly, Fenno concluded from a study of a large number of appropriations bills from 1946 to 1962 that the Senate conferees won 57 percent of the time and the House conferees 31 percent, with an even split in the remaining cases. Stephen Horn found a similar ratio of senatorial victories in an intensive study of the appropriations process in 1965. Fenno and Horn suggest that the breadth of influence and committee responsibilities of senators serving on the Appropriations Committee give them a broader base of support than their counterparts in the House have, and that this strengthens their bargaining position in the conference committee.[52] Vogler found that the balance between the Senate and the House varied substantially from one committee to another and that a few of the House committees (including the important Interstate and Foreign Commerce, Judiciary, and Interior and Insular

Affairs committees) were more often successful than their Senate counterparts. He did not discover any consistent explanation for the variations in conference influence from one committee to another.[53]

Theoretically, conference committees may not consider any provisions of a bill except those in disagreement between the two houses; they may not add provisions on their own initiative or exclude or modify provisions agreed on by the two houses. For many years, the rules and precedents of both houses have imposed such restrictions. However, when one house has rewritten a bill passed by the other house in substantially different form, the conference committee has wide discretion in further rewriting the bill. This often occurs in the passage of major pieces of legislation. Conference committee reports that appear to violate these rules are subject to a point of order in either house, but such points of order are rarely endorsed in either branch. The House has adopted a rule, however, in response to the Senate practice (prohibited by House rules) of adopting amendments that are not germane to the bill. When such a nongermane amendment is accepted by the conference committee, a point of order can be raised in the House against it. If the House votes to sustain the point of order, then (after brief debate) a separate vote is taken on the amendment. As a consequence, the House may send the conference committee's version of a bill back to the Senate to reconsider any such amendments that it has rejected. This is an exception to the general principle that both houses must accept or reject the conference committee report as a whole.[54]

Limited Use in the States

When there are differences in state legislatures between the versions of bills passed in the two houses, some machinery is necessary for resolving the differences. Often, when minor bills or trivial amendments are involved, the amendments of the second house will be accepted by the first, perhaps because this is the only way to ensure passage in the hurried closing days of a session. When differences remain, the task of resolving them may be delegated to a conference committee, or it may be handled, perhaps more informally, by the leadership of the two houses. It is evident that conference committees are used much more frequently in some state legislatures than in others, but the reasons for these variations are obscure, and little research has been done on conference committees. A recent study of procedures in thirteen western states showed that conference committees are used in most of these states. Some states give such committees the right to revise any part of a bill (including parts that are not in dispute), and a few provide that if a conference committee fails to reach agreement after one or two efforts, it will have such freedom on subsequent efforts. In Arizona and Hawaii, the conferences get instructions from the caucus.[55]

Appropriations measures are sent to conference committees more often than other categories of bills. In some states, appropriations bills are regularly sent to conference; in others, this is the only type of bill that is likely to require a conference. In states where the committees play a decisive part in the decision-making process, conference committees are likely to be used, at least on the most important and controversial legislation in a session. In states where there is strong party leadership, the conference committee may simply ratify the decisions made by these leaders; on other occasions, the party leaders or the governor may be unwilling to delegate (even formally) the settlement of controversies to a conference committee. In 1974 there were seven states that made no use of conference committees, including several with strong party leadership—Connecticut, Rhode Island, New York, and New Jersey. The move to open up committee meetings and publicize them has not yet had much effect on conference committees. In 1974 there were twenty states in which conference committees were open in theory, but in only eight of these were the meetings scheduled in advance with enough publicity so that they were effectively public. Because conference committees are often scheduled on short notice in the closing days, or even hours, of a session, it is difficult to devise rules that will guarantee their accessibility to the public.[56]

NOTES

1. See John W. Baker, ed., *Member of the House: Letters of a Congressman by Clem Miller* (New York, 1962), p. 8

2. For an excellent, detailed description of hearings, see Bertram M. Gross, *The Legislative Struggle* (New York, 1953), chap. 15.

3. *Congressional Quarterly Weekly Report* 34 (January 24, 1976):152–155.

4. Ralph K. Huitt, "The Congressional Committee: A Case Study," *American Political Science Review* 48 (1954):345. Huitt's article provides the best analysis of committee roles as revealed in hearings. The roles we have delineated are derived in part from his descriptions.

5. Bernard C. Cohen, *The Political Process and Foreign Policy: The Making of the Japanese Peace Settlement* (Princeton, N.J., 1957), pp. 155–156.

6. Huitt, "The Congressional Committee: A Case Study," pp. 345–346.

7. Ibid., p. 347.

8. Charles O. Jones, "The Role of the Congressional Subcommittee," *Midwest Journal of Political Science* 6 (1962):327–344.

9. Huitt, "The Congressional Committee: A Case Study," p. 348.

10. Citizens Conference on State Legislatures, *Legislative Openness* (Kansas City, Mo., 1974), pp. 88–91.

11. Kenneth T. Palmer, "The Legislative Committee System in Pennsylvania" (Ph.D. diss., Pennsylvania State University, 1964), pp. 105–108; Eagleton Institute of Politics, *Studies of the New Jersey Legislature* (New Brunswick, N.J., 1970), pp. 111–112; Sidney Wise, *The Legislative Process in Pennsylvania* (Washington, D.C., 1971), pp. 39–41.

12. See Stephen Horn, *Unused Power: The Work of the Senate Committee on Appropriations* (Washington, D.C., 1970), pp. 135–140.

13. Richard F. Fenno, Jr., "The House Appropriations Committee as a Political System: The Problem of Integration," *American Political Science Review* 56 (1962):310–324.

14. Ibid., pp. 311–315.

15. Ibid., pp. 315–317.

16. Richard F. Fenno, Jr., *Congressmen in Committees* (Boston, 1973), pp. 97–101; David Price, *Who Makes the Laws?* (Cambridge, Mass., 1972), chap. 7.

17. Fenno, *Congressmen in Committees*, p. 102.

18.   Ibid., pp. 94–114, 184–190; Price, *Who Makes the Laws?*, chap. 3; Peter H. Schuck, *The Judiciary Committees* (Ralph Nader Congress Project, New York, 1975), pp. 16–23.

19.   James W. Dyson and John W. Soule, "Congressional Committee Behavior on Roll Call Votes: The U.S. House of Representatives, 1955–64," *Midwest Journal of Political Science* 14 (1970):626–647.

20.   Fenno, *Congressmen in Committees*, p. 84. Data on the Public Works Committee comes from James T. Murphy, "Political Parties and the Porkbarrel: Party Conflicts and Cooperation in House Public Works Committee Decision Making," *American Political Science Review* 68 (1974):169–185, 172.

21.   Fenno, *Congressmen in Committees*, p. 84.

22.   See ibid., chaps. 3 and 4; and Randall B. Ripley, *Power in the Senate* (New York, 1969), pp. 146–149.

23.   Fenno, *Congressmen in Committees*, pp. 75, 86–87.

24.   Jones, "The Role of the Congressional Subcommittee," pp. 329, 332, 340–344.

25.   Murphy, "Political Parties and the Porkbarrel," pp. 169–185.

26.   John F. Manley, "The House Committee on Ways and Means: Conflict Management in a Congressional Committee," *American Political Science Review* 59 (1965):927.

27.   Ibid.

28.   Fenno, *Congressmen in Committees*, p. 84.

29.   Ibid., p. 88.

30.   Alan Rosenthal, *Legislative Performance in the States* (New York, 1974) chap. 2.

31.   Ibid., chap. 3.

32.   Citizens Conference on State Legislatures, *Legislative Openness*, pp. 78–85.

33.   Donald R. Matthews, *U.S. Senators and Their World* (Chapel Hill, N.C., 1960), pp. 169–171.

34.   Dyson and Soule, "Congressional Committee Behavior on Roll Call Votes," pp. 626–647.

35.   Ibid.; Fenno, *Congressmen in Committees*, p. 197.

36.   Murphy, "Political Parties and the Porkbarrel," pp. 181–182.

37.   See Arthur G. Stevens, Jr., "Informal Groups and Decision-Making in the U.S. House of Representatives" (Ph.D. diss., University of Michigan, 1970), chap. 4.

38.   Fenno, *Congressmen in Committees*, p. 204. See also John Manley, *The Politics of Finance* (Boston, 1970), pp. 246–247.

39.   Murphy, "Political Parties and the Porkbarrel," p. 182.

40.   See Douglas C. Chaffey, "The Institutionalization of State Legislatures: A Comparative Study," *Western Political Quarterly* 23 (1970):180–196.

41.   Dean E. Mann, "The Legislative Committee System in Arizona," *Western Political Quarterly* 14 (1961):925–941; quotation at 938.

42.   Gilbert Y. Steiner and Samuel K. Gove, *Legislative Politics in Illinois* (Urbana, Ill., 1960), p. 82; Palmer, "The Legislative Committee System in Pennsylvania," pp. 199–201. For information on the proportion of committee-reported bills passed in the legislatures of several states, see Rosenthal, *Legislative Performance in the States*, pp. 28–31, 139.

43.   See Ada C. McCown, *The Congressional Conference Committee* (New York, 1927), pp. 254–257. This is the best source of information on the early history of conference committees.

44.   George Goodwin, Jr., *The Little Legislatures* (Amherst, Mass., 1970), p. 243.

45.   David J. Vogler, *The Third House* (Evanston, Ill., 1971), pp. 38–41. This is the most recent comprehensive study of conference committees. For an excellent survey containing fifty-six case studies over an earlier period, see Gilbert Y. Steiner, *The Congressional Conference Committee* (Urbana, Ill., 1957).

46.   Goodwin, *The Little Legislatures,* p. 245; and David L. Paletz, "Influence in Congress: An Analysis of the Nature and Effects of Conference Committees" (Paper presented at the 1970 annual meeting of the American Political Science Association), p. 3.

47.   *Congressional Quarterly Weekly Report* 33 (February 8, 1975):293.

48.   David J. Vogler, "Flexibility in the Congressional Seniority System: Conference Representation," *Polity* 2 (1970):494–507. This study includes only votes on the bill itself and not on amendments to it that might be in dispute between the two houses.

49.   *Congressional Quarterly Weekly Report* 33 (February 8, 1975), p. 293.

50.   Ibid., pp. 290–291.

51.   Vogler, *The Third House,* pp. 55–58.

52.   Richard D. Fenno, Jr., *The Power of the Purse* (Boston, 1966), pp. 663–664; Horn, *Unused Power,* pp. 160–163.

53.   Vogler, *The Third House,* pp. 64–74.

54.   *Congressional Quarterly Weekly Report* 33 (February 8, 1975):294.

55.   Council of State Governments, *Lawmaking in the West,* vol. 1 (San Francisco, 1967), pp. 79–82.

56.   Citizens Conference on State Legislatures, *Legislative Openness,* pp. 91–93.

CHAPTER EIGHTEEN

The Legislature and the Executive: Oversight, Supervision, Control

In Chapter 11, we viewed the executive as an actor in the legislative system. In this chapter, we examine the legislature as an institution engaged in the policy activity of overseeing, supervising, or controlling executive agencies. The terms *oversight, supervision,* and *control,* although they are not unambiguous, tend to denote analytically distinct degrees of legislative influence upon agencies of administration. When an individual legislator observes closely and becomes familiar with the organization and policy implementation of an administrative agency, or when a legislative committee by contact, observation, or investigation places itself in the posture of a watchdog over agency activities, we speak of these legislative-executive relationships in terms of *oversight.* When the influence of individual legislators or legislative committees constitutes substantial involvement in the formulation or implementation of administration policy, producing changes in policy emphasis or priority, we speak of these relationships as legislative *supervision.* When the legislature directs administrative organization and policy or requires legislative clearance for administrative decisions, it is meaningful to talk of the legislative-executive relationship as one of *control.* In effect, these terms crudely demarcate cutoff points on a continuum of variable legislative-executive relations, ranging from little legislative influence upon administrative policy to substantial legislative control over executive agencies. The real virtue of the distinctions among oversight, supervision, and control is the fairly important one of maintaining alertness to rather wide variations in the relationships between legislatures and executive agencies. Thus, legislative committees could be classified as primarily engaged in oversight, supervision, or control. In the Congress, for instance, the House Armed Services Committee could, as we shall demonstrate, be typed as an oversight committee; the appropriations committees, as mainly supervisory; and the Joint Committee on Atomic Energy, as a control committee. We shall illustrate these variations in legislative influence upon administration later in this chapter.

Legislative influence upon administrative agencies fulfills at least three purposes from the point of view of the legislative branch. The varied relationships between legislative institutions and executive agencies provide mechanisms by means of which the legislature can test and attempt to secure the compliance of administrative agencies with legislative policy and can hold agencies accountable to legislative intentions. Again, legislative investigation, review, and even involvement in administrative policy-making provide the legislature with mechanisms for the evaluation and assessment of legislative policy, exposing gaps between expected and actual performance and providing legislative policy-makers with cues to needed changes in law or informal legislative-executive agreements. Finally, legislative oversight, supervision, and control provide relationships between legislators and administrators that facilitate reciprocal and sustaining support for public policy. Administrative agencies need legislative support, both to maintain their existence and to legitimize their programs; legislative support tends to facilitate support for administrative policies in the larger political community.[1]

PROBLEMS OF LEGISLATIVE-EXECUTIVE RELATIONS

Because the web of government is far too complex, it is impossible to treat legislative-executive relations in the United States in detail here. Legislative surveillance of administrative agencies is highly decentralized, and at all levels of American government, administration has become enormously large and far-flung. In our discussion, it is necessary to select major problems to deal with in order to focus upon the most useful among a wide variety of examples of legislative-executive relations. It is possible to consider the relationships between legislative bodies and administrative agencies in terms of the problems that these relationships raise for legislatures.

Atomization

Legislative innovation and response to executive agencies are highly atomized. Not only are a very large number of legislative committees and subcommittees typically involved, but individual legislators who regularly have interpersonal contacts with individual bureaucrats are persistently involved in the administrative process. Analyses of legislative-executive relations ordinarily focus attention upon legislative committee activities, but the contacts between legislators and administrators, usually stimulated by constituency demands, may constitute the most pervasive and fundamental form of legislative oversight. These interpersonal relations have a mutual cognitive and affective value. They permit legislators and bureaucrats to become knowledgeable about each other's work ways, and they tend to facilitate mutual understanding. In addition, the reciprocity made possible by many opportunities for mutual aid at this level of interpersonal relations probably makes a significant contribution to the functional integration of the legislative and executive branches of government in the face of constitutional, or formal, separation of powers.

Since American legislators are predominantly constituency-oriented, legislator-bureaucrat contact tends to be motivated by demands from the legislators' constituents. As one Democratic congressman said of his dealings with the National Labor Relations Board: "We never think twice about calling the Board and asking for a little special handling of some cases; not just to speed things up but to look a little differently at the case."[2] But beyond the legislator making demands upon the administrator in behalf of his constituents, legislator influence upon agency policy may very frequently be informal, interpersonal, and individual. For instance, in describing relations between members of congressional appropriations committees and the War Department in the early 1940s, Elias Huzar points out that "many controls which might have been included in statutes are contained, instead, in understandings between members of the Appropriations Committees and officials of the War Department." These "administrators have a well-recognized responsibility to take legislators into their confidence about their operating plans," and "they have a recognized obligation to adhere to the plans Congress approves not only by formal legislation but also by gentlemen's agreements."[3]

Congressional and state legislative institutions are thus highly atomized with respect to their relations with executive agencies. The legislatures are characterized by multiple focal points of influence and intervention in administrative activity. All legislators and a host of committees and subcommittees are involved, and legislative influence is thereby dispersed and decentralized. This dispersal and decentralization create serious problems for coordinated and integrated surveillance of the executive branch.

Strategic Conditions

As a result of his observation of relationships between congressional committee members and independent regulatory agencies, Seymour Scher has identified several strategic conditions for legislative oversight, supervision, and control. He suggests that a congressman, faced with the problem of deciding whether to devote his time and energy to reviewing agency procedure and policies or engaging in new legislative activity, can be expected to ask himself: "What's in it for me?" The decision to get involved may be governed by the following strategic considerations:

1. Congressmen tend to see opportunities for greater rewards in the things they value from involvement in legislative and constituent-service activity than from participation in oversight activity.
2. Committee members tend to view the agencies as impenetrable mazes and to believe that any serious effort at penetrating them poses hazards for the inexpert Congressman which outweigh any conceivable gain to him.
3. Congressmen who have established mutually rewarding relationships with agency people tend to be reluctant to initiate or become actively engaged in a close review of that agency's affairs.
4. Congressmen tend to view their personal contacts with the agencies as more efficient than committee investigations for serving constituent and group needs.
5. Committee members will tend to avoid agency review if they expect it will

provoke costly reprisals from powerful economic interests regulated by the agencies.

6. Congressmen who perceive that gains to themselves can be had by loyalty to the President can be expected to avoid close examination of the performance of agency officials appointed by the Executive.

7. As committee routines become fixed, for all of the foregoing reasons, in ways that make no regular provision for agency oversight, in the absence of powerful external stimuli they tend to resist change.[4]

Scher found congressional oversight of federal regulatory agencies to be intermittent, characterized by long periods of inactivity punctuated by bursts of oversight. He concluded that "committee leaders can be expected to involve committee resources in studies of agency performance if and when the likely gain in things valued by Congressmen is gauged as greater than any prospective loss in those things."[5] These strategic conditions are then pertinent:

1. When the leadership of the majority party in Congress believes it can cause sufficient embarrassment, with accompanying profit for itself, to a past or current opposition President who is held responsible for the performance of his agency appointees, committee oversight tends to be used for this purpose.

2. When the committee leadership or powerful committee members believe that constituent or group interests important to them cannot be satisfied by the routine personal intercessions between Congressman and agency, committee review tends to be used as a substitute.

3. When Congressmen perceive a threat, particularly from the President, to their traditional prerogatives of primacy in relation to the regulatory agencies, committee interest in the agencies is a likely response.

4. When, periodically, interest builds in Congress for revising regulatory policy, committee attention to the regulatory agency tends to occur as a by-product.

5. When the committee leadership becomes convinced that interests to which it is opposed can be substantially advanced by the exposure of dramatic evidence of agency failure, it can be expected to move first to neutralize or minimize these gains by initiating its own inquiry.[6]

In general, American legislatures are today better equipped to evaluate, to assess, and even sometimes to develop and integrate ideas, than they are to innovate or stimulate the invention of ideas. Strategically, legislatures are better able to "check and balance when there are, within the politically alert public, sets of ideas and interests which check and balance each other, thus creating a situation within which [they are] able to *sift, winnow,* and *judge.*"[7]

Generalist-Specialist Tension

We referred in Chapter 15 to some of the occupational role strains experienced by the American legislator in his relationships with bureaucrats. It is appropriate to refer here to potential problems of legislative-executive relations that arise in the contact between citizen legislators and administrative experts. At least three aspects of this problem can be pursued. On the one hand, legislators may regard the work of administrative agencies as simply too complex and technical for effective legislative supervision. As one United States House committee member said of the work of overseeing the federal regulatory agencies: "The [regulatory] agencies' work is pretty technical. Most of us just don't know enough about it to even begin to ask intelligent questions."[8] Again, legislators may themselves define technical and nontechnical questions in a way that confines their involvement in administration to manageable and desirable proportions, from their own point of view. Lewis A. Dexter, in describing the oversight activities of the House Committee on Armed Services, points out that "Congressmen tend to regard as 'technical' such questions for 'professional' military men as the nature of war plans" but that "they regard as 'non-technical' and fit subjects for their consideration such matters as the way in which oil is stored at overseas installations or how service credit shall be allocated for ROTC or military academy training."[9] Congressmen "will evaluate or try to evaluate the efficiency of given types of rifles or waste in the procurement of military overcoats," but "they have recently shown little interest in stimulating the invention and development of newer types of weapons or innovations in 'grand strategy.' "[10] That is left up to the experts.

Finally, of course, legislators may resent the greater knowledge of administrators or may be suspicious of their credentials as experts. Legislators may understand different versions of the facts and tend to substitute what they consider to be their own expertise for that of administrators. Thus, J. Leiper Freeman, in explaining some of the factors in the receptivity of members of the congressional committees on Indian affairs to the policy viewpoints of the Bureau of Indian Affairs, points out that committee members came to view the administrators as attempting to secure and expand their own administrative structure and, in their arguments before the committees, to rationalize their own interests and challenge the members of the committees for the loyalty of their Indian constituents.

> By this light, personnel of the Bureau became "theorists" who knew too little at first hand about either Indians or the law. Reflected in the frames of reference of some committee members were those ancient criteria of practical knowledge and ability, whereby bureaucratic attorneys are deemed impractical if they have "never tried a case," and public servants are written off if they have "neither carried a precinct nor met a payroll." A great deal of time was spent in trying to show that the Commissioner could not know as much about the needs of Indians in the various states as did the legislators from those states.[11]

Legislative Role Perceptions

The legislator's response to executive agencies will depend upon how he perceives his job as a representative. He may be agency-oriented in a positive direction and take the posture of defending the agency from attacks upon it, or he may play a hostile role. Whether the legislator plays the role of *agency defender* or *agency detractor* is likely to depend upon a variety of factors in the situation, including the partisan affiliation of the President who appointed the agency officials, the comity of interpersonal relations between the legislator and the agency chiefs,[12] his satisfaction with the information furnished about administration policy,[13] and the legislator's perception of constituency expectations and demands.

The latter is likely to be especially compelling in the American legislator's view of his role as an *agency overseer.* Legislators are likely to become heavily involved in administrative processes on behalf of explicit demands made upon them by their constituents.[14] For example, witness the views of United States Senator Everett Dirksen (R-Ill.) about communication with agency officials on behalf of his constituents:

> Ever since 1933, when I came here as a freshman Congressman, I have been calling every agency in Government in the interest of my constituents. I expect I am going to continue to do it whether this becomes law or not, and I am afraid this bill [to bar *ex parte* communications by "any person" in adjudicatory proceedings] is not going to become law with my sanction, because I don't go that far.
>
> I make the case just as clear as crystal, so the whole world may know. But now let's get the specific examples. There is an airline, let us say X, based in Chicago. I know the president and all the personnel and a good many of the pilots. There is another airline based in Missouri, my neighboring State. I don't know very much about it. But there is a petition or an application pending before CAB [Civil Aeronautics Board], and they both want to be certified for a stop in Iowa, so I call up this Chairman of the CAB and I say: "Look, Mr. _____, X Airlines has an application pending. I know these people, they are good, reliable operators; they are good, solid citizens. I just want to know what the status of the matter is."[15]

The legislative oversight role will also bear a relationship to the perceptions the legislator has toward the administration and the obligations and responsibilities of his committee. Some committees, such as the space and aeronautics committees and small business committees of the House and Senate, take a very paternalistic posture toward the agencies they deal with. Some legislative committees are hardly involved in oversight activities at all because the committee chairmen or powerful committee members conceive their role in a way that eschews oversight activities on the part of their committee. Such was the case in the late 1950s and early 1960s with the United States Senate Committee on Banking and Currency, whose chairman, Senator A. Willis Robertson (D-Va.), "used his powers primarily as a restraining influence on his committee. . . . His conception of the proper function of a committee places little emphasis on oversight. . . . He feels that the committee should not, in the words of a colleague, 'be poking around the agencies and stirring things up.' "[16]

Some legislative committees engage in what might be called *selective* oversight. Their members conceive their role to be that of observing and reviewing selected or limited aspects of agency operation. The United States House Committee on Armed Services is perhaps the best available illustration. Not only does this committee tend to defer to the appropriate appropriations subcommittee in the matter of review of important substantive policy issues regarding the military establishment, but within its own purview, the committee tends to select a substantively narrow range of oversight interests.[17] The committee members have little inclination to raise or consider broad issues of military policy involving weapons, personnel, appropriations, military objectives, organization, or administration. The main concern of the House Armed Services Committee is the location of military, air, and naval installations and the purchase, sale, or transfer of properties by the Department of Defense. As one of the members of the committee staff said: "Our committee is a real estate committee. Don't forget that. If you study our committee, you are studying real estate transactions."[18]

The appropriations committees of the Congress, especially the House committee, exemplify a more pervasive role conception on the part of committee members vis-à-vis the administrative agencies. In their posture of guardians of the federal treasury, members of the House committee tend to engage in the most detailed and sweeping oversight of the general government, largely with the object of reducing budgetary requests.[19]

No greater control over executive policy-making and implementation exists than that of the Joint Committee on Atomic Energy. Members of this congressional committee conceive their job as that of recommending programs and policies both to the agencies responsible for the use of nuclear energy and to Congress. The joint committee is so heavily involved in atomic energy policy formulation and execution that it is difficult to tell where the legislative process leaves off and the administrative process begins. "The Joint Committee on Atomic Energy is, in terms of its sustained influence in Congress, its impact and influence on the Executive, and its accomplishments, probably the most powerful Congressional committee in the history of the nation."[20]

Legislative Organization

Two aspects of legislative organization can be developed here with respect to legislative oversight, supervision, and control of the administration. One has to do with the *jurisdiction* of legislative committees to engage in surveillance over executive agencies. At the congressional level, the Legislative Reorganization Act of 1946 endowed all congressional standing committees with wide jurisdiction to engage in oversight activities. Section 136 of the act provides that "each standing committee of the Senate and the House of Representatives shall exercise continuous watchfulness of the execution by the administrative agencies concerned of any laws, the subject matter of which is within the jurisdiction of such committee." Furthermore, the act especially gave the committees on government operations authority to investigate and oversee federal agencies. The Committee Reform Amendments of 1974 represented an effort to strengthen congressional oversight by requiring standing committees of the House of Representatives to formulate and report specific plans for oversight activities during each Congress. Under these new arrangements, the Committee on Government Operations in the House not only has substantial oversight authority in its own right, but also is required to supervise and coordinate the oversight activities of other House committees. State legislative committees seldom have such pervasive jurisdiction. Again, the specific jurisdiction of each congressional standing committee varies considerably. Where more than one committee has jurisdiction over legislation affecting the same executive agency, the agency may be able to develop multiple sources of support in Congress and thus benefit from the dispersion of congressional resources for oversight. Thus, the military and defense establishment may utilize its support from the House Armed Services Committee to bolster its efforts before the Defense Appropriations Subcommittee for increased appropriations. Both cooperation and conflict between legislative committees may benefit the administrative agency whose budget or program is under review.[21] The congressional Joint Committee on Atomic Energy is perhaps a unique legislative committee in the pervasiveness of its jurisdiction and in the importance of its statutory basis as an institutional factor in its unusual accretion of power. The Atomic Energy Act of 1954 empowered the joint committee to take jurisdiction over "all bills, resolutions or other matters in the Senate or the House of Representatives relating primarily to the Commission or to the development, use, or control of atomic energy."[22] This broad committee jurisdiction both enhances the committee's position with regard to other congressional committees that might claim jurisdiction over particular programs and makes it clear to the Energy Research and Development Administration and the Nuclear Research Commission that they must deal with the committee. These agencies have not been able to develop competing bases of support in other congressional committees. When the joint committee's authority to use executive facilities, authorize appropriations, veto proposed agency actions, and require information from the executive branch is added to its sweeping jurisdiction, it becomes easy to understand the substantial control that the joint committee exercises over the agencies.[23]

The second relevant problem of legislative organization involves the structural-constitutional factor of *bicameralism,* a factor to be reckoned with in the case of the Congress and of every state legislature except that of Nebraska (where, as a matter of fact, little is known of the variable effects of unicameralism). One aspect of the problem that bicameral legislative organization raises has to do with the nature and extent of cooperation and conflict between house and senate committees engaged in oversight activities. The generally low level of coordination between house and senate committees is likely to impinge upon the effectiveness of the legislature in the performance of its oversight tasks.

In the supervision of administration through the budgetary process, the respective committees of the United States House and Senate take quite different positions, and their members play different roles. The House committee members, as we have already suggested, tend to play the role of guardian of the exchequer, cutting the budgets of administrative agencies whenever possible. The Senate Appropriations Committee, on the other hand, takes the position of an appellate court with respect to executive agencies, and its members tend to play the role of hearing appeals from House committee budget cuts. The difference in the perspectives of the two congressional committees is illustrated very well by the remarks of Senator Dirksen. Referring to a House committee decision to cut the number of employees for a particular agency from ten to six, Dirksen said: "It was great, good fun when I was on the House Appropriations Committee to cut four [positions]. Too often you discover that the six positions depend in large measure on the four. You just wasted the money for the six. I would rather give you nothing or whatever it takes to do a good job."[24]

A second problem that bicameralism raises for legislative oversight, although closely related to the first, involves the position taken by the respective legislative houses on administrative agency programs. The case of the reduction of the RS-70 bomber program that occurred in 1962 is an example. In preparing the federal military budget for the 1963 fiscal year, Secretary of Defense McNamara, with the support of the President, proposed drastic cuts in funds for the development of a supersonic reconnaissance strike bomber (the RS-70) and the elimination altogether of plans for the mass production of these bombers. Although only a relatively small amount of money was involved, this proposal stimulated substantial opposition on the part of powerful individuals in Congress and in the Defense Department. The principal congressional opponent of the cutback plan was Representative Carl Vinson (D-Ga.), venerable chairman of the House Committee on Armed Services. In the Department of Defense, Air Force Chief of Staff General Curtis LeMay vocally supported the buildup of manned bombers and opposed the RS-70 reduction. However, Secretary McNamara won the support of Congressman George Mahon (D-Tex.), chairman of the Defense Appropriations Subcommittee, and under his guidance, the House of Representatives supported the Defense Department in its final appropriations bill. The Senate did not support the RS-70 reduction and appropriated the $491 million that Representative Vinson and General LeMay wanted for the bomber program. The conference committee finally agreed upon the spending of $362 million, but Secretary McNamara privately negotiated a tacit agreement with the House conferees that he would not spend all that the conference committee had authorized. The defense secretary stood on his constitutional prerogative of refusing to spend money on a program with which he disagreed, even though Congress had appropriated the necessary funds. Thus, "Congress may authorize expenditure, but it can do little to bring it about unless it is able to persuade the President and the administrative agencies concerned that its policy position is appropriate. A united Congress has a good chance for success in this endeavor, but a divided legislature has little hope."[25]

An extremely important factor in congressional policy initiation, especially in attempting to counter the policy position of an executive agency supported by the President, is that of the fragmentation of the policy processes of Congress in relation to the administration. When the two houses of a legislature are divided and the chief executive supports the bureaucracy, imposing legislative policy on an executive agency is very difficult, and legislative oversight is thereby substantially vitiated.

Staff Involvement

A further problem of legislative-executive relations is the extent to which the legislative committee or individual staffs are involved.[26] At the state levels, if effective legislative oversight exists, some legislative staff person is likely to be the one who does it. Almost all states have staffs for the specific purpose of budgetary and fiscal review, and this tends to be the major, if not the only, continuing legislative oversight of the state executive agencies.[27] At the congressional level, however, the staffs of some committees have a very prominent place in the oversight process.

The staff of the congressional Joint Committee on Atomic Energy, one of the most effective operations, maintains very close contact with the operating personnel of the atomic energy agencies, including its field personnel.[28] The committee staff has been described as being more knowledgeable about the commission's field activities than the agencies' own Washington staffs. One of the major purposes of the joint committee's staff has been to keep committee members informed, although it has also played the more creative role of suggesting problem areas for exploration and initiating committee investigations.

The well-integrated and nonpartisan staffs of the congressional appropriations committees play a more significant part in oversight activities than most committee staffs do. Reciprocal confidence between the Appropriations Committee staff and budget officers of executive agencies is made necessary by their mutual dependence, and "many agencies choose to keep subcommittee staff informed months and sometimes years ahead on new developments."[29] When hearings are in progress, contact between committee staff and agency budget officers may be as frequent as several times a day; clearly, the staff plays an important part in the budgetary oversight process.

At the same time, legislative staff aides are by no means a match for the enormous pool of experts upon whom an executive officer can call for intelligence and information. The personnel of executive agencies not only are more numerous but also have a greater opportunity to specialize; they are free of the necessity of periodic exposure to the electorate and have a tremendous advantage over the congressional committee staff in knowledge of and experience with the operating end of agency activity. Even an enlarged legislative committee staff would be required to get much of its information about agency activities from the agency personnel themselves.

Anticipated Reactions

A number of students of legislative-executive relations have noted the phenomenon of anticipated reactions (sometimes called *feedback*, or *strategic sensitivity*) in the relationships between legislative committees and executive agencies.[30] It involves the bureaucrats' abilities "to anticipate or to recognize the expectations of committee members, to gauge the timeliness of a request, and to be cognizant of the claims, demands, and expectations which others direct at committee members immediately, but which are ultimately directed at the bureau itself."[31] The bureau officer who learns to take a role in his relationships with legislators that is formulated in terms of legislators' expectations about the proper behavior of representatives of administrative agencies maximizes his chances of successful legislative-executive relations. Administrators get many cues about the behavior expected of them by legislators through legislative committee hearings, personal contacts between legislators and agency leaders, or contacts with a committee staff. American legislators tend to expect bureaucrats to be hard-working, economy-minded, honest, straightforward, trustworthy, well-informed, friendly, and respectful of the legislative body. The complexity of modern government requires considerable mutual confidence between legislators and administrators, and such confidence "is achieved by gearing one's behavior to fit in with the expectations of committee people."[32]

A good illustration of administrators anticipating the reactions of legislators about their behavior is provided by the budget process. Because the principal objective of members of the appropriations committees has been to reduce governmental expenditures or at least to keep them to a minimum, the budget officer from an executive agency "needs to show that he is also a guardian of the treasury: sound, responsible, not a wastrel; he needs to be able to defend his presentations with convincing evidence and to at least appear to be concerned with protecting the taxpayer."[33]

> Like the lady who gets a "bargain" and tells her husband how much she has saved, so the administrator is expected to speak of economies. Not only is there no fat in his budget, there is almost no lean. Witness Dewey Short, a former Congressman, speaking on behalf of the Army: "We think we are almost down to the bone. It is a modest request . . . a meager request. . . ." Agency people soon catch on to the economy motif: "I have already been under attack . . . for being too tight with this money."[34]

LEGISLATIVE CONTROL OF EXECUTIVE ORGANIZATION

American legislatures can, and many do, exercise considerable control over administrative organization and reorganization, personnel recruitment and policy, and administrative procedures and rules.[35] Executive agencies and their programs must have authorization in the laws enacted by legislatures. The detail of statutory authorization varies a great deal, although there is an increasing tendency for legislatures to prescribe administrative organization, procedures, and programs in greater detail.[36] By appropriations and civil service legislation, controls are imposed by legislatures upon the recruitment, loyalty, promotions, salaries, duties, and numbers of administrative personnel. And in the last three decades, with the increasing necessity for legislative delegation of wide discretionary authority to administrative agencies, legislatures have attempted to devise adequate mechanisms for controlling the use of administrative discretion.

A potentially important method of control is legislative approval of executive appointments. The United States Senate gives its advice and consent to thousands of appointments, most of them routine. Out of more than 134,000 presidential nominations between 1947 and 1970, only 14 were rejected by the Senate, although 2,400 were withdrawn and 24,000 were left unconfirmed.[37] Of course, many of these presidential nominations are appointments of military officers. Traditionally, with respect to more important appointments, senators questioned the competence of a nominee or possible conflicts of interest arising from the appointment, but rarely did doubts lead to rejection of a nominee. On some historic occasions, Senate rejection of a presidential nominee had significant policy implications—as in 1949 where the Senate's rejection of Leland Olds for appointment to the Federal Power Commission (nominated by President Truman) involved differences over the scope of the commission's regulatory authority, or when in 1959 Eisenhower-nominee Lewis Strauss was rejected as a member of the Atomic Energy Commission partly because of disagreement with his views on public power.[38]

However, the events of Watergate during the Nixon administration touched off a sequence of confrontations between the Senate and the President over nominations. In its first few months, the Ford administration withdrew nominees for two ambassadorships, a nomination of a federal energy administrator, and a nominee to the Federal Power Commission. In 1975, serious objection was raised in the Senate to a number of President Ford's nominees, and in one case—a nominee to the board of the legal services corporation for the poor—a negative vote by the Senate Committee on Labor and Public Welfare brought about the withdrawal of the nomination.[39] Nevertheless, on the whole the overwhelmingly Democratic Ninety-fourth Congress approved the appointments of the Republican President. The greater scrutiny of nominees by Senate committees since Watergate has, perhaps, largely reflected partisan conflict, but it does represent a very real source of legislative control in some circumstances.

The chief executive's power to dismiss his appointees is obviously a vital part of his executive authority, but the extent of senatorial control over dismissals was long an unsettled constitutional question. The impeachment proceedings against President Andrew Johnson resulted from his refusal to abide by a law that required senatorial approval of dismissals. In the 1926 *Myers* case, the Supreme Court held that the President has exclusive authority to dismiss administrative officials, a decision modified in 1935 to provide that Congress might limit presidential authority to remove members of independent regulatory commissions.[40] In a number of states, there are constitutional or statutory limitations on the governor's power to remove, except for cause, numerous officials and members of commissions who are appointed for fixed terms. Although control of the legislature by the opposition party sometimes leads to rejection of gubernatorial appointments, it is these limitations on the removal power that constitute the most serious restrictions on governors.

Perhaps the most direct and visible legislative control over administrative organization and procedure has been that of the so-called legislative veto. In the early New Deal days, when economic crisis made necessary the delegation of what was then thought to be sweeping discretionary power to administrative agencies, Congress sought to retain some check upon the procedures, rulings, and organization of the new federal agencies. In the field of executive reorganization, for instance, in the 1932 reorganization law, Congress required that a President's reorganization plans be submitted to Congress sixty days before going into effect, subject to disapproval by a resolution of either house. This precedent has been followed in subsequent legislation dealing with executive reorganization. Under such legislation, Congress twice rejected reorganization plans submitted by President Truman to create a Department of Health, Education and Welfare (finally accepted shortly after President Eisenhower took office) and rejected a reorganization plan of President Kennedy that would have created a Department of Urban Affairs.

Formal statutory requirements for legislative committee clearance of administrative procedures, rules, or decisions began with the passage by Congress in 1944 of a naval public works statute that authorized the Secretary of the Navy to acquire land for the establishment of naval shore facilities, but only after review and approval by the naval affairs committees.[41] Congress has used the veto technique on a variety of matters, especially on government purchases, land acquisition, sale of surplus property, conservation and reclamation projects, deportation, and exchange of military information and atomic energy materials.[42] The most all-encompassing legislative veto powers are those in the hands of the members of the Joint Committee on Atomic Energy.[43]

Somewhat similar developments have been occurring in some of the states. Administrative procedures acts in several states contain legislative review provisions. In these states, administrative regulations must be submitted to legislative review, and rules disapproved by the legislature are void. The Michigan statute, which has been in effect longest (since 1947), states: "The legislature reserves the right to approve, alter, suspend or abrogate any rule promulgated pursuant to the provisions of this act." It requires that all rules promulgated by executive agencies be submitted to each member of the legislature prior to the regular session; those disapproved by concurrent resolution are void. Between sessions, the clearance process is performed by a joint committee on administrative rules that has the power to suspend rules until the next legislative session. In practice, this joint committee performs a continuous clearance of administrative rules. One significant result of the Michigan law has been to reduce the issuance of formal rules by Michigan administrative agencies.[44]

Legislative clearance is a method of control over administration with considerable appeal to legislators who wish to secure or maintain current supervision of the uses of delegated authority. The usual mechanisms of legislative oversight—reporting, budget review, investigation—tend to be ex post facto in nature, and they are therefore somewhat limited in usefulness. Furthermore, legislative clearance may be appealing to administrative officers who desire the favorable reaction of the legislature to their use of delegated authority. "Committee clearance helps to decrease the guesswork in such calculations and predictions," and thus "promotes security and stability." Requiring that each use of administrative discretion be accompanied by legislative committee acceptance "assures the agencies of approval and support by the most influential units of the legislative branch."[45] At the same time, legislative committee clearance does tend to reduce the supervisory capacity of the chief executive and to some extent of the legislative body as a whole.

OVERSIGHT BY INVESTIGATION

One of the most important and sometimes the most spectacular devices for legislative oversight of administration is the committee investigation. Legislative committee investigations came into public prominence after World War II largely because of the improprieties in state legislative and congressional committee investigations of internal Communist or allegedly subversive activities.[46] Although the loyalty of officials in the executive agencies of government was at least the original focus of most of these inquiries, committees investigating un-American activities have seldom limited themselves to the narrow confines of legislative-executive relations; these investigations have almost invariably broadened their scope. Perhaps the most bizarre legislative investigation in American history was the so-called Army-McCarthy Hearings in the spring of 1954, which involved the erratic Senator Joseph McCarthy of Wisconsin.[47] Peculiar as the McCarthy investigations were, and significant as they were for understanding the temper of American society in the 1950s, they reveal little about legislative-executive relations beyond indicating legislative excesses, the failure of legislatures to impose restraints upon investigating committees under some circumstances, and the extent to which investigations of certain kinds can distort and inflate individual legislators' reputations. In marked contrast to the anti-communist investigations of the 1950s, the most recent widely publicized congressional investigations—those of the 1972 campaign activities of Richard Nixon, and the impeachment investigation—already are pointed to as models of congressional probity and courage. During most of 1973, the Senate Select Committee on Presidential Campaign Activities, led by Chairman Sam Ervin (D-N.C.), conducted an extensive investigation into the so-called Watergate affair. Its televised public hearings contributed mightily to constructing a public record that led to the inquiry by the House Judiciary Committee into the impeachment of the President. The Judiciary Committee held hearings and conducted investigations through most of 1974, holding historic televised hearings and debate in July. In early August, the Committee voted three articles of impeachment against President Nixon, including the charges that he (1) obstructed and impeded the administration of justice, (2) "repeatedly engaged in conduct violating the constitutional rights of citizens," and (3) failed to produce papers and other evidence required by Congress in the exercise of its power of impeachment. On August 8, 1974, President Nixon resigned, saying in a televised speech that "it has become evident to me that I no longer have a strong enough political base in Congress to justify continuing" the effort to stay in office.

The impeachment investigation by the House Judiciary Committee was virtually without precedent in many respects. In general, members of the committee were well aware of the extraordinary, historic character of the inquiry. The televising of the impeachment debate by the committee brought members into the limelight and gave them a public visibility rare for congressmen. The committee approached its constitutional responsibility with great caution, engaging in a prudent debate about the nature of impeachable offenses. Amendments to the articles of impeachment were debated with care, and many of the committee votes on amendments were bipartisan. On the final vote on Article I, adopted twenty-seven to eleven, the twenty-one Committee Democrats voted "aye," along with six of the seventeen Republicans. Article II was adopted on a final vote of twenty-eight to ten, supported by seven Republicans. The final vote on Article III was twenty-one to seventeen, with nineteen Democrats and two Republicans voting "aye," and two Democrats and fifteen Republicans voting "nay." By the time the committee reported the three articles of impeachment to the House, the incriminating revelations of the tape recordings of President Nixon's conversations had become public, and it was clear that the House would vote the impeachment of the President and that he would be convicted by the Senate.

But the highly publicized congressional investigations should not obscure the fact that many kinds of investigations of executive agencies and activities have been undertaken. Accentuated concern about congressional oversight by investigation is indicated by the enactment by the House of Representatives in 1974 of House Resolution 988, which encouraged standing committees to create oversight subcommittees and to conduct investigations.[48] In the Ninety-fourth Congress, the Committee on Agriculture's Subcommittee on Department Operations, Investigation and Oversight undertook a major investigation of the Food Stamp Program. The Surveys and Investigations Staff of the Appropriations Committee, which conducted ninety-five investigative studies during the Ninety-third Congress, planned forty-four investigations and reviews during 1975. The Committee on Banking, Currency and Housing projected major investigations of federal monetary policy, the New Communities Program of the Department of Housing and Urban Development, bank failures, and the Export-Import Bank; the Committee on Interior and Insular Affairs' Subcommittee on Public Lands conducted an inquiry into the Alaska pipeline construction. Both House and Senate established select committees on intelligence operations and conducted extensive investigations of the Central Intelligence Agency and the Federal Bureau of Investigation.

State legislative investigating committees have been subjected to very little study, although they appear to operate only sporadically and irregularly. But congressional investigations have increased significantly in number since standing congressional committees obtained wider investigative authority and greater resources with the enactment of the 1946 Legislative Reorganization Act. Since 1950, Congress has conducted some 200 investigations each year, covering a very wide range of subjects. Most of these investigations have a distinct and legitimate legislative purpose and bear some relation to specific legislative enactments that are, in part at least, their result. Some congressional committee investigations, rather than having a direct lawmaking purpose, provide a means by which the committees can supervise executive agencies by examining their implementation of delegated power in particular circumstances. Also, investigations may have a primarily informational purpose, simply helping legislators to keep up with events.

Legislative investigations of executive agencies may be generated by many motives. Partisan advantage is often involved: "When the Republicans captured control of Congress in 1946, it was virtually a political obligation to set about discrediting the Democratic administration through investigations—with an eye to the 1948 election."[49] Investigations may be instigated by legislators because of the anticipated personal profit in the form of national publicity and popularity. Suspicion or evidence of malfeasance, wrongdoing, illegal activity, or improper conduct on the part of administration officials may trigger congressional investigations. And investigations may be forthcoming because legislative leaders have come to feel that administrative agencies are not doing the job that the legislature intended.

If legislative investigations are often designed to curb executive agencies by means of probing and public disclosure, it is clear that there are great institutional and interpersonal restraints upon penetrating investigations of the behavior and conduct of administrative officials. In addition, as often as not, legislative committee investigations seem to be designed to help the chief executive or an executive agency, and congressional-administrative cooperation in the development (or squelching) of investigations is not uncommon. In some cases, legislative inquiries have been designed primarily to reinforce the recommendations of the President for major legislation. Thus, "exposures in 1933 and 1934 by the Senate committee investigating stock exchange practices and banking, for example, contributed markedly to the enactment of such Administration-supported legislation as the Banking Acts of 1933 and 1935, the Securities Act of 1933, and the Securities and Exchange Act of 1934."[50] Cooperation between a congressional committee and an administration agency may occur when the agency wishes to get information that only an investigating committee can acquire by using its subpoena power. Thus, it is said that "the Senate Committee on Interstate Commerce conducted an inquiry into the financing of railroads partly for the purpose of acquiring information which the Interstate Commerce Commission felt it did not have the power to obtain."[51] Finally, congressional leaders may initiate an investigation by a committee or subcommittee led by congressmen friendly to the administration in order to circumvent an investigation by hostile members, a factor that appears to have been important in the authorization of the so-called Truman committee, created in 1941 to investigate defense mobilization.[52]

One of the important sources of conflict between legislative investigating committees and executive agencies comes in connection with the right of committee access to the papers and files of executive agencies and the correlative right of executive agencies, under presidential authority, to withhold information that the President regards as contrary to the public interest. Congressional dependence upon information from executive agencies is acute, and congressional reaction is often heated when information is denied. Especially since 1954, presidential claims of "executive privilege" have touched off serious disputes between Congress and the President. A great controversy over the meaning of executive privilege arose during the Nixon administration, inasmuch as President Nixon set records for the withholding of information from Congress. One celebrated instance was the withholding of the Pentagon Papers, describing failures of American policy in Vietnam, from the Senate Foreign Relations Committee. An even more celebrated case was the assertion by President Nixon that he could, on grounds of executive privilege, withhold from Congress information having to do with criminal activities—the so-called Watergate cover-up.[53]

AUTHORIZATION AND APPROPRIATIONS

The most substantial and detailed legislative supervision of executive agencies is in the area of fiscal control, the central processes of which are the authorization for the expenditure of funds, the appropriation of funds, and the audit or review of their actual expenditure. At the congressional level, the primary units for fiscal supervision are the appropriations committees, although the budget committees, the Joint Economic Committee, the committees on government operations, and the General Accounting Office also have important parts in the fiscal review process.[54] Although it is not possible to examine congressional fiscal surveillance in detail, some of its main characteristics can be described.

Authorization-Appropriations Tension

A fundamental characteristic of the congressional budget process is the distinction between *authorization* and *appropriation*. Authorization is accomplished by the substantive legislative committees (Agriculture, Interstate and Foreign Commerce, International Relations, and so forth) and involves setting a ceiling on expenditures for substantive governmental programs. Substantive committee authorizations for programs "may be open-ended, requiring no further action by the legislative committee; they may be multi-year or lump sum, expiring when either the time or expenditure limitation is exceeded; or they may be annual—i.e., requiring action by the legislative committee concerned *each* fiscal year."[55] Programs must be authorized before funds can be appropriated for their implementation. The appropriations committees allocate funds to be expended for programs already authorized. But the control of the appropriations committees over the purse strings gives them a crucial opportunity to make policy. This control, when they wish to exercise it, frequently leads to tension between the appropriations committees and the substantive committees. Such tension is clearly indicated by the following comments of a member of the House:

> Theoretically the weapons system is authorized by the Committee on Armed Services, but that is only in theory. On the missile programs that have been permitted to go ahead, decision is made by the Appropriations Committee through the language of reports and through riders. The committee which heard all the testimony and is presumed to have special competence is not the one which makes the decisions. If we are going to take the trouble to develop men with specialized knowledge in a given field, then we should give them the right to sit in and second guess on Appropriations. There is no point in having hearings before Armed Services and then have the final decision made by Appropriations.[56]

Appropriations-authorization tension is mitigated to some extent in the Senate, where members of the Appropriations Committee serve on a larger number of other committees, where the Senate committee is not so much inclined as the House committee is toward budget reduction, and where ex-officio members from substantive committees participate in Appropriations subcommittee deliberations.[57]

In the last ten years, tension between the appropriations committees and the authorizing committees has, on the whole, increased, and the balance of power probably has shifted in the direction of the authorizing committees. The enormous increases in federal expenditures (from $118 billion in 1965 to $325 billion in 1975) have affected the status of the appropriations committees in serving as guardians of the treasury, inasmuch as spending pressures have weakened the capacity of the appropriations committees to engage in budgetary control. And, increasingly, techniques to evade the appropriations process—so-called "backdoor spending"—have grown in importance. Thus, the authorizing committees bring about spending obligations for the federal treasury by authorizing agencies to borrow, conferring contract authority on federal agencies, or enacting legislation entitling a person or government agency to a certain level of benefits (e.g., social security benefits, government retirement programs). By and large, authorizations of these kinds incur spending obligations without the participation of the appropriations committees. Provisions of the Congressional Budget and Impoundment Control Act of 1974 are designed to regain for the appropriations committees some jurisdiction over back-door spending and to alter the timing of authorization bills to the advantage of the appropriations committees; but it remains to be seen whether or not the new budget procedures will mitigate or, in fact, exacerbate authorization-appropriations tension. And the creation of the new House and Senate budget committees constitutes a potential threat to the primacy of the appropriations committees in the congressional appropriations process.[58]

Decentralization of Decision Making

The atomization of legislative control of administrative agencies is nowhere more clearly illustrated than in the appropriations process. That appropriations decisions are highly decentralized is primarily a function of the congressional norms of specialization and reciprocity. The crucial unit of appropriations decision making is the subcommittee. The subcommittees of the House and Senate Appropriations committees are highly independent and autonomous and subject to very little direction or coordination from the parent committees. As Arthur W. Macmahon observed a good many years ago:

> It is not the Congress, not the House or Senate, not even the appropriations committee as a whole that should be thought of as abstractions, set against administration. The reality is a handful of men from particular states or districts, working with a particular committee clerk on a multitude of details.[59]

Perhaps the most notable example of decentralization is to be found in the case of the Senate Appropriations' Central Intelligence Agency Subcommittee. According to Stephen Horn, "the appropriations decisions made by the CIA Subcommittee are not ratified by the full committee," and "no formal hearing records are kept." So secret was this subcommittee's work thought to be that its existence was not even a matter of record until 1969; Horn adjudges it "the most powerful unit of the full committee."[60]

Subcommittees of the House Committee on Appropriations are independent and autonomous in the extreme and especially guard their independence from one another. As Richard F. Fenno has said:

> Each subcommittee works in virtual isolation from every other one. "We tend to be," says Chairman Mahon, "more an aggregation of autonomous subcommittees than a cohesive Appropriations Committee." Members participate in the labors of those, and only those, subcommittees of which they are official members. . . . Members of one subcommittee will not lend their "justification books" to Committee members not on the subcommittee. And nothing save the incapacitation of an official subcommittee member will bring a nonsubcommittee member into the group's crucial markup session. . . . The Committee at work is the Committee compartmentalized.[61]

In 1974, Congress sought to reduce the decentralized character of the congressional appropriations process in the enactment of the Congressional Budget and Impoundment Control Act. This legislation created budget committees in the House and Senate, and established a Congressional Budget Office to provide Congress with staff assistance in budgetary planning and decision making. The budget committees are intended under the Act to set overall spending and tax goals within which the appropriations committees are to operate.

Budgetary Restraint and Complexity

Budgeting for a modern government is extremely complex, and the armada of officials in executive agencies who prepare and justify the President's budget far outnumbers the congressional subcommittees and their small staffs. Ranking subcommittee members have had long experience in supervising budget items within their jurisdiction, but they must, of necessity, concentrate their attention on a few details. The question of how much money should be spent for a government program is often without a determinate answer. The amounts of money that executive agencies request and the amounts Congress appropriates are not, however, unrestrained. As Fenno points out with regard to the relationships between the House Committee on Appropriations and executive agencies:

> How to increase certainty by winning and keeping the confidence of the House Appropriations Committee becomes the central agency preoccupation. Their formulas involve obedience to Committee reports, careful preparation for Committee hearings, confidence-producing behavior in the hearing room, and the maintenance of informal contacts through the year. . . .
>
> Committee members wish to support the various programs for which they appropriate. . . . They consider, however, that their own particular function should be a negative rather than a positive one. . . . The Committee feels that it must exercise the power of the purse by subjecting agency activity to constant scrutiny and by ferreting out unnecessary expenditures wherever they exist. . . .
>
> The Committee perceives its oversight and budget-reducing tasks as essentially incremental operations. When the Committee makes its annual inquiry into agency appropriations, it does not normally range throughout the length and breadth of agency activities.[62]

Although conflict and uncertainty characterize committee-agency relationships, both agency and subcommittee strategies in their encounter are grounded in the assumptions of incremental budgeting and that disputation will occur over agency requests for increases in their budgets.[63] The executive agencies develop their figures and justifications with an eye to what Congress will approve, and the subcommittees operate in a climate of expectation about what the agencies want and will spend. Once House action on agency budget requests is completed, agencies must endure the scrutiny of their requests by the appropriate subcommittee of the Senate Committee on Appropriations. There, "agency heads generally view the various Senate Appropriations subcommittees as more interested in appeals from House actions than in a thorough review," and Senate subcommittees do often serve as "courts of appeals" for agencies from budget cuts made by the House committee.[64]

Inasmuch as the actual costs of programs authorized by Congress are seldom known for certain, and because Congress has sometimes attached conditions to the receipt of Treasury funds, the executive-branch agencies have traditionally withheld appropriated funds from actual expenditure in a variety of circumstances. Some so-called "impoundments" have occurred to effect savings and encourage good management of programs; sometimes changes in the course of events require that appropriated funds not be spent; funds may be impounded to prevent abuses or corruption; Congress may require the executive to impound funds to avoid exceeding spending ceilings or going beyond the limit on the public debt, or when there is racial discrimination, when states refuse to adopt federal standards, or when foreign governments seize property of American corporations without reasonable compensation. Thus, impoundment in itself has not been illegal or unusual, although occasionally a presidential impoundment order has stirred congressional controversy. However, the Nixon Administration claimed powers to impound congressionally appropriated funds on an unprecedented scale. Ultimately, a series of federal court cases required the Nixon Administration to release the full allotment of funds for a number of programs for which funds had been impounded, and Congress made ad hoc efforts in several of enactments to require the full release of appropriated funds. Finally, in the 1974 Budget and Impoundment Control Act, Congress attempted to restrict impoundments by the executive branch. The new legislation requires the executive to report all impoundments to Congress, permits one house of Congress to disapprove a deferral or delay of program funding within sixty days of such a deferral, and requires a recision, or cancellation, of budget authority to be approved within sixty days by both House and Senate. However, the impoundment control legislation has not proved to be entirely workable; the reporting requirements brought about an avalanche of reports, and ambiguities in the Act ironically seem to give the President new authority for impounding funds. As Louis Fisher has said, "Members of Congress, under the impression that they had curbed impoundment, awoke months later to find that the number of policy impoundments under President Ford had actually increased."[65]

Reduction of Budget Estimates

It is part of the prevailing normative structure of the congressional appropriations committees to economize. The resulting behavior can be fairly easily observed by looking at Fenno's tabulations of the action of the House Appropriations Committee on executive budget requests, and the Senate committee's action on the decisions made by the House committee, as shown in Table 18.1. It is apparent that executive budget requests were reduced by the House Appropriations Committee an overwhelming proportion of the time in the two periods analyzed (74 percent from 1947–1962 and 92 percent from 1958–1965). Of course, House Appropriations subcommittees do increase expenditures some of the time; programs that have strong congressional support are sometimes appropriated greater amounts than the executive agencies request. Furthermore, reduction in an ap-

TABLE 18.1   Action of House and Senate Appropriations Committees on Executive
Budget Requests, 1947–1965 (In percentages)

COMMITTEE DECISIONS	HOUSE COMMITTEE ACTION ON BUDGET REQUESTS		SENATE COMMITTEE ACTION ON HOUSE DECISIONS	
	1947–1962	1958–1965	1947–1962	1958–1965
Increase	8	2	56	78
Same	18	6	34	12
Decrease	74	92	10	11
Total	100	100	100	101*
Number	575	130	575	130

*More than 100% because of rounding off.
SOURCE: Richard F. Fenno, Jr., *Congressmen in Committees* (Boston, 1973), pp. 194, 201.

propriation for an agency may be followed by a deficiency or supplementary appropriation that awards the agency as much as, or more than, it originally requested. The Appropriations Committee may endeavor "to keep the total appropriation figure down for a while to demonstrate that it was economizing," and then make restitution of the funds later.[66] Furthermore, the Senate Appropriations Committee is more prone to increase agency funding than the House Committee is, as Table 18.1 shows.

Defense spending has, in recent decades, constituted the single major area of government expenditures. In that realm, the appropriations committees have not abjectly accepted the budget requests of the administration. From 1960 to 1970, the President's defense budget requests were reduced in seven fiscal years, although not by large proportions. Although congressional changes in amounts appropriated for defense personnel have not been great, congressional control over the defense budget in regard to weapons procurement and research and development has been substantial. In short, "the widely held notion that an uncritical Congress passively grants whatever appropriations are requested by the President and the Pentagon does not do justice to the reality of the pattern of the congressional changes in the defense budget, nor does it illuminate the past and potential congressional role in influencing the content of defense policy."[67]

Adoption of Committee Recommendations

It is uncommon for the recommendations of appropriations subcommittees to be rejected or fundamentally altered by the full committees. In addition, as is indicated in Table 18.2, the recommendations of the appropriations committees are overwhelmingly adopted without change on the floor of the House and the Senate. Members of the subcommittees are regarded as men with special expertise, whose judgment really ought not to be questioned on the floor. Such an attitude is suggested by the remarks made on the House floor by Representative Carl Vinson, long-time chairman of the Armed Services Committee, in urging the adoption of the defense appropriation bill in the form reported by the Appropriations Committee: "They [the subcommittee] deserve the support of every member of this House because they are in a far better position to know the needs and

TABLE 18.2   Floor Adoption of Appropriations Committee Recommendations, 1947–1962 (In percentages)

HOUSE OR SENATE ACTION	SENATE COMMITTEE DECISIONS	HOUSE COMMITTEE DECISIONS
Accept recommendations	88	90
Decrease recommendations	3	5
Increase recommendations	9	5
Total	100	100
Number	575	576

SOURCE: Fenno, *The Power of the Purse: Appropriations Politics in Congress* (Boston, 1966), pp. 450, 597.

necessities of national defense than you and I, who have not given . . . [the bill] the complete and detailed study it should have."[68]

That the appropriations committees make public policy along with allocating funds can hardly be questioned. The committee hearings provide a public opportunity for members of the committees to give cues to executive officials and to extract promises from them about policy, and committee reports may contain specific expressions of the agreements and understandings between subcommittees and officials about the manner of spending funds.[69] Holbert N. Carroll's observations of the relations between officials of the Department of State and the appropriations subcommittees led him to conclude:

> Prudent administrators carefully read the hearings and reports of the committee because they know they will be questioned on their compliance with the advice the next time they appear before the subcommittee. These subcommitteemen, so free with advice, control the lifeblood of any policy—money—and the administrators are acutely aware of this simple fact. It is often wiser to please the money committee than to placate the legislative committee which authorized the policy, if the two do not agree.[70]

In addition, policy decisions and directives may actually be written into appropriations acts. It is not uncommon for appropriations bills to earmark funds for specified purposes and to contain detailed restrictions on the salaries and employment of personnel, on spending without prior committee approval or other congressional action, and on administrative expenditures.[71] Finally, the committees engage in year-round surveillance of executive agencies through studies and investigations of the expenditure of appropriated funds conducted by committeemen and members of the committee staffs.

In addition to its controls over executive agencies through budget authorization, allocation, and review, Congress created its own staff agency to audit federal expenditures when it enacted the Budget and Accounting Act of 1921. The General Accounting Office, headed by the comptroller general, was authorized to investigate the receipt and disbursement of public funds and to report to Congress. In addition to auditing reports, the comptroller general may recommend ways of achieving greater economy and efficiency in governmental expenditures and report on fiscal control practices in executive agencies or on violations of law in expending funds. The staff of the General Accounting Office may be used to help congressional committees conduct investigations or prepare analyses of budgetary implementation and execution.[72]

State Legislative Fiscal Control

As we suggested earlier in this chapter, legislative review of the state budget is the major instrument for oversight of the executive branch at the state level. The governor is the budget-making authority in most American states; only in Arkansas does the budget-making authority reside exclusively with a legislative agency. In a number of states, however, legislative committees or staff personnel participate to some degree in the process of budget formulation. In New York, for example, the chairmen of the house and senate appropriations committees and their staffs participate in executive budget hearings and are usually consulted by the governor before he submits his budget, which then is customarily considered briefly without legislative hearings and passed without change. In Texas, New Mexico, and Georgia both an executive and a legislative budget are submitted to the legislature. The legislative budget is prepared by an interim committee and its permanent staff. The staff prepares budget estimates, conducts investigations, holds hearings on budget requests, and prepares a draft budget for the committee. The committee reports to the legislature independently of the executive.[73]

Almost all the state legislatures have available to them some kind of fiscal oversight machinery, although only thirty-four states have specialized agencies for budget review and analysis, continuous study of revenue and expenditures, and legislative postauditing. In some states, one or more of these activities are engaged in by the legislative interim committees; in others, permanent fiscal review committees and staffs are provided.[74] But in many state legislatures, budgetary control is minimal. Commonly, the governor and executive agencies prepare the budget. Legislative committees and staffs, because of their small numbers and limited time, can engage in only circumscribed review of the executive budget, which may be enacted without opportunity for much review and often without significant change; there is also restricted oversight following statutory enactment, although the scope and effectiveness of postauditing services have grown. Illinois is a fairly typical state. There, hearings before the appropriations committees provide some opportunity for legislators and citizens to become better informed about executive agency policy, but they are largely perfunctory. Only a very short time is available for budgetary consideration. Seldom are objections raised to executive agency budgetary items; legislative consideration constitutes little danger to the integrity of the governor's estimates.[75] Similarly, in California, the role of the legislature in the budgetary process is largely managed by the governor. The governor's part in the selection of the chairman of the Appropriations Committee in the lower house is great, and he has some role in the selection of the senate committee chairman as well. Analysis of the executive budget by the Joint Legislative Budget Committee and the legislative analyst has tended to focus on specific details, rather than on larger questions of public policy. In the end, the legislature makes little change in the governor's budget request; the average net change by the legislature in the governor's budget from 1943 to 1962 was less than 4 percent.[76]

Ira Sharkansky has analyzed the effects of incrementalism and legislative reliance on gubernatorial budget recommendations for 592 executive agencies in nineteen states, and he also conducted a detailed analysis of legislative support for the budget recommendations of the governors in Georgia and Wisconsin. From these analyses, he concludes:

> A favorable recommendation from the governor seems essential for agency budget success in the legislature. The agency may influence both the governor's recommendation and the legislature's appropriation by the nature of its request. Acquisitive requests generally receive severe short-run treatment from the governor and the legislature, but an acquisitive strategy appears to be essential for a significant budget expansion. On the basis of separate causal analyses for each of the 19 states, it appears that the governor's recommendation is more directly important for the legislature of more states than is the acquisitiveness of agency requests.[77]

Aggressive executive agencies seeking substantial budgetary increases face short-run difficulties arising from the general tendency of incremental budgeting to favor agencies seeking little or no increase over current budgets and from the reluctance of governors and legislatures to innovate in behalf of highly acquisitive agencies. Thus:

> chief executives and legislators have surrendered much of their innovative potential for a more limited role as reviewers of administrators' requests. And state legislators seem to have accepted a more limited supervisory role than the governors. The findings of greater importance for the governor's recommendation (rather than the agency's request) in the legislature's decisions indicates the legislature's dependence upon the governor's budget cues.[78]

Of course, deviations from the normal budgetary processes, in which incrementalism and gubernatorial influence play a major part, may come about in unusual circumstances, for example, when there is especially sharp conflict between the governor and the legislative leadership, where substantial new programs are unavoidable, or where substantial tax increases can most easily be justified by sizable budget growth.[79]

A significant factor in state legislative supervision, oversight, and control of the budgetary process is the fairly widespread use of segregated or earmarked funds. This results when state revenue legislation specifically pledges the expenditure of revenues for a designated purpose, for example, when gasoline taxes or motor vehicle license fees are specifically earmarked for the highway fund to be spent for highway construction and maintenance, rather than going into the general funds of the state for regular government operating expenses. Where they are used often, such earmarked funds tie revenues to specified programs, and leave little flexibility or initiative to either the executive or the legislative branch for fiscal planning and management. Where, as in thirty-six states, 25 to 75 percent of the state money is earmarked, the sphere and scope of legislative control are obviously very limited.[80]

CONGRESS AND FOREIGN POLICY

Although the foreign policy of the United States is often seen to be a province of the President, in which Congress mainly authorizes, where necessary, actions recommended by the President and the Secretary of State, in fact the foreign policy role of Congress has been substantial, if episodically so. Traditionally, the Senate has had a special capacity to oversee the executive through its constitutional prerogative of giving advice and consent to treaties with foreign countries. Although ratification of treaties is by no means an inconsequential weapon of congressional control of the executive, the pervasiveness of its utility was diluted by the rapid post–World War II increase in the use of executive agreements in presidential negotiations with other nations, which are not subject to senatorial approval. The number of treaties and executive agreements put into effect since the New Deal is as follows:[81]

	Treaties	Executive Agreements
President Franklin D. Roosevelt (1933–1944)	131	369
President Harry S Truman (1945–1952)	132	1,324
President Dwight D. Eisenhower (1953–1960)	89	1,834
Presidents John F. Kennedy and Lyndon B. Johnson (1961–1968)	104	1,896
President Richard M. Nixon (1969–1974)	93	1,317

Most executive agreements have dealt with routine matters of foreign relations (such as food deliveries or customs enforcement), but congressional efforts to curb their use without approval by Congress date back to the early 1950s (focused around the so-called Bricker Amendment, which was introduced in 1953 by Senator John W. Bricker (R-Ohio), but failed to pass in 1954).[82] In 1975, a number of proposals were introduced in the House and Senate to require congressional approval of executive agreements, an indication of renewed interest in a stronger role for Congress in foreign policy matters.[83]

During the 1960s, many commentators observed and reacted critically to the quiescence of Congress and deplored executive dominance in the foreign policy field. In particular, it was often concluded that the failure to end the Vietnam war until 1974 illustrated the impotence of Congress. But, as Gary Orfield has pointed out:

> The fact is that Congress did not even try to end the war, because there was no congressional majority opposed to the war. In the House of Representatives there was a consistent majority, including the leadership of both parties, that supported the general presidential policy toward Vietnam. Even in the Senate the division was

very close. The fact that a majority of Congress may have been wrong does not show that it was impotent, or even that it was unrepresentative. Indeed, polls show deep contradictions in public attitudes toward the war. When a particular presidential action stirred up strong public and congressional protests, such as the 1970 invasion of Cambodia, the threat of congressional restrictions on the White House was sufficiently serious to bring a rapid presidential retreat.[84]

Probably it can be said that from about 1955 to 1965 Congress did depend heavily upon executive leadership in foreign policy. Nevertheless, in recent years Congress has taken quite an aggressive posture, particularly in regard to war policy, foreign aid, and international trade.

Congress contributed to the termination of American involvement in Vietnam by voting in 1973 to prohibit further bombing and other forms of military action in Cambodia, Laos, and South Vietnam. Then, Congress adopted legislation, overriding President Nixon's veto, limiting the President's exercise of the constitutional war-making powers. The War Powers Act of 1973 put a limit of sixty days of any commitment of American combat forces abroad by the President without a specific congressional authorization. In addition, the war powers legislation made it possible for Congress to terminate a commitment of American forces before the sixty-day limit by concurrent resolution, not requiring the President's signature.

The most spectacular involvement by Congress in foreign policy often has been in the field of foreign aid legislation, an area in which congressional consideration is vital inasmuch as the appropriation of money is indispensable. Most recently, the Turkish invasion of Cyprus in mid-1974 in violation of United States foreign assistance laws brought Congress to suspend foreign aid to Turkey. The embargo imposed by Congress lasted eight months, in spite of vigorous objection by President Ford and his advisors. Relations between the United States and Turkey deteriorated, with Turkey closing some American military bases. Finally, in October 1975 both House and Senate voted to end the embargo to the extent of permitting shipment of military equipment regarded as necessary for Turkey's continued responsibilities to the North Atlantic Treaty Organization.

Legislation providing for the regulation of international trade was considered by Congress in 1974 when there was substantial congressional concern over policies of the Soviet Union regarding the emigration of Soviet Jews and over those of the Arab oil countries, which had effected an oil embargo. Senator Henry M. Jackson (D-Wash.) offered an amendment to the trade bill that effectively linked trade concessions to the Soviet Union to the adoption by the Soviets of more liberal emigration policies. Also, the Jackson amendment prohibited granting tariff preferences to members of the Organization of Petroleum Exporting Countries (OPEC), whether they had participated in the oil embargo or not. This amendment was adopted in the Trade Act of 1974 over the very strong objection of President Ford and Secretary of State Henry Kissinger.

Because the conduct of the foreign policy of the United States almost invariably requires the expenditure of money, the role of the Congress in the formulation and implementation of foreign policy, real and potential, is very considerable. Accordingly, the authorizing committees and the appropriations committees routinely get involved in foreign policy decision making. And periodically, congressional initiatives, such as those represented by the attempt to limit executive agreements, the War Powers Act, the Turkish aid embargo, and the trade bill, indicate responses to pressures for a direct congressional role in making foreign policy. Nevertheless, the direct congressional policy-making role tends to be a negative one—reducing appropriations for specific programs, prohibiting trade concessions, or attaching various kinds of conditions to authority granted to the executive branch. As Senator Adlai E. Stevenson III (D-Ill.) said during Senate consideration of the weapons bill in mid-1975:

> This debate is useful because it demonstrates that Congress is, as we all know, unfit to formulate foreign policy or to effectively oversee its implementation in all parts of a diverse, fast moving world. . . . The formulation of foreign policy is by law and the order of things uniquely within the authority and competence of the executive branch. . . . [Congress] can act, as it has, to halt the misconduct of policy as well as to support policies of which it approves. It can do no more. . . .[85]

The emphasis of this chapter has been upon some of the salient characteristics of the legislative process of sifting, winnowing, and judging the organization, programs, policies, practices, and spending of executive agencies. We have dealt primarily with the activities of Congress for two reasons: In most state legislatures, oversight (except perhaps for the budget) has been minimal; furthermore, descriptive literature on legislative-executive relations is much more adequate at the national than at the state level. The paucity of systematic research is, however, much more impressive than the plethora of descriptive and frequently repetitive commentaries. Here is an area of legislative research that is badly in need of expansion.

NOTES

1. See Roland Young, *The American Congress* (New York, 1958), pp. 165–167.
2. Seymour Scher, "Congressional Committee Members as Independent Agency Overseers: A Case Study," *American Political Science Review* 54 (1960):919.
3. Elias Huzar, *The Purse and the Sword* (Ithaca, N.Y., 1950), p. 354; and William W. Boyer, *Bureaucracy on Trial* (Indianapolis, Ind., 1964), pp. 44–46.
4. Seymour Scher, "Conditions for Legislative Control," *Journal of Politics* 25 (1963): 526–540.
5. Ibid., p. 541.
6. Ibid., pp. 541–550.
7. Lewis A. Dexter, "Congressmen and the Making of Military Policy," in *New Perspectives on the House of Representatives,* ed. Robert L. Peabody and Nelson W. Polsby (Chicago, 1963), p. 312.
8. Scher, "Conditions for Legislative Control," p. 533.
9. Dexter, "Congressmen and the Making of Military Policy," p. 321.
10. Ibid.
11. J. Leiper Freeman, *The Political Process: Executive Bureau–Legislative Committee Relations* (Garden City, N.Y., 1955), p. 59.
12. A good example is the well-known antagonism that existed between United States Senator Clinton Anderson (D-N.M.) and Admiral Lewis Strauss when Strauss was chair-

man of the Atomic Energy Commission. Senator Anderson served on the Joint Committee on Atomic Energy. "Much of the Joint Committee's history between 1954 and June, 1958, was colored by the personal enmity between Anderson and Strauss." See Harold P. Green and Alan Rosenthal, *Government of the Atom* (New York, 1963), pp. 59–60.

13. For example, James A. Robinson, "Process Satisfaction and Policy Approval in State Department-Congressional Relations," *American Journal of Sociology* 67 (1961): 278–283.

14. See Scher, "Congressional Committee Members as Independent Agency Overseers," p. 919. See also Aaron Wildavsky, *The Politics of the Budgetary Process* (Boston, 1964), pp. 47–51.

15. Quoted in Scher, "Conditions for Legislative Control," p. 536.

16. John F. Bibby, "Legislative Oversight of Administration: A Case Study of a Congressional Committee" (Ph.D. diss., University of Wisconsin, 1963), p. 146. For examples of fairly passive and paternalistic committee-agency relations, see Thomas P. Jahnige, "The Congressional Committee System and the Oversight Process: Congress and NASA," *Western Political Quarterly* 21 (1968):227–239; and Dale Vinyard, "The Congressional Committees on Small Business: Pattern of Legislative Committee–Executive Agency Relations," *Western Political Quarterly* 21 (1968):391–399. See also John F. Bibby, "Committee Characteristics and Legislative Oversight of Administration," *Midwest Journal of Political Science* 10 (1966):78–98.

17. See Bernard K. Gordon, "The Military Budget: Congressional Phase," *Journal of Politics* 23 (1961):689–710; and Dexter, "Congressmen and the Making of Military Policy," pp. 305–324.

18. Dexter, "Congressmen and the Making of Military Policy," p. 312.

19. See Wildavsky, *The Politics of the Budgetary Process,* pp. 47–62; and Richard F. Fenno, Jr., "The House Appropriations Committee as a Political System: The Problem of Integration," *American Political Science Review* 56 (1962):310–324.

20. See Green and Rosenthal, *Government of the Atom,* p. 266.

21. Jurisdictional conflicts between committees may, of course, make for disadvantages from the point of view of the executive agency. For an interesting discussion of this possibility in connection with legislative authorization of military weapons systems, see Raymond H. Dawson, "Congressional Innovation and Intervention in Defense Policy: Legislative Authorization of Weapons Systems," *American Political Science Review* 56 (1962):42–57.

22. Quoted in Green and Rosenthal, *Government of the Atom,* p. 79.

23. Ibid., pp. 79–103.

24. Wildavsky, *The Politics of the Budgetary Process,* p. 52; and Huzar, *The Purse and the Sword,* p. 39.

25. Peter Woll, *American Bureaucracy* (New York, 1963), p. 128.

26. Various kinds of staff oversight activities are briefly described in Kenneth Kofmehl, *Professional Staffs of Congress* (West Lafayette, Ind., 1962), pp. 127–131.

27. See Council of State Governments, *State Legislative Appropriations Process* (Lexington, Ky., 1975), pp. 19–28.

28. This paragraph is based upon Green and Rosenthal, *Government of the Atom,* pp. 67–70, 107.

29. Wildavsky, *The Politics of the Budgetary Process,* pp. 55–56, 83–84; quotation at pp. 55–56.

30. See Boyer, *Bureaucracy on Trial,* p. 42; Freeman, *The Political Process,* pp. 34–35; Wildavsky, *The Politics of the Budgetary Process,* pp. 41–42, 74–83; and William E. Rhode, *Committee Clearance of Administrative Decisions* (East Lansing, Mich., 1959), pp. 67–68.

31. Freeman, *The Political Process,* p. 34.

32. Wildavsky, *The Politics of the Budgetary Process,* p. 74.

33. Ibid., p. 75.

34. Ibid.

35. Judicial organization and rule-making are, of course, subject to legislative oversight, supervision, and control as well, although these are much more sporadic than oversight of the executive. The process does not differ greatly, but oversight of the judiciary may generate more ideological conflict. On the attempt of one state legislature to reorganize the state judiciary, see Gilbert Y. Steiner and Samuel K. Gove, *Legislative Politics in Illinois* (Urbana, Ill., 1960), pp. 164–198. See also C. Herman Pritchett, *Congress Versus the Supreme Court* (Minneapolis, 1961); and Walter F. Murphy, *Congress and the Court* (Chicago, 1962).

36. This general subject is treated by Joseph P. Harris, *Congressional Control of Administration* (Washington, D.C., 1964), pp. 15–45, 163–248. Few studies have been made of the activities of state legislatures in state administrative reorganization, but see Steiner and Gove, *Legislative Politics in Illinois,* pp. 134–163, for a treatment of the efforts of the Illinois legislature to reorganize that state's financial administration; and Thomas H. Eliot, *Reorganizing the Massachusetts Department of Conservation* (University, Ala., 1953).

37. Randall B. Ripley, *Congress: Process and Policy* (New York, 1975), p. 256.

38. See James N. Rosenau, *The Nomination of "Chip" Bohlen* (New York, 1962); and Joseph P. Harris, "The Senatorial Rejection of Leland Olds: A Case Study," *American Political Science Review* 45 (1951):674–692.

39. *Congressional Quarterly Weekly Report* 32 (December 7, 1974):3254–3256, and 33 (June 21, 1975):1303.

40. *Myers* v. *United States,* 272 U.S. 52 (1926); and *Humphrey's Executor* v. *United States,* 295 U.S. 602 (1935).

41. See Rhode, *Committee Clearance of Administrative Decisions,* pp. 9–10.

42. See Harris, *Congressional Control of Administration,* pp. 204–248; and Rhode, *Committee Clearance of Administrative Decisions,* pp. 8–49.

43. Green and Rosenthal, *Government of the Atom,* pp. 87–89.

44. See Ferrel Heady, *Administrative Procedure: Legislation in the States* (Ann Arbor, Mich., 1952), pp. 49–62. See also Glendon A. Schubert, Jr., Helenan Sonnenberg, and George Kantrowitz, *The Michigan Athletic Awards Rule* (University, Ala., 1955).

45. Rhode, *Committee Clearance of Administrative Decisions,* p. 68.

46. For congressional investigations, see Alan Barth, *Government by Investigation* (New York, 1955); Robert K. Carr, *The House Committee on Un-American Activities* (Ithaca, N.Y., 1952); and Telford Taylor, *Grand Inquest* (New York, 1955). For state legislative investigations, see Edward L. Barrett, *The Tenney Committee: Legislative Investigation of Subversive Activities in California* (Ithaca, N.Y., 1951); and Vern Countryman, *Un-American Activities in the State of Washington: The Work of the Canwell Committee* (Ithaca, N.Y., 1951).

47. See Emile de Antonio and Daniel Talbot, *Point of Order! A Documentary of the Army-McCarthy Hearings* (New York, 1964); and Richard H. Rovere, *Senator Joe McCarthy* (New York, 1959).

48. U.S. House of Representatives, Committee on Government Operations, *Oversight Plans of the Committees of the U.S. House of Representatives.* House Report No. 94–61, 94th Congress, 1st Session (Washington, D.C., 1975).

49. Harris, *Congressional Control of Administration,* p. 263.

50. M. Nelson McGeary, "Congressional Investigations: Historical Development," *University of Chicago Law Review* 18 (1951):431.

51. Ibid.

52. See Donald H. Riddle, *The Truman Committee* (New Brunswick, N.J., 1964), p. 14.

53. See Raoul Berger, *Executive Privilege: A Constitutional Myth* (Cambridge, Mass., 1974).

54. An excellent brief review of the budgetary process is found in John S. Saloma III, *The Responsible Use of Power: A Critical Analysis of the Congressional Budget Process* (Washington, D.C., 1964), pp. 1–21. See also Robert A. Wallace, *Congressional Control of Federal Spending* (Detroit, 1960).

55. Saloma, *The Responsible Use of Power,* p. 15.

56. Charles L. Clapp, *The Congressman: His Work as He Sees It* (Washington, D.C., 1963), p. 220. See the detailed discussion in Richard F. Fenno, Jr., *The Power of the Purse* (Boston, 1966), pp. 113–124.

57. See Stephen Horn, *Unused Power: The Work of the Senate Committee on Appropriations* (Washington, D.C., 1970), pp. 50–52, 60–62.

58. For an excellent treatment of these questions, see Allen Schick, "The Appropriations Committees Versus Congress" (Paper presented at the 1975 annual meeting of the American Political Science Association).

59. Arthur W. Macmahon, "Congressional Oversight of Administration: The Power of the Purse," *Political Science Quarterly* 58 (1943):181.

60. Horn, *Unused Power,* pp. 39–40.

61. Fenno, *The Power of the Purse,* p. 135.

62. Ibid., pp. 313–316.

63. For an analysis of agency and subcommittee strategies and activities in regard to the work of one House Appropriations subcommittee, see Ira Sharkansky, "Four Agencies and an Appropriations Subcommittee: A Comparative Study of Budget Strategies," *Midwest Journal of Political Science* 9 (1965):254–281; and "An Appropriations Subcommittee and Its Client Agencies: A Comparative Study of Supervision and Control," *American Political Science Review* 59 (1965):622–628.

64. Horn, *Unused Power,* p. 81.

65. Louis Fisher, *Presidential Spending Power* (Princeton, N.J., 1975), p. 200.

66. Holbert N. Carroll, *The House of Representatives and Foreign Affairs* (Pittsburgh, 1958), p. 155.

67. Arnold Kanter, "Congress and the Defense Budget: 1960–1970," *American Political Science Review* 66 (1972):129–143; quoted at p. 142.

68. Quoted in Harris, *Congressional Control of Administration,* p. 69.

69. See Fenno, *The Power of the Purse,* pp. 324–341; and Horn, *Unused Power,* pp. 115–127.

70. Carroll, *The House of Representatives and Foreign Affairs,* p. 162. See also Fenno, *The Power of the Purse,* pp. 291–293; and Horn, *Unused Power,* pp. 186–192.

71. See Harris, *Congressional Control of Administration,* pp. 93–97.

72. Ibid., pp. 128–152; and Horn, *Unused Power,* pp. 110–114. On the work of the General Accounting Office, see Richard E. Brown, *The GAO: Untapped Source of Congressional Power* (Knoxville, Tenn., 1970).

73. See Council of State Governments, *State Legislative Appropriations Processes* (Lexington, Ky., 1975).

74. A detailed summary and tabulation of fiscal services available in the states is provided in the Council of State Governments, *The Book of the States, 1974–1975* (Lexington, Ky., 1974), pp. 62–63.

75. Steiner and Gove, *Legislative Politics in Illinois,* pp. 78–81.

76. D. Jay Doubleday, *Legislative Review of the Budget in California* (Berkeley, Calif., 1967).

77.　Ira Sharkansky, "Agency Requests, Gubernatorial Support and Budget Success in State Legislatures," *American Political Science Review* 62 (1968):1230.

78.　Ibid., p. 1231. Also, see Alan Rosenthal, *Legislative Performance in the States* (New York, 1974), pp. 66–83.

79.　See Ira Sharkansky and Augustus B. Turnbull III, "Budget-Making in Georgia and Wisconsin: A Test of a Model," *Midwest Journal of Political Science* 13 (1969): 631–645.

80.　Council of State Governments, *State Legislative Appropriations Process,* p. 16.

81.　*Congressional Quarterly Weekly Report* 33 (August 2, 1975):1714.

82.　Louis Fisher, *President and Congress: Power and Policy* (New York, 1972), p. 225.

83.　*Congressional Quarterly Weekly Report* 33 (August 2, 1975):1712–1717.

84.　Gary Orfield, *Congressional Power: Congress and Social Change* (New York, 1975), p. 259.

85.　*Congressional Quarterly Weekly Report* 33 (June 28, 1975):1349–1350.

CHAPTER NINETEEN

The Courts and
the Legislative Process

The term "separation of powers" that describes the American constitutional system is a familiar one to students, but it can be a misleading one if taken too literally. We have already described the very important part that the executive branch—and particularly the chief executive—plays in the legislative process. In this chapter we are concerned with the influence of the courts on the legislative process. That influence is less direct and obvious than the influence of a President or governor. Judges do not normally submit a list of legislative recommendations to the legislature, or stand in the corridors of the capitol trying to persuade members to pass or defeat bills. In fact the courts have no opportunity to act on legislation until after it has been passed. There is a clear distinction between the legislative process and the judicial process. The legislative bodies pass laws. The courts apply laws to specific cases, and in the course of doing so they interpret the meaning of these laws and occasionally declare them to be unconstitutional. Nevertheless, the actors in the legislative process are frequently influenced in their behavior by judicial decisions that have been made in the past or that may be anticipated in the future.

From the point of view of interest groups, the courts offer an alternative arena in which to try to accomplish their objectives if they have failed in the legislative arena. The decisions of courts may alter the input into the legislative system by affecting election or apportionment laws. Previous judicial decisions may limit the options available to the legislature in its efforts to achieve policy goals through legislation. The decisions of the courts may provoke efforts by the legislature to change the direction of judicial decisions or restrict the authority of the courts. It is important to remember that interactions between the courts and legislatures take place within the context of the federal system, that state legislatures are affected by both state and federal courts.

THE COURTS AS ALTERNATIVE
POLITICAL ARENAS

The American system of government is characterized by multiple points of access for interest groups that are trying to bring about—or block—the adoption of a particular policy. The diffusion of power within Congress means that an interest group can concentrate its efforts at those points within the system where its influence is likely to be greatest; a subcommittee or committee in either branch, or particular party leaders, for example. It also means that it is more difficult to pass legislation than to defeat it because it is necessary to win support at so many different points in the system. But Congress is only one part of the national system of government. If an interest group fails to achieve its goal in Congress, it may turn its attention to other parts of that system. It may turn to the President or to administrative agencies for help in persuading Congress to pass a bill, or it may ask the President to veto it. After legislation is passed, the group may try to influence how it is administered or who is chosen to administer it in an agency, and it may try to influence administrative and legislative decisions on budgetary support for programs created by the legislation. At the state level a group that fails to gain its objectives in the legislature may similarly turn to the executive branch for help, or it may turn its attention to the national government and try to get action by Congress or the President either to fill the void left by state legislatures or to reverse the effect of state legislation.[1]

The group that loses its battle in the legislative branch, and fails to get adequate assistance from the executive, may try to achieve its goals in the courts. It should be obvious that some policy goals are beyond the power of the judicial branch. The courts cannot raise taxes or appropriate money if the legislature fails to do so, nor can they directly initiate programs of action that will require funding. To a large degree the authority of the courts is negative—to block governmental programs or forms of taxation. The range of possible judicial action is not unlimited, but it is substantial. If legislation has been passed, the courts have the authority to interpret its meaning, and an interest group may seek a ruling from a court that strengthens or weakens the effect of legislation. A group that has failed to defeat a bill may try to persuade the courts that it is unconstitutional or that some part of the bill is unconstitutional. (Similarly a group that supported the bill may seek a prompt, favorable ruling on its constitutionality to remove any doubts about it.) When the legislative branch has failed to act positively on legislation, an interest group may try to achieve similar objectives by judicial action, although we have noted that there are serious limits on the authority of the courts to initiate policy. An interest group at the state level normally turns to the state courts for assistance, but it may seek a remedy in the federal courts if either the state legislation or the situation that the state legislature had failed to correct appears to violate rights guaranteed by the federal Constitution.

It is the job of the courts to interpret the law. When a case arises that involves statutory law, the court must decide exactly what the law means and how it applies to specific cases. This may be difficult to do for a number of reasons.

The task of draftsmanship is difficult enough when only a single person is endeavoring to give precise form to his thoughts. It is infinitely more difficult when many legislators with widely differing points of view are involved, and when their task is to find formulas on which a majority of the participants can agree. Given the legislative problem, a considerable amount of ambiguity in the product is a necessity, not a consequence of bad draftsmanship.

... Sometimes the ambiguity is a result of compromises required to obtain a majority. Sometimes the legislators are subjected to such pressure that something must be done, but no one is sure just what. Then an ambiguous statute will be an expedient way of shifting the pressure to the courts.[2]

Another source of difficulty in interpretation is that the situation giving rise to a case before the court may be one that was not anticipated by the legislature but which seems to fall within the scope of the law. The more general the language of the statute, of course, the more uncertainty there will be about whether and how it applies to a particular case.

In interpreting a statute, the court may try to determine what the legislature had in mind when it was adopted. This may require an examination of the "legislative history" of a bill: committee reports, amendments adopted or defeated, and speeches made during debates—a record that is sometimes rather thin in the case of state legislatures. The courts often fail to find any clear statement of legislative intent in the record, or else discover that various legislators had different viewpoints about the meaning of the law. The less clear the intent of the legislature, the greater freedom the court has to use its own judgment and, at times, to follow its own value judgments in interpreting the law.

Although the courts are usually cautious and conservative about interpreting the meanings of laws, they have sometimes made decisions regarding interpretation that have had a profound impact on the law, and in some cases the courts have aroused strong criticism from the legislators who had originally enacted it. Two cases pertaining to subversion can be used as illustrations. In the 1957 *Yates* case, the Supreme Court reversed the convictions of fourteen Communist leaders, and the basis for its decision was a very narrow interpretation of the term "organize" in the Smith Act, which made it a crime (among other things) to organize for the purpose of teaching or advocating the forceful overthrow of the government. The Court said that the intent of Congress was unclear, and therefore the term should be construed narrowly to include only the original establishment of the Communist party in 1945.[3] In another case *(Pennsylvania* v. *Nelson)* that illustrates the importance of interpretation, the Supreme Court held in 1955 that by passing the Smith Act and other legislation on sedition, Congress could be presumed to have preempted the field, and consequently state legislation pertaining to sedition against the federal government was unconstitutional. In both cases many congressmen vigorously insisted that the Court had misinterpreted the intent of Congress and the meaning of legislation.[4]

When opponents of a bill fail to prevent its enactment by the legislature, they may try to get it declared unconstitutional by the courts. Congressional legislation can be challenged in the federal courts; state legislation might be challenged in either the state or federal courts (or both) depending on whether it was alleged to have violated the state or national constitution. Whether a group that has opposed a bill decides to challenge its constitutionality in the courts depends on several factors: the intensity of its opposition, the availability of resources to support a legal battle, and the prospects for winning in the courts. If previous court decisions suggest that the bill is vulnerable to constitutional attack, opponents are more likely to take the issue to the courts.

The authority of the United States Supreme Court to declare acts of Congress unconstitutional was established by Justice John Marshall in 1803 in the famous case of *Marbury* v. *Madison*. But the Court invalidated only one other act of Congress before the Civil War; that was in the famous *Dred Scott* decision in 1857. Beginning in about 1890 the Supreme Court began to play a very active and very conservative part in the political system, striking down economic and social legislation passed by Congress. The Court used a narrow interpretation of the interstate commerce power and a substantive interpretation of the "due process" clause to invalidate legislation regulating the economy and protecting the economic welfare of individuals. Between 1890 and 1939 the Supreme Court handed down fifty-seven decisions declaring congressional acts unconstitutional. This period of judicial activism culminated in decisions invalidating some of the most important New Deal legislation enacted in the early years of the Roosevelt administration. Since 1940, as a result of major changes in the personnel and philosophy of the Court, relatively few important acts of Congress have been invalidated; the total number ruled unconstitutional was six in the 1940s and 1950s and fourteen in the 1960s.[5]

During the 1890 to 1939 period the United States Supreme Court was just as rigidly conservative in opposing economic and social welfare legislation at the state level as at the national level, and some 400 state legislative acts were voided during this period. Since that time the Supreme Court has rarely interfered with state legislation affecting economic issues or property rights, but it has frequently invalidated state and local legislation and administrative actions that interfered with individual rights and liberties protected by the United States Constitution. Examples include state laws perpetuating segregation and those placing restrictions on the right to vote. In other words, opponents of state legislation have little chance of overturning it in a federal court unless the law impinges on individual rights or has a discriminatory impact on some group such as a racial minority.

The rise of judicial activism at the state-court level in most states came in the early years of the twentieth century. This was a period of rapid increase in the volume of economic and social legislation, which was often overruled by state courts. Equally important is the fact that in the late nineteenth and early twentieth centuries many new state constitutions were adopted that imposed much more rigid restrictions on the powers of state legislatures.[6] The more specific the constitution, the more litigation is likely to arise concerning the constitutionality of legislation. It is difficult to generalize about the frequency with which state courts invalidate legislation today or the types of laws that are overruled because the details of constitutional provisions differ so much from state to state. Legislation that is vulnerable to attack in the courts in some states includes tax laws, laws regulating relationships between local governments, and those authorizing local governments to levy taxes or carry out certain functions.

The courts may be used not only by groups that have failed to block action in the legislature but also by those that failed to persuade the legislature to take positive action. For example, a group that had been unable to get the legislature to repeal old laws on abortion or segregation might try to get these laws declared unconstitutional. If the legislature has failed to adopt new legislation to deal with some problem, it may be possible to achieve the same goal through judicial action, though the positive steps that the courts can take are clearly limited. Any group that has been unsuccessful in its legislative efforts may decide to turn to the courts, but such a tactic is particularly attractive to a group that for some reason lacks access to or influence in the legislature. A good example of such a group would be the black citizens of southern states, at least prior to the mid-1960s. Many black citizens were unable to vote in Southern states; there were no black members of the legislatures; and most white legislators were unwilling even to give a hearing to the demands of black citizens. Consequently, efforts to repeal legislation that perpetuated segregation in the 1940s and 1950s or to remove discriminatory provisions in registration and voting laws were doomed to failure. Black citizens, though they constituted one-fifth to one-third of the population in most Southern states, had no effective representation in the legislature. As a result, organizations such as the NAACP went to the courts, particularly at the federal level, to challenge the constitutionality of the legislation that guaranteed segregation and restricted voting, and they were largely successful in achieving their objectives. After the initial victories in the courts, these groups began to gain passage of some remedial legislation in Congress.

The experience of black interest groups points up an important difference between legislative and judicial bodies. Any group seeking effective access to the legislature must have political strength that is recognized by legislators—particularly if it is seeking controversial changes in major policies. Groups seeking access to the courts do not need political strength, though they may need substantial financial resources to carry on an extensive legal battle. It is also noteworthy that the challenge to segregation and discriminatory voting laws was more successful in the federal than in the state courts, presumably because federal judges were more sensitive to constitutional principles and less sensitive to political pressures than state judges in southern states.[7] Groups who believe that state laws violate federal constitutional guarantees of civil rights are more likely to appeal to federal than to state courts.

THE IMPACT OF JUDICIAL DECISIONS ON THE LEGISLATURE

The courts do not make demands on the legislature in the same sense that demands are made by members of the executive branch or by lobbyists. But the decisions of courts have various impacts on the operation of the legislature and on the decisions it makes. Judicial decision may directly affect the political input into the legislative system by changing the electoral or apportionment laws that affect who gets elected to the legislature. On rare occasions a court may place restrictions on the procedures used by the legislature. Decisions on the meaning and constitutionality of legislation previously passed by the legislative branch influence the actions of legislators in a variety of ways. Judicial findings that certain types of legislation are unconstitutional may deter the legislature from adopting such laws in the future. Legislators may adopt laws designed to implement policy goals adopted by the courts. Alternatively, judicial decisions may trigger legislative action designed to reverse or evade judicial decisions.

Judicial rulings on congressional and state legislative apportionment provide the best examples of decisions having a direct impact on the selection of legislators; these are discussed in detail in the next section. Some judicial decisions pertaining to elections have had incidental effects on legislative elections. Court decisions, as well as congressional legislation, gradually eliminated the obstacles to black registration and voting in southern states and thereby enlarged the electorate for congressional and legislative elections—as well as others—in those states. Occasionally judicial decisions determine whether a particular legislative candidate is eligible to be on the ballot. Contested legislative elections may be settled in the courts, although Congress and state legislatures generally have the authority to pass final judgment on the election returns and qualifications of their members, and also to expel them.

Recent court decisions have indicated that neither Congress nor state legislatures have absolute control over admitting or expelling members. The United States House voted in 1967 to expel Adam Clayton Powell from the Ninetieth Congress. After Powell was reelected in a special election, he filed suit in the federal courts, and in 1969 the Supreme Court held that the House did not have the authority to expel Powell because he met the constitutional requirements for holding a congressional seat.[8] (In the meantime he had been readmitted by the House to the Ninety-first Congress.) In 1966 the Supreme Court also overruled the Georgia House of Representatives, which had excluded one of its first black members, Julian Bond, because of antiwar statements that he had made. The Supreme Court asserted that the basis of the exclusion violated Bond's right to freedom of speech under the First Amendment.[9]

In an unusual case involving the New Jersey legislature, a federal district judge in 1975 ruled that the senate Democratic caucus in that state had no right to exclude a Democratic senator from meetings of the caucus. The case involved a woman senator who had charged many of her colleagues with conflicts of interest and had reported secret deliberations of the caucus to the press. The judge asserted that her exclusion violated her right to freedom of speech and deprived her constituents of equal protection of the laws. He not only ordered her to be admitted to caucus meetings but ordered all twenty-eight Democratic senators to stand trial on charges of having violated her constitutional rights.[10]

Most of the examples of judicial interference with the procedures used by legislative bodies have concerned investigations carried out by congressional and state legislative committees. In 1927 the Supreme Court unanimously upheld the right of Congress to carry out investigations to gather information necessary for passing laws. The Court held that "the power of inquiry—with process to enforce it—is an essential and appropriate auxiliary to the legislative function."[11] In recent years, however, the Supreme Court has placed limits on that power in cases where committees have questioned individuals, often about alleged Communist or subversive activities. In 1957, in two such cases involving the United States House Un-American Activities Committee and an investigation authorized by the New Hampshire legislature, the Court declared that witnesses could not be punished for refusing to testify unless the committee's jurisdiction was clearly defined, the investigation had a valid legislative purpose, and the questions asked were clearly pertinent to that purpose.[12] The Court said, "There is no general authority to expose the private affairs of individuals without justification in terms of the functions of Congress."[13] Since that time, in a number of cases, the Court has attempted to define more precisely the limits of the legislative power to investigate, but the narrow margin of several of these decisions (often five to four) has contributed to uncertainty about just what Congress and state legislatures may do.[14] It is obvious that the generally broad legislative authority to carry out investigations must be implemented under procedures that provide as much protection as possible to the rights of individuals.

REAPPORTIONMENT: A CASE STUDY OF JUDICIAL IMPACT ON THE LEGISLATURE

During the 1960s the representational base of most American state legislatures was fundamentally changed as a result of decisions made by the United States Supreme Court, and a less dramatic change was made in the districting of the United States House of Representatives, in response to the Court's decree. An examination of the Court's decisions and their impact will demonstrate how the courts can affect the framework of legislative decisions. It will also show how groups that fail to achieve their goals in the legislature can carry their battle to the courts, sometimes successfully; and it will illustrate the variety of tactics that may be used by those in the legislature who oppose the decisions of the courts.

Before the Supreme Court acted, most state legislatures had been seriously malapportioned for many years.[15] The rapid growth of cities in the years after the Civil War had provoked efforts by rural legislators to preserve their majority control because they perceived significant conflicts of interest between urban and rural areas. During the late nineteenth century in rural America, there was often a deep suspicion of the city, which was heavily populated by immigrants and often dominated by political machines. In later years conservative rural interests feared the power of labor unions and ethnic minorities, whose strength was usually concentrated in the cities. The conflict was sharpest and rural fears greatest in states where a single metropolitan center constituted a majority or near majority of the state's population. By the middle of the twentieth century it was the exploding suburbs within the metropolitan areas that were most seriously under-represented; and although urban-rural conflicts had become less significant factors in legislative politics, the nonmetropolitan majority in the legislatures continued to resist reapportionment. In a substantial number of states one of the political parties had a stake in preserving the existing apportionment. In the Northeast and Midwest, where Democratic strength was concentrated in the large cities, malapportionment helped the Republican party to maintain legislative control even when a Democratic governor was elected. In some of the border and southwestern states, malapportionment had the similar effect of helping the Democratic party to hold on to the legislature. In recent decades partisan interests have usually been more salient than urban or rural interests in many state legislatures.

As the population migration from rural to urban and suburban areas continued, the population inequalities in the districts of many state legislatures became very large. In 1961 the citizens of the five largest cities in Connecticut, with one-fourth of the state's population, elected only 10 of the 294 members in the lower house. The 6 million citizens of Los Angeles County, almost 40 percent of California's population, had only 1 of 40 seats in the state senate. Not every state had such severe malapportionment, but there were fourteen states in which a majority of the members in one house or both could be elected by as few as 20 percent of the electorate from the most rural areas; and there were very few legislatures in which serious disparities could not be found.[16]

Before 1964 it was rare for a state legislature to change congressional district lines unless there was a change in the number of congressmen assigned to the state, and even when this occurred, urban areas were usually discriminated against in redistricting. As a result, the rapidly growing sections of states, both urban and suburban, were underrepresented in Congress. In the 1962 election there were twenty-one states in which congressional districts varied in population by a ratio of more than two to one, though only a few had variations as large as three to one. Congress had provided by law that after every decennial census the Bureau of the Census should determine how many congressional seats each state should have, but it had done nothing to force the decennial redistricting within the states.

This was the background for the judicial decisions of the 1960s that established rigid standards for apportionment and brought about drastic changes in the rural-urban-suburban balance in state legislatures. In the 1962 *Baker* v. *Carr* decision, the Supreme Court declared that the courts had responsibility for determining whether, in specific cases, the rights of citizens to equal protection of the laws under the Fourteenth Amendment were being abridged by malapportionment.[17] Two years later, in *Reynolds* v. *Sims,* the Supreme Court held that "the Equal Protection Clause requires both houses of a state legislature to be apportioned on a population basis."[18] Also in 1964, in *Wesberry* v. *Sanders,* the Court held that "as nearly as is practicable one man's vote in a congressional election is to be worth as much as another's."[19] Subsequent decisions have had the effect of establishing increasingly strict, though slightly different, standards of population equality for both congressional and state legislative districts. By the end of the 1960s, the gross inequalities in state legislative districts had been eliminated, and there were no systematic differences between the population of rural and urban or suburban districts. Differences in the population of congressional districts within states had become negligible.

The Courts as Agents of Change

Throughout the decades prior to the 1960s, urban interests in a number of states made periodic efforts to bring about changes in state constitutions or laws that would provide the cities with a fair share of legislative seats. Most of these efforts failed, simply because rural interests continued to control one or both of the legislative houses in most states. Blocked in the legislature, urban interests began to turn their efforts to the courts, both state and federal. Prior to 1962 the state courts offered little or no relief. They were unwilling to force reapportionment, and when they occasionally invalidated a legislative reapportionment law, it had the effect of resurrecting an earlier and even less equitable apportionment. The leading federal decision was *Colegrove* v. *Green* (1946), in which the Supreme Court refused to intervene in a controversy over congressional districts in Illinois. Justice Frankfurter's opinion, in which he argued that "it is hostile to a democratic system to involve the judiciary in the politics of the people," was interpreted by most lower courts to mean that the federal courts would be unwilling to provide relief for malapportioned legislatures.[20] In 1960, however, in the case of *Gomillion* v. *Lightfoot,* the Supreme Court invalidated a change of municipal boundaries in Tuskegee, Alabama, because it was designed to disenfranchise black voters.[21] The stage was set for a new look by the Supreme Court at the Fourteenth Amendment's guarantee of "equal protection of the laws" and its pertinence to the problems of apportionment.[22]

The Tennessee legislature, the subject of the Supreme Court's scrutiny in the case of *Baker* v. *Carr,* was a prime example of an inequitable apportionment system. In the sixty years since the last apportionment, the uneven growth of population had led to major inequalities not only between metropolitan and rural counties, but among rural counties as well.[23] The Court's decision in *Baker* v. *Carr* dealt only with a single issue: the right to equal protection under apportionment laws is "within the reach of judicial protection under the Fourteenth Amendment."[24] The Court did not establish standards of population equality or explain what factors might justify deviations from such equality. The limited scope of the Court's decision left doubts about the fate of apportionment systems in other states that were not so inequitable or irrational as that in Tennessee.

The answers came from state and federal courts with surprising speed but without unanimity. In some states, suits had already been filed; and in many states, hearings were held quickly because of the urgency imposed by impending elections. Judges in the various courts were sharply divided on mathematical standards of equality and even on the question of whether the population principle should be applied to one or both houses. Some courts deferred to decisions on apportionment made at the polls; others scorned them as irrelevant. The courts sometimes approved imperfect plans as temporary expedients for the next election until a subsequent legislature could do better, but occasionally the courts ordered alternative plans put into effect.

In June, 1964, the Supreme Court handed down decisions affecting apportionment in fifteen states and providing authoritative answers to many of the unanswered questions. In every case, the result of the Court's decision was to strike down apportionments that gave too little weight to population or to uphold judicially imposed apportionments that had been challenged by rural interests. The Court's views were most fully expressed in the Alabama case, *Reynolds* v. *Sims.* In the *Reynolds* decision, the Court articulated a clear goal for the state: it must "make an honest and good faith effort to construct districts, in both houses of its legislature, as nearly of equal population as is practicable." At the same time, the Court did not require "mathematical exactness or precision." The Court explicitly rejected any analogy to the federal system as irrelevant, and it declared that there was "no constitutional difference" between the two houses and that consequently both must be apportioned according to population. It upheld the principle of periodic reapportionment, approved the decennial period as a reasonable one, and indicated that it would look with suspicion on any plan for less frequent reapportionment.[25] The Court refused to give any weight to popular votes on apportionment: "A citizen's constitutional rights can hardly be infringed simply because a majority of the people chose to do so."[26] The Court refused to establish any precise mathematical tests for population equality, but suggested that certain circumstances might permit differences in standards from state to state. In particular, the Court approved the use of political subdivisions (cities and counties) as a basis for forming district boundaries but warned that in some states, rigid adherence to existing political boundaries would not be possible because it would result in "total subversion of the equal-population principle."[27]

Although the *Baker* case pertained to state legislatures, the Court's decision that apportionment cases were justiciable led to the filing of a number of suits challenging congressional districts. In February, 1964, in the case of *Wesberry* v. *Sanders,* which involved Georgia's congressional districts, the Supreme Court decided that the "one man—one vote" principle applied to Congress. In a decision that reviewed in some detail speeches made at the Constitutional Convention and in the debates over ratification, the Court based its conclusion on the intent of the framers that the House should be the branch of Congress in which the people were directly and equally represented. The Court acknowledged that "it may not be possible to draw congressional districts with mathematical precision" but insisted that "that is no excuse for ignoring our Constitution's plain objective" of equal representation in the House.[28]

The judicial decisions regarding reapportionment stirred up little response from an apathetic public. There was no evidence of the bitter public resentment that had greeted the decisions on desegregation or prayer in the public schools. In the urban areas, there was strong support from the newspapers and other leaders of public opinion. In states where referendums were held on constitutional amendments involving apportionment, there was no consistent pattern of voting; and it appeared that many of the voters had little understanding of their stake in legislative representation.

Despite the lack of public interest, the *Reynolds* decision provoked vigorous criticism from many congressmen and state legislators. At both the congressional and state legislative levels, a series of efforts to reverse or limit the effects of that decision came close to success but in the end fell short. During the 1964 session of Congress, the House passed a bill that would have withdrawn all jurisdiction over apportionment from both the federal district courts and the Supreme Court. The Senate rejected that drastic approach, but it gave serious consideration to a proposal directing federal courts to delay implementation of the apportionment decisions in order to prevent disruption of state election machinery, a proposal that failed because of a prolonged filibuster by northern liberal Democrats.

During the Eighty-ninth Congress, the debate continued, with attention focused on a constitutional amendment proposed by Senator Dirksen that was designed to ease the rigid requirements of the *Reynolds* decision. There were several versions of the Dirksen amendment, but most provided that one house of a state legislature might be apportioned on the basis of geography and political subdivisions as well as population, if such an apportionment plan were approved by the voters as an alternative to a strict population plan. The Dirksen amendment won a majority vote in the Senate in both 1965 and 1966, but both times it fell seven votes short of the two-thirds required for a constitutional amendment. Northern liberal Democrats continued to be the strongest opponents.[29]

In an effort to force some form of congressional action, the supporters of the Dirksen amendment organized a campaign to get state legislatures to pass petitions asking Congress to call a constitutional convention for the purpose of passing the Dirksen amendment or something approximating it. Congress is supposed to call a constitutional convention if two-thirds of the legislatures (thirty-four) adopt petitions. By early 1967, such petitions had been adopted by thirty-two state legislatures, twenty-six of which were under court order to reapportion at the time they adopted the amendment. Although the supporters of the Dirksen amendment came within two of the required number of states, they were clearly losing in the race with the courts. Reapportionment was changing the urban-rural balance so rapidly that many legislatures which had originally petitioned for the Dirksen amendment would have been unlikely to ratify it even if Congress had approved it. Finally, Dirksen's death in 1969 put an end to the campaign to curtail the judicial reform of apportionment standards.

Standards of Population Equality

In the 1964 *Reynolds* decision, Chief Justice Warren, speaking for the Court, declared that legislative districts must be "as nearly of equal population as is practicable." But he also said: "We realize that it is a practical impossibility to arrange legislative districts so that each one has an identical number of residents, or citizens, or voters. Mathematical exactness or precision is hardly a workable constitutional requirement."[30] The Court has never been willing to specify, in percentage or absolute terms, how much deviation from perfect population equality it would permit, and some of its decisions during the 1960s created considerable uncertainty about the standards that it would enforce. In more recent decisions, the Court has established several clear guidelines for the states to follow:

1. The standards to be used in state legislative apportionment are more flexible than those required for congressional districting.[31]
2. In congressional cases the Court recognizes "no excuse for the failure to meet the objective of equal representation for equal numbers of people in congressional districting other than the practical impossibility of drawing equal districts with mathematical precision."[32]
3. In state legislative apportionment cases the states may legitimately take into account several relevant factors and interests other than mathematical equality, as part of a "rational state policy."[33]
4. Specifically, "a State can rationally consider according political subdivisions some independent representation in at least one body of the state legislature, as long as the basic standard of equality of population among districts is maintained. ... And a State may legitimately desire to construct districts along political subdivision lines to deter the possibilities of gerrymandering."[34]

This means that the states can follow the common practice of basing legislative district lines on boundaries of counties, cities, and other subdivisions, although exceptions will have to be made to avoid serious disparities in the population of districts. It also means that state apportionment plans passed by legislatures cannot be successfully challenged in the courts simply because it is possible to devise a plan that comes closer to mathematical equality in the population of districts. It seems likely that in the years ahead the final decisions on apportionment will be made more often in legislative than in judicial bodies. In fact the Supreme Court has emphasized that it does not favor apportionment standards "so difficult to satisfy that the reapportionment task is recurringly removed from legislative hands and performed by federal courts who themselves must make the political decisions necessary to formulate a plan. ... That the Court was not deterred by the hazards of the political thicket when it undertook to adjudicate the reapportionment cases does not mean that it should become bogged down in a vast, intractable apportionment slough, particularly when there is little, if anything, to be accomplished by doing this."[35]

Questions of Minority Representation

When the Supreme Court decided, in the *Baker* case, that apportionment laws were subject to judicial scrutiny under the equal protection clause, Justice Frankfurter, in a dissenting opinion, warned that the Court was being asked "to choose among competing bases of representation—ultimately, really, among competing theories of political philosophy."[36] For a number of years the Court concentrated on defining standards for population equality of districts, and avoided more fundamental questions about the fairness of representational systems. In more recent years the Supreme Court and other judicial bodies have begun to grapple with the question of whether specific features of representative systems, notably gerrymandered districts and the use of multimembered districts, unconstitutionally discriminate against particular minorities. The groups most obviously handicapped by these methods are partisan and racial minorities. The courts have shown little interest in protecting voters who belong to minority parties, but they do show a growing interest in protecting those who belong to minority races.

The term *gerrymandering* can be defined in a variety of ways. We will use partisan gerrymandering to describe the tactic of drawing district boundaries in a way that minimizes the effective voting strength of the minority political party. Racial gerrymandering is the same tactic applied to a racial minority. In the past, partisan or racial gerrymandering often accompanied large population inequalities. But the elimination of these inequalities does not guarantee the elimination of gerrymandering.

Any single-member district system wastes votes, and more votes are usually wasted by the minority party. The purpose of any gerrymander carried out by the majority party is to waste as many votes of the minority party as possible. This can be done by splitting up areas of minority party strength among districts controlled by the majority party and/or creating a few districts which the minority party will carry by an overwhelming majority in order to assure majority party control—by smaller margins—of a large number of districts. Partisan gerrymandering is a hazardous strategy, one that is sometimes upset by rapidly changing political tides or highly mobile populations. Other factors that may discourage gerrymandering are the fear of retribution should the other party win a legislative majority and legislative norms that discourage blatant efforts to maximize partisan advantage.

A legislative majority may also use the strategy of gerrymandering to reduce the political effectiveness of a racial minority. It is possible for a white legislative majority to minimize the chances for election of black legislators, either by concentrating black voters in one or a few districts or by scattering them thinly among a number of districts that are predominantly white. If black voters are highly concentrated geographically, however, it may be difficult to avoid creating heavily black districts. Although black political leaders usually prefer a districting plan that creates the maximum possible number of districts with black majorities, black voters normally have considerable political power and sometimes elect black legislators in districts where they constitute no more than a large minority. In this sense the implications of racial and partisan gerrymandering are somewhat different.

It is often difficult to recognize gerrymandering in practice and to measure its effects precisely. It is much easier to understand the impact of multimember districts on minorities, whether partisan or racial, or any other kind. The mathematics of multimember districting was described briefly in Chapter 4. The larger the number of legislators elected at large in a district, the greater the impact of multimember districting. If a large metropolitan county chooses ten state legislators at large, and if a majority of the voters are white Democrats, they are likely to elect ten white, Democratic legislators. Black or Republican legislators are much more likely to be elected in such a county under a single-member district system, assuming some geographic concentration of voters belonging to those minorities. (It is worth recalling that no state except Illinois uses proportional representation in multimember districts.)

In some of the states that used multimember districts for metropolitan areas, the reapportionment laws passed in the 1960s drastically increased the number of legislators to be elected at large in those areas. One consequence was that the voters were burdened with a long list of candidates. In Cuyahoga County, Ohio, for example, there were often as many as a hundred candidates in the Democratic primary for the seventeen house seats chosen at large. Another consequence was that the increase in the number of seats in metropolitan counties only benefited the majority party and racial group in each of these counties. During the 1960s a number of states (including Michigan, Ohio, Colorado, Tennessee, Georgia, Texas, and Pennsylvania) replaced at-large elections with either smaller multimember or single-member districts. Nevertheless, in 1970 about one-half of the upper houses and two-thirds of the lower houses of legislatures made some use of multimember districts, although such districts seldom were used to choose more than two or three members. The proportion of legislators in all fifty states elected from multimember districts in 1970 was 29 percent in the state senates and 50 percent in the lower houses (higher percentages than applied in 1962).[37]

The Supreme Court has never directly ruled on the question of partisan gerrymandering in either congressional or legislative apportionment cases, although several lower courts have held that it is not an appropriate question for judicial determination.[38] Perhaps the clearest statement of the Supreme Court's attitude is found in a decision involving the Connecticut legislature in which political gerrymandering was charged. The Court recognized that, "Politics and political considerations are inseparable from districting and apportionment," and pointed out that the Court has not "attempted the impossible task of extirpating politics from what are the essentially political processes of the sovereign States."[39] On several occasions, beginning in 1965, the Supreme Court has acknowledged that the use of multimember districts might have the effect of underrepresenting or minimizing the voting strength of minority political parties, but the Court has rejected the argument that multimember districts are inherently discriminatory, and it has insisted that there must be proof that such a districting system has denied a party access to the political process.[40] In no case has the Court invalidated the use of multimember districts because of their discriminatory effects on minority parties.

The Supreme Court and other federal courts have been much more sensitive to the discriminatory effects of gerrymandering and multimember districts on racial minorities. In general this reflects a long-standing concern of federal courts —the prevention of efforts by state and local governments to undermine or dilute the voting rights of black voters, a concern that was first extended to districting matters in the 1960 *Gomillion* decision, cited earlier. More specifically, the federal courts have dealt with these issues in part because Section 5 of the 1965 Voting Rights Act provides that state or local governments in a number of southern states must submit changes in voting laws or procedures for approval to the United States Attorney General or to the United States District Court for the District of Columbia, for judgment on whether they are racially discriminatory in purpose or effect.[41] In a 1969 case the Supreme Court held that multimember districts were subject to scrutiny under that law because they might have a discriminatory effect.[42]

Although the Supreme Court has not dealt directly with the question of racial gerrymandering of single-member districts, there have been several cases in which other federal courts (or in some cases the Attorney General) have invalidated state apportionment laws because of a judgment that boundary lines were drawn with the intent and the effect of minimizing the voting strength of black voters.[43]

There have been a larger number of decisions by the Supreme Court and other courts regarding the effects of multimember districts on racial (black and Mexican-American) minorities. Without going into the complicated details of these cases, we can list several of the major conclusions that can be drawn from them:

1. The courts are most likely to reject the use of multimember districts when they are convinced that their use is part of a pattern of deliberate efforts to minimize the voting strength of racial minorities.
2. The courts are most likely to invalidate multimember district plans if it can be shown that these, perhaps in combination with other electoral devices and political practices, have the effect of excluding racial minorities from full participation in the political process. This was the reason given by the Supreme Court for invalidating multimember legislative districts in several

counties in Texas where they discriminated against black and Mexican-Americans.[44]

3. Even if there is no evidence of discrimination against racial or political minorities, federal district courts should avoid imposing multimember districts on state legislatures, particularly if single-member districts have been traditionally used.[45]

It remains true that the Supreme Court has never grappled with the fundamental issues of legislative representation. But it has acknowledged that the principle of "one person, one vote" is inadequate to deal with all aspects of inequality in voting for the legislature. It has recognized that some districting methods may have both the intent and the effect of diluting the effective vote of racial minorities. Spurred on by Congress, which passed the 1965 Voting Rights Act, the federal courts have forced the legislatures of several states to change both district boundaries and at-large multimember districts when it could be proved that these undermined effective participation by racial minorities in the political process.

LEGISLATIVE RESPONSE TO JUDICIAL DECISIONS

Implementation of Judicial Decisions

The previous rulings of courts on the constitutionality of legislation are carefully studied by legislators who are trying to write new laws that will stand up under judicial scrutiny. State legislators may pay attention not only to decisions of the state court but also to federal court rulings on similar legislation passed in other states if federal constitutional issues are involved. Sometimes a court will not only explain why provisions of a law are unconstitutional but will also provide guidelines that will help the legislature to achieve its objectives by constitutional means. Just as judges often have difficulty interpreting the meaning of statutes, legislators often have difficulty interpreting the meanings of judicial decisions and their implications for bills pending in the legislature. Both supporters and opponents of bills frequently cite the opinions of judges to support their arguments. During debates over apportionment legislation, legislators have paid particular attention to the standards established by federal and state courts, and arguments over these standards have often overshadowed debate over the merits of such legislation.

Some of the most important decisions of the courts, and particularly of the United States Supreme Court, have charted new policies for the national and state governments. Two obvious examples are the decisions requiring the desegregation of schools and other public facilities and voiding restrictions on the political rights of racial minorities. Although such decisions often arouse strong opposition from some legislators and interest groups, they also generate strong support from others. If the supporters of such court decisions are strong enough, they may be able to pass legislation that implements and supports the policies initiated by the judicial branch. Congress in recent years has adopted amendments to appropriations bills denying funds to state institutions and agencies, such as school districts, that have failed to desegregate their facilities. The consequence of such legislation has been more rapid compliance with the spirit of the Supreme Court's desegregation mandate than would have resulted from judicial decisions alone. During the late 1950s and 1960s Congress passed a series of laws that had the effect of eliminating the remaining barriers to voting in southern states by black citizens. The Supreme Court had led the way in removing some of these obstacles at a time when Congress was unwilling to act. After the Court provided the impetus and set the goals for political equality, Congress passed legislation that was extensive and effective enough to achieve the goal.

Efforts to Reverse Judicial Decisions

A controversial judicial decision may trigger efforts in a legislative body to evade or overrule the decision. These efforts may take a number of forms, depending on the nature of the decision and the political strength and tactics of the opponents. If a judicial decision interprets the meaning of a law in a fashion that a legislative majority believes is wrong, the legislature can pass a new law to clarify its intentions and correct the mistake. Between 1945 and 1957 one study showed that Congress passed new laws that had the effect of overruling the Supreme Court's interpretation of statutes in twenty-one instances.[46] In a 1944 decision, for example, the Supreme Court ruled that insurance companies operate in interstate commerce and are therefore subject to the provisions of the federal antitrust law. Because of the political strength of insurance companies and a long-established pattern of state regulation of insurance, Congress reversed the decision and made it clear that insurance companies were exempt from antitrust legislation.

During the 1950s and 1960s the Supreme Court handed down a number of decisions, particularly those enlarging the rights of defendants in criminal cases and overruling the conviction of Communist leaders, that provoked strenuous opposition and led to prolonged efforts in Congress to pass legislation reversing or modifying several of the decisions. The House on three separate occasions passed a bill to overturn the 1957 *Yates* decision (described earlier) by broadening the meaning of the term "organize" in the Smith Act, and it finally became law in 1962 when the Senate also passed the bill. There were unsuccessful efforts in Congress to reverse the *Nelson* decision and make it clear that Congress had not preempted the field of sedition. Some of the Supreme Court decisions expanding the procedural rights of defendants in criminal cases have pertained to federal courts and others have covered cases in state courts. The procedures in federal criminal cases can be changed by congressional legislation, and there have been many attempts to do so. In 1957, after a protracted battle, Congress passed legislation that modified but did not completely reverse the Court's decision in the *Jencks* case concerning the right of the defense to examine written statements made by witnesses for the government.[47] Several Supreme Court decisions, particularly those in the *Mallory* case (1957) and the *Miranda* case (1966), concerned a prisoner's rights during interrogation by police and his right to prompt arraignment. There were repeated efforts to reverse the effects of the *Mallory* case, with such bills passing one house or the other on several occasions. Finally, in 1968 Congress passed the Omnibus Crime Control and Safe Streets Act, which included a section designed to modify these decisions and permit a defendant's confession to be used against him in a federal criminal case under conditions less rigid than those that the Supreme Court had imposed.[48]

When the courts declare a federal or state law to be unconstitutional, it is more difficult for Congress or a state legislature to reverse the effects of the decision, but it may not be impossible. Sometimes it may be possible to accomplish the same goal by changing the wording of legislation or basing the new law on a different section of the Constitution. One authority has concluded that in almost one-third of the cases where provisions of congressional legislation have been declared unconstitutional, "Congress passed legislation that has had the effect of reversing the Court either totally or in substantial measure."[49] During the New Deal, when the Supreme Court was striking down a number of the most important parts of President Roosevelt's program, Congress was kept busy trying to find legislative alternatives that might accomplish the objectives of the original legislation. Most of these alternatives were upheld by the Court, but only after changes in its membership led to basic changes in the direction of its policies.

The prolonged struggle over child-labor legislation provides a classic example of congressional efforts to find means of accomplishing its objectives that would meet judicial standards of constitutionality. In 1916 Congress passed a law restricting child labor and used the interstate commerce power as the basis for the legislation, but two years later the Supreme Court declared the law unconstitutional. In 1919 Congress tried to accomplish the same objective by imposing a 10 percent tax on the profits of companies violating federal standards for child labor. In 1922 the Supreme Court invalidated this law. Congress adopted a new strategy in 1924 when it passed a constitutional amendment authorizing Congress to regulate or prohibit child labor, but the amendment was not adopted by enough states to become part of the Constitution. During the New Deal Congress included child-labor provisions in the National Industrial Recovery Act, which was declared invalid by the Court in 1935. Congress finally achieved its purpose when the Supreme Court in 1941 upheld the Fair Labor Standards Act of 1938.[50]

Legislative bodies may try to evade the effects of court decisions by trying to do indirectly what the courts will not permit them to do directly. After the Supreme Court ruled in 1927 that the Texas "white primary" law (which barred blacks from participating) was unconstitutional, the Texas legislature tried to get around the decision by authorizing the state Democratic party to prescribe qualifications for party membership; but the Supreme Court eventually decided (in 1945) that the state party could not ban black voters from the primary. South Carolina tried to evade the effects of this decision by repealing all statutory references to state primaries, but a federal court invalidated that device as well.[51] The poll tax and the literacy test for voting in some Southern states were often legislative devices to discourage voting by blacks after more direct devices had been rejected by the courts on constitutional grounds. In the long battle over school desegregation, a number of states tried a variety of legislative tactics in an effort to preserve the substance of segregation. One example that was eventually invalidated by the courts was the use of "private schools" subsidized directly or indirectly by the state or local government as a substitute or supplement for public schools.

Another example, unrelated to racial questions, illustrates the use of indirect legislative tactics to reverse the effect of a judicial decision. In the 1960s Kentucky educational groups that were seeking stronger local financial support for schools challenged the low and uneven local property *assessment rates* in court. The state Court of Appeals declared that the Kentucky constitution required property to be assessed at 100 percent of its actual value. Since property in most counties was assessed at less than one-third of its value, this decision would have made possible vastly increased levels of support for education in districts, without any increase in the *tax rate* which was limited by the constitution. But the Kentucky legislature blocked any increase in the revenue available for schools (with a few exceptions) by adopting a law requiring that *tax rates* be rolled back far enough in each school district so that the total revenue produced would not be greater than that produced under the lower *assessment rate.* The opponents of larger spending for education had won back in the legislature what they had lost in the courts.

The surest way to reverse a court decision declaring a law unconstitutional is to amend the constitution. It is also likely to be the most difficult, because in Congress and in most states constitutional amendments require an extraordinary legislative majority and ratification beyond the legislative branch (by state legislatures for national constitutional amendments and by the voters for state amendments). If the issue is a controversial one, it is likely to be difficult to overcome the obstacles to constitutional amendment. Several amendments to the United States Constitution were adopted in reaction to judicial determinations that congressional legislation was unconstitutional. The Eleventh Amendment overturned a 1793 decision ruling that states could be sued by citizens of other states. The Thirteenth and Fourteenth Amendments after the Civil War had the incidental effect of negating the *Dred Scott* decision. In 1895 the Supreme Court ruled that Congress could not adopt an income tax. Repeated efforts to override this decision finally produced the Sixteenth Amendment in 1913. The 1970 Voting Rights Act provided that the voting age should be lowered to eighteen for all national, state, and local elections, but later that year the Supreme Court ruled, in a divided opinion, that Congress had the authority to lower the voting age only for national elections. In 1971 Congress passed the Twenty-sixth Amendment to lower the voting age to eighteen for all elections, and the required three-fourths of the state legislatures passed the amendment in record time.

Several of the most controversial Supreme Court decisions in recent years have provoked vigorous but unsuccessful efforts to pass constitutional amendments. The Supreme Court's decision in 1962 and 1963 cases that prayers and Bible reading in the public schools are unconstitutional provoked a public reaction that was stronger than that in any other modern case except for that on school desegregation. Congressmen were bombarded with mail demanding that they take action to restore prayer to the schools. During the Eighty-eighth Congress almost 150 resolutions were introduced proposing constitutional amendments to accomplish that goal, and the House Judiciary Committee held extensive hearings. The hearings demonstrated that there was also strong opposition to such an amendment, with most leaders of major church groups speaking out against it.

The House committee, after six weeks of hearings, took no action. In 1966, however, the Senate took up an amendment by Senator Dirksen to permit "voluntary prayer" in the schools. The proposal won a majority in the Senate, but it fell short of the required two-thirds vote, and its failure signaled the end of serious efforts to adopt a school-prayer amendment.[52]

Earlier we described Senator Dirksen's extensive campaign first to delay and then to modify the effect of the Supreme Court's decisions in state legislative apportionment cases. It was the most elaborate campaign in recent years for such a constitutional amendment, and it came close to succeeding. If it had succeeded, it would have modified, if not completely blocked, massive reapportionment. Although there was little reason to believe that the average citizen was either seriously concerned about the Court's policy on apportionment or was opposed to it, the effort to modify that policy had broad support in both Congress and the state legislatures. Senator Dirksen led a two-pronged campaign on behalf of his amendment to permit one branch of a state legislature to be apportioned on the basis of factors other than population. His amendment came to a vote in the Senate in both 1965 and 1966, and each time nearly got the necessary two-thirds vote. At the same time the number of state legislatures petitioning Congress to call a constitutional convention on the Dirksen amendment continued to grow until it reached thirty-two, two less than the required number. Dirksen expected that the pressure from state legislatures would force Congress either to call such a convention or to adopt the amendment itself. In the last analysis the campaign fell short because a substantial minority in Congress and legislators of some of the most urbanized states remained opposed to it.[53]

CONGRESSIONAL EFFORTS TO CONTROL OR RESTRICT THE COURT

When decisions of the judicial branch arouse strong opposition among legislators, it is not surprising that they should make efforts not only to reverse specific decisions but also to change the course of the court's decisions or to limit its power. Conflicts between the legislative and judicial branches of government are as common and probably as inevitable as conflicts between either of these branches and the executive. We will concentrate our attention on congressional efforts to control the Supreme Court because these are more familiar to students and because Congress has more constitutional authority over the personnel and jurisdiction of the federal courts than most state legislatures have over state courts.

The Constitution provides for "one Supreme Court" and "such inferior courts as the Congress may from time to time ordain and establish." Congress has established district courts, courts of appeals, and several specialized courts. Congress also has the authority to determine the size of the various federal courts and to determine the appellate jurisdiction of the Supreme Court and the jurisdiction of other courts, in addition to the Senate's power to approve the appointment of federal judges and the rarely used congressional power of impeachment.

Control over Appointments

One of the most direct ways of influencing the courts is to influence the choice of judges. Several times during the nineteenth century the size of the Supreme Court was increased or decreased for political or policy reasons. In 1937 President Franklin Roosevelt proposed that the size of the Supreme Court be increased by providing an additional justice for each of the justices then on the Court who was over seventy. It was a deliberate effort to "pack the Court" with new members who would outvote the conservative majority and put an end to the series of decisions that had limited the federal government's authority to regulate the economy. Although a majority of senators and representatives supported most of the New Deal program, a majority was not willing to pack the Court, and Roosevelt's effort failed.

The Senate can influence the policy directions of the federal courts by approving or rejecting presidential nominees to the judiciary. Members of the Judiciary Committee have sometimes questioned prospective justices about their viewpoints, but nominees have usually been unwilling to commit themselves on issues likely to come before the Court. From time to time, a judicial nominee—usually nominated to the Supreme Court—has aroused opposition from those senators who disagreed with his viewpoint or ideological orientation.

One of the most distinguished justices in the history of the Court, Louis Brandeis, who was appointed by Woodrow Wilson, was vigorously opposed by conservative Republicans and was confirmed only after long delay and a narrow vote in the Judiciary Committee.[54] Liberal senators defeated one of Herbert Hoover's nominees to the Supreme Court, John J. Parker, because he was too conservative. In 1968 the Senate failed to confirm President Johnson's nomination of Justice Abe Fortas as Chief Justice to replace the retiring Earl Warren. (The President withdrew the nomination after the Senate failed to pass a cloture motion that was necessary to halt a filibuster on the nomination.) Some of the opposition came from Republicans who expected Richard Nixon to be elected and wanted to give him the chance (which he got) to choose a chief justice, and some senators raised ethical questions about Fortas's behavior as a justice. But some of the opposition came from conservatives who were critical of the policies of the Warren Court and expected Fortas to try to continue those policies.[55] Nixon's nominee for Chief Justice, Warren Burger, was confirmed with no difficulty. But after Fortas resigned under pressure from the Court, two men whom Nixon nominated to replace him—Clement Haynsworth, Jr., and Harrold Carswell—were rejected by the Senate, and in both cases much of the opposition came from liberal senators who disagreed with the conservative political philosophies of the nominees.[56] Haynsworth and Carswell were the only nominees, other than John Parker, to be rejected by the Senate since 1900.

Senators play a major role in the selection of other federal judges (below the Supreme Court level), but the criteria for selection have little to do with judicial policy. When a vacancy occurs, the senators from the state where the vacancy exists submit names to the Justice Department for nomination. A senator belonging to the President's party is particularly influential, but a senator of the other party may have what amounts to a veto on the selection. Senators get advice from political leaders and lawyers in a state and pay particular attention to the political and legal qualifications of those who are suggested. The advice of senators is usually followed if they can agree on a candidate who belongs to the President's party and who has been declared qualified by a committee of the American Bar Association. When a nomination reaches the Senate Judiciary Committee, it is normally reviewed and approved in perfunctory fashion by a subcommittee and the full committee, with questions seldom being raised about either the qualifications or viewpoint of the candidate.[57] Legislative influence over the selection of judges at the state level is minimal. Many states elect judges; in those where judges are appointed, the governor and advisory committees of lawyers dominate the selection process.

It is possible for federal or state judges to be impeached, but it rarely occurs. At the federal level, only nine judges have been impeached by the House and only four convicted by the Senate, with the last conviction occurring in 1936. Data on impeachments at the state level indicate that only a handful of judges have been convicted in recent years.[58] Impeachment is not a method for settling legislative-judicial disputes over policy, but a device for removing judges who have demonstrated gross incompetence or dishonesty.

Control over the Scope of Judicial Jurisdiction

Because Congress has authority over the appellate jurisdiction of the Supreme Court, it is possible for Congress to remove particular subject-matter areas from the Court's jurisdiction. Efforts to do so have been common in Congress when a series of Court decisions in a particular area has aroused strong opposition. Over a century ago, in 1868, Congress removed the Supreme Court's appellate jurisdiction under the Habeas Corpus Act; the action was taken while the Court was considering a case brought under that act, and its purpose was to prevent a decision by the Court that might have undermined the Reconstruction policies of Congress.[59]

There have been a number of recent efforts, none successful, to deprive the Supreme Court of jurisdiction over specific areas in which its decisions have been unpopular with some members of Congress. One of the best examples is a bill introduced by Senator Jenner in 1957 that would have removed the Court's appellate jurisdiction over five distinct areas that were directly or indirectly related to the problem of subversion and Communist party membership. After some modification, the bill was narrowly defeated in the Senate.[60] Early in the controversy over the Court's reapportionment decisions, in 1964, the House passed a bill that would have withdrawn from the entire federal court system all jurisdiction over state legislative apportionment. The bill never became law, and the Senate never gave serious consideration to such a drastic step.[61]

Congress's authority to curb the appellate jurisdiction of the Supreme Court would seem to be potentially one of its most powerful weapons in any conflict with the Court.[62] It is a weapon that can be applied selectively, so that the Court's authority can be restricted in precisely those fields where its decisions have met with congressional disfavor. If this is such a potent weapon, why has it so seldom been used, particularly in recent years when so many of the Court's decisions have been under attack? One explanation is that there is widespread respect in Congress for the Court as an institution. There is a recognition that the selective withdrawal of jurisdiction would weaken the Court's independence and might lead to efforts in the future to remove the Court's jurisdiction in other fields. Moreover, some of the most controversial decisions of the Court have many staunch defenders among congressmen. Their votes, along with the votes of those who are concerned about maintaining judicial independence, have been sufficient to preserve the Court's jurisdictional authority.[63] In 1954 the Senate passed a constitutional amendment (which died in the House) that would have eliminated congressional authority to control the size or the jurisdiction of the Supreme Court. Although Congress has not been willing to surrender such power over the Court, it has demonstrated great caution in recent years, as it did during the New Deal period, about exercising that power.

NOTES

1. See David B. Truman, *The Governmental Process* (New York, 1951), chaps. 9, 11, 15.

2. Walter F. Murphy and C. Herman Pritchett, *Courts, Judges, and Politics* (New York, 1961), p. 401. See also the comments of Justice Felix Frankfurter on interpreting statutes, from the *Record of the Association of the Bar of the City of New York* 213 (1947), included in Murphy and Pritchett, *Courts, Justices, and Politics,* pp. 407–412.

3. Walter F. Murphy, *Congress and the Court* (Chicago, 1962), p. 103.

4. Ibid., p. 85.

5. William J. Keefe and Morris S. Ogul, *The American Legislative Process* (Englewood Cliffs, N.J., 1973, 3d ed.), pp. 448–449.

6. Ibid., pp. 451–452; Oliver P. Field, *Judicial Review of Legislation in Ten Selected States* (Bloomington, Ind., 1943).

7. Herbert Jacob and Kenneth Vines, eds., *Politics in the American States* (Boston, 1965, 1st ed.), p. 253.

8. *Powell* v. *McCormack,* 395 U.S. 486 (1969). See "Comments on *Powell* v. *McCormack,*" *UCLA Law Review* 17 (1969):1–191.

9. *Bond* v. *Floyd,* 385 U.S. 116 (1966).

10. *New York Times,* Jan. 21, Feb. 1, Feb. 19, 1975.

11. *McGrain* v. *Daugherty,* 273 U.S. 135 at 174 (1927).

12. *Watkins* v. *United States,* 354 U.S. 178 (1957); *Sweezy* v. *New Hampshire,* 354 U.S. 234 (1957).

13. *Watkins* v. *United States,* 354 U.S. 178 at 187 (1957).

14. See especially *Barenblatt* v. *United States,* 360 U.S. 109 (1959); *Braden* v. *United States,* 365 U.S. 431 (1961); *Yellin* v. *United States,* 374 U.S. 109 (1963).

15. Technically, *apportionment* refers to the apportioning of seats among existing political units, such as states or counties, and *districting* means the creation of districts, whether they are formed by combinations of units, within units, or without regard to existing units. In common usage, the term *apportionment* has been used more often for state legislatures, and the term *districting,* for Congress.

16. Robert G. Dixon, Jr., *Democratic Representation* (New York, 1968), pp. 589–628.

17. 369 U.S. 186.

18. 377 U.S. 533 at 576.

19. 376 U.S. 1 at 7–8.

20. 328 U.S. 549 at 553–554.

21. 364 U.S. 339.

22. The cases leading up to *Baker* v. *Carr* are carefully analyzed in Dixon, *Democratic Representation,* chap. 5; and Anthony Lewis, "Legislative Apportionment and the Federal Courts," *Harvard Law Review* 71 (1958):1057–1098.

23. For background to the case see the article by Wilder Crane, "Tennessee: Inertia and the Courts," in *The Politics of Reapportionment,* ed. Malcolm E. Jewell (New York, 1965), pp. 314–325.

24. *Baker* v. *Carr,* 369 U.S. 186 at 237.

25. 377 U.S. 533 at 571–584.

26. *Lucas* v. *Colorado General Assembly,* 377 U.S. 713 at 736–737.

27. 377 U.S. 533 at 578–581.

28. 376 U.S. 1 at 7–8.

29. For a full description of the congressional efforts, see Dixon, *Democratic Representation,* chaps. 15 and 16.

30. 377 U.S. 533 at 568, 577.

31. *Mahan* v. *Howell,* 93 S.Ct. 979 at 983.

32. Ibid. at 984. See also *Kirkpatrick* v. *Preisler,* 394 U.S. 526, and *Wells* v. *Rockefeller,* 394 U.S. 542.

33. *Gaffney* v. *Cummings,* 37 L Ed 2d 298 at 305, 309.

34. *Reynolds* v. *Sims,* 377 U.S. 533 at 580–581, cited in *Mahan* v. *Howell,* 93 S. Ct. 979 at 983–984.

35. *Gaffney* v. *Cummings,* 37 L Ed 2d 298 at 310.

36. 369 U.S. 186 at 300.

37. See Paul T. David and Ralph Eisenberg, *State Legislative Redistricting* (Chicago, 1962), p. 20; 1970 data from unpublished material provided by the Citizens Conference on State Legislatures.

38. For excellent analyses of gerrymandering as a political issue, see Dixon, *Democratic Representation,* chap. 18; and Gordon E. Baker, "Gerrymandering: Privileged Sanctuary or Next Judicial Target?" in *Reapportionment in the 1970s,* ed. Nelson W. Polsby (Berkeley and Los Angeles, 1971), pp. 121–141.

39. *Gaffney* v. *Cummings,* 37 L Ed 2d 298 at 312, 313.

40. See *Fortson* v. *Dorsey,* 379 U.S. 433 at 439; and *Whitcomb* v. *Chavis,* 403 U.S. 124 at 159–160.

41. For analyses of decisions under this act, see Armand Derfner, "Multi-Member Districts and Black Voters," *Black Law Journal* 2 (1972):120; and Stanley A. Halpin, Jr., and Richard L. Engstrom, "Racial Gerrymandering and Southern State Legislative Redistricting: Attorney General Determinations Under the Voting Rights Act," *Journal of Public Law* 22 (1973):37.

42. *Allen* v. *State Board of Elections,* 393 U.S. 544.

43. See Halpin and Engstrom, "Racial Gerrymandering and Southern State Legislative Redistricting."

44. *White* v. *Regester,* 37 L Ed 2d 314 at 324–326.

45. See *Connor* v. *Johnson,* 402 U.S. 690, and *Chapman* v. *Meier,* 43 *Law Week* 4199.

46. "Congressional Reversal of Supreme Court Decisions, 1945–1957," *Harvard Law Review* 71 (1958):1326, 1336.

47. Murphy, *Congress and the Courts,* chap. 6.

48. Congressional Quarterly, *Congress and the Nation, 1965–1968,* II:323–326.

49. Henry J. Abraham, *The Judicial Process* (New York, 1968, 2d ed.), p. 334.

50. *Hammer* v. *Dagenhart,* 247 U.S. 251 (1918); *Bailey* v. *Drexel Furniture Co.,* 259 U.S. 20 (1922); *Schechter Poultry Corp.* v. *United States,* 295 U.S. 495 (1935): *United States* v. *Darby Lumber Co.,* 312 U.S. 100 (1941).

51. See *Nixon* v. *Herndon,* 273 U.S. 536; *Smith* v. *Allright,* 321 U.S. 649; *Elmore* v. *Rice,* 72 F. Supp. 516 (1947).

52. *Congress and the Nation,* II: 410–411.

53. Dixon, *Democratic Representation,* chaps. 15 and 16.

54. Alpheus T. Mason, *Brandeis* (New York, 1946), chaps. 30 and 31.

55. The Fortas case is analyzed in John R. Schmidhauser and Larry L. Berg, *The Supreme Court and Congress* (New York, 1972), pp. 103–128.

56. For a detailed study of the Carswell case, see Richard Harris, *Decision* (New York, 1971).

57. Peter H. Schuck, *The Judiciary Committees* (Ralph Nader Congress Project, New York, 1975), chap. 10.

58. Abraham, *The Judicial Process,* pp. 43–45; George Brand, "Discipline of Judges," *American Bar Association Journal* 46 (1960):1315.

59. Murphy, *Congress and the Court,* pp. 38–40. Dixon discusses the question of whether Congress has authority to limit the Supreme Court's appellate jurisdiction in *Democratic Representation,* pp. 385–397.

60. Murphy, *Congress and the Court,* chaps. 7 and 9.

61. Dixon, *Democratic Representation,* pp. 385–397.

62. See C. Herman Pritchett, *Congress Versus the Supreme Court* (Minneapolis, 1961), p. 122.

63. See ibid., pp. 119–121; Murphy, *Congress and the Court,* chap. 11. For a study that compares congressional voting patterns on bills to reverse the Court's statutory interpretations and on bills to weaken the authority of the Court, see Schmidhauser and Berg, *The Supreme Court and Congress,* chap. 7.

Bibliography

The bibliography contains a selection of books and articles most likely to be of use to those who want to explore particular aspects of legislative processes and behavior in greater depth. The bibliography is not intended to be comprehensive, nor does it repeat all the references already listed in the footnotes. It is organized according to the structure of the volume. At the end of this bibliography, we have included (as Section VII) several citations for advanced students who wish to consult sources on legislative behavior research.

General

Few attempts have been made to include both national and state legislative bodies in a comprehensive study. The major substantial effort is William J. Keefe and Morris S. Ogul, *The American Legislative Process: Congress and the States,* 4th ed. (Englewood Cliffs, N.J., 1976). Two anthologies include materials about both Congress and state legislatures: John C. Wahlke and Heinz Eulau, eds., *Legislative Behavior* (Glencoe, Ill., 1959); and Samuel C. Patterson, ed., *American Legislative Behavior* (Princeton, N.J., 1968).

Among the older standard works on Congress are two by George B. Galloway, *The Legislative Process in Congress* (New York, 1953); and *History of the House of Representatives* (New York, 1961). The latter contains a wealth of historical information. More recent general studies are Randall B. Ripley, *Congress: Process and Policy* (New York, 1975); and Leroy N. Rieselbach, *Congressional Politics* (New York, 1973).

The seminal congressional analyses by Ralph K. Huitt are presented in Ralph K. Huitt and Robert L. Peabody, *Congress: Two Decades of Analysis* (New York, 1969). The emphasis in this study is upon the roles of congressional committee members and leaders. Charles L. Clapp, *The Congressman: His Work as He Sees It* (Washington, D.C., 1963); and Lewis A. Dexter, *The Sociology and Politics of Congress* (Chicago, 1969), deal with the congressional way of life. These two studies are based upon informal interviews with congressmen. A valuable assessment of the role of Congress in national policy is Gary Orfield, *Congressional Power: Congress and Social Change* (New York, 1975). For a very different kind of evaluation see Thomas P. Murphy, *The New Politics Congress* (Lexington, Mass., 1974). Two very useful books on the Senate are Donald R. Matthews, *U.S. Senators and Their World* (New York, 1960), which combines statistical and interview data, and Randall B. Ripley, *Power in the Senate* (New York, 1969), based upon group interviews with senators and staff members. Under the direction of Ralph K. Huitt, the Study of Congress project sponsored by the American Political Science Association has produced a useful set of studies, including: Lewis A. Froman, Jr., *The Congressional Process* (Boston, 1967); Charles O. Jones, *The Minority Party in Congress* (Boston, 1970); John F. Manley, *The Politics of Finance* (Boston, 1970); Randall B. Ripley, *Majority Party Leadership in*

Congress (Boston, 1969); John S. Saloma III, *Congress and the New Politics* (Boston, 1969); and Richard F. Fenno, Jr., *Congressmen in Committees* (Boston, 1973), and Robert L. Peabody, *Leadership in Congress,* (Boston, 1976). A good general treatment of Congress, with informative case studies, is provided by John F. Bibby and Roger H. Davidson, *On Capitol Hill,* 2d ed. (New York, 1972). Finally, there are a variety of anthologies that include a wide range of congressional studies, perhaps the most valuable of which are: Leroy N. Rieselbach, ed., *The Congressional System* (Belmont, Calif., 1970); Nelson W. Polsby, ed., *Congressional Behavior* (New York, 1971); Norman J. Ornstein, ed., *Congress in Change* (New York, 1975); and Theodore J. Lowi and Randall B. Ripley, eds., *Legislative Politics U.S.A.,* 3d ed. (Boston, 1973).

General works on state legislative politics include a brief study by Malcolm E. Jewell, *The State Legislature,* 2d ed. (New York, 1969); and the American Assembly collection edited by Alexander Heard, *State Legislatures in American Politics* (Englewood Cliffs, N.J., 1966). Evaluations of the state legislatures are made in the Citizens Conference on State Legislatures volume, *State Legislatures: An Evaluation of Their Effectiveness* (New York, 1971), and in James A. Robinson, ed., *State Legislative Innovation* (New York, 1973). For a small but slowly growing number of states, there are studies of the legislatures that are analytical and not merely descriptive and procedural. Among the best examples are William Buchanan, *Legislative Partisanship: The Deviant Case of California* (Berkeley and Los Angeles, 1963); William C. Havard and Loren P. Beth, *The Politics of Misrepresentation: Rural-Urban Conflict in the Florida Legislature* (Baton Rouge, La., 1962); Alan G. Hevesi, *Legislative Politics in New York State: A Comparative Analysis* (New York, 1975); Frank J. Sorauf, *Party and Representation: Legislative Politics in Pennsylvania* (New York, 1963); Gilbert Y. Steiner and Samuel K. Gove, *Legislative Politics in Illinois* (Urbana, Ill., 1960); Marvin Harder and Carolyn Ramphey, *The Kansas Legislature* (Lawrence, Kansas, 1972); and James B. Kessler, ed., *Empirical Studies of Indiana Politics* (Bloomington, Ind., 1970). An excellent comparative study of state legislative policy making is Wayne L. Francis, *Legislative Issues in the Fifty States* (Chicago, 1967).

Some of the most valuable sources of information on Congress are the publications of Congressional Quarterly, Inc.: its annual *Almanac,* its *Weekly Report,* its series of volumes on *Congress and the Nation,* and *The Guide to Congress* (1972). Also *The National Journal* provides detailed reporting of congressional activities. These publications provide data on roll calls, the legislative histories of bills, and current information in great detail on the organizational structure and political controversies in Congress. Two specialized journals focus on legislative analysis: *Legislative Studies Quarterly,* and the *Harvard Journal on Legislation.* Information about congressional districts can be found in the U.S. Bureau of Census publication, *Congressional District Data Book;* and biographical information about members of Congress can be found in the *Congressional Directory* and the *Biographical Directory of the American Congress.* Comprehensive descriptive data on state legislatures can be found in a number of the publications of the Council of State Governments; see especially, *The Book of the States,* issued biennially and containing many comparative tables on legislative organization. State blue books and manuals pertaining to legislative organization, rules, and elections vary widely in scope and detail. Their contents have been summarized by Charles Press and Oliver Williams in *State Manuals, Blue Books,* and *Election Results* (Berkeley, Calif., 1962).

There are a number of case studies concerning passage of legislation in Congress. Among the most informative are: Stephen K. Bailey, *Congress Makes a Law* (New York, 1950); Daniel M. Berman, *A Bill Becomes a Law,* 2d ed. (New York, 1966); Eugene Eidenberg and Roy D. Morey, *An Act of Congress* (New York, 1969); J. W. Anderson, *Eisenhower, Brownell, and the Congress* (University, Ala., 1964); Dennis W. Brezina and Allen Overmyer, *Congress in Action: The Environmental Education Act* (New York, 1974); Eric Redman, *The Dance of Legislation* (New York, 1973); Bruce I. Oppenheimer, *Oil and the Congressional Process* (Lexington, Mass., 1974).

I. The Legislative System

The only extensive investigation of American legislative systems remains the four-state study by John C. Wahlke et al., *The Legislative System* (New York, 1962). The most comprehensive exposition of notions about political representation is Hanna F. Pitkin, *The Concept of Representation* (Berkeley and Los Angeles, 1967).

The pioneering effort to analyze the development of legislatures is Polsby's work on the United States House of Representatives: Nelson W. Polsby, "The Institutionalization of the U.S. House of Representatives," *American Political Science Review* 62(1968):144–168. Interesting and useful historical studies of Congress include: George H. Haynes, *The Senate of the United States,* 2 vols. (Boston, 1938); and *The Election of Senators* (New York, 1906); Woodrow Wilson, *Congressional Government* (New York, 1956; first published in 1885); Paul D. Hasbrouck, *Party Government in the House of Representatives* (New York, 1927); Ralph V. Harlow, *The History of Legislative Methods in the Period before 1825* (New Haven, Conn., 1917); and the indispensable history of the House by DeAlva Stanwood Alexander, *History and Procedure of the House of Representatives* (Boston, 1916). The early development of Congress is analyzed by James S. Young, *The Washington Community, 1800–1828* (New York, 1966); and Rudolph M. Bell, *Party and Faction in American Politics: The House of Representatives, 1789–1801* (Westport, Conn., 1973). An excellent study of the late nineteenth-century House is Davis W. Brady, *Congressional Voting in a Partisan Era* (Lawrence, Kans., 1973).

OTHER SOURCES

Bogue, Allan G. "The Radical Voting Dimension in the U.S. Senate During the Civil War." *Journal of Interdisciplinary History* 3 (1973):449–474.

Clubok, Alfred B., and Wilensky, Norman M. "Family Relationships, Congressional Recruitment, and Political Modernization." *Journal of Politics* 31 (1969):1035–1062.

de Grazia, Alfred. *Public and Republic: Political Representation in America.* New York, 1951.

Eulau, Heinz. "Bases of Authority in Legislative Bodies: A Comparative Analysis." *Administrative Science Quarterly* 7 (1962):309–321.

———. "Changing Views of Representation." In *Contemporary Political Science: Toward Empirical Theory,* edited by Ithiel de Sola Pool. New York, 1967, pp. 53–85.

Patterson, Samuel C. "Party Opposition in the Legislature: The Ecology of Legislative Institutionalization." *Polity* 4 (1972):344–366.

Pennock, J. Roland, and Chapman, John W., eds. *Representation.* New York, 1968.

Polsby, Nelson W., Gallaher, Miriam, and Rundquist, Barry S. "The Growth of the Seniority System in the U.S. House of Representatives." *American Political Science Review* 63 (1969):787–807.

Prewitt, Kenneth, and Eulau, Heinz. "Political Matrix and Political Representation: Prolegomenon to a New Departure from an Old Problem." *American Political Science Review* 63 (1969):427–441.

Shade, William G., Hopper, Stanley D., Jacobson, David, and Moiles, Stephen E. "Partisanship in the United States Senate: 1869–1901." *Journal of Interdisciplinary History* 4 (1973):185–205.

Witmer, T. Richard. "The Aging of the House." *Political Science Quarterly* 79 (1964): 526–541.

II. Selection of Legislators

The study of the recruitment of legislators owes a great deal to the work of Donald R. Matthews. His *The Social Background of Political Decision-Makers* (Garden City, N.Y., 1954), and his analysis of U.S. Senators, in *U.S. Senators and Their World* (New York, 1970), still provide valuable material. An excellent analysis of the recruitment and role of lawyers in American state legislatures is David R. Derge, "The Lawyer as Decision-Maker in the American State Legislature," *Journal of Politics* 21 (1959):408–433. Samuel C. Patterson and G. R. Boynton, "Legislative Recruitment in a Civic Culture," *Social Science Quarterly* 59 (1969):243–263, compares recruitment of legislators in one state with other segments of the political elite. Lester G. Seligman, Michael R. King, Chong Lim Kim, and Roland E. Smith, in *Patterns of Recruitment* (Chicago, 1974), provide a thorough analysis of legislative recruitment in Oregon.

Compilations of the congressional vote can be found in: Cortez A. M. Ewing, *Congressional Elections, 1896–1944* (Norman, Okla., 1947); the biennial volumes of *America Votes* (Washington, D.C.), published since 1952; the *Congressional Directory;* and the *Congressional Quarterly Weekly Report.* Legislative election statistics are published in some states in manuals, in reports by the secretary of state, or in publications by state universities (which contain historical data). There have been few published analyses of American legislative elections. The most comprehensive work is Milton C. Cummings, Jr., *Congressmen and the Electorate* (New York, 1966). Two studies that use survey research data are Angus Campbell and Homer C. Cooper, *Group Differences in Attitudes and Votes: A Study of the 1954 Congressional Election* (Ann Arbor, Mich., 1956); and William N. McPhee and William A. Glaser, eds., *Public Opinion and Congressional Elections* (New York, 1962). Charles O. Jones has analyzed "The Role of the Campaign in Congressional Politics," in *The Electoral Process,* ed. Harmon Zeigler and Kent Jennings (Englewood Cliffs, N.J., 1966). The starting point for research in state legislative elections is V. O. Key, Jr., *American State Politics* (New York, 1956).

OTHER SOURCES

Eulau, Heinz, and Sprague, John D. *Lawyers in Politics: A Study in Professional Convergence.* Indianapolis, Ind., 1964.

Fishel, Jeff. *Party and Opposition.* New York, 1973.

Huckshorn, Robert J., and Spencer, Robert C. *The Politics of Defeat: Campaigning for Congress.* Amherst, Mass., 1971.

Kingdon, John W. *Candidates for Office: Beliefs and Strategies.* New York, 1968.

Kirkpatrick, Jeane J. *Political Women.* New York, 1974.

Kostroski, Warren L. "Party and Incumbency in Postwar Senate Elections: Trends, Patterns, and Models." *American Political Science Review* 67 (1973):1213–1234.

Leuthold, David A. *Electioneering in a Democracy.* New York, 1968.

McCann, James C. "Differential Mortality and the Formation of Political Elites: The Case of the U.S. House of Representatives." *American Sociological Review* 37 (1972): 689–700.

Mezey, Michael L. "Ambition Theory and the Office of Congressmen." *Journal of Politics* 32 (1970):563–579.

Mileur, Jerome M., and Sulzner, George T. *Campaigning for the Massachusetts Senate.* Amherst, Mass., 1974.

Ray, David. "Membership Stability in Three State Legislatures: 1893–1969." *American Political Science Review* 68 (1974):106–112.

Sullivan, John L., and O'Connor, Robert E. "Electoral Choice and Popular Control of Public Policy: The Case of the 1966 House Elections." *American Political Science Review* 61 (1972):1256–1268.

Tufte, Edward R. "Determinants of the Outcomes of Midterm Congressional Elections." *American Political Science Review* 69 (1975):812–826.

———. "The Relationship Between Seats and Votes in Two-Party Systems." *American Political Science Review* 62 (1973):540–554.

Werner, Emmy E. "Women in Congress: 1917–1964." *Western Political Quarterly* 19 (1966):16–30.

———. "Women in the State Legislatures." *Western Political Quarterly* 21 (1968): 40–50.

III. Legislative Organization and Procedure

Most of the works cited in the General section give a substantial amount of attention to this topic, especially the Study of Congress contribution by Lewis A. Froman, Jr. In addition to the studies by Jones and Ripley noted in the General section, party organization in Congress is the focus of Hugh A. Bone, *Party Committees and National Politics* (Seattle, Wash., 1958), especially pp. 126–196; and Charles O. Jones, *Party and Policymaking: The House Republican Policy Committee* (New Brunswick, N.J., 1964). Randall B. Ripley has contributed to knowledge about congressional party leadership in "The Party Whip Organization in the United States House of Representatives," *American Political Science Review* 58 (1964):561–576; *Party Leaders in the House of Representatives* (Washington, D.C., 1967); and *Power in the Senate* (New York, 1969). A classic study of Senate party leadership is Ralph K. Huitt, "Democratic Party Leadership in the Senate," *American Political Science Review* 55 (1961):333–344.

A number of general analyses of congressional committees are now available, including: George Goodwin, Jr., *The Little Legislatures: Committees of Congress* (Amherst, Mass., 1970); and William L. Morrow, *Congressional Committees* (New York, 1969). Barbara Hinckley has done an excellent study of congressional seniority in *The Seniority System in Congress* (Bloomington, Ind., 1971). The most comprehensive study of congressional staffing is Kenneth Kofmehl, *Professional Staffs of Congress* (West Lafayette, Ind., 1962). Of the several studies dealing with the legislative council movement in the states, the best analytical volume is by William J. Siffin, *The Legislative Council in the American States* (Bloomington, Ind., 1959).

Since 1959, Charles B. Brownson, a former congressman, has compiled and edited an annual volume on congressional staffs, the *Congressional Staff Directory,* which contains biographical material on key congressional staff personnel, as well as a great deal of detailed information on the personnel and organization of committee and member staffs.

OTHER SOURCES

Abram, Michael, and Cooper, Joseph. "The Rise of Seniority in the House of Representatives." *Polity* 1 (1968):52–85.

Bullock, Charles S. III. "Committee Transfers in the United States House of Representatives." *American Political Science Review* 35 (1973):85–120.

———. "Freshmen Committee Assignments and Re-election in the United States House of Representatives." *American Political Science Review* 61 (1972):996–1007.

Chaffey, Douglas C., and Jewell, Malcolm E. "Selection and Tenure of State Legislative Party Leaders: A Comparative Analysis." *Journal of Politics* 34 (1972):1278–1286.

Deckard, Barbara. "State Party Delegations in the U.S. House of Representatives: A Comparative Study of Group Cohesion." *Journal of Politics* 34 (1972):199–222.

Dodd, Lawrence C. "Committee Integration in the Senate: A Comparative Analysis." *Journal of Politics* 34 (1972):1135–1171.

Eulau, Heinz. "The Informal Organization of Decisional Structures in Small Legislative Bodies." *Midwest Journal of Political Science* 13 (1969):341–366.

Fiellin, Alan. "The Group Life of a State Delegation in the House of Representatives." *Western Political Quarterly* 23 (1970):305–320.

Froman, Lewis A., Jr., and Ripley, Randall B. "Conditions for Party Leadership: The Case of the House Democrats." *American Political Science Review* 59 (1965):52–63.

Hinckley, Barbara. "Congressional Leadership Selection and Support: A Comparative Analysis." *Journal of Politics* 32 (1970):268–287.

Jones, Charles O. "Joseph G. Cannon and Howard W. Smith: An Essay on the Limits of Leadership in the House of Representatives." *Journal of Politics* 30 (1968):617–646.

———. "The Minority Party and Policy-Making in the House of Representatives." *American Political Science Review* 62 (1968):481–493.

Manley, John F. "Congressional Staff and Public Policy-Making: The Joint Committee on Internal Revenue Taxation." *Journal of Politics* 30 (1968):1046–1067.

Masters, Nicholas A. "House Committee Assignments." *American Political Science Review* 55 (1961):345–357.

Monsma, Stephen V. "Integration and Goal Attainment as Functions of Informal Legislative Groups." *Western Political Quarterly* 22 (1969):19–28.

Patterson, Samuel C. "Legislative Leadership and Political Ideology." *Public Opinion Quarterly* 27 (1963):399–410.

———. "Patterns of Interpersonal Relations in a State Legislative Group: The Wisconsin Assembly." *Public Opinion Quarterly* 23 (1959):101–109.

———. "The Professional Staffs of Congressional Committees." *Administrative Science Quarterly* 15 (1970):22–37.

Peabody, Robert L. "Party Leadership Change in the United States House of Representatives." *American Political Science Review* 61 (1967):675–693.

Price, David E. "Professionals and 'Entrepreneurs': Staff Orientations and Policy Making on Three Senate Committees." *Journal of Politics* 33 (1971):316–336.

Rohde, David W., and Shepsle, Kenneth A. "Democratic Committee Assignments in the House of Representatives: Strategic Aspects of a Social Choice Process." *American Political Science Review* 67 (1973):889–905.

Stevens, Arthur G., Jr., Milller, Arthur H., and Mann, Thomas E. "Mobilization of Liberal Strength in the House, 1955–1970: The Democratic Study Group." *American Political Science Review* 68 (1974):667–681.

Tacheron, Donald G., and Udall, Morris K. *The Job of the Congressman,* 2d ed. Indianapolis, Ind., 1970.

Uslaner, Eric M. *Congressional Committee Assignments: Alternative Models for Behavior.* Beverly Hills, Calif., 1974.

Westefield, Louis P. "Majority Party Leadership and the Committee System in the House of Representatives." *American Political Science Review* 68 (1974):1593–1604.

IV. Participants in the Legislative Process

The President's role as a legislative leader has not been subjected to very full inquiry. The most lucid and thorough contribution is Nelson W. Polsby, *Congress and the Presidency,* 2d. ed. (Englewood Cliffs, N.J., 1971). Several recent books on the Presidency provide a variety of perspectives on executive-legislative relations, including Arthur M. Schlesinger, Jr., *The Imperial Presidency* (Boston, 1973); and Rexford G. Tugwell and Thomas E. Cronin, eds., *The Presidency Reappraised* (New York, 1974). Two books that cover the cabinet and its legislative involvement are Stephen Horn, *The Cabinet and Congress* (New York, 1960); and Richard F. Fenno, Jr., *The President's Cabinet* (New York, 1959). There are a number of chapters touching on the governor's role in Thad Beyle and J. Oliver Williams, eds., *The American Governor in Behavioral Perspective* (New York, 1972).

There are three systematic studies of lobbyists, two on lobbying in Congress and one on state legislatures. Lester W. Milbrath, in *The Washington Lobbyists* (Chicago, 1963), presents evidence based on interviews with a sample of 100 lobbyists in Washington, D.C. The results of an extensive survey of opinion formation and lobbying by business interests in connection with reciprocal-trade legislation are analyzed in an excellent study by Raymond A. Bauer, Ithiel de Sola Pool, and Lewis A. Dexter, *American Business and Public Policy: The Politics of Foreign Trade* (New York, 1963). Finally, Harmon Zeigler and Michael A. Baer, in *Lobbying: Interaction and Influence in American State Legislatures* (Belmont, Calif., 1969), provide an analysis of relationships between legislators and lobbyists in Massachusetts, North Carolina, Oregon, and Utah.

The pioneering effort to analyze relationships between legislators and constituents is found in the work of Warren E. Miller and Donald E. Stokes; their main report is "Constituency Influence in Congress," *American Political Science Review* 57 (1963):45–56. This research has been extended by Charles F. Cnudde and Donald J. McCrone in "The Linkage Between Constituency Attitudes and Congressional Voting Behavior: A Causal Model," *American Political Science Review* 60 (1966):66–72. The work on constituents' support for the legislature was developed at the University of Iowa and is reported in Samuel C. Patterson, Ronald D. Hedlund, and G. Robert Boynton, *Representatives and Represented: Bases of Public Support for the American Legislatures* (New York, 1975).

OTHER SOURCES

Barber, James D. "Leadership Strategies for Legislative Party Cohesion." *Journal of Politics* 28 (1966):347–367.

Davidson, Roger H., and Parker, Glenn R. "Positive Support for Political Institutions: The Case of Congress." *Western Political Quarterly* 25 (1972):600–612.

Erikson, Robert S., Luttbeg, Norman R., and Holloway, William V. "Knowing One's District: How Legislators Predict Referendum Voting." *American Journal of Political Science* 19 (1975):231–246.

Fisher, Louis. *President and Congress.* New York, 1972.

Freeman, J. Leiper. *The Political Process: Executive Bureau–Legislative Committee Relations.* Garden City, N.Y., 1955.

Hedlund, Ronald D., and Friesema, H. Paul. "Representatives' Perceptions of Constituency Opinion." *Journal of Politics* 34 (1972):730–752.

Holtzman, Abraham. *Legislative Liaison: Executive Leadership in Congress.* Chicago, 1970.

Kingdon, John W. "Politicians' Beliefs About Voters." *American Political Science Review* 61 (1967):137–145.

Kolasa, Bernard D. "Lobbying in the Nonpartisan Environment: The Case of Nebraska." *Western Political Quarterly* 14 (1971):65–78.

Lane, Edgar. *Lobbying and the Law.* Berkeley and Los Angeles, 1964.

Sarah P. McNally. "The Governor and His Legislative Party." *American Political Science Review* 60 (1966):923–942.

Miller, Warren E. "Majority Rule and the Representative System of Government." In *Mass Politics: Studies in Political Sociology,* eds. Erik Allardt and Stein Rokkan. New York, 1970, pp. 284–311.

Moe, Ronald, and Teel, Steven C. "Congress as Policy Makers: A Necessary Reappraisal." *Political Science Quarterly* 85 (1970):433–470.

Olson, David M. "District Party Organization and Legislative Performance in Congress." *Journal of Politics* 36 (1974):482–486.

Patterson, Samuel C., and Boynton, G. R. *Citizens, Leaders, and Legislators: Perspectives on Support for the American Legislature.* Beverly Hills, Calif., 1974.

Ripley, Randall B. and Franklin, Grace A., *Congress, the Bureaucracy, and Public Policy.* Homewood, Ill., 1976.

Teune, Henry. "Legislative Attitudes Toward Interest Groups." *Midwest Journal of Political Science* 11 (1967):489–504.

V. The Legislature as a Social System

Only a few attempts have been made to view the legislative body as a social system and to examine legislative roles and norms. The most definitive is the comparative analysis of legislative behavior in Ohio, Tennessee, New Jersey, and California presented in John C. Wahlke et al., *The Legislative System* (New York, 1962). Senate norms have been analyzed by Donald R. Matthews in *U. S. Senators and Their World* (New York, 1960); and the norms of the House Appropriations Committee by Richard F. Fenno, Jr., in *The Power of the Purse* (Boston, 1966). The roles of members of the United States House of Representatives have been investigated by Roger H. Davidson, *The Role of the Congressman* (New York, 1969). An assessment of the usefulness of legislative-role studies is carried forth by Malcolm E. Jewell in "Attitudinal Determinants of Legislative Behavior: The Utility of Role Analysis," in *Legislatures in Developmental Perspective,* ed. Allan Kornberg and Lloyd D. Musolf (Durham, N.C., 1970), pp. 460–500.

OTHER SOURCES

Asher, Herbert B. "The Learning of Legislative Norms." *American Political Science Review* 67 (1973):499–513.

Barber, James D. *The Lawmakers: Recruitment and Adaptation to Legislative Life.* New Haven, Conn., 1965.

Bell, Charles G., and Price, Charles M. "Pre-legislative Sources of Representational Roles." *Midwest Journal of Political Science* 13 (1969):254–270.

Dexter, Lewis A. "The Representative and His District." *Human Organization* 16 (1957):2–13.

Eulau, Heinz, et al. "The Role of the Representative: Some Empirical Observations on the Theory of Edmund Burke." *American Political Science Review* 53 (1959):742–756.

Francis, Wayne L. "The Role Concept in Legislatures: A Probability Model and a Note on Cognitive Structure." *Journal of Politics* 27 (1965):567–585.

Hebert, F. Ted, and McLemore, Lelan E. "Character and Structure of Legislative Norms: Operationalizing the Norm Concept in the Legislative Setting." *American Journal of Political Science* 17 (1973):506–527.

Jones, Bryan D. "Competitiveness, Role Orientations, and Legislative Responsiveness." *Journal of Politics* 35 (1973):924–947.

Prewitt, Kenneth, Eulau, Heinz, and Zisk, Betty H. "Political Socialization and Political Roles." *Public Opinion Quarterly* 30 (1966–1967):569–582.

Price, Charles M., and Bell, Charles G. "The Rules of the Game: Political Fact or Academic Fancy?" *Journal of Politics* 32 (1970):839–855.

Rosen, Corey M. "Legislative Influence and Policy Orientation in American State Legislatures." *American Journal of Political Science* 18 (1974):681–691.

Smith, T. V. *The Legislative Way of Life.* Chicago, 1940.

VI. The Legislature in Action

The pioneering investigations of congressional voting behavior were those of Turner, Truman, and MacRae. Using indexes of party unit, cohesion, and likeness, Julius Turner (and subsequently Edward V. Schneier, Jr., who expanded the study and brought it up to date) correlated partisan and area factors with roll-call voting in *Party and Constituency: Pressures on Congress,* rev. ed. (Baltimore, 1970). Concentrating on the Eighty-first Congress, David B. Truman analyzed roll-call clusters in *The Congressional Party* (New York, 1959); and Duncan MacRae, Jr., in *Dimensions of Congressional Voting* (Berkeley, Calif., 1958), submitted roll calls to cumulative scale analysis. Examples of similar work at the state legislative level are Thomas A. Flinn, "Party Responsibility in the States: Some Causal Factors," *American Political Science Review* 58 (1964):60–71; and Hugh L. Le-Blanc, "Voting in State Senates: Party and Constituency Influences," *Midwest Journal of Political Science* 13 (1969):33–57. Recent major studies of legislative voting include: Aage R. Clausen, *How Congressmen Decide: A Policy Focus* (New York, 1973); Morris P. Fiorina, *Representatives, Roll Calls, and Constituencies* (Lexington, Mass., 1974); John E. Jackson, *Constituencies and Leaders in Congress: Their Effects on Senate Voting Behavior* (Cambridge, Mass., 1974); John W. Kingdon, *Congressmen's Voting Decisions* (New York, 1973); and Donald R. Matthews and James A. Stimson, *Yeas and Nays: Normal Decision-Making in the U.S. House of Representatives* (New York, 1975).

Considerable information about the work of some congressional committees is available. Outstanding works on this subject are Richard F. Fenno, Jr., *The Power of the Purse: Appropriations Politics in Congress* (Boston, 1966); John F. Manley, *The Politics of Finance: The House Committee on Ways and Means* (Boston, 1970); and Richard F. Fenno, Jr., *Congressmen in Committees* (Boston, 1973). These studies were based upon extensive interviews with committee members; they probe the committee leadership and attitudes of members of the committees. Two studies of Senate committees are Stephen Horn, *Unused Power: The Work of the Senate Committee on Appropriations* (Washington, D.C., 1970), and David Price, *Who Makes the Laws? Creativity and Power in the Senate Committees* (Cambridge, Mass., 1972). As the entries in the bibliographic listing below indicate, there are also available studies of the House and Senate foreign policy committees, the House Committee on Government Operations, the House Committee on Agriculture, the Joint Committee on Atomic Energy, the Senate Committee on Banking and Currency (now Banking, Housing, and Urban Affairs), the committees dealing with education legislation, and the House Committee on Rules. Most of these studies of congressional committees deal with oversight, supervision, or control of executive agencies; the only general treatment of the subject is Joseph Harris, *Congressional Control of Administration* (Washington, D.C., 1964). The best recent study of legislative committees at the state level is Alan Rosenthal, *Legislative Performance in the States: Explorations of Committee Behavior* (New York, 1974).

There are two general studies of relations between Congress and the United States Supreme Court: C. Herman Pritchett, *Congress Versus the Supreme Court* (Minneapolis, 1961); and Walter F. Murphy, *Congress and the Court* (Chicago, 1962). A detailed analysis of congressional response to Supreme Court decisions is found in John R. Schmidhauser and Larry L. Berg, *Congress and the Court: The Post War Era, 1945–1968* (New York, 1971).

The literature on legislative apportionment and districting has grown to be voluminous. A very useful and comprehensive entry into this literature is provided by Robert G. Dixon, Jr., *Democratic Representation* (New York, 1968). Methods of apportionment are analyzed very carefully by Laurence F. Schmeckebier, *Congressional Apportionment* (Washington, D.C., 1964). A recent volume with a variety of viewpoints is Nelson W. Polsby, ed., *Reapportionment in the 1970s* (Berkeley and Los Angeles, 1971). Finally, some valuable theoretical and empirical work is available in L. Papayanopoulos, ed., *Democratic Representation and Apportionment* (New York, 1973).

OTHER SOURCES

Asher, Herbert B. *Freshman Representatives and the Learning of Voting Cues.* Beverly Hills, Calif., 1973.

Bibby, John F. "Committee Characteristics and Legislative Oversight of Administration." *Midwest Journal of Political Science* 10 (1966):78–98.

Carmines, Edward G. "The Mediating Influence of State Legislatures on the Linkage Between Interparty Competition and Welfare Policies." *American Political Science Review* 68 (1974):1118–1124.

Carroll, Holbert N. *The House of Representatives and Foreign Affairs,* rev. ed. Pittsburgh, 1966.

Cherryholmes, Cleo H., and Shapiro, Michael J. *Representatives and Roll Calls.* Indianapolis, Ind., 1969.

Cimbala, Stephen J. "Foreign Policy as an Issue Area: A Roll Call Analysis." *American Political Science Review* 63 (1969):148–156.

Clotfelter, James. "Senate Voting and Constituency Stake in Defense Spending." *Journal of Politics* 32 (1970):979–983.

Cobb, Stephen A. "Defense Spending and Foreign Policy in the House of Representatives." *Journal of Conflict Resolution* 13 (1969):358–369.

Doubleday, Douglas J. *Legislative Review of the Budget in California.* Berkeley, Calif., 1967.

Erickson, Robert S. "The Electoral Impact of Congressional Roll Call Voting." *American Political Science Review* 65 (1971):1018–1032.

———. "The Partisan Impact of State Legislative Reapportionment." *Midwest Journal of Political Science* 15 (1971):57–71.

———. "Malapportionment, Gerrymandering, and Party Fortunes in Congressional Elections." *American Political Science Review* 61 (1972):1234–1245.

Farnsworth, David N. *The Senate Committee on Foreign Relations.* Urbana, Ill., 1961.

Ferejohn, John A. *Pork Barrel Politics: Rivers and Harbors Legislation, 1947–1968.* Stanford, Calif., 1974.

Francis, Wayne L. "Influence and Interaction in a State Legislative Body." *American Political Science Review* 56 (1962):953–960.

Green, Harold P., and Rosenthal, Alan. *Government of the Atom.* New York, 1963.

Hahn, Harlan. "Leadership Perceptions and Voting Behavior in a One-Party Legislative Body." *Journal of Politics* 32 (1970):140–155.

Hedlund, Ronald D. "Perceptions of Decisional Referents in Legislative Decision-Making." *American Journal of Political Science* 19 (1975):527–542.

Hinckley, Barbara. "Coalitions in Congress: Size and Ideological Distance." *Midwest Journal of Political Science* 16 (1972):197–207.

Jewell, Malcolm E. *Senatorial Politics and Foreign Policy.* Lexington, Ky., 1962.

———. *Metropolitan Representation: State Legislative Districting in Urban Counties.* New York, 1969.

———. ed. *The Politics of Reapportionment.* New York, 1965.

Jones, Charles O. "Representation in Congress: The Case of the House Agriculture Committee." *American Political Science Review* 55 (1961):358–367.

Koehler, David H. "Legislative Coalition Formation: The Meaning of Minimal Winning Size with Uncertain Participation." *American Journal of Political Science* 19 (1975): 27–39.

Kovenock, David. "Influence in the U.S. House of Representatives: A Statistical Analysis of Communications." *American Politics Quarterly* 1 (1973):407–464.

Manley, John F. "The Conservative Coalition in Congress." *American Behavioral Scientist* 17 (1973):223–247.

Mayhew, David R. *Party Loyalty Among Congressmen.* Cambridge, Mass., 1966.

Morehouse, Sally M. "The State Political Party and the Policy-Making Process." *American Political Science Review* 67 (1973):55–72.

Patterson, Samuel C. "Dimensions of Voting Behavior in a One-party State Legislature." *Public Opinion Quarterly* 26 (1962):185–200.

Rieselbach, Leroy N. *The Roots of Isolationism.* Indianapolis, Ind., 1966.

Robeck, Bruce W. "Legislative Partisanship, Constituency and Malapportionment: The Case of California." *American Political Science Review* 61 (1972):1246–1255.

Scher, Seymour. "Conditions for Legislative Control." *Journal of Politics* 25 (1963): 526–551.

Shannon, W. Wayne. *Party, Constituency, and Congressional Voting.* Baton Rouge, La., 1968.

Sharkansky, Ira. "An Appropriations Subcommittee and Its Client Agencies: A Comparative Study of Supervision and Control." *American Political Science Review* 59 (1965): 622–628.

Strom, Gerald S. "Congressional Policy Making: A Test of a Theory." *Journal of Politics* 37 (1975):711–735.

Vogler, David J. *The Third House: Conference Committees in the United States Congress.* Evanston, Ill., 1971.

Welch, Susan, and Carlson, Eric H. "The Impact of Party on Voting Behavior in a Nonpartisan Legislature." *American Political Science Review* 67 (1973):854–867.

VII. Legislative Behavior Research

Two very thorough essays summarize developments in legislative behavior research in recent years: John C. Wahlke, "Behavioral Analyses of Representative Bodies," in *Essays on the Behavioral Study of Politics,* ed. Austin Ranney (Urbana, Ill., 1962), pp. 173–190; and Heinz Eulau and Katherine Hinckley, "Legislative Institutions and Processes," in *Political Science Annual,* vol. 1, ed., James A. Robinson (Indianapolis, Ind., 1966), pp. 85–189. Both describe in some detail the various types of research that have been pursued on legislatures. For those contemplating roll-call analysis, two methodological studies are very helpful: Lee F. Anderson, Meredith W. Watts, and Allen R. Wilcox, *Legislative Roll-Call Analysis* (Evanston, Ill., 1965); and Duncan MacRae, Jr., *Issues and Parties in Legislative Voting: Methods of Statistical Analysis* (New York, 1970).

Comparative legislative research is beginning to develop as a major analytical strategy, stimulated by the publication of John C. Wahlke et al., *The Legislative System* (New York, 1962). Some problems of comparative research on state legislative behavior are discussed in that work. Problems of cross-national comparative legislative research are discussed in Allan Kornberg and Lloyd D. Musolf, eds., *Legislatures in Developmental Perspective* (Durham, N.C., 1970); Allan Kornberg, ed., *Legislatures in Comparative Perspective* (New York, 1971); Samuel C. Patterson and John C. Wahlke, eds., *Comparative Legislative Behavior: Frontiers of Research* (New York, 1972); and John G. Grumm, *A Paradigm for the Comparative Analysis of Legislative Systems* (Beverly Hills, Calif., 1973).

OTHER SOURCES

Clausen, Aage R. "Measurement of Identity in the Longitudinal Analysis of Legislative Voting." *American Political Science Review* 61 (1967):1020–1035.

―――――. "The Measurement of Legislative Group Behavior." *Midwest Journal of Political Science* 11 (1967):212–224.

Coleman, James S. "Collective Decisions." *Sociological Inquiry* 34 (1964):166–181.

Eulau, Heinz. "Logics of Rationality in Unanimous Decision-making." In *Rational Decisions,* ed. Carl J. Friedrich. New York, 1964, pp. 26–54.

Eulau, Heinz, and Abramowitz, Alan. "Recent Research on Congress in a Democratic Perspective." *Political Science Review* 2 (1972):1–38.

Grumm, John G. "A Factor Analysis of Legislative Behavior." *Midwest Journal of Political Science* 7 (1963):336–356.

———. "The Systematic Analysis of Blocs in the Study of Legislative Behavior." *Western Political Quarterly* 18 (1965):350–362.

Hunt, William H., Crane, Wilder W., Jr., and Wahlke, John C. "Interviewing Political Elites in Cross-cultural Comparative Research." *American Journal of Sociology* 70 (1964): 59–68.

Jackson, John E. "Statistical Models of Senate Roll Call Voting." *American Political Science Review* 65 (1971):451–470.

Morrison, Richard J. "A Statistical Model for Legislative Roll Call Analysis." *Journal of Mathematical Sociology* 2 (1972):235–247.

Patterson, Samuel C. "Comparative Legislative Behavior: A Review Essay." *Midwest Journal of Political Science* 12 (1968):599–616.

Price, H. Douglas. "Are Southern Democrats Different? An Application of Scale Analysis to Senate Voting Patterns." In *Politics and Social Life,* eds. Nelson W. Polsby, Robert A. Dentler, and Paul A. Smith. Boston, 1963, pp. 740–756.

Wahlke, John C. "Policy Determinants and Legislative Decisions." In *Political Decision-Making,* ed. S. Sidney Ulmer. New York, 1970, pp. 76–120.

Wainer, Howard, Gruveus, Gunnar, and Zill, Nickolas II. "Senatorial Decision Making." *Behavioral Science* 18 (1973):7–26.

Weisberg, Herbert F. "Scaling Models for Legislative Roll-Call Analysis." *American Political Science Review* 61 (1972):1306–1315.

Index

ABOUT THE AUTHORS

MALCOLM E. JEWELL received his B.A. *cum laude* from Harvard University in 1949, and his M.A. from Columbia University the following year. After receiving his Ph.D. from Pennsylvania State University in 1958, he joined the political science department of the University of Kentucky where, focusing on legislative processes and American political parties and politics, he continues to teach. Professor Jewell is active in the American Political Science Association, the Midwest Political Science Association, the Southern Political Science Association, and the Kentucky Conference of Political Scientists. Editor of the *Midwest Journal of Political Science* from 1966 to 1970 and currently editor of a new journal, *Legislative Studies Quarterly,* he has authored, coauthored, and edited numerous books and monographs and has contributed articles and book reviews to several journals. His current research interests include a study into legislative and political developments in Korea, Kenya, and Turkey and a coauthored book-length study of American state parties and elections.

SAMUEL C. PATTERSON received his B.A. from the University of South Dakota in 1953 and then did graduate work at the University of Wisconsin, obtaining his Ph.D. there in 1959. He taught at Oklahoma State University before joining the political science department of the University of Iowa in 1961, where he has been department chairman since 1973. Dr. Patterson has been visiting professor at the University of Wisconsin (1962), the University of Oklahoma (1968–1976), and the University of Essex in England (1969–1970). Past editor of the *American Journal of Political Science* (1970–1973), he now serves on the editorial boards of the *American Journal of Political Science, American Political Science Review, British Journal of Political Science,* and *Legislative Studies Quarterly.* Professor Patterson has authored, coauthored, and edited numerous books, monographs, and articles and has contributed chapters to several anthologies. He is currently director of the Social Science Research Council.